DATE			
OCT 2 5 1988			

© THE BAKER & TAYLOR CO.

NEW ESSAYS ON HUMAN UNDERSTANDING

Manuscript draft, in Leibniz's handwriting, of pp. 50f of the *Nouveaux essais*.

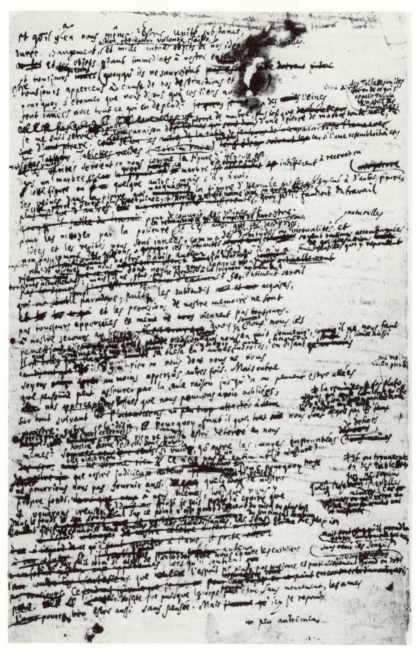

G. W. LEIBNIZ

NEW ESSAYS ON
HUMAN UNDERSTANDING

Translated and edited by
Peter Remnant
and
Jonathan Bennett

CAMBRIDGE UNIVERSITY PRESS

CAMBRIDGE

LONDON   NEW YORK   NEW ROCHELLE
MELBOURNE   SYDNEY

Published by the Press Syndicate of the University of Cambridge
The Pitt Building, Trumpington Street, Cambridge CB2 1RP
32 East 57th Street, New York, NY 10022, USA
296 Beaconsfield Parade, Middle Park, Melbourne 3206, Australia

First published 1981

Printed in Great Britain at the
University Press, Cambridge

British Library Cataloguing in Publication Data
Leibniz, Gottfried Wilhelm von
New essays on human understanding
1. Locke, John. Essay concerning human understanding
2. Knowledge, Theory of
I. Title
121'.092'4   B1294   79-42668
ISBN 0 521 23147 7 hard covers
ISBN 0 521 29836 9 paperback

CONTENTS

Frontispiece   *page* ii
Key to abbreviations   viii
EDITORS' INTRODUCTION
  i The history of the *Nouveaux essais*   xi
 ii A brief description of the work   xiii
iii Procedures adopted in this translation   xvii
 iv Explanatory apparatus   xx
  v Acknowledgements   xxi
 vi Corrigenda   xxii

NEW ESSAYS ON
HUMAN UNDERSTANDING

PREFACE   43

BOOK I: OF INNATE NOTIONS
Ch. i   Whether there are innate principles in the mind of
             man   69
Ch. ii   That there are no innate practical principles   88
Ch. iii   Other considerations concerning innate principles,
             both speculative and practical   101

BOOK II: OF IDEAS
Ch. i   In which we discuss ideas in general, and incidentally
             consider whether the soul of man thinks always   109
Ch. ii   Of simple ideas   120
Ch. iii   Of ideas of one sense   121
Ch. iv   Of solidity   122
Ch. v   Of simple ideas of divers senses   128
Ch. vi   Of simple ideas of reflection   128
Ch. vii   Of ideas of both sensation and reflection   129
Ch. viii   Some farther considerations concerning simple ideas   129
Ch. ix   Of perception   133
Ch. x   Of retention   140
Ch. xi   Of discerning, or the faculty of distinguishing ideas   141
Ch. xii   Of complex ideas   145

Ch. xiii   Of simple modes; and first, of the simple modes of
            space   146
Ch. xiv   Of duration, and its simple modes   151
Ch. xv   Of duration and expansion, considered together   154
Ch. xvi   Of number   155
Ch. xvii   Of infinity   157
Ch. xviii   Of other simple modes   159
Ch. xix   Of the modes of thinking   160
Ch. xx   Of modes of pleasure and pain   162
Ch. xxi   Of power and freedom   168
Ch. xxii   Of mixed modes   212
Ch. xxiii   Of our complex ideas of substances   217
Ch. xxiv   Of collective ideas of substances   226
Ch. xxv   Of relation   226
Ch. xxvi   Of cause and effect, and other relations   228
Ch. xxvii   What identity or diversity is   229
Ch. xxviii Of certain other relations, especially moral relations   247
Ch. xxix   Of clear and obscure, distinct and confused ideas   254
Ch. xxx   Of real and chimerical ideas   263
Ch. xxxi   Of complete and incomplete ideas   266
Ch. xxxii   Of true and false ideas   268
Ch. xxxiii Of the association of ideas   269

BOOK III: OF WORDS

Ch. i   Of words or language in general   273
Ch. ii   Of the signification of words   278
Ch. iii   Of general terms   288
Ch. iv   Of the names of simple ideas   296
Ch. v   Of the names of mixed modes and of relations   300
Ch. vi   Of the names of substances   304
Ch. vii   Of particles   329
Ch. viii   Of abstract and concrete terms   333
Ch. ix   Of the imperfection of words   334
Ch. x   Of the abuse of words   340
Ch. xi   Of the remedies of the foregoing imperfections and
            abuses   351

BOOK IV: OF KNOWLEDGE

Ch. i   Of knowledge in general   355
Ch. ii   Of the degrees of our knowledge   361
Ch. iii   Of the extent of human knowledge   375
Ch. iv   Of the reality of our knowledge   391
Ch. v   Of truth in general   396
Ch. vi   Of universal propositions, their truth and certainty   398

Ch. vii	Of the propositions which are named maxims or axioms	406
Ch. viii	Of trifling propositions	428
Ch. ix	Of our knowledge of our existence	433
Ch. x	Of our knowledge of the existence of God	434
Ch. xi	Of our knowledge of the existence of other things	443
Ch. xii	Of ways of increasing our knowledge	448
Ch. xiii	Some farther considerations concerning our knowledge	456
Ch. xiv	Of judgment	456
Ch. xv	Of probability	457
Ch. xvi	Of the degrees of assent	459
Ch. xvii	Of reason	475
Ch. xviii	Of faith and reason, and their distinct provinces	495
Ch. xix	Of enthusiasm	503
Ch. xx	Of error	509
Ch. xxi	Of the division of the sciences	521
Notes		xxiii
Bibliography		lxxxi
Index of names		lxxxiv
Index of topics		lxxxvii
List of examples		xcv

KEY TO ABBREVIATIONS

References to the edition of Leibniz's *Sämtliche Schriften und Briefe* by the Akademie-Verlag of Berlin consist of the series and volume numbers, usually followed by page numbers, without further identification (e.g. 'VI.6, pp. 43–527'). In the Introduction and in the footnotes to the text we occasionally refer to the Akademie-Verlag edition of the *Nouveaux essais* as the 'Academy edition', and to the text it contains as the 'Academy text'.

Bodemann = Eduard Bodemann, *Der Briefwechsel des Gottfried Wilhelm Leibniz*, Hanover, 1895.

CB = *Correspondance de Bossuet*, Paris, 1909–25.

Child = *The Early Mathematical Manuscripts of Leibniz*, tr. J. M. Child, Chicago, 1920.

Couturat = *Opuscules et fragments inédits de Leibniz*, ed. Louis Couturat, Paris, 1903.

DNB = *Dictionary of National Biography*, London, 1908– .

Dutens = *Gothofredi Guillelmi Leibnitii . . . opera omnia*, ed. Louis Dutens, Geneva, 1768.

Edwards = *The Encyclopedia of Philosophy*, ed. Paul Edwards, New York, 1967.

Encyc. Brit. = *The Encyclopaedia Britannica*, 11th edn, Cambridge, 1910–11.

Foucher de Careil = *Oeuvres de Leibniz*, ed. A. Foucher de Careil, Paris, 1859–75 (vols. I and II in the 2nd edn of 1867–9).

Freudenthal = *Die Lebensgeschichte Spinoza's*, ed. J. Freudenthal, Leipzig, 1899.

Gerland = *Leibnizens nachgelassene Schriften physikalischen, mechanischen und technischen Inhalts*, ed. Ernst Gerland, Leipzig, 1906.

Grua = Leibniz, *Textes inédits*, ed. Gaston Grua, Paris, 1948.

HOC = *Oeuvres complètes de Christiaan Huygens*, The Hague, 1888–1950.

Klopp = *Die Werke von Leibniz*, ed. Onno Klopp, Hanover, 1864–84.

LBG = *Der Briefwechsel von Gottfried Wilhelm Leibniz mit Mathematikern*, ed. C. I. Gerhardt, Berlin, 1899.

Leibniz–Arnauld = *The Leibniz–Arnauld Correspondence*, ed. H. T. Mason, Manchester, 1967. French text ed. Geneviève Lewis, Paris, 1952.

Leibniz–Clarke = *The Leibniz–Clarke Correspondence*, ed. H. G. Alexander, Manchester, 1956. Also ed. *Loemker* pp. 675–717 (but omits Clarke's final letter). French (Leibniz) and English (Clarke) text ed. André Robinet, Paris, 1957.

LMG = *Leibnizens mathematische Schriften*, ed. C. I. Gerhardt, Berlin and Halle, 1849–63 (re-issued as Leibniz, *Mathematische Schriften*).

LPG = *Die philosophischen Schriften von Gottfried Wilhelm Leibniz*, ed. C. I. Gerhardt, Berlin, 1875–90.

Loemker = Leibniz, *Philosophical Papers and Letters*, ed. Leroy E. Loemker, Dordrecht, 1969.

Morris and Parkinson = Leibniz, *Philosophical Writings*, tr. Mary Morris and G. H. R. Parkinson, London, 1973.

Müller = Kurt Müller and Gisela Krönert, *Leben und Werk von G. W. Leibniz*, Frankfurt, 1969.

NC = *The Correspondence of Isaac Newton*, Cambridge, 1959–.

OC = *The Correspondence of Henry Oldenburg*, Madison and London, 1965– .

OED = *The Oxford English Dictionary*, Oxford, 1933.

Parkinson = Leibniz, *Logical Papers*, ed. G. H. R. Parkinson, Oxford, 1966.

Pertz = *Leibnizens gesammelte Werke*, ed. G. H. Pertz, Hanover, 1843–47 (re-issued as Leibniz, *Gesammelte Werke*).

Riley = *The Political Writings of Leibniz*, ed. Patrick Riley, Cambridge, 1972.

SB = *Briefwechsel der Herzogin Sophie von Hannover mit ihrem Bruder*, Leipzig, 1885.

Schrecker = Leibniz, *Monadology and other Philosophical Essays*, ed. Paul Schrecker, Indianapolis, 1965.

Stein = Ludwig Stein, *Leibniz und Spinoza*, Berlin, 1890.

Struik = *A Source Book in Mathematics, 1200–1800*, ed. D. J. Struik, Cambridge, Mass., 1969.

Wiener = *Leibniz Selections*, ed. Philip P. Wiener, New York, 1951.

INTRODUCTION

I   The history of the *Nouveaux essais*

1. Within five years of the first appearance of Locke's *Essay Concerning Human Understanding* (1690), Leibniz had read at least some of it, and had written several pages of comments – some appreciative, some mildly critical – upon parts of the work, allowing an intermediary to pass them on to Locke.[1] The latter received them sourly, writing to a friend with a sceptical allusion to Leibniz's 'great name', and concluding that 'even great parts will not master any subject without great thinking, and even the largest minds have but narrow swallows' (Locke to Molyneux, April 1697). The letter containing that remark was published in 1708, and Leibniz later wrote: 'I am not surprised by it: we differed rather too much in principles' (Leibniz to Rémond, March 1714).

Leibniz's interest in Locke's work is abundantly shown by his correspondence in the 1690s, by his re-working the comments mentioned above, and by his writing a fresh set of remarks on Books I and II of the *Essay*, as well as (in 1698) a longer commentary on the controversy which the *Essay* had stirred up between Locke and Stillingfleet, the Bishop of Worcester.

The English language must have been something of a barrier between Leibniz and Locke's long, difficult book. In a letter admitting the imperfections in his French, he wrote: 'I only wish I had the same knowledge of the English language; but not having had the occasion for it, the most I can manage is a tolerable understanding of books written in that language';[2] and on p. 462 of the present work there is a small but striking indication of his not being at home with English. Still, he did sometimes grapple directly and effectively with Locke's text. Whether he read the entire *Essay* in English, and if so how thoroughly, we do not know. His own copy of the first edition has about seventy underlinings and

---

[1] This, like most of our historical remarks, is backed by references in the Introduction to the Academy edition of the *Nouveaux essais* (see §5 below), which also supplies full details of references which we give in truncated form.

[2] Leibniz to Burnett, 27 July 1696, in *LPG* III, p. 181. (That date was 17 July in England. The Gregorian calendar, which was adopted by Roman Catholic countries in 1582, was adopted by the German Lutheran states only in 1700 and by Britain in 1752; we have adjusted all dates to conform to the new calendar.)

marginal marks, and about thirty marginal notes (most of them now undecipherable); all of these being in Book II, Chapters 1–21.

2. The situation changed in 1700 with the publication of Pierre Coste's French version of the *Essay*, under the title *Essai philosophique concernant l'entendement humain* etc., based primarily on the fourth edition. Nidditch rightly praises this as being, 'almost everywhere, admirably clear, readable, and reliable', though it does contain some mistakes and a good number of minor liberties. Leibniz had known it was coming: in 1696 it was proposed that his critical comments might serve as an introduction to the Coste translation (and though he very properly declined, there was a muddle through which Locke was given to understand that the proposal was Leibniz's own). Leibniz apparently did not seriously start reading Coste until about mid-1703; and at about that time he also began writing the more extensive critical commentary which eventually became the *New Essays on Human Understanding*. In this, he relied heavily on Coste's version, and probably had little further recourse to the English text. Where Coste diverges from Locke, Leibniz usually follows suit; the only clear exceptions to this are described in III.2 below. Even of the passages which Leibniz underlined in his own copy of the English work, two are non-trivially misrepresented in the *New Essays*: once wholly because of Coste (p. 134 in the present volume), and once – a complete reversal of meaning – partly because of him (p. 171).

3. The writing was done, Leibniz says, hastily and with many interruptions. The first draft was finished in May 1704. Between then and August of that year Leibniz did a good deal of revising, and recast the first two Books into dialogue form (the third and fourth were dialogues from the outset). Linguistic and stylistic changes were also being made: the Academy editors (see §5 below) report traces of interventions by eight correctors.

The preparation of a fair copy, embodying the revisions and corrections of Leibniz and others, was completed at just about the time Locke died (November 1704). Leibniz heard the news before the month was out. In January 1705 he solicited further linguistic help from a French writer, and expressed an intention to have the work published; and he was certainly tinkering with it as late as May 1705 (on p. 286 he mentions the recent death of J. Schilter, who died in that month). But he probably did little with it after learning of Locke's death.

Nor is there any evidence that he had intended to re-work it in its philosophical aspects. Locke's death somehow aborted the plan to have the work published, and probably also cut short the process of stylistic improvement; but there is no reason to think that it also inhibited changes which would otherwise have been made to the philosophical content. In that respect, it seems, we have before us a virtually completed work.

4. Why did Locke's death affect Leibniz's plans? His earliest extant statement about this is in a letter to Lady Masham in July 1705, where he says that he is discouraged, implying that a main purpose of the *New Essays* was to elicit replies from Locke; and he said similar things to others. There is indeed ample evidence of Leibniz's long-standing desire to engage in philosophical discussion with Locke. Still, that may not be the whole explanation. To another correspondent Leibniz wrote that it would be unfair to publish extensive criticism of a man who could no longer defend himself. To yet another he seems – judging from the reply – to have expressed the rather different fear that if he published he would be accused of unfairness or cowardice.[1]

5. Leibniz died in 1716, and the *New Essays* did not see the light of day until 1765, when it was published by R. E. Raspe, the author of the Baron Munchausen tales. (Kant's reading of this in about 1769 seems to have given him his first direct knowledge of Leibniz's philosophy, and to have marked an important stage in the development of his own thought.) There have been several subsequent editions, but the only acceptable text is the one published in 1962 by the Akademie-Verlag in Berlin, and edited by André Robinet and Heinrich Schepers; we refer to this throughout as the Academy edition, and to the text which it contains as the Academy text.

The *New Essays* has been translated into German and Italian, three times each, and also into Czech, Polish, Hungarian, Russian, Spanish, Japanese, and English – the last by A. C. Langley (New York, 1896). It has never been accessible to English speakers who cannot cope with Leibniz's often quite difficult French. The Langley version is almost unreadable for stylistic reasons, and also remarkably inaccurate: in literally hundreds of places Langley gives renderings from which no one could discover what thought is expressed in the French text.

About a sixth of the work appears in English in a volume of Leibniz extracts edited by P. Wiener. This, though better than the Langley version, seems to be based on it and is still very imperfect. The Preface of the *New Essays* is well translated in the Everyman Leibniz collection by Mary Morris and G. H. R. Parkinson.

II   A brief description of the work

1. There are in English two extended philosophical discussions of the *New Essays*, assessing its philosophical significance, judging the main points of contention between Locke and Leibniz, and so on. They are John Dewey's *Leibniz's New Essays Concerning Human Understanding: a Critical*

---

[1] Naudé to Leibniz, 13 October 1706, unpublished. There is a full archival reference in the Academy edition; but it is from Nicholas Jolley that we known of the letter's reassurances about accusations of unfairness or cowardice.

Exposition (Chicago, 1888), and two chapters of James Gibson's *Locke's Theory of Knowledge and its Historical Relations* (Cambridge, 1917). We hope that our translation will stimulate further work of this sort; but our own efforts have been of a different kind, and have not equipped us to offer a commentary on or philosophical assessment of the *New Essays* – and certainly not one deserving to be included in an edition of the work itself. In what follows we offer some descriptive and evaluative remarks of a less ambitious sort, in the belief that they may interest readers and those who are wondering whether to become readers.

2. The principal defects of the *New Essays* are conspicuous and notorious. Let them be admitted at once.

The work is in the form not of 'essays' but of an extended conversation, and Leibniz's handling of the dialogue form is disappointing – especially when compared with Plato, Berkeley and Hume. Instead of two real people seriously arguing with one another, we have a mechanical spokesman for Locke (Philalethes) who dutifully serves up portions of the *Essay* so that Leibniz's spokesman (Theophilus) can pass judgment on them. Sometimes Philalethes abjectly backs down from Locke's position, but usually he just passes on, without comment, to the next topic; rarely is he allowed anything like an effective reply. The dialogue form does no great harm to the work, but it constitutes a promise which is unfulfilled. This was inevitable: as Leibniz ruefully says in his Preface (p. 48), if you are going to follow through a book which has already been written, you cannot also have the charms (*agréments*) of life-like conversation.

If the dialogue form had been fully utilized, there might have been more fairness to Locke. Not that the unfairness is extreme. Leibniz reproduces some things from the *Essay* just because he likes them so much. And some fairness is achieved even at points of conflict: Philalethes does usually present Locke's main arguments on anything on which the two philosophers disagree; and Leibniz's contributions to the disagreements are often thorough and candid enough to exhibit difficulties in his position as well as in Locke's. An example of this is his discussion on pp. 394f of the classification of creatures whose status as human is in doubt, this being Locke's test case in the battle between nominalism and realism regarding the ontological status of species or kinds. Still, this falls short of letting Philalethes make some effective replies.

It is also a defect in the work that Theophilus tends to ramble, especially in the second half. His digressions are made harder to manage by the fact that the sentences and paragraphs are often, as Leibniz's friends complained, very badly constructed. We have tried by conservative means to keep the structure of each passage clear, sometimes re-ordering clauses. But we have resisted the temptation to intrude further, e.g. by imposing paragraph breaks other than the few supplied by Leibniz himself.

The third and gravest defect is that Leibniz does not try to give a comprehensive understanding of the main outlines of Locke's way of thinking, or of his own. Had he attempted both, the result would have been a synoptic view, through the eyes of the greatest rationalist, of how his way of thinking relates to empiricism. In the event, we get something less than that. Although he sometimes criticizes Locke on internal grounds of inconsistency, Leibniz does not try to enter into the Lockean manner of thinking. Nor does he properly introduce the reader to his own. His comments on Locke constantly rely on aspects of his own philosophical system – a wide-ranging ontology, theology, logic, and philosophy of mind – which was firmly settled in his mind by the time he wrote the *New Essays*. This material is frequently mentioned in the work, and sometimes a few details are sketched in; but no attempt is made to lay the main outlines of Leibniz's thought before the reader's eyes. The work is thus less self-contained than one would like. We try to remedy that somewhat, through explanatory notes; but the fact remains, and cannot be much helped by editorial interventions, that Leibniz did not take the great opportunity he had created for himself.

In assessing all these defects, however, and especially the inadequate handling of the dialogue form, one should bear in mind that if Leibniz's hopes had been realized the *New Essays* would have been only a prelude to the real debate between Locke and himself.

3. The work as it stands is absorbingly interesting and brilliantly illuminating. If it does not offer a systematic confrontation between empiricism and rationalism, it does present a lively clash between certain aspects of the two traditions. This includes a clash between two kinds of intellectual temperament which have historically tended to be associated with empiricism and rationalism respectively: Locke's inclination to keep theorizing in check by means of common sense, and Leibniz's much stronger preparedness to sacrifice surface plausibility to theoretic strength and unity. On almost every page, the *New Essays* manifests Leibniz's passion for system, order, definition, rigorous formality, and clarity; and in this respect he is in strong contrast with Locke (and even more so with Philalethes). For a tiny but vivid example – one of hundreds – see the dashing account of 'affinity' on p. 249. For a much larger one, which affects various parts of the work, consider the difference between Locke's attitude and Leibniz's to the question 'What, basically, *is* there?' Locke speaks of minds and of bodies, but makes no attempt to give them any kind of conceptual unity. And as regards bodies: he says that infinite divisibility is inconceivable, and yet he does not explicitly affirm atomism and explore its consequences. Leibniz, on the other hand, insists that an issue of this kind requires a strong, clear theory, and he does indeed have one. Sometimes he tries to save Locke from himself: where Locke has

'substances', Philalethes is often made to say 'substantial entities' instead, so as not to prejudge the question of whether the items in question are further divisible.

The confrontation has other roots as well, in differences of basic doctrine rather than of intellectual temperament. Locke's starting-point is always the particular datum of experience, which he calls an 'idea'; and he is generally agreed to have been unable to get from there to a satisfactory general account of the mind. Much of Book I discusses one aspect of this problem, namely the question of how, if all knowledge comes from what is given in experience, we can know that a given proposition is necessarily true. But Leibniz's attacks on this aspect of Locke's thought are broader and deeper than that. The central point is that Locke tries to use 'idea' in such a way that an 'idea of x' may be a sense-presentation of it or something like a concept or notion of it; and Leibniz repeatedly insists that these are wholly different and should not be given the same name. In his terminology, the datum of the senses is an 'image', and an 'idea' is an intellectual item which is involved in understanding, judging, defining, and so on. One wishes that Hume had been saved from Locke's conflation by reading this salutary corrective.

The serious student of Leibniz's thought will find in these pages significant and interesting treatments of many philosophical topics: innate ideas, personal identity, infinity, freedom, impenetrability, mind–body relationships, self-consciousness, scepticism about the external world, the nature of necessary truth, vacuum, the mental powers of beasts, the causes of human actions, mechanism and mentality, and others.

4. As well as large issues, there are hundreds of small ones. Any attentive reader of the *New Essays* must receive a dominant impression of being in the presence of a powerful, restless, superbly sharp intelligence. See for example the beautifully crisp handling on p. 384 of Locke's supposedly necessary truth that where there is no property there can be no injustice. Leibniz snaps down on this: if 'property' is restricted to objects, then there can be injustice – e.g unfair imprisonment – in a society which lacks property; and if 'property' also includes one's actions, then there could not be a society in which there was no property. There is an aesthetic pleasure in seeing the thing so well done. Hosts of other examples might be cited, including: the perfect treatment of the Molyneux problem (pp. 136–8); the superb comparison between spatial and temporal vacuum on p. 155; the sharp, accurate handling of the problem of cohesion on p. 223; the elegant use of a duplicate-world fiction to challenge Locke's theory of personal identity on p. 245; the defence of the notion of a 'hidden constitution' for modes as well as for substances on pp. 346f; the effective refutation of the idea that 'affirm' and 'negate' can be explained purely in terms of combining or separating signs, on p. 396; the incisive criticism

of Locke's form of the cosmological argument for God's existence on p. 436; the explaining away of apparently prophetic dreams on p. 445.

5. The rambling quality in the work, noted in §2 above, has its positive side. The style is the man himself. In the *New Essays* we are given a generous slice of the real Leibniz: busy, friendly, didactic, endlessly curious, full of personal memories and impersonal political plans, in touch with a good proportion of Europe's leading thinkers, and possessed of inexhaustible intellectual energy.

The reader will look in vain for the 'avaricious' and 'unprincipled' Leibniz of some commentators. We do not find that Leibniz anywhere in our material. What emerges from the primary sources is a kindly, honest, candid, and generous man, strongly motivated by a concern for human progress, and pursuing his own self-interest only in the furtherance of the work that enthralled him.

There is a human charm in some of the *idées fixes* which are revealed: for example, the advocacy of state-supported medical research at p. 317 (see also pp. 426f and 454), the doomed, cherished theory about the meanings of vowels and consonants on pp. 282–5, the recurrent interest in the possibility of becoming a good (pp. 185–91) or a bad (p. 511) person through training, the thought of inter-planetary travel (p. 314). Also, as we try to bring out in the Notes at the end, many of Leibniz's glancing references to individuals are connected with significant episodes in his life (e.g. Witsen at p. 103, Pomponne at p. 509); and some of the non-philosophical topics on which he touches – such as horology, librarianship, historiography, mathematics, literary criticism, church union, political decision-making – reflect some of his own real-life activities.

III Procedures adopted in this translation

1. We have used the text and the page numbering of the Academy edition, that is, the edition of the *Nouveaux essais sur l'entendement humain* edited by André Robinet and Heinrich Schepers, and published in 1962 by the Akademie-Verlag of Berlin. For Locke's *Essay* we have gratefully used the edition by Peter Nidditch, published in 1975 by the Oxford University Press. For Coste's translation of the *Essay*, we have used a photocopy of the first edition which was kindly supplied to us by Peter Nidditch.

Our deliberate departures from the Academy text are few and minor. Twice for clarity's sake, and twice for accuracy, we resort to an earlier version of the work than is given in the Academy text, indicating each departure in a footnote. And we are freer than the Academy editors in restoring words and phrases omitted by Leibniz's copyists. The former restore, within square brackets, only things whose omission they say would 'harm the understanding of the text'; we restore a few other expressions which have some slight philosophical interest. This occurs ten times in pp. 54–68, and once each on pp. 120, 137, 308, 313, 314, 330, 332. For the information upon which our departures are based, as for much else, we are indebted to the Academy editors.

Relative to Locke's *Essay*, many of Leibniz's section numbers are misplaced, as is one of his chapter breaks. We silently correct these.

2. Leibniz purports to indicate which parts of Philalethes' remarks are and which are not drawn from Locke's text. Since these indications are often inaccurate and are at best coarse-grained and incomplete, we have substituted our own, which are now described.

In our renderings of Philalethes' remarks, and of the headings of Books and Chapters, anything under quotation marks is quoted directly from Locke's *Essay*, following Nidditch's edition in everything except spelling, italics and capitals. Within these passages, three-point ellipses and square brackets are used in the conventional manner, for omissions and interpolations respectively. When an omission and an interpolation occur at the same place, brackets only are used, even if what is omitted is quite lengthy: the loss of information which this procedure involves is compensated for, we think, by the improvement it brings to the appearance of the text. Also for aesthetic reasons, we never put seven full points in a row. On the dozen occasions when something is omitted from the end of one sentence and from the beginning of the next, only one omission is indicated.

When two quoted passages occur in this work in a different order from the one they have in the *Essay*, quotation marks are closed around the first of them and then re-opened around the second. Apart from those rare cases, there is no information to be got from the difference between cases where quotation marks are closed and then re-opened and cases where square brackets occur under a single pair of quotation marks: the choice was based in each case on aesthetic considerations.

These quotation marks, brackets and ellipses are not part of the text, and should be omitted in quoting from it. They are our attempt to report facts about the provenance of Philalethes' share of the text. The principles governing them are these. We do not enclose any remark by Philalethes within quotation marks unless *both* (1) the corresponding text of Leibniz's exactly copies Coste, or differs only in ways which apparently have no considered intention behind them, *and* (2) Coste's version does not depart from Locke's meaning in any way that matters. Thus, where Leibniz departs from Coste with evident deliberation, even if only for stylistic or expository reasons, we follow him rather than reverting to Locke's wording, except in the nine places where he diverges from Coste because, clearly, he worked directly from Locke's text (pp. 163f, 170, 200, 251, 263, 269, 331, 370, 393f). Three possible further cases (pp. 342, 404, 443) are signalled in footnotes.

Most of the Philalethes material not enclosed in quotation marks also represents material in Locke's *Essay*; and much more could have been handled by the quotation system, but only with more brackets etc. than we were prepared to inflict on the reader. In the non-quoted material, we have been guided by Locke's choice of vocabulary and, often, of phrasing.

Enormous amounts of the *Essay* make no appearance in the *New Essays* and we cannot sign-post these. But we do indicate, in footnotes, the most interesting omissions, additions, and alterations pertaining to words and short phrases. Where such a footnoted variation is not explicitly attributed to Coste, it is due to Leibniz. Where it is attributed to Coste without mention of Leibniz, this of course means that Coste made the change and that Leibniz retained it. (Of the variations which we judge not to be worth a footnote, many are Coste's and many are Leibniz's; we do not distinguish them.) Footnotes of the form 'Added by...' have maximum scope: that is, the added portion runs from the footnote indicator back to the immediately preceding closing quotation mark or opening square bracket, or, if these do not occur, back to the start of the section or paragraph.

Whenever Philalethes shows awareness of Theophilus as a person, or mentions Locke or his followers, or expresses less than perfect confidence in Locke's views, some dialogue has been composed for him by Leibniz; it is usually clear how much. These passages are not footnoted.

When Theophilus announces that he is quoting from Locke's *Essay*, or when Leibniz does so in the Preface, we adopt the same principles as in Philalethes' speeches. A similar procedure is followed with the material quoted in the Preface from Locke's letters to Stillingfleet: here the touchstone has been the first published versions of those letters.

3. Most of our uses of quotation marks in Theophilus' speeches are of the conventional sorts – to give a quotation, to mention a word, to display a word while using it, and so on – usually on the strength of an indication from Leibniz, but sometimes on our own initiative. One class of cases needs special mention: sometimes Theophilus uses an expression which (or a cognate of which) has been used by Philalethes shortly before; where we think that this is a deliberate echo which might otherwise be missed, we highlight it by enclosing the expression in quotation marks, whether or not Leibniz has underlined it. Except where otherwise indicated, these 'echo' uses of quotation marks all relate not to Locke's text or to Coste's, but to the speeches of Philalethes. On a few occasions Theophilus clearly purports to be echoing Philalethes although he does not quote him exactly: here too we use quotation marks without turning the echo into an exact quotation.

4. Since we have not tried to write seventeenth-century pastiche, Locke's prose combines with ours to make an uneven mixture. To lessen this effect, and for other obvious reasons, we have tried in rendering both

Philalethes and Theophilus to avoid serious anachronism in vocabulary and idiom. At the same time, we have tried to avoid archaisms: the translation purports to be in that part of contemporary English which was also English in 1704.

We translate material in Greek and Latin except when there is special reason not to do so, e.g. because Leibniz goes on to give his own translation. We also put book titles into English when they are informative and are not already well established, in their original form, in the English literature.

IV Explanatory apparatus

1. On pp. xxiii–lxxx there is a system of explanatory Notes, arranged in alphabetical order of key words or phrases. When something in the text particularly requires a reference to one of these notes, there is in the text an asterisk at the start of the key word or phrase; or of a word which is cognate and alphabetically close – e.g. an asterisk on 'likelihood' points to the note headed 'likely'. A given note may also be relevant to passages which are not linked to it by an asterisk.

A few of the notes give needed explanation of the meanings of certain technical or out-of-the-way words. Some explain aspects of Leibniz's philosophy which need to be grasped for an understanding of the text. A third category deal with certain recurrent translation problems. But the vast majority of them are concerned with people and events and schools of thought alluded to in the text and of significance in Leibniz's career. Most of the people dealt with were friends or acquaintances or correspondents of Leibniz's; a few others influenced him only through their published writings, but are now sufficiently forgotten to require some introduction: Comenius, Gassendi, Ramus; at least one – Descartes – although by no means forgotten, was so pervasively influential that, again, some account of his doctrines seemed justified.

The over-all purpose of the Notes – apart from those which are strictly needed for the comprehension of the text – is to help the reader to grasp the astonishing richness of the *New Essays* as a resource not only in philosophy but also in the history of ideas.

2. When we need to refer to parts of the *New Essays* or of the *Essay*, either for our editorial purposes or in rendering references by Leibniz, we use the system by which 'III.ii.3' means 'Book III, chapter ii, section 3', and 'ii.3' means 'this Book, chapter ii, section 3', and '§3' means 'this chapter, section 3'. Where Leibniz cross-alludes without detailed references, we supply the latter by page numbers.

Where Leibniz alludes to other works of his own, we insert a reference which can be unpacked by means of the Bibliography on pp. lxxxiff. Page numbers in these inserted references refer to the version of the work listed

in the Bibliography, or to the first-mentioned version if there are several –
with one exception which is noted as it occurs.

Allusions to works by others which we judge to be of sufficient interest
are explained in the Notes, except that in the case of works by well-known
philosophers references are interpolated in the text in the same manner as
for Leibniz's works.

We sometimes interpolate the name of a Latin author, primarily to
indicate a passage's status as a classical quotation. Complete references for
these passages can be found in the Academy edition.

Everything inserted by us is placed within square brackets; and these
are used for no other purpose except in passages quoted from Locke's
Essay, as explained in III.2 above.

3. The Bibliography lists works by Leibniz alluded to in the text or in
the Notes. If a work is currently available in English translation,
references are given; Leibniz's own title, if any, is given and, if Leibniz
published the work, the place and date of publication – if not, the date of
the work's completion; finally, we indicate the best available edition known
to us of the original work.

The abbreviated references employed in the Notes and the Bibliography
are explained in the Key to Abbreviations on pp. viii f.

Readers are reminded that the Notes contain, in what we hope is an
accessible form, much bibliographical information about non-Leibnizian
works. References to works we ignore, and some amplification of most of
our non-Leibnizian references, can be found in the Academy edition.

V Acknowledgements

For help with problems of French, we are indebted to Laurence Bongie,
François Duchesneau, Normand Lacharité, Margret Jackson, and Sylvana
Tomaselli. For assistance with many philosophical and linguistic problems
we owe thanks to Hidé Ishiguro, G. H. R. Parkinson, David Shwayder,
and Margaret Wilson. For indispensable guidance on specialized matters,
we are grateful to Ronald Riddell and D. T. Whiteside (mathematics),
John Yolton (Locke), Peter Stein (law), Richard Bauckham (theology),
H. W. Janson (fine arts), and John Butterworth (bookkeeping). We have
also had good help from Anthony Barrett, Lewis White Beck, Elizabeth
Bongie, Gerd Buchdahl, Anne Dybikowski, Frederick Grover, Ian
Hacking, Jaakko Hintikka, and Walter Ong.

Secretarial and other expenses were covered by research grants from the
University of British Columbia, here gratefully acknowledged.

The writing of the first draft of the translation was done in a level
collaboration. The Bibliography and most of the Notes are primarily
Remnant's work; Bennett did correspondingly more in revising the

translation and preparing the footnotes, though the translation was the subject of consultation at every stage. There is no senior partner, and the order of our names was decided by the spin of a coin.

VI Corrigenda

We hope within a few years to issue an amended edition in which the most serious localized defects in the translation, and errors and omissions in the explanatory apparatus and the indexes, are set right. Readers who find such faults are urged to send their findings to one of us.

Jonathan Bennett
Department of Philosophy
Syracuse University
Syracuse, N.Y. 13210
U.S.A.

Peter Remnant
Department of Philosophy
University of British Columbia
Vancouver, B.C. V6T 1W5
Canada

NEW ESSAYS ON
HUMAN UNDERSTANDING

PREFACE

The *Essay on the Understanding*, produced by an illustrious Englishman, is one of the finest and most admired works of the age. Since I have thought at length about the same subject and about most of the topics which are 44 dealt with in it, I have decided to comment upon it. I thought that this would be a good opportunity to publish something entitled *New Essays on the Understanding* and to gain a more favourable reception for my thoughts by putting them in such good company. I thought too that I might benefit 45 from someone else's labour, not only to lessen mine (since it is easier to follow the thread of a good author than to do everything by one's own efforts), but also to add something to what he has produced for us, which 46 is always easier than to start from the beginning. It is true that my opinions frequently differ from his, but far from denying the merit of this famous writer I testify in his favour by showing where and why I differ from him, 47 when I find that on certain significant points I have to prevent his authority from prevailing over reason.

Indeed, although the author of the *Essay* says hundreds of fine things which I applaud, our systems are very different. His is closer to Aristotle and mine to Plato, although each of us parts company at many points from the teachings of both of these ancient writers. He is more popular whereas 48 I am sometimes forced to be a little more esoteric and abstract – which is no advantage for me, particularly when writing in a living language. However, I think that by using two speakers, one of whom presents opinions drawn from that author's *Essay* and the other adds my comments, the confrontation will be more to the reader's taste than a dry commentary from which he would have to be continually turning back to the author's book in order to understand mine. Nevertheless it would be well to compare our writings from time to time, and to judge of his opinions only from his own book even though I have usually retained its wording. I am afraid that the obligation to follow the thread, when commenting on someone else's treatise, has shut out any hope of my attaining to the charms of which dialogue is capable; but I hope that the matter will make up for the shortcomings of the manner.

Our disagreements concern points of some importance. There is the question whether the soul in itself is completely blank like a writing tablet on which nothing has as yet been written – a *tabula rasa* – as Aristotle and the author of the *Essay* maintain, and whether everything which is inscribed there comes solely from the senses and experience; or whether the soul inherently contains the sources[1] of various notions and doctrines, which external objects merely rouse up on suitable occasions, as I believe and as do Plato and even the Schoolmen and all those who understand in this sense the passage in St Paul where he says that God's law is written in our hearts (*Romans*, 2: 15). The Stoics call these sources Prolepses, that is fundamental assumptions or things taken for granted in advance. Mathematicians call them common notions or *koinai ennoiai*. Modern philosophers give them other fine names and Julius Scaliger, in particular, used to call them 'seeds of eternity' and also '*zopyra*' – meaning living fires or flashes of light hidden inside us but made visible by the stimulation of the senses, as sparks can be struck from a steel. And we have reason to believe that these flashes reveal something divine and eternal: this appears especially in the case of necessary truths. That raises another question, namely whether all truths depend on experience, that is on induction and instances, or if some of them have some other foundation. For if some events can be foreseen before any test has been made of them, it is obvious that we contribute something from our side. Although the senses are necessary for all our actual knowledge, they are not sufficient to provide it all, since they never give us anything but instances, that is particular or singular truths. But however many instances confirm a general truth, they do not suffice to establish its universal necessity; for it does not follow that what has happened will always happen in the same way. For instance, the Greeks and Romans and all the other nations on earth always found that within the passage of twenty-four hours day turns into night and night into day. But they would have been mistaken if they had believed that the same rule holds everywhere, since the contrary was observed during a stay in Novaya Zemlya. And anyone who believed that it is a necessary and eternal truth at least in our latitudes would also be mistaken, since we must recognize that neither the earth nor even the sun exist necessarily, and that there may come a time when this beautiful star no longer exists, at least in its present form, nor its whole system. From this it appears that necessary truths, such as we find in pure mathematics and particularly in arithmetic and geometry, must have principles whose proof does not depend on instances nor, consequently, on the testimony of the senses, even though without the senses it would never occur to us to think of them. This distinction must be thoroughly observed, and Euclid understood that so well that he demonstrates by reason things that experience and sense-images make very evident. Logic also abounds in such truths, and so do metaphysics and ethics, together with their respective products, natural theology and natural jurisprudence; and so the *proof of them can only come from

---

[1] '*principes*'.

inner principles, which are described as innate. It would indeed be wrong to think that we can easily read these eternal laws of reason in the soul, as the Praetor's edict can be read on his notice-board, without effort or inquiry; but it is enough that they can be discovered within us by dint of attention: the senses provide the occasion, and successful experiments also serve to corroborate reason, somewhat as checks in arithmetic help us to avoid errors of calculation in long chains of reasoning. It is in this same respect that man's knowledge differs from that of beasts: beasts are sheer empirics and are guided entirely by instances. While men are capable of demonstrative knowledge [*science*], beasts, so far as one can judge, never manage to form necessary propositions, since the faculty by which they make sequences is something lower than the reason which is to be found in men. The sequences of beasts are just like those of simple empirics who maintain that what has happened once will happen again in a case which is similar in the respects that they are impressed by, although that does not enable them to judge whether the same reasons are at work. That is what makes it so easy for men to ensnare beasts, and so easy for simple empirics to make mistakes. Even people made cunning by age and experience are not proof against this when they trust too much to their past experience; as has happened to various people engaged in civil or military affairs, through their not taking sufficiently to heart that the world changes and that men become cleverer and find hundreds of new tricks – whereas the deer and hares of our time are not becoming craftier than those of long ago. The sequences of beasts are only a shadow of reasoning, that is, they are nothing but a connection in the imagination – a passage from one image to another; for when a new situation appears similar to its predecessor, it is expected to have the same concomitant features as before, as though things were linked [*liaison*] in reality just because their images are linked in the memory. It is true, moreover, that reason counsels us to expect ordinarily that what we find in the future will conform to long experience of the past; but even so, this is no necessary and infallible truth, and it can fail us when we least expect it to, if there is a change in the reasons which have been maintaining it. This is why the wisest men do not trust it so implicitly that they neglect to probe somewhat, where possible, into the reason for such regularities, in order to know when they will have to allow exceptions. For only reason is capable of establishing reliable rules, of making up the deficiencies of those which have proved unreliable by allowing exceptions to them, and lastly of finding unbreakable links in the cogency of necessary inferences. This last often provides a way of foreseeing events without having to experience sensible links between images, as beasts must. Thus what shows the existence of inner sources of necessary truths is also what distinguishes man from beast.

Perhaps our gifted author will not entirely disagree with my view. For

51

after devoting the whole of his first book to rejecting innate illumination, understood in a certain sense, he nevertheless admits at the start of his second book, and from there on, that ideas which do not originate in sensation come from reflection. But reflection is nothing but attention to what is within us, and the senses do not give us what we carry with us already. In view of this, can it be denied that there is a great deal that is innate in our minds, since we are innate to ourselves, so to speak, and since we include Being, Unity, Substance, Duration, Change, Action, Perception, Pleasure, and hosts of other objects of our intellectual ideas? And since these objects are immediately related to our understanding and always present to it (although our distractions and needs prevent us being always aware of them), is it any wonder that we say that these ideas, along with what depends on them, are innate in us? I have also used the analogy of a veined block of marble, as opposed to an entirely homogeneous block of marble, or to a blank tablet – what the philosophers call a *tabula rasa*. For if the soul were like such a blank tablet then truths would be in us as the shape of *Hercules is in a piece of marble when the marble is entirely neutral as to whether it assumes this shape or some other. However, if there were veins in the block which marked out the shape of Hercules rather than other shapes, then that block would be more determined to that shape and Hercules would be innate in it, in a way, even though labour would be required to expose the veins and to polish them into clarity, removing everything that prevents their being seen. This is how ideas and truths are innate in us – as inclinations, dispositions, tendencies, or natural potentialities, and not as actions; although these potentialities are always accompanied by certain actions, often insensible ones, which correspond to them.

52

Our gifted author seems to claim that there is nothing *potential* in us, in fact nothing of which we are not always actually aware. But he cannot hold strictly to this; otherwise his position would be too paradoxical, since, again, we are not always aware of our acquired dispositions [*habitude*] or of the contents of our memory, and they do not even come to our aid whenever we need them, though often they come readily to mind when some idle circumstance reminds us of them, as when hearing the opening words of a song is enough to bring back the rest. So on other occasions he limits his thesis to the statement that there is nothing in us of which we have not at least previously been aware. But no one can establish by reason alone how far our past and now perhaps forgotten awarenesses may have extended, especially if we accept the Platonists' doctrine of recollection which, though sheer myth, is entirely consistent with unadorned reason. And furthermore, why must we acquire everything through awareness of outer things and not be able to unearth anything from within ourselves? Is our soul in itself so empty that unless it borrows

53

images from outside it is nothing? I am sure that our judicious author could not approve of such a view. Where could tablets be found which were completely uniform? Will a perfectly homogeneous and even surface ever be seen? So why could we not also provide ourselves with objects of thought from our own depths, if we take the trouble to dig there? Which leads me to believe that fundamentally his view on this question is not different from my own or rather from the common view, especially since he recognizes two sources of our knowledge, the senses and reflection.

I doubt if it will be so easy to make him agree with us and with the *Cartesians when he maintains that the mind does not think all the time, and in particular that it has no perceptions during dreamless sleep, arguing that since bodies can be without movement souls can just as well be without thought. But my response to this is a little different from the usual one. For I maintain that in the natural course of things no substance can lack activity, and indeed that there is never a body without movement. Experience is already on my side, and to be convinced one need only consult the distinguished Mr *Boyle's book attacking absolute rest. But I believe that reason also supports this, and that is one of my proofs that there are no atoms. Besides, there are hundreds of indications leading us to conclude that at every moment there is in us an infinity of perceptions, unaccompanied by *awareness or reflection; that is, of alterations in the soul itself, of which we are unaware because these impressions are either too *minute and too numerous, or else too unvarying, so that they are not sufficiently distinctive on their own. But when they are combined with others they do nevertheless have their effect and make themselves felt, at least confusedly, within the whole. This is how we become so accustomed to the motion of a mill or a waterfall, after living beside it for a while, that we pay no heed to it. Not that this motion ceases to strike on our 54 sense-organs, or that something corresponding to it does not still occur in the soul because of the harmony between the soul and the body; but these impressions in the soul and the body, lacking the appeal of novelty, are not forceful enough to attract our attention and our memory, which are applied only to more compelling objects. Memory is needed for attention: when we are not alerted, so to speak, to pay heed to certain of our own present perceptions, we allow them to slip by unconsidered and even unnoticed. But if someone alerts us to them straight away, and makes us take note, for instance, of some noise which we have just heard, then we remember it and are aware of just having had some sense of it. Thus, we were not straight away aware of these perceptions, and we became aware of them only because we were alerted to them after an interval, however brief. To give a clearer idea of these minute perceptions which we are unable to pick out from the crowd, I like to use the example of the roaring noise of the sea which impresses itself on us when we are standing on the shore. To hear this noise as we do, we must hear the parts which make up this whole, that is the noise of each wave, although each of these little noises makes itself known only when combined confusedly with all the others, and would not be noticed if the wave which made it were by itself. We must be affected slightly by the motion of this wave, and have some perception of each of these noises, however faint they may be; otherwise there would be no perception of a hundred thousand waves, since a hundred thousand nothings cannot make something. Moreover, we never sleep so soundly that we do not have some feeble and confused *sensation; and the loudest noise in the world would never waken us if we did not have some perception of its start, which is small, just as the strongest force in the world would never break a rope unless the least force strained it and stretched it slightly, even though that little lengthening which is produced is imperceptible.

These minute perceptions, then, are more effective in their results than has been recognized. They constitute that *je ne sais quoi*, those flavours, those images of sensible qualities, vivid in the aggregate but confused as to the parts; those impressions which are made on us by the bodies around us and which involve the infinite; that connection that each being has with all the rest of the universe. It can even be said that by virtue of these minute perceptions the present is big with the future and burdened with the past, that all things harmonize – *sympnoia panta*, as *Hippocrates put it – and that eyes as piercing as God's could read in the lowliest substance the universe's whole sequence of events – 'What is, what was, and what will soon be brought in by the future' [Virgil].

These insensible perceptions also indicate and constitute the same individual, who[1] is characterized by the vestiges or expressions which the perceptions preserve from the individual's former states, thereby connecting these with his present state. Even when the individual himself has no sense of the previous states, i.e. no longer has any explicit memory of them, they could be known by a superior mind. But those perceptions also provide the means for recovering this memory at need, as a result of successive improvements which one may eventually undergo. That is why death can only be a sleep, and not a lasting one at that: the perceptions merely cease to be sufficiently distinct; in animals they are reduced to a state of confusion which puts awareness into abeyance but which cannot last for ever; and I shall not here discuss the case of man, who must in this regard have special prerogatives for safeguarding his personhood.

It is also through insensible perceptions that I account for that marvellous *pre-established harmony between the soul and the body, and indeed amongst all the *monads or simple substances, which takes the place of

---

[1] Or 'which', and so throughout the rest of this sentence and the next.

an untenable influence of one on another and, in the opinion of the author of the finest of dictionaries [*Bayle], exalts the greatness of divine perfection beyond anything previously conceived. It would not be adding much to that if I said that it is these minute perceptions which determine our behaviour in many situations without our thinking of them, and which deceive the unsophisticated with an appearance of *indifference of equilibrium* – as if it made no difference to us, for instance, whether we turned left or right. I need not point out here, since I have done so in the work itself [pp. 164–6, 188f], that they cause that disquiet which I show to consist in something which differs from *suffering only as small from large, and yet which frequently causes our desire and even our pleasure, to which it gives a dash of spice. They are also the insensible parts of our sensible perceptions, which bring it about that those perceptions of colours, warmth and other sensible qualities are related to the motions in bodies which correspond to them; whereas the Cartesians (like our author, discerning as he is), regard it as arbitrary what perceptions we have of these qualities, as if God had given them to the soul according to his good pleasure, without concern for any essential relation between perceptions and their objects. This is a view which surprises me and appears unworthy of the wisdom of the author of things, who does nothing without harmony and reason.

In short, insensible perceptions are as important to *pneumatology as insensible corpuscles are to *natural science, and it is just as unreasonable to reject the one as the other on the pretext that they are beyond the reach of our senses. Nothing takes place suddenly, and it is one of my great and best confirmed maxims that *nature never makes leaps*. I called this the Law of Continuity when I discussed it formerly in the *Nouvelles de la république des lettres* ['Letter on a general principle useful in explaining the laws of nature']. There is much work for this law to do in natural science. It implies that any change from small to large, or vice versa, passes through something which is, in respect of degrees as well as of parts, in between; and that no motion ever springs immediately from a state of rest, or passes into one except through a lesser motion; just as one could never traverse a certain line or distance without first traversing a shorter one. Despite which, until now those who have propounded the laws of motion have not complied with this law, since they have believed that a body can instantaneously receive a motion contrary to its preceding one. All of which supports the judgment that noticeable perceptions arise by degrees from ones which are too minute to be noticed. To think otherwise is to be ignorant of the immeasurable fineness of things, which always and everywhere involves an actual infinity.

I have also pointed out that in consequence of imperceptible variations no two individual things could be perfectly alike, and that they must always

56

57

differ more than numerically [e.g. 'On nature itself' pp. 505f]. This puts an end to the blank tablets of the soul, a soul without thought, a substance without action, empty space, atoms, and even to portions of matter which are not actually divided, and also to absolute rest, completely uniform parts of time or place or matter, perfect spheres of the *second element which take their origin from perfect cubes, and hundreds of other fictions which have arisen from the incompleteness of philosophers' notions. They are something which the nature of things does not allow of. They escape challenge because of our ignorance and our neglect of the insensible; but nothing could make them acceptable, short of their being confined to abstractions of the mind, with a formal declaration that the mind is not denying what it sets aside as irrelevant to some present concern. On the other hand if we meant literally that things of which we are unaware exist neither in the soul nor in the body, then we would fail in philosophy as in politics, because we would be neglecting *to mikron*, imperceptible changes. Whereas abstraction is not an error as long as one knows that what one is pretending not to notice, is *there*. This is what mathematicians are doing when they ask us to consider perfect lines and uniform motions and other regular effects, although matter (i.e. the jumble of effects of the surrounding infinity) always provides some exception. This is done so as to separate one circumstance from another and, as far as we can, to trace effects back to their causes and to foresee some of their results; the more care we take not to overlook any circumstance that we can control, the more closely practice corresponds to theory. But only the supreme Reason, who overlooks nothing, can distinctly grasp the entire infinite and see all the causes and all the results. All we can do with infinities is to know them confusedly and at least to know distinctly that they are there. Otherwise we shall not only judge quite wrongly as to the beauty and grandeur of the universe, but will be unable to have a sound natural science which explains the nature of things in general, still less a sound *pneumatology, comprising knowledge of God, souls and simple substances in general.

58   This knowledge of insensible perceptions also explains why and how two souls of the same species, human or otherwise, never leave the hands of the Creator perfectly alike, each of them having its own inherent relationship to the points of view which it will have in the universe. But that follows from what I have already said about two individuals, namely that the difference between them is always more than numerical. There is another significant point on which I must differ, not only from our author, but from most of the moderns: I agree with most of the ancients that every *Spirit, every soul, every created simple substance is always united with a body and that no soul is ever entirely without one. I have *a priori* reasons for this doctrine, but it will be found to have the further merit of solving all the philosophical difficulties about the state of souls, their perpetual pre-

servation, their immortality, and their mode of operation. Their changes of state never are and never were anything but changes from more to less sensible, from more perfect to less perfect, or the reverse, so that their past and future states are just as explicable as their present one. Even the slightest reflection shows that this is reasonable, and that a leap from one state to an infinitely different one cannot be natural. I am surprised that the Schoolmen – unreasonably abandoning nature – deliberately plunged into the greatest difficulties and provided free-thinkers with apparent cause for triumph. The latters' arguments are pulled down all at once by my account of things, in which there is no more difficulty in conceiving the preservation of the soul (or rather, on my view, of the *animal) than in conceiving the transformation of a caterpillar into a butterfly, or the preservation of thought during sleep–to which Jesus Christ has sublimely compared death. I have also said already that no sleep could last for ever; and in the case of rational souls it will be of even briefer duration or almost none at all. These souls are destined always to preserve the *persona*[1] which they have been given in the city of God, and hence to retain their memories, so that they may be more susceptible of punishments and rewards. I further add that in general no disruption of its visible organs can reduce an animal to total confusion, or destroy all the organs and deprive the soul of its entire organic body and of the ineradicable vestiges of its previous traces. But people's readiness to abandon the ancient doctrine of the rarefied bodies annexed to angels (which was confused with the corporeality of the angels themselves), the inclusion among created things of alleged separate intelligences (and notably the ones which in Aristotle's doctrine make the heavens revolve), and lastly the misconception to which some have been subject, that preservation of the souls of beasts would lead one to metempsychosis and to their transmigration from body to body – the perplexity that people have been in through not knowing what they should do about all this has resulted, in my opinion, in their overlooking the natural way to explain the preservation of the soul. This has done great harm to natural religion, and has led some to believe that our immortality is just a miraculous gift from God; even our distinguished author displays some doubt about this, as I shall point out shortly. But I wish that all who are of this opinion would discuss it as wisely and candidly as he does; for I am afraid that some who speak of immortality through grace do so only for the sake of appearances, and are fundamentally not far from those *Averroists and certain wicked *Quietists who imagine that the soul is absorbed into and reunited with the sea of divinity; my system is perhaps the only one which properly shows the impossibility of this notion.

We also seem to disagree about matter: our author thinks that motion requires a vacuum, because he believes that the tiny parts of matter are

[1] '*personnage*'; a standard word for a character in a play, one of the *dramatis personae*.

rigid. I admit that if matter were composed of such parts, motion in a plenum would be impossible – imagine a container full of little pebbles without the least empty space. But this assumption is not granted; and there appears to be no reason for it either, although this gifted author goes so far as to believe that rigidity or the cohesion of its tiny parts constitutes the essence of body. Rather, we should think of space as full of matter which is inherently fluid, capable of every sort of division and indeed actually divided and subdivided to infinity; but with this difference, that how it is divisible and divided varies from place to place, because of variations in the extent to which the movements in it run the same way. That is what brings it about that matter has everywhere some degree of rigidity as well as of fluidity, and that no body is either hard or fluid in the ultimate degree – we find in it no invincibly hard atoms and no mass which is entirely unresistant to division. The order of nature, and in particular the law of continuity, equally pull down both alternatives.

60

I have also shown that *cohesion* which was not itself the result of *impulse or motion would cause *traction* strictly so-called [e.g. 'Confession of nature against atheists' p. 112]. For given an inherently rigid body, e.g. an Epicurean atom, part of which stuck out in the form of a hook (since we can imagine atoms of every kind of shape), then pressure on this hook would draw the rest of the atom with it – that is, would draw the part on which there was no pressure and which did not lie in the line of the impulse. Yet our gifted author is himself opposed to these 'philosophic' tractions, such as those which used to be ascribed to the fear of a vacuum; he reduces them to impulses, maintaining with the moderns that one part of matter operates immediately on another only by pushing against it. I think that they are right about that, since otherwise the process would be unintelligible [*centripetal force].

I must admit noticing, though, that our excellent author somewhat retracts what he has said about this, and I cannot refrain from praising his modesty and candour about it, just as I have admired his great penetration of mind in other matters. His retraction occurs on p. 408 of his reply to the second letter of the late Bishop of Worcester [*Stillingfleet], published in 1699. In defending the view he had upheld against this learned prelate, namely that matter might think, he says among other things: 'It is true, I say (*Essay* II.viii.11), "that bodies operate by impulse, and nothing else." And so I thought when I writ it, and can yet conceive no other way of their operation. But I am since convinced by the judicious Mr. Newton's incomparable book, that it is too bold a presumption to limit God's power [by our]¹ narrow conceptions. The gravitation of matter towards matter, by ways inconceivable to me, is not only a demonstration that God can, if he pleases, put into bodies powers and ways of operation, above what

¹ Locke: 'to limit God's power, in this point, by my'.

can be derived from our idea of body, or can be explained by what we know of matter, but also an unquestionable...instance, that he has done so. And therefore in the next edition of my book, I shall take care to have that passage rectified.' I find that in the French version of this book, undoubtedly made from the most recent editions, §11 reads as follows:[1] It is manifest, at least in so far as we can conceive it, that it is 'by impulse, and nothing else' that 'bodies operate one upon another.... It being impossible to conceive, that body should operate on what it does not touch, (which is all one as to imagine it can operate where it is not)'. 61

I cannot but praise our renowned author's modest piety here, when he acknowledges that God can do what is beyond our understanding and hence that there may be inconceivable mysteries among the articles of faith. But I would not like to be compelled to resort to miracles in the ordinary course of nature, or to admit absolutely inexplicable powers and operations. For, with the aid of 'what God can do', we may give too much leeway to bad philosophy by admitting these 'centripetal powers' and 'immediate attractions' at a distance, without being able to make them intelligible; I do not see what is to prevent our Scholastics from saying that everything simply comes about through 'faculties', and from promoting their 'intentional species' which travel from objects to us and find their way into our souls. If that is acceptable, 'Everything will now happen whose possibility I used to deny' [Ovid]. So it seems to me that our author, judicious as he is, is here going rather too much from one extreme to the other. He is captious about the operations of *souls* when it is merely a matter of admitting what is not *sensible*, and here he is granting to *bodies* what is not even *intelligible*, granting them powers and activities which in my opinion transcend anything that a created mind could do or understand; for he grants attraction to them, even at great distances and without limitation to any sphere of activity, merely so as to uphold a view which is equally inexplicable, namely the possibility of matter thinking in the natural course of events.

The issue between him and the eminent bishop who had attacked him is *whether matter can think*. Since this is an important question, for the present work also, I feel bound to enter into it a little and take cognizance of their debate. I shall present the substance of their disagreement on this topic, and shall take the liberty of saying what I think about it. The late Bishop of Worcester, fearing (in my opinion without much cause) that our author's doctrine of ideas might be open to certain abuses prejudicial to the Christian faith, undertook to examine certain aspects of it in his 62

---

[1] From the third edition of the *Essay*, though mainly Coste worked from the fourth (which was still in preparation at the time). In the third, §11 says nothing about what 'we can conceive'. In the fourth, §11 reads in its entirety: 'The next thing to be considered is how bodies can produce ideas in us, and that is manifestly by impulse, the only way which we can conceive bodies operate in.'

Vindication of the Doctrine of the Trinity. After rightly giving this distinguished writer credit for maintaining that the existence of mind is as certain as that of body, even though the one substance is as little known as the other, he asks (pp. 241 ff) how reflection can assure us of the existence of mind if God can, as our author claims (*Essay* IV.iii), give matter the faculty of thought; since then the way of ideas, which should distinguish what is proper to the soul as opposed to the body, would become useless; whereas it was said in the *Essay* II.xxiii.15, 27, 28 that the operations of the soul provide us with the idea of mind, and that the understanding and the will together make this idea as intelligible to us as solidity and impulse make the nature of body. In his first letter, our author gives the following reply (pp. 65ff): I believe that I have proved that there is a spiritual substance in us, for 'we experiment in ourselves thinking.' This action or mode cannot be the object of the idea of a self-subsistent thing and therefore this mode requires 'a support or subject of inhesion[, and] the idea of that support is what we call substance. . . . The general idea of substance being the same every where,' it follows that when the modification which is called thought or power of thinking is joined to it, that 'makes it a spirit, without considering what other modifications it has, [i.e.][1] whether it has. . .solidity or no. As on the other side, substance, that has the modification [which is called] solidity, is matter, whether it has' thought or not. But if by spiritual substance you mean 'an immaterial substance, I grant I have not proved, nor upon my principles can it be proved' demonstratively that there is such within us. But what I have said about the systems of matter (*Essay* IV.x.16) in demonstrating that God is immaterial makes it 'in the highest degree probable, that the thinking substance in us is immaterial.' . . . However, I have shown (the author adds on p. 68) that 'the great ends of religion and morality are secured. . .by the immortality of the soul, without a necessary supposition that the soul is immaterial'.

63

The learned Bishop, in his answer to this letter, in order to show that our author held a different view when he wrote the second book of the *Essay*, quotes (p. 51) the following passage from it: 'By the simple ideas we have taken from those operations of our own minds. . .we are able to frame the complex idea of [a][2] spirit. And. . .by putting together the ideas of thinking, perceiving, liberty, and power of moving [our body], we have as clear a. . .notion of immaterial substances, as we have of material.' (*Essay* II.xxiii.15) He adduces still other passages to show that the author contrasted mind [*spirit] with body. He says (p. 54) that the end of religion and morality is better secured by proving that the soul is by its nature immortal, that is, immaterial. He also quotes (p. 70) this passage: That 'all the ideas we have of particular distinct sorts of substances, are nothing but several combinations of simple ideas' (*Essay* II.xxiii.6); which he says

---

[1] Locke: 'as', meaning 'e.g.'.   [2] Locke: 'an immaterial'.

indicates that the author believed that the ideas of thinking and willing gave a different substance from that given by the ideas of solidity and impulse. And he says that in §17 the author remarks that the latter ideas constitute body as opposed to mind.

The Bishop of Worcester could have added that even if the *general idea* of substance is present in both body and mind, it does not follow, as our author asserts in the part of his first letter which I have presented, that their *differentiae* are modifications of a single thing. Modifications must be distinguished from attributes. The faculties for having perception and for acting, together with extension and solidity, are attributes, i.e. permanent main predicates; whereas thought, impetus, shape, and motion are modifications of these attributes. Furthermore one should distinguish between ***physical** (or rather real) genus and *logical* (or ideal) genus. Things which are of the same physical genus, or which are 'homogeneous', are so to speak of the same *matter* and can often be transformed from one into the other by changing their modifications – circles and squares for instance. But two heterogeneous things can belong to a common logical genus, and then their *differentiae* do not consist in mere accidental modifications of a single subject or of a single metaphysical or physical matter. For instance, time and space are very heterogeneous things, and it would be a mistake to think that they have resulted from modifications of who knows what real common subject, characterized only by continuous quantity in general. Yet their common logical genus is continuous quantity. Perhaps people will laugh at these philosophers' distinctions: two genera, one merely logical, the other real as well; and two matters, one physical (which is that of bodies), the other merely metaphysical or general – as if someone were to say that two parts of space have a single matter, or that two hours share a single matter. Yet these are not merely distinctions among terms but among things themselves, and they seem very apposite here, where confusing them has led to a false conclusion. These two genera share a common notion, and the notion of real genus is common to both matters; so that their genealogy will be like this:

64

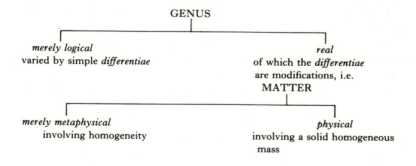

I have not seen the author's second letter to the Bishop, and the prelate's reply to it hardly mentions the topic of thinking matter. But our author's reply to this second response returns to this topic. What he says, in nearly these words,[1] is this (p. 397): God adds to the essence of matter what qualities and perfections he pleases: to some parts simple motions alone, but to plants vegetation and to animals sense. Those who agree to this much immediately protest when we go one step further and say that God can give thought, reason and volition to matter, as though that destroyed the essence of matter. To prove this they urge that thought and reason are not included in the essence of matter; but that proves nothing, since motion and life are not included in it either. They also urge that we cannot conceive that matter can think; but our conception is not the measure of God's power. He then cites the example of the attraction of matter on p. 399, and especially on p. 408 where he speaks of the gravitation of matter to matter, 65 attributed to Mr Newton, in the words which I have quoted above, acknowledging that we will never be able to understand how it comes about. This amounts to a return to qualities which are occult and, what is more, inexplicable. He adds (p. 401) that nothing is more likely to favour the sceptics than denying what we do not understand, and (p. 402) that we do not even conceive how the soul thinks. He maintains (p. 403) that, since the two substances, material and immaterial, can be conceived in their bare essence, devoid of all activity, it is at God's discretion to bestow the power of thought on one or the other. And he tries to take advantage of a confession by his adversary, who had conceded sense to the beasts while not allowing them any immaterial substance. He claims that liberty and self-consciousness (p. 408) and the power of abstracting (p. 409) can be given to matter, not as matter but as enriched by divine power. Finally he repeats (p. 434) the remark – made by no less eminent and judicious a travel-ler than M. de *La Loubère – that the pagans of the East know the immor-tality of the soul even though they cannot understand its immateriality.

I shall comment on all of this before expounding my own views. Certainly, as our author agrees, matter cannot mechanically produce sense, any more than it can reason. I acknowledge that we must not deny what we do not understand, but I add that we are entitled to deny (within the natural order at least) whatever is absolutely unintelligible and inexplicable. I also maintain that substances (material or immaterial) cannot be conceived in their bare essence, devoid of activity; that activity is of the essence of substance in general; and, finally, that although what creatures conceive is not the measure of God's powers, their 'conceptivity' or power of conceiving is the measure of nature's powers: everything which is in accord with the natural order can be conceived or understood by some creature. Those who come to understand my system will realize that I cannot

---

[1] What follows is a compressed but accurate version of Locke's argument.

entirely agree with either of these excellent authors, although their dispute is very instructive. But to explain myself distinctly: it must be borne in mind above all that the modifications which can occur to a single subject naturally and without miracles must arise from limitations and variations of a real genus, i.e. of a constant and absolute inherent nature. For that is how philosophers distinguish the modes of an absolute being from that being itself; just as we know that size, shape and motion are obviously limitations and variations of corporeal nature (for it is plain how a limited extension yields shapes, and that changes occurring in it are nothing but motion). Whenever we find some quality in a subject, we ought to believe that if we understood the nature of both the subject and the quality we would conceive how the quality could arise from it. So within the order of nature (miracles apart) it is not at God's arbitrary discretion to attach this or that quality haphazardly to substances. He will never give them any which are not natural to them, that is, which cannot arise from their nature as explicable modifications. So we may take it that matter will not naturally possess the attractive power referred to above, and that it will not of itself move in a curved path, because it is impossible to conceive how this could happen – that is, to explain it mechanically – whereas what is natural must be such as could become distinctly conceivable by anyone admitted into the secrets of things. This distinction between what is natural and explicable and what is miraculous and inexplicable removes all the difficulties. To reject it would be to uphold something worse than occult qualities, and thereby to renounce philosophy and reason, giving refuge to ignorance and laziness by means of an irrational system which maintains not only that there are qualities which we do not understand – of which there are only too many – but further that there are some which could not be comprehended by the greatest intellect if God gave it every possible opportunity, i.e. [qualities] which are either miraculous or without rhyme or reason. And indeed it would be without rhyme or reason for God to perform miracles in the ordinary course of events. So this idle hypothesis would destroy not only our philosophy which seeks reasons but also the divine wisdom which provides them.

As for thought, it is certain, as our author more than once acknowledges, that it cannot be an intelligible modification of matter and be comprehensible and explicable in terms of it. That is, a sentient or thinking being is not a mechanical thing like a watch or a *mill: one cannot conceive of sizes and shapes and motions combining mechanically to produce something which thinks, and senses too, in a mass where [formerly] there was nothing of the kind – something which would likewise be extinguished by the machine's going out of order. So sense and thought are not something which is natural to matter, and there are only two ways in which they could occur in it: through God's combining it with a substance to which thought is natural, or through his putting thought into it by a miracle. On this topic I am therefore entirely in agreement with the Cartesians, except that I include the beasts and believe that they too have sense, and souls which are properly described as immaterial and are as imperishable as atoms are according to Democritus and *Gassendi; whereas the Cartesians have been needlessly perplexed over the souls of beasts. Not knowing what to do about them if they are preserved (since they have failed to hit on the idea of the preservation of the animal in miniature), they have been driven to deny – contrary to all appearances and to the general opinion of mankind – that beasts even have sense. But if someone said that God could at least join the faculty of thought to a machine which was made ready [for it], I should reply that if that were done, and if God added this faculty to matter without at the same time infusing into it a substance in which this same faculty inhered (which is how I conceive it) – i.e. without joining an immaterial soul to it – the matter would have had to be miraculously exalted in order to receive a power of which it is not naturally capable. Similarly some Scholastics claim that God exalts fire to the point where it is able, without any intermediary, to burn spirits separated from bodies, which would be a sheer miracle. Suffice it to say that we cannot maintain that matter thinks unless we put into it either an imperishable soul or a miracle; and thus that the immortality of our souls follows from what is natural, since we can only maintain their extinction by means of a miracle, whether through the exaltation of matter or through the annihilation of the soul. For we know very well that although our souls are immaterial and, in the ordinary course of nature, immortal, God's omnipotence could make them mortal since he can annihilate them.

68   Now, there is no doubt that this truth about the immateriality of the soul is important. For in our day especially, when many people have scant respect for pure revelation and miracles, it is infinitely more useful to religion and morality to show that souls are naturally immortal, and that it would be miraculous if they were not, than to maintain that it is of their nature to die but that, thanks to a miraculous grace resting solely on God's promise, they will not die. It has long been known that those who have sought to destroy natural religion and reduce everything to revelation, as if reason had nothing to teach us in this area, have been under suspicion, and not always without reason. But our author is not one of these; he upholds the demonstration of the existence of God and he accords the immateriality of the soul a 'probability in the highest degree', which can therefore be regarded as a *moral certainty*. Therefore, since his sincerity is as great as his insight, I should think he could thoroughly accommodate himself to the doctrine which I have just set forth and which is fundamental in any rational philosophy. Otherwise I do not see how one could keep from relapsing into philosophy which is either fanatical, like *Fludd's *Mosaicall*

Philosophy which saves all the phenomena by ascribing them immediately and miraculously to God, or barbarous, like that of certain philosophers and physicians of the past, who still reflected the barbarism of their own times and are today rightly scorned; these saved the appearances by fabricating faculties or occult qualities, just for the purpose, and fancying them to be like little demons or imps which can without ado perform whatever is wanted, as though pocket watches told the time by a certain horological faculty without needing wheels, or as though mills crushed grain by a fractive faculty without needing anything in the way of millstones. As for the difficulty which some nations have had in conceiving an immaterial substance: this will simply disappear (in large part at least) when it stops being a question of substance separated from matter; and indeed I do not believe that such substances ever occur naturally among created things. There are still other subjects on which the author of the *Essay* and I agree and disagree, such as infinity and freedom.

BOOK I
'OF INNATE NOTIONS'

Chapter i[1]
Whether there are innate principles in the mind of man.[2]

PHILALETHES. When I re-crossed the Channel after finishing my business in England, my first thought was of visiting you, sir, to renew our old friendship and also to discuss some things which are important to us both and about which I think I have gained new insights during my stay in London. When we were neighbours in Amsterdam, we used to enjoy exploring first principles, and ways of searching into the inner natures of things; and although we often differed in our views, this added to the pleasure of our discussions, because there was nothing unpleasant in our occasional conflicts. You sided with *Descartes, and with the opinions of the famous author of the *Search after Truth* [*Malebranche]; and I found the views of *Gassendi, as expounded by M. Bernier, more plausible and natural. I now feel that I am put in a much stronger position by the fine work which a distinguished Englishman whom I have the honour to know personally has since published – a book which has had several reprintings in England under the modest title *Essay Concerning Human Understanding*. Happily, it was recently published in Latin and in French, so that it can be even more widely useful. I have profited greatly from reading this book, and indeed from conversation with its author, with whom I talked often in London and sometimes at Oates, the home of Lady *Masham. She is a daughter worthy of her father, Mr Cudworth, the great English philosopher and theologian and author of the *Intellectual System*; and she has inherited his reflective temper and love of fine knowledge, as is shown especially in the friendship she maintains with the author of the *Essay*. When he was attacked by several worthy scholars, I enjoyed reading a defence of him by a judicious and insightful young lady [*Trotter] as well as the defences he wrote himself. This author is pretty much in agreement with M. Gassendi's system, which is fundamentally that of Democritus: he supports vacuum and atoms, he believes that matter could think, that

---

[1] In Book I, each chapter number is one lower than the number of the corresponding chapter in any English edition of the *Essay*. Coste rendered Locke's Chapter i as an unnumbered 'Introduction'.

[2] Locke: 'No innate principles in the mind.'

there are no innate ideas, that our mind is a *tabula rasa*, and that we do not think all the time; and he seems inclined to agree with most of M. Gassendi's objections against M. Descartes. He has enriched and strengthened this system with hundreds of fine thoughts; and I am sure that our side will now overwhelm their opponents, the *Peripatetics and the Cartesians. So if you have not already read the book, please do; and if you have read it, I beg you to tell me what you think of it.

THEOPHILUS. I am glad to see you back after all this time, with your   71 important business satisfactorily concluded, your health good, your friendship towards me unchanged, and still prompted by the same eagerness for inquiry into the most important truths. I have also carried on with my meditations, in the same spirit; and I believe that I have profited too, as much as you and perhaps more, if I am not mistaken. But then I needed to, because you were further ahead. You had more to do with the speculative philosophers, while I was more inclined towards moral questions. But I have been learning, more and more, how greatly morality can be strengthened by the solid principles of true philosophy; which is why I have lately been studying them more intensively, and have started on some quite new trains of thought. So we have all we need to give each other a long period of mutual pleasure by explaining our positions to one another. But I should tell you the news that I am no longer a Cartesian, and yet have moved further than ever from your Gassendi, learned and worthy though I acknowledge him to be. I have been impressed by a new system, of which I have read something in the learned *journals of Paris, Leipzig and Holland, and in M. *Bayle's marvellous *Dictionary*, in the article entitled 'Rorarius'; and now I think I see a new aspect of the inner nature of things. This system appears to unite Plato with Democritus, Aristotle with Descartes, the Scholastics with the moderns, theology and morality with reason. Apparently it takes the best from all systems and then advances further than anyone has yet done. I find in it something I had hitherto despaired of – an intelligible explanation of the union of body and soul. I find the true principles of things in the substantial unities which this system introduces, and in their harmony which was *pre-established by the *primary substance. I find in it an astounding simplicity and uniformity, such that everything can be said to be the same at all times and places except in degrees of perfection. I now see what Plato had in mind when he took matter to be an imperfect and transitory being; what Aristotle meant by his *'entelechy'; in what sense even Democritus could promise another life, as Pliny says he did; how far the sceptics were right in decrying the senses; why Descartes thinks that animals are   72 automata, and why they nevertheless have souls and sense, just as mankind thinks they do. How to make sense of those who put life and perception into everything – e.g. of Cardano, Campanella, and (better than them) of the late Platonist Countess of *Conway, and our friend the late M. Franciscus Mercurius van *Helmont (though otherwise full of meaningless paradoxes) together with his friend the late Mr Henry *More. How the laws of nature – many of which were not known until this system was developed – derive from principles higher than matter, although in the material realm everything does happen mechanically. The spiritualizing authors I have just mentioned went wrong about that with their *'archei', and so did even the Cartesians, by believing that immaterial substances at least change the direction or determination, if not the force, of the motions of bodies. Whereas according to the new system the soul and the body each perfectly observes its own laws, and nevertheless they obey one another as much as they should. Finally, since thinking about this system I have discovered why the immortality of human souls is not damaged by the fact that the beasts have souls and sensations; or, rather, why the best possible basis for our natural immortality is the view that all souls are immortal ('souls are exempt from death' [Ovid]), and that this need not create fears about metempsychosis, for it is not merely souls but animals which live, sense and act, and will continue to do so; everywhere it is just as it is here – always and everywhere as it is with us – as follows from what I have already told you. The only difference is that the states of animals are more or less perfect and developed, with never any need for completely separated souls; whereas we have spirits which are as pure as may be, despite our bodily organs, since these could not interfere in the slightest with the laws of our spontaneity. What excludes vacuum and atoms, I find, is something entirely different from the faulty Cartesian argument founded on the alleged coincidence of the idea of body with that of extension. I see everything to be regular and rich beyond what anyone has previously conceived; with matter everywhere organic – nothing empty, sterile, idle –

73   nothing too uniform, everything varied but orderly; and, what surpasses the imagination, with the entire universe being epitomized, though always from a different point of view, in each of its parts and even in each of its substantial unities. Besides this new *analysis of things, I have understood better the analysis of notions or ideas, and of truths. I understand what it is for an idea to be true, vivid [*claire], distinct and – if I may adopt this term – adequate. I understand which are the *primary truths and the true axioms; and how to distinguish necessary truths from truths of fact, and human reasoning from its shadow – the thought-sequences of beasts. Well, sir, you will be surprised at all I have to tell you, especially when you grasp how much it elevates our knowledge of the greatness and perfection of God. I have always been open with you, and I cannot hide how possessed I now am by admiration and (if we may venture to use the word) by love of this sovereign source of things and of beauties, since I have

found that those which are revealed by the new system surpass everything that has hitherto been conceived. You know that I once strayed a little too far in another direction, and began to incline to the *Spinozist view which allows God infinite power only, not granting him either perfection or wisdom, and which dismisses the search for final causes and explains everything through brute necessity. But these new insights cured me of that; and since then I have sometimes taken the name Theophilus. I have read the famous Englishman's book of which you have just spoken. I think very well of it, and have found fine things in it. But it seems to me that we should go deeper, and that we should even part company from his opinions when he adopts ones which limit us unduly, and somewhat lower not only the condition of man but also that of the universe.

PHIL. I am indeed astonished by your list of wonders, though your account is somewhat too favourable to be accepted easily. Still, I am ready to hope there will be something solid among all these novelties you wish to spread before me; and if there is, you will find me very teachable. You know that I have always been disposed to yield to reason, and that I have sometimes used the name Philalethes. So let us now use these two very suitable names. We have a way of coming to grips: since you have read the famous Englishman's book which I find so satisfying, and since it deals with a large proportion of the topics you have just mentioned, and especially with the analysis of our ideas and our knowledge, the simplest procedure will be to follow the thread of the book and see what you have to say about it.

THEO. I agree to your proposal. Here is the book.

PHIL. I have read the book so carefully that I can recall its very words,   74
which I shall be careful to follow. Thus, I shall not need to consult it except in certain cases where we think it necessary. We shall discuss first the origin of ideas or notions (Book I), then the different sorts of ideas (Book II) and the words which serve to express them (Book III), and then finally the knowledge and truths which result from them (Book IV). That last part will take the most time.

   As for the origin of ideas, I share the belief of this author and many able people that there are no innate ideas, nor any innate principles either. §1. And to refute the error of those who do allow them, it would be sufficient to show that – as will emerge later on – there is no need for them, and that men 'may attain to all the knowledge they have, without the help of any innate impressions'.

THEO. You know, Philalethes, that I have long held a different view: that I always did and still do accept the innate idea of God, which M. Descartes upheld, and thus accept other innate ideas which could not come to us from the senses. Now the new system takes me even further; and – as you will see later on – I believe indeed that all the thoughts and actions of our soul come from its own depths and could not be given to it by the senses. But in the meantime I shall set aside the inquiry into that, and shall conform to accepted ways of speaking, since they are indeed sound and justifiable, and the outer senses can be said to be, in a certain sense, partial causes of our thoughts. I shall thus work within the common framework, speaking of the action of the body on the soul, in the way that the Copernicans quite justifiably join other men in talking about the movement of the sun; and I shall look into why, even within this framework, one should in my opinion say that there are ideas and principles which do not reach us through the senses, and which we find in ourselves without having formed them, though the senses bring them to our awareness. I suppose that your able author has been made hostile to the doctrine of innate principles because he has noticed that people often maintain their prejudices under the name of innate principles, wanting to excuse themselves from the trouble of discussing them. He will have wanted to fight the laziness and the shallowness of thought of those who use the specious pretext of innate ideas and truths, naturally engraved on the mind and readily assented to, to avoid serious inquiry into where our *items of knowledge come from, how they are connected, and what certainty they have. I am entirely on his side about that, and I would go even further. I would like no limits to be set to our analysis, definitions to be given of all terms which admit of them, and demonstrations – or the means for them – to be provided for all axioms which are not primary, without reference to men's opinions about them and without caring whether they agree to them or not. This would be more useful than might be thought. But it seems that our author's zeal, highly praiseworthy though it is, has carried him too far in another direction. In my opinion he has not adequately distinguished the origin of necessary truths, whose source is in the understanding, from that of truths of fact, which are drawn from sense-experience and even from confused perceptions within us. So you see, sir, that I do not accept what you lay down as a fact, namely that we can acquire all our knowledge without the need of innate impressions. We shall see which of us is right.

PHIL. We shall indeed. I grant you, my dear Theophilus, that §2. 'there is nothing more commonly taken for granted, than that there are certain principles...universally agreed upon by all mankind', which are therefore called common notions, *koinai ennoiai*;[1] 'which therefore they argue, must needs be...impressions, which the [minds] of men receive in their first beings'. §3. But if it were certain that there are principles[2] 'wherein all mankind agreed, it would not prove them innate, if there can be any other way shewn, how men may come to that universal agreement...; which I

---

[1] Added by Leibniz.
[2] Locke: 'if it were true in matter of fact, that there were certain truths'. The change from 'true...' to 'certain' is Coste's.

presume may be done.' **§4.** But, what is worse, this universal agreement is hardly to be found, not even with regard to those two famous speculative principles (we shall come to practical principles later) that *Whatever is, is*; and that *It is impossible for something to be and not be at the same time*. For although you will doubtless take these two propositions to be necessary truths, and to be axioms, to a great part of mankind they are not even known.

THEO. I do not rest the certainty of innate principles on universal consent; for I have already told you, Philalethes, that I think one should work to find ways of proving all axioms except primary ones. I grant you also that a very general but not universal agreement could come from a transmission diffused throughout the whole of mankind; the practice of smoking tobacco has been adopted by nearly all nations in less than a century, though some island races have been found who are not even acquainted with fire and thus are far from being smokers. Some able people – even some theologians, though only *Arminians – have believed knowledge of the Divinity came in that way from a very old and very widespread trans- 76 mission; and I am willing to believe that such knowledge has indeed been confirmed and amended by teaching. But it appears that nature has helped to bring men to it without doctrine: the wonders of the universe have made them think of a higher power. A child deaf and dumb from birth has been seen to worship the full moon. And nations have been found which fear invisible powers, though they seem not to have learned anything else from any other societies. I grant you, my dear Philalethes, that this is not yet the idea of God which we have and require; but that idea too is in the depth of our souls, without being put there, as we shall see. And some of God's eternal laws are engraved there in an even more legible way, through a kind of instinct. But these are practical principles, which we shall have occasion to speak about later. You must admit, though, that the inclination we have to recognize the idea of God is part of our human nature. Even if the first teaching of it were attributed to revelation, still men's receptiveness to this doctrine comes from the nature of their souls. But we shall decide later that the teaching from outside merely brings to life what was already in us. I conclude that a principle's being rather generally accepted among men is a sign, not a demonstration, that it is innate; and that the way for these principles to be rigorously and conclusively *proved is by its being shown that their certainty comes only from what is within us. As for your point that there is not universal approval of the two great speculative principles which are the best established of all: I can reply that even if they were not known they would still be innate, because they are accepted as soon as they have been heard. But I shall further add that fundamentally everyone does know them; that we use the principle of contradiction (for instance) all the time, without paying distinct attention to it; and that the conduct of a liar who contradicts himself will be upsetting to anyone, however uncivilized, if the matter is one which he takes seriously. Thus, we use these maxims without having them explicitly in mind. It is rather like the way in which one has potentially in mind the suppressed premisses in *enthymemes, which are omitted in our thinking of the argument as well as in our outward expression of it.

PHIL. I am surprised by what you say about potential knowledge and about these inner suppressions. §5. For it seems 'to me near a contradiction, to say, that there are truths imprinted on the soul, which it perceives...[1] not'.

THEO. If you have that prejudice, I am not surprised that you reject innate knowledge. But I am surprised that it has not occurred to you that we know an infinity of things which we are not *aware of all the time, even when we need them; it is the function of memory to store them, and of recollection to put them before us again, which it does often – but not always – when there is need for it to do so. Well might this be called *souvenir* (*subvenire*),[2] for recollection needs some assistance [*mnemonics]. Something must make us revive one rather than another of the multitude of items of knowledge, since it is impossible to think distinctly, all at once, about everything we know.

PHIL. I believe you are right about that. And my too general assertion that *we are always aware of*[3] *all the truths that are in our soul* is one which I let slip without having thought enough about it. But you will not find it quite so easy to deal with the point I am about to put to you. It is that if one can maintain the innateness of any particular proposition, then one will be able to maintain by the same reasoning that all propositions which are reasonable,[4] and which the mind will ever be able to regard as such, are already imprinted on the soul.

THEO. I grant you the point, as applied to pure ideas, which I contrast with images of sense, and as applied to necessary truths or truths of reason, which I contrast with truths of fact. On this view, the whole of arithmetic and of geometry should be regarded as innate, and contained within us in a potential way, so that we can find them within ourselves by attending carefully and methodically to what is already in our minds, without employing any truth learned through experience or through being handed on by other people. Plato showed this, in a dialogue where he had Socrates leading a child to abstruse truths just by asking questions and without

77

---

[1] Locke: 'or understands'. Coste's omission.

[2] Here a French word meaning 'come to mind' or 'remember' is followed by a cognate Latin word meaning 'come to the assistance of'.

[3] '*nous nous apercevons de*'; but Locke and Philalethes have spoken only of what '*nous apercevons*', what we perceive.

[4] Locke: 'true'.

teaching him anything [*Meno* 82^b]. So one could construct these sciences in one's study and even with one's eyes closed, without learning from sight or even from touch any of the needed truths; although it is true that if one had never seen or touched anything, one would not bring to mind the relevant ideas. For it is an admirable arrangement on the part of nature that we cannot have abstract thoughts which have no need of something sensible, even if it be merely symbols such as the shapes of letters, or sounds; though there is no necessary connection between such arbitrary *symbols and such thoughts. If sensible traces were not required, the *pre-established harmony between body and soul, which I shall later have an opportunity to talk to you about more fully, would not obtain. But that does not preclude the mind's obtaining necessary truths from within itself. It is sometimes evident how far it can go through a purely natural logic and arithmetic, with no help: for instance, the Swedish boy who – if I remember rightly what I was told about the case – has developed his natural arithmetic to the point where he can do complex calculations on the spot, in his head, without having learned the standard methods of calculation nor even to read and write. It is true that he cannot solve inverse problems, such as ones which require the finding of roots. But that does not preclude there being some further trick of the mind by which he could have found even those solutions within himself; so it proves only that, of the things which are in us, some are harder to become aware of than others. Some innate principles are common property, and come easily to everyone. Some theorems are also discovered straight away; these constitute natural *sciences, which are more extensive in some people than in others. Finally, in a larger sense, which is a good one to use if one is to have notions which are more comprehensive and determinate, any truths which are derivable from primary innate knowledge may also be called innate, because the mind can draw them from its own depths, though often only with difficulty. But if someone uses the terms differently, I would not argue about words.

PHIL. I have conceded that there could be something in the soul which one did not perceive there; for one does not at any given moment remember everything one knows. But whatever is known must have been learned, and must at some earlier stage have been explicitly known. So 'if any one can be said to be in the mind, which it never yet knew, it must be only because' it has the capacity or faculty for knowing it.[1]

THEO. Why couldn't it be because of something different, such as that the soul can contain things without one's being aware of them? Since an item of acquired knowledge can be hidden there by the memory, as you admit that it can, why could not nature also hide there an item of unacquired

---

[1] Locke: 'it is capable of knowing it'. Coste's change.

knowledge? Must a self-knowing substance have, straight away, actual knowledge of everything which belongs to its nature? Cannot – and should not – a substance like our soul have various properties and states which could not all be thought about straight away or all at once? The Platonists thought that all our knowledge is recollection, and thus that the truths which the soul brought with it when the man was born – the ones called innate – must be the remains of an earlier explicit knowledge. But there is no foundation for this opinion; and it is obvious that if there was an earlier state, however far back, it too must have involved some innate knowledge, just as our present state does: such knowledge must then either have come from a still earlier state or else have been innate or at least created with [the soul]; or else we must go to infinity and make souls eternal, in which case these items of knowledge would indeed be innate, because they would never have begun in the soul. If anyone claimed that each previous state took something from a still earlier state which it did not pass on to its successors, the reply is that obviously some self-evident truths must have been present in all of these states. On any view of the matter, it is always manifest in every state of the soul that necessary truths are innate, and that they are proved by what lies within, and cannot be established by experience as truths of fact are. Why could one not have in the soul something which one had never used? Is having something which you do not use the same as merely having the faculty for acquiring it? If that were so, our only possessions would be the things we make use of. Whereas in fact it is known that for a faculty to be brought to bear upon an object there must often be not merely the faculty and the object, but also some disposition in the faculty or in the object, or in both.[1]

PHIL. On that view of the matter, one will be able to say that there are truths engraved in the soul[2] which it has never known, and even ones which it will never know; and that appears strange to me.

THEO. I see no absurdity in that – though one cannot say confidently that there are such truths. For things which are higher than any we can know in our present course of life may unfold in our souls some day when they are in a different state.

PHIL. But suppose that 'truths can be imprinted on the understanding without being perceived' by it: I do not see how they can differ, so far as their origin is concerned, from ones which the understanding is merely capable of coming to know.

THEO. The mind is capable not merely of knowing them, but also of finding them within itself. If all it had was the mere capacity to receive those items of knowledge – a passive power to do so, as indeterminate as the power

[1] Taking '*et dans toutes les deux*' to be a slip for '*ou dans tous les deux*'.
[1] Locke: 'imprinted on the mind'. Coste's change.

of wax to receive shapes or of a blank page to receive words – it would not be the source of necessary truths, as I have just shown that it is. For it cannot be denied that the senses are inadequate to show their necessity, and that therefore the mind has a disposition (as much active as passive) to draw them from its own depths; though the senses are necessary to give the mind the opportunity and the attention for this, and to direct it towards certain necessary truths rather than others. So you see, sir, that these people who hold a different view, able though they are, have apparently failed to think through the implications of the distinction between necessary or eternal truths and truths of experience. I said this before, and our entire debate confirms it. The fundamental proof of necessary truths comes from the understanding alone, and other truths come from experience or from observations of the senses. Our mind is capable of knowing truths of both sorts, but it is the source of the former; and however often one experienced instances of a universal truth, one could never know inductively that it would always hold unless one knew through reason that it was necessary. 80

PHIL. But if the words 'to be in the understanding' have any positive content, do they not signify *to be perceived and comprehended by the understanding*?[1]

THEO. They signify something quite different to us. It suffices that what is 'in the understanding' can be found there, and that the sources or fundamental proofs of the truths we are discussing are only 'in the understanding'. The senses can hint at, justify and confirm these truths, but can never demonstrate their infallible and perpetual certainty.

PHIL. §11. However, all 'those who will take the pains to reflect with a little attention on the operations of the understanding, will find, that this ready assent of the mind to some truths, depends' on the faculty of the human mind.[2]

THEO. Yes indeed. But what makes the exercise of the faculty easy and natural so far as these truths are concerned is a special affinity which the human mind has with them; and that is what makes us call them innate. So it is not a bare faculty, consisting in a mere possibility of understanding those truths: it is rather a disposition, an aptitude, a preformation, which determines our soul and brings it about that they are derivable from it. Just as there is a difference between the shapes which are arbitrarily given to a stone or piece of marble, and those which its veins already indicate or are disposed to indicate if the sculptor avails himself of them.

PHIL. But truths are subsequent to the ideas from which they arise, are they not? And ideas all come from the senses.[3] 81

---

[1] Locke: 'If [they] have any propriety, they signify to be understood.' Coste's change.

[2] Locke: 'depends not, either on native inscription, or the use of reason; but on a faculty of the mind quite distinct from both of them'.

[3] Added by Leibniz, perhaps based on Locke's §§15–16.

THEO. Intellectual ideas, from which necessary truths arise, do not come from the senses; and you acknowledge that some ideas arise from the mind's reflection when it turns in on itself. Now, it is true that explicit knowledge of truths is subsequent (in temporal or natural order) to the explicit knowledge of ideas; as the nature of truths depends upon the nature of ideas, before either are explicitly formed, and truths involving ideas which come from the senses are themselves at least partly dependent on the senses. But the ideas that come from the senses are confused; and so too, at least in part, are the truths which depend on them; whereas intellectual ideas, and the truths depending on them, are distinct, and neither [the ideas nor the truths] originate in the senses; though it is true that without the senses we would never think of them.

PHIL. But according to you, the ideas of numbers are intellectual ones; and yet the difficulties about numbers arise from the difficulty of explicitly forming the requisite ideas. §16. For example, 'a man knows that eighteen and nineteen, are equal to thirty-seven, by the same self-evidence, that he knows one and two to be equal to three: yet, a child knows this, not so soon as the other;...because the ideas the words eighteen, nineteen, and thirty-seven stand for, are not so soon got, as those, which are signified by one, two, and three.'

THEO. I can grant you that the difficulty about explicitly forming truths often arises from a difficulty about explicitly forming ideas. I think that in your example, however, it is rather a matter of using ideas which have already been formed. For anyone who has learned to count to 10, and the procedure for going on from there by a certain repetition of tens, easily grasps what 18, 19 and 37 are, namely one or two or three times 10, plus 8 or 9 or 7. But to infer from this that 18 plus 19 make 37, requires more attention than is needed to know that 2 plus 1 are three, which really amounts only to a definition of *three*.

PHIL. §18. It is not 'the prerogative of numbers alone', or of the ideas which you call intellectual, to 'afford propositions, which are sure to meet with assent, as soon as they are understood.' They are encountered also in 'natural philosophy, and all the other sciences', and even the senses provide some.[1] For example, the proposition 'that two bodies cannot be in the same place [at the same time],[2] is a truth, that no body any more sticks at, than at this maxim, That it is impossible for the same thing to be, and not to be [at the same time]; That white is not [red], That a square is not a circle, That yellowness is not sweetness'.

82

---

[1] Added by Leibniz.
[2] Whenever 'at the same time' occurs in parentheses, the addition is Coste's. Future occurrences will not be noted.

THEO. There is a difference between these propositions. The first of them, which claims that bodies cannot interpenetrate, needs proof. Indeed, it is rejected by all those who believe in condensation and rarefaction, strictly and properly so-called, such as the Peripatetics and the late Sir Kenelm Digby; not to mention Christians, most of whom think that the opposite – namely the *penetration of dimensions – is possible for God. But the other propositions are *identities*, or nearly so; and identical or immediate propositions do not admit of proof. The ones pertaining to what the senses provide, such as that 'yellowness is not sweetness', merely apply the general maxim of identity to particular cases.

PHIL. 'Every proposition, wherein one different idea is denied of another,' e.g. that the square is not a circle, and that to be yellow is not to be sweet, will just as certainly be accepted as indubitable[1] 'at first...understanding the terms, as this general one, *It is impossible for the same to be, and not to be [at the same time]*'.

THEO. That is because one (namely the general maxim) is the principle, while the other (namely the negation of an idea by an opposed idea) is the application of it.

PHIL. It seems to me rather that the maxim rests on that negation, 'which is the foundation of it', and that it is even easier to grasp that '*The same is not different*' than to grasp the maxim which rejects contradictions. By your account, then, we shall have to admit as innate truths an infinite number of propositions of this kind, in which one idea is denied of another, not to mention other truths. Furthermore, 'since no proposition can be innate, unless the ideas [which make it up][2] be innate, this will be, to suppose all our ideas of colours, sounds, tastes, figures, etc. innate'.

THEO. I cannot really see how the proposition *The same is not different* is the origin of the principle of contradiction, and 'easier' than it: for it appears to me that one goes further in asserting that A is not B than in saying that A is not non-A; and it is *because* B contains non-A that A is prevented from being B. Furthermore, the proposition that *The sweet is not the bitter* is not 'innate' in the sense we have given to the term 'innate truth'; for the *sensations of sweet and bitter come from the outer senses, so that the proposition is a mixed conclusion (*hybrida conclusio*), in which the axiom is applied to a sensible truth. But as for the proposition *The square is not a circle*: it might be called innate, for in thinking it one applies the principle of contradiction to materials which the understanding itself provides, as soon as one becomes aware that these ideas – which are innate – contain incompatible notions.

83

---

[1] Locke: 'as certainly find assent'. Coste's change.
[2] Locke: 'ideas, about which it is'. Coste's change.

PHIL. §19. When you maintain 'that those...particular self-evident propositions, which are assented to at first hearing, as...that green is not red,...are received as the consequences of those more universal propositions, which are looked on as innate principles', you seem to overlook the fact, sir, that these particular propositions are accepted as indubitable truths by people who know nothing of those more general maxims.

THEO. I have answered that already [p. 76]. We rely on those general maxims, as we rely on the major premises which are suppressed when we reason in enthymemes; for although we are very often not thinking distinctly about what we are doing when we reason, any more than about what we are doing when we walk or jump, it remains the case that the cogency of the inference lies partly in what is being suppressed; there is nowhere else it can come from, as one will discover in trying to defend the inference.

PHIL. §20. But 'those general and abstract ideas' seem to be 'more strangers' to our minds than are particular truths and notions; so these particular truths will be more natural to the mind than is the principle of contradiction, and yet you say that they are just applications of it.

THEO. The truths that we start by being aware of are indeed particular ones, just as we start with the coarsest and most composite ideas. But that doesn't alter the fact that in the order of nature the simplest comes first, and that the reasons for particular truths rest wholly on the more general ones of which they are mere instances. And when one wants to think about what is in us potentially, before all awareness, it is right to start with the simplest. For general principles enter into our thoughts, serving as their inner core and as their mortar. Even if we give no thought to them, they are necessary for thought, as muscles and tendons are for walking. The mind relies on these principles constantly; but it does not find it so easy to sort them out and to command a distinct view of each of them separately, for that requires great attention to what it is doing, and the unreflective majority are hardly capable of that. Do not the Chinese have articulate sounds, just as we do? And yet, since they have adopted a different system of writing, it has not yet occurred to them to make an alphabet of these sounds. It is in that way that many things are possessed without the possessor's knowing it.

PHIL. §21. If the mind agrees so readily to certain truths, might that not be because the very 'consideration of the nature of...things' will not let it judge otherwise, rather than because these propositions are naturally engraved in the mind?

THEO. Both are true: the nature of things and the nature of the mind work together. And since you contrast the consideration of the thing with the awareness of what is engraved in the mind, this very objection shows, sir, that those with whom you ally yourself take 'innate truths' to be merely whatever one would naturally accept, as though by instinct, even if one knows it only in a confused way. There are truths like that, and we shall have occasion to discuss them. But the *light of nature*, as it is called, involves distinct knowledge; and quite often a 'consideration of the nature of things' is nothing but the knowledge of the nature of our mind and of these innate ideas, and there is no need to look for them outside oneself. Thus I count as innate any truths which need only such 'consideration' in order to be verified. I have already replied (§5) [p. 79] to the objection (§22) which maintains that when it is said that innate notions are 'implicitly' in the mind, that should signify only that the mind has a faculty for knowing them; for I have pointed out that it has in addition a faculty for finding them in itself, and the disposition, if it is thinking about them properly, to accept them.

PHIL. **§23.** You seem then to be maintaining, sir, that those who hear these general maxims for the first time learn nothing which is entirely new to them. But it is clear that they do learn – first the names, and then the truths and even the ideas on which these truths depend.

THEO. Names are not in question here. They are in a way arbitrary, whereas ideas and truths are natural. But with regard to these ideas and truths, you attribute to me, sir, a doctrine which I am far from accepting; for I quite agree that we learn innate ideas and innate truths, whether by paying heed to their source or by verifying them through experience. So I do not suppose, as you say I do, that in the case you have mentioned we learned nothing new. And I cannot accept the proposition that *whatever is learned is not innate*. The truths about numbers are in us; but still we learn them, whether by drawing them from their source, in which case one learns them through demonstrative reason (which shows that they are innate), or by testing them with examples, as common arithmeticians do. The latter, not knowing the underlying principles, learn their rules merely through their being handed on; at best, before teaching them they confirm their rules, as far as they judge appropriate, by trying them out.[1] Sometimes even a very able mathematician, not knowing the proof of some result obtained by someone else, has to be satisfied with examining it by that inductive method. That is what was done by a well-known writer in *Paris while I was there: he tested my arithmetical tetragonism rather hard by comparing it with Ludolph's numbers, expecting to find something wrong in it; and he was right to go on being sceptical until he was sent the demonstration of it [*quadrature]. Demonstration spares us from having to make these tests, which one might continue endlessly without

85

---

[1] '*par l'expérience*'.

ever being perfectly certain. And it is just that – namely the imperfection of inductions – that *can* be verified through the trying out of particular cases.[1] For there are progressions which one can follow a very long way before grasping the changes, and the laws that they involve.

PHIL. But might it not be that not only the terms or words that we use, but also our ideas, come from outside us?

THEO. If they did, we too should have to be outside ourselves; for intellectual ideas, or ideas of reflection, are drawn from our mind. I would like to know how we could have the idea of *being* if we did not, as beings ourselves, find being within us.

86

PHIL. What do you say, sir, to this challenge which a friend of mine has offered? If anyone can find a proposition whose ideas are innate, let him name it to me (he says); he could not please me more.

THEO. I would name to him the propositions of arithmetic and geometry, which are all of that nature; and among necessary truths no other kind is to be found.[2]

PHIL. Many people would find that strange. Can we really say that the deepest and most difficult *sciences are innate?

THEO. The actual knowledge of them is not innate. What is innate is what might be called the potential knowledge of them, as the veins of the marble outline a shape which is in the marble before they are uncovered by the sculptor.

PHIL. §25. But is it possible that children 'receive and assent to adventitious[3] notions, and [are] ignorant of those, which are supposed' to be innate in them and to be as it were parts of their mind, in which they are said to be 'imprinted[4]...in indelible characters, to be [a] foundation ...? This would be, to make Nature take pains to no purpose; or, at least, to [engrave][5] very ill; since its characters could not be read by those eyes, which saw other things very well'.

THEO. To be aware of what is within us, we must be attentive and methodical. Now, it is not only possible but appropriate that children should attend more to the notions of the senses, because attention is governed by need. However, we shall see later that nature has not 'taken pains to no purpose' in imprinting us, innately, with items of knowledge; for without these there would be no way of achieving actual knowledge of

---

[1] '*par les instances de l'expérience*'.
[2] '*on n'en saurait trouver d'autres*'.
[3] Taking '*au dehors*' to be a slip for Coste's '*de dehors*'.
[4] Locke: 'supposed woven into the very principles of their being, and imprinted'. Coste's change.
[5] Locke: 'write'. Coste's change.

necessary truths in the demonstrative sciences, or of learning the reasons for facts; and we should have nothing over the beasts.

PHIL. §26. If there are innate truths, must there not be innate thoughts?

THEO. Not at all. For thoughts are actions, whereas items of knowledge (or truths), in so far as they are within us even when we do not think of them, are tendencies or dispositions; and we know many things which we scarcely think about.

PHIL. It is very hard to conceive of 'a truth in the mind, that it has never thought on.' 87

THEO. That is like saying that it is hard to conceive how there can be veins in the marble before they have been uncovered. Also, this objection seems to come rather too close to begging the question. Everyone who admits innate truths, without founding them on Platonic recollection, admits some which have not yet been thought of. Furthermore, your argument proves too much: for if truths are thoughts, we shall lose not only truths which we have never thought of but also those which we have thought of but are no longer thinking of at this moment. And if truths are not thoughts but tendencies and aptitudes, natural or acquired, there is no obstacle to there being within us truths which have never and will never be thought about by us.

PHIL. §27. If general maxims were innate they 'should appear fairest and clearest in those persons, in whom yet we find no footsteps of them'. I allude to 'children, idiots, savages,' who are of all men those whose minds are the least spoiled and corrupted by custom or by the influence of borrowed opinions.

THEO. I believe that the argument at this point should run quite differently. Innate maxims make their appearance only through the attention one gives to them; but those people have almost no attention to give, or have it only for something quite different. They think about little except their bodily needs; and it is appropriate that pure and disinterested thoughts should be the reward for having nobler concerns. It is true that the minds of children and savages are less 'spoiled by customs', but they are also less improved by the teaching which makes one attentive. It would be very unjust if the brightest lights had to shine better in minds which are less worthy of them and are wrapped in the thickest clouds. People as learned and clever as you, Philalethes, or your excellent author, should not flatter ignorance and barbarism; for that would be to disparage the gifts of God. It may be said that the less one knows the closer one comes to sharing with blocks of marble and bits of wood the advantage of being 88 infallible and faultless. But unfortunately that is not the respect in which one comes close to them; and in so far as one is capable of knowledge, it is a sin to neglect to acquire it, and the less instruction one has had the easier it is to fail in this.

Chapter ii
That there are 'no innate practical principles'.

PHILALETHES. §1. Morality is a demonstrative science, and yet it has no innate principles. Indeed 'it will be hard to instance [a] moral rule, which can pretend to so general and ready an assent[1] as, *What is, is*'.

THEOPHILUS. It is absolutely impossible that there should be truths of reason which are as evident as *identities* or immediate truths. Although it is correct to say that morality has indemonstrable principles, of which one of the first and most practical is that we should pursue joy and avoid sorrow, it must be added that that is not a truth which is known solely from reason, since it is based on inner experience – on confused knowledge; for one only senses[2] what joy and sorrow are.

89 PHIL. It is only through 'reasoning and discourse, and some exercise of the mind,' that one can be sure of practical truths.[3]

THEO. Even so, that would not make them any less innate. However, the maxim which I have just advanced seems to be of a different nature; it is not known by reason but by an *instinct*, so to speak. It is an innate principle, but it does not share in the natural light since it is not known in a luminous way. Given this principle, though, one can derive scientific conclusions from it, and I warmly applaud what you have just said, sir, about morality as a demonstrative science. So we observe that it teaches truths so evident that robbers, pirates and bandits are compelled to observe them among themselves.

PHIL. §2. But thieves 'keep...rules of justice one with another', without taking them to be innate principles.

THEO. What does that show? Do people in general trouble themselves about these theoretical issues?

PHIL. They practise the maxims of justice only as 'rules of convenience' which they absolutely must observe if they are to preserve their confederacy.[4]

THEO. Very good; and if you were speaking generally of all mankind, you could not improve on that. This is how these laws are engraved in the soul, namely as necessary for our survival and our true welfare. Are we supposed to be maintaining that truths are in the understanding independently of one another, as the Praetor's edicts used to be on his notice-board – his

---

[1] Preferring '*reçue*', from an earlier version, to the Academy edition's '*résolue*'.
[2] Taking '*on ne sent pas*' ('one does not sense') to be a slip. In drafting the passage, Leibniz first wrote '*on ne sait pas assez*' ('one does not really know').
[3] Locke: 'moral principles'.
[4] Added by Coste.

album? I set aside for now the *instinct* which leads one human being to love another; I will speak of it shortly, but for the moment I wish to confine myself to truths in so far as they are known through *reason*. I recognize too that certain rules of justice can be demonstrated in their full extent and perfection only if we assume the existence of God and the immortality of the soul, and that those to which the instinct of humanity does not impel us are engraved in the soul only as other derivative truths are. However, those for whom justice is founded only on the necessities of this life and on their own need for justice – rather than on the satisfaction which they ought to take in it, which is one of the greatest satisfactions when God is its foundation – are apt to resemble a community of thieves. 'If there is a hope of escaping detection, they will contaminate the sacred with the profane' [Horace].

PHIL. §3. 'Nature, I confess [to you], has put into man a desire of happiness, and a [strong] aversion to misery: these indeed are innate practical principles, which (as practical principles ought) do continue constantly to influence all our actions[;] but these are inclinations of the [soul] to good, not impressions of' some truth which is engraved in our understanding.[1]

THEO. I am delighted, sir, to find that you do after all acknowledge innate truths, as I will shortly maintain. This principle agrees well enough with the one which I have just pointed out, which leads us to pursue joy and avoid sorrow. For happiness is nothing but lasting joy. However, what we incline to is not strictly speaking happiness, but rather joy, i.e. something in the present; it is reason which leads us to the future and to what lasts. Now, an inclination which is expressed by the understanding becomes a *precept* or practical truth; and if the inclination is innate then so also is the truth – there being nothing in the soul which is not expressed in the understanding, although not always in distinct actual thinking, as I have sufficiently shown. Nor do instincts always pertain to practice: some of them contain theoretical truths – the in-built principles of the sciences and of reasoning are like that when we employ them through a natural instinct without knowing the reasons for them. You cannot avoid ac-knowledging some innate principles, in this sense, even if you wanted to deny that derivative truths are 'innate'. Such a denial would be merely a matter of a name, given my explanation of what I call 'innate'; and if any-one wishes to restrict the application of this term to the truths which are accepted straight away, by instinct, I shan't dispute the point with him.

---

[1] Locke: 'of the appetite to good, not impressions of truth on the understanding.' Coste's changes.

91 PHIL. That is well enough; but if there were certain characters engraved naturally in our soul,[1] 'as the principles of knowledge, we could not but perceive them constantly operate in us,' as we feel the influence of the two principles which are always at work in us, namely the desire to be happy and the fear of being miserable.

THEO. There are principles of knowledge which enter into our reasonings as constantly as practical ones do into our volitions; for instance, everyone makes use of the rules of inference through a *natural logic*, without being aware of them.

PHIL. **§4.** 'Moral rules need a proof, *ergo* [they are] not innate'[2] – for instance that rule which is the 'foundation of all social virtue, *That one should do* [only][3] *as he would be done unto*'.

THEO. You keep facing me with an objection which I have already refuted. I grant you, sir, that some moral rules are not innate principles; but that does not preclude their being innate truths, since a derivative truth will be innate if we can derive it from our mind. But there are two ways of discovering innate truths within us: by illumination and by instinct. Those to which I have just referred are demonstrated through our ideas, and that is what the natural light is. But there are things which follow from the natural light, and these are principles in relation to instinct. This is how we are led to act humanely: by instinct because it pleases us, and by reason because it is right. Thus there are in us instinctive truths which are innate principles that we sense and that we approve, even when we have no proof of them – though we get one when we explain the instinct in question. This is how we employ the laws of inference, being guided by a confused knowledge of them, as if by instinct, though the logicians demonstrate the reasons for them; as mathematicians explain what we do unthinkingly when we walk or jump. As regards the rule to the effect that we should do to others only what we are willing that they do to us, it requires not only proof but also elucidation. We would wish for more than our share if we had our own way; so do we also owe to others more than their share?

92 I will be told that the rule applies only to a just will. But then the rule, far from serving as a standard, will need a standard. The true meaning of the rule is that the right way to judge more fairly is to adopt the point of view of other people.

PHIL. **§9.** People frequently perform misdeeds without any remorse: for instance when a town is taken by storm the soldiers have no compunction about doing the wickedest things. Civilized nations have exposed their children. 'The Caribs were wont to geld their children, on purpose to fat

---

[1] Locke: 'imprinted by nature on the understanding'. Coste's change.
[2] Locke's marginal summary.
[3] Added by Coste.

and eat them. And Garcilasso de la Vega tells us of a people in Peru, which were wont to fat and eat the children [when they reached the age of thirteen][1] they got on their female captives, whom they kept as concubines for that purpose; and when they were past breeding the mothers themselves were killed too and eaten.' In Baumgarten's *Voyage* it is related that there was an Egyptian fakir who was regarded as a holy man because he never lay with women or boys but only with she-donkeys and mules.[2]

THEO. Setting aside instincts, like the one which makes us pursue joy and flee sorrow, moral knowledge [*science*] is innate in just the same way that arithmetic is, for it too depends upon demonstrations provided by the inner light. Since demonstrations do not spring into view straight away, it is no great wonder if men are not always aware straight away of everything they have within them, and are not very quick to read the characters of the natural law which, according to St Paul, God has engraved in their minds. However, since morality is more important than arithmetic, God has given to man instincts which lead, straight away and without reasoning, to part of what reason commands. Similarly we walk in conformity with the laws of mechanics without thinking about them; and we eat not only because is it necessary for us to, but also and much more because eating gives us pleasure. But these instincts do not irresistibly impel us to act: our passions lead us to resist them, our prejudices obscure them, and contrary customs distort them. Usually, though, we accede to these instincts of conscience, and even follow them whenever stronger feelings do not overcome them. The largest and soundest part of the human race bears witness to them. The Orientals, the Greeks and the Romans, the Bible and the Koran agree in that; the Mahommedan authorities customarily punish what Baumgarten reports; and one would have to be as brutalized as the American savages to approve of their customs which are full of a cruelty surpassing even that of the beasts. However, these same savages have a good sense of what justice is in other situations; and although there may be no wicked custom which is not permitted somewhere and in some circumstances, nonetheless most of them are condemned most of the time and by the great majority of mankind. This did not come about for no reason; and since it has not come about through unaided reasoning it must in part be related to natural instincts. Custom, tradition and discipline play their part, but natural feeling[3] is what causes custom to veer mainly in the right direction as regards our duties. Again it is *natural* feeling that has brought about the *tradition* that there is a God. Nature instils in man and even in most of the animals an affection and gentleness towards the members of their own species. Even the tiger 'spares those of kindred stripe' [Juvenal]; whence

93

---

[1] Added by Coste.
[2] Locke and Coste give this anecdote – and Leibniz gives its 'because' clause – in Latin.
[3] '*le naturel*'.

the apt remark of a Roman jurist that since nature has established kinship among all mankind, it is wrong for one man to entrap another. Spiders are almost the only exception: they consume each other, even to the point that the female devours the male after mating with him. In addition to this general social instinct, which can be called 'philanthropy' in man, there are more particular ones such as the affection between male and female, the love of fathers and mothers for their offspring, which the Greeks called *storge*, and other similar inclinations. These make up that natural law, or rather that semblance of law, which the Roman jurists say that nature has taught to the animals. But in man in particular there is a certain concern for dignity and propriety which induces us to conceal things which degrade us, to value modesty, to loathe incest, to bury corpses, and not to eat men at all or beasts when they are alive. It also leads us to look after our

94   reputations, even beyond the point where this serves our needs and beyond the end of life; to be subject to remorse and to feel those *laniatus et ictus* – those tortures and agonies – which Tacitus speaks of (following Plato [*Gorgias* 524^e]), in addition to the fear, which also comes naturally enough, of a hereafter and of a supreme power. There is something real in all this; but these natural impressions, of whatever sort they may be, are fundamentally no more than aids to reason and indications of nature's plan. Custom, education, tradition, reason contribute a great deal, but still human nature plays its part; though without reason these aids would not suffice to make morality completely certain. Finally, will we deny that men are naturally led to avoid what is sordid, for example, on the grounds that some people enjoy talking of nothing but filth, that there are even some whose way of life requires them to handle excrement, and that among the people of Bhutan that of their king is considered to be fragrant? I take it, sir, that you fundamentally agree with me about these natural instincts for what is upright and good; although you will perhaps say, as you did about the instinct which leads [us] towards joy and happiness, that these impressions are not innate truths. But I have already replied [p. 90?] that every feeling is the perception of a truth, and that natural feeling[1] is the perception of an innate truth, though very often a confused one as are the experiences of the outer senses. Thus *innate truths* can be distinguished from the *natural light* (which contains only what is distinctly knowable) as a genus should be distinguished from its species, since innate truths comprise instincts as well as the natural light.

PHIL. §11. A person who knew the 'natural measures of right and wrong' and still confounded them together could not 'but be looked on, as the professed enemy of [the] peace and happiness' of the society of which he

---

[1] '*le sentiment naturel*'.

was a member. But men continually confound them; therefore they do not know them.

THEO. You are treating the matter a little too theoretically. It is a daily occurrence for men to act against what they know; they conceal it from themselves by turning their thoughts aside, so as to follow their passions. Otherwise we would not find people eating and drinking what they know will make them ill or even kill them. They would not neglect their affairs; they would not do what whole nations did, in certain ways, a few years 95 ago.[1] The future and reasoning seldom strike as forcefully as do the present and the senses. There was an Italian who knew this very well: when he was going to be tortured he resolved to keep the gallows continually before his mind's eye, the better to bear up under his agonies; he was heard from time to time saying 'I see you', and he explained what he meant later on, after his deliverance. Unless we resolve firmly to keep our minds on true good and true evil, so as to pursue the one and avoid the other, we find ourselves carried away, and the most important needs of this life are treated in the same way as heaven and hell are, even by their truest believers:

> We sing of this and praise it,
> We tell and hear about it,
> We write of it and read of it...
> And then we do without it.

PHIL. 'Whatever...principle is [supposed to be][2] innate, cannot but be known to every one, to be just and good.'

THEO. That is still reverting to the assumption, which I have time after time refuted, that every innate truth is known always and by everyone.

PHIL. §12. 'But the generally allowed breach of [a law] is a proof, that it is not innate'. For example, the law of love and care for children was violated by the ancients when they permitted exposing them.

THEO. Granting this violation, all that follows is that we have not always correctly read the characters which, though nature has engraved them in our souls, are sometimes veiled by our licentiousness. In any case, to have a compelling view of the necessity of one's duties one would have to grasp a demonstration of it, which seldom happens. If geometry conflicted with our passions and our present concerns as much as morality does, we would dispute it and transgress it almost as much – in spite of all Euclid's and Archimedes' demonstrations, which would be treated as fantasies and deemed to be full of fallacies – and Joseph Scaliger, *Hobbes and others who have written against Euclid and Archimedes would not find so few supporters as they do in fact. Only a lust for glory, which these authors 96

---

[1] Incorporating 'depuis quelques années' from the last version in Leibniz's hand.
[2] Added by Coste.

thought they could get from squaring the circle and solving other knotty problems, could have blinded such worthy men to such an extent [*quadrature]. If others had as much incentive, they would behave in the same way.

PHIL. All duty must carry with it the idea of law,[1] and a law cannot 'be known, or supposed without a law-maker, or without reward and punishment'.

THEO. There can be natural rewards and punishments without a law-maker; intemperance, for instance, is punished by illness. However, since it does not always do its damage straight away, I admit that there is hardly any rule which would be unavoidably binding if there were not a God who leaves no crime unpunished, no good action unrewarded.

PHIL. Then the ideas of a God and of an after-life must also be innate.

THEO. I agree with that, in the sense which I have explained.

PHIL. But these ideas are so far from being naturally engraved in the minds of all men that they appear not to be very 'clear and distinct' even in the minds of many studious men, who profess to examine matters with some precision, let alone being known to every human creature.

THEO. You are reverting again to the same assumption, according to which if something is not known it is not innate, in spite of my having refuted it so often. Because something is innate it does not follow that it can be known clearly and distinctly straight away; one must often be very attentive and orderly to become aware of it, which 'studious men' do not always achieve, still less 'every human creature'.

PHIL. §13. But 'if men can be ignorant or doubtful of what is innate,' it is in vain to talk to us about innate principles and to claim to show their necessity;[2] far from their being able to instruct us about the truth and certainty of things, as is claimed, we would be in the same uncertainty with these principles as if we did not have them.

THEO. One cannot 'be doubtful' of all innate principles. You agreed about that, sir, in the case of identities or the principle of contradiction, and admitted that there are indubitable principles, although at that time you did not recognize them as innate. But it does not follow that everything which is innate and connected necessarily with these innate principles is also straight away evident beyond doubt.

PHIL. §14. 'No body, that I know, has ventured yet to give a catalogue' of these principles.

THEO. Has anyone yet given us a full and accurate list of the axioms of geometry?

---

[1] Locke: 'what duty is, cannot be understood without a law'. Coste's change.
[2] Locke: 'innate principles are insisted on, and urged to no purpose'. Coste's change.

PHIL. §15. Lord Herbert has attempted to indicate some of these principles, as follows: (1) That there is a supreme God. (2) That He must be served. (3) That virtue joined with piety is the best worship. (4) That we must repent of our sins. (5) That there are penalties and rewards in the hereafter. 'I allow these to be clear truths, and such as, if rightly explained, a rational creature can hardly avoid giving his assent to'. But, my friends say, they fall far short of being innate impressions. §16. And if these five propositions are 'common notions' engraved in our souls[1] by the finger of God, then there are a good many others which belong in the same class.

THEO. I agree with that, sir, since I deem all necessary truths to be innate, and I even add in the instincts. But I grant you that those five propositions are not innate principles, since I maintain that they can and should be proved.

PHIL. §18. In the third proposition, that virtue is the worship most acceptable to God, it is not clear what is meant by *virtue*. If it is understood in the sense which is most commonly given to it, I mean the sense of that which 'according to the different opinions of several countries, [is] accounted laudable, [this proposition] will be...so far from being certain, that it will not be true. If *virtue* be taken for actions conformable to God's will,' then this proposition will be almost an identity and will not teach us very much, since it will amount to no more than that God is pleased with what is conformable to his will. §19. The same holds with regard to the notion of *sin* in the fourth proposition.

THEO. I do not remember finding that virtue is 'commonly' taken to be something that depends on opinion; philosophers at least do not present it like that. It is true that the word 'virtue' depends on the opinions of those who apply it to different dispositions [*habitudes*] and actions, according to whether they judge well or badly and whether they use their reason; but all men agree pretty well on the general notion of virtue even though they differ in how they apply it. According to Aristotle and various others, 'virtue' is a general disposition to moderate the passions by means of reason, or more simply still a disposition to act in accordance with reason. And that cannot fail to be pleasing to him who is the supreme and ultimate reason of all things, to whom nothing is unimportant, least of all the actions of rational creatures.

PHIL. §20. It is often said that the principles of morality which are supposed to be innate[2] 'may, by education, and custom, and the general opinion of those, amongst whom we converse, be darkened.... Which assertion of theirs, if true, quite takes away the argument of universal

---

[1] Locke: 'writ on our minds'. Coste's change.
[2] Locke: 'the innate principles of morality'. Coste's change.

consent'. The argument which many people employ amounts only to this: the principles which are admitted by men of good sense[1] are innate; 'we and those of our mind, are men of [good sense]; therefore... our principles are innate: which is a very pretty way of arguing, and a short cut to infallibility'!

THEO. Speaking for myself, I employ universal consent not as a main proof, but as a confirmation. Innate truths, considered as the natural light of reason, bear their distinguishing marks with them, as in geometry for instance, since they are contained in immediate principles – and even you acknowledge these to be unquestionable. But I admit that it is more difficult to distinguish instincts and some other natural dispositions from customs, although it seems that this can usually be done. Further, it appears to me that nations which have cultivated their minds have some grounds for crediting themselves with using good sense and savages with not doing so, since they plainly show their superiority to savages by subduing them almost as easily as they do the beasts. If we cannot always get the upper hand it is because they – again like the beasts – escape into the depths of the forests where it is hard to conquer them and the game 99 is not worth the candle. A cultivated mind is certainly an advantage; and if we are allowed to take the side of savagery against cultivation, we shall also have the right to attack reason on behalf of the beasts, and to take seriously M. Despréaux's witty lines in one of his *Satires* where, as a challenge to man's superiority over animals, he asks:

> Is the bear afraid of the traveller, or the traveller afraid of the bear?
> And can an edict of the shepherds of Libya
> Banish lions from the folds of Numidia?

However, it must be admitted that savages surpass us in some important ways, especially in bodily vigour. Even with regard to the soul, their practical morality can be said to be in some respects better than ours, because they have neither greed for the accumulation of goods nor ambition to dominate. And one might even add that intercourse with Christians has made them worse in many respects: it has taught them drunkenness (by providing them with strong drink), swearing, blasphemy, and other vices formerly little known to them. With us there is more good and more evil than with them: a wicked European is more wicked than a savage – he is punctilious in his evil. There is, however, nothing to prevent men from combining the advantages which nature gives to these people with those which reason gives to us.

PHIL. But what answer will you give, sir, to the dilemma posed by one of my friends? I would like (he says) the defenders of innate ideas to tell

---

[1] Locke: 'men of right reason'. Coste's change.

me whether these principles 'can, or cannot, by education and custom, be ...[1] blotted out: if they cannot, we must find them in all mankind', and they must appear clearly in the mind of each individual man;[2] 'and if they may suffer variation from adventitious notions, we must then find them clearest and most [sparkling][3] nearest the fountain, in children and illiterate people, who have received least impression from foreign opinions. Let them take which side they please, they will [he says] certainly find it inconsistent with [uniform facts][4] and daily observation.'

THEO. I am amazed that your astute friend should confuse 'obscured' with 'blotted out', just as your allies confuse 'non-existent' with 'not appearing'. Innate ideas and truths could not be effaced, but they are obscured in all men (in their present state) by their inclination towards the needs of their bodies and often still more by supervening bad habits. These writings in inner light would sparkle continuously in the understanding, and would give warmth to the will, if the confused perceptions of the senses did not monopolize our attention. Holy scripture speaks of this conflict no less than does philosophy, ancient and modern.   100

PHIL. And so we find ourselves in as deep a darkness and as great an uncertainty as if there were no such illumination.

THEO. God forbid! We would have neither sciences nor laws, and would not even have reason.

PHIL. §§21–3. I hope at least that you will agree about the influence of prejudice. It often passes off as natural the results of the bad teaching to which children are subjected, and the bad habits which education and social intercourse have given them.

THEO. I acknowledge that the distinguished author whom you are following says some very fine things on that score, and that taken in the right way they are worthwhile; but I do not believe that they are inconsistent with the doctrine of natural feeling[5] or innate truths, correctly understood. And I am convinced that he would not want to push his comments too far. For I am sure that many opinions are taken for truths which are merely the result of custom and credulity, and equally sure that others which certain philosophers would like to dismiss as prejudices are in fact grounded in right reason and in nature. There is at least as much reason, indeed more, to beware of those who claim – usually from ambition – to be breaking new ground as there is to distrust long-standing impressions. Having diligently considered both the old and the new. I have found that most accepted

---

[1] Locke: 'blurred and'. Coste's omission.
[2] Locke: 'must be clear in every body'. Coste's change.
[3] Locke: 'perspicuous'. Coste's change.
[4] Locke: 'visible matter of fact'. Coste's change.
[5] 'du naturel'.

doctrines can bear a sound sense. So I wish that men of intellect would seek to gratify their ambition by building up and moving forward, rather than by retreating and destroying. I would rather they emulated the Romans who built fine public works than that Vandal king whose mother advised him that since he could not hope for renown by rivalling those magnificent structures he should seek to destroy them.

PHIL. §§24–7. When able men have fought against innate truths, their aim has been to prevent others from passing off prejudices and concealing laziness under a high-sounding name.

THEO. We agree about this; for, far from approving the acceptance of doubtful principles, I want to see an attempt to demonstrate even Euclid's axioms, as some of the ancients tried to do. If it be asked how one can know and investigate innate principles, I reply in conformity with what I have said above: apart from the instincts the reason for which is unknown, we must try to reduce them to first principles (i.e. to identical or immediate axioms) by means of definitions, which are nothing but a distinct setting out of ideas. I do not doubt that even your friends, opposed as they have so far been to innate truths, are in favour of this method, which appears to conform to their chief aim.

Chapter iii
'Other considerations concerning innate principles, both speculative and practical.'

PHILALETHES. §3. You would have truths reduced to first principles; and I grant you that if there is any innate principle it is undeniably this: '*It is impossible for the same thing to be, and not to be* [*at the same time*]'. But it appears hard to maintain that this is innate, since we must also be convinced 'that impossibility and identity, are two innate ideas'.

THEOPHILUS. Those who support innate truths must indeed maintain and be convinced that those ideas are also innate – I acknowledge that that is my own opinion. The ideas of *being*, *possible* and *same* are so thoroughly innate that they enter into all our thoughts and reasoning, and I regard them as essential to our minds. But I have already said that we do not always pay particular attention to them, and that it takes time to sort them out. I have said too that we are so to speak innate to ourselves; and since we are beings, being is innate in us – the knowledge of being is comprised in the knowledge that we have of ourselves. Something very like this holds of other general notions.

PHIL. §4. If the idea of identity is natural,[1] 'and consequently so clear and obvious to us, that we must needs know it even from our cradles; I would

---

[1] Locke: 'If identity...be a native impression'. Coste's change.

gladly be resolved, by one of seven, or seventy years old, whether a man, being a creature, consisting of soul and body, be the same man, when his body is changed?' And whether, on the supposition of metempsychosis, Euphorbus would be the same as Pythagoras?

THEO. I have said often enough that what is natural to us need not therefore be known from the cradle. Furthermore we can know an idea without being able to settle straight away all the questions which can be raised about it. As if someone were to argue that a child cannot know what a square and its diagonal are because it will have trouble grasping that the diagonal is incommensurable with the side of the square. As for the question itself, it appears to me to be demonstratively settled by the doctrine of *monads which I have published elsewhere [e.g. 'On nature itself']; but we shall discuss this matter more fully later [pp. 232 ff].

PHIL. §6. I see that it would be useless to object to you that the axiom according to which 'the whole is bigger than a part' is not innate, on the grounds that the ideas of whole and part are 'relative', and depend on those of number and extension; for you would be likely to maintain that there are logically derivative innate ideas,[1] and that those of number and extension are innate too.

103

THEO. You are right. Indeed my view is rather that the idea of extension is posterior to those of whole and part.

PHIL. §7. What do you say about the truth 'that God is to be worshipped' – is it innate?

THEO. I believe that the duty to worship God implies that at certain times one should indicate that one honours him beyond any other object, and that this follows necessarily from the idea of him and from his existence, which on my theory signifies that this truth is innate.

PHIL. §8. But atheists seem to prove by their example that the idea of God is not innate. Apart from the ones which were 'taken notice of amongst the ancients,' have not whole nations been discovered – such as at the Bay of Saldanha, and in Brazil, the Caribee Islands, and Paraguay – who had no idea of God[2] nor any names standing for God or the soul?

THEO. The late M. *Fabricius, the well-known Heidelberg theologian, wrote an *Apology* for the human race, to clear it of the charge of atheism. He was a very careful writer and quite above many prejudices. However, I have no intention of getting into this debate about the facts. I will concede that there are whole peoples who have never thought of the supreme substance or of what the soul is. I remember when, at my request, seconded by the distinguished M. *Witsen, someone attempted to obtain for me in

---

[1] '*idées innées respectives*'.
[2] Locke: 'no notion of a God'. Coste's change.

Holland a version of the Lord's Prayer in the language of Barantola, he got no further than 'hallowed be thy name', because it was impossible to make the Barantolans understand the meaning of 'holy'. I remember too that in the *Credo* written for the Hottentots, it was necessary to use their words for a gentle and pleasant wind to translate 'Holy Spirit'. This is not unreasonable since our Greek and Latin words *pneuma, anima, spiritus* primarily signify simply the air or wind which one breathes, as being one of the most rarefied things that our senses acquaint us with; one starts with the senses in order to lead men gradually to what is above the senses. However, all these difficulties in the way of attaining abstract knowledge count not at all against innate knowledge. There are people who have no word corresponding to 'being'; does anyone suspect that they do not know what it is to be, granted that they hardly ever think of *being* in isolation? Before I finish, what I have read in our distinguished author about the idea of God is so fine and so much to my liking that I cannot forbear quoting it: 'Men...can scarce avoid having some kind of ideas of those things, whose names, those they converse with, have occasion frequently to mention to them: and if it carry with it the notion of excellency, greatness, or something extraordinary' which engages some part of one's being and is impressed upon the mind under the idea of an absolute and irresistible power which one cannot help fearing (or, I would add, an ultimate goodness which one cannot help loving),[1] then 'the idea is likely to sink the deeper, and spread the farther; especially if it be such an idea, as is agreeable to the [simplest lights][2] of reason, and naturally deducible from every part of our knowledge, as that of...God is. For the [brilliant] marks[3] of extraordinary wisdom and power, appear so plainly in all the works of the creation, that a rational creature, who will but seriously reflect on them, cannot miss the discovery of [the author of all these wonders]:[4] and the influence, that the discovery of such a being must [naturally have on the soul][5] of all, that have but once heard of it, is so great, and carries' with it thoughts which are so weighty and so fit to be propagated in the world,[6] 'that it seems stranger to me, that a whole nation of men should be any where found so brutish, as to want the notion of a god; than that they should be without any notion of numbers, or fire.' (*Essay* I.iv.9) I wish that I might copy word for word many other excellent passages from our author which we are obliged to pass over. All I shall say at this point is that this author when he speaks of 'the simplest lights of reason' which are 'agreeable to'

[1] Parenthetical clause added by Leibniz. The unquoted clauses preceding it represent an expansion by Coste.
[2] Locke: 'common light'. Coste's change.
[3] Locke: 'of a God is. For the visible marks'. Coste's changes.
[4] Locke: 'discovery of a deity'. Coste's change.
[5] Locke: 'necessarily have on the minds'. Leibniz's adverb, Coste's noun.
[6] Locke: 'carries such weight of thought and communication with it'. Coste's change.

the idea of God, and of what is 'naturally deducible' from them, appears to differ hardly at all from my own views about innate truths. When he says that it seems to him as strange that there should be men with no idea of God as it would be surprising to find men who had no idea of number or of fire, I would point out that the inhabitants of the Mariana Islands – named after the Queen of Spain, who supported missions to them – had no knowledge of fire at the time that they were discovered. My source is the account which Father *Le Gobien, the French Jesuit in charge of missions to distant lands, has presented to the public and sent to me.

PHIL. §15. 'If it be a reason to think the notion of God innate, because all wise men had it, virtue too must be...innate; for wise men have always had' a genuine idea of it.

THEO. It is not virtue but the idea of virtue that is innate. Perhaps that is all that you mean.

PHIL. §16. ''Tis as certain, that there is a god, as that the opposite angles, made by the intersection of two straight lines, are equal. There was never any rational creature, that set himself sincerely to examine the truth of these propositions, that could fail to assent to them: though yet it be past doubt, that there are many men, who having not applied their thoughts that way, are ignorant both of the one and the other.'

THEO. I grant it, but that does not stop them from being innate, i.e. one's being able to find them within oneself.

PHIL. §18. It would be useful also to have an innate idea of *substance*; but in fact we have that neither as innate nor as acquired, since we have it neither by sensation nor by reflection.

THEO. It is my opinion that reflection enables us to find the idea of substance within ourselves, who are substances. And this is an extremely important notion. But perhaps we shall speak of it at greater length later in our discussion.

PHIL. §20. 'If there be any innate ideas...[1] in the mind, which the mind does not actually think on; they must [at least] be lodged in the memory, and from thence must be brought into view by remembrance; i.e. must be known, when [the memory of them is conjured up], to have been perceptions in the [*soul] before, unless remembrance can be without remembrance.' For this inner conviction[2] that such an idea has been in our mind before is strictly 'that, which distinguishes remembering from all other ways of thinking.'

THEO. Knowledge, ideas and truths can be in our minds without our ever having actually thought about them. They are merely natural tendencies,

---

[1] Locke: 'any innate ideas, any ideas'. Coste's omission.
[2] Locke: 'this consciousness'. Coste's change.

that is dispositions and attitudes, active or passive, and more than a *tabula rasa*. However, the Platonists did indeed believe that we have already actually thought about everything that we find again within us; to say that we do not remember doing so will not refute them, since certainly countless thoughts come back to us which we have forgotten having had. It once happened that a man thought that he had written original verses, and was then found to have read them word for word, long before, in some ancient poet. And we often have an unusual capacity to conceive certain things because we have conceived them formerly without remembering doing so. A child who has become blind may forget having ever seen light and colours; this is what happened to the famous Ulrich Schönberg at the age of two and a half, as a result of smallpox. He was born in Weiden, in the Upper Palatinate, and died at Königsberg in Prussia in 1649; he taught philosophy and mathematics there and was universally admired. Such a man may well retain the effects of former impressions without remembering them. I think that dreams often revive former thoughts for us in this way. After Julius Scaliger had extolled the eminent men of Verona in verse, a certain man calling himself Brugnolus, who came from Bavaria but had settled in Verona, appeared to him in a dream and complained of having been overlooked. Scaliger, who could not remember having ever before heard of him, nevertheless wrote an elegy in his honour on the authority of this dream. Later his son, Joseph Scaliger, while travelling in Italy, learned in more detail that there had formerly been in Verona a famous grammarian or scholarly critic of this name who had contributed to the restoration of literature in Italy. This story can be found in the elder Scaliger's poems, which include the elegy, and in his son's letters. It is also presented in *Scaligerana*, which has been put together from Joseph Scaliger's conversations. It is very likely that Julius Scaliger had had some knowledge of Brugnol and no longer remembered it, and that his dream had in part consisted in reviving a former idea – although there had not occurred that 'remembering', strictly so-called, which makes us know that we have had that same idea before. At least, I see nothing which compels us to insist that no traces of a perception remain just because there are not enough left for one to remember that one has had it.

107

PHIL. I must acknowledge that you reply naturally enough to the objections which we have made to innate truths. Perhaps, then, our authors do not deny them in the same sense in which you maintain them. So I shall merely reiterate, sir, that §24. there has been some reason to fear that the belief in innate truths may serve as an excuse to ease 'the lazy from the pains of search,' and may let masters and teachers, for their own convenience, 'make this the principle of principles, that principles must not be questioned'.

THEO. I have already said that if *that* is your friends' purpose, to urge us to look for the proofs of truths which admit of them, whether or not they are innate, then I entirely agree. The belief in innate truths, taken in my way, should not distract anyone from that; not only is it good to look for the explanation of instincts, but it is one of my chief maxims that it is good to look for the demonstrations even of axioms. I remember that in Paris, when they laughed at the late M. *Roberval, who was old by then, because he wanted to demonstrate Euclid's axioms following the examples of Apollonius and Proclus, I showed the importance of such an inquiry. 108 As for the 'principle' of those who say that we should never argue with people who deny principles, it does not wholly apply to any principles except those which can be neither doubted nor proved. Of course, restrictions may be imposed on public disputes and certain other assemblies, in order to prevent outrages and disturbances; and under these it may be forbidden to question certain established truths. But this is a matter of public order rather than of philosophy.

BOOK II
'OF IDEAS'

Chapter i
In which we discuss 'ideas in general', and incidentally consider whether the soul of man thinks always.

PHILALETHES. §1. Having examined whether ideas are innate, let us consider what they are like and what varieties of them there are. Is it not true that an 'idea is the object of thinking'?[1]

THEOPHILUS. I agree about that, provided that you add that an idea is an immediate inner object, and that this object expresses the nature or qualities of things. If the idea were the *form* of the thought, it would come into and go out of existence with the actual thoughts which correspond to it, but since it is the *object* of thought it can exist before and after the thoughts. Sensible outer objects are only *mediate*, because they cannot act immediately on the soul. God is the only *immediate outer* object. One might say that the soul itself is its own immediate inner object; but that is only to the extent that it contains ideas, i.e. something corresponding to things. For the soul is a little world where distinct ideas represent God and confused ones represent the universe.

PHIL. §2. Our gentlemen who take the soul to be initially a blank page,[2] 'void of all characters, without any ideas; [ask] How comes it to be furnished? Whence comes it by that vast store...? To this [they] answer, in one word, from experience'.

THEO. This *tabula rasa* of which one hears so much is a fiction, in my view, which nature does not allow and which arises solely from the incomplete notions of philosophers – such as vacuum, atoms, the state of rest (whether absolute, or of two parts of a whole relative to one another), or such as that prime matter which is conceived without any form. Things which are uniform, containing no variety, are always mere abstractions: for instance, time, space, and the other entities of pure mathematics. There is no body whose parts are at rest, and no substance which does not have something which distinguishes it from every other. Human souls differ not only from other souls but also from one another, though the latter differences are

---

[1] Locke's marginal summary.
[2] Locke: 'white paper'. Coste: '*tabula rasa*'. Leibniz: '*une table rase*'.

not of the sort that we call specific. And I think I can demonstrate that every substantial thing, be it soul or body, has a unique relationship to each other thing; and that each must always differ from every other in respect of *intrinsic *denominations*. Not to mention the fact that those who hold forth about the 'blank page' cannot say what is left of it once the ideas have been taken away – like the Scholastics who leave nothing in their prime matter. It may be said that this 'blank page' of the philosophers means that all the soul possesses, naturally and inherently, are bare faculties. But inactive faculties – in short, the pure powers of the Schoolmen – are also mere fictions, unknown to nature and obtainable only by abstraction. For where will one ever find in the world a faculty consisting in sheer power without performing any act? There is always a particular disposition to action, and towards one action rather than another. And as well as the disposition there is an *endeavour towards action – indeed there is an infinity of them in any subject at any given time, and these endeavours are never without some effect. Experience is necessary, I admit, if the soul is to be given such and such thoughts, and if it is to take heed of the ideas that are within us. But how could experience and the senses provide the ideas? Does the soul have windows? Is it similar to writing-tablets, or like wax? Clearly, those who take this view of the soul are treating it as fundamentally corporeal. Someone will confront me with this accepted philosophical axiom, that there is nothing in the soul which 111 does not come from the senses. But an exception must be made of the soul itself and its states. *Nihil est in intellectu quod non fuerit in sensu, excipe : nisi ipse intellectus.* Now the soul includes being, substance, one, same, cause, perception, reasoning, and many other notions which the senses cannot provide. That agrees pretty well with your author of the *Essay*, for he looks for a good proportion of ideas in the mind's reflection on its own nature.

PHIL. I hope then that you will concede to this able author that all ideas come through sensation or through reflection; that is, through 'our observation employed either about external, sensible objects; or about the internal operations of our' soul.

THEO. In order to keep away from an argument upon which we have already spent too long, let me say in advance, sir, that when you say that ideas come from one or other of those causes, I shall take that to mean the actual perception of the ideas; for I believe I have shown that in so far as they contain something distinct they are in us before we are aware of them.

PHIL. With that in mind, let us see when the soul should be said to start perceiving and actually thinking of ideas. §9. 'I know it is an opinion, that the soul always thinks,...and that actual thinking is as inseparable from the soul, as actual extension is from the body'. §10. But I cannot 'conceive it any more necessary for the soul always to think, than for the body always to move; the perception of ideas being...to the soul, what motion is to the body'. That appears to me quite reasonable, at least; and I would be very pleased, sir, to have your opinion on it.

THEO. You have said it, sir: action is no more inseparable from the soul than from the body. For it appears to me that a thoughtless state of the soul and absolute rest in a body are equally contrary to nature, and never occur in the world. A substance which is in action at some time will be so forever after, for all the impressions linger on, merely being mixed with new ones. When one strikes a body one causes or rather induces[1] an infinity of swirls, as in a liquid – for fundamentally every solid is in some degree liquid, every liquid in some degree solid – and there is no way of ever entirely stopping this internal turbulence. Now you may believe that since the body is never without movement, the soul which corresponds to it will never be without perception either.

PHIL. But 'that, perhaps, is the privilege of the...Author and Preserver' of all things, that being infinite in his perfections he 'never[2] slumbers nor sleeps; but is not competent to any finite being, at least not to [a being such as] the soul of man.'

THEO. Certainly, we slumber and sleep, and God has no need to. But it does not follow that when asleep we have no perceptions; rather, if the evidence is considered carefully it points the other way.

PHIL. 'There is something in us, that has a power to think'. But that does not imply that thinking is always occurring in us.

THEO. True powers are never simple possibilities; there is always endeavour, and action.

PHIL. But 'that the soul always thinks [is not] a self-evident proposition'.

THEO. I do not say that it is either. It cannot be found without a little attention and reasoning: the common man is no more aware of it than of the pressure of the air or the roundness of the earth.

PHIL. ''Tis doubted whether I thought all last night'; this is a question 'about a matter of fact,' and it must be settled 'by sensible experience'.

THEO. One settles it in the same way that one *proves that there are imperceptible bodies and invisible movements, though some people make fun of them. In the same way there are countless inconspicuous perceptions, which do not stand out enough for one to be aware of or to remember them but which manifest themselves through their inevitable consequences.

---

[1] '*excite ou détermine plutôt*'.
[2] Locke: 'Preserver of things, who never'. Coste's expansion.

PHIL. A certain author has objected that we maintain that the soul goes out of existence because we are not sensible of its existence during sleep. But that objection can only arise from a strange prejudice. For we 'do not say there is no soul in a man, because he is not sensible of it in his sleep; but [we] do say, he cannot think...without being' aware of it.[1] 113

THEO. I have not read the book where that objection occurs. But there would have been nothing wrong with objecting against you simply that thought need not stop just because one is not aware of it; for if it did, then by parity of argument we could say that there is no soul while one is not aware of it. To meet that objection, you must show that it is of the essence of thought in particular that one be aware of it.

PHIL. §11. It is 'hard to conceive, that any thing should think, and not be conscious of it.'

THEO. That is undoubtedly the crux of the matter – the difficulty by which able people have been perplexed. But here is the way to escape from it. Bear in mind that we do think of many things all at once, but pay heed only to the thoughts that stand out most distinctly. That is inevitable; for if we were to take note of everything, we should have to direct our attention on an infinity of things at the same time – things which impress themselves on our senses and which are all sensed by us. And I would go further: something remains of all our past thoughts, none of which can ever be entirely wiped out. When we are in dreamless sleep, or when we are dazed by some blow or a fall or a symptom of an illness or other mishap, an infinity of small, confused *sensations occur in us. Death itself cannot affect the souls of animals in any way but that; they must certainly regain their distinct perceptions sooner or later, for in nature everything is orderly. I admit, though, that in that confused state the soul would be without pleasure and pain, for they are noticeable perceptions.

PHIL. §12. Is it not true that 'the men [we] have here to do with,' namely the *Cartesians who believe that the soul always thinks,[2] 'allow life, without a thinking [and knowing][3] soul to all other animals'? And that they see no difficulty about saying that the soul can think without being joined to a body?

THEO. Speaking for myself, my view is different; for although I share the Cartesians' view that the soul always thinks, I part company with them on the other two points. I believe that beasts have imperishable souls, and 114 that no soul – human or otherwise – is ever without some body. I hold that God alone is entirely exempt from this because he is pure act.

[1] Locke: 'sensible of it'. Coste's change.
[2] Added by Leibniz.   [3] Added by Coste.

PHIL. If you had accepted the Cartesian view, I would have drawn the following conclusion from it. Since the bodies of Castor and of Pollux can stay alive while sometimes having a soul and sometimes not; and since a soul can stay in existence while sometimes being in a given body and sometimes out of it; it could be supposed that Castor and Pollux shared a single soul which acted in their bodies by turn, with each being asleep while the other was awake. In that case, it would make two persons as distinct as Castor and Hercules could be.

THEO. I in turn shall offer you a different supposition which appears to be more real. Must it not be agreed that after some passage of time or some great change one may suffer a total failure of memory? They say that Sleidan before his death forgot everything he knew, and there are plenty of other examples of this sad phenomenon. Now, suppose that such a man were made young again, and learned everything anew – would that make him a different man? So it is not memory that makes the very same man. But as for the fiction about a soul which animates different bodies, turn about, with the things that happen to it in one body being of no concern to it in the other: that is one of those fictions which go against the nature of things – like space without body, and body without motion – which arise from the incomplete notions of philosophers, and which vanish when one goes a little deeper. For it must be borne in mind that each soul retains all its previous impressions, and could not be separated into two halves in the manner you have described: within each substance there is a perfect bond between the future and the past, which is what creates the identity of the individual. Memory is not necessary for this, however, and is sometimes not even possible, because of the multitude of past and present impressions which jointly contribute to our present thoughts; for I believe that each of a man's thoughts has some effect, if only a confused one, or leaves some trace which mingles with the thoughts which follow it. One may forget many things, but one could also retrieve them, much later, if one were brought back to them in the right way.

115

PHIL. §13. Those 'who do at any time sleep without dreaming, can never be convinced, that their thoughts are...busy'.

THEO. While sleeping, even without dreams, one always has some faint sensing going on. Waking up is itself a sign of this: the easier someone is to awaken, the more sense he has of what is going on around him, though often this sense is not strong enough to cause him to wake.

PHIL. §14. 'That the soul in a sleeping man should be this moment busy a thinking, and the next moment in a waking man, not remember, [appears][1] very hard to be conceived'.

---

[1] Locke: 'is'. Coste's change.

THEO. Not only is it easy to conceive, but something like it can be observed during every day of our waking lives. For there are always objects which strike our eyes and ears, and therefore touch our souls as well, without our paying heed to them. For our attention is held by other objects, until a given object becomes powerful enough to attract it, either by acting more strongly upon us or in some other way. It is as though we had been selectively asleep with regard to that object; and when we withdraw our attention from everything all together, the sleep becomes general. It is also a way of getting to sleep – dividing one's attention so as to weaken it.

PHIL. 'I once knew a man, that was bred a scholar, and had no bad memory, who told me, he had never dreamed in his life, till he had that fever, he was then newly recovered of, which was about the five or six and twentieth year of his age.'

THEO. I have also been told of a scholar, much older than that, who had never dreamed. But the case for saying that the soul perceives continually does not rest entirely on dreams, since I have shown how even when asleep it has some perception of what is happening around it.

PHIL. §15. 'To think often, and never to retain [the memory of what one thinks] so much as one moment, is a...useless sort of thinking'.

THEO. Every impression has an effect, but the effects are not always noticeable. When I turn one way rather than another, it is often because of a series of tiny impressions of which I am not aware but which make one movement slightly harder than the other. All our undeliberated actions result from a conjunction of minute perceptions; and even our customs and passions, which have so much influence when we do deliberate, come from   116
the same source; for these tendencies come into being gradually, and so without the *minute perceptions we would not have acquired these noticeable dispositions. I have already remarked [p. 56] that anyone who excluded these effects from moral philosophy would be copying the ill-informed people who exclude insensible corpuscles from natural science; and yet I notice that among those who speak of liberty there are some who, ignoring these insensible impressions which can suffice to tilt the balance, fancy that moral actions can be subject to sheer indifference like that of Buridan's ass half-way between two pastures. We shall discuss that more fully later on [pp. 166, 197f]. I admit, though, that these impressions tilt the balance without necessitating.

PHIL. Perhaps it will be said that in a man who is awake, his body plays a part in his thinking, and that the memory is preserved by traces in the brain; whereas when he sleeps the soul has its thoughts separately, in itself.

THEO. I would say nothing of the sort, since I think that there is always a perfect correspondence between the body and the soul, and since I use bodily impressions of which one is not aware, whether in sleep or waking states, to prove that there are similar impressions in the soul. I even maintain that something happens in the soul corresponding to the circulation of the blood and to every internal movement of the viscera, although one is unaware of such happenings, just as those who live near a water-mill are unaware of the noise it makes. The fact is that if during sleep or waking there were impressions in the body which did not touch or affect the soul in any way at all, there would have to be limits to the union of body and soul, as though bodily impressions needed a certain shape or size if the soul was to be able to feel them. And that is indefensible if the soul is incorporeal, for there is no relation of proportion between an incorporeal substance and this or that modification of matter. In short, many errors can flow from the belief that the only perceptions in the soul are the ones of which it is aware.

PHIL. §16. Most of the dreams which we remember are extravagant and incoherent...So we should have to say either that the soul owes its capacity for rational thinking to the body or else that it retains none of its 'rational soliloquies'.

THEO. The body has counterparts of all the thoughts of the soul, rational or otherwise, and dreams have traces in the brain just as much as do the thoughts of those who are awake.

117 PHIL. §17. Since you are so confident 'that the soul always actually thinks, I [wish that you could tell me] what those ideas are, that are in the soul of a child, before, or just at the union with the body, before it hath received any by sensation.'

THEO. It is easy to satisfy you on my principles. The perceptions of the soul always correspond naturally to the state of the body; and when there are many confused and indistinct motions in the brain, as happens with those who have had little experience, it naturally follows that the thoughts of the soul cannot be distinct either. But the soul is never deprived of the aid of 'sensation'; for it always expresses its body, and this body is always affected in infinitely many ways by surrounding things, though often they provide only a confused impression.

PHIL. §18. But here is yet another question posed by the author of the *Essay*. 'I would be glad [he says] to learn from these men, who so confidently pronounce, that the human soul, or which is all one, that a man always thinks, how they...know it'.

THEO. I suggest that it needs even more 'confidence' to deny that anything happens in the soul of which we are not aware. For anything which is noticeable must be made up of parts which are not: nothing, whether thought or motion, can come into existence suddenly. In short, it is as though someone were to ask, these days, how we know about insensible particles.

PHIL. §19. 'They who tell us, that the soul always thinks, do never, that I remember, [tell us] that a man always thinks.'

THEO. I suppose that that is because they are talking about the separated soul too, and that they would readily admit that the man always thinks while his soul and body are united. As for my own views: since I have reason to hold that the soul is never completely separated from all body, I think it can be said without qualification that the man does and will always think. 118

PHIL. To say that a body is extended without having parts, and that anything thinks without being aware that it does so, are two assertions which seem equally unintelligible.

THEO. Forgive me, sir, but I must point out that when you contend that there is nothing in the soul of which it is not aware, you are begging the question. That contention has already held sway all through our first meeting, when you tried to use it to tear down innate ideas and truths. If I conceded it, I would not only be flying in the face of experience and of reason, but would also be gratuitously relinquishing my own view, for which I think I have made a good enough case. My opponents, accomplished as they are, have adduced no proof of their own firmly and frequently repeated contention on this matter; and what is more, there is an easy way of showing them that they are wrong, i.e. that it is impossible that we should always reflect explicitly on all our thoughts; for if we did, the mind would reflect on each reflection, *ad infinitum*, without ever being able to move on to a new thought. For example, in being aware of some present feeling, I should have always to think that I think about that feeling, and further to think that I think of thinking about it, and so on *ad infinitum*. It must be that I stop reflecting on all these reflections, and that eventually some thought is allowed to occur without being thought about; otherwise I would dwell for ever on the same thing.

PHIL. But could one not 'with as much reason . . . say, that a man is always hungry,' adding that he can be hungry without being aware of it?

THEO. There is a great deal of difference: hunger arises from special conditions which do not always obtain. Still, it is true that even when one is hungry one does not think about the hunger all the time; but when one thinks about it, one is aware of it, for it is a very noticeable disposition: there are always disturbances in the stomach, but they do not cause hunger unless they become strong enough. One should always observe this distinction between thoughts in general and noticeable thoughts. Thus, a point which was offered in mockery of my view really serves to confirm it.

119 PHIL. §23. It may be asked now 'when a man begins to have any ideas' in his thought.[1] And it seems to me that one ought to reply that it is 'when he first has any sensation.'

THEO. That is my view too, though only for a somewhat special reason. For I believe that we are never without ideas, never without thoughts, and never without sensations either. But I distinguish ideas from thoughts. For we always have all our pure or distinct ideas independently of the senses, but thoughts always correspond to some sensation.

PHIL. §25. But the mind is 'merely passive' in the perception of simple ideas, which are the 'beginnings [or] materials of knowledge'; whereas in the forming of composite ideas it is active.[2]

THEO. How can it be wholly passive with respect to the perception of all simple ideas, when by your own admission some simple ideas are perceived through reflection? The mind must at least give itself its thoughts of reflection, since it is the mind which reflects. Whether it can shut them out is another matter; no doubt it cannot do so unless some circumstance prompts it to turn aside.

PHIL. So far we seem to have been in open disagreement. Now that we are moving on to consider ideas in detail, I hope that we shall find more to agree on and that our disagreements will be restricted to minor matters.

THEO. I shall be delighted to see able people accepting views which I hold to be true, for they can cause the views to be appreciated and can show them in a good light.

120
Chapter ii
'Of simple ideas.'

PHILALETHES. §1. I hope then that you will still agree, sir, that some ideas are simple and some composite.[3] Thus, the warmth and softness of wax, the hardness and coldness of ice, provide simple ideas; for of these the soul has a uniform conception which is not distinguishable into different ideas.

THEOPHILUS. It can be maintained, I believe, that these sensible ideas appear simple because they are confused and thus do not provide the mind with any way of making discriminations within what they contain; just like distant things which appear rounded because one cannot discern their angles, even though one is receiving some confused impression from them. It is obvious that green, for instance, comes from a mixture of blue and

---

[1] Added by Leibniz.   [2] Added by Leibniz.
[3] Locke: 'complex'. Coste's change.

yellow; which makes it credible that the idea of green is composed of the ideas of those two colours, although the idea of green appears to us as simple as that of blue, or as that of warmth. So these ideas of blue and of warmth should also be regarded as simple only in appearance. I freely admit that we treat them as simple ideas, because we are at any rate not aware of any divisions within them; but we should undertake the *analysis of them by means of further experiments, and by means of reason in so far as they can be made more capable of being treated by the intellect.

Chapter iii
'Of ideas of one sense.'

PHILALETHES. §1. Now we can classify simple ideas according to how we come to perceive them, namely (1) by one sense only, (2) by more senses than one, (3) by reflection, or (4) by all the ways of sensation and reflection. As for those 'which have admittance only through one sense, which is peculiarly adapted to receive them[,] light and colours...come in only by the eyes: all kinds of noises, sounds, and tones only by the ears:' the several tastes by the palate, and smells by the nose.[1] The organs or nerves convey them to the brain, and if some of the organs become disordered, those sensations have no side-entrance to be admitted by. 'The most considerable of those, belonging to the touch, are heat and cold, and solidity'. The rest consist either in the arrangement of sensible parts, 'as smooth and rough; or else [in the] adhesion of the parts, as hard and soft, tough and brittle'.

THEOPHILUS. I am pretty much in agreement with what you say, sir. But I might remark that, judging by the late Monsieur *Mariotte's experiment on the blind spot in the region of the optic nerve, it seems that membranes receive the *sensation more than nerves do; and that there is a side-entrance for hearing and for taste, since the teeth and the cranium contribute to the hearing of sounds, and tastes can be experienced in a fashion through the nose because the organs are connected. But none of that makes any fundamental difference as regards the elucidation of ideas. As for tactile qualities: smooth and rough, like hard and soft, can be described as mere modifications of resistance or solidity.

Chapter iv
'Of solidity.'

PHILALETHES. §1. No doubt you will also agree that the *sensation[1] of solidity 'arises from the resistance which we find in body, to the entrance

---

[1] Locke: 'the several tastes and smells, by the nose and palate.' Coste's change.
[1] Locke: 'idea'.

of any other body into the place it possesses, till it has left it. [Accordingly, that which] hinders the approach of two bodies, when they are moving one towards another, I call solidity. ... If any one think it better to call it impenetrability, he has my consent. [But I think that] *solidity*...carries something more of positive in it[. This idea appears the] most intimately connected with, and essential to body,' and one can find it only in matter.

THEOPHILUS. It is true that we find resistance in the sense of touch, when there is difficulty in getting another body to give way to our own. It is true also that bodies are reluctant[1] jointly to occupy a single place. Yet some people are not convinced that this reluctance is unconquerable; and it is worth bearing in mind that the resistance which occurs in matter arises from it in more than one way, and for rather different reasons. One body resists another when it either has to leave the place it is already in or fails to enter the place it was about to enter, because the other body exerts itself to enter there too; and in that case it can happen, if neither yields, that each brings the other to a halt or pushes it back. The resistance is manifested in the change in the body which is resisted – whether a loss of force or a change of direction or both at once. Now, it can be said in a general way that this resistance comes from the reluctance of two bodies to share the same place, which can be called impenetrability; for when one exerts itself to enter the place, it also exerts itself to drive the other out or prevent it from entering. But having granted that there is this kind of incompatibility which makes one or both of them yield, there are in addition several other sources for a body's resistance to another body which tries to make it give way. Some lie in the body itself, the others in neighbouring bodies. Within the body itself there are two – one passive and constant, and the other active and changing. The former is what I follow Kepler and *Descartes in calling *inertia*. This renders matter resistant to motion, so that force must be expended to move a body, independently of its having weight or being bonded to other things. Thus a body which seeks to drive another along must encounter such resistance as a result. The other cause – the active and changing one – consists in the body's own impetus: the body will not yield without resistance at a time when its own impetus is carrying it to a given place. These sources of resistance recur in the neighbouring bodies when the resisting body cannot yield without making others yield in their turn. But now a new element enters the picture, namely *firmness* or the bonding of one body to another. This bonding often results in one's being unable to push one body without at the same time pushing another which is bonded to it, so that there is a kind of *traction* of the second body. Because of this bonding, there would be resistance even if there were

[1] Leibniz's '*répugnance*' could mean either 'reluctance' or 'logical impossibility', but the latter does not fit the context. There are other indications, too, that Leibniz wants this passage to have an anthropomorphic tone.

no inertia or manifest impetus. For if space is conceived as full of perfectly fluid matter which has neither inertia nor impetus, and a single hard body is placed in it, there will be no resistance to the body's being moved; but if space were full of small cubes, a hard body would encounter resistance to its being moved among them. This is because the little cubes – just because they were hard, i.e. because their parts were bonded together – would be difficult to split up finely enough to permit circular movement $\quad$ 124 in which the position being evacuated by the moving body would at once be refilled by something else. But if two bodies were simultaneously inserted into the two open ends of a tube into which each of them fitted tightly, the matter which was already in the tube, however fluid it might be, would resist just because of its sheer impenetrability. So the phenomenon of resistance which we are considering involves the impenetrability of bodies, inertia, impetus, and bonding. It is true that in my opinion this bonding of bodies results from more attenuated movements of bodies towards one another; but since the point is disputable, it ought not to be assumed from the start. Nor, for the same reason, should it be initially assumed that there is an inherent, essential solidity which makes the place occupied always equal to the thing which occupies it, i.e. that the incompatibility (or, to put it more accurately, the *disagreement*) of two bodies in one place is a matter of perfect impenetrability, not admitting of degrees; since some people say that perceptible solidity may be due to a body's having a certain reluctance – but not an unconquerable one – to share a place with another body. For all the ordinary Peripatetics and some others believe that what they call rarefaction and condensation can occur, i.e. that the very same matter could occupy more or less space: not merely in appearance (as when water is squeezed out of a sponge), but really, as the Schoolmen think is the case with air. I do not hold this view, but I do not think that one ought to assume its contradictory from the start; for the senses unaided by reasoning do not suffice to establish that perfect impenetrability which I hold obtains in the natural realm but which is not apprehended by mere sensation. And someone could claim that bodies' resistance to compression is due to an effort by their parts to spread out when they are subject to confinement. Two final points. In detecting these qualities, the eyes can very usefully come to the aid of the sense of touch. And solidity, in so far as there is a distinct notion of it, is fundamentally conceived through pure reason, though the senses provide a basis for reasoning to prove that solidity occurs in nature.

PHIL. §4. We are in agreement, at least, that a body's 'solidity consists in repletion, and so an utter exclusion of other bodies out of the space it possesses' unless it can find some new space for itself;[1] but hardness (or

---

[1] Added by Leibniz, as is the following parenthetical phrase.

125 rather stability, which some call firmness) is 'a firm cohesion of the parts of matter, making up masses of a sensible bulk, so that the whole does not easily change its figure.'

THEO. As I have already remarked, the special function of rigidity is to make it difficult to move one part of a body without also moving the remainder, so that when one part is pushed the other is also taken in the same direction by a kind of *traction*, although it is not itself pushed and does not lie on the line along which the endeavour is exercised; and, furthermore, if the latter part meets an obstacle which holds it still or forces it back, it in turn will pull back or hold still the former part – this is always reciprocal. The same thing happens sometimes with two bodies which are not in contact and are not contiguous parts of a single continuous body; for even then it can happen that the one, on being pushed, makes the other move without pushing it, in so far as our senses can tell. Examples of this are provided by the magnet, electrical attraction, and the attraction which used to be attributed to nature's fear of a vacuum.

PHIL. It seems that in general 'hard and soft are names that we give to things, only in relation to the constitutions of our own bodies'.

THEO. But then there would not be many philosophers attributing hardness to their 'atoms'. The notion of hardness does not depend on the senses: the possibility of it can be conceived through reason, although it is the senses which convince us that it also actually occurs in nature. However, rather than the word 'hardness' I would prefer 'firmness', if I may be allowed to use it in this sense, for there is always some firmness even in soft bodies. I would even look for a broader and more general word such as 'stability' or *'cohesion'. Thus, I would contrast hard with soft, and firm with fluid; for wax is soft, but unless melted by heat it is not fluid and retains its boundaries; and even in fluids there is usually some cohesion, as can be seen in drops of water and of mercury. My opinion is that all bodies have a degree of cohesion; just as I think that there are none which are entirely without fluidity or possessed of a cohesion which cannot be overcome; so that in my view the atoms of Epicurus, which are supposed to be unconquerably hard, cannot exist, any more than can the rarefied and perfectly fluid matter of the Cartesians. But this is not the place to defend this view or to explain what gives rise to cohesion.

126

PHIL. There seems to be experimental proof that bodies are perfectly solid. For example, in Florence a golden globe filled with water was put into a press; the water could not give way, and so it passed out through the pores of the globe.

THEO. There is something to be said about the conclusion you draw from what happened to the water in that experiment. Air is a body just as much as water is, and yet the same thing would not happen to air, since it is – at least so far as the senses can tell – compressible. And those who hold with genuine rarefaction and condensation will say that water is already too compressed to yield to our machines, just as very compressed air resists further compression. But I admit on the other hand that if some tiny change were noticed in the volume of the water, that could be ascribed to the air which it contains; but I shall not now discuss the question of whether pure water is itself compressible, as it is found to be expansible when it evaporates. Still, fundamentally I share the view of those who think that bodies are perfectly impenetrable, and that there is only apparent rarefaction and condensation. But this cannot be proved by the sort of experiment you have described, any more than the *Torricellian tube or *Guericke's machine suffices to prove a perfect vacuum.

PHIL. If body could be strictly rarefied or compressed, it could change its volume or its extension; but since that cannot happen, a body will always be equal to the same space.[1] §5. Yet its extension will always be distinct from the extension of the space.

THEO. Body could have its own extension without that implying that the extension was always determinate or equal to the same space. Still, although it is true that in conceiving body one conceives something in addition to space, it does not follow that there are two extensions, that of space and that of body. Similarly, in conceiving several things at once one conceives something in addition to the number, namely the things numbered; and yet there are not two pluralities, one of them abstract (for the number) and the other concrete (for the things numbered). In the same way, there is no need to postulate two extensions, one abstract (for space) and the other concrete (for body). For the concrete one is as it is only by virtue of the abstract one: just as bodies pass from one position in space to another, i.e. change how they are ordered in relation to one another, so things pass also from one position to another within an ordering or enumeration – as when the first becomes the second, the second becomes the third, etc. In fact, time and place are only kinds of order; and an empty place within one of these orders (called 'vacuum' in the case of space), if it occurred, would indicate the mere possibility of the missing item and how it relates to the actual.

PHIL. I am still very pleased that you are fundamentally in agreement with me that matter does not alter its volume. But when you refuse to allow that there are two extensions, sir, you seem to go too far, and to come close to the Cartesians, who do not distinguish space from matter. Now, it seems to me that if there are people who do not have these distinct ideas of space and of the solidity which fills it, but rather confound them and turn the two ideas into one, it is impossible to see how such people can communicate

---

[1] Added by Leibniz.

with anyone else. They are as a blind man would be, in relation to someone who was telling him about the colour scarlet, if the blind man believed that it is like the sound of a trumpet.

THEO. But I also hold that the ideas of extension and solidity do not consist in a *je ne sais quoi*, like the idea of the colour scarlet. I distinguish extension from matter, opposing the Cartesians' view, but I do not believe that there are two extensions. Also, since those who dispute about the difference between extension and solidity do agree on some truths in this area, and have some distinct notions, they should be able to find a way of resolving their conflict, and so the alleged differences in their ideas ought not to serve as an excuse for letting the debate go on for ever; though I know that certain Cartesians – very able ones too – are given to sheltering behind ideas which they claim to have. But if they would avail themselves of means which I formerly presented ['Meditations on knowledge, truth and ideas'] for telling true ideas from false – means which we shall also say something about later on [p. 269] – they would withdraw from their untenable position.

128

Chapter v
'Of simple ideas of divers senses.'

PHILALETHES. The ideas the perception of which comes to us 'by more than one sense, are of space, or extension, figure, rest, and motion'.

THEOPHILUS. These ideas which are said to come from more than one sense – such as those of space, figure, motion, rest – come rather from the common sense, that is, from the mind itself; for they are ideas of the pure understanding (though ones which relate to the external world and which the senses make us perceive), and so they admit of definitions and of demonstrations.

Chapter vi
'Of simple ideas of reflection.'

PHILALETHES. §§ 1–2. The simple ideas which come through reflection are the ideas of the understanding and of the will; for we are aware of these when we reflect upon ourselves.

129 THEOPHILUS. It is doubtful whether these are all simple ideas; for it is evident for instance that the idea of the will includes that of the understanding, and that the idea of movement contains the idea of figure.

Chapter vii
'Of…ideas of both sensation and reflection.'

PHILALETHES. §1. There are simple ideas which come to be perceived in[1] 'the mind, by all the ways of sensation and reflection, viz. Pleasure …Pain…Power…Existence…Unity.'

THEOPHILUS. It seems that the senses could not convince us of the existence of sensible things without help from reason. So I would say that the thought of existence comes from reflection, that those of power and unity come from the same source, and that these are of a quite different nature from the perceptions of pleasure and pain.

Chapter viii
'Some farther considerations concerning…simple ideas.'

PHILALETHES. §2. What shall we say about privative qualities? It seems to me that the ideas of rest, darkness and cold are just as positive as those of motion, light and heat. §6. However, 'the privative causes I have here assigned of positive ideas, are according to the common opinion; but in truth it will be hard to determine, whether there be really any ideas from a privative cause, till it be determined, whether rest be any more a privation than motion.'

130

THEOPHILUS. I had never thought there could be any reason to doubt the privative nature of rest. All it involves is a denial of motion in the body. For motion, on the other hand, it is not enough to deny rest; something else must be added to determine the degree of motion, for it is essentially a matter of more and less, whereas all states of rest are equal. It is different when the cause of rest is in question, for that must be positive in secondary matter, i.e. mass. But I should still think that the *idea* of rest is privative, that is, that it consists only in negation. It is true that the act of denial is something positive.

PHIL. §8. The *qualities* of things are their faculties for producing the perception of ideas in us. §9. We should make a distinction within them. There are primary and secondary qualities. Extension, solidity, figure, number, and mobility are what I call 'primary' qualities: they are the original qualities of body and are inseparable from it. §10. And I designate as 'secondary qualities' the faculties or powers which bodies have to produce certain sensations in us, or certain effects in other bodies, as for example the effect of the fire on the wax which it melts.

THEO. I think it could be said that when a power is intelligible and admits of being distinctly explained, it should be included among the primary

---

[1] Locke: 'which convey themselves into'.

qualities, but when it is merely sensible and yields only a confused idea it should be put among the secondary qualities.

PHIL. §11. These primary qualities show 'how bodies operate one upon another'. Bodies act only by *impulse, at least so far as we can conceive, 'it being impossible to [understand], that body should operate on what it does not touch, (which is all one as to imagine it can operate where it is not)'.[1]

THEO. I am also of the opinion that bodies act only by impulse, but there is a problem for the argument you have just given. For attraction sometimes involves touching: one can touch something and draw it along apparently without impulse, as I showed earlier in discussing hardness [pp. 60, 125]. If one part of an Epicurean atom (supposing there were such things) were pushed, it would draw the rest along with it, being in contact with it while setting it into motion without impulse; and when there is an attraction between two contiguous things, the one which draws the other along with it cannot be said to 'operate where it is not'. This argument would be valid only against attraction at a distance, such as would be involved in the so-called *centripetal force which some worthy people have advanced.

PHIL. §13. Now, when certain particles strike our organs in various ways, they cause in us certain *sensations of colours or of tastes, or of other secondary qualities which have the power to produce those *sensations. 'It being no more impossible, to conceive, that God should annex such ideas [as that of heat] to such motions, with which they have no similitude; than that he should annex the idea of pain to the motion of a piece of steel dividing our flesh, with which that idea hath no resemblance.'

THEO. It must not be thought that ideas such as those of *colour and pain are arbitrary and that between them and their causes there is no relation or natural connection: it is not God's way to act in such an unruly and unreasoned fashion. I would say, rather, that there is a resemblance of a kind – not a perfect one which holds all the way through, but a resemblance in which one thing expresses another through some orderly relationship between them. Thus an ellipse, and even a parabola or hyperbola, has some resemblance to the circle of which it is a projection on a plane, since there is a certain precise and natural relationship between what is projected and the projection which is made from it, with each point on the one corresponding through a certain relation with a point on the other. This is something which the Cartesians have overlooked; and on this occasion, sir, you have deferred to them more than is your wont and more than you had grounds for doing.

[1] The content of this paragraph was dropped after the third edition of the *Essay*, but retained by Coste.

131

PHIL. I tell you what appears to me true; and it appears to be the case that §15. 'the ideas of primary qualities of bodies, are resemblances of [those qualities]; but the ideas, produced in us by [the] secondary qualities, have no resemblance of them at all.'

THEO. I have just pointed out how there is a resemblance, i.e. a precise relationship, in the case of secondary qualities as well as of primary. It is thoroughly reasonable that the effect should correspond to the cause; and how could one ever be sure that it does not, since we have no distinct knowledge either of the sensation of blue (for instance) or of the motions which produce it? It is true that pain does not resemble the movement of a pin; but it might thoroughly resemble the motions which the pin causes in our body, and might represent them in the soul; and I have not the least doubt that it does. That is why we say that the pain is in our body and not in the pin, although we say that the light is in the fire;[1] because there are motions in the fire which the senses cannot clearly detect individually, but which form a confusion – a running together – which is brought within reach of the senses and is represented to us by the idea of light.

PHIL. §21. But if the relation between the object and the *sensation were a natural one, how could it happen, as we observe it to do, that the same water can appear cold to one hand and warm to the other? That phenomenon shows that the warmth is no more in the water than pain is in the pin.

THEO. The most that it shows is that warmth is not a sensible quality (i.e. a power of being sensorily detected) of an entirely absolute kind, but rather depends upon the associated organs; for a movement in the hand itself can combine with that of warmth, altering its appearance. Again, light does not appear to malformed eyes, and when eyes are full of bright light they cannot see a dimmer one. Even the primary qualities (as you call them), such as unity and number, can fail to appear as they should; for, as M. *Descartes has already reported [*Optics* VI], a globe appears double when it is touched with the fingers in a certain way, and an object is multiplied when seen in a mirror or through a glass into which facets have been cut. So, from the fact that something does not always appear the same, it does not follow that it is not a quality of the object, or that its image does not resemble it. As for warmth: when our hand is very warm, the lesser warmth of the water does not make itself felt, and serves rather to moderate the warmth of the hand, so that the water appears to us to be cold; just as salt water from the Baltic, when mixed with water from the Sea of Portugal, lessens its degree of salinity even though it is itself saline. So there is a sense in which the warmth can be said to inhere in the water in a bath, even if the water appears cold to someone; just as we describe honey in

___
[1] This refers to Locke's §16.

132

absolute terms as sweet, and silver as white, even though to certain invalids one appears sour and the other yellow; for things are named according to what is most usual. None of this alters the fact that when the organ and the intervening medium are properly constituted, the internal bodily motions and the ideas which represent them to the soul resemble the motions of the object which cause the colour, the warmth, the pain etc.; or – what is here the same thing – they express the object through some rather precise relationship; though this relation does not appear distinctly to us, because we cannot disentangle this multitude of minute impressions, whether in our soul or in our body or in what lies outside us.

PHIL. §24. The qualities which the sun has of blanching and softening wax, or hardening mud, we consider only as simple powers, without conceiving anything in the sun which resembles this whiteness and this softness, or this hardness. Yet warmth and light 'are commonly thought real qualities [of] the sun.... Whereas, if rightly considered, these qualities of light and warmth, which are perceptions in me..., are no otherwise in the sun, than the changes made in the wax, when it is blanched or melted, are in the sun.'

THEO. Some have pushed this doctrine so far that they have tried to persuade us that if someone could touch the sun he would find no heat in it. The counterfeit sun which can be felt at the focus of a mirror or a burning glass should disabuse them of that. But as for the comparison between the warming faculty and the melting one: I would venture to say that if the melted or blanched wax were sentient, it too would feel something like what we feel when the sun warms us, and it would say if it could that the sun is hot. This is not because the wax's whiteness resembles the sun, for in that case the brown of a face tanned by the sun would also resemble it; but because at that time there are motions in the wax which have a relationship with the motions in the sun which cause them. There could be some other cause for the wax's whiteness, but not for the motions which it has undergone in receiving whiteness from the sun.

Chapter ix
'Of perception.'

PHILALETHES. §1. This brings us specifically to ideas of reflection. 'Perception, as it is the first faculty of the [soul], exercised about our ideas; so it is the first and simplest idea we have from reflection[. *Thinking* often] signifies that sort of operation of the mind about its ideas, wherein the mind is active; where it with some degree of voluntary attention, considers any thing. [But in what is called] *perception*, the mind is, for the most part, only passive; and what it perceives, it cannot avoid perceiving.'

THEOPHILUS. It might perhaps be added that beasts have perception, and that they don't necessarily have thought, that is, have reflection or anything which could be the object of it. We too have minute perceptions of which we are not aware in our present state. We could in fact become thoroughly aware of them and reflect on them, if we were not distracted by their multiplicity, which scatters the mind, and if bigger ones did not obliterate them or rather put them in the shade.

PHIL. §4. I admit that while the 'mind is intently employed in the contemplation of some objects; [it is no way aware][1] of impressions of [certain] bodies, made upon the organ of hearing. . . . A sufficient impulse there may be. . . ; but it not reaching the observation of the [soul], there follows no perception'.

THEO. I would prefer to distinguish between *perception* and *being *aware*. For instance, a perception of light or colour of which we are aware is made up of many minute perceptions of which we are unaware; and a noise which we perceive but do not attend to is brought within reach of our awareness by a tiny increase or addition. If the previous noise had no effect on the soul, this minute addition would have none either, nor would the total. (I have already touched on this point at II.i.11, 12, 15 etc.)

PHIL. §8. This is a good time to remark that the ideas which are received by sensation are often altered by the judgment of the mind in grown people, without their being aware of it. The idea of a 'globe, of any uniform colour, . . . is of a flat circle variously shadowed' and lighted. But as we are accustomed to distinguish the appearances of bodies, and the alterations in the reflections of light according to the shapes of their surfaces, we substitute the cause of the image for what actually appears to us, and confound judging with seeing.[2]

THEO. That is perfectly true: this is how a painting can deceive us, by means of an artful use of perspective. When bodies have flat surfaces they can be depicted merely by means of their outlines, without use of shading, painting them simply in the Chinese manner but with better proportions. This is how drawings of medallions are usually done, so that the draftsman can stay closer to the precise lineaments of the ancient originals. But such a drawing, unaided by shading, cannot distinguish definitely between a flat circular surface and a spherical surface – since neither contains any distinct points or distinguishing features – and yet there is a great difference

135

---

[1] Locke: 'it takes no notice'. Coste: '*il ne s'aperçoit en aucune manière*'.
[2] Locke: 'the judgment. . .alters the appearances into their causes'. Coste: '*nous mettons . . .à la place de ce qui nous paraît, la cause même de l'image. . .joignant à la vision un jugement que nous confondons avec elle*'. The clause '*joignant. . .elle*', which may be based on Locke's §9, is contracted by Leibniz to '*et confondons le jugement avec la vision*'.

between them which ought to be marked. That is why M. *Desargues has offered rules about the effects of hue and shading.

So when we are deceived by a painting our judgments are doubly in error. First, we substitute the cause for the effect, and believe that we immediately see the thing that causes the image, rather like a dog barking at a mirror. For strictly we see only the image, and are affected only by rays of light. Since rays of light need time – however little – to reach us, it is possible that the object should be destroyed during the interval and no longer exist when the light reaches the eye; and something which no longer exists cannot be the present object of our sight. Secondly, we are further deceived when we substitute one cause for another and believe that what comes merely from a flat painting actually comes from a body. In such cases our judgments involve both metonymy and metaphor (for even figures of rhetoric turn into sophisms when they mislead us). This confusion of the effect with the real or the putative cause frequently occurs in other sorts of judgments too. This is how we come to believe that it is by an immediate real influence that we sense our bodies and the things which touch them, and move our arms, taking this influence to constitute the interaction between the soul and the body; whereas really all that we sense or alter in that way is what is within us.

PHIL. Here is a problem for you, which 'that very ingenious and studious promoter of real knowledge, the learned and worthy Mr *Molyneux,' sent to the distinguished Mr Locke. This is more or less how he worded it: 'Suppose a man born blind, and now adult, and taught by his touch to distinguish between a cube, and a sphere of the same metal, and nighly of the same bigness, so as to tell, when he felt one and t'other, which is the cube, which the sphere. Suppose then the cube and sphere placed on a table, and the blind man to be made to see. *Quaere*, whether by his sight, before he touched them, he could now distinguish, and tell, which is the globe, which the cube.' Now, sir, please tell me what your view is about this.

136

THEO. The question strikes me as a rather interesting one. I would need to spend time thinking about it; but since you urge me to reply at once I will risk saying, just between the two of us, that I believe that if the blind man knows that the two shapes which he sees are those of a cube and a sphere, he will be able to identify them and to say without touching them that this one is the sphere and this the cube.

PHIL. I am afraid I have to include you among the many who have given Mr Molyneux the wrong answer. In the letter containing this question he recounts that having, on the occasion of Mr Locke's *Essay*, 'proposed this to divers very ingenious men, he hardly ever met with one, that at first gave the answer to it, which he thinks true, [although after] hearing his reasons they were convinced' of their mistake. The answer which this 'acute and judicious proposer' gives is negative. For, he says, though this blind man 'has obtained the experience of, how a globe, how a cube affects his touch; yet he [does not yet know] that what affects his touch so or so, must affect his sight so or so; or that a protuberant angle in the cube, that pressed his hand unequally, shall appear to his eye, as it does in the cube.' The author of the *Essay* declares that he entirely agrees.

THEO. It may be that Mr Molyneux and the author of the *Essay* are not as far from my opinion as at first appears, and that the reasons for their view – contained in Mr Molyneux's letter, it appears, and successfully used by him to convince people of their mistake – have been deliberately suppressed by our author in order to make his readers exercise their minds the harder. If you will just consider my reply, sir, you will see that I have included in it a condition which can be taken to be implicit in the question: namely that it is merely a problem of telling which is which, and that the blind man knows that the two shaped bodies which he has to discern are before him and thus that each of the appearances which he sees is either that of a cube or that of a sphere. Given this condition, it seems to me past question that the blind man whose sight is restored could discern them by applying rational principles to the sensory knowledge which he has already acquired by touch. I am not talking about what he might actually do on the spot, when he is dazzled and confused by the strangeness – or, one should add, unaccustomed to making inferences. My view rests on the fact that in the case of the sphere there are no distinguished points on the surface of the sphere taken in itself, since everything there is uniform and without angles, whereas in the case of the cube there are eight points which are distinguished from all the others. If there were not that way of discerning shapes, a blind man could not learn the rudiments of geometry by touch, nor could someone else learn them by sight without touch. However, we find that men born blind are capable of learning geometry, and indeed always have some rudiments of a natural geometry; and we find that geometry is mostly learned by sight alone without employing touch, as could and indeed must be done by a paralytic or by anyone else to whom touch is virtually denied. These two geometries, the blind man's and the paralytic's, must come together, and agree, and indeed ultimately rest on the same ideas, even though they have no images in common. Which shows yet again how essential it is to distinguish *images* from *exact ideas* which are composed of definitions. It would indeed be very interesting and even informative to investigate thoroughly the ideas of someone born blind, and to hear how he would describe shapes. For he could achieve that, and could even understand optical theory in so far as it rests on distinct mathematical ideas, though he would not be able to achieve a conception of the *vivid-confused*, i.e. of the image of light and colours. That is why one man born blind, who had heard lessons in optics and appeared to understand them quite well, when he was asked what he believed light was, replied that he supposed it must be something pleasant like sugar. Similarly, it would be very important to investigate the ideas which a man born deaf and dumb can have about things without shapes: we ordinarily have the description of such things in words, but he would have to have it in an entirely different manner – though it might be equivalent to ours, just as Chinese writing produces an effect equivalent to that of our alphabet although it is utterly different from it and might appear to have been invented by a deaf man. I am indebted to a great Prince for the report of a man in Paris who was born deaf and dumb and whose ears have finally begun to perform their function. He has now learned the French language (the report came from the French court, not long ago), and will be able to tell very interesting things about his conceptions during his previous state and about how his ideas have changed since beginning to exercise his sense of hearing. Men born deaf and dumb can accomplish more than one might think. There was one at Oldenburg, during the time of the last Count, who had become a good painter and also proved himself to be a very intelligent man. A most learned Breton has told me that around 1690 in Blain – a town belonging to the Duke de Rohan, ten leagues from Nantes – there was a poor man, born deaf and dumb, who lived in a hut near the chateau, outside the town; he would carry letters and so on to the town, and would be guided to the right houses by certain signs made to him by people who were used to employing him. Eventually the poor man became blind as well, yet he still made himself useful taking letters to the town, wherever was indicated to him by touch. He had a board in his hut, running from the door to the spot where his feet rested, and the movements of this would announce to him when someone was coming in. Men are very remiss in not informing themselves accurately about how such people think. If he is no longer alive there is likely to be someone on the spot who could still give us some information about him and explain how people indicated to him the tasks he was to carry out.

But to return to the man born blind who begins to see, and to what he would judge about the sphere and the cube when he saw but did not touch them: as I said a moment ago, I reply that he will know which is which if he is told that, of the two appearances or perceptions he has of them, one belongs to the sphere and the other to the cube. But if he is not thus instructed in advance, I grant that it will not at once occur to him that these paintings of them (as it were) that he forms at the back of his eyes, which could come from a flat painting on the table, represent bodies. That will occur to him only when he becomes convinced of it by the sense of touch or when he comes, through applying principles of optics to the light rays, to understand from the evidence of the lights and shadows that there is something blocking the rays and that it must be precisely the same thing that resists his touch. He will eventually come to understand this when he sees the sphere and cube rolling, with consequent changes in their appearances and in the shadows they cast; or when, with the two bodies remaining still, the source of the light falling on them is moved or the position of his eyes changes. For these are pretty much the means that we do have for distinguishing at a distance between a picture or perspective representing an object and the real object.

PHIL. §11. Let us return to perception in general. It 'puts the distinction betwixt the animal kingdom, and the inferior' beings.

THEO. The great analogy which exists between plants and animals inclines   139
me to believe that there is some perception and appetite even in plants; and if there is a vegetative soul, as is generally thought, then it must have perception. All the same, I attribute to mechanism everything which takes place in the bodies of plants and animals except their initial formation. Thus I agree that the movements of what are called 'sensitive' plants result from mechanism,[1] and I do not approve of bringing in the soul when plant and animal phenomena have to be explained in detail.

PHIL. §§13-14. Indeed, 'I cannot but think, there is some small dull perception' even in such animals as oysters and cockles. For 'quickness of sensation [would only] be an inconvenience to an animal, that must lie still, where chance has once placed it; and there receive the afflux of colder or warmer, clean or foul water, as it happens to come to it'.

THEO. Very good, and I believe that almost the same could be said about plants. In man's case, however, perceptions are accompanied by the power to reflect, which turns into actual reflection when there are the means for it. But when a man is reduced to a state where it is as though he were in a coma, and where he has almost no *feeling, he does lose reflection and awareness, and gives no thought to general truths. Nevertheless, his faculties and dispositions, both innate and acquired, and even the impressions which he receives in this state of confusion, still continue: they are not obliterated though they are forgotten. Some day their turn will come to contribute to some noticeable result; for nothing in nature is useless, all confusion must be resolved, and even the animals, which have sunk into a condition of stupidity, must return at last to perceptions of a higher degree. Since simple substances endure for ever it is wrong to judge of eternity from a few years.

Chapter x   140
'Of retention.'

PHILALETHES. §1. 'The next faculty of the mind, whereby it makes a farther progress towards knowledge [of things than it does through simple

---

[1] Locke says this in §11.

perception],[1] is that which I call retention,' or the preserving of those items of knowledge[2] which the mind has received through the senses or through reflection. This is done in two ways: by keeping the idea actually in view, which is called contemplation; and **§2.** by keeping the power to bring ideas back before the mind, which is what is called memory.

THEOPHILUS. We also retain and contemplate innate knowledge, and very often we cannot distinguish the innate from the acquired. There is also perception of images, both those we have had for some time and those which have newly come into being in us.

PHIL. But it is believed by our party that these images or ideas 'cease to be any thing, when there is no perception of them, [and that] this laying up of . . . ideas in the repository of the memory, signifies no more but this, that the [soul] has a power, in many cases, to revive perceptions, which it has once had,' accompanied by a feeling which convinces it that it has had these sorts of perceptions before.[3]

THEO. If ideas were only the forms or manners of thoughts, they would cease with them; but you yourself have acknowledged, sir, that they are the inner objects of thoughts [p. 109], and as such they can persist. I am surprised that you can constantly rest content with bare 'powers' and 'faculties', which you would apparently not accept from the scholastic philosophers. What is needed is a somewhat clearer explanation of what this faculty consists in and how it is exercised: that would show that there are dispositions which are the remains of past impressions, in the soul as well as in the body, but which we are unaware of except when the memory has a use for them. If nothing were left of past thoughts the moment we ceased to think of them, it would be impossible to explain how we could keep the memory of them; to resort to a bare faculty to do the work is to talk unintelligibly.

141

Chapter xi
Of discerning, or the faculty of distinguishing ideas.[4]

PHILALETHES. **§1.** On the faculty of 'discerning' ideas 'depends the evidence and certainty' of various propositions which are taken to be innate truths.

THEOPHILUS. I grant that it requires discernment to think of these innate ideas and to sort them out, but they are no less innate on that account.

[1] Added by Coste.
[2] Locke: 'those simple ideas'.
[3] Locke: 'with this additional perception annexed to them, that it has had them before.' Coste's change.
[4] Locke: 'Of discerning, and other operations of the mind.'

PHIL. §2. Quickness of wit[1] consists in the ready recall of ideas, but there is judgment in setting them out precisely and separating them accurately.

THEO. It may be that each of those is quickness of imagination, and that judgment consists in the scrutiny of propositions in accordance with reason.

PHIL. I pretty much agree with this distinction between wit and judgment. And sometimes there is judgment in not over-using judgment. For instance, 'it is a kind of an affront [to a witty remark] to go about to examine it, by the severe rules of truth, and good reason'.

THEO. That is a good point. Witty thoughts must at least appear to be grounded in reason, but they should not be scrutinized too minutely, just as we ought not to look at a painting from too close. It seems to me that Father *Bouhours, in his *Right Thinking in the Exercise of Wit*, has gone wrong on this count more than once; for instance in his scorn for Lucan's epigram: 'The winning cause pleased the Gods, but the losing one pleased Cato.'

PHIL. §4. 'The comparing them one with another, in respect of extent, degrees, time, place, or any other circumstances, is another operation of the mind about its ideas, and is that upon which depends all that large tribe of ideas, comprehended under relation.'

THEO. I take relation to be more general than comparison. Relations divide 142 into those of *comparison* and those of *concurrence*. The former concern *agreement* and *disagreement* (using these terms in a narrower sense), and include resemblance, equality, inequality etc. The latter involve some *connection*, such as that of cause and effect, whole and parts, position and order etc.

PHIL. §6. The 'composition' of simple ideas to make complex ones is another operation of our mind. This may be taken to cover the faculty of 'enlarging' ideas by putting together several of the same kind, as in forming a dozen out of several units.

THEO. No doubt one is as much composition as the other, but the composition of like ideas is simpler than that of different ideas.

PHIL. §7. 'A bitch will nurse, play with, and be fond of young foxes, as much as…of her puppies, if you can but get them once to suck her so long, that her milk may go through them. And those animals, which have a numerous brood of young ones at once, appear not to have any knowledge of their number'.

---

[1] '*esprit*', which means both 'wit' and 'mind'. Locke in §2 is contrasting 'judgment' with 'wit'.

THEO. The affection of animals arises from a pleasure which is increased by familiarity. But as for precise numbers, even human beings can know the numbers of things only by means of some artifice, such as using numerals for counting, or arranging things in patterns so that it can be seen at a glance, without counting, if one is missing.

PHIL. §10. The beasts do not make abstractions either.

THEO. That is my view too. They apparently recognize whiteness, and observe it in chalk as in snow; but this does not amount to abstraction, which requires attention to the general apart from the particular, and consequently involves knowledge of universal truths, which beasts do not possess. It is also very well said that beasts which talk do not use speech to express general ideas, and that men who are incapable of speech and of words still make other general signs.[1] I am delighted to see you so well aware, here and elsewhere, of the privileges of human nature.

143   PHIL. §11. However, if beasts 'have any ideas at all, and are not bare machines (as some would have them) we cannot deny them to have [a certain degree of] reason. It seems as evident to me, that they...[2] reason, as that they have sense; but it is only in particular ideas, just as they received them from their senses.'

THEO. Beasts pass from one imagining to another by means of a link between them which they have previously experienced. For instance, when his master picks up a stick the dog anticipates being beaten. In many cases children, and for that matter grown men, move from thought to thought in no other way but that. This could be called 'inference' or 'reasoning' in a very broad sense. But I prefer to keep to accepted usage, reserving these words for men and restricting them to the knowledge of some *reason* for perceptions' being linked together. Mere sensations cannot provide this: all they do is to cause one naturally to expect once more that same linking which has been observed previously, even though the reasons may no longer be the same. Hence those who are guided only by their senses are frequently disappointed.

PHIL. §13. Imbeciles[3] are lacking in 'quickness, activity, and motion, in the intellectual faculties, whereby they are deprived of reason: whereas mad men,...seem to suffer by the other extreme. For they do not appear to me to have lost the faculty of reasoning: but having joined together some ideas very wrongly, they mistake them for truths; and they err as men do, that argue right from wrong principles....Thus you shall find a distracted

---

[1] Presumably referring to Locke's §11, though that speaks of beasts which can 'pronounce words distinctly enough', not of ones which can 'talk'.

[2] Locke: 'do some of them in certain instances'. Coste's omission.

[3] Locke uses the now obsolete word 'naturals'.

man fancying himself a king, with a right inference, require suitable attendance, respect, and obedience'.

THEO. Imbeciles don't exercise reason at all. They differ from the stupid, whose judgment is sound but who are looked down on and are a nuisance because they are so slow to grasp things – as someone would be who insisted on playing cards with important people and then spent too long, too often, deciding how to play his hand. I recall that an able man who had lost his memory through using certain drugs was reduced to that condition, but his judgment continued to be evident. A complete madman lacks judgment in almost every situation, yet the quickness of his imagination can make him entertaining. But there are people who are selectively mad: they acquire a false conviction about some important aspect of their lives and then reason correctly from it, as you have rightly pointed out. A man of this kind is well known at a certain court; he believes that he is destined to re-establish the Protestants and to put France to rights, and that to this end God has caused the most eminent personages to pass through his body in order to ennoble it. He seeks to marry all the marriageable princesses that he meets, but only after having sanctified them, in order to establish a holy lineage to govern the earth. He blames all the miseries of the war on the lack of respect paid to his counsels. When he speaks to a sovereign he takes all necessary measures to preserve his dignity. And when anyone engages in reasoning with him he defends himself so skillfully that more than once I have suspected that he is only feigning madness, since he does very well out of it. However, those who know him more intimately assure me that it is quite genuine.

PHIL. §17. 'The understanding is not much unlike a closet wholly shut from light, with only some little openings left, to let in external visible [images];[1] would the [images][2] coming into such a dark room but stay there, and lie so orderly as to be found upon occasion, it would very much resemble the understanding of a man'.

THEO. To increase the resemblance we should have to postulate that there is a screen in this dark room to receive the species,[3] and that it is not uniform but is diversified by folds representing items of innate knowledge; and, what is more, that this screen or membrane, being under tension, has a kind of elasticity or active force, and indeed that it acts (or reacts) in ways which are adapted both to past folds and to new ones coming from impressions of the species. This action would consist in certain vibrations or oscillations, like those we see when a cord under tension is plucked and

144

145

---

[1] Locke: 'resemblances'. Coste's change.
[2] Locke: 'pictures'. Coste's change.
[3] '*espèces*' – i.e. the 'sensible species' which Leibniz declares on p. 343 to be tolerable when understood as here.

gives off something of a musical sound. For not only do we receive images and traces in the brain, but we form new ones from them when we bring 'complex ideas' to mind; and so the screen which represents our brain must be active and elastic. This analogy would explain reasonably well what goes on in the brain. As for the soul, which is a simple substance or *'monad': without being extended it represents these various extended masses and has perceptions of them.

Chapter xii
'Of complex ideas.'

PHILALETHES. §3. Complex ideas are either of modes or of substances or of relations.

THEOPHILUS. This division of the objects of our thoughts into substances, modes and relations is pretty much to my liking. I believe that qualities are just modifications of substances, and that the understanding adds relations. More follows from this than people think.

PHIL. §5. Modes are either *simple* (such as a dozen, a score, which are made from simple ideas of the same kind, i.e. from units), or *mixed* (such as beauty) which contain simple ideas of different kinds.

THEO. It may be that *dozen* and *score* are merely relations and exist only with respect to the understanding. The units are separate and the understanding takes them together, however scattered they may be. However, although relations are the work of the understanding they are not baseless and unreal. The primordial understanding is the source of things; and the very reality of all things other than simple substances consists only in there being a foundation for the perceptions or phenomena of simple substances. Often the same holds with regard to mixed modes, i.e. they ought to be treated rather as relations.

PHIL. §6. 'The ideas of substances are such combinations of simple ideas, as are taken to represent distinct particular things subsisting by themselves;' in which the obscure notion of substance is always considered to be the first and chief, and is supposed without being known, whatever it may be in itself.[1]

THEO. The idea of substance is not as obscure as it is thought to be. We can know about it the things that have to be the case, and the ones that are found to be the case through other things; indeed knowledge of concrete things is always prior to that of abstract ones – hot things are better known than heat.

---

[1] Locke: 'in which the supposed, or confused idea of substance, such as it is, is always the first and chief.' Coste's change.

PHIL. 'Of substances also, there are two sorts of ideas; one of single   146
substances,...as of a man, or a sheep; the other of several of those put
together, as an army of men, or flock of sheep'. These collections also form
a single idea.

THEO. This unity of the idea of an aggregate is a very genuine one; but
fundamentally we have to admit that this unity that collections have is
merely a respect or relation, whose foundation lies in what is the case within
each of the individual substances taken alone. So the only perfect unity
that these 'entities by aggregation' have is a mental one, and consequently
their very being is also in a way mental, or *phenomenal, like that of the
rainbow.

Chapter xiii
'Of simple modes; and first, of the simple modes of space.'

PHILALETHES. §3. 'Space considered [in relation to the] length between
any two beings,...is called distance: if considered in [relation to] length,
breadth, and thickness,...it may be called capacity'.

THEOPHILUS. To put it more clearly, the distance between two fixed
things – whether points or extended objects – is the size of the shortest
possible line that can be drawn from one to the other. This distance can
be taken either absolutely or relative to some figure which contains the two
distant things. For instance, a straight line is absolutely the distance
between two points; but if these two points both lie on the same spherical
surface, the distance between them on that surface will be the length of
the smaller arc of the great circle that can be drawn from one to the other.
It is also worth noticing that there are distances not only between bodies
but also between surfaces, lines and points. And we can speak of the
'capacity', or rather the 'interval', between two bodies or two other
extended things, or between an extended thing and a point, as being the   147
space constituted by all the shortest lines which can be drawn between the
points of the one and of the other. This interval will be a solid, except in
the case where the two fixed things lie on a single surface and the shortest
lines between their points either do lie on this surface or are expressly
required to be drawn upon it.

PHIL. §4. In addition to what nature provides,[1] men have settled in their
minds the ideas of certain determinate[2] lengths, such as an inch and a foot.

THEO. That they cannot do, for it is impossible to have the idea of an exact
determinate length: no one can say or grasp in his mind what an inch or
a foot is. And the signification of these terms can be retained only by means
of real standards of measure which are assumed to be unchanging, through

---

[1] Added by Leibniz.   [2] Locke: 'stated'. Coste's change.

which they can always be re-established. An English mathematician, Mr Greaves, wanted to make use of the Egyptian pyramids, which have lasted for a rather long time and are apparently going to last a while longer, to preserve our units of measurement, by indicating to posterity the proportions of the units to certain designated lengths on one of these pyramids. Indeed it has recently been discovered that pendulums can be used to preserve measurements ('those measures of things which should be passed on to posterity'); M. *Huygens, M. Mouton and M. Buratini (the former mint-master of Poland) have shown this by recording the proportions of our lengths to the length of a pendulum which, for instance, has a period of exactly one second – that is, the 86 400th part of one revolution of the fixed stars or of one astronomical day. M. Buratini devoted a treatise to this topic, which I saw in manuscript. But this pendulum standard of measurement has this drawback that it must be restricted to certain countries, for if pendulums are to swing at the same rate at the Equator they must be shorter. And it would still be necessary to assume the constancy of the fundamental real measure, namely the length of a day or of a rotation of the earth on its axis, and even the constancy of the cause of gravity, not to mention other factors.

PHIL. §5. Observing how the extremities are bounded[1] either by straight lines which meet at distinct angles, or by curved lines in which no angles can be perceived, we form the idea of shape.[2]

148   THEO. A shape on a surface is bounded by a line or lines, but the shape of a body can be limited[3] without determinate lines, as in the case of a sphere. A single straight line or plane surface cannot enclose a space or form any shape. But a single line can enclose a shape on a surface – a circle or oval, for instance – just as a single curved surface can enclose a solid shape such as a sphere or spheroid. Still, not only several straight lines or plane surfaces, but also several curved lines or several curved surfaces can meet and can even form angles with each other when one is not tangent to the other. It is difficult to give a general definition of 'shape' as geometers use the term. To say that it is extended and limited would be too general, since a straight line, for instance, though bounded by its two ends, is not a shape; nor, for that matter, can two straight lines form a shape. To say that it is what is extended and limited by something extended is not general enough, since a whole spherical surface is a shape and yet it is not limited by anything extended. Again, one might say that 'shape' is what is extended and limited and contains an infinite number of paths from one point to another. This includes limited surfaces lacking boundary

---

[1] 'se terminent'.

[2] Locke: 'figure'; but here and in some other passages we prefer to render 'figure' by 'shape'.   [3] 'bornée'.

lines, which the previous definition did not cover, and it excludes lines, because from one point to another on a line there is only one path or a determinate number of paths. But it would be better still to say that a shape is what is extended and limited and has an extended cross-section, or simply that it has 'breadth', another term whose definition has not been given until now.

PHIL. §6. All shapes, at least, are nothing but 'simple modes of space'.

THEO. Simple modes, on your account, repeat the same idea; but shapes do not always involve repetition of the same thing. Curves are quite different from straight lines and from one another. So I do not see how the definition of simple mode can apply here.

PHIL. Our definitions should not be taken too strictly.[1] But let us move on from shape to 'place'. §8. When we find all the chess-men 'standing on the same squares of the chess-board, where we left them, we say they are all in the *same place*,...though, perhaps, the chess-board hath been [moved]. The chess-board, we also say, is in the *same place*...if it remain in the same part of the cabin, though, perhaps, the ship which it is in [has set sail]: and the ship is [also] said to be in the *same place*, supposing it kept the same distance with the parts of the neighbouring land; though, perhaps, the earth hath turned'.

149

THEO. 'Place' is either *particular*, as considered in relation to this or that body, or *universal*; the latter is related to everything, and in terms of it all changes of every body whatsoever are taken into account. If there were nothing fixed in the universe, the place of each thing would still be determined by reasoning, if there were a means of keeping a record of all the changes or if the memory of a created being were adequate to retain them – as the Arabs are said to play chess on horseback by memory. However, what we cannot grasp is nevertheless determinate in the truth of things.

PHIL. §15. 'If any one ask me, what [space][2] is? I will tell him, when he tells me what...[3] extension is.'

THEO. I wish I could say what fever is, or some other illness, as well as I believe the nature of extension[4] can be explained. Extension is an abstraction from the extended, and the extended is a continuum whose parts are coexistent, i.e. exist at the same time.

PHIL. §17. If anyone asks 'whether...space void of body, be substance or accident, I shall readily answer, I know' nothing about it.[5]

---

[1] Added by Leibniz.   [2] Locke: 'this space, I speak of'.
[3] Locke: 'his'. Coste's omission.
[4] Taking '*l'espace*' to be a slip for '*l'étendue*'.
[5] Locke: 'I know not'. Coste's change.

THEO. I have reason to fear being accused of vanity in trying to settle what you, sir, admit you do not know. But there are grounds for thinking that you know more about it than you say or believe that you do. Some people have thought that God is the place of objects: Lessius and M. Guericke, if I am not mistaken, held this view; but it makes place involve something over and above what we attribute to space, to which we deny any agency. Thus viewed, space is no more a substance than time is, and if it has parts it cannot be God. It is a relationship: an order, not only among existents, but also among possibles as though they existed. But its truth and reality are grounded in God, like all eternal truths.

150 PHIL. I am not far from your view. You know the passage in St Paul which says that in God we live, move and have our being. So that, depending on how one looks at the matter, one could say that space is God or that it is only an order or relation.[1]

THEO. Then the best way of putting it is that space is an order but that God is its source.

PHIL. To know whether space is a substance, however, we should have to know the nature of substance in general. **§18.** That raises the following difficulty. If 'God, [finite] spirits, and body [participate] in the same common nature of substance,' will it not follow that they differ only in the 'different modification of that substance'?

THEO. If that inference were valid, it would also follow that since God, finite spirits and bodies 'participate in the same common nature' of being, they will differ only in the 'different modification' of that being.

PHIL. **§19.** 'They who first ran into the notion of accidents, as a sort of real beings, that needed something to inhere in, were forced to find out the word substance, to support them.'

THEO. Do you then believe, sir, that accidents can exist out of substance? Or do you not regard them as real beings? You seem to be creating needless problems; as I have already pointed out, substances and concrete things are conceived before accidents and abstractions are [p. 145].

PHIL. **§20.** In my opinion the words 'substance' and 'accident' are not of much use in philosophy.

THEO. I confess to holding a different view. I believe that the consideration of substance is of the greatest importance and fruitfulness for philosophy.

PHIL. We have been discussing substance only incidentally, in asking whether space is a substance. But all that matters here is that it is not a body. **§21.** Thus no one will venture to affirm that body, like space, is infinite.

---

[1] Paragraph based on Locke's §26.

THEO. Yet M. Descartes and his followers, in making the world out to be indefinite so that we cannot conceive of any end to it, have said that matter has no limits. They have some reason for replacing the term 'infinite' by 'indefinite', for there is never an infinite whole in the world, though there are always wholes greater than others *ad infinitum*. As I have shown elsewhere, the universe itself cannot be considered to be a whole [e.g. 'Quelques remarques sur le livre de M. Locke intitulé *Essay of Understanding*' p. 7]. 151

PHIL. Those who take matter and the extended to be one and the same thing claim that the inner surfaces of an empty hollow body would touch. But the space which lies between two bodies is enough to prevent their mutual contact.[1]

THEO. I agree with you; for although I deny that there is any vacuum, I distinguish matter from extension, and I grant that if there were a vacuum inside a sphere the opposite poles within the hollow would still not touch. But I believe that divine perfection does not permit such a situation to occur.

PHIL. §23.[2] Yet it seems that motion proves the existence of vacuum. 'Where the least particle of the body divided, is as big as a mustard-seed, a void space equal to the bulk of a mustard-seed [is] requisite to make room for the free motion of the parts of the divided body[. The same will hold] where the particles of matter are 100,000,000 less'.

THEO. If the world were full of hard particles which could be neither bent nor divided, as atoms are represented, then motion would indeed be impossible. But in fact hardness is not fundamental; on the contrary fluidity is the fundamental condition, and the division into bodies is carried out – there being no obstacle to it – according to [our] need. That takes all force away from the argument that there must be a vacuum because there is motion.

Chapter xiv
'Of duration, and its simple modes.'

PHILALETHES. §1. Corresponding to extension there is duration. §10. And 'a part of duration...wherein we perceive no succession [of ideas][3] is that which we may call an instant'.

THEOPHILUS. This definition of 'instant' ought (I believe) to be taken 152 as applying to the everyday notion, like the ordinary man's notion of a

---

[1] Paragraph based on Locke's §16.
[2] Numbered 22 in the first five editions of the *Essay*.
[3] Added by Leibniz.

'point'. For strictly speaking, points and instants are not parts of time or space, and do not have parts either. They are only termini.

PHIL. §16. It is not 'motion, but [a][1] constant train of ideas..., that furnishes us with the idea of duration'.

THEO. A train of perceptions arouses the idea of duration in us, but it does not create it. Our perceptions never provide a sufficiently constant and regular train to correspond to the passage of time, which is a simple and uniform continuum like a straight line. Changes in our perceptions prompt us to think of time, and we measure it by means of uniform changes. But even if nothing in nature were uniform, time could still be determined, just as place could still be determined even if there were no fixed and motionless bodies. Knowing the rules governing non-uniform motions, we can always bring them back to comprehensible uniform motions, and by this means predict what will happen through various motions in combination. In this sense time is the measure of motion, i.e. uniform motion is the measure of non-uniform motion.

PHIL. §21. One cannot know for certain that two 'parts of duration' are equal; and it must be admitted that astronomical observations can only yield approximations. Exact research has 'discovered inequality in the diurnal revolutions of the sun, and we know not whether the annual also be not unequal'.

THEO. The pendulum has revealed the inequality between days, as measured from one noon to the next – 'it dares to accuse the sun of lying' [adapted from Virgil]. We already knew this of course, and that there are rules governing the inequality. As for the annual rotation, which evens out the inequalities of the solar days, it could change in the course of time. The earth's rotation on its axis, which is popularly attributed to the prime mover, is the best measure we have so far, and clocks and watches enable us to divide it up. Yet this same daily rotation of the earth could also change in the course of time; and if some pyramid could last long enough or were replaced by newly built ones, men could be aware of that change through keeping records – in terms of the pyramids – of the length of pendulums which now swing a known number of times during one rotation. We could also learn about the change, in a fashion, by comparing this rotation with others – those of Jupiter's moons, for example – since it is unlikely that if they too underwent change it would always be at a corresponding rate.

153

PHIL. Our measurement of time would be more accurate if we could keep a past day for comparison with days to come, as we keep measures of spaces.

THEO. Instead of which we have to keep and consult bodies which go through their motions in more or less equal times. But we certainly cannot

---

[1] Locke: 'the'. Coste's change.

say, either, that a measure of space, such as a yard, which is kept in wood or metal, remains perfectly the same.

PHIL. §22. Since[1] 'all men manifestly measured time by the motion of the [heavenly] bodies', it is very strange that '*time* yet should be defined to be the *measure of motion*'.

THEO. I have just explained (§16) how that should be understood. In fact, Aristotle said that time is the 'number of motion', not its measure [*Physics* IV, 219^{b}1]. Indeed we could say that a duration is known by the number of equal periodic motions, each beginning when the preceding one ceases, for instance by so many revolutions of the earth or the stars.

PHIL. §24. And yet we anticipate these revolutions: 'should one say, that Abraham was born in the 2712 year of the Julian period, it is altogether as intelligible, as reckoning from the beginning of the world,...[2] though the Julian period be supposed to begin several hundred years, before there were really either days, nights, or years, marked out by any revolutions of the sun'.

THEO. This vacuum which can be conceived in time indicates, along with that in space, that time and space pertain as much to possibles as to existents. I would add that counting years from the beginning of the world is the least suitable of all systems of dating, if only because of the great disparity between the Septuagint and the Hebrew text, not to mention other reasons.

PHIL. §26. One can conceive the beginning of motion, though one cannot understand[3] the beginning of all duration. Similarly, one 'may set limits to body,...but not to space'.

THEO. As I have just said, time and space indicate possibilities beyond any that might be supposed to be actual. Time and space are of the nature of eternal truths, which equally concern the possible and the actual.

PHIL. §27. The ideas of time and of eternity really have a common source, for 'we can, in our thoughts, add [certain] lengths of duration to one another, as often as we please'.

THEO. But to derive the notion of *eternity* from this we must also conceive that the same principle[4] applies at every stage, letting one go a stage further. It is this thought of principles which yields the notion of the infinite, or the indefinite, in possible progressions. Thus the senses unaided cannot

---

[1] Locke: 'whilst', meaning 'although'. Coste's '*pendant*' is wrong, and Leibniz's '*puisque*' is even more so. Through this error, and through omission of what Locke goes on to say, his point is seriously misrepresented.

[2] Locke: 'though there were so far back no motion of the sun, nor any other motion at all'.

[3] Locke uses 'conceive' for both clauses. Coste's change. Leibniz emphasizes '*concevoir*' and '*comprendre*'.

[4] '*raison*', which can also mean 'reason' and 'ratio'.

enable us to form these notions. Ultimately one can say that the idea of the *absolute* is, in the nature of things, prior to that of the *limits* which we contribute, but we come to notice the former only by starting with whatever is limited and strikes our senses.

Chapter xv
'Of duration and expansion, considered together.'

PHILALETHES. §4. An infinite duration of time is allowed more easily than an infinite expanse of place, because we 'conceive in God infinite duration,' but we attribute extension 'only to matter, which is finite,' and we term spaces 'beyond the limits of the universe, imaginary'. §2. But 'Solomon ...seems to have other thoughts, when he says [speaking of God], *Heaven, and the heaven of heavens, cannot contain thee*: and he, I think, very much magnifies to himself the capacity of his own understanding, who persuades himself, that he can extend his thoughts farther than [the place where]¹ God exists'.

155

THEOPHILUS. If God were extended he would have parts. But duration confers parts only on his operations. However, where space is in question we must attribute immensity to God, and this also gives parts and order to his immediate operations. He is the source of possibilities and of existents alike, the one by his essence and the other by his will. So that space like time derives its reality only from him, and he can fill up the void whenever he pleases. It is in this way that he is omnipresent.

PHIL. §11. 'What spirits have to do with space, or how they [partake]² in it, we know not.' But we do know that they partake in duration.

THEO. Every finite spirit is always joined to an organic body, and represents other bodies to itself by their relation to its own body. Thus it is obviously related to space as bodies are. Finally, before leaving this topic, I will add a comparison of my own to those that you have given between time and space. If there were a vacuum in space (for instance, if a sphere were empty inside), one could establish its size. But if there were a vacuum in time, i.e. a duration without change, it would be impossible to establish its length. It follows from this that we can refute someone who says that if there is a vacuum between two bodies then they touch, since two opposite poles within an empty sphere cannot touch – geometry forbids it. But we could not refute anyone who said that two successive worlds are contiguous in time so that one necessarily begins as soon as the other ceases, with no possible interval between them. We could not refute him, I say, because that interval is indeterminable. If space were

¹ Added by Coste.
² Locke: 'communicate'. Coste: '*participent*'. Locke uses 'partake in' earlier in §11.

only a line, and if bodies were immobile, it would also be impossible to establish the length of the vacuum between two bodies.

Chapter xvi
'Of number.'

PHILALETHES. **§4.** 'The ideas of numbers are more precise, and distinguishable than in extension; where every equality and excess are not so easy to be observed, or measured; because our thoughts cannot in space arrive at [a certain] determined smallness beyond which it cannot go,' comparable to a unit of number.

THEOPHILUS. That applies to *whole* numbers. For *number in the broad sense* – comprising fractions, irrationals, *transcendental numbers and everything which can be found between two whole numbers – is analogous[1] to a line, and does not admit of a minimum any more than the continuum does. So this definition of 'number' as a multitude of units is appropriate only for whole numbers. Precise distinctions amongst ideas of extension do not depend upon size: for we cannot distinctly recognize sizes without having recourse to whole numbers, or to numbers which are known through whole ones; and so, where distinct knowledge of size is sought, we must leave continuous quantity and have recourse to discrete quantity. So if one does not use numbers, one can distinguish amongst the modifications of extension only through *shape* – taking that word broadly enough to cover everything which prevents two extended things from being [geometrically] similar to one another.

PHIL. **§5.** 'By the repeating...of the idea of an unit, and joining it to another unit, we make thereof one collective idea, marked by the name *two*. And whosoever can do this, and proceed on, still adding one more to the last collective idea,...and give a name to it, may count...as far as he hath a series of names...and a memory to retain that series'.

THEO. One could not get far by that method alone. For the memory would become overloaded if it had to retain a completely new name for each addition of a new unit. For that reason there has to be a certain orderliness in these names – a certain repetitiveness, with each new start conforming to a certain progression.

PHIL. 'The several...[2] modes of numbers [are not] capable of any other difference, but more or less'. That is why they are simple modes, like those of extension.[3]

---

[1] '*proportionel*' – meaning 'ordinally similar' in the contemporary sense.
[2] Locke: 'simple'. Coste's omission.
[3] Sentence based on Locke's xiii.1, 4.

THEO. That may be said of time, and of a straight line, but not at all of shapes and still less of numbers; for these are subject not only to differences of size but also to dissimilarities. An even number can be divided into two equal parts, but an odd one cannot; three and six are triangular numbers, four and nine are squares, eight is a cube, etc. This obtains with numbers even more than with shapes, for two non-congruent shapes can be perfectly similar, which two numbers can never be. But I am not surprised that people so often go wrong about this, because most people have no distinct idea of 'similar' and 'dissimilar'. So you see, sir, that your idea of 'simple' and of 'mixed' modifications, or your way of applying it, stands in great need of amendment.

157

PHIL. **§6.** You are right in your comment that numbers should be given names which are apt to be remembered. So it would be a good idea, I believe, if in counting we abbreviated 'million of millions' to 'billion', and abbreviated 'million of millions of millions' or 'million of billions' to 'trillion', and so on up to 'nonillions'; for one is hardly likely to have a use for anything higher.

THEO. These names are acceptable. Let x be equal to 10; then a million will be x^6, a billion x^{12}, a trillion x^{18}, etc. and a nonillion x^{54}.

Chapter xvii
'Of infinity.'

PHILALETHES. **§1.** One extremely important notion is that of finite and infinite, which are 'looked upon...as the modes of quantity'.

THEOPHILUS. It is perfectly correct to say that there is an infinity of things, i.e. that there are always more of them than one can specify. But it is easy to demonstrate that there is no infinite number, nor any infinite line or other infinite quantity, if these are taken to be genuine wholes. The Scholastics were taking that view, or should have been doing so, when they allowed a 'syncategorematic' infinite, as they called it, but not a 'categorematic' one. The true infinite, strictly speaking, is only in the *absolute*, which precedes all composition and is not formed by the addition of parts.

PHIL. 'When we apply to [the] first...being our idea of infinite,...we do it primarily in respect of his duration and ubiquity; and...more figuratively to his power, wisdom, and goodness, and other attributes'.

THEO. Not more figuratively, but less immediately, because the magnitude of the other attributes is known only by reference to the ones which do involve the thought of parts.

PHIL. §2. I have been taking it as established that the mind looks on finite   158
and infinite 'as modifications of expansion and duration'.

THEO. I do not consider that to have been established. The thought of finite
and infinite is appropriate wherever there is magnitude or multiplicity.
And the genuine infinite is not a 'modification': it is the absolute; and
indeed it is precisely by modifying it that one limits oneself and forms a
finite.

PHIL. §3. It has been our belief that the mind gets its idea of infinite space
from the fact that no change occurs in its power to go on enlarging its idea
of space by further additions.

THEO. It is worth adding that it is because the same principle can be seen
to apply at every stage. Let us take a straight line, and extend it to double
its original length. It is clear that the second line, being perfectly similar
to the first, can be doubled in its turn to yield a third line which is also
similar to the preceding ones; and since the same principle is always
applicable, it is impossible that we should ever be brought to a halt; and
so the line can be lengthened to infinity. Accordingly, the thought of the
infinite comes from the thought of likeness, or of the same principle, and
it has the same origin as do universal necessary truths. That shows how our
ability to carry through the conception of this idea comes from something
within us, and could not come from sense-experience; just as necessary
truths could not be proved by induction or through the senses. The idea
of the absolute is internal to us, as is that of being: these absolutes are
nothing but the attributes of God; and they may be said to be as much
the source of ideas as God himself is the principle of beings. The idea of
the absolute, with reference to space, is just the idea of the immensity of
God and thus of other things. But it would be a mistake to try to suppose
an absolute space which is an infinite whole made up of parts. There is
no such thing: it is a notion which implies a contradiction; and these
infinite wholes, and their opposites the infinitesimals, have no place except
in geometrical calculations, just like the use of imaginary roots in algebra.

PHIL. One can also conceive a magnitude without taking it to consist of
parts lying side by side.[1] §6. 'To the perfectest idea I have of the whitest
whiteness, if I add another of a less or equal whiteness, (and of a whiter
than I have [which I take to be the most brilliant of which I have any
present conception],[2] I cannot add the idea,) it makes no increase, and
enlarges not my idea at all; and therefore the different ideas of whiteness
...are called degrees.'

THEO. I cannot see that this reasoning is cogent, for nothing prevents one   159
from having the perception of a whiteness more brilliant than one at present

---

[1] Added by Leibniz.   [2] Added by Coste.

conceives. The real reason why one has grounds for thinking that whiteness could not be increased to infinity is that it is not a fundamental quality: the senses provide only a confused knowledge of it; and when we do achieve a distinct knowledge of it we shall find that it depends upon structure, and that its limits are set by the structure of the visual organs. But where fundamental or distinctly knowable qualities are concerned, there are ways of going to infinity, not only in contexts involving *extent* or (if you will) *spread*[1] or what the Schoolmen call *partes extra partes* [parts beside parts], e.g. time and space, but also in ones involving *intensity* or *degrees*, e.g. with regard to speed.

PHIL. §7. We do not have the idea of a space which is infinite; §8. and 'nothing [is] more evident, than the absurdity of the actual idea of an infinite number.'

THEO. That is my view too. But it is not because we cannot have the idea of the infinite, but because an infinite cannot be a true whole.

PHIL. §16. By the same token, we have no positive idea of an infinite duration, i.e. of eternity, §18. nor one of immensity.[2]

THEO. I believe that we have a positive idea of each of these. This idea will be true provided that it is conceived not as an infinite whole but rather as an absolute, i.e. as an attribute with no limits. In the case of eternity, it lies in the necessity of God's existence: there is no dependence on parts, nor is the notion of it formed by adding times. That shows once again that, as I have already remarked, the notion of infinity comes from the same source as do necessary truths.

Chapter xviii
'Of other simple modes.'

PHILALETHES. §1. There are many other simple modes, which are formed out of simple ideas. For example §2. the modes of motion such as sliding and rolling; §3. those of sounds, which are modified by notes and tunes, §4. as colours are by shades; §5. not to mention tastes and smells. §6. There are not always measures and distinct names, any more than there are with complex modes,[3] §7. because we are guided by what is useful. We shall discuss this more fully when we come to consider words [pp. 300ff].

160

THEOPHILUS. Most modes are not so very simple, and could be classified as complex. For example, to explain what sliding or rolling is, one would have to take into account not just motion but also surface friction.

[1] '*diffusion*', apparently not a rendering of any word used by Locke.
[2] Locke: 'infinite space'.
[3] Apart from an entry in the Index, the phrase 'complex mode' does not occur in the *Essay*.

Chapter xix
'Of the modes of thinking.'

PHILALETHES. §1. Let us pass on from modes which come from the senses to those which reflection gives us. 'Sensation...is, as it were, the actual entrance of any idea into the understanding by the senses. [When] the same idea...again recurs [in the mind] without the operation of the like object on the external sensory, [that act of the mind is called] *remembrance*:[1] if it be sought after by the mind, and with pain and endeavour found, and brought again in view, 'tis [*self-communion*]:[2] if it be held there long under attentive consideration, 'tis *contemplation*: when ideas float in our mind, [as it were,] without any reflection or regard of the understanding, it is [what is called *reverie*]: when the ideas that offer themselves...are taken notice of, and, as it were, registered in the memory, it is *attention*: when the mind with great earnestness...fixes its view on any idea, considers it on all sides, and will not be called off by the...solicitation of other ideas, it is that we call [concentration of mind],[3] or *study*: sleep, without dreaming, is [a cessation of] all these. And *dreaming*...is the having of ideas, (whilst the outward senses are stopped, so that they receive not [the impression of] outward objects with their usual quickness,) in the mind, not suggested by any external objects, or known occasion; nor under any choice or conduct of the understanding at all: and whether that, which we call *ecstasy*, be not dreaming with the eyes open, I leave to be examined.'

THEOPHILUS. It is good to sort out these notions, and I shall try to help. 161 I shall say then that it is *sensation* when one is aware of an outer object, and that *remembrance* is the recurrence of it[4] without the return of the object; but when one knows that one has had it[5] before, this is *memory*. *Self-communion* is usually understood not in your sense but rather as naming a state in which one disengages oneself from practical matters in order to engage in meditation. But since there is no word that I know which does fit your notion, sir, yours could be adapted for the purpose. We exercise *attention* on objects which we pick out in preference to others. When attention is continued in the mind, whether or not the outer object continues [to be observed], and whether or not it even continues to exist, it is *consideration*; and when the latter is directed towards knowledge without reference to action, that is *contemplation*. Attention which aims at *learning* – i.e. acquiring knowledge in order to keep it – is *study*. To consider

---

[1] Locke: 'the same idea, when it again recurs..., is remembrance'. Coste's change.
[2] Locke: 'recollection'. Coste: '*recueillement*'.
[3] Locke: 'intention', now obsolete in this sense.
[4] That is, of the perception which is involved: an earlier draft said that sensation is the '*perception*' of an outer object etc.
[5] As previous note.

with a view to planning some project is to *meditate ;* but to engage in *reveries* seems to consist merely in following certain thoughts for the sheer pleasure of them and with no other end in view. That is why reverie can lead to madness: one forgets oneself, forgets one's goals, drifts towards dreams and fantasies, builds castles in Spain. We can distinguish *dreams* from sensations only because they are not connected with sensations – they are like a separate world. *Sleep* is a cessation of sensations, and thus *ecstasy* is a very profound sleep from which the subject cannot easily be waked, arising from a temporary internal cause. That [last condition] is added so as to exclude the deep sleep which arises from a drug or – as in a coma – from some prolonged impairment of one's functions. Ecstasies are sometimes accompanied by *visions*, but the latter can also occur without ecstasy; and it seems that a vision is nothing but a dream which is taken for a sensation as though it conveyed something true about objects. Divine visions do indeed contain truth, as can be discovered for instance when they contain detailed prophecies which are justified by events.

PHIL. §4. From the differences in degree of concentration and relaxation of the mind it follows 'that thinking is the action, and not the essence of the soul'.

THEO. No doubt thinking is an action, and cannot be the essence; but it is an essential action, and such actions occur in all substances. I have shown above [pp. 115f] that we always have an infinity of minute perceptions 162 without being aware of them. We are never without perceptions, but necessarily we are often without *awareness, namely when none of our perceptions stand out. It is because that important point has been neglected that so many good minds have been conquered by a loose philosophy – one as ignoble as it is flimsy – and that until very recently we have been ignorant of all that is finest in the soul. And that is why people have found so plausible the erroneous doctrine that souls are by nature perishable.

Chapter xx
'Of modes of pleasure and pain.'

PHILALETHES. §1. As bodily sensations, like the thoughts of the mind, may be either indifferent or followed by pleasure or pain, 'these like other simple ideas cannot be described, nor their names defined'.[1]

THEOPHILUS. I believe that there are no perceptions which are matters of complete indifference to us; but a perception can be so described if it is not a notable one, for *pleasure* and *pain* appear to consist in notable helps

---

[1] Locke does not present the first clause as implying the second. Leibniz has changed the sense by altering Coste's punctuation.

and hindrances. I concede that this definition of them is not a nominal one, and that that cannot be given.

PHIL. §2. The *good* is that 'which is apt to cause or increase pleasure, or diminish [or cut short][1] pain in us [. *Evil*] is apt to produce or increase any pain, or diminish any pleasure in us'.

THEO. That is my opinion too. The good is divided into the virtuous, the pleasing, and the useful; though I believe that fundamentally something good must either be pleasing in itself or conducive to something else which can give us a pleasant feeling. That is, the good is either pleasing or useful; and virtue itself consists in a pleasure of the mind.

PHIL. §3. From pleasure and pain come the passions. §4. One has love for something which can produce pleasure, and §5. 'the thought of the [sorrow or][2] pain which any thing present or absent is apt to produce [is hatred.] But hatred or love, to beings capable of happiness or misery, is often [a displeasure or a contentment][3] which we find in our selves arising from a consideration of their very being,' or of the happiness which they enjoy.

THEO. That definition of *love is almost the same as the one I gave, when expounding the principles of justice in the Preface to my *Codex juris gentium*, where I said that to love is to be disposed to take pleasure in the perfection, well-being or happiness of the object of one's love. And this invòlves not thinking about or asking for any pleasure of one's own except what one can get from the happiness or pleasure of the loved one. On this account, whatever is incapable of pleasure or of happiness is not strictly an object of love; our enjoyment of things of that nature is not love of them, unless by a kind of personifying, as though we fancied that they could themselves enjoy their perfection. When one says that one loves a fine painting, because of the pleasure one gets from taking in its perfections, that is not strictly love. But it is permissible to extend the sense of a term, and in our present case usage varies. Philosophers, and even theologians, distinguish two kinds of love: the love which they call 'concupiscence', which is merely the desire or the feeling we bear towards what gives pleasure to us, without our caring whether it receives any pleasure; and the love of 'benevolence', which is the feeling we have for something by whose pleasure or happiness we are pleased or made happy. The former fixes our view on our own pleasure; the latter on the pleasure of others, but as something which produces or rather constitutes our own pleasure – for if it did not reflect back on us somehow we could not care about it, since it is impossible (whatever they say) to disengage from a concern for one's own good. That is the way to understand 'disinterested' or non-mercenary

163

---

[1] Added by Coste.　　　　[2] Added by Coste.
[3] Locke: 'the uneasiness or delight'. Coste's change.

love, if we are properly to grasp its nobility and yet not succumb to fantasies about it.

PHIL. §6. 'The uneasiness[1] a man finds in himself upon the absence of any thing, whose present enjoyment carries the idea of delight with it, is that we call desire.... The chief if not only spur to human industry and action is uneasiness. For whatever good is proposed, if its absence carries no displeasure nor pain with it; if a man be easy and content without it, there is no desire of it, nor endeavour after it; there is no more but a bare velleity, the term used to signify the lowest degree of desire' – which is next to the state the soul is in regarding a thing towards which it is wholly indifferent[2] – 'when there is so little [displeasure[3] caused by] the absence of any thing, that it carries a man no farther than some faint wishes for it, without any...use of the means to attain it. Desire also is stopped or abated by the opinion of the...unattainableness of the good proposed, as far as the uneasiness [of the soul] is cured or allayed by that consideration.' I should add that these remarks about uneasiness [*inquiétude*] come from the famous English author whose views I have frequently reported to you. I have been in some difficulty about what the English word 'uneasiness' signifies; but the French translator, whose skill indisputably fits him for this task, remarks in a footnote that the English writer uses this word to designate the state of a man who is not at his ease – a lack of *ease* or tranquillity in the soul, the latter being in this respect purely passive; and that he had to translate it by *inquiétude*, which does not express exactly the same idea but which comes closest to doing so. This warning is especially necessary, he adds, in connection with the next chapter, on Power, where this kind of *inquiétude* plays a large role in the argument; for if one did not associate the word with the idea just indicated, one could not properly understand the contents of this chapter, which are the subtlest and most important in the whole work.

THEO. The translator is right; as I have seen from reading his good author for myself, this treatment of *inquiétude* is an important matter in which the author makes especially evident the depth and penetration of his mind. So I have given it some thought; and after thorough reflection I am now almost inclined to think that the word *inquiétude*, even if it does not express very well what the author has in mind, nevertheless fits pretty well the nature of the thing itself, and that *uneasiness* – if that indicated a displeasure, an irritation, a discomfort, in short an actual *suffering – would *not* fit it.[4] For

[1] '*inquiétude* (uneasiness *en anglais*)'.
[2] Locke: 'which is next to none at all'. Coste's omission.
[3] Locke: 'uneasiness'. Coste: '*déplaisir*'.
[4] From now on, '*inquiétude*' will be rendered by 'disquiet': in Theophilus' speeches so as not to make him use 'uneasiness', which he condemns, and in Philalethes' for the sake of uniformity.

164

I would prefer to say that a desire in itself involves only a disposition to suffering, a preparation for it, rather than suffering itself. It is true that this perception sometimes differs only in degree from what is involved in suffering; but it is of the essence of suffering to be of a certain degree, for it is a notable perception. That emerges also in the difference between appetite and hunger, for when the disturbance of the stomach becomes too strong it causes discomfort. So this is another case requiring our doctrine about perceptions which are too minute for us to be aware of them; for if what goes on in us when we have appetite and desire were sufficiently 165 amplified, it would cause suffering. That is why the infinitely wise Author of our being was acting in our interests when he brought it about that we are often ignorant and subject to confused perceptions – so that we could act the more quickly by instinct, and not be troubled by excessively distinct sensations of hosts of objects which, necessary though they are to nature's plan, are not entirely agreeable to us. How many insects we swallow without being aware of it, how many people we observe who are inconvenienced by having too fine a sense of smell, and how many disgusting objects we would see if our eyesight were keen enough! By the same device, nature has given us the spurs of desire in the form of the rudiments or elements of suffering, semi-suffering one might say, or (to put it extravagantly just for the sake of emphasis) of minute sufferings of which we cannot be aware. This lets us *enjoy the advantage of evil* without enduring its inconveniences; for otherwise, if this perception were too distinct, one would always be miserable when looking forward to something good; whereas our continual victory over these semi-sufferings – a victory we feel when we follow our desires and somehow satisfy this or that appetite or itch – provides us with many semi-pleasures; and the continuation and accumulation of these (as with the continuing thrust of a heavy body gaining impetus as it falls) eventually becomes a whole, genuine pleasure. In fact, without these semi-sufferings there would be no pleasure at all, nor any way of being aware that something is helping and relieving us by removing obstacles which stand between us and our ease. This also exhibits that affinity of pleasure with suffering which Socrates comments on in Plato's *Phaedo* [606ᶜ], when his feet are itching. This account of tiny aids, imperceptible little escapes and releases of a thwarted *endeavour, which finally generate notable pleasure, also provides a somewhat more distinct knowledge of our inevitably confused ideas of pleasure and of pain; just as the *sensation of warmth or of light results from many tiny motions which, as I said earlier (viii.13), express the motions in objects, and are different from them only in appearance, and that only because we are not aware of this analysed multiplicity. As against this view, some contemporaries believe that our ideas of sensible qualities differ entirely from motions and from what occurs in the objects, and are something *primary 166 and inexplicable and even arbitrary; as though God had made the soul sense whatever he had a whim that it should sense, rather than whatever happens in the body – which is nowhere near the right analysis of our ideas. But to return to *disquiet*, i.e. to the imperceptible little urges which keep us constantly in suspense: these are confused stimuli, so that we often do not know what it is that we lack. With *inclinations* and *passions*, on the other hand, we at least know what we want; though confused perceptions come into their way of acting too, and though passions give rise further to the disquiet or itch which is under discussion. These impulses are like so many little springs trying to unwind and so driving our machine along. And I have already remarked [pp. 55f, 115f] that that is why we are never indifferent, even when we appear to be most so, as for instance over whether to turn left or right at the end of a lane. For the choice that we make arises from these insensible stimuli, which, mingled with the actions of objects and of our bodily interiors, make us find one direction of movement more comfortable than the other. In German, the word for the balance of a clock is *Unruhe* – which also means disquiet; and one can take that for a model of how it is in our bodies, which can never be perfectly at their ease. For if one's body were at ease, some new effect of objects – some small change in the sense-organs, and in the viscera and bodily cavities – would at once alter the balance and compel those parts of the body to exert some tiny effort to get back into the best state possible; with the result that there is a perpetual conflict which makes up, so to speak, the disquiet of our clock; so that this [German] appellation is rather to my liking.

PHIL. §7. 'Joy is a delight [which the soul feels], from the consideration of the present or assured approaching possession of a good; and we are then possessed of any good, when we have it so in our power, that we can use it when we please.'

THEO. Languages do not have terms which are specific enough to distinguish neighbouring notions. Perhaps this definition of joy comes nearer to the Latin *gaudium* than to *laetitia*; the latter is also translated as 'joy', but then joy appears to me to signify a state in which pleasure predominates in us; for during the deepest sorrow and amidst sharpest anguish one can have some pleasure, e.g. from drinking or from hearing music, although displeasure predominates; and similarly in the midst of the most acute agony the mind can be joyful, as used to happen with martyrs.

167 PHIL. §8. 'Sorrow is [a disquiet of the soul] upon the thought of a good lost, which might have been enjoyed longer; or' upon being tormented by a present evil.[1]

---

[1] Locke: 'or the sense of a present evil.' Coste's change.

THEO. Not only a present evil but also the fear of a future one can bring sorrow; and so I believe that the definitions I have just given of *joy* and *sorrow* are more true to common usage. As for disquiet: there is something further in suffering, and consequently in sorrow. Also, there is disquiet even in joy, for the latter makes a man alert, active, and hopeful of further success. Joy has been able to kill people, through excess of emotion, and those cases involved something more than mere disquiet.

PHIL. §9. Hope is the contentment of the soul which thinks 'of a probable future enjoyment of a thing, which is apt to delight' it. §10. Fear is a disquiet of the soul, 'upon the thought of future evil' which may occur.

THEO. If disquiet signifies a displeasure, I grant that it always accompanies fear; but taking it for that undetectable spur which urges us on, it is also relevant to hope. The Stoics took the passions to be beliefs: thus for them hope was the belief in a future good, and fear the belief in a future evil. But I would rather say that the passions are not contentments or displeasures or beliefs, but endeavours – or rather modifications of *endeavour* – which arise from beliefs or opinions and are accompanied by pleasure or displeasure.

PHIL. §11. 'Despair is the thought of the unattainableness of any good,' which can cause distress and sometimes causes lassitude.

THEO. Despair, viewed as passion, will be a kind of strong endeavour which is utterly thwarted, resulting in violent conflict and much displeasure. But when the despair is accompanied by lassitude and indolence, it will be a belief rather than a passion.

PHIL. §12. Anger is that disquiet or 'discomposure' which we feel 'upon the receipt of any injury, with a present [desire for][1] revenge.'

THEO. Anger seems to be something simpler and more general than that, since it can occur in beasts, which cannot be subjected to injury.[2] Anger involves a violent effort to rid oneself of an evil. The desire for vengeance can remain when one is cool, and when the emotion one has is hatred rather than anger.

PHIL. §13. Envy is the disquiet (the displeasure)[3] of the soul which comes from 'the consideration of a good we desire, obtained by one, we think should not have had it before us.'

THEO. According to that notion of it, envy would always be a commendable passion, and would always be legitimate, at least in one's own opinion. But I suspect that envy is often directed towards someone else's acknowledged merit, which one would not care to vilify if it were one's own. One may

168

---

[1] Locke: 'purpose of'. Coste's change.
[2] '*injure*', meaning 'injustice' or 'insult'.
[3] Parenthetical phrase added by Leibniz.

even envy people's possession of a good which one would not care to possess for oneself: one would merely like to see them deprived of it, without thought of benefiting by their loss – and even with no possible hope of such benefit, for some goods are like paintings in fresco, which can be destroyed but cannot be removed.

PHIL. §17. 'The passions...have most of them in [many][1] persons operations on the body, and cause various changes in it: which [are not] always sensible'. For instance, shame, which is a disquiet of the soul which one feels 'upon the thought of having done something, which is indecent, or will lessen the...esteem which others have for us, has not always blushing accompanying it.'

THEO. If men were more thorough in observing the overt movements which accompany the passions, it would be hard to disguise them. As for shame, it is worth thinking about the fact that modest people sometimes feel agitations like those of shame merely upon witnessing an indecent action.

Chapter xxi
'Of power' and freedom.[2]

PHILALETHES. §1. The mind, noticing how one thing ceases to be, and how another comes to exist which did not exist before, and concluding that in the future similar things[3] will be produced by similar agents, 'considers in one thing the possibility of having any of its simple ideas changed, and in another the possibility of making that change;' and so the mind comes by the idea of power.

169

THEOPHILUS. If 'power' corresponds to the Latin *potentia*, it is contrasted with 'act', and the transition from power into act is 'change'. That is what Aristotle means by the word 'movement', when he says that movement is the act – or perhaps the actualizing – of that which has the power to be [*Physics* III, 201ª10]. Power in general, then, can be described as the possibility of change. But since change – or the actualization of that possibility – is action in one subject and passion in another, there will be two powers, one active and one passive. The active power can be called 'faculty', and perhaps the passive one might be called 'capacity' or 'receptivity'. It is true that active power is sometimes understood in a fuller sense, in which it comprises not just a mere faculty but also an *endeavour*; and that is how I take it in my theorizing about dynamics [e.g. 'Dynamics: a summary' pp. 435f]. One could reserve the word 'force' for that. Force would divide into 'entelechy' and 'effort'; for although Aristotle takes 'entelechy' so generally that it comprises all action and all

----

[1] Locke: 'most'. Coste's change.
[2] Added by Leibniz.   [3] Locke: 'the like changes'.

effort, it seems to me more suitable to apply it to *primary acting forces*, and 'effort' to *derivative* ones. There is, furthermore, a more special kind of passive power which carries more reality with it: it is a power which matter 170 has, for matter has not only mobility (i.e. the capacity for or receptivity to movement) but also *resistance*, which includes both impenetrability and inertia. When an entelechy – i.e. a primary or substantial endeavour – is accompanied by perception, it is a soul.

PHIL. §3. The idea of power expresses something relative. But 'which of our ideas, of what kind soever,...does not? For our ideas of extension, duration, and number, do they not all contain in them a secret relation of the parts? Figure and motion have something relative in them much more visibly: and sensible qualities..., what are they but the powers of different bodies, in relation to our perception, [and in] themselves,[1] do they not depend on the bulk, figure, texture, and motion of the parts? [Which puts some kind of relation amongst them.][2] Our idea therefore of power, I think, may well have a place amongst other simple ideas'.

THEO. The ideas which you have just listed are fundamentally composite: those of sensible qualities retain their place among the simple ideas only because of our ignorance; and the others, which are distinctly known, keep their place there only through an indulgence which it would be better not to grant them. It is not unlike the case of those commonly accepted 'axioms' which, though they could be and deserve to be demonstrated along with the rest of the theorems, are allowed to count as axioms as though they were primary truths. This indulgence does more harm than you might think. It is true that one is not always in a position to avoid it.

PHIL. §4. 'If we will consider it attentively, bodies, by our senses, do not afford us so clear and distinct an idea of active power, as we have from [our] 171 reflection on the operations of our minds. [There are, I believe,] but two sorts of action, whereof we have any idea, viz., thinking and motion.... Of thinking, body affords us no idea at all; it is only from reflection that we have that.... Neither have we from body any idea of the beginning of motion.'

THEO. These are very good points; and although 'thought' is here being construed so generally that it covers all perception, I do not want to quarrel about the use of words.

PHIL. When a body is itself in motion, this motion is an action on its part rather than a passion; but[3] 'when [a] ball obeys the stroke of a billiard-stick, it is not any action of the ball, but bare passion'.

[1] Locke: 'and if considered in the things themselves'.
[2] Locke: 'All which include some kind of relation in them.' Coste's change.
[13] Locke: 'when it is set in motion it self, that motion is rather a passion, than an action in it. For'. Coste rendered 'is set in motion' by '*est en mouvement*', which presumably made Leibniz conjecture that '*action*' and '*passion*' had been switched.

THEO. There is something to be said about that, namely that bodies would not receive motion with the stroke, in conformity to the laws they are observed to obey, unless they already contained motion within themselves; but let us not dwell on that point now.

PHIL. Similarly, 'when by impulse it sets another ball in motion, that lay in its way, it only communicates the motion it had received from another, and loses in it self so much, as the other received'.

THEO. This erroneous opinion that bodies lose as much motion as they give, which was made fashionable by the Cartesians, is now refuted by experiment and by theoretical considerations; and it has been abandoned even by the distinguished author of the *Search after Truth*, who published an article just for the purpose of retracting it [*Malebranche]. I see, however, that the view can still mislead able people into building their theories on ruinous foundations.

PHIL. The transfer of motion 'gives us but a very obscure idea of an active power of moving in body, whilst we observe it only to transfer, but not produce...motion'.

THEO. I am not sure whether you are contending that motion passes from subject to subject, and that the numerically same motion is taken across. I do know that some people, including the Jesuit Father Casati, have gone that way, despite all the Scholastics. But I doubt that this is your view, or that of your able friends, who usually stay well clear of such fantasies. However, if the very same motion does not go across, it must be admitted that a new motion is produced in the body which is set into motion; and so the body which gives the motion is truly active, although at the same time it passively undergoes a loss of force. For although it is not true that a body always loses as much motion as it gives, it does always lose some motion, and it always loses as much force as it gives, as I have explained elsewhere [e.g. 'Brief demonstration of a notable error of Descartes']. Thus, we must always allow that it has force or active power, taking 'power' in the more elevated sense which I explained a little way back, in which there is endeavour as well as faculty [p. 169]. I still agree with you, though, that the clearest idea[1] of active power comes to us from the mind. So active power occurs only in things which are analogous to minds, that is, in entelechies; for strictly matter exhibits only passive power.

PHIL. §5. 'We find in our selves a power to begin or forbear, continue or end several actions of our [soul], and motions of our bodies, barely by a thought or preference of the mind ordering, or as it were commanding the doing or not doing such...a particular action. This power...is that which we call the *will*. The actual exercise of that power [is called] *volition....*

---

[1] Locke said 'clear and distinct', rendered by Coste as '*claire et distincte*'; and here Leibniz selects '*claire*'. He may mean 'the most vivid idea'. Cf. *clair*.

The forbearance or performance of that action, consequent to such...
command of the [soul] is called *voluntary*. And whatsoever action is
performed without such a [direction of the soul][1] is called *involuntary*.'

THEO. That all strikes me as sound and true. However, to speak more
directly and perhaps to go a little deeper, I shall say that volition is the
effort or endeavour (*conatus*) to move towards what one finds good and
away from what one finds bad, the endeavour arising immediately out of
one's awareness of those things. This definition has as a corollary the
famous axiom that from will and power together, action follows; since any
endeavour results in action unless it is prevented. So it is not only the   173
voluntary inner acts of our minds which follow from this *conatus*, but outer
ones as well, i.e. voluntary movements of our bodies, thanks to the union
of body and soul which I have explained elsewhere [e.g. 'New system of
the nature and communication of substances' pp. 457f]. There are other
efforts, arising from insensible perceptions, which we are not aware of; I
prefer to call these 'appetitions' rather than volitions, for one describes
as 'voluntary' only actions one can be aware of and can reflect upon when
they arise from some consideration of good and bad; though there are also
appetitions of which one can be aware.

PHIL. 'The power of [perceiving][2] is that which we call...under-
standing': there is 'the perception of ideas', 'the perception of the
signification of signs', and finally 'the perception of the...agreement or
disagreement, that there is between any of our ideas.'

THEO. We are *aware of many things, within ourselves and around us,
which we do not understand; and we *understand* them when we have
distinct ideas of them accompanied by the power to reflect and to derive
necessary truths from those ideas. That is why the beasts have no
understanding, at least in this sense; although they have the faculty for
awareness of the more conspicuous and outstanding impressions – as
when a wild boar is aware of someone who is shouting at it, and goes
straight at that person, having previously had only a bare perception of him,
a confused one like its perceptions of all the objects which stand before
its eyes and reflect light-rays into the lenses. So 'understanding' in my
sense is what in Latin is called *intellectus*, and the exercise of this faculty
is called 'intellection', which is a distinct perception combined with a
faculty of reflection, which the beasts do not have. Any perception which
is combined with this faculty is a thought, and I do not allow thought to
beasts any more than I do understanding. So one can say that intellection
occurs when the thought is distinct. A final point: the perception of the

---

[1] Locke: 'thought of the mind'. Coste's change.
[2] Locke: 'perception'. Coste: '*apercevoir*'.

signification of signs does not need here to be distinguished from the perception of the ideas which are signified.

174   PHIL. **§6.** 'The ordinary way of speaking is, that the understanding and will are two *faculties* of the [soul]; a word proper enough, if it be used as all words should be, [with a care] not to breed any confusion in men's thoughts,' as I suspect has happened in this matter of the soul. And when we are told[1] that 'the will is [that] superior faculty of the soul [which rules and commands all things]; that it is, or is not free; that it determines the inferior faculties; that it follows the dictates of the understanding[, though these expressions] may be understood in a clear and distinct sense', yet I am afraid that they have misled many people into a confused idea of so many agents acting separately in us.[2]

THEO. The question of whether there is a real distinction between the soul and its faculties, and whether one faculty is really distinct from another, has long exercised the Scholastics. The *realists have said Yes, the nominalists No; and the same question has been debated concerning the reality of various other *abstract beings* which must stand or fall with faculties. But I do not think that we need here plunge into the brambles in an attempt to settle this question, despite the fact that Episcopius, I remember, attached such importance to it that he thought that if the faculties of the soul were real beings then human freedom would be untenable. However, even if they were real, distinct beings, it would still be extravagant to speak of them as real *agents*. Faculties or qualities do not act; rather, substances act through faculties.

PHIL. **§8.** 'So far as a man has [the] power to think, or not to think; to move, or not to move, according to the preference or direction of his own mind, so far is a man free.'

175   THEO. The term 'freedom' is highly ambiguous. There is freedom in law, and freedom in fact. In law, a slave is not free, and a subject is not entirely free; but a poor man is as free as a rich one. Freedom in fact, on the other hand, consists either in the power to do what one wills or in the power to will as one should.[3] Your topic, sir, is *freedom to do*, and there are different degrees and varieties of this. Speaking *generally*, a man is free to do what he wills in proportion as he has the means to do so; but there is also a *special* meaning in which 'freedom' is a matter of having the use of things which are customarily in our power, and above all with the free use of our body; and so prison and illness, which prevent us from moving our bodies and

---

[1] Locke: 'when we say'.

[2] Locke: 'so many distinct agents in us'. Coste: '*autant d'agents qui existent distinctement en nous*'. Leibniz: '*agissent*' for '*existent*'.

[3] Or 'to do what one wants or...want what one should'. In this chapter the verbs 'will' and 'want' are virtually interchangeable, each being a fair rendering of '*vouloir*'.

our limbs as we want to and as we ordinarily can, detract from our freedom. It is in that way that a prisoner is not free, and that a paralytic does not have the free use of his limbs. The *freedom to will* is also understood in two different senses: one of them stands in contrast with the imperfection or bondage of the mind, which is an imposition or constraint, though an inner one like that which the passions impose; and the other sense is employed when freedom is contrasted with necessity. Employing the former sense, the Stoics said that only the wise man is free; and one's mind is indeed not free when it is possessed by a great passion, for then one cannot will as one should, i.e. with proper deliberation. It is in that way that God alone is perfectly free, and that created minds are free only in proportion as they are above passion; and this is a kind of freedom which pertains strictly to our understanding. But the freedom of mind which is contrasted with necessity pertains to the bare will, in so far as this is distinguished from the understanding. It is what is known as 'free will':[1] it consists in the view that the strongest reasons or impressions which the understanding presents to the will do not prevent the act of the will from being contingent, and do not confer upon it an absolute or (so to speak) metaphysical necessity. It is in this sense that I always say that the understanding can determine the will, in accordance with which perceptions and reasons prevail, in a manner which, although it is certain and infallible, *inclines without necessitating.

PHIL. §9. It is well to note also that 'a tennis-ball, whether in motion by the stroke of a racquet, or lying still at rest, is not by any one taken to be a free agent. [This] is, because we conceive not a tennis-ball to think, [nor][2] to have any volition [which would make it prefer][3] motion to rest'.

THEO. If everything which acts without impediment were therefore 'free', a ball which had been set in motion along a smooth trajectory would then be a free agent. But Aristotle has rightly noted that we are not prepared to call an action 'free' unless as well as being unconstrained it is also deliberate [*Nic. Ethics* III, 1111ᵇ6].   176

PHIL. That is why the ball's 'motion and rest, come under our idea of *necessary*'.

THEO. The term 'necessary' should be handled just as circumspectly as 'free'. This conditional truth – *If the ball is in motion in a smooth trajectory without any impediment, it will continue the same motion* – may be regarded as in a way necessary though fundamentally it depends not just on geometry but also on an assumption, for it is founded on the wisdom of

---

[1] Leibniz here uses the specialized phrase '*le franc arbitre*'. Ordinarily he uses '*libre*' for 'free', and '*la volonté*' for 'will'.

[2] Locke: 'and consequently not'.

[3] Locke: 'have any volition, or preference of'. Coste's change.

God, who does not change his influence unless he has some reason to do so, and there is assumed to be no such reason in the case in question. But this non-conditional proposition – *This ball is now in motion in this plane* – is an entirely contingent truth, and in this sense the ball is a contingent unfree agent.

PHIL. §10. 'Suppose a man be carried, whilst fast asleep, into a room, where is a person he longs to see and speak with; and be there locked fast in': he awakes, is glad to find himself with this person, and thus remains in the room with pleasure.[1] I do not think it will be doubted that he stays there voluntarily; and yet 'he has not freedom to be gone [if he wishes]. So that liberty is not an idea belonging to volition'.

THEO. This strikes me as a most apt example for bringing out that there is a sense in which an action or state can be 'voluntary' without being free. Still, when philosophers and theologians dispute about 'free will'[2] they have a quite different sense in mind.

PHIL. §11. If paralysis should hinder someone's 'legs from obeying the determination of his mind,...there is want of freedom, though the sitting still even of a paralytic, whilst he prefers it to a removal, [may be][3] voluntary. Voluntary then is not opposed to necessary; but to involuntary.'

THEO. This preciseness of expression would suit me well enough, but ordinary usage does not conform to it. And when people contrast freedom with necessity they mean to talk not about outer actions but about the very act of willing.

PHIL. §12. 'A waking man...is not at liberty to think, or not to think; no more than he is at liberty' to prevent or not prevent his body from touching any other.[4] 'But whether he will remove his contemplation from one idea to another, is many times in his choice; and then he is in respect of his ideas, as much at liberty, as he is in respect of bodies he rests on: he can at pleasure remove himself from one to another. But yet some ideas', like some motions, are so fixed in the mind that[5] 'in certain circumstances it cannot...obtain their absence by the utmost effort it can use. A man on the rack, is not at liberty to lay by the idea of pain...: and sometimes a boisterous passion hurries our [mind], as a hurricane does our bodies'.

THEO. Thoughts are ordered and interconnected, as motions are, for the one corresponds perfectly to the other. This is despite the fact that the determination to which motions are subject is blindly compelling; whereas it is free, i.e. accompanied by choice, in a thinking being, who is only

---

[1] Locke: 'willingly'. Coste's change.
[2] '*le libre arbitre*'.
[3] Locke: 'is truly'. Coste dropped the adverb; Leibniz changed the modality.
[4] Locke: 'at liberty, whether his body shall touch any other, or no'. Coste's change.
[5] Coste is chiefly responsible for this garbling of Locke's point.

inclined and not forced by considerations of good and bad. For the soul keeps its perfections while representing the body; and although in involuntary actions the mind depends on the body (to put the matter accurately), in other actions the mind is independent and even makes the body depend upon it. But this dependence is only a *metaphysical* one, which consists in God's taking account of one of them in regulating the other, or taking more account of one than of the other depending upon the inherent perfections of each; whereas *real* dependence would consist in an immediate influence which the dependent one would receive from the other. A further point: involuntary thoughts come to us partly from without, through objects' affecting our senses, and partly from within, as a result of the (often undetectable) traces left behind by earlier perceptions, which continue to operate and mingle with new ones. We are passive in this respect; and even when we are awake we are visited by images – which I take to include representations not only of shapes but also of sounds and other sensible qualities – which come to us unbidden, as in dreams. In German they are called *fliegende Gedanken*, meaning 'flying thoughts'; they are not within our power, and they are sometimes full of irrationalities which provide upright people with moments of moral unease, and provide much work for casuists and directors of consciences. It is like a magic lantern, with which one can make figures appear on the wall by turning something on the inside. But our mind on becoming aware of some image which occurs in it can say Stop! and bring it to a halt, so to speak. What is more, the mind embarks as it sees fit on certain trains of thought which lead it to others. But that applies when neither kind of impression prevails – those from within or those from without. This is a matter in which people differ very much, according to their temperaments and according to the use they have made of their powers of self-control; so that one may be able to rise above impressions by which another would be swept along.

PHIL. §13. 'Wherever thought is wholly wanting, ...there necessity takes place. This in an agent capable of volition, when the beginning or continuation of any action is contrary to that preference of his mind, [is what I call *constraint*];[1] when the hindering or stopping any action is contrary to his volition, [let me call it][2] *restraint*. Agents that have no thought, no volition at all, are in every thing necessary agents.'

THEO. It seems to me that even though volitions are contingent, strictly speaking *necessity* should be contrasted not with volition but with *contingency*, as I have already pointed out in §9; and that determination should not be confused with necessity: there is just as much connection or

178

---

[1] Locke: 'is called compulsion'. Coste's change.
[2] Locke: 'it is called'. Coste's change.

determination amongst thoughts as amongst motions (since being determined is not at all the same as being forced or pushed in a constraining way). If we do not always notice the reason which determines us, or rather by which we determine ourselves, it is because we are as little able to be aware of all the workings of our mind and of its usually confused and imperceptible thoughts as we are to sort out all the mechanisms which nature puts to work in bodies. If by 'necessity' we understood a man's being inevitably determined, as could be foreseen by a perfect Mind provided with a complete knowledge of everything going on outside and inside that man, then, since thoughts are as determined as the movements which they represent, it is certain that every free act would be necessary; but we must distinguish what is necessary from what is contingent though determined. Not only are contingent truths not necessary, but the links between them are not always absolutely necessary either; for it must be admitted that when one thing follows from another in the contingent realm, the kind of determining that is involved is not the same as when one thing follows from another in the realm of the necessary. Geometrical and metaphysical 'followings' necessitate, but *physical and moral ones incline without necessitating. There is even a moral and voluntary element in what is physical, through its relation to God, since the laws of motion are necessitated only by what is best. God chooses freely, even though he is determined to choose the best. But since bodies do not choose for themselves, God having chosen for them, they have come to be called 'necessary agents' in common usage. I have no objection to this, provided that no one confounds the necessary with the determined and goes on to suppose that free beings act in an undetermined way – an error which has prevailed in certain minds, and destroys the most important truths, even the fundamental axiom that *nothing happens without reason*, without which the existence of God and other great truths cannot be properly demonstrated. As for 'constraint', it is useful to distinguish two sorts: *physical*, as when a man is imprisoned against his will or thrown off a precipice; and *moral*, as for example the fear of a greater evil, in which case the action, although in a way compelled, is nevertheless voluntary. One can also be compelled by the thought of a greater good, as when a man is tempted by the offer of a too great benefit, although this is not usually called constraint.

179

PHIL. §14. Let us see if we cannot now 'put an end to that long agitated, and, I think, unreasonable, because unintelligible, question, viz. *whether man's will be free, or no.*'

THEO. There is good reason to exclaim at the strange behaviour of men who torment themselves over misconceived questions: 'They seek what they know already, and they know not what they seek.'

PHIL. 'Liberty, which is but a power, belongs only to agents, and cannot be an attribute or modification of the will, which is [itself nothing] but a power.'

THEO. You are right, sir, if the words are used properly. Still, the accepted way of talking can be defended in a fashion. Just as we customarily attribute a power to heat or to other qualities, that is to a body in so far as it has this quality, so here the intention is to ask whether a man is free when he wills.

PHIL. §15. 'Liberty...is the power a man has to do or forbear doing any ...action...according as he...wills it.'

THEO. If that were all that people meant by freedom [*liberté*] when they   180
ask if the will or choice[1] is free, then the question would be truly absurd. But we shall soon see what they are really asking, and indeed I have already touched on it. It is true, but for another reason, that what they are asking for – many of them at least – is after all absurd and impossible: that is, an utterly imaginary and futile freedom of equilibrium, which would not be of use to them even if it were possible that they should have it, i.e. could have the freedom to will contrary to all the impressions which may come from the understanding – which would destroy true liberty, and reason with it, and would bring us down below the beasts.

PHIL. §17. Someone who said 'that the power of speaking directs the power of singing, [and that] the power of singing obeys or disobeys the power of speaking', would be expressing himself in 'as proper and intelligible' a manner as one who said – as it often *is* said – 'that the will directs the understanding [and that] the understanding obeys, or obeys not the will'. §18. 'This way of talking, nevertheless, has prevailed, and, as I guess, produced great confusion'; although the power of thinking no more operates on the power of choosing, or vice versa, than does the power of singing on that of dancing. §19. 'I grant, that this or that...thought may [provide] the occasion of...exercising the power a man has to choose; [and that the] choice of the mind [may be] the cause of [his actually] thinking on this or that thing: as the actual singing of such a tune, may be the occasion of dancing such a dance'.

THEO. Rather more is involved here than the providing of occasions: there is also an element of dependence. For we can only will what we think good, and the more developed the faculty of understanding is the better are the choices of the will. And, in the other direction, in so far as a man wills *vigorously*, he determines his thoughts by his own choice instead of being determined and swept along by involuntary perceptions.

PHIL. 'Powers are relations, not agents'.

---

[1] '*la volonté ou l'arbitre*'.

THEO. If the essential faculties are merely relations, and add nothing further to the essence [of the mind], qualities and faculties which are accidental or subject to change are something else again.[1] *They* can be said often to depend on one another in the performance of their functions.

181 PHIL. §21. 'I think the question is not proper, whether the will be free, but whether a man be free. Thus, I think...that so far as any one can, by the direction or choice of his mind, [prefer] the existence of any action, to the non-existence of that action, and *vice versa*, [that is, can] make it to exist, or not exist[12] [as he wills], so far he is free. . . . And we can scarce tell how to imagine any being freer, than to be able to do what he wills. So that in respect of actions, within the reach of such a power in him, a man seems as free, as 'tis possible for freedom to make him', if I may so put it.[3]

THEO. In reasonings about the freedom of the will, or about 'free will',[4] the question is not whether a man can do what he wills to do but whether his will itself is sufficiently independent. It is not a question about whether his legs are free or whether he has room to move about, but whether he has a free mind and what that consists in. On this way of looking at things, intelligences will differ in how free they are, and the supreme Intelligence will possess a perfect freedom of which created beings are not capable.

PHIL. §22. 'But the inquisitive mind of man, willing to shift off from himself, as far as he can, all thoughts of guilt, though it be by putting himself into a worse state, than that of fatal necessity, is not content with this: freedom, unless it reaches farther than this, will not serve the turn: and it passes for a good plea, that a man is not free at all, if he be not as free to will, as he is to act, what he wills.' §23. As to that, I believe that a man cannot be free in respect of a particular act of willing an action which is in his power, when once that action has been 'proposed to his [mind].[5] The reason whereof is very manifest: for it being unavoidable that the action depending on his will, should exist, or not exist; and its existence, or not existence, [having to follow] perfectly the determination, and [choice][6] of his will, he cannot avoid willing the existence, or not existence, of that action'.

THEO. I should have thought that we can and very frequently do suspend choice, particularly when other thoughts break into our deliberations. So that, although the action about which we are deliberating must exist or

---

[1] In an earlier draft Leibniz wrote: 'I agree that faculties are only relations, but qualities are something else again.' Cf. p. 226.

[2] Locke writes of the ability to make an act exist or not as one prefers, but does not equate the ability to make etc. with the ability to prefer. Coste's change.

[3] Added by Coste.   [4] '*le franc arbitre*'.

[5] Locke: 'to his thoughts as presently to be done'. Coste's change.

[6] Locke: 'preference'. Coste's change.

not exist, it does not follow that we must necessarily *decide* on its existence or non-existence; for its non-existence may come about for want of a decision. This is how the Areopagites in effect acquitted a man whose case they had found too difficult to decide: they adjourned it to a date in the distant future, giving themselves a hundred years to think about it.

PHIL. 'To make a man free after this manner, by making the action of willing to depend on his will, there must be another antecedent will [or faculty of willing],[1] to determine the acts of this will, and another to determine that, and so *in infinitum*: for wherever one stops, the actions of the last will cannot be free'.

182

THEO. We certainly speak very incorrectly when we speak of willing to will. We do not will to will, but rather will to do; and if we did will to will, we should will to will to will, and so on *ad infinitum*. However, we must recognize that by our voluntary actions we often indirectly prepare the way for other voluntary actions; and that although we cannot will what we want to, just as we cannot judge what we want to, we can nevertheless act ahead of time in such a way that we shall eventually judge or will what we would like to be able to judge or will today. We attach ourselves to people, reading material and ways of thinking which are favourable to a certain faction, and we ignore whatever comes from the opposite faction; and by means of these and countless other devices, which we usually employ unwittingly and without set purpose, we succeed in deceiving ourselves or at least changing our minds, and so we achieve our own conversion or perversion depending on what our experience has been.

PHIL. §25. Since, then, it is plain that a man is not at liberty to will to will[2] 'or no; the next thing demanded is, whether a man be at liberty to will which of the two he pleases, [for instance] motion or rest. [But] this question carries the absurdity of it so manifestly in it self, that [anyone who reflects on it] might[3] thereby sufficiently be convinced, that liberty concerns not the will. For to ask, whether a man be at liberty to will either motion, or rest; speaking, or silence; which he pleases, is to ask, whether a man can will, what he wills; or be pleased with what he is pleased with. A question, which, I think, needs no answer'.

THEO. For all that, people do have a difficulty about this which deserves to be resolved. They say that after everything is known and taken account of, it is still in their power to will not only what pleases them most but also the exact opposite, just to show their freedom. But what has to be borne in mind is that even this whim or impulse, or at least this reason which

---

[1] Added by Coste.
[2] Locke: 'plain, that in most cases a man is not at liberty, whether he will will'. Coste's change.
[3] Locke: 'that one might'. Coste's expansion.

prevents them following the other reasons, weighs in the balance and makes pleasing to them something which would otherwise not be; so that their choice is always determined by their perception. So we do not will what we wish to,[1] but what pleases us; though the will can contribute indirectly, as though from a distance, to make something pleasing to us or the reverse, as I have already noted. Since men mainly fail to sort out all these separate considerations, it is not surprising that they are in such a muddle about this question, with all its hidden twists and turns.

PHIL. §29. 'To the question, what is it determines the will? the true and proper answer is, The mind.... If this answer satisfies not, 'tis plain the meaning of [that] question [amounts only to] this, What moves the mind, in every particular instance, to determine its general power of directing [its faculties towards motion or towards rest],[2] to this or that particular motion or rest? And to this I answer, [what makes us continue] in the same state or action, is only the present satisfaction in it; the motive to change, is always some' disquiet.[3]

THEO. As I have shown in the preceding chapter, this disquiet is not always a displeasure, just as one's state of ease is not always a satisfaction or a pleasure. Often it is an insensible perception which we can neither discern nor single out, and which makes us lean one way rather than the other without being able to say why.

PHIL. §30. Will and desire should not be confused: a man desires to be relieved of the gout, but realizing 'that the removal of the pain may translate the noxious humour to a more vital part, his will is never determined to any...action, that may serve to remove this pain.'

THEO. Such a desire is a kind of *velleity*, as contrasted with a complete volition: one would will, if a greater evil were not to be feared from obtaining what one wants, or perhaps a greater good to be hoped for by forgoing it. However, we could say that the man does will to be rid of his gout, with a certain intensity of volition but not one which ever rises to full strength. When a volition contains some imperfection or impotence, it is called 'velleity'.

PHIL. §31. It is as well to bear in mind, though, that what determines the will to action 'is not, as is generally supposed, the greater good...:[4] but some (and for the most part the most pressing)' disquiet. This can be called desire, which is a disquiet of the mind caused by the lack of some absent good – or the desire to be relieved of pain. 'All absent good does not,

---

[1] '*ce qu'on voudrait*', literally meaning 'what one would will to'.
[2] Added by Coste.
[3] Locke: 'uneasiness'. Coste: '*inquiétude*'. See p. 164.
[4] Locke: 'the greater good in view'. Coste's '*le plus grand bien*', here and later in the speech, could as well mean 'the greatest good'.

according to the greatness it has, or is acknowledged to have, cause pain equal to that greatness; [whereas] all pain causes desire equal to it self: because the absence of good is not always [an evil],[1] as the presence of pain is. And therefore absent good may be looked on, and considered without [pain].[2] But so much as there is any where of desire, so much there is of' disquiet. **§32.** 'Who is there, that has not felt in desire, what the wise man says of hope [*Proverbs* 13: 12], that it being *deferred makes the heart sick*'? Rachel cries (*Genesis* 30: 1) '*give me children...or I die*'. **§34.** 'When a man is perfectly content with the state he is in, which is when he is perfectly [free of all disquiet], what will is there left, but to continue in it?.... And thus...our all-wise Maker...has put into man the [discomfort][3] of hunger and thirst, and other natural desires...to move and determine their wills, for the preservation of themselves, and the continuation of their species....*It is better to marry than to burn*, says St Paul [I *Corinth.* 7: 9; so true it is that] a little burning felt pushes us more powerfully, than greater pleasures in prospect draw or allure.' **§35.** Indeed, 'it seems so established and settled a maxim...that good, the greater good, determines the will, that I do not at all wonder, that [formerly] I took it for granted.... But yet upon a [strict][4] inquiry, I am forced to conclude, that good, the greater good, though apprehended and acknowledged to be so, does not determine the will, until our desire, raised proportionably to [its excellence], makes us [unquiet] in the want of it.... Let a man be never so well persuaded of the advantages of virtue, that it is...necessary to a man, who has any great aims in this world, or hopes in the next...: yet till he *hungers and thirsts after righteousness...*, his *will* will not be determined to any action in pursuit of this' excellent good; and any other disquiet which presents an obstacle will carry his will to other things. 'On the other side, let a drunkard see, that his health decays, his estate wastes; discredit and diseases, and the want of all things, even of his beloved drink, attends him in the course he follows: yet the returns of [disquiet] to miss his companions' drives him to the tavern at his usual time, 'though he has in his view the loss of health and plenty, and perhaps of the joys of another life' – joys which he cannot regard as inconsiderable, and which on the contrary he confesses to be far better than the pleasure of drinking 'or the idle chat of a soaking club'. It is not for want of viewing the sovereign[5] good that he persists in his dissolute ways: he sees it and acknowledges its excellence, 'and in the intervals of his drinking hours, will take resolutions to pursue [this sovereign][5] good; but when the [disquiet] to miss his accustomed delight returns' to torment him, the good which he acknowledges to be better than that of drinking loses its hold on

185

---

[1] Locke: 'a pain'. Coste 's change.   [2] Locke: 'desire'.

[3] Locke: 'uneasiness'. Coste's change.   [4] Locke: 'stricter'.

[5] Locke: 'the greater'. Coste's change.

his mind, 'and the present [disquiet] determines the will to the accustomed action; which thereby gets stronger footing to prevail against the next occasion, though he at the same time makes secret promises to himself, [so to speak,] that he will do so no more; this is the last time he will act against the attainment of those greater goods. And thus he is, from time to time, [reduced to saying] *Video meliora proboque, deteriora sequor'* – I see and esteem the better; I follow the worse [Ovid] – 'which sentence, allowed for true, and made good by constant experience, may this, and possibly no other, way be easily made intelligible.'

THEO. There is merit and substance in these thoughts. However, I would not want them to encourage people to believe they should give up the old axioms that the will pursues the greatest good, and flees the greatest evil, of which it is sensible. The neglect of things that are truly good arises largely from the fact that, on topics and in circumstances where our senses are not much engaged, our thoughts are for the most part what we might call *'blind' – in Latin I call them *cogitationes caecae*. I mean that they are empty of perception and sensibility, and consist in the wholly unaided use of *symbols, as happens with those who calculate algebraically with only intermittent attention to the geometrical figures which are being dealt with. Words ordinarily do the same thing, in this respect, as do the symbols of arithmetic and algebra. We often reason in words, with the object itself virtually absent from our mind. But this sort of knowledge cannot influence us – something livelier is needed if we are to be moved. Yet this is how people usually think about God, virtue, happiness; they speak and reason without explicit ideas – it is not that they cannot have the ideas, for they are there in their minds, but that they do not take the trouble to carry the analysis through. Sometimes they have the idea of an absent good or evil, but only very faintly, so it is no wonder that it has almost no influence on them. Thus, if we prefer the worse it is because we have a sense of the good it contains but not of the evil it contains or of the good which exists on the opposite side. We assume and believe – or rather we tell ourselves, merely on the credit of someone else's word or at best of our recollection of having thought it all out in the past – that the greater good is on the better side and the greater evil on the other. But when we do not have them actively in mind, our thoughts and reasonings which oppose our sentiments are a kind of parrotting which adds nothing to the mind's present contents; and if we do not take steps to improve them they will come to nothing, as I have already pointed out (ii.11); the finest moral precepts and the best prudential rules in the world have weight only in a soul which is as sensitive to them as to what opposes them – if not directly sensitive (which is not always possible), then at least indirectly sensitive, as I shall explain shortly. Cicero somewhere makes the good remark that if our eyes could see the beauty of virtue we would love it ardently. Since neither that nor anything like it is the case, it is not surprising that, in the struggle between flesh and *spirit, spirit so often loses, because it fails to make good use of its advantages. This struggle is nothing but the conflict between different endeavours – those that come from confused thoughts and those that come from distinct ones. Confused thoughts often make themselves vividly sensed, whereas distinct ones are usually only potentially vivid: they could be actually so, if we would only apply ourselves to getting through to the senses of the words or symbols; but since we do not do that, through lack of care or lack of time, what we oppose lively sentiments with are bare words or at best images which are too faint. I knew a man, eminent in both church and state, whose ill-health had made him resolve to diet, but who confessed that he had been unable to resist the smell of food being taken past his quarters to other people – a shameful weakness, no doubt, but that is the way men are! However, if the mind made good use of its advantages it would triumph nobly. The first step would have to be in education, which should be conducted in such a way that true goods and evils are made as thoroughly sensible as they can be, by clothing one's notions of them in details which are more appropriate to this end. And a grown man who missed this excellent education should still – better late than never – begin to seek out enlightened and rational pleasures to bring against the confused but potent pleasures of the senses. And indeed divine grace itself is a pleasure which brings enlightenment. Thus when a man is in a good frame of mind he ought to make himself laws and rules for the future, and then carry them out strictly, drawing himself away – abruptly or gradually, depending on the nature of the case – from situations which are capable of corrupting him. A lover will be cured by a voyage undertaken just for that purpose; a period of seclusion will stop us from keeping company with people who confirm some bad disposition in us. Francisco Borgia, the General of the Jesuits, who has at last been canonized, was given to drinking heavily when he was a member of fashionable society; when he was considering withdrawing from the world, he retrenched gradually to almost nothing, by each day letting a drop of wax fall into the flagon which he was accustomed to drinking dry. To dangerous interests[1] we will oppose innocent ones like farming or gardening; we will avoid idleness, will collect curiosities, both natural and artificial, will carry out experiments and inquiries, will take up some compelling occupation if we do not already have one, or engage in useful and agreeable conversation or reading. In short, we should take advantage of our good impulses to make effective resolutions, as though they were the voice of God calling us. Since we cannot always analyse the notions of true good and true evil to the point where we can see the pleasures and pains which they involve, so as to be

187

---

[1] 'sensibilités'.

188 influenced by them, we must make this rule for ourselves once and for all: wait till you have the findings of reason and from then on follow them, even if they are ordinarily retained only as 'blind thoughts' devoid of sensible charms. We need this rule so as finally to gain control both of our *passions* and of our *insensible inclinations*, or disquiets, by acquiring that custom of acting in conformity with reason which makes virtue a pleasure and second nature to us. But it is not my purpose here to offer and instil moral precepts, or spiritual procedures and skills for the practice of true piety. It will be enough if by thinking about how our souls operate we see the source of our frailties; knowledge of the source provides knowledge of the remedies.

PHIL. §36. The present disquiet that we are in 'alone operates on the will, and...does naturally determine [it] in order to that happiness which we all aim at in all our actions', because everyone regards pain and uneasiness[1] – i.e. that disquiet or rather discomfort which prevents us from being at our ease – as 'inconsistent with happiness;...a little pain serving to mar all the pleasure we [rejoice][2] in. And therefore that, which of course determines the choice of our will to the next action, will always be the removing of pain, as long as we have any left, as the first and necessary step towards happiness.'

THEO. If you take 'uneasiness'[3] or disquiet to be a genuine displeasure, then I do not agree that it is all that spurs us on. What usually drives us are those minute insensible perceptions which could be called *sufferings that we cannot become aware of, if the notion of suffering did not involve awareness. These minute impulses consist in our continually overcoming small obstacles – our nature labours at this without our thinking about it. This is the true character of that disquiet which we sense without taking cognizance of it; it makes us act not only when we are impassioned but also when we appear most calm – for we are never without some activity and motion, simply because nature continually labours to be more completely at ease. And it is what determines us also, without any question being raised, in those cases which appear to us the most indifferent; because we are never completely in equilibrium and can never be evenly balanced between two options. Now if these elements of suffering (which

189 do sometimes degenerate into suffering, or genuine displeasure, when they grow too strong) were real suffering, we would be continually wretched as long as we pursued our own good restlessly[4] and zealously. However, quite the opposite is the case. As I said earlier (xx.6), nature's accumulation of continual little triumphs, in which it puts itself more and more at ease – drawing closer to the good and enjoying the image of it, or reducing

---

[1] Leibniz uses the English word.
[2] Locke: 'rejoiced'. Coste's change.
[3] Again, Leibniz uses the English word.
[4] Or 'with disquiet'.

the feeling of suffering – is itself a considerable pleasure, often better than the actual enjoyment of the good. Far from such disquiet's being inconsistent with happiness, I find that it is essential to the happiness of created beings; their happiness never consists in complete attainment, which would make them insensate and stupified, but in continual and uninterrupted progress towards greater goods. Such progress is inevitably accompanied by desire or at least by constant disquiet, but of the kind I have just explained: it does not amount to discomfort, but is restricted to the elements or rudiments of suffering, which we cannot be aware of in themselves but which suffice to act as spurs and to stimulate the will. That is what a healthy man's appetite does, unless it amounts to that discomfort which unsettles us and gives us a tormenting obsession with the idea of whatever it is that we are without. These 'appetitions', whether small or large, are what the Scholastics call *motus primo primi, and they are truly the first steps that nature makes us take; not so much towards happiness as towards joy, since in them one looks only to the present; but experience and reason teach us to govern and moderate them so that they can lead us to happiness. I have already said something about this (1.ii.3). Appetitions are like a stone's *endeavour to follow the shortest but not always the best route to the centre of the earth; it cannot foresee that it will collide with rocks on which it will shatter, whereas it would have got closer to its goal if it had had the wit and the means to swerve aside. In the same way, by rushing straight at a present pleasure we sometimes fall into the abyss of misery. That is why reason opposes appetition with images of greater goods or evils to come, and with a firm policy and practice of thinking before acting and then standing by whatever is found to be best, even when the sensible grounds which lead to it are no longer present to the mind, and consist in little but faint images or even in the 'blind thoughts' which are generated by words or signs which have no concrete interpretation. So it is all a matter of 'Think about it carefully' and 'Remember' – by the first 190 to make laws, and by the second to follow them even when we do not remember the reasons from which they sprang. It is wise to keep those reasons in mind as much as possible, though, so that one's soul may be filled with rational joy and enlightened pleasure.

PHIL. §37. These precautions are undoubtedly the more necessary since the idea of an absent good cannot counterbalance the feeling of any disquiet or displeasure which is presently troubling us, until this good raises our desire. 'How many are to be found, that have...lively representations set before their minds of the unspeakable joys of Heaven, which they acknowledge both possible and probable too, who yet would be content to take up with their happiness here?' And so the disquiets of their present desires, getting the upper hand and being carried swiftly towards the pleasures of this life, determine their wills to seek those pleasures; and all the while they are entirely insensitive[1] towards the good things of another life.

THEO. This is partly because men are very often not really convinced: whatever they say, a secret doubt prevails in the depths of their souls. They lack one or other of the two things which are required for conviction: either they have never understood the sound reasons which confirm that immortality of the soul which is worthy of divine justice and is the foundation of true religion; or they no longer remember having understood them. Few people even conceive that the future life, as true religion and even true reason represent it, is *possible*; so far are they from conceiving its *probability*, not to mention its *certainty*. Their thoughts about it are all mere parrotting or else crude and shallow imagery, Moslem fashion. Even they find little plausibility in the imagery, for they are far from being influenced by it, as the soldiers of the Prince of the Assassins, the Lord of the Mountain, are said to have been influenced: they were transported while deeply asleep into a delightful setting; thinking they were in Mahomet's paradise, they absorbed from sham angels and saints the opinions their Prince wished them to have; and then, having been made drowsy again, they were returned to the place they had been brought from. This gave them courage thereafter to undertake anything, including attempts on the lives of princes hostile to their master. I suspect that this is unfair to that Lord or Old Man[2] of the Mountain: we don't know of many great princes whom he had assassinated; although we do find English historians trying to exonerate King Richard I of the assassination of a count or prince of Palestine, by reproducing a letter, allegedly written by the Lord of the Mountain, in which he admits having had this count killed in revenge for an insult. Be that as it may, it is possible that religious zeal made this Prince of the Assassins wish to give people a beneficial idea of paradise – one which would always accompany their thoughts and prevent the latter from being 'blind' – without intending them to believe that they had actually been in paradise. But even if he had so intended, it would not have been surprising if those pious frauds had had more effect than the truth badly presented. Still, nothing would be more powerful than the truth if we set ourselves to know it thoroughly and to show it off to good advantage; without doubt there are ways of disposing men powerfully towards it. When I consider how great an effect ambition and avarice have on all those who once enter into that way of life, which is almost devoid of present sensible charms, I give up no cause for lost. And I believe that virtue would have infinitely more effect, accompanied as it is by so many substantial

191

[1] Locke: 'not one jot moved'. Coste: *'entièrement insensibles'*.
[2] *'ce Seigneur ou* Senior (*vieux*)'.

benefits, if some happy transformation in human kind brought it at last into favour – made it fashionable, so to speak. It is quite certain that young people could be made accustomed to getting their greatest pleasure from the exercise of virtue. And even grown men could make laws for themselves and make a practice of following them, so that they would be powerfully disposed to them, and as prone to disquiet when deflected from them as a drunkard is when prevented from going to the tavern. I am pleased to add these thoughts about how such remedies for our ills are possible and even easily available, instead of helping to discourage men from pursuing true goodness by merely expounding on our frailties.

PHIL. It is almost entirely a matter of making them constantly desire the true good.[1] §39. It seldom happens that any voluntary action is produced in us 'without some desire accompanying it; which...is...why the will and desire are so often confounded. But yet we are not to look upon the [disquiet] which [is a part or at least a result of][2] most of the other passions, as wholly excluded in the case. Aversion, fear, anger, envy, shame,...have each their [disquiet] too, and thereby influence the will.' I doubt that any of these passions exists simple and alone. 'Nay there is, I think, scarce any of the passions to be found without desire joined with it. I am sure, wherever there is [disquiet] there is desire'. As our eternity does not depend upon the present moment, we look beyond, no matter what pleasures we are now enjoying,[3] 'and desire goes with our foresight, and that still carries the will with it. So that even in joy it self, that which keeps up the action, whereon the enjoyment depends, is the desire to continue it, and fear to lose it: and whenever a greater [disquiet] than that takes [hold of][4] the mind, the [mind][5] presently is by that determined to some new action, and the present delight neglected.'

THEO. Various perceptions and inclinations combine to produce a complete volition: it is the result of the conflict amongst them. There are some, imperceptible in themselves, which add up to a disquiet which impels us without our seeing why. There are some which join forces to carry us towards or away from some object, in which case there is desire or fear, also accompanied by a disquiet but not always one amounting to pleasure or displeasure. Finally, there are some impulses which are accompanied by actual pleasure or suffering. All these perceptions are either new sensations or the lingering images of past ones (whether or not accompanied by memory): these images revive the charms which were associated with them in those earlier sensations, and thereby also revive the former

192

---

[1] Sentence based loosely on Locke's §38.
[2] Locke: 'makes up, or at least accompanies'. Coste's change.
[3] This sentence up to here reflects mistranslation by Coste.
[4] Locke: 'place in'. Coste's change.
[5] Locke: 'will'.

impulses in proportion to the liveliness of the imagining. The eventual result of all these impulses is the prevailing effort, which makes a full volition. However, desires and endeavours of which we are aware are often called 'volitions' too, though less complete ones, whether or not they prevail and take effect. So it is easy to see that volition can hardly exist without *desire* and without *avoidance*, which I suggest as a name for the opposite of desire. Disquiet occurs not merely in uncomfortable passions such as 'aversion, fear, anger, envy, shame', but also in their opposites, love, hope, calmness, generosity, and pride. It can be said that wherever there is desire there will be disquiet; but the converse does not always hold, since one is often in a state of disquiet without knowing what one wants, in which case there is no fully developed desire.

193 PHIL. §40. The disquiet which determines the will to action is 'that ordinarily, which is the most pressing of those, that are judged capable of being then removed.'

THEO. Since the final result is determined by how things weigh against one another, I should think it could happen that the most pressing disquiet did not prevail; for even if it prevailed over each of the contrary endeavours taken singly, it may be outweighed by all of them taken together. The mind can even avail itself of the trick of 'dichotomies', to make first one prevail and then another; just as in a meeting one can ensure that one faction prevails by getting a majority of votes, through the order in which one puts the questions to the vote. The mind should make provision for this from a distance, for once battle has been engaged there is no time left to make use of such artifices: everything which then impinges on us weighs in the balance and contributes to determining a *resultant direction*, almost as in mechanics; so that without some prompt diversion we will be unable to stop it. 'The charioteer is carried away by the horses, nor does the chariot heed the reins' [Virgil].

PHIL. §41. 'If it be farther asked, what 'tis moves desire? I answer happiness and that alone. *Happiness* and *misery* are the names of two extremes, the utmost bounds whereof we know not; 'tis what *eye hath not seen, ear hath not heard, nor hath it entered into the heart of man to conceive.*' But of both we have lively impressions, made by various kinds of delight and joy, of torment and sorrow, 'which, for shortness sake, I shall comprehend under the names of pleasure and pain, there being pleasure and pain of the mind, as well as the body. . . . Or to speak [more accurately], they are all of the mind; though some have their rise in the mind from thought, others in the body from certain modifications of motion. §42. Happiness then [taken] in its full extent is the utmost pleasure we are capable of, and misery [taken in the same way]¹ the utmost pain: and the

¹ Coste's addition, Leibniz's formulation of it.

lowest degree of what can be called happiness, is' that state in which, being freed from all pain, one enjoys a level of present pleasure such that one cannot be content with less. 'What has an aptness to produce pleasure in us, is that we call *good*, and what is apt to produce pain in us, we call *evil* .... Yet it often happens, that we do not call it so,' when one or other of these goods or evils comes into competition with a greater good or greater evil.

THEO. I doubt that a greatest pleasure is possible; I am inclined to believe that it can increase *ad infinitum*, for we do not know how far our knowledge and our organs can be developed in the course of the eternity which lies before us. So I would think that *happiness* is a lasting pleasure, which cannot occur without a continual progress to new pleasures. Thus of two people, one of whom progresses incomparably faster and by way of greater pleasures than the other, each will be happy in himself and considered by himself, although their happiness is very unequal. We might say, then, that happiness is a pathway through pleasures and that pleasure is only a single step: it is the most direct move towards happiness that our present impressions indicate, but not always the best, as I said near the end of §36. We can miss the right road by trying to follow the shortest one, just as the stone by falling straight down may too soon encounter obstacles which prevent it getting at all close to the centre of the earth. This shows that it is reason and will that lead us towards happiness, whereas sensibility and appetite lead us only towards pleasure. Now, although pleasure cannot be given a nominal definition, any more than light or heat can, it can like them be defined causally: I believe that fundamentally pleasure is a sense of perfection, and pain a sense of imperfection, each being notable enough for one to become aware of it. For the minute insensible perceptions of some perfection or imperfection, which I have spoken of several times and which are as it were components of pleasure and of pain, constitute inclinations and propensities but not outright passions. So there are insensible inclinations of which we are not aware. There are sensible ones: we are acquainted with their existence and their objects, but have no sense of how they are constituted; these are confused inclinations which we attribute to our bodies although there is always something corresponding to them in the mind. Finally there are distinct inclinations which reason gives us: we have a sense both of their strength and of their constitution. Pleasures of this kind, which occur in the knowledge and production of order and harmony, are the most valuable. Our author is right to say that in general these inclinations, passions, pleasures, and pains belong only to the mind, or to the soul; to which I will add that in metaphysical strictness the origin of each of them is in the soul, but that nevertheless one is justified in saying that confused thoughts come from the body, since it is by considering the body and not by considering the mind that we can discover something distinct and intelligible concerning them. *Good* is what provides or conduces to pleasure, as *evil* is what conduces to pain; but when we sacrifice a greater good to a lesser one which conflicts with it, the latter can become really an evil in so far as it contributes to the pain which must result.

PHIL. §47. The soul has 'a power to suspend the...satisfaction of any of its desires,' and is thus at liberty to consider them one after another, and to compare them. 'In this lies the liberty man has' – 'which is (as I think improperly) called free will' – 'and from the not using of it right comes all that variety of mistakes, errors, and faults which we run into' when we are too precipitate in determining our wills.

THEO. The execution of our desire is suspended or prevented when it is not strong enough to arouse us and to overcome the difficulty or discomfort involved in satisfying it. This difficulty sometimes consists merely in an insensible laziness or slackness which inhibits us without our paying heed to it; it is greatest in people brought up in indolence, in those of phlegmatic temperament, and in those discouraged by old age or failure. Even when the desire is strong enough in itself to arouse us if nothing hinders it, it can be blocked by contrary inclinations, either consisting in a mere propensity, like the germ or beginning of a desire, or amounting to an actual desire. But as these contrary inclinations, propensities and desires must already exist in the soul, it does not have them within its power; and consequently it could not resist them in any free and voluntary way in which reason could play a part, if it did not have another method, namely to turn the mind in a different direction. But how can we ensure that it occurs to us to do this whenever the need arises? – that is the problem, especially when one is in the grip of a strong passion. Hence what is required is that the mind be prepared in advance, and be already stepping from thought to thought, so that it will not be too much held up when the path becomes slippery and treacherous. It helps with this if one accustoms oneself in general to touching on certain topics only in passing, the better to preserve one's freedom of mind. Best of all, we should become accustomed to proceeding methodically and sticking to sequences of thoughts for which reason, rather than chance (i.e. insensible and fortuitous impressions), provides the thread. It helps with this if one becomes accustomed to withdrawing into oneself occasionally, rising above the hubbub of present impressions – as it were getting away from one's own situation and asking oneself 'Why am I here?', 'Where am I going?', 'How far have I come?', or saying 'I must come to the point, I must set to work!' Men often need an appointed official to interrupt them and call them back to their duties, like the one who did this for Philip, the father of Alexander the Great. Lacking such an official,

196

we would profit from being disciplined to perform this function for
ourselves. Once we are in a position to stop our desires and passions from
taking effect, i.e. to suspend action, we can find ways of fighting against
them, either by contrary desires and inclinations or by diversion, that is
by occupying ourselves with other matters. It is through these methods
and stratagems that we become masters of ourselves, and can bring it about
that we have certain thoughts and that when the time comes we shall will
according to our present preference and according to reason's decrees.
However, this always takes place in determinate ways and never without
reasons[1] – never by the fictitious principle of total indifference or equilibrium. Some people would claim the latter to be the essence of freedom,
as if one could determine oneself without reasons and even against all
reasons, going directly contrary to the prevalent impressions and propensities. 'Without reasons', I say, i.e. without other inclinations going the
opposite way, without being already in the process of turning the mind to
other matters, and without any other such intelligible means. If we allow
this, we are having recourse to such chimeras as the Scholastics' bare
faculties and occult qualities, in which there is neither rhyme nor reason.

PHIL. I too am in favour of this intellectual determination of the will by
what is contained in perception and in the understanding. ''Tis not a fault,
but a perfection of our nature to...will, and act according to the last result
of a fair examination. §48. This is so far from being a restraint or
diminution of freedom, that it is the very improvement and benefit of it:
...and the farther we are removed from such a determination, the nearer
we are to misery and slavery. [Indeed, if you suppose] a perfect [and
absolute][2] indifferency in the mind, not determinable by its last judgment
of...good or evil,' you will put it into a very imperfect state.

THEO. I like all that very much. It shows that the mind has no complete
and direct power to block its desires at any time; if it did, it would never
be settled,[3] whatever investigation it might make and whatever good
reasons or effective sentiments it might have, and would remain forever
irresolute, fluctuating endlessly between fear and hope. So it must
eventually be settled, and thus it must be able to oppose its desires only
indirectly, by preparing weapons in advance with which to combat them
when necessary, as I have just explained.

PHIL. However, 'a man is at liberty to lift up his hand to his head, or let
it rest quiet: he is perfectly indifferent in either; and it would be an
imperfection in him, if he wanted that power'.

[1] In this passage, the plural 'reasons' is used to render '*sujet*', which can mean 'reason',
'basis', 'cause', 'determining factor', etc.
[2] Added by Coste.
[3] In this speech and in Theophilus' next, 'settle' etc. translates '*déterminer*' etc. which
is often rendered by 'determine' etc.

THEO. Strictly speaking, one is never indifferent with regard to two alternatives, of whatever kind, for instance whether to turn right or left, or to put the right foot forward (as was required at Trimalchio's) or the left. For we do one or the other without thinking about it, which is a sign that a confluence of internal dispositions and external impressions – all of them insensible – settles us on the alternative which we adopt. Its predominance is very slight, however, and we are bound to seem indifferent about the matter, since the slightest sensible consideration which arises for us can easily determine us to go one way rather than the other: even though there is a little difficulty in raising an arm to put a hand on one's head, it is so small that we easily overcome it. I concede that it would be a great imperfection in man if he were less indifferent than he is, and lacked the power easily to determine himself to lift or not to lift his arm.

PHIL. 'But it would be as great an imperfection, if he had the same indifferency' in all situations, e.g. when he would like to[1] 'save his head or eyes from a blow he sees coming' – that is, if it were as easy to prevent this movement as those of which we were just speaking, where it is almost a matter of indifference – for in that case he would not be brought to move vigorously or swiftly enough when he needs to. Thus, determination is frequently useful and necessary to us; and if we were only weakly determined in every sort of situation, and more or less insensitive to reasons drawn from perceptions of good and bad, we would be without effective choice.[2] 'Were we determined by any thing but the last result of our own minds, judging of the good or evil of any action, we were not free'.

THEO. Nothing could be more true; those who seek some other kind of freedom do not know what they are asking for.

PHIL. §49. 'Those superior beings...who enjoy perfect happiness...are more steadily determined in their choice of good than we; and yet we have no reason to think they are...less free, than we are.'

THEO. Theologians say for this reason that those blessed substances are confirmed in goodness and are exempt from all danger of falling.

PHIL. I even think that 'if it were fit for such poor finite creatures as we are, to pronounce what infinite wisdom and goodness could do,...we might say, that God himself cannot choose what is not good; the freedom of the Almighty hinders not his being determined by what is best.'

THEO. I am so convinced of this truth that I believe we can assert it boldly, poor finite creatures though we are, and indeed that we would be very wrong to doubt it. In doing so we would detract from his wisdom, his

---

[1] Locke: 'indifferency whether he would prefer the lifting up his hand, or its remaining in rest, when it would'. Coste's change.

[2] Added by Leibniz.

goodness and his other infinite perfections. But choice, however much the will is determined to make it, should not be called absolutely and in the strict sense necessary: a predominance of goods of which one is aware inclines without necessitating, although, all things considered, this inclination is determining and never fails to have its effect.

PHIL. To be determined by reason to the best is to be most free.[1] §50. Would anyone wish to be an imbecile[2] because an imbecile 'is less determined, by wise considerations, than a wise man?' If to shake off reason's yoke is liberty, then 'mad men and fools are the only freemen: but yet, I think, no body would choose to be mad for the sake of such liberty, but he that is mad already.

THEO. Some people these days believe that it is clever to decry reason and to treat it as intolerable pedantry. I see little pamphlets whose self-congratulating authors have nothing to say, and sometimes I even see verses so fine that they should not be used to express such false thoughts. In fact, if those who make fun of reason were speaking in earnest this would be a new kind of absurdity, unknown in past centuries. To speak against *reason* is to speak against the truth, for reason is a chain of truths. This is to speak against oneself, and against one's own good, since the principal use of reason consists in knowing the good and pursuing it.

PHIL. §51. 'As therefore the highest perfection of [an] intellectual [being] lies in a careful and constant pursuit of true...happiness; so the care of our selves, that we mistake not imaginary for real happiness, is the... foundation of our liberty. The stronger ties, we have, to an unalterable pursuit of happiness in general, which...our desires always follow, the more are we free from any necessary determination of our will [by] our desire, set upon any particular...good, till we have duly examined, whether it [agrees with][3] or be inconsistent with our real happiness'.

THEO. True happiness ought always to be the object of our desires, but there is some reason to doubt that it is. For often we hardly think of it, and, as I have more than once pointed out here, unless appetite is directed by reason it endeavours after present pleasure rather than that lasting pleasure which is called happiness – although it does endeavour to make the pleasure last (see §36 and §41).

PHIL. §53. 'If any extreme disturbance...possesses our whole [soul], as ...the pain of the rack,...we are not masters enough of our own minds'. But in order, so far as possible, to moderate our passions, we should 'suit the relish of our minds to the true intrinsic good or ill,...and not permit a...great and weighty good to slip out of our thoughts, without leaving

[1] Based on Locke's §48.
[2] Locke uses the now obsolete 'changeling'.
[3] Locke: 'has a tendency to'. Coste's change.

any relish,' until we have formed desires[1] in our minds suitable to its excellence, and made ourselves disquieted 'in the want of it, or in the fear of losing it' when we do have it.

THEO. That agrees pretty well with what I have just said in §§31–5, and with what I have said more than once about enlightened pleasures; we can understand how they perfect us without exposing us to the danger of some greater imperfection, as do the confused pleasures of the senses. The latter should be avoided, especially when one has not discovered by experience that one can safely enjoy them.

PHIL. 'Nor let any one say, he cannot govern his passions, nor hinder them from breaking out, and carrying him into action; for what he can do before a prince, or a great man, he can do alone, or in the presence of God, if he will.'

THEO. That is an excellent point and worthy of frequent reflection.

PHIL. §54. Yet 'the various and contrary choices, that men make in the world [show] that the same thing is not good to every man alike.... Were all the concerns of man terminated in this life,' the explanation of this variety – some men choosing luxury and debauchery for example, and others preferring sobriety to sensuality[2] – would be merely that 'their happiness was placed in different things.'

THEO. That is the explanation of it, even as things actually are – though they all do or should have that common goal of a future life in front of their eyes. It is true that a regard for real happiness, even in this life, would require us to prefer virtue to sensuality, which takes us away from happiness; although the requirement would not then be as strong or as decisive. It is also true that men's tastes differ, and it is said that one should not argue about matters of taste. However, since tastes are only confused perceptions, we should rely on them only when their objects have been examined and are acknowledged to be insignificant and harmless. If someone acquired a taste for poisons which would kill him or make him wretched, it would be absurd to say that we ought not to argue with him about his tastes.

PHIL. §55. 'If there be no prospect beyond the grave, the inference is certainly right, *Let us eat and drink*, let us enjoy what we delight in, *for to morrow we shall die*.'

THEO. To my mind something can be said about this inference. Aristotle and the Stoics and various other ancient philosophers held a different view, and in fact I believe that they were right. If there were nothing beyond this life, tranquillity of soul and bodily health would still be preferable to

201

---

[1] Locke: 'appetites'. Coste's change.
[2] Locke: '[choosing] sobriety and riches'. Coste: '*préférant la tempérance à la volupté*'.

pleasures incompatible with them. And the fact that a good is not going to last for ever is not a reason to disregard it. But I admit that in some cases there would be no way of demonstrating that the most honourable thing is also the most useful. So that only a regard for God and immortality makes the obligations of virtue and justice absolutely binding.

PHIL. §58. It seems to me that 'our judgment of present good or evil [is] always right.'[1] And 'as to present happiness and misery, when that alone comes in consideration, and the consequences are quite removed, a man never chooses amiss'.

THEO. That is, if everything were restricted to this present moment, there would be no reason to refuse any pleasure which is offered. As things are, although every pleasure is a sense of perfection, as I noted earlier [p. 194], there are certain perfections which bring with them greater imperfections. If someone devoted his entire life to throwing peas at pins, trying to get the knack of skewering them every time – emulating the man who was rewarded by Alexander the Great with the gift of a bushel of peas – he would achieve a sort of perfection, but a very trivial one which could not stand comparison with all the essential perfections which he had let go. In the same way, the perfection involved in certain present pleasures should be made to yield, above all, to the cultivation of perfections which are needed if one is not to be plunged into misery, which is the state of going from imperfection to imperfection, from suffering to suffering. But if there were only the present, one would have to settle for the perfections which it offered, i.e. for present pleasure.

202

PHIL. §62. No one would willingly make his state miserable except through wrong judgments. I am not speaking of those mistakes which are consequences of invincible error, and which hardly deserve[2] 'the name of wrong judgment; but of that wrong judgment, which every man must' confess to himself[3] to be so. §63. Firstly, then, the soul makes mistakes when we compare present pleasure or pain with a future pleasure or pain, measuring them according to the different distances at which they stand from us. We are like a spendthrift heir who renounces a great inheritance which was certain to come to him, in exchange for some small present gain. Everyone must acknowledge that this is a wrong judgment; for the future will become present and will then have 'the same advantage of nearness .... Were the pleasure of drinking accompanied, the very moment a man takes off his glass, with that sick stomach, and aching head, which [will] follow not many hours after, [he would not] ever let wine touch his lips'.

[1] Locke's marginal summary of §§58, 59.
[2] Locke writes of 'a wrong judgment' and of 'that mistake, which is the consequence' etc. One pluralization by Coste, the others by Leibniz.
[3] Locke: 'himself confess'. Coste's change.

If a small interval of time can produce such a great illusion, there is all the stronger reason to expect a larger distance to have the same effect.

THEO. Distances between times are in this respect somewhat like distances between places. But there is also this difference: the effect which a visible thing has on our eyesight is inversely proportional, more or less, to its distance from us, but the same does not hold for the effect on our minds and imaginations of things in the future. Light rays are straight lines, and move apart at a steady rate. But there are curves which after some distance appear to meet a straight line, and are no longer perceptibly separated from it. That is what happens with a curve which asymptotically approaches a straight line – the apparent distance between the two disappears, though in reality they remain apart for ever. We find that even the apparent size of objects eventually stops decreasing in proportion to their distance from us, because before long the appearance disappears entirely although the object is not infinitely distant. That is how a small distance of time can completely hide the future from us, just as though the object had disappeared. Often nothing remains of it in the mind but the name, together with thoughts of a kind I have already mentioned – 'blind' thoughts which cannot influence anyone unless he has made provision for them through being methodical and through practice.

PHIL. 'I mention not here the [kind of] wrong judgment, whereby the absent are not only lessened, but reduced to perfect nothing' in the minds of men,[1] when they enjoy whatever they can get in the present, concluding that no harm to them will ensue.

THEO. It is another kind of wrong judgment that occurs when the expectation of good or evil is abolished through one's denying or doubting what will in fact arise out of the present; but setting that case aside, the error which reduces to nothing the sense of the future is just the same as the false judgment which I have discussed already, the one which results from having too weak a representation of the future and paying little attention to it or none whatsoever. Also, perhaps we might here distinguish false judgment from defective taste; for often one does not so much as raise the question of whether the future good is preferable – one acts solely on impressions, with no thought of bringing them under scrutiny. When someone does give thought to the future, one of two things happens: either he is not thorough enough in his thinking, and drops the question he has embarked upon, without having followed it through; or he pursues his critical scrutiny and forms a conclusion. Either way, there is sometimes a certain lingering sense of wrongdoing; but sometimes there are absolutely no scruples, no deterrent fears – whether because the mind sheers right away from them or because it is hoodwinked by its preconceptions.

[1] Added by Coste.

PHIL. §64. 'The cause of our judging amiss, when we compare [goods or evils, is the] narrow constitution of our minds. We cannot well enjoy two pleasures at once, much less any pleasure...,[1] whilst pain possesses us. ...A little bitter mingled in our cup, leaves no relish of the sweet.... The pain that any one actually feels, is still of all other the worst; and...they cry out, *Any rather than this*'.

THEO. That varies a great deal according to individual temperament, the intensity of what one feels, and the habits one has acquired. A man with gout may be overjoyed because a great fortune has come to him, and a man who bathes in pleasure and could live at his ease on his estates is deep in sorrow because of a disgrace at court. When pleasure is mixed with pain, the occurrence of joy or sorrow is a result – it depends upon which component prevails in the mixture. Leander, drawn by the attractions of the lovely Hero, disregarded the difficulty and danger of swimming across the sea at night. There are people who have some infirmity or disorder which causes them great pain whenever they eat or drink, or when they satisfy other appetites; and yet they satisfy those appetites, even going beyond what they need and what is proper. Others are so soft or delicate that they reject any pleasure which is mixed with any pain, nastiness or discomfort. There are people who rise right above the minor pleasures and pains of the present, and act almost entirely on the basis of hope and fear; others are so effeminate that they complain of the slightest discomfort and chase after the slightest of present sensible pleasures – almost like children. To these people, the pain or sensual pleasure of the present always seems to be the greatest; they are like those extravagant preachers or panegyrists for whom – as the proverb has it – the saint of the day is always the greatest saint in heaven. Still, despite all these individual differences, it remains true that everyone acts only according to his present perceptions: when the future affects someone, it does so either through his image of it or else through his having made a policy and practice of being guided by the mere name or some other arbitrary symbol of the future without any image or natural sign of it. The latter case depends on the fact that one cannot go against a policy one has firmly adopted – still less against one's established practice – without a certain disquiet and sometimes a certain feeling of distress.

204

PHIL. §65. 'Men are apt enough to lessen [future pleasure]; and conclude with themselves, that when it comes to trial, it may possibly not answer [their hopes or the] opinion, that generally passes of it, they having often found' through their own experience not only that what others have magnified has appeared very insipid to them, but also that what they have

---

[1] Locke: 'almost'.

themselves been delighted by at one time has shocked and displeased them at another.

THEO. That is how the sensualist reasons, for the most part, but the ambitious man and the miser are usually found to think quite differently about honours and riches – though when they acquire honours or riches they get but feeble pleasure from them and often almost none at all, because their thoughts are always on the next move. Nature the Architect did very well, it seems to me, making men so sensitive to things which have so little effect on the senses. If we were incapable of becoming ambitious or miserly, it would be hard for us – in the present state of human nature – to become virtuous and rational enough to work towards our own perfection in face of the present pleasures which distract us from it.

PHIL. §66. 'As to things good or bad in their consequences, and by the aptness is in them to procure us good or evil..., we judge amiss[1] several ways[: either] when we judge that so much evil does not really depend on them, as in truth there does [or] when we judge, that though the consequence be of [importance], yet it is not of that certainty, but that it may otherwise fall out; or else by some means be avoided, as by industry, address, change [of conduct], repentance'.

THEO. If by the importance of the 'consequence' you mean that of the result, i.e. the amount of good or evil which may ensue, then this must be that kind of false judgment, discussed earlier, in which future good or evil is badly represented. So all that remains, that concerns us at present, is the second kind of false judgment, namely the one where it is doubted that the result will ensue.

PHIL. That these evasions which I have mentioned 'are wrong ways of judging, were easy to show in every particular...: but I shall only mention this in general, viz. that it is a very wrong, and irrational way of proceeding, to venture a greater good, for a less,' or to expose oneself to misery in order to achieve a small good or avoid a small harm, 'upon uncertain guesses, and before a due examination be made'.

THEO. The question of how inevitable a result is[2] is heterogeneous from – i.e. cannot be compared with – the question of how good or bad it is.[3] So in trying to compare them, moralists have become muddled, as can be seen from writings on *probability. The fact is that in this as in other assessments which are disparate, heterogeneous, having more than one dimension (so to speak), the magnitude of the thing in question is made up proportionately out of two estimates; as with a rectangle, where two things have to be considered, namely its length and its breadth. As for the

---

[1] Taking the omission of Coste's 'faussement' to be a slip.
[2] 'la grandeur de la conséquence'.   [3] 'la grandeur du conséquent'.

inevitability of the result, and degrees of probability, we do not yet possess *that branch of logic* which would let them be estimated. And most casuists who have written on probability [*probabilism] have not so much as understood the nature of it: they have sided with Aristotle in founding it upon authority, rather than upon *likelihood as they ought to have, authority being only one of the reasons for something's likelihood.

PHIL. Here are some of 'the usual causes of this wrong judgment'. §67. The first is ignorance. The second is heedlessness,[1] 'when a man overlooks even that, which he does know. This is an affected[2] and present ignorance, which misleads our judgments,' as well as our wills.[3]

THEO. It is always present, but it is not always affected: sometimes when a person needs to think of something which he knows, and which he would call to mind if he had perfect control of his memory, it does not occur to him to do so. Affected ignorance always involves some heeding for as long as it is affected, though commonly there can be heedlessness later on. If someone discovered *the art of bringing to mind at the right time* the things that one knows, it would be of prime importance; but so far as I can see, no one has so far thought of constructing the rudiments of such an art [*mnemonics]. Plenty of people have written about the art of memory, but that is quite different.

PHIL. 'If therefore [the reasons on][4] either side be huddled up in haste, and several of the sums, that should have gone into the reckoning, be overlooked, and left out, this precipitancy causes as [many wrong judgments][5] as if it were a perfect ignorance.'

THEO. Indeed, for the right decision to be made in a case where reasons have to be weighed against one another, many things are needed. That is much the way it is with merchants' account books. For in those one must not ignore any amount, each separate amount must be carefully ascertained, and they must be put in good order and then listed accurately. But some items are omitted, either because they escape one's mind or because one passes too quickly over them. And some are not given their correct values – as in the case of the book-keeper who carefully adds up the columns on each page but incorrectly computes the individual amounts of each line or entry before extending them into the column; which he does in order to deceive the auditors, who mainly check what is in the columns.

207

---

[1] Locke uses 'inadvertency'.
[2] Nidditch conjectures that Locke is using 'affected' in its now obsolete sense of 'afflicted, tainted'. Coste's '*affectée*' could not mean that; and Leibniz seems to take it in the sense of the medieval '*ignorantia affectata*', wilful ignorance.
[3] Locke: 'as much as the other.'
[4] Added by Leibniz.
[5] Locke: 'wrong a judgment'. Coste's change.

Lastly, after having taken every care, one can still make an error in listing the column totals, and even in the final list where the grand total is to be found. So if we are to make good use of the *art of inference, we need an art of bringing things to mind, another of estimating probabilities, and, in addition, knowledge of how to evaluate goods and ills; and we need to be attentive, and, on top of all that, to have the patience to carry our calculations through. Finally, we need to be firmly and steadily resolved to act on our conclusions; and we need skills, methods, rules of thumb, and well-entrenched habits to make us true to our resolve later on, when the considerations which led us to it are no longer present to our minds. God has seen to it that in regard to what matters most – what concerns the most important thing, namely happiness and misery – one does not need as great an array of knowledge, aids and skills as would be needed for sound judgment in a council of state or of war, in a court of law, in a medical consultation, in a theological or historical debate, or in a problem of mathematics or mechanics. But as against that, where the great matter of happiness and virtue is concerned one needs more firmness and regularity of conduct [*habitude] if one is always to make good resolves and to abide by them. In short, true happiness requires less knowledge but greater strength and goodness of will, so that the dullest idiot can achieve it just as easily as can the cleverest and most educated person.

PHIL. So it can be seen that 'without liberty the understanding would be to no purpose: and without understanding, liberty...[1] would signify nothing.' If a man could see what would do him good or harm, without being able to move one step towards the one or away from the other, what advantage would it be to him that he could see? It would only make him more miserable still, for he would yearn uselessly for the good and fear the harm which he saw to be unavoidable.[2] And he who is at liberty to ramble in perfect darkness, how is he better off than if he were driven up and down by the force of the wind?

THEO. He would satisfy his whims a little better, yet he would be no better placed to encounter good and avoid harm.

PHIL. §68. Another source of false judgment: being satisfied with the first pleasure that comes to hand or that custom has endeared to us, we look no further. 'This is another occasion to men of judging wrong, when they take not that to be necessary to their happiness, which really is so.'

THEO. It seems to me that this false judgement falls under the previous heading of error about what will result.

PHIL. §69. 'The last inquiry...is, whether it be in a man's power to change the pleasantness, and unpleasantness, that accompanies [some

208

---

[1] Locke: '(if it could be)'.   [2] Sentence added by Leibniz.

particular]¹ action?... In many cases he can. Men may and should correct
their palates,' and make them appreciate things. The soul's tastes can be
altered too, by 'a due consideration[,] practice, application, and custom'.
That is how one becomes accustomed to tobacco, which eventually
becomes enjoyable through use and familiarity. It is the same with regard
to virtue: habits have great charms, and cannot be given up without
disquiet. It will perhaps be thought a paradox that men can make things
or actions more or less pleasing to themselves, so greatly neglected is this
task.

THEO. That is what I said too, near the end of §37 above and again near
the end of §47. One can induce oneself to want something and to develop
a taste for it.

PHIL. §70. 'Morality, established upon its true foundations, cannot but
determine' one to be virtuous: all that is needed is the possibility of infinite
happiness or misery in an after-life. It must be admitted that a virtuous
life, with the expectation of possible everlasting bliss, is to be preferred
to a vicious one, with the fear of a dreadful state of misery 'or at best the
terrible uncertain hope of annihilation. This is evidently so, though the
virtuous life here had nothing but pain, and the vicious continual pleasure:
which yet is for the most part quite otherwise' – because I believe that the
wicked, all things considered, fare worse than others even in this life.

THEO. So even if there were nothing beyond the tomb, an Epicurean life
would not be the most rational one. I am very pleased, sir, that you are
now correcting the contrary claim which you seemed to make in §55 above.

PHIL. Who would be so mad as to decide (if he thought hard about it) to
expose himself to a possible danger of being infinitely miserable, so that
there was nothing for him to gain except sheer annihilation;² rather than
putting himself in the position of the good man, who has nothing to fear
but annihilation and can hope for eternal happiness? 'I have forborne to
mention any thing of the certainty, or probability of a future state,
designing here only to show the wrong judgment, that any one must allow,
he makes upon his own principles'.

THEO. The wicked are powerfully drawn to the belief that there cannot
be an after-life. But their only reason for this is that we should not go
beyond what we learn from our senses, and that no one they know has
returned from the other world. There was a time when by that argument
one could have denied the existence of the Antipodes, if one were not
prepared to augment popular notions with mathematical ones; and that

¹ Locke: 'any sort of'. Coste's change.
² Locke: 'Who in his wits would choose to come within a possibility of infinite misery, which
 if he miss, there is yet nothing to be got by that hazard?' Coste's changes, except for
 the parenthetical clause which is Leibniz's.

209

would have been every bit as justifiable as it is now to deny the after-life because one refuses to augment the notions of imagination with true metaphysics. You see, there are three levels of notions or ideas – popular, mathematical, and metaphysical. The first were not enough to make people believe in the Antipodes, and the first two still do not suffice to make one believe in the other world, though even they create a presumption in its favour. Notions of the second kind conclusively established the existence of the Antipodes in advance of our present experience of them (I am referring not to the inhabitants but to the place which geographers and geometers assigned to them, from their knowledge of the roundness of the earth); and notions of the third kind can provide just as much certainty that there is an after-life – doing this right now, before we have gone to see.

PHIL. This chapter is supposed to have power as its general topic, freedom being merely one species, though a most important one. Let us return to 210 power. §72. It will 'be to our purpose, and help to give us clearer conceptions about power, if we' take a more exact survey of what is called *action*.[1] I have said at the beginning of our discussion of power 'that we have ideas but of two sorts of action, viz. motion and' thought.[2]

THEO. One might, I believe, replace 'thought' by a more general term, 'perception', attributing thought only to minds whereas perception belongs to all entelechies. But still I would not challenge anyone's right to use 'thought' with that same generality, and I may sometimes have carelessly done so myself.

PHIL. But although these two things are given the name 'action', it will not be found always to be perfectly suitable to them: there are instances which will be recognized rather to be passions. 'For in these instances, the substance that hath motion, or thought, receives the impression whereby it is put into that action purely from without, and so acts merely by the capacity it has to receive' that impression, which is a mere passive power. 'Sometimes the substance, or agent, puts it self into action by its own power, and this is properly *active* power.'

THEO. As I have already said, anything which occurs in what is strictly a substance must be a case of 'action' in the metaphysically rigorous sense of something which occurs in the substance spontaneously, arising out of its own depths; for no created substance can have an influence upon any other, so that everything comes to a substance from itself (though ultimately from God). But if we take 'action' to be an endeavour towards perfection, and 'passion' to be the opposite, then genuine substances are active only when their perceptions (for I grant perceptions to all of them)

[1] Locke: 'make our thoughts take a little more exact survey of action.' Coste's change.
[2] Locke: 'thinking'. Coste's change.

are becoming better developed and more distinct, just as they are passive only when their perceptions are becoming more confused. Consequently, in substances which are capable of pleasure and pain every action is a move towards pleasure, every passion a move towards pain. As for motion: it has only *phenomenal reality, because it belongs to matter or mass, which is not strictly speaking a substance. Still, there is a semblance[1] of action in motion, as there is a semblance of substance in mass. From that point of view a body can be said to 'act' when there is spontaneity in its change, and to 'undergo passively' when it is pushed or blocked by another body; just as with the true action or passion of a true substance, we can take to be its 'action', and attribute to the substance itself, any change through which it comes closer to its own perfection; and can take to be its 'passion', and attribute to an outside cause (though not an immediate one), any change in which the reverse happens; because the change can be explained in an intelligible way by reference to the substance itself in the former case and by reference to outer things in the latter. I give to bodies only a semblance of substance and of action, because something made up of parts cannot, strictly speaking, be accounted *a* substance, any more than a herd can; though a body may be granted to involve something substantial, whose unity – which makes it like *one* being – comes from thought.

PHIL. It has been my view that 'a power to receive ideas, or thoughts, from the operation of any external substance, is called a power of thinking: [although fundamentally] this is but a passive power, or [a mere][2] capacity.' (I here abstract from the reflections and inner changes which always accompany the image which is received, for the expression that occurs in the soul is like what there would be in a living mirror.)[3] 'But to be able to bring into view ideas out of sight, at one's own choice, and to compare which of them one thinks fit, this is [truly] an active power.'

THEO. That involves a transition to a more perfect state, so what you say about it agrees with the notions I have just been putting forward. Yet I should have thought that sensations also involve action, in as much as they present us with perceptions which stand out more, and thus with opportunities for observation and for self-development, so to speak.

PHIL. §73. Now I believe that our primary, 'original' ideas appear to be reducible to the following few. Extension, Solidity, Mobility (i.e. passive power or capacity to be moved),[4] which come to us by our senses; then 'Perceptivity' and 'Motivity' (i.e. active power or faculty of moving),[5] which come into our minds by way of reflection; and finally Existence, Duration, Number, which come to us by both ways, from sensation and

----

[1] '*une image*'.
[2] Added by Coste. [3] Added by Leibniz.
[4] Locke: 'Mobility, or the power of being moved'.
[5] Locke: 'Motivity, or the power of moving'.

212 from reflection. 'For by these, I imagine, might be explained the nature of colours, sounds, tastes, smells, and all other ideas we have, if we had but faculties acute enough to perceive the [different] motions, of these minute bodies, which produce those...sensations'.

THEO. To speak frankly, I believe that few of those ideas are thoroughly original and primary, as they are here claimed to be: in my opinion most of them admit of further decomposition. Yet I don't blame you, sir, for stopping there and not pushing the analysis back further. There is another point: although by further analysis we could reduce the number of ideas, I think we could also increase it by adding others which are just as original if not more so. As for how they should be arranged: if we are to follow the order of analysis, I think we should put existence before the others, number before extension, and duration before 'motivity' and mobility; not that this analytic order is the usual order in which events prompt us to think of these ideas. The senses provide us with materials for reflections: we could not think even about thought if we did not think about something else, i.e. about the particular facts which the senses provide. I am convinced that created minds and souls never lack organs and never lack sensations, as they cannot reason without symbols. Some people have wanted to maintain a complete separation [of body from soul], and to endow the separated soul with thought-processes which could not be explained by anything we know, and which would be remote not only from our present experience but also – and far more important – from the general order of things. They have given too much of an opening to those who profess to be free-thinkers, and have made many people sceptical about the finest and greatest truths; since their position deprives them of various good ways of *proving those truths – ways which are provided by the general order of things.

Chapter xxii
'Of mixed modes.'

PHILALETHES. §1. Let us turn to mixed modes. 'I...distinguish them from the more simple modes, which consist only of simple ideas of the same
213 kind. These mixed modes being...such combinations of simple ideas, as are not looked upon to be...characteristical marks of any real beings that have a steady existence, but scattered and independent ideas, put together by the mind, are thereby distinguished from the complex ideas of substances.'

THEOPHILUS. To understand this properly, we ought to run over your earlier divisions. You divide ideas into simple and complex, and the latter are ideas of substances, modes, and relations. Modes are either simple (composed of simple ideas of the same kind) or mixed. So according to you there are simple ideas, ideas of simple modes and of mixed ones, ideas of substances, and ideas of relations. We could also divide terms, i.e. the objects of ideas, into abstract and concrete, the abstract into absolute and relational, the absolute into attributes and modifications, and each of these last two into simple and composite; and concrete terms could be divided into substances and substantial things which are composed of or result from true, simple substances.

PHIL. §2. 'The mind, in respect of its simple ideas, is wholly passive, and receives them...as sensation or reflection offers them'. But it is often active, of its own accord, with regard to mixed modes, for it can combine simple ideas to make 'complex ideas, without examining whether they exist so together in nature.' That is why these ideas are called 'notions'.

THEO. But reflection, which makes one think of simple ideas, is often voluntary too; and, moreover, combinations which nature has not made may occur in our minds as though of their own accord in dreams and reveries – simply through memory and with no more activity on the mind's part than in the case of simple ideas. As for the word 'notion': many people apply it to all sorts of ideas or conceptions, original as well as derivative.

PHIL. §4. The mark of the union of several ideas into a single one is the name.

THEO. That assumes that they can be combined; but often they cannot.

PHIL. The crime of killing an old man, not having a name as parricide does, is not taken for a complex idea. 214

THEO. The reason why there is no name for the murder of an old man is that such a name would be of little use, since the law has not assigned a special penalty for that crime. However, ideas do not depend upon names. If a moralizing writer did invent a name for that crime and devoted a chapter to 'Gerontophony', showing what we owe to the old and how monstrous it is to treat them ungently, he would not thereby be giving us a new idea.

PHIL. §6. It is still true that since the manners and customs of a people create combinations[1] which are familiar to them, each language contains particular terms which could not always be given word-for-word translations. Thus *ostracism* amongst the Greeks, and *proscription* amongst the Romans, were words which other languages cannot express by equivalent words. §7. This is why change of customs creates new words.

THEO. There is an element of chance as well. For instance, the French use horses just as much as their neighbours; and yet they have abandoned their old word corresponding to the Italians' *cavalcar*, and must make shift with the phrase *aller à cheval*.

[1] Locke: 'combinations of ideas'.

PHIL. §9. We get the ideas of mixed modes by observation, as when one sees two men wrestling; we get them also by invention (or voluntary putting together of simple ideas) – thus the man who invented printing had an idea of that art before it existed. Finally, we get them by the explanation of terms which are reserved for actions which have never been seen.[1]

THEO. One can also get them in dreams and reveries without the combination being a voluntary one – for instance seeing golden palaces in a dream without having thought of them before.

PHIL. §10. The simple ideas which 'have been most modified' are those of thinking, of motion, and of power, from which actions are conceived to flow. 'For action [is] the great business of mankind'; all actions are thoughts or movements. The 'power or ability in man, of doing any thing, when it has been acquired by frequent doing the same thing, is that idea, we name *habit*; when it is...ready upon every occasion, to break into action, we call it *disposition*'. Tenderness, for instance, is a disposition to be friendly or loving.[2]

THEO. By 'tenderness' I suppose you here mean soft-heartedness. But in other contexts, it seems to me, 'tenderness' is taken to be a quality which someone has while in love, making the lover sensitive to whatever good or harm comes to the beloved. It appears to me that it is this quality that 'the map of Tenderness' fits, in that fine novel *Clelia* [*Scudéry]. Also, as charitable people love their neighbour with some measure of tenderness, they are sensitive to the good or harm of others. Furthermore, it is true on the whole that those who are soft-hearted will be somewhat disposed to be tender when in love.

PHIL. 'Boldness is the power to speak or do what we intend, before others, without' being intimidated;[3] and to the former kind of confidence – confidence in speaking – the Greeks give a special name of its own.

THEO. It would be good to reserve some word for the notion which you attach to 'boldness', but the latter is often used quite differently, as when people spoke of 'Charles the Bold'. The ability not to be intimidated is a strength of the mind, but scoundrels misuse it when they carry it to the point of impudence; just as shame is a weakness which is nevertheless pardonable and even praiseworthy in certain circumstances. As for the word *parrhesia*, which may be the Greek word you have in mind:[4] this is applied also to writers who tell the truth fearlessly, although since they are not speaking in front of people they have no reason to be intimidated.

215

---

[1] Locke: 'names of actions we never saw'.
[2] Locke: 'testiness is a disposition...to be angry'. Coste's change.
[3] Locke: 'fear or disorder'. Coste: '*craindre ou se décontenancer en aucune manière*'. Leibniz: '*se décontenancer*'.
[4] The Greek word occurs in Locke's text, but Coste relegates it to the margin.

PHIL. §11. 'Power being the source from whence all action proceeds, the substances wherein these powers are, when they exert this power into act, are called *causes*; and the substances which thereupon are produced, or [rather]¹ the simple ideas [–i.e. the objects of simple ideas –]² which are introduced into any subject by the exerting of that power, are called *effects*. The *efficacy* whereby the new substance or idea [(quality)]³ is produced, is called, in the subject exerting that power, *action*; but in the subject, wherein any simple idea [(quality)]⁴ is changed or produced, it is called *passion*'.

THEO. If 'power' is taken to be the source of action, it means more than the aptitude or ability in terms of which power was explained in the preceding chapter. For, as I have more than once remarked [pp. 169, 172], it also includes endeavour. It is in order to express this sense that I appropriate the term 'entelechy' to stand for power. An entelechy may be either *primary*, corresponding to the soul considered as something abstract, or *derivative*, such as is involved in the conception of conatus, and of force and impetus. The term 'cause' is understood here only in the sense of 'efficient cause'; but it is also taken to mean 'final' cause or motive, not to mention matter and form, which the Scholastics also call causes. I am not convinced that we should say that the very same *item is called action in the agent and passion in the thing which is acted upon, so that it exists in two subjects at once, like a relation; and that it would not be better to say that there are two items, one in the agent and the other in the thing which is acted upon.

PHIL. 'Many words, which seem to express some action, signify nothing [but the cause and the effect]; v.g. *creation*, *annihilation*, contain in them no idea of the action or manner . . ., but barely of the cause, and the thing' which is produced.⁵

THEO. I admit that in thinking of the creation one does not – and indeed cannot – conceive of any process in detail. But one thinks of something in addition to God and the world, for one thinks that God is the cause and the world the effect, i.e. that God has produced the world. So obviously one does also think of action.

Chapter xxiii
'Of our complex ideas of substances.'

PHILALETHES. §1. The mind takes notice that a certain number of 'simple ideas go constantly together; which being presumed to belong to

---

¹ Added by Coste.   ² Added by Leibniz.
³ Added by Leibniz.   ⁴ Added by Leibniz.
⁵ Locke: 'the thing done.' Coste's change.

one thing,...are called so united in one subject, by one name; which [through heedlessness][1] we are apt afterward to talk of...as one simple idea, which indeed is a complication of many ideas together'.

THEOPHILUS. I see nothing in the ordinary ways of talking which deserves to be accused of 'heedlessness'. We do take it that there is one subject, and one idea, but not that there is one simple idea.

PHIL. 'Not imagining how these simple ideas can subsist by themselves, we accustom our selves to suppose some *substratum* [– some thing which supports them –] wherein they do subsist, and from which they do result, which therefore we call substance.'

THEO. I believe that this way of thinking is correct. And we have no need to 'accustom' ourselves to it, or to 'suppose' it; for from the beginning we conceive several predicates in a single subject, and that is all there is to these metaphorical words 'support' and 'substratum'. So I do not see why it is made out to involve a problem. On the contrary, what comes into our mind is the *concretum* conceived as wise, warm, shining, rather than[2] *abstractions* or qualities such as wisdom, warmth, light etc., which are much harder to grasp. (I say 'qualities', for what the substantial object contains are qualities, not ideas.) It can even be doubted whether these accidents are genuine entities at all, and indeed many of them are only relations. We know, too, that it is abstractions which cause the most problems when one tries to get to the bottom of them. Anyone knows this who is conversant with the intricacies of scholastic thought: their thorniest brambles disappear in a flash if one is willing to banish abstract entities, to resolve that in speaking one will ordinarily use only concrete terms and will allow no terms into learned demonstrations except ones which stand for substantial subjects. So to treat qualities or other abstract terms as though they were the least problematic, and concrete ones as very troublesome, is to 'look for a knot in a bullrush' [Plautus], if you will allow me the phrase, and to put things back to front.

PHIL. §2. A person's only notion of pure substance in general is that of I know not what subject of which he knows nothing at all but which he supposes to be the support of qualities. 'We talk like children; who, being questioned, what such a thing is, which they know not, readily give this [to them] satisfactory answer, that it is *something*; which in truth signifies ..., when so used,...that they know not what' it is.

THEO. If you distinguish two things in a substance – the attributes or predicates, and their common subject – it is no wonder that you cannot conceive anything special in this subject. That is inevitable, because you have already set aside all the attributes through which details could be

---

[1] Locke uses 'inadvertency'.   [2] Or: 'before'.

conceived. Thus, to require of this 'pure subject in general' anything beyond what is needed for the conception of 'the same thing' – e.g. it is the same thing which understands and wills, which imagines and reasons – is to demand the impossible; and it also contravenes the assumption which was made in performing the abstraction and separating the subject from all its qualities or accidents. The same alleged difficulty could be brought against the notion of *being*, and against all that is plainest and most primary. For we may ask a philosopher what he conceives when he conceives 'pure being in general'; since the question excludes all detail, he will have as little to say as if he had been asked what 'pure substance in general' is. So I do not believe that it is fair to mock philosophers, as your author does [xiii.19] when he compares them to an Indian philosopher who was asked what supported the world, to which he replied that it was a great elephant; and then when he was asked what supported the elephant he said that it was a great tortoise; and finally when he was pressed to say what the tortoise rested on, he was reduced to saying that it was 'something, he knew not what'. Yet this conception of substance, for all its apparent thinness, is less empty and sterile than it is thought to be. Several consequences arise from it; these are of the greatest importance to philosophy, to which they can give an entirely new face.

PHIL. §4. We have 'no clear idea of substance in general.'[1] §5. And we have as clear an idea of spirit[2] as of body, because 'the idea of [a] corporeal substance in matter is as remote from our conceptions...[3] as that of spiritual substance'. It is rather like the story about the graduation ceremony in which the chief examiner said solemnly 'I pronounce you Doctor of Law', and the candidate interrupted him to shout 'Of two kinds!' – meaning civil law and canon law – to which the examiner replied: 'You are right, sir, for you are as learned in one as in the other.'[4]

THEO. My own view is that this opinion about what we don't know springs from a demand for a way of knowing which the object does not admit of. The true sign of a clear and distinct notion is one's having means for giving *a priori* proofs of many truths about it. I showed this in a paper about truths and ideas which was published in 1684 in the *Acta* of Leipzig ['Meditations on knowledge, truth and ideas'].

PHIL. §11. If our senses were acute enough, sensible qualities such as 'the yellow colour of gold, would then disappear, and instead of it we should see an admirable texture of parts.... This microscopes plainly discover to us'. §12. Our present knowledge is suited to the condition we are now in. Perfect knowledge of the things around us is perhaps beyond the reach

219

---

[1] Locke's marginal summary.
[2] Locke: 'of the substance of spirit'.
[3] Locke: 'and apprehensions'. Coste's omission.
[4] Leibniz's anecdote. This rendering borrows from a fuller version in an earlier draft.

'of any finite being. We are furnished with faculties [which suffice] to lead us to the knowledge of the Creator, and the knowledge of our duty .... But were our senses altered, and made much quicker and acuter, [this change][1] would be inconsistent with our being'.

THEO. That is all true, and I said something about it earlier [p. 165]. But the colour yellow is a reality, all the same, like the rainbow. Also we are apparently destined to achieve a much higher state [of knowledge] than we are now in, and may even go on rising for ever, since corporeal nature does not contain elementary particles. If there were atoms, as our author appeared elsewhere to believe that there are [i.15? ii.2?], perfect knowledge of bodies could not be 'beyond any finite being'. Lastly: if our eyes became better equipped or more penetrating, so that some colours or other qualities disappeared from our view, others would appear to arise out of them, and we should need a further increase in acuity to make them disappear too; and since matter is actually divided to infinity, this process could go on to infinity also.

220 PHIL. §13. I suspect that 'one great advantage' which some spirits have over us is 'that they can so...shape to themselves organs of sensation ...as to suit them to their present design'.

THEO. We do that too, when we 'shape' microscopes; but other creatures can take it further than we can. If we could transform our eyes themselves – as we actually do, in a way, according as we want to see close up or far away[2] – we should need to shape them by means of something belonging to us even more intimately than they do; for all this would at least have to occur mechanically, because the mind cannot act immediately on bodies. Furthermore, I am of the opinion that Spirits perceive things in a manner comparable with ours, even if they have the pleasing advantage with which the imaginative Cyrano [*moon] endows certain animate inhabitants of the sun: they are composed of an infinity of tiny flying creatures which move at the command of a dominant soul and thus take all sorts of bodily shapes. Nothing is so wonderful that it could not be produced by nature's mechanism. And I think that the wise Fathers of the Church were right to attribute bodies to angels.

PHIL. §15. The ideas 'of thinking, and moving [the] body,' which we find in the idea of spirit, can be conceived just as clearly and distinctly as can 'the ideas of extension, solidity, and being moved', which we find in matter.

THEO. I concur, so far as the idea of thought is concerned, but I do not hold that view about the idea of moving the body. For according to my system of pre-established harmony, bodies are so made that once they have

[1] Locke: 'the appearance and outward scheme of things'. Coste's change.
[2] An earlier draft says: 'If we could transform our eyes more than we do at present....'

been set into motion they continue of their own accord, as the actions of the mind require. This hypothesis makes sense; the other does not.

PHIL. 'Every act of sensation...gives us an equal view of...the corporeal and [of the] spiritual. For whilst I know, by seeing or hearing,...that there is some corporeal being without me,...I do more certainly know, that there is some spiritual being within me, that sees and hears.'

THEO. Well said, and very true! The existence of spirit is indeed 'more certain' than that of sensible objects.

PHIL. §19. 'Spirits, as well as bodies, cannot operate, but where they are;' 221 and at various times and¹ various places. Therefore 'I cannot but attribute change of place to all finite spirits'.

THEO. I think that that is right, since space is only an order of coexisting things.

PHIL. §20. One has only to think about the separation of the soul from the body by death to become convinced of the motion of the soul.

THEO. The soul could stop operating in this visible body; and if it could stop thinking altogether, as our author earlier maintained, it could be separated from this body without being united with another; and so its separation would not involve motion. My own view is that the soul always thinks and *feels, is always united with some body, and indeed never suddenly and totally leaves the body with which it is united.

PHIL. §21. 'If it be said by any one, that...the spirits are not' *in loco sed in aliquo ubi*,² I do not suppose that much weight will now be given to that way of talking. But if anyone thinks it can be given a reasonable sense, 'I desire him to put it into intelligible [ordinary language];³ and then from thence draw a reason to show that...spirits are not capable of motion.'

THEO. The Scholastics have three sorts of *ubiety*, or ways of being somewhere. The first is called *circumscriptive*. It is attributed to bodies in space which are in it point for point, so that measuring them depends upon being able to specify points in the located thing corresponding to points in space. The second is the *definitive*. In this case, one can 'define' – i.e. determine – that the located thing lies within a given space without being able to specify exact points or places which it occupies exclusively. That is how some people have thought that the soul is in the body, because they have not thought it possible to specify an exact point such that the soul or something pertaining to it is there and at no other point. Many competent people still take that view. (It is true that M. Descartes sought

---

¹ Locke: 'in'.
² Meaning 'are not *in a place* but are *somewhere*'. Locke: 'are not *in loco*, but *ubi*' – are not *in a place* but *where*.
³ Locke: 'English'. Coste: '*français*'. Leibniz: '*langage commun*'.

to impose narrower limits on the soul by locating it specially in the pineal gland; but since he did not venture to say that it is restricted to some one point in that gland, he achieved nothing, and it would have made no difference if he had given the soul the run of its whole bodily prison.) What should be said about angels is, I believe, about the same as what is said about souls. The great Thomas Aquinas believed that an angel can be in a place only through its operations [upon what is there], which on my theory are not immediate and are just a matter of the pre-established harmony. The third kind of ubiety is the *repletive*. God is said to have it, because he fills the entire universe in a more perfect way than minds fill bodies, for he operates immediately on all created things, continually producing them, whereas finite minds cannot immediately influence or operate upon them. I am not convinced that this scholastic doctrine deserves the mockery which you seem to be trying to bring down on it. However, one can always attribute a sort of motion to the soul, if only by reference to the body with which it is united or by reference to the sort of perceptions it has.

PHIL. §23. 'If any one says, he knows not...how he thinks; I answer, neither knows he how...the solid parts of body are [joined] together to make' an extended whole.[1]

THEO. It is indeed rather hard to explain cohesion. But this cohesion of parts appears not to be necessary to make an extended whole, since perfectly rarefied and fluid matter may be said to make up an extended thing, without its parts being joined to one another. In fact, though, I think that perfect fluidity is appropriate only to *primary matter* – i.e. matter in the abstract, considered as an original quality like motionlessness. But it does not fit *secondary matter* – i.e. matter as it actually occurs, invested with its derivative qualities – for I believe that no mass is ultimately rarefied and that there is some degree of bonding everywhere. This is produced by motions, when they all run the same way so that any division would have to set up cross-currents, which cannot happen without some turbulence and resistance. I would add that the nature of perception, and secondly of thought, provides us with a notion of [qualities of] an extremely original kind. On this, however, I believe that the doctrine of substantial unities – monads – will throw a good deal of light.

PHIL. As for cohesion, some people explain it by saying that the surfaces at which two bodies touch are pressed together by something (e.g. air) surrounding them. §24. It is quite true that the pressure of an 'ambient fluid...may hinder the [separation][2] of two polished superficies, one from another in a line perpendicular to them[; but it could not] hinder the

---

[1] Locke: 'extension'. Coste's change.
[2] Locke uses the now obsolete 'avulsion'.

separation by a motion, in a line parallel to those surfaces.... Therefore, if there were no other cause of cohesion, all parts of bodies must be easily separable by such a lateral sliding motion [in any plane you like] intersecting any mass of matter'.

THEO. Yes, no doubt, if all the contiguous flat parts lay in the same plane or in parallel planes. But that is not and cannot be the case. Obviously, then, in trying to make some parts slide one will be acting in some quite different way on infinitely many others whose planes are at an angle with the plane of the former. It must be understood that there is difficulty in separating two congruent surfaces, not only when the line of motion is perpendicular but also when it is at an oblique angle to them. This suggests the conjecture that in polyhedral bodies which nature constructs, in minerals and elsewhere, there are flakes laid over one another in all directions. I concede, however, that an explanation of the basis of all cohesion could not be given just in terms of the pressure of the surroundings on flat contiguous surfaces; for that explanation tacitly assumes that there is already cohesion within these contiguous faces.

PHIL. §27. It has been my view that the 'extension of body...is nothing but the cohesion of solid parts'.

THEO. That appears to me to conflict with your own earlier explanations. It seems to me that if a body has (as I believe all bodies always do have) internal movements going on in it, i.e. if its parts are engaged in pulling away from one another, it is still extended for all that. So the notion of extension appears to me to be totally different from that of cohesion.

PHIL. §28. 'Another idea we have of body, is the power of communication of motion by impulse; and [another we have] of our souls [is] the power of exciting of motion by thought. These ideas...every day's experience clearly furnishes us with: but if [we want further to] inquire how this is done, we are equally in the dark. For in the communication of motion ..., wherein as much motion is lost to one body, as is got to the other, which is the ordinariest case, we can have no other conception, but of the passing of motion out of one body into another; which, I think, is as obscure and unconceivable, as how our minds move or stop our bodies by thought.... The increase of motion by impulse, which is observed or believed sometimes to happen, is yet harder to be understood.' 224

THEO. I am not surprised that you encounter insurmountable problems when you seem to be entertaining something as inconceivable as an accident's passing from one subject to another; but I see no reason why we have to suppose such a thing. It is almost as strange as the Scholastics' notion of accidents which are not in any subject; though they are careful to attribute theirs solely to the miraculous workings of divine omnipotence, whereas this passage would be an ordinary occurrence. I have already said something about it (xxi.4), also making the point that it is not true that a body loses as much motion as it gives to another body. That seems to be your conception of it, as though motion were something substantial, like salt dissolved in water; if my memory serves me, this analogy was actually used by M. Rohault. I now add that it [sc. the case where a body loses as much motion as it gives] is not even 'the ordinariest case': I have demonstrated elsewhere [e.g. 'Explanation of the new system of the communication of substances' pp. 129f] that the same quantity of motion is conserved only when the two colliding bodies are moving in the same direction before the collision, and still moving in the same direction after it. The fact is that the real laws of motion depend upon a cause which is higher than matter. As for 'the power of exciting motion by thought': I don't think that we have any idea of this, or any experience of it either. The Cartesians themselves admit that the soul cannot give any new force to matter, but they claim that it can give a new determination – i.e. direction – to the force which the matter has already. I on the other hand maintain that souls can make no change in the force or in the direction of bodies, that one of these would be as inconceivable and irrational as the other, and that to explain the union of soul and body we must avail ourselves of the pre-established harmony.

225 PHIL. 'It is worth our consideration, whether active power be not the proper attribute of spirits, and passive power of [bodies].[1] Hence may be conjectured, that created spirits are not totally separate from matter, because they are both active and passive. Pure spirit, viz. God, is only active; pure matter is only passive; those beings that are both active and passive we may judge to partake of both.'

THEO. These thoughts are greatly to my liking, and perfectly express my own views, just so long as the word 'spirit' is construed broadly enough to cover all souls or rather – to put it more generally still – all entelechies or substantial unities, which have some analogy to spirits.

PHIL. §31. 'I would fain have instanced any thing in our notion of spirit more perplexed, or nearer a contradiction, than the very notion of body includes in it; [I mean] divisibility *in infinitum*'.

THEO. What you say yet again here [see pp. 222, 224], in order to show that we understand the nature of spirit as well as or better than that of body, is true indeed. When *Fromondus devoted a whole book to the composition of the continuum, he was right to call it *The Labyrinth*. But that comes from a false idea that people have of the nature of body as well as of space.

---

[1] Locke: 'matter'. Coste's change.

PHIL. §33. Even the idea of God comes to us as the others do: our complex idea of God is made up of the simple ideas which we receive from reflection and which we enlarge by our idea of the infinite.

THEO. As to that, I would direct you to what I have said in several places in order to show that all these ideas, and especially that of God [pp. 103–5?], are within us from the outset; that all we do is to come to pay heed to them; and that the idea of the infinite, above all, is not formed by extending finite ideas [p. 159].

PHIL. §37. 'Most of the simple ideas, that make up our complex ideas of substances, when truly considered, are only powers, however we are apt to take them for positive qualities'.

THEO. I think that powers which are not essential to substance, and which include not merely an aptitude but also a certain endeavour, are exactly what are or should be meant by 'real qualities'.   226

Chapter xxiv
'Of collective ideas of substances.'

PHILALETHES. §1. After simple substances, let us look at collective ones. Is not 'the idea of such a collection of men as make an army...as much one idea, as the idea of a man'?

THEOPHILUS. It is right to say that this aggregate (*ens per aggregationem*, to say it in Scholastic) makes up a single idea, although strictly speaking such a collection of substances does not really constitute a true substance. It is something resultant, which is given its final touch of unity by the soul's thought and perception. However, it can be said to be something substantial, in a way, namely as containing substances.

Chapter xxv
'Of relation.'

PHILALETHES. §1. Ideas of relations, which are in reality the most tenuous ideas, still remain to be considered. When the mind compares one thing with another this is '*relation* and *respect*', and the relative terms or denominations which are made from it serve 'as marks to lead the thoughts beyond the subject...to something distinct from it'; and these two are called subjects of the relation (*relata*).

THEOPHILUS. Relations and orderings are to some extent 'beings of reason', although they have their foundations in things; for one can say that their reality, like that of eternal truths and of possibilities, comes from the Supreme Reason.   227

PHIL. **§5.** However, a change of relation can occur without there having been any change in the subject: Titius, 'whom I consider to day as a father, ceases to be so to morrow, only by the death of his son, without any alteration made in himself.'

THEO. That can very well be said if we are guided by the things of which we are aware; but in metaphysical strictness there is no wholly extrinsic denomination (*denominatio pure extrinseca*), because of the real connections amongst all things.

PHIL. **§6.** I believe that there is 'relation only betwixt two things.'[1]

THEO. But there are instances of relations between several things at once, as occurs in an ordering or in a genealogical tree, which display the position and the connections of each of their terms or members. Even a figure such as a polygon involves the relation among all its sides.

PHIL. **§8.** It is worth noticing that 'the ideas of relations [are] clearer often, than of the subjects related.'[2] Thus the idea[3] of *father* is clearer than that of *man*.

THEO. That is because this relation is so general that it can also apply to other substances. Besides, as there can be something *clear and something obscure in a subject, a relation can be grounded in what is clear. But if the very form of the relation involved knowledge of what is obscure in the subject, the relation would share in this obscurity.

PHIL. **§10.** Terms which 'necessarily lead the mind to... other ideas, than are supposed really to exist in that thing, to which the [term or] word is applied, are relative', and the others are absolute.

228 THEO. It is a good thing you put in 'necessarily', and you could also have added 'explicitly' or 'straight away', for we can think of black, for instance, without thinking of its cause, but that involves staying within the limits of the knowledge which comes to one straight away, which is either confused (when one has no analysis of the idea) or distinct but incomplete (when one has only a limited analysis). But there is no term which is so absolute or so detached that it does not involve relations and is not such that a complete analysis of it would lead to other things and indeed to all other things. Consequently, we can say that 'relative terms' *explicitly* indicate the relationship which they contain. I am here contrasting 'absolute' with 'relative': when I earlier contrasted it with 'limited' [pp. 154, 157f] that was in a different sense.

---

[1] Locke's marginal summary.   [2] Locke's marginal summary.
[3] Taking '*relation*' to be a slip.

Chapter xxvi
'Of cause and effect, and other relations.'

PHILALETHES. §1. *Cause* is 'that which produces any simple or complex idea', and *effect* is 'that which is produced'.

THEOPHILUS. I notice, sir, that you frequently understand by 'idea' the objective reality of the idea, i.e. the quality which it represents. You only define *efficient cause*, as I pointed out earlier [p. 216]. It must be admitted that in saying that 'efficient cause' is what produces and 'effect' is what is produced, you are merely dealing in synonyms. I have, it is true, heard you say somewhat more distinctly that 'cause' is what makes another thing begin to exist [pp. 168f]; although the word 'makes' also leaves the main difficulty intact. But this will become clearer later.

PHIL. §4. To mention some other relations, let me point out that there are 'other words of time, that ordinarily are thought to stand for positive ideas, which yet [are] relative, such as are *young, old*, etc.'; for they involve a relation to the ordinary duration of the substance of which we predicate them. Thus 'a man is called young at twenty years, and very young at seven years old: but yet a horse we call old at twenty, and a dog at seven years'. But we do not say that the sun and stars, or a ruby or a diamond, are old or young, because we do not know how long such things usually last. §5. It is the same thing with place and extension; for instance when we say that a thing is high or low,[1] large or small. 'That will be a great horse to a Welshman, which [appears a very] little one to a Fleming', since each of them thinks of the horses which are raised in his own country.

THEO. These remarks are excellent. But we do sometimes depart somewhat from this approach, as when we say that a thing is old, not in comparison with things of its own kind, but of other kinds. For instance we say that the world or the sun is very old. When someone asked Galileo if he thought that the sun was eternal, he answered: 'Not eternal, but very old.'

Chapter xxvii
What identity or diversity is

PHILALETHES. §1. A relative idea of the greatest importance is that of identity or of diversity.[2] We never find, nor can we conceive it 'possible, that two things of the same kind should exist in the same place at the same time[. That is why, when] we demand, whether any thing be the same or no, it refers always to something that existed such a time in such a place

[1] Locke: 'above, below'.
[2] Locke speaks of 'the ideas of identity and diversity'.

.... From whence it follows, that one thing cannot have two beginnings of existence, nor two things one beginning...in time and place'.

230 THEOPHILUS. In addition to the difference of time or of place there must always be an internal *principle of distinction*: although there can be many things of the same kind, it is still the case that none of them are ever exactly alike. Thus, although time and place (i.e. the relations to what lies outside) do distinguish for us things which we could not easily tell apart by reference to themselves alone, things are nevertheless distinguishable in themselves. Thus, although diversity in things is accompanied by diversity of time or place, time and place do not constitute the core of identity and diversity, because they [sc. different times and places] impress different states upon the thing.[1] To which it can be added that it is by means of things that we must distinguish one time or place from another, rather than *vice versa*; for times and places are in themselves perfectly alike, and in any case they are not substances or complete realities. The method which you seem to be offering here as the only one for distinguishing among things of the same kind,[2] is founded on the assumption that interpenetration is contrary to nature. This is a reasonable assumption; but experience itself shows that we are not bound to it when it comes to distinguishing things. For instance, we find that two shadows or two rays of light interpenetrate, and we could devise an imaginary world where bodies did the same. Yet we can still distinguish one ray from the other just by the direction of their paths, even when they intersect.

PHIL. §3. What is called the *principle of individuation* in the Schools, where it 'is so much inquired after,...is existence it self, which determines a being...to a particular time and place incommunicable to two beings of the same kind.'

THEO. The 'principle of individuation' reduces, in the case of individuals, to the principle of distinction of which I have just been speaking. If two individuals were perfectly similar and equal and, in short, *indistinguishable* in themselves, there would be no principle of individuation. I would even venture to say that in such a case there would be no individual distinctness, no separate individuals. That is why the notion of atoms is chimerical and arises only from men's incomplete conceptions. For if there were atoms, i.e. perfectly hard and perfectly unalterable bodies which were incapable of internal change and could differ from one another only in size and in

231 shape, it is obvious that since they could have the same size and shape they would then be indistinguishable in themselves and discernible only by means of external denominations with no internal foundation; which is contrary to the greatest principles of reason. In fact, however, every body

---

[1] '*parce qu'ils amènent avec eux des impressions différentes sur la chose*'.
[2] Locke implies this in §2.

is changeable and indeed is actually changing all the time, so that it differs in itself from every other. I remember a great princess [*Sophie], of lofty intelligence, saying one day while walking in her garden that she did not believe there were two leaves perfectly alike. A clever gentleman who was walking with her believed that it would be easy to find some, but search as he might he became convinced by his own eyes that a difference could always be found. One can see from these considerations, which have until now been overlooked, how far people have strayed in philosophy from the most natural notions, and at what a distance from the great principles of true metaphysics they have come to be.

PHIL. §4. What constitutes the *unity* (identity) of a single plant[1] is having 'such an organization of parts in one...[2] body, partaking of one common life,' which lasts as long as the plant exists, even though it changes its parts.

THEO. Organization or configuration alone, without an enduring principle of life which I call 'monad', would not suffice to make something remain numerically the same, i.e. the same individual. For the configuration can continue specifically[3] without continuing individually. When an iron horse-shoe changes to copper in a certain mineral water from Hungary, the same kind of shape remains but not the same individual: the iron dissolves, and the copper, with which the water is impregnated, is precipitated and imperceptibly replaces it. But the shape is an accident, which does not pass from one subject to another (*de subjecto in subjectum*). So we must acknowledge that organic bodies as well as others remain 'the same' only in appearance, and not strictly speaking. It is rather like a river whose water is continually changing, or like Theseus's ship which the Athenians were constantly repairing. But as for substances which possess in themselves a genuine, real, substantial unity, and which are capable of actions which can properly be called 'vital'; and as for substantial beings, *quae uno spiritu continentur* as one of the ancient jurists says, meaning that a certain indivisible spirit animates them: one can rightly say that they remain perfectly 'the same individual' in virtue of this soul or spirit which makes the *I* in substances which think.

232

PHIL. §5. 'The case is not so much different in brutes' from how it is in plants.

THEO. If plants and brutes have no souls, then their identity is only apparent, but if they do have souls their identity is strictly genuine, although their organic bodies do not retain such an identity.

---

[1] Locke speaks of what '[is] one plant', Coste of '*l'unité d'une plante*', and Leibniz of '*l'unité (identité) d'une même plante*'.
[2] Locke: 'coherent'. Coste's omission.
[3] '*spécifiquement*', cognate with '*espèce*' which in this context is rendered by 'kind'.

PHIL. **§6.** 'This also shows wherein the identity of the same man consists; viz. in nothing but' his enjoying the same life, which is continued[1] 'by constantly fleeting particles of matter, in succession vitally united to the same organized body.'

THEO. That can be understood in my way. In fact, an organic body does not remain the same for more than a moment; it only remains equivalent. And if no reference is made to the soul, there will not be the same life, nor a 'vital' unity, either. So the identity in that case would be merely apparent.

PHIL. 'He that shall place the identity of man in any thing else, but. . . in one fitly organized body taken in any one instant, and from thence continued under one organization of life in several successively fleeting particles of matter, united to it, will find it hard, to make an embryo, one of years, mad, and sober, the same man,' without its following from this supposition that it is 'possible for Seth, Ishmael, Socrates, Pilate, St Augustine. . . to be the same man. [This] would agree yet worse with the notions of those philosophers, who allow of transmigration, and are of opinion that the souls of men may, for their miscarriages, be detruded into the bodies of beasts. . . . But yet I think no body, could he be sure that the soul of Heliogabalus were in [a hog], would yet say that hog were a man [, and the same man as] Heliogabalus.'

THEO. We have here both a question about the name and a question about the thing. As regards the thing, a single individual substance can retain its identity only by preservation of the same soul, for the body is in
233 continual flux and the soul does not reside in certain atoms which are reserved for it or in some little indestructible bone, like the *luz* of the rabbins. However, there is no 'transmigration' in which the soul entirely abandons its body and passes into another. Even in death it always retains an organic body, part of its former one, although what it retains is always subject to wasting away insensibly and to restoring itself, and even at a given time to undergoing a great change. Thus, instead of transmigration of the soul there is reshaping, infolding, unfolding, and flowing, in the soul's body. M. van *Helmont the younger believed that souls pass from body to body, but always within the same species. This implies that there will always be the same number of souls of a given species – the same number of men or of wolves, so that if the wolves have been reduced or wiped out in England they must have correspondingly increased elsewhere. Certain meditations published in France seemed to take the same view [*Lannion]. If transmigration is not taken strictly, i.e. if anyone thought that souls remain in the same rarefied bodies and only change their coarse bodies, that would be possible, even to the extent of the same soul's passing

[1] Locke: 'nothing but a participation of the same continued life,'. Coste's change.

into a body of another species in the Brahmin or Pythagorean manner. But not everything which is possible is therefore in conformity with the order of things. If such a transformation did occur, however, and assuming in accordance with rabbinical doctrine that Cain, Ham and Ishmael had the same soul, the question of whether they ought to be called the same man is merely a question of a name. I have noticed that the distinguished author whose opinions you have supported recognizes this and sets it forth very clearly (in the final paragraph of this chapter). There would be identity of substance but, if there were no connection by way of memory between the different *personae*[1] which were made by the same soul, there would not be enough moral identity to say that this was a single person. And if God wished a human soul to pass into the body of a hog and to forget the man and perform no rational acts, it would not constitute a man. But if while in the body of the beast it had the thoughts of a man, and even of the man whom it had animated before the change, like the golden ass of Apuleius, perhaps no one would object to saying that the same Lucius, who had come to Thessaly to see his friends, remained inside the skin of the ass where Photis had inadvertently put him, and wandered from master to master until by eating the roses he was restored to his natural shape.

234

PHIL. §8. 'I think I may be confident, that whoever [of us] should see a creature of his own shape and make, though it [gave no more appearance of]² reason all its life, than a cat or a parrot, would call him still a man; or whoever should hear...³ a parrot discourse, reason, and philosophize, would call or think it nothing but...a parrot; and say, the [first of these animals] was a dull irrational man, and the [second] a very intelligent rational parrot.'

THEO. I agree more with the second point than with the first, although something needs to be said about that too. Few theologians would be bold enough to decide straight away and without qualification to baptize an animal of human shape, lacking the appearance of reason, which⁴ had been found as an infant in the woods. A priest of the Roman Church might say conditionally 'If you are a man I baptize you'. For it would not be known whether it belonged to the human race and whether there was a rational soul in it; it might be an orang-outang – a monkey closely resembling a man in external features – like the one *Tulp speaks of having seen, and the one whose anatomy has been published by a learned physician. It is certain, I admit, that a man can become as stupid as an orang-outang; but the inner being of the rational soul would remain despite the suspending of the exercise of reason, as I have already explained. So that is the essential

---

¹ '*personnages*'; see footnote on p. 58.
² Locke: 'had no more'. Coste's change.
³ Locke: 'a cat or'. Coste's omission.
⁴ Or 'who': the French leaves the question open.

point, and it cannot be settled by appearances. As to the second case, there is no obstacle to there being rational animals of some other species than ours, like the poet's birds who had their kingdom in the sun, where a parrot who had gone there from this world after his death saved the life of a traveller who had been kind to him on earth [*moon]. However if, as happens in fairy-land and in Mother Goose, a parrot were the transformed daughter of a king and revealed itself as such by speaking, no doubt the father and mother would caress it as their daughter and would believe that they had her back though concealed in that alien form. Still, I would not quarrel with someone who said that in the Golden Ass there is still the same 'self' or individual (because of the same immaterial spirit), as well as the same Lucius or person (because of his awareness of this *I*), but that it is no longer a man. Indeed it does seem that we have to add something about the shape and constitution of the body to the definition of man, when he is said to be a rational animal; otherwise, according to my views, *Spirits would also be men.

PHIL. §9. The word *person* stands for 'a thinking intelligent being, that has reason and reflection, and can consider it self as it self, the same thinking thing in different times and places; which it does only by' the sense that it has of its own actions.[1] And this knowledge[2] always accompanies our present sensations and perceptions – when they are sufficiently distinct, as I have remarked more than once already – 'and by this every one is to himself, that which he calls *self*: it not being considered in this case, whether the same self be continued in the same, or divers substances. For since consciousness[3] always accompanies thinking, and 'tis that, that makes every one to be, what he calls *self*; and thereby distinguishes himself from all other thinking things, in this alone consists personal identity, i.e. [what makes] a rational being [always the same]: and as far as this consciousness can be extended backwards to any past action or thought, so far reaches the identity of that person; it is the same self now [as] it was then'.

THEO. I also hold this opinion that consciousness or the sense of *I* *proves moral or personal identity. And that is how I distinguish the *incessancy* of a beast's soul from the *immortality* of the soul of a man: both of them preserve *real, *physical identity*; but it is consonant with the rules of divine providence that in man's case the soul should also retain a moral identity which is apparent to us ourselves, so as to constitute the same person, which is therefore sensitive to punishments and rewards. You seem to hold, sir, that this apparent identity could be preserved in the absence of any real

235

236

---

[1] Locke: 'only by...consciousness.' Coste's change.
[2] Locke: 'consciousness'. Coste's change.
[3] '*conscience* (*consciousness, *consciosité*)'.

identity. Perhaps that could happen through God's absolute power; but I should have thought that, according to the order of things, an identity which is apparent to the person concerned – one who senses himself to be the same – presupposes a real identity obtaining through each immediate [temporal] transition accompanied by reflection, or by the sense of I; because an intimate and immediate perception cannot be mistaken in the natural course of things. If a man could be a mere machine and still possess consciousness, I would have to agree with you, sir; but I hold that that state of affairs is not possible – at least not naturally. I would not wish to deny, either, that 'personal identity' and even the 'self' persist in us, and that I am that I who was in the cradle, merely on the grounds that I can no longer remember anything that I did at that time. To discover one's own moral identity unaided, it is sufficient that between one state and a neighbouring (or just a nearby) one there be a mediating bond of consciousness, even if this has a jump or forgotten interval mixed into it. Thus, if an illness had interrupted the continuity of my bond of consciousness, so that I did not know how I had arrived at my present state even though I could remember things further back, the testimony of others could fill in the gap in my recollection. I could even be punished on this testimony if I had done some deliberate wrong during an interval which this illness had made me forget a short time later. And if I forgot my whole past, and[1] needed to have myself taught all over again, even my name and how to read and write, I could still learn from others about my life during my preceding state; and, similarly, I would have retained[2] my rights without having to be divided into two persons and made to inherit from myself. All this is enough to maintain the moral identity which makes the same person. It is true that if the others conspired to deceive me (just as I might deceive myself by some vision or dream or illness, thinking that what I had dreamed had really happened to me), then the appearance would be false; but sometimes we can be morally certain of the truth on the credit of others' reports. And in relation to God, whose social bond with us is the cardinal point of morality, error cannot occur. As regards 'self', it will be as well to distinguish it from the appearance of self and from consciousness. The 'self' makes real physical identity, and the appearance of self, when accompanied by truth, adds to it personal identity. So, not wishing to say that personal identity extends no further than memory, still less would I say that the 'self', or physical identity, depends upon it. The existence of real personal identity is proved with as much certainty as any matter of fact can be, by present and immediate reflection; it is proved conclusively enough for ordinary purposes by memories across intervals[3]

237

---

[1] Replacing '*je serais*' by '*et fusse*' from an earlier version.
[2] Or: 'and [learn about] how I had retained'. Or: 'just as I have retained'.
[3] '*par notre souvenir d'intervalle*'.

and by the concurring testimony of other people. Even if God were to change the real identity in some extraordinary manner, the personal identity would remain, provided that the man preserved the appearances of identity – the inner ones (i.e. the ones belonging to consciousness) as well as outer ones such as those consisting in what appears to other people. Thus, consciousness is not the only means of establishing personal identity, and its deficiencies may be made up by other people's accounts or even by other indications. But difficulties arise when there is a conflict between these various appearances. Consciousness may stay silent, as in loss of memory; but if it spoke out plainly in opposition to the other appearances, we would be at a loss to decide and would sometimes be suspended between two possibilities: that the memory is mistaken or that outer appearances are deceptive.

PHIL. §11. It will be said that the limbs of each man's body are parts of himself; and that therefore, since his body is in constant flux, the man cannot remain the same.

238 THEO. I would rather say that the *I* and the *he* are without parts, since we say, quite correctly, that he continues to exist as really the same substance, the same physical *I*; but we cannot say – with complete fidelity to the truth of things – that the same whole continues to exist if a part of it is lost. And what has bodily parts cannot avoid losing some of them at every moment.

PHIL. §13. 'The consciousness of [one's] past actions [could not] be transferred from one thinking substance to another' – and our having a sense of ourselves as the same would render it certain that the same substance remained[1] – if 'the same consciousness [were] the same individual action', that is, if there were no difference between the action of reflecting and the action on which one reflected in being aware of it.[2] 'But it being but a present representation of a past action, why it may not be possible, that that may be represented to the mind to have been, which really never was, will remain to be shown.'

THEO. We can be deceived by a memory across an interval – one often experiences this and one can conceive of a natural cause of such an error. But a present or immediate memory, the memory of what was taking place immediately before – or in other words, the consciousness or reflection which accompanies inner activity – cannot naturally deceive us. If it could, we would not even be certain that we are thinking about such and such a thing; for this too [sc. 'I think...' as well as 'I remember...'] is silently said only about past actions, not about the very action of saying it. But if the immediate inner experience is not certain, we cannot be sure of any truth of fact. I have already said that there can be an intelligible reason for the element of error in perceptions which are mediate and outer,

_____
[1] Added by Leibniz.　　　　[2] Added by Leibniz.

but with regard to immediate inner ones such a reason could not be found except by having recourse to God's omnipotence.

PHIL. §14. 'As to the...question, whether the same immaterial substance remaining, there may be two distinct persons; which question seems to me to be built on this, whether, the same immaterial being...may be... stripped of all [sense][1] of its past existence, and lose it beyond the power of ever retrieving again: and so as it were beginning a new account from a new period, have a consciousness that cannot reach beyond this new state. All those who hold pre-existence [of souls] are evidently of this mind.... I once met with one, who was persuaded his had been the soul of Socrates (...I know, that in the post he filled, which was no inconsiderable one, he passed for a very rational man, and [his published works have] shown, that he wanted not parts or learning).... Souls being, as far as we know any thing of them in their nature, indifferent to any parcel of matter, the supposition [of a single soul's passing from one body to another] has no apparent absurdity in it.... But he, now having no' sense of anything at all that Nestor or Socrates ever did or thought,[2] 'does, or can he, conceive himself the same person with either of them? Can he be concerned in either of their actions? Attribute them to himself, or think them his own more than the actions of any other man, that [already] existed?...He is no more one [person][3] with either of them, than if the soul [which is now in] him, had been created...when it began to inform his present body.... This would no more make him the same person with Nestor, than if some of the particles of matter, that were once a part of Nestor, were now a part of this man, the same immaterial substance without the same consciousness, no more making the same person by being united to any body, than the same' particles of matter united to any body without a common consciousness can make[4] 'the same person.'

239

THEO. An immaterial being or spirit cannot 'be stripped of all' perception of its past existence. It retains impressions of everything which has previously happened to it, and it even has presentiments of everything which will happen to it; but these states of mind[5] are mostly too minute to be distinguishable and for one to be aware of them, although they may perhaps grow some day. It is this continuity and interconnection[6] of perceptions which make someone really the same individual; but our awarenesses – i.e. when we are aware of past states of mind[7] – *prove a

---

[1] Locke: 'consciousness'. Coste: '*sentiment*', with '*ou con-science*' in the margin.
[2] Locke: 'no consciousness of any of the actions either of Nestor or Thersites'. Coste's changes, except for Leibniz's 'Socrates'.
[3] Locke: 'self'. Coste's change.
[4] Locke: 'particle of matter without consciousness united to any body, makes'. Coste's change.   [5] '*sentiments*'.
[6] '*liaison*'.   [7] '*sentiments*'.

moral identity as well, and make the real identity appear. The pre-existence of souls does not appear to us through our perceptions. But if it really were the case, it could some day make itself known. So it is unreasonable to suppose that memory should be lost beyond any possibility of recovery, since insensible perceptions, whose usefulness I have shown in so many other important connections, serve a purpose here too – preserving the seeds of memory. The late Mr Henry *More, the Anglican theologian was convinced of the pre-existence of the soul and wrote in support of it. The late M. van Helmont the younger went further, as I have just said, and believed in the transmigration of souls, although always between bodies of the same species, so that in his opinion human souls always animate men. He believed, like certain rabbins, that the soul of Adam passed into the Messiah as the new Adam. For all I know he may, clever man though he was, have believed himself to be one of the ancients. I have explained earlier [p. 233] a way in which the migration of souls is possible (though it does not appear likely), namely that souls might, while retaining rarefied bodies, pass suddenly into other coarse bodies. If migration really did occur – at least, if it occurred in that manner – then the same individual would exist throughout, in Nestor, in Socrates and in some modern; and it[1] could even let its identity be known to someone who penetrated deeply enough into its nature, by means of the impressions or records of all that Nestor or Socrates had done, which remained in it and could be read there by a sufficiently acute mind. Yet if the modern man had no way, inner or outer, of knowing what he has been, it would from a moral point of view be as though he had never been it. But it appears that nothing in the world lacks significance – moral significance, indeed – since God reigns over the world and his government is perfect. On my hypotheses souls are not 'indifferent to any parcel of matter', as it seems to you that they are; on the contrary they inherently express those portions with which they are and must be united in an orderly way. So if they passed into a new coarse or sensible body, they would still retain the expression of everything of which they had had any perception in the old one; and indeed the new body would have to feel the effects of it, so that there will always be real marks of the continuance of the individual. But whatever our past state may have been, we cannot always be aware of the effect which it leaves behind. The able author of the *Essay on Understanding*, whose views you had adopted, remarks (xxvii.27) that his suppositions or fictions about the migration of souls – considered as being possible – rest partly on the fact that the mind is commonly regarded not merely as 'independent' of matter but also as 'indifferent' to every kind of matter. But I hope, sir, that what I have said to you on this topic, in one place and another, will clear up this uncertainty and will give a better grasp of what can naturally happen. It shows in what

[1] Or 'he', and so throughout the rest of the sentence.

way the actions of an ancient would belong to a modern who possessed the same soul, even though he was unaware of them. But if it did come to be known, that would imply personal identity in addition. What makes the same human individual is not 'a parcel of matter' which passes from one body to another, nor is it what we call *I*; rather, it is the soul.

PHIL. §16. However, it is true that I am 'as much concerned, and as justly accountable for any action was done a thousand years since, appropriated to me now by this self-consciousness'[1] which I now have, as having been done by myself,[2] 'as I am, for what I did the last moment.'

THEO. This belief that we have done something can deceive us if the action was long ago. People have mistaken their dreams for reality, and have come to believe their own stories by constantly repeating them. Such a false belief can cause perplexity, but it cannot make one liable to punishment if there are no other beliefs which confirm it. On the other hand, one can be accountable for what one has done, even if one has forgotten it, provided that there is independent confirmation of the action.

PHIL. §17. 'Every one finds [daily] that whilst comprehended under that consciousness, the little finger is as much a part of it self [(of him)][3] as what is most so.'

THEO. I have said (§11) why I would not wish to maintain that my finger is part of *me*; but it is true that it belongs to me and is a part of my body.

PHIL. Those who hold a different view will say: 'Upon separation of this little finger, should this consciousness go along with the little finger, and leave the rest of the body, 'tis evident the little finger would be the person, the same person; and self then would have nothing to do with the rest of the body.'

THEO. Nature does not permit these fictions, which are eliminated by the system of harmony, i.e. of the perfect correspondence between soul and body.

242

PHIL. §18. It seems, though, that 'if the same body should still live, and ...have its own peculiar consciousness, whereof the little finger knew nothing' – and if, nevertheless, the soul was in the finger – the finger could not acknowledge any of the actions of the rest of the body, nor could one impute them to it.

THEO. Nor would the soul which was in the finger belong to this body. I admit that if God brought it about that consciousnesses were transferred to other souls, the latter would have to be treated according to moral notions as though they were the same. But this would disrupt the order of things for no reason, and would divorce what can come before our

[1] Leibniz and Coste use '*conscience*' and the English word.
[2] Added by Coste.   [3] Added by Leibniz.

awareness from the truth – the truth which is preserved by insensible perceptions. That would not be reasonable, since perceptions which are at present insensible may grow some day: nothing is useless, and eternity provides great scope for change.

PHIL. §20. 'Human laws [do not punish] the mad man for the sober man's actions, nor the sober man for what the mad man did, [and so they make] them two persons[. Thus] we say such an one...is *besides himself'*.

THEO. The laws threaten punishment and promise reward in order to discourage evil actions and encourage good ones. But a madman may be in a condition where threats and promises barely influence him, since his reason is no longer in command; and so the severity of the penalty should be relaxed in proportion to his incapacity. On the other hand, we want the criminal to have a sense of the effects of the evil he has done, in order to increase people's fear of committing crimes; but since the madman is not sufficiently sensitive, we are content to postpone for some time carrying out the sentence by which we punish him for what he did while in his right mind. Thus what laws and judges do in these cases is not the result of their supposing that two persons are involved.

PHIL. §22. Indeed, those whose views I am presenting to you have raised this objection against themselves: if a man who is drunk and who then becomes sober is not the same person, he ought not to be punished for what he did while drunk, since he no longer has any sense of it. To this it is replied that he is 'just as much the same person, as a man that walks, and does other things in his sleep, is the same person, and is answerable for any mischief he shall do in it.'

243

THEO. There is a great deal of difference between the actions of a drunk man and of a true and acknowledged sleepwalker. We punish drunkards because they could stay sober and may even retain some memory of the punishment while they are drunk. But a sleepwalker is less able to abstain from his nocturnal walk and from what he does during it. Still, if it were true that a good birching on the spot would make him stay in bed, we would have the right to carry it out – and we would carry it out, too, although this would be a remedy rather than a punishment. Indeed, this remedy is reported to have been effective.

PHIL. 'Human laws punish both with a justice suitable to [men's] way of knowledge [of things]: because in these [sorts of] cases, they cannot distinguish certainly what is real, what counterfeit; and so the ignorance in drunkenness or sleep is not admitted as a plea....The fact is proved against him, but want of consciousness cannot be proved for him.'

THEO. The real question is not so much that as what to do when it has been well established – as it can be – that the drunkard or the sleepwalker really was beside himself. In that case the sleepwalker can only be regarded as victim of a mania; but since drunkenness is voluntary and sickness is not, we punish the one rather than the other.

PHIL. 'But in the great [and fearful day of judgment], wherein the secrets of all hearts shall be laid open, [we are entitled][1] to think, no one shall be made to answer for what he knows nothing of; but shall receive his doom, his conscience accusing or excusing him.'

THEO. I doubt that man's memory will have to be raised up on the day of judgment so that he can remember everything which he had forgotten, and that the knowledge of others, and especially of that just Judge who is never deceived, will not suffice. One could invent the fiction, not much in accord with the truth but at least possible, that a man on the day of judgment believed himself to have been wicked and that this also appeared true to all the other created spirits who were in a position to offer a judgment on the matter, even though it was not the truth. Dare one say that the supreme and just Judge, who alone knew differently, could damn this person and judge contrary to his knowledge? Yet this seems to follow from the notion of 'moral person' which you offer. It may be said that if God judges contrary to appearances, he will not be sufficiently glorified and will bring distress to others; but it can be replied that he is himself his own unique and supreme law, and that in this case the others should conclude that they were mistaken. 244

PHIL. §23. If we could suppose either that two distinct incommunicable consciousnesses might act alternately in the same body, the one constantly by day, the other by night; or that the same consciousness might act by intervals in two distinct bodies; 'I ask in the first case, whether the *day* and the *night*-man, [if I may express myself in this way,][2] would not be two as distinct persons, as Socrates and Plato; and whether in the second case, there would not be one person in two distinct bodies'? It is not relevant that this single consciousness which affects two different bodies, and these consciousnesses which affect the same body at different times, belong in the one case to the same immaterial substance, and in the other to two distinct immaterial substances, which introduce those different consciousnesses into those bodies; since 'the personal identity would equally be determined by the consciousness, whether that consciousness were annexed to some individual immaterial substance or no. [Furthermore,] that immaterial thinking thing may sometimes [lose sight of] its past consciousness, and [recall] it again[3].... Make these intervals of memory and forgetfulness to take their turns regularly by day and night, and you

---

[1] Locke: 'it may be reasonable'. Coste's change.
[2] Added by Coste.
[3] Locke: 'part with its past consciousness, and be restored to it again'. Coste's change.

have two persons with the same immaterial spirit....So that *self* is not determined by identity or diversity of substance, which [one] cannot be sure of, but only by identity of consciousness.'

THEO. I acknowledge that if all the appearances of one mind were transferred to another, or if God brought about an exchange between two minds by giving to one the visible body of the other and its appearances and states of consciousness, then personal identity would not be tied to the identity of substance but rather would go with the constant appearances, which are what human morality must give heed to. But these appearances would not consist merely in states of consciousness: God would have to exchange not only the states of awareness or consciousness of the individuals concerned, but also the appearances which were presented to others; otherwise what the others had to say would conflict with the consciousnesses of the individuals themselves, which would disturb the moral order. Still, it must be granted to me that the divorce between the insensible and sensible realms, i.e. between the insensible perceptions which remained in the same substances and the states of awareness which were exchanged, would be a miracle – like supposing God to create a vacuum. For I have already explained why this is not in conformity with the natural order. Here is something we could much more fittingly suppose: in another region of the universe or at some other time there may be a sphere in no way sensibly different from this sphere of earth on which we live, and inhabited by men each of whom differs sensibly in no way from his counterpart among us. Thus at one time there will be more than a hundred million pairs of similar persons, i.e. pairs of persons with the same appearances and states of consciousness. God could transfer the minds, by themselves or with their bodies, from one sphere to the other without their being aware of it; but whether they are transferred or left where they are, what would your authorities say about their persons or 'selves'? Given that the states of consciousness and the inner and outer appearances of the men on these two spheres cannot yield a distinction between them, are they two persons or are they one and the same? It is true that they could be told apart by God, and by minds which were capable of grasping the intervals [between the spheres] and their outer relations of space and time, and even the inner constitutions, of which the men on the two spheres would be insensible. But since according to your theories consciousness[1] alone distinguishes persons, with no need for us to be concerned about the real identity or diversity of substance or even about what would appear to other people, what is to prevent us from saying that these two persons who are at the same time in these two similar but inexpressibly distant spheres, are one and the same person? Yet that would be a manifest absurdity. I will add

[1] Taking *'conscienciosité'* to be a slip for *'consciosité'*.

that if we are speaking of what can naturally occur, the two similar spheres and the two similar souls on them could remain similar only for a time. Since they would be numerically different, there would have to be a difference at least in their insensible constitutions, and the latter must unfold in the fullness of time.

246

PHIL. §26. 'Supposing a man punished now, for what he had done in another life, whereof he could be made to have no consciousness at all, what difference is there between' such treatment and the treatment he would get in being created miserable?[1]

THEO. Platonists, Origenists, certain Hebrews and other defenders of the pre-existence of souls have believed that the souls of this world were put into imperfect bodies to make them suffer for crimes committed in a former world. But the fact is that if one does not know the truth of the matter, and will never find it out either by recalling it through memory or from traces or from what other people know, it cannot be called punishment according to the ordinary way of thinking. If we are to speak quite generally of punishment, however, there are grounds for questioning whether it is absolutely necessary that those who suffer should themselves eventually learn why, and whether it would not quite often be sufficient that those punishments should afford, to other and better informed Spirits, matter for glorifying divine justice. Still, it is more likely, at least in general, that the sufferers will learn why they suffer.

PHIL. §§28-9.[2] Perhaps, all things considered, you can agree with my author when he concludes his chapter on identity by saying that the question of whether 'the same man' remains is a question of name, depending on whether by 'a man' we understand just a rational spirit, or just a body of the form we call human, or, finally, a spirit united with such a body. On the first account, the spirit which is separated (from the coarse body at least) will still be a man; on the second, an orang-outang which was exactly like us apart from reason would be a man, and if a man were deprived of his rational soul and given the soul of a beast he would remain the same man. On the third account both must remain, still united to one another: the same spirit, and the same body too in part – or at least its equivalent as regards sensible bodily form. Thus one could remain the same being *physically and morally, that is the same substance and the same person, without remaining a man, if we follow the third account in regarding this shape as essential to the identity of the man.

THEO. I admit that there is a question of name involved here. And the third account is like the same animal being at one time a caterpillar or silk-worm and at another a butterfly; or, as some have imagined, the angels of this

247

---

[1] Locke: 'between that punishment, and being created miserable?' Coste's change.
[2] This paragraph is very loosely based upon Locke.

world having been men in a former world. But we have met to discuss more important matters than the signification of words. I have shown you the basis of true physical identity, and have shown that it does not clash with moral identity or with memory either. And I have also shown that although they [sc. moral identity and memory][1] cannot always indicate a person's physical identity either to the person in question or to his acquaintances, they never run counter to physical identity and are never totally divorced from it. Finally, I have shown that there are always created spirits who know or can know the truth of the matter, and that there is reason to think that things which make no difference from the point of view of the persons themselves will do so only temporarily.

Chapter xxviii
Of certain 'other relations', especially moral relations.

PHILALETHES. §1. Besides the relations founded upon time, place, and causality, which we have just been discussing, there are 'infinite others, some whereof I shall mention. [Any simple idea which is] capable of parts or degrees, affords an occasion of comparing the subjects wherein it is ..., v.g. *whiter*' or less white or equally white.[2] This relation may be called 'proportional'.

THEOPHILUS. But there is a way in which one thing can be greater than another although they are not proportional. They then differ by what I call an 'imperfect' magnitude. An example is provided when it is said that the angle which a radius makes with the arc of its circle is less than a right angle; for it is impossible for those two angles to stand in any proportion to one another, or for either of them to stand in any proportion to the angle of contingence, i.e. the difference between them.

PHIL. §2. 'Another occasion of comparing things [is provided by] the circumstances of their origin', upon which are founded the relations father and child, brothers, cousins, compatriots. It would hardly occur to any speaker of our language to say: this bull is the grandfather of that calf, or these two pigeons are first cousins. That is because languages are adapted for common use. But 'in some countries..., where they are more careful of the pedigrees of their horses, than of their own,...they...have not only names for particular horses, but also of their several relations of kindred one to another.'

THEO. The ideas and names pertaining to family could be brought in here, along with those of kindred. In fact, there is no evidence that under the Empire of Charlemagne, or for a good while before and after, there were any family names in Germany or France or Lombardy. It was not so long

248

---

[1] Taking '*elles*' to be a slip for '*ils*'.   [2] Added by Leibniz.

ago that some families in the north, including noble ones, had no name; so that a man was identified in the place of his birth by the use of his name and his father's, and if he moved to somewhere else the name of his place of origin was added to his own. The Arabs and the Turcomans still use that system, I understand. They have virtually no names for individual families, so they are content to use the name of the person's father, grandfather etc.; and they also honour their prize horses in this way, naming each by its own name and its father's name and even further back. That is how the horses were spoken of which the Turkish Monarch sent to the Emperor after the peace of Carlowitz. And the last Count of Oldenburg, now dead after a long life but in his time the owner of studs which were famous, had genealogical trees of his horses so that he could prove their 'nobility'; and he even went to the lengths of having portraits of their ancestors – like the *imagines majorum* [effigies of one's forebears] which were so prized by the Romans. But to return to mankind: the Arabs and the Tartars have names for *Tribes*, which are like enormous families which have increased tremendously through the years. Some of these names are taken from the progenitor of the tribe, just as in Moses' time; others come from the place where the tribe lives, or from some other circumstance. Mr Worsley, an observant traveller who has spent some time in desert Arabia and is well informed about the present state of things there, tells us that in the whole region between Egypt and Palestine – the region which Moses crossed – there are today only three tribes, which might run to five thousand men altogether; and that one of these tribes is called Salih, after its founder (I understand), whose tomb his descendants revere as 249 though it were that of a saint, by collecting the dust from it which they sprinkle Arab-fashion on their own heads and on those of their camels. It remains to say that 'blood-relationship' is what you have when the two people whose relationship is in question have a common origin, and one could say that alliance or affinity[1] is what obtains between two people if they can be blood-related to some one person without thereby being blood-related to one another – which can happen through the intervention of marriages. But affinity is not ordinarily said to obtain between husband and wife, although their marriage causes affinities between others; so perhaps it would be better to say that affinity is what obtains between two people who would be blood-related if some husband and wife were taken to be a single person.

PHIL. §3. Sometimes a relationship is founded on a 'moral right': the relationship of General of an army, for instance, or that of citizen. These relations, since they depend upon agreements that men have made among

---

[1] '*alliance ou affinité*', each word meaning a relatedness between two people because of intermarriage between their families.

themselves, 'I call *instituted, or voluntary; and may be distinguished from the natural'. Sometimes there is a name for each of the two relata, as with *patron* and *client*, *general* and *soldier*; but that is not always the case – for instance there is no name for those who have the relevant relationship to a *chancellor*.

THEO. We sometimes furbish and enrich natural relations by associating them with moral ones. For example, offspring have the right to claim their legitimate inherited share of their parents' estates; young people are subjected to certain restraints, and the old are granted certain immunities. It can also happen, though, that something is taken to be a natural relation which is not so, as when the law says that the father of a child is the man who was wedded to the mother of the child at a time which makes it possible to regard the child as his. This replacement of a natural relation by an instituted one sometimes merely expresses a presumption, i.e. a judgment which makes something which may be false pass for true so long as its falsity is not proved. That is the way in which the maxim 'The father is the one whom the nuptials indicate' is understood in Roman law and in most societies where it is accepted. But I have been told that in England it is no use proving an alibi, just so long as you were in one of the three kingdoms at the relevant time; which turns the presumption into a fiction, or what some scholars call 'a legal presumption with the force of law'.

PHIL. §4. Moral relation 'is the conformity, or disagreement, men's voluntary actions have to a rule' which lets them be judged 'morally good, or bad'. §5. Moral good and moral evil is 'the conformity or disagreement of our voluntary actions to some law, whereby [natural][1] good or evil is drawn on us, from the will and power of the lawmaker' or of someone seeking to uphold the law;[2] which is what 'we call *reward* and *punishment*.'

THEO. Writers as able as the one whose views you are presenting, sir, are entitled to adapt terms as they see fit. But all the same, according to that account a single action could be morally good and morally bad at the same time under different legislators. Similarly, in an earlier passage our good author took virtue to be whatever is praised [p. 97], so that the very same action would be virtuous or not, according to men's opinions. Since that is not the ordinary sense of 'morally good' and of 'virtuous' as applied to actions, I for one would prefer to measure moral worth and virtue by the unchanging rule of reason which God has undertaken to uphold. We can then be certain that through his instrumentality every moral good becomes a natural good, or, as the ancient authors used to put it, whatever is good is useful. But to express our author's notion of it, we would have to say that moral good or evil is an instituted good or evil – something imposed on us, which he who has the reins of power in his hand tries

250

---

[1] *'physique', added by Leibniz. [2] Added by Leibniz.

through rewards and punishments to make us seek or avoid. It is a curious circumstance[1] that whatever is instituted by God's general commands also conforms to nature, i.e. to reason.

PHIL. §7. There are three sorts of laws. 'The *divine* law.... The *civil* law .... The law of *opinion* or *reputation*'. The first is the standard for 'sins, or duties', the second for 'criminal, or innocent' actions, the third for 'virtues or vices'.

THEO. In the ordinary senses of the terms, virtues differ from duties and vices from sins only as general dispositions [*habitude*] differ from actions. Nor are virtue and vice ordinarily taken to be matters which depend upon opinion. A grave sin is called a 'crime'; and 'innocent' is contrasted not with 'criminal' but with 'guilty'. There are two sorts of divine law: natural and *positive. Civil law is positive. The 'law of reputation' cannot properly be called 'law' unless it is included in the natural law – as one might speak of the 'law of health', the 'law of business', in areas where one's actions naturally bring various goods and evils, such as the approval of others, health, monetary gain.

PHIL. §10. 'Virtue and vice are names pretended... every where to stand for actions in their own nature right and wrong: and as far as they really are so applied,' virtue to that extent agrees perfectly with the natural divine law.[2] 'But yet, whatever is pretended, this is visible, that these names, [considered] in the particular instances of their application,... are constantly attributed only to such actions, as in each country [or] society are in reputation or discredit.' Otherwise, men 'would condemn themselves'. Thus the measure of what is called 'virtue and vice is this approbation or dislike, [esteem][3] or blame, which by a secret and tacit consent establishes it self.... For though men uniting into politic societies, have resigned up to the public the disposing of all their force, so that they cannot employ it against any fellow-citizen, any farther than the law [permits]: yet they retain still the power of thinking well or ill; approving or disapproving'.

THEO. If the able author whom you expound in that way, sir, were to declare that he has chosen to give this as an arbitrary nominal definition of the names 'virtue' and 'vice', one could only say that he is entitled to do that in his theory if it helps him to express himself, e.g. for lack of other terms; but one would be compelled to add that that signification does not square with ordinary usage, and is not very edifying, and that if anyone

251

---

[1] '*Le bon est*', which in Leibniz's day could mean 'It is a strange coincidence' or 'The irony of the situation is' or, almost, 'The cream of the jest is'. For Leibniz, what follows is morally necessary; '*Le bon est*' ironically expresses the attitude which he thinks Locke must take to it.

[2] Locke: 'they so far are co-incident with the divine law above-mentioned.' Coste's change up to 'with', Leibniz's thereafter.

[3] Locke: 'praise'. Coste's change.

tried to get it accepted in daily life and daily speech, it would 'sound ill' to many people – as the author himself seems to acknowledge in his Preface.[1] But what we are offered here is something more: although you admit that men profess to be speaking of what is virtuous or vicious according to immutable laws, you allege that they really mean to speak only of something which is a matter of opinion. But it seems to me that by parity of argument one could maintain that truth and reason and everything we could adduce as most real are also matters of opinion, on the grounds that people make erroneous judgments about them. Would it not be altogether better to say that people do understand virtue – like truth – as something conforming to nature, but that they often go wrong in the application [of the term]? At that, they are not as wrong as they are thought to be, for what they praise usually deserves it in some respects. The drinker's virtue, i.e. the ability to hold one's wine, is an advantage which enabled Bonosus to ingratiate himself with the barbarians and extract their secrets from them. The nocturnal powers which that same Bonosus claimed to share with Hercules were equally a perfection. The Spartans praised the cunning of thieves; and there is nothing blameworthy in that skill, but only in the misuse of it. Some of those who are broken on the wheel in peace-time could make excellent irregular soldiers in time of war. Thus, all of that depends upon application, and on the good or bad use of the advantages that one has. Also, the idea that men 'condemn themselves' should not be thought of as very strange: they do it very often, as when they do things which they condemn others for doing. There are often public scandals concerning contradictions between words and actions, in cases where no one can help seeing that a magistrate or preacher is doing what he forbids to be done.

252

PHIL. §11. What counts as[2] 'virtue is everywhere that, which is thought praiseworthy. . . . Virtue and praise. . . are called often by the same name.' 'Even here praiseworthy deeds[3] have their rewards,' says Virgil (*Aeneid* I, 461); and Cicero says 'Nature knows nothing more excellent than honesty, praise, dignity, honour,' and a little further on he adds: 'By these various terms I wish to indicate one and the same thing' (*Tusculan Disputations* II, 20).

THEO. It is true that in the ancient world virtue was called 'honesty', as when they praised 'a breast burning with noble honesty' [Persius]; and it is also true that honesty is called 'honour' or 'praise'. But what that

---

[1] This refers to a phrase in Locke's prefatory 'Epistle to the Reader'. The passage containing it became, in the fifth and later editions, a long footnote to II.xxviii.11.

[2] Added by Coste.

[3] '*laudi*', literally meaning 'praises'. Locke gives this quotation and the next in Latin, and the final one in *oratio obliqua*.

means is not that virtue is whatever is praised, but that it is whatever is worthy of praise, and that depends on the truth and not on opinion.

PHIL. §12. Many people give no serious thought to the law of God, or else they hope that they will some day be reconciled with its Author; and they 'flatter themselves with the hopes of impunity' with respect to the law of the state. But no man thinks that he can escape 'the punishment of their censure and dislike, who offends against the...opinion of the company he keeps, and would recommend himself to.' Nobody that has any sense of his own nature can live in society constantly despised.[1] Such is the force of the law of reputation.

253

THEO. I have already said that that is not so much a legal punishment as a natural one which is brought on by the action itself. In fact, though, many people hardly care about it, because if they are despised by those who condemn something they have done, they usually find accomplices or at least allies who do not despise them – just so long as they do in some other way deserve a measure of respect, however small. Even the most infamous actions are forgotten; and often the culprit has only to be sufficiently bold and shameless, like Terence's character Phormio, for everything to pass away. If excommunication gave rise to enduring and universal disdain, it would be as compelling as the 'law' of which our author speaks; and it really did have that force among the first Christians – they had no legal powers to punish the guilty and used excommunication instead. In somewhat the same way, craftsmen uphold certain customs amongst themselves, in defiance of the law, through the disdain they exhibit towards those who do not conform. That is also why duelling has been kept up although it is illegal. One could wish that the populace were in agreement with each other and with reason in the distribution of praise and blame; and in particular that people of rank would refrain from sheltering villains by treating bad actions as a joke in which – most of the time, it seems – it is not the malefactor but the victim who is punished by disdain and made to look ridiculous. No less commonly, men will be found to despise not so much vice as weakness and misfortune. Thus the law of reputation needs to be thoroughly reformed and also to be better obeyed.

PHIL. §19. Before leaving the topic of relations,[2] I would remark that we usually have as clear a notion of the relation as we have of its foundation, or a clearer one. 'If I believed, that Sempronia [took Titus from under a cabbage][3], (as they use to tell children,) and thereby became his mother; and that afterwards [she had Caius] in the same manner,...I had as clear

---

[1] Locke: 'under...constant dislike'. Coste's 'mépriser' (despise) is cognate to the noun 'mépris' which in the next paragraph we render by 'disdain'.

[2] 'rapports' – ways of referring things to other things.

[3] Locke: 'digged Titus out of the parsley-bed'. Coste's change, accompanied by a careful marginal note.

a notion of the relation of brothers between them, as if I had all the skill of a midwife'.

254 THEO. Yet one time when a child was told that his new-born brother had been drawn from a well (which is how the Germans satisfy children who are curious about this matter), the child replied that he was surprised they did not throw the baby back into the same well when it troubled its mother by crying so much. The point is that that account gave him no explanation for the love the mother showed towards the baby. It can be said, then, that if someone does not know the foundation of a relation, his thoughts about it are partly of the kind I call blind, and are also insufficient, even though they may suffice in some respects and in some situations.

Chapter xxix
'Of *clear and obscure, distinct and confused ideas.'

PHILALETHES. §2. Let us now turn to certain differences among ideas. 'Our simple ideas are *clear*, when they are such as the objects themselves, from whence they were taken, did or might, [with all the circumstances required for]¹ a well-ordered sensation or perception, [represent]² them. Whilst the memory retains them thus, . . . they are clear ideas. So far as they either want any thing of that original exactness, or have lost any of their first freshness, and are, as it were, faded or tarnished by time, so far are they obscure. Complex ideas . . . are clear, when the [simple] ideas that go to their composition, are clear; and the number and order of those simple ideas . . . is determinate'.

THEOPHILUS. In a short discussion of ideas – true and false, clear and obscure, distinct and confused – which appeared in 1684 in the *Acta* of Leipzig ['Meditations on knowledge, truth and ideas'], I gave a definition of 'clear idea' which applied both to simple and to composite ideas; and it provides an explanation for what is said about them here. I say, then, that an idea is clear when it enables one to recognize the thing and distinguish it from other things. For example, when I have a really clear idea of a colour I shall not accept some other colour in place of it; and if I have a clear idea of a plant, I shall pick it out from others which are close 255 to it – if I cannot, the idea is obscure. I believe that we have hardly any perfectly clear ideas of sensible things: some colours are alike in such a way that one cannot tell them apart in memory but will sometimes tell them apart when they are laid side by side. Again, when we think we have thoroughly described a plant, someone may bring from the Indies a plant which exactly fits everything we have put into our description and which

¹ Locke: 'in'. Coste: '*avec toutes les circonstances requises à*'.
² Locke: 'present'.

nevertheless can be seen to belong to a different species. So we can never perfectly determine *species infimae* – lowest species.

PHIL. §4. 'As a *clear* idea is that whereof the mind has such a full and evident perception, as it does receive from an outward object operating duly on a well-disposed organ, so a *distinct* idea is that wherein the mind perceives a difference from all other; and a *confused* idea is such an one, as is not sufficiently distinguishable from another, from which it ought to be different.'

THEO. On this account of what a 'distinct' idea is, I do not see how to distinguish it from a 'clear' one. So in this matter I always follow M. Descartes's language: for him an idea can be at once *clear and confused, as are the ideas of sensible qualities which are associated with particular organs, e.g. the ideas of colour and of warmth. They are clear, because we recognize them and easily tell them from one another; but they are not distinct, because we cannot distinguish their contents. Thus, we cannot define these ideas: all we can do is to make them known through examples; and, beyond that, until their inner structure has been deciphered we have to say that they are a *je ne sais quoi*. Thus, although according to us distinct ideas distinguish one object from another, so also do ideas which are clear though in themselves confused; so we do not call 'distinct' all the ideas which are distinguishing (i.e. which distinguish objects), but only those which are distinguished, i.e. which are in themselves distinct and which distinguish in the object the marks which make it known, thus yielding an analysis or definition. Ideas which are not like this we call 'confused'. On this view, we are not to blame for the confusion which reigns among our ideas, for this is an imperfection in our nature: to be able to pick out the causes of odours and tastes, for instance, and the content of these qualities, is beyond us. But I am to blame for the confusion in a case where distinct ideas are within my power and it matters that I should have them, for example if I accept spurious gold as genuine because I have not conducted the tests which bring out the marks of real gold.

256

PHIL. §5. But it will be said that no idea is confused (or, as you would say, *obscure*) in itself, since 'it can be no other but such as the mind perceives it to be; and that...sufficiently distinguishes it from all other ideas'. §6. To remove this difficulty, we must consider that the faultiness of ideas 'is in reference to...names',[1] and that 'that which makes it [faulty][2] is, when it is such, that it may as well be called by another name, as that which it is expressed by'.

THEO. It should not be made a matter of names, it seems to me. Alexander the Great is reported to have seen in a dream a plant which he dreamed

---

[1] Locke's marginal summary: 'Confusion of ideas, is in reference to their names.'
[2] Locke: 'confused'.

would cure his friend Lysimachus (and so it did, subsequently being named *Lysimachia*). He had many plants brought to him, among which he recognized the one he had seen in his dream. But suppose that by bad luck his idea of the plant had not sufficed for it to be recognized, so that like Nebuchadnezzar he needed a Daniel to take him back over the dream itself: obviously in that case his idea would have been imperfect and 'obscure' (which I prefer to calling it 'confused'), not for want of the right relation to some name, for he had no name for it, but for want of a relation to the thing, i.e. to the medicinal plant. It would be a case where Alexander had remembered some details while being unsure about others. Names serve to designate things, which is why someone who goes wrong in relating an idea to a name will usually go wrong about the thing he wants the name to stand for.

PHIL. §7. As composite[1] ideas are most liable to this imperfection, it can result from an idea's being 'made up of too small a number of simple ideas,' as for example the 'idea...of a beast with spots,' which is too general and does not suffice to distinguish amongst the lynx, the leopard and the panther, although each of these is distinguished by its own particular name.

THEO. Our ideas could still be defective in this way even if we were in the same position as Adam was before he had named the animals. If one knew that among the spotted beasts there was one with extraordinarily penetrating vision, but did not know whether it was the tiger or the lynx or some other species, that inability to distinguish it would be an imperfection. So it's not so much a matter of a name as of that [reality] which can provide a subject for the name, and which makes the animal worthy of its own particular name. What emerges from this is that the idea of a beast with spots is good in itself, and not at all confused or obscure, if it has only to mark the genus; but if in combination with some other insufficiently remembered idea it has to designate the species, then the idea which is made up from it is obscure and imperfect.

PHIL. §8. An opposite defect occurs when the simple ideas which make a composite one are numerous enough but are too jumbled and disorderly;[2] like a picture which seems so confused that it is fit only to represent a cloudy sky. If it *did*, then it would not be said to involve confusion, any more than would a second picture which was made in imitation of the first. But if the picture is said to be a portrait, then it can rightly be called confused, because one cannot tell whether it depicts a man or a monkey or a fish.

---

[1] Locke: 'complex'. Wherever Philalethes uses 'composite' ('*composé*'), Locke has 'complex'. Future occurrences will not be footnoted. Sometimes '*composé*' is rendered by 'made up'.

[2] Phrase based on Locke's marginal summary.

257

But it may be that when the picture is viewed in a cylindrical mirror the confusion disappears and one sees that it is a Julius Caesar. Thus, none of these mental pictures (if I may so express myself)[1] can be called confused, however its parts are put together; for the pictures, whatever they are like, can be plainly discerned from all others so long as they are not ranked under some ordinary name to which, as far as one can see, they do not belong any more than they do to some other name with a different signification.

THEO. This picture whose parts one sees distinctly, without seeing what they result in until one looks at them in a certain way, is like the idea of a heap of stones, which is truly confused – not just in your sense but also in mine – until one has distinctly grasped how many stones there are and some other properties of the heap. If there were thirty-six stones, say, one would not know just from looking at them in a jumble that they could be arranged in a triangle or in a square – as in fact they could, because thirty-six is both a square number and a triangular one. Similarly, in looking at a thousand-sided figure one can have only a confused idea of it until one knows the number of its sides, which is the cube of 10. So what matters are not names but the *distinct properties* which the idea must be found to contain when one has brought order into its confusion. It is sometimes hard to find the key to the confusion – the way of viewing the object which shows one its intelligible properties; rather like those pictures which Father *Niceron has shown how to construct, which must be viewed from a special position or by means of a special mirror if one is to see what the artist was aiming at.

PHIL. §9. Still, it cannot be denied that ideas may be defective in a third way which really does depend on the misuse of names, namely when our ideas are 'uncertain [or][2] undetermined. Thus we may observe [as a daily occurrence] men, who not forbearing to use the ordinary words of their language, till they have learned their precise signification, change the idea[s] they make' them stand for almost as often as they use them in their discourse. §10. Thus it can be seen 'how much names...are the occasion of denominating ideas *distinct* or *confused*....Without taking notice of ...distinct names, as the signs of distinct things, it will be hard to say what a confused idea is.'

THEO. Yet I have just explained it, without bringing in names, both when 'confusion' is taken in your sense to stand for what I call 'obscurity', and when it is taken in my sense to stand for the lack of an analysis of a notion which one has. I have also shown that every obscure idea is in fact indeterminate or uncertain – as in the case where one has seen a beast with

258

259

---

[1] Locke: 'mental draughts'. Coste: '*peintures mentales (si j'ose m'exprimer ainsi)*'.
[2] Locke: 'and'.

spots and one knows that something must be combined with this general
notion but does not clearly remember what. So the first and third defects
which you have listed amount to the same thing. Still, it is certainly true
that many mistakes do arise from the abuse of words, for it results in a
kind of error in calculation – as though in calculating one failed to note
carefully the position of each counter, or wrote the numerals so badly that
one could not tell a 2 from a 7, or carelessly changed or omitted something.
This abuse of words may consist either in not associating a word with any
idea at all, or else in associating it with an imperfect one of which a part
is empty, left blank so to speak; and in either of these cases the thought
contains a gap or a 'blind' part which is filled only by the name. Or the
defect may consist in associating several different ideas with a word; one
may be unsure which idea should be selected (in which case the idea is
obscure, just as much as when a part of it is blind); or it may be that one
selects them turn about, ignoring the discrepancies amongst them and
using first one and then another as the sense of a single word in a single
argument, in a way that is apt to generate error. Uncertain thought, then,
either is empty and lacks ideas, or floats amongst two or more ideas. This
does harm, if we want to indicate something determinate, or if we want
to hold a word to one particular sense which we have previously given it
or in which it is used by others – especially in the ordinary language of the
populace at large or of the experts. It generates no end of pointless,
shapeless disputes in conversations, in lecture-halls and in books. People
sometimes try to settle such disputes by means of distinctions; but usually
that merely tangles them further, replacing vague and obscure terms by
others which are even vaguer and obscurer – as are many of the ones which
philosophers use, without having good definitions of them, in drawing their
distinctions.

PHIL. §12. 'If there be any other confusion of ideas' than that which has
'a secret reference to names', at least it is the latter which, more than any
other, 'disorders men's thoughts and discourses'.

THEO. I agree about that; but some notion of the thing, and of one's
purpose in using the name, is usually involved as well. For instance, when
people speak of 'the Church' some have in mind a government while
others think of doctrinal truth.

PHIL. The way to prevent such confusion is to 'apply steadily the same
name' to a certain collection of simple ideas 'united in a determinate
number and order.... But this neither accommodating men's ease or
vanity, or serving [for anything but discovering and defending the] truth,[1]
which is not always the thing aimed at, such exactness, is rather to be
wished, than hoped for.... The loose application of names, to undeter-

260

[1] Locke: 'or serving any design, but that of naked truth'. Coste's change.

mined, variable, and [in blind thoughts]¹ almost no ideas, serves both to cover our own ignorance, as well as to perplex and confound others,' which counts as real learnedness and as a mark of superiority in knowledge.

THEO. These language troubles also owe much to people's straining to be elegant and fine in their use of words. If it will help them to express their thoughts in an attractive way they see no objection to employing figures of speech in which words are diverted slightly from their usual senses. The new sense may be narrower or wider than the usual one (this is called *synecdoche*); it may be a transferred sense, where two things have had their names exchanged because of some relation between the things, either a concomitance (*metonymy*) or a similarity (*metaphor*); and then there is *irony*, which replaces an expression by its opposite. That is what such changes [of sense] are called when they are noticed; but they are rarely noticed. Given this indeterminacy in the use of language, a situation where we want some kind of laws governing the signification of words (something along those lines occurs in the *Digest* of Roman law, in the part entitled 'Of the Significations of Words'), what is a judicious person to do? If he is writing for ordinary readers, he will deprive himself of the means for giving charm and emphasis to what he writes if he abides strictly by fixed significations for the terms he uses. What he must do – and this is enough – is to be careful not to let the variations generate errors or fallacious reasoning. The ancients distinguished the 'exoteric' or popular mode of exposition from the 'esoteric' one which is suitable for those who are seriously concerned to discover the truth; and that distinction is relevant here. If anyone wants to write like a mathematician in metaphysics or moral philosophy there is nothing to prevent him from rigorously doing so; some have announced that they would do this, and have promised us mathematical demonstrations outside mathematics, but it is extremely seldom that anyone has succeeded. I believe that people are repelled by the amount of trouble they would have to take for a tiny number of readers: like the question in Persius, 'Who will read this?', with its answer 'Either two people or no one'. Yet I think that if anyone did go about it in the right way, he would have no reason to regret his labour. I have been tempted to try it myself.

261

PHIL. §13. You will agree with me, though, that composite ideas may 'be very clear and distinct in one part, and very obscure and confused in another.'

THEO. There are no grounds for questioning that. For instance, we have very distinct ideas of a good proportion of the solid, visible parts of the human body, but we have almost none of the bodily fluids.

---

¹ Added by Leibniz.

PHIL. 'In a man who speaks of a...body of a thousand sides, the idea of the figure may be very [obscure in his mind],[1] though that of the number be very distinct' in it.

THEO. That is not an apt example. A regular thousand-sided polygon is known just as distinctly as is the number one thousand, because in it one can discover and demonstrate all sorts of truths.

PHIL. But one has no precise idea of a thousand-sided figure, such that one could distinguish it from one that has only nine hundred and ninety-nine sides.

THEO. That example shows that the idea is being confounded with the image. If I am confronted with a regular polygon, my eyesight and my imagination cannot give me a grasp of the thousand which it involves: I have only a *confused* idea both of the figure and of its number until I *distinguish* the number by counting. But once I have found the number, I know the given polygon's nature and properties very well, in so far as they are those of a chiliagon. The upshot is that I have this idea of a chiliagon, even though I cannot have the image of one: one's senses and imagination would have to be sharper and more practised if they were to enable one to distinguish such a figure from a polygon which had one side less. But knowledge of figures does not depend upon the imagination, any more than knowledge of numbers does, though imagination may be a help; and a mathematician may have precise knowledge of the nature of nine- and ten-sided figures, because he has means for constructing and studying them, yet not be able to tell one from the other on sight. The fact is that a labourer or an engineer, perhaps knowing little enough of the nature of the figures, may have an advantage over a great geometrician in being able to tell them apart just by looking and without counting; just as there are porters and pedlars who will say what their loads weigh, to within a pound – the world's ablest expert in statics could not do as well. It is true that this empiric's kind of knowledge, gained through long practice, can greatly facilitate swift action such as the engineer often needs in emergencies where any delay would put him in danger. Still, this *clear image* that one may have of a regular ten-sided figure or of a 99-pound weight – this accurate sense that one may have of them – consists merely in a *confused idea*: it does not serve to reveal the nature and properties of the figure or the weight; that requires a *distinct idea*. The point of this example is to bring out the difference between ideas, or rather between ideas and images.

PHIL. **§15.** Again, 'we are apt to think, we have a positive comprehensive idea of [eternity], which is as much as to say, that there is no part of that duration, which is not clearly [known][2] in our idea.' But however great a

---

[1] Locke: 'confused'. Coste's change.
[2] Locke: 'contained'. Coste: '*contenue*'. Leibniz: '*connue*'.

262

duration someone represents to himself, since what is in question is a boundless extent there must always remain a 'part of his idea, which is still beyond [what] he represents to [himself, and which] is very obscure and undetermined. And hence it is, that in disputes and reasonings concerning eternity, or any other infinite, we are very apt to [tangle] our selves in manifest absurdities.'

THEO. This example does not appear to me to suit your purpose either, but it is very apt to mine, which is to disabuse you of your notions about this topic. There reigns here that same confusion of the image with the idea. We have a 'comprehensive', i.e. accurate, idea of eternity, since we have the definition of it, although we have no image of it at all. But ideas of infinites are not formed by the assembling of 'parts'; and the mistakes people make when reasoning about the infinite do not arise from their having no image of it.

PHIL. §16. But is it not true that 'when we talk of the divisibility of matter *in infinitum*, though we have clear ideas of division[,] we have but very obscure, and confused ideas of corpuscles[?] For I ask any one, whether taking the smallest atom of dust he ever saw, he has any distinct idea... betwixt the 100 000, and the 1 000 000 part of it.'   263

THEO. This is that same mistake of taking the *image* for the *idea*; I am amazed to see them so confounded. The having of an image of something so small is utterly beside the point. Such an image is impossible, given how our bodies are now constituted. If we could have it, it would be pretty much like the images of things which now appear to us as within range of our awareness; but we should have to pay a price, for the present object of our imagination would be lost to us, becoming too large to be imagined. There are no images of size, in itself; and the images of it which we do have depend merely on comparing things with our organs and with other objects. Here the employment of imagination is useless. So what emerges from your latest remarks is that you are expending your ingenuity on creating needless difficulties for yourself by asking for too much.

Chapter xxx
Of real and chimerical[1] ideas.

PHILALETHES. §1. Ideas, in reference to things, are either real or chimerical, complete or incomplete,[2] true or false. 'By *real* ideas, I mean such as have a foundation in nature [and] have a conformity with [a real

---

[1] Locke: 'fantastical'. Coste's change.
[2] Locke: 'adequate, or inadequate'. Coste's change.

being, with the]¹ existence of things, or with...archetypes.' Otherwise they are 'fantastical or chimerical'.

THEOPHILUS. There is a slight unclearness in that explanation: an idea can have a foundation in nature without 'conforming' to that foundation, as when it is said that our *sensations of colour and warmth do not resemble any pattern or archetype. An idea is real, also, if it is possible, even when nothing actual corresponds to it. Otherwise the idea of a species would become 'chimerical' if all the members of the species went out of existence.

PHIL. §2. 'Simple ideas are all real, [for] though whiteness and coldness are no more in snow, than pain is' – according to some people –² yet the ideas of them are 'in us the effects of powers in things without us'; and these 'constant effects' serve us just as well in distinguishing things as they would if they were 'exact resemblances of something in the things themselves'.

264

THEO. This is the point I inquired into above [p. 263], and now it appears that you do not insist there always be conformity with an archetype. According to the opinion (which I do not approve, though) of those who conceive of God as having arbitrarily settled what ideas we are to have to indicate the qualities of objects, with no resemblance and not even a natural relationship, our ideas would no more conform to their archetypes than the words which are employed in languages through *institution conform to ideas or to things themselves.

PHIL. §3. The mind is passive in respect of its simple ideas; but when it combines them to form a composite idea in which several simple ideas are brought together under one name, there is a voluntary element. For one man will include in the complex idea of gold, or of justice, simple ideas which another man leaves out of it.

THEO. The mind also deals actively with simple ideas when it teases them apart so as to scrutinize them separately. This is just as voluntary as is the combining of several ideas, whether the mind does this so as to examine the resulting composite idea or whether its purpose is to bring those ideas together under the name bestowed on their combination. And the mind cannot go wrong in this, provided that it does not join incompatible ideas, and provided that the name in question is still virgin, so to speak, i.e. has not already been associated with some notion. If it has, that could cause the latter notion to become mingled with the one which is newly being associated with the name, and could generate impossible notions by joining ideas which could not be exemplified together, or generate superfluous

¹ Locke: 'the real being, and'. Coste's change.
² Added by Leibniz.

notions – containing veiled redundancies – by joining ideas one of which can and should be demonstratively derived from the other.

PHIL. §4. 'Mixed modes and relations, having no other reality, but what they have in the minds of men, [all that is] required to those kind of ideas, to make them real [is the] possibility of existing' or of being mutually compatible.[1]

THEO. The reality of relations is dependent on mind, as is that of truths; but they do not depend on the human mind, as there is a supreme intelligence which determines all of them from all time. Mixed modes, which are distinct from relations, are sometimes real accidents; but whether or not they are dependent on mind, the ideas of them are real just so long as the modes are *possible*, or – what is the same thing – distinctly conceivable. And that requires that its constituent ideas be *compossible*, i.e. be able to be in mutual agreement. 265

PHIL. §5. But composite 'ideas of substances, being made all of them in reference to things existing without us, and intended to be representations of substances, as they really are, are no farther real, than as they are such combinations of simple ideas, as are really united, and co-exist in things [which exist][2] without us. On the contrary, those are [chimerical] which are made up of such collections of simple ideas, as were really never united, never were found together in any substance' – such as the ideas which constitute a centaur, or a body which resembles gold except that it weighs less than water, or a body which appears to the senses to be homogeneous all through but which is endowed with perception and voluntary motion, etc.

THEO. You give one account of the real/chimerical distinction for ideas of modes, and a different one for ideas of substantial things: you have two distinctions, with nothing in common between them that I can see. You regard modes as real when they are possible, but you do not allow the reality of ideas of substantial things unless the things are existent. But if we try to bring in questions of existence, we shall hardly be able to discover whether a given idea is chimerical or not; for if something is possible but happens not to occur in the place or the time that we occupy, it may have existed previously or be going to exist in the future, or it may exist now in some other world, or even in our own world without our knowing about it – like the idea Democritus had of the Milky Way, which has been verified by telescopes. So it seems best to say that possible ideas become merely chimerical when the idea of actual existence is groundlessly attached to them – as is done by those who think they can find the Philosopher's Stone, 266

---

[1] Locke: 'existing conformable to them.' Coste: '*d'exister et de compatir ensemble.*' Leibniz: '*ou*' for Coste's '*et*'.

[2] Taking '*coexistent*' to be a slip for Coste's '*existent*'.

and would be done by anyone who thought that there was once a race of centaurs. If on the other hand one takes what exists as one's only guide, one will needlessly diverge from accepted ways of speaking; for these do not allow one to say that someone who speaks of roses or carnations in winter-time is speaking about a chimera, unless he thinks that he can find such flowers in his garden – like the story that is told about *Albert the Great or some other would-be magician.

Chapter xxxi
Of complete and incomplete ideas.

PHILALETHES. §1. Real ideas are *complete* when they 'perfectly represent those archetypes, which the mind supposes them taken from; which [they represent],[1] and to which it refers them.' *Incomplete* ideas represent them only partially. §2. All our simple ideas are complete. The idea of whiteness or sweetness which is observed in sugar is complete, because all that is needed for completeness is that the idea should correspond fully to the powers which God has put into that body to produce those sensations.

THEOPHILUS. I see, sir, that you call ideas 'complete' and 'incomplete' where your favoured author calls them 'adequate' and 'inadequate'.[2] One might also call them 'perfect' and 'imperfect'. I once defined 'adequate idea' (or 'perfect idea') as one which is so distinct that all its components are distinct ['Meditations on knowledge, truth and ideas' p. 292]; the idea of a number is pretty much like that. But even if an idea is distinct, and does contain the definition or criteria[3] of the object, it can still be inadequate or 'imperfect' – namely if these criteria or components are not all distinctly known as well. For example, gold is a metal which resists *cupellation and is insoluble in aquafortis; that is a distinct idea, for it gives the criteria or the definition of 'gold'. But it is not a perfect idea, because we know too little about the nature of cupellation and about how aquafortis operates. The result of having only an imperfect idea of something is that the same subject admits of several mutually independent definitions: we shall sometimes be unable to derive one from another, or see in advance that they must belong to a single subject, and then mere experience teaches us that they do belong to it together. Thus, 'gold' can be further defined as the heaviest body we have, or the most malleable, and other definitions could also be constructed; but only when men have penetrated more deeply into the nature of things will they be able to see why the capacity to be separated out by the above two assaying procedures is something that

267

---

[1] Locke: 'which it intends them to stand for'. Coste changed the second verb, Leibniz dropped the first.

[2] This divergence is due to Coste.

[3] '*marques réciproques*', necessary and sufficient conditions.

belongs to the heaviest metal. Whereas in geometry, where we do have perfect ideas, it is another matter. We can prove that closed plane sections of cones and of cylinders are the same, namely ellipses; and we cannot help knowing this if we give our minds to it, because our notions pertaining to it are perfect ones. I regard the perfect/imperfect division as merely a subdivision within distinct ideas; and it does not appear to me that confused ideas such as the idea we have of sweetness (which you spoke of, sir) deserve the name. For although they express the power which produces the sensation, they do not fully express it; or at any rate we cannot know that they do – if we understood the content of our idea of sweetness we could then judge whether the idea suffices to explain everything that experience shows us about sweetness.

PHIL. So much for simple ideas; now let us turn to complex ones. They are either of modes or of substances. §3. Those 'of modes, being voluntary collections of simple ideas, which the mind puts together, without reference to any real archetypes, or standing patterns, existing any where, are, and cannot but be [complete] ideas. Because they not being [copies but][1] archetypes made by the mind, to rank and denominate things by, cannot want any thing; they having each of them that combination of ideas [which the mind wished to make], and thereby that perfection which [it] intended they should'. One does not conceive that the understanding could have a more 'complete or perfect idea' of a triangle than that of three sides and three angles. He that 'put together the idea[s] of danger..., absence of disorder[2] from fear, sedate consideration of what was justly to be done, and executing of that without...being deterred by the danger', thereby formed the idea of *courage*. And he achieved what he wanted to, namely a complete idea conforming to his 'good-liking and will'. It is otherwise with ideas of substances, in which we aim to copy[3] what really exists.

268

THEO. The ideas of *triangle* and of *courage* have their archetypes in the possibility of things, just as much as the idea of gold. It makes no difference to the nature of an idea whether it was invented in advance of experience or whether it is something one has retained after perceiving a combination which nature had made. The combining of ideas to form modes is not entirely 'voluntary' or arbitrary either, for one might bring together incompatible elements, as do the people who design perpetual motion machines. On the other hand, someone may invent a sound, practical machine, with no other archetype for it in our world but the inventor's idea, which in turn has as its archetype a real possibility, or a divine idea. Those machines are something substantial; but one can also fabricate

[1] Locke: 'intended for copies...but for'.
[2] Following Coste's '*l'exemption du trouble*' rather than Leibniz's '*l'exécution, du trouble*'.
[3] Taking the omission of Coste's '*de copier*' to be a slip.

impossible modes – for example when the parallelism of parabolas is contemplated, through the delusion that two parabolas can be found which are parallel to one another, like two straight lines or two circles. So whether it be of a mode or of something substantial, an idea can be complete or incomplete, depending on whether one has a good or a poor grasp of the partial ideas which go to make up the whole idea. One mark of a perfect idea is that it shows conclusively that the object is possible.

Chapter xxxii
'Of true and false ideas.'

PHILALETHES. §1. Since truth and falsehood belong only to propositions, it follows that when ideas are termed true or false, there is some tacit proposition or affirmation.[1] §4. There is, namely, 'a tacit supposition of their conformity' to something. §5. Above all, to what others designate by the same name (as when they speak of 'justice'); also to what really exists (as with *man* and not with *centaur*); also to the 'essence of any thing, whereon...its properties depend' – and taken in this way our ordinary ideas of substances are false when we have the delusion of certain substantial forms.[2] §26. I would add that it would be better to call ideas 'right' and 'wrong' rather than 'true' and 'false'.

THEOPHILUS. I believe that one could understand 'true' and 'false', as applied to ideas, in that way; but as these different senses are mutually discordant, and cannot conveniently be brought under a common notion, I would prefer to call ideas 'true' or 'false' by reference to another 'tacit affirmation' which they all include, namely the affirmation of a possibility. Thus, possible ideas are 'true' and impossible ideas are 'false'.

Chapter xxxiii
'Of the association of ideas.'

PHILALETHES. §1. One often notices oddities in the thinking of others, and no one is free from them. §2. This does not come wholly from obstinacy or self-love, for 'men of fair minds...are frequently guilty' of this fault. §3. It is sometimes not even sufficient to attribute it to 'education and prejudice'.[3] It is rather a sort of 'madness', §4. and anyone who always behaved in that manner *would* be mad. §5. This defect comes from a non-natural 'connection of ideas' which originates in 'chance or custom'. §6. Inclinations and interests are involved. The tracks followed

---

[1] '*ou affirmation*' added by Leibniz.
[2] Locke: '[taken in this way,] the greatest part, if not all our ideas of substances, are false.'
[3] Mainly based on Coste's marginal summary.

by repeated movements of the animal spirits 'are worn into a smooth path'. If a tune is familiar, one retrieves it as soon as one is given a start. §7. This is the source of such 'sympathies and antipathies' as are not 'born with us'. A child is made sick by eating too much honey; then when he grows up he cannot hear the name of honey without nausea. §8. Children are very susceptible of such impressions, and one ought to guard against them. §9. This unruly association[1] of ideas has great influence in all our actions and passions, 'as well moral as natural'. §10. Darkness recalls the idea of ghosts to children, because of the stories they have been told about them.   270
§11. One does not think of somebody one hates without thinking of the harm that he did or might inflict on one. §12. One avoids a room where one has seen a friend die. §13. It sometimes happens that a mother who has lost a much-loved child thereby loses all her joy, until time erases from her mind the imprint of that idea – which in some cases does not happen. §14. A man perfectly cured of madness by an extremely painful operation acknowledged all through his life his indebtedness to the man who had performed the operation, and yet he was quite unable to bear the sight of him. §15. Some people hate books all their lives because they were badly treated at school. When someone once gets the upper hand over someone else, he never loses it. §16. There was a man who had learned to dance well, but who could not perform unless the room contained a trunk like one which had stood in the room where he had had his dancing-lessons. §17. This same non-natural connection occurs in our intellectual habits: *being* is linked with *matter*, as though there were nothing immaterial.[2] §18. In philosophy, religion and politics, we combine sectarian loyalties with our opinions.

THEOPHILUS. I am wholly in sympathy with this important observation, which could be confirmed by endless examples. M. Descartes when he was young was fond of a person who had a squint, and throughout his life he could not help being drawn to people with that affliction. Another great philosopher, Mr Hobbes, could not (they say) remain alone in the dark without being terrified by visions of ghosts; he did not believe in ghosts, but the impression of them had stayed with him from children's stories. There are learned and thoroughly sensible people, quite above superstition, who cannot bring themselves to make thirteen at table without being extremely distressed, because their imaginations were once captured by the thought that one of them must die within the year. There was a gentleman who could not see a badly fastened pin without feeling faint, because he had once been hurt by one, perhaps as a baby. A first minister who bore the name of 'President' in his master's court took offence at the title-page of Ottavio Pisani's *Lycurgus Italicus*, and arranged for the book to be   271

[1] Locke: 'This wrong connection'. Coste's adjective, Leibniz's noun.
[2] Locke: no 'separate spirits'.

attacked; the reason was that its author included 'presidents' in his list of legal officials whom he regarded as superfluous; and although this term, as applied to the minister, signified something quite different, he had so thoroughly tied the word to his own person that he was 'wounded in this word'.[1] And it's one of the commonest examples of a non-natural association which can generate error – this associating of words with things despite the presence of an ambiguity. For a better understanding of the source of the non-natural connecting of ideas, you should note what I said earlier (xi.11) when discussing the reasoning of beasts, namely that men as well as beasts are apt to join in their memory and imagination anything which they have found to be joined in their perceptions and their experiences. That is all there is to the 'reasoning' of beasts, if I may call it that; and there is often nothing more to it with men, in so far as they are empirics, governing themselves only by their senses and by particular instances without inquiring into whether the same principles are still at work. We often do not know what principles are involved, and so to the extent that the instances are frequent we must take them seriously; for then it is reasonable to anticipate or recall one perception upon the occurrence of another which is ordinarily linked with it, especially when it is a matter of taking precautions. But a single very strong impression may, by its very intensity, instantly have as much effect as could be had by a repetition of mild impressions over a long period of time; and so this intensity may etch into the imagination[2] as deep and vivid an image as prolonged experience produces. That is how it comes about that one casual but violent impression brings together in our imagination and memory a pair of ideas which were both there already, binding them every bit as strongly and durably, and making us just as inclined to link them and to expect one to follow the other, as if the connection between them had been verified for us by long familiarity. In such a case there is the same effect, namely an association of ideas, though not for the same reason. Authority, sectarian allegiance, and custom also produce the same effect as do experience and reason, and it is not easy to free oneself from these inclinations. But it would not be very difficult to protect oneself from false judgments in these matters, if men devoted themselves sufficiently seriously to the pursuit of truth, and proceeded methodically in cases where they recognized that it is important to them that the truth be found.

[1] '*blessé dans ce mot*', analogous to '*blessé dans son orgueil*' ('wounded in his pride').
[2] '*fantaisie*'; the only occurrence of the word in this passage.

BOOK III
'OF WORDS'

Chapter i
'Of words or language in general.'

PHILALETHES. §1. 'God having designed man for a sociable creature, made him not only with an inclination, and under a necessity to have fellowship with those of his own kind; but furnished him also with [the faculty of speaking],[1] which was to be the great instrument, and common tie of society.' This is the origin of words, which serve to represent and even to explicate ideas.[2]

THEOPHILUS. I am happy to find you far removed from Mr *Hobbes's view. He did not agree that man was designed for society, and imagined that we have merely been forced into it by necessity and by the wickedness of the members of our species. But he did not take into account that the best of men, free from all wickedness, would join together the better to accomplish their goal, just as birds flock together the better to travel in company. Or as beavers congregate by the hundreds to construct great dams, which could not be achieved by a small number of them: they need these dams to create reservoirs or ponds, in which they build their lodges and catch the fish on which they feed. That is the foundation of society amongst social animals, and not fear of their kind, which hardly occurs among the beasts.

PHIL. Just so; and, the better to promote such society, man 'had by nature his organs so fashioned, as to be fit to frame articulate sounds, which we call words.'

THEO. As regards organs, those of monkeys are apparently just as well adapted as ours for forming speech, yet they show not the slightest progress in this direction. Hence they must lack something invisible. We must also bear in mind that one could 'speak' – i.e. make oneself understood by sounds from one's mouth – without forming 'articulate sounds', by employing musical tones for this purpose. But it would take great skill to devise a language of tones, whereas a language of words has been able to be formed and perfected gradually by people in a state of natural simplicity.

[1] Locke: 'with language'. Coste's change.
[2] Added by Leibniz.

Yet there are peoples, such as the Chinese, who use tones and accents to vary their words, of which they have only a small number. So it was the opinion of Golius, the noted mathematician and great authority on languages, that their language is artificial – that is, it was invented all at once by some ingenious man in order to bring about verbal communication between the many different peoples occupying the great land we call China, although this language might by now be changed through long usage.

275 PHIL. Just as orang-outangs and other monkeys possess the organs but do not form words,[1] parrots and certain other birds may be said to have words but no language. For these birds and several others 'will be taught to make...sounds distinct enough, which yet, by no means, are capable of language.' §2. Only man is in a position 'to use these sounds, as signs of internal conceptions;...whereby they might be made known to others'.

THEO. I believe that without the desire to make ourselves understood we would indeed never have created language. Once created, however, it also enables man to reason to himself, both because words provide the means for remembering abstract thoughts and because of the usefulness of symbols and *blind thoughts in reasoning, since it would take too long to lay everything out and always replace terms by definitions.

PHIL. §3. But since 'the multiplication of words would have perplexed their use, had every particular thing need of a distinct name to be signified by[,] language had yet a farther improvement [by] the use of general terms, [when they] stand for general ideas'.

THEO. General terms do not merely improve languages but are required for their essential structure. If by 'particular things' you mean individual ones, then if we only had words which applied to them – only *proper names* and no *appellatives* – we would not be able to say anything. This is because new ones are being encountered at every moment – new individuals and accidents and (what we talk about most) actions. But if by 'particular things' you mean the lowest species (*species infimae*), then, apart from the fact that it is often difficult to determine them, it is obvious that they are themselves universals, founded on similarity. And then, since it is just a matter of more or less widespread similarity, depending on whether one is speaking of genera or of species, it is natural to mark all sorts of similarities or agreements, and thus to employ terms having every degree of generality. Indeed those of greatest generality, though they have a wider spread over individuals with which they agree, carry a lighter load of ideas or essences; they were very often the easiest to form, and are the most

276 useful. Thus you will see children and people who are trying to speak an unfamiliar language, or to speak about unfamiliar matters, employ general terms like 'thing', 'plant', 'animal', in place of the more specific terms

---

[1] Added by Leibniz.

which they do not have. And it is certain that all proper or individual names were originally appellative or general.

PHIL. §4. There are even 'words which men make use of, not to signify any idea, but the want or absence of some ideas', such as *nothing*, '*ignorance* and *barrenness*.'

THEO. I don't see why we cannot say that there are *privative ideas*, just as there are negative truths, since the act of denial is positive. I have already mentioned this [p. 130].

PHIL. §5. Without disputing over that, it will be more useful, in order to 'lead us a little towards the original of all our notions and knowledge, if we remark...how those [words] which are made use of to [conceive][1] actions and notions quite removed from sense, have their rise from... sensible ideas[, from which they] are transferred to more abstruse significations'.

THEO. The situation is that our [specifically human] needs have forced us to abandon the natural order of ideas, for that order would be common to angels and men and to intelligences in general. It would be the one for us to follow if we had no concern for our own interests. However, we have had to hold fast to the order which was provided by the incidents and accidents to which our species is subject; this order represents the history of our discoveries, as it were, rather than the origin of notions.

PHIL. Just so; and this historical order, which cannot be provided by the analysis of notions, for the reason you have given, can be learned from names themselves by means of the analysis of words. Thus the following words: '*imagine*,...*comprehend, adhere, conceive, instil, disgust, disturbance, tranquillity*, etc. are all words taken from the operations of sensible things, and applied to certain modes of thinking. *Spirit*, in its primary signification, is breath; *angel*, a messenger.... By which we may give some kind of guess, what kind of notions they were...which filled their minds, who were the first beginners of languages; and how nature...unawares suggested to men the originals and principles of all their knowledge' by means of the names themselves.

THEO. I have already called to your attention [p. 104] that in the Hottentots' *Creed* the Holy Spirit is called by a word of theirs which signifies a mild, gentle puff of air. It is the same with most other words – sometimes 277 without its even being recognized, because most of the true etymologies are lost. A certain Dutchman [*Koerbagh] who had no great love of religion, exaggerated this truth (that the terms of theology, moral philosophy and metaphysics are originally derived from earthy things) in order to hold Christian theology and the Christian faith up to ridicule. He wrote a little

---

[1] Locke: 'stand for'. Coste: '*signifier*'. Leibniz: '*former*'.

Flemish dictionary in which he defined or explained the terms in accordance
not with their use but with what the original sense of the words seemed
to imply, and gave them a malicious twist. Since he had shown other signs
of impiety, he is said to have been punished in the *Raspelhuys*. Still, this
analogy between sensible and insensible things, which has served as the
foundation for figures of speech, is worth exploring. We will understand
it better if we consider the very widespread examples afforded by the use
of prepositions, such as 'to', 'with', 'of', 'before', in', 'out', 'by',
'for', 'upon', 'toward', which are all derived from place, distance and
motion and subsequently transferred to all kinds of changes, orders,
sequences, differences, and conformities. 'To' signifies approach, as when
we say: I am going *to* Rome. But also, to tie something down we make it
approach the thing we want to join it to, and so we say that one thing is
tied *to* another. Furthermore, since there is an immaterial tie, so to speak,
when one thing follows from another according to moral reasons, we say
that what results from someone's movements or decisions belongs or
attaches *to* him, as if it tended to cling to and go along with him. One body
is *with* another when they are in the same place; but we also say that one
thing is *with* whatever occurs at the same time, or belongs to the same
ordering or part of an ordering, or co-operates in one and the same action.
If someone is *of* [*from*]¹ a certain place, the place has been an object for
him by virtue of the sensible things with which it has confronted him, and
it is still an object of his memory, which continues to be full of it; and that
has the result that objects [of thought] are signified by the preposition *of*,
as when we say: it is a question *of* this, he is speaking *of* that; as though
the person were *of* [*from*] the item in question. And just as what is shut
278 up somewhere or is *in* some whole, is supported by it and goes where it
goes, so accidents are thought of similarly as *in* the subject – *sunt in subjecto*,
inhaerent subjecto. The particle *on* is also applied to objects [of thought]:
we say that someone's mind is *on* such and such a topic, much as a
craftsman works *on* the wood or stone which he is cutting or shaping. Since
these analogies are extremely variable .and do not depend upon any
determinate notions, languages vary greatly in their use of these particles
and of the cases which prepositions govern – or rather which implicitly
contain the prepositions as something tacitly understood.

Chapter ii
'Of the signification of words.'

PHILALETHES. §1. Now, since words are 'made use of by men, as the signs
of their ideas', we can begin by asking how these words came to be settled
as such. It is agreed that it is 'not by any natural connection, that there

¹ '*de*', which means both 'of' and 'from'.

is between particular articulate sounds and certain ideas, for then there would be but one language amongst...men; but by [an arbitrary] imposition, whereby such a word is made [voluntarily]¹ the mark of such an idea.'

THEOPHILUS. I know that the Scholastics and everyone else are given to saying that the significations of words are arbitrary (*ex instituto*), and it is true they are not settled by natural necessity; but they are settled by reasons – sometimes natural ones in which chance plays some part, sometimes moral ones which involve choice. Perhaps there are some artificial languages which are wholly chosen and completely arbitrary, as that of China is believed to have been, or like those of George Dalgarno and the late Bishop Wilkins of Chester. But those which we know to have been made up out of already known languages involve a mixture of chosen features and natural and chance features of the languages upon which they are built. It is like that with the languages which robbers have made up so as not to be understood except by those of their band, which the Germans call *Rothwelsch*, the Italians *lingua zerga* and the French *narquois*; usually they develop them from the ordinary languages which are known to them, either by replacing the accepted significations of the words by metaphorical ones or by compounding or deriving new words according to their fancy. Languages are also formed through intercourse among different peoples, either by the haphazard mingling of neighbouring languages or, more often, by taking one language as a base and – through neglecting or changing its rules² and even by grafting new words onto it – mangling and garbling and mixing and corrupting it. The *lingua franca* which is employed in Mediterranean trade is derived from Italian, with no regard for rules of grammar. An Armenian Dominican with whom I talked in Paris had constructed, or perhaps learned from his colleagues, a kind of *lingua franca* derived from Latin which I found intelligible enough even though it employed no cases, tenses or other inflections; he was familiar with it and spoke it fluently. A very learned French Jesuit, Father Labbé, who was well known from his many other works, devised a language with Latin as its base which is simpler and less constrained than our Latin but more regular than the *lingua franca*. He wrote a book all about it. As for existing languages which were devised long ago, most of them are now very much altered. This becomes obvious when we compare them with the ancient books and monuments which survive. Old French was more like Provençal and Italian. And the state of Teutonic as well as French – or rather Romance (formerly called *lingua romana rustica*) – in the ninth century A.D. can be seen from the wording of the oaths sworn by the sons of the Emperor

279

¹ Locke: 'a voluntary imposition...made arbitrarily'. Coste's change. Coste translates 'imposition' by *'institution'*.
² '*en négligeant et changeant ce qu'elle observe*'.

Louis the Pious, which were preserved for us by their kinsman Nithard. There is hardly any other example of French, Italian or Spanish which is so old. However, in the case of Teutonic or old German there is the Gospel of Otfrid, a monk of Weissenburg at that same time, which was published by Flacius and which M. Schilter intended to re-issue. The Saxons who crossed over to Great Britain have left us still older books: there is a version or paraphrase of the beginning of Genesis and of some other parts of Sacred History, done by a certain Caedmon who lived early enough to be mentioned by Bede. But the oldest book in any Germanic language, or indeed in any European language except Greek or Latin, is the Gospel of the Black Sea Goths, known as the *Codex argenteus and written in characters entirely its own; it was found in the Benedictine monastery of Werden in Westphalia and was taken to Sweden where they keep it with as much care as the original of the *Pandects* is kept in Florence, as though of right, despite the fact that this version was made for the Ostrogoths and in a dialect very different from the Germanic language of Scandinavia. But the reason for that is that they believe, not improbably, that the Black Sea Goths came originally from Scandinavia or at least from the Baltic. Now, the language or dialect of these ancient Goths is very different from modern Germanic, although it is of the same linguistic stock. Ancient Gallic was even more different from it, to judge from the language closest to true Gallic, namely that of Wales, Cornwall and western Brittany; but Irish differs from it further still, and gives us a glimpse of a yet more ancient Britannic, Gallic and Germanic language. Still, these languages all come from one source and can be regarded as variants of a single language which could be called 'Celtic' – just as the ancients called the Germans as well as the Gauls 'Celts'. If we go even further back in order to understand the origins of Celtic, as well as of Latin and Greek[1] which have many roots in common with the Germanic or Celtic languages, we can conjecture that this results from the common origin of all the peoples descended from the Scythians who came from the Black Sea and crossed the Danube and the Vistula; some could have gone to Greece while the rest will have occupied Germania and Gaul. This is a consequence of the hypothesis that the Europeans came from Asia. Sarmatian – assuming that it is a Slavonic language – is at least half descended from Germanic or from some common ancestor with Germanic. Much the same appears to be true of Finnish, which is the language of the earliest Scandinavians, before the Germanic peoples (i.e. the Danes, Swedes and Norwegians) had occupied the best parts of the country, nearest the sea. Proto-Finnic, which was the language of the north-east of our continent and still is that of the Lapps, stretched from the German or rather the Norwegian Sea to the Caspian, though cut

[1] Taking 'tant de celtique et latin que du grec' as a slip for 'tant du celtique que du latin et grec'.

in two by the Slavic peoples who have squeezed themselves in between; it is related to Hungarian, which comes from countries which are now in part under the Muscovites. But the Tartar language which pervades north-east Asia appears, with its variations, to have been that of the Huns and Cumans, just as it is of the Uzbeks or Turks, the Kalmucks and the Mongols. Now, all these Scythian languages have many roots in common with one another and with ours; even Arabic (in which Hebrew, ancient Punic, Chaldean, Syriac, and the Ethiopian of the Abyssinians should be included) has so many roots in common with our languages and shows such a striking agreement with them, that this cannot be attributed to mere chance or even to mere interaction, but rather to the migrations of people. Thus, in all of this there is nothing which conflicts with – indeed there is nothing which does not support – the belief in the common origin of all nations and in a primitive root-language. If Hebrew or Arabic are closest to it, then it must have changed a great deal, to say the least; and Teutonic seems to have remained more natural – or as Jacob Boehme would have said, more Adamic. If we had the primitive language in its pure form, or well enough preserved to be recognizable, the reasons for the connections [it involved] – whether they were grounded in reality[1] or came from a wise 'arbitrary imposition' worthy of the first author – would be bound to appear. But granted that our languages are derivative so far as origins are concerned, nevertheless considered in themselves they have something primitive about them. This has come to them along the way, in connection with new root words created in our languages by chance but for reasons which are grounded in reality. Examples of this are provided by words which signify the sounds of animals or are derived from them. Thus the Latin *coaxare*, applied to frogs, corresponds to the German *couaquen* or 282 *quaken*. It would seem that the noise these animals make is the primordial root of other words in the Germanic language. Since these animals make a great deal of noise, we connect it with chatterers and babblers, whom we call by the diminutive *quakeler*; though it seems that this same word *quaken* used to be taken in a favourable sense to signify all kinds of sounds made with the mouth, even including speech. And since those sounds or noises of animals testify to the presence of life, and tell us that something living is there before we can see it, in old German *quek* signified life or living; we can find this word in the oldest books, and vestiges of it still remain in the modern language, for *quek-silber* is quicksilver,[2] and *erquicken* is to succour – i.e. revive or enliven after some weakening or great exertion. In Low German certain weeds are called *Quäken*, that is, alive and running, as they say in German, spreading and seeding themselves easily in the fields to the detriment of the grain; and in English *quickly* means

[1] '*raisons *physiques*'.
[2] Leibniz: '*vif-argent*'. In French, '*vif*' means 'alive', as 'quick' used to in English.

promptly and in a lively manner. Thus, as far as these words are concerned the Germanic language can be considered primitive; after all, the ancient Germans had no need to borrow from another language a sound which imitates the sound of frogs. And there are many other instances where it shows just as well. It seems that by a natural instinct the ancient Germanic peoples, Celts, and other related peoples have used the letter R to signify violent motion and a noise like the sound of this letter. This is found in *rheo* (*fluo*), *rinnen, rüren* (*fluere*), *ruhr* (dysentery), the *Rhine, Rhône, Ruhr* (*Rhenus, Rhodanus, Eridanus, Rura*), *rauben* (*rapere*, to ravish), *radt* (*rota*), *radere* (scrape), *rauschen* (a difficult word to translate into French: it signifies the sort of noise made by leaves or trees when disturbed by the wind or by a passing animal, or made by a trailing dress), *reckken* (to stretch violently) – whence it comes about that *reichen* is to reach; that *der rick*, in the version of Low German or Low Saxon spoken in the vicinity of Brunswick, signifies a long rod or pole for hanging things on; that *rige, reihe, recta, regula, regere* all have to do with a length or a straight path; and that *reck* used to signify a very long, broad thing or person and in particular a giant, and later a powerful and rich man, as it now shows up as the Germans' *reich* and as the *riche* or *ricco* of the semi-Latins. In Spanish, *ricos hombres* signified nobles or chiefs. This also shows how words have passed by means of metaphors, synecdoches and metonymies from one signification to another, without our always being able to follow the trail. We find the same sort of noise and violent motion in *Riss* (rupture), which has a connection with the Latin *rumpo*, the Greek *rhegnymi*, the French *arracher*, and the Italian *straccio*. Now, just as the letter R naturally signifies a violent motion, the letter L signifies a gentler one. Thus we see that children and others who find R too harsh and difficult to pronounce replace it with the letter L – and ask their palish pliest to play for them.[1] This gentle motion appears in *leben* (to live); *laben* (to comfort or give life to); *lind ; lenis ; lentus* (slow); *lieben* (to love); *lauffen* (to glide swiftly, like water flowing); *labi* (to glide, *labitur uncta vadis abies*[2]); *legen* (to set down gently), from which comes *liegen* (to lie down), *lage* or *laye* (a bed, of stones for instance – thus *lay-stein*, covering-stone, slate), *lego, ich lese* (I take up what has been put down, taking up being the opposite of putting down, and then I read [*je lis*] and finally if I am a Greek I speak [*lego*]); *laub* (leaf – something easily moved, to which *lap, lid* and *lenken* are related); *laube* (roof of foliage); *luo; lyo* (*solvo*); *leien* (Low Saxon), to dissolve, to melt like snow – which is how Hanover's river Leine gets its name: it rises in a mountainous region and is greatly swollen by melted snow. I could mention any number of similar terms which *prove that there is something natural in the origin of words – something which reveals a

283

---

[1] '*comme disant par exemple* mon lévélend pèle'.
[2] 'The sleek ship glides over the waves' (Virgil).

relationship between things and the sounds and motions of the vocal organs. This is also the reason why adding the letter L to other names produces diminutives in Latin, semi-Latin and High German. I cannot claim that this principle applies universally, however, since the lion, the lynx and the leopard[1] are anything but gentle. But perhaps people seized upon another of their characteristics, namely their speed (*lauf*), which makes them feared or which compels flight, as if anyone who saw such an animal coming would shout to the others *Lauf*! (Run!); besides which, various accidents and transformations have left most words greatly changed and far removed from their original pronunciation and signification.

PHIL. A further example would make it clearer.

THEO. Here is one that is plain enough and includes several others. Take the word *oeil* and its ancestry. To set it out I will go pretty far back. *A* – the first letter of the alphabet – followed by a little aspiration makes *Ah*, and since this is an emission of air making a sound which begins fairly loudly and then fades away, this sound naturally signifies a mild breath (*spiritus lenis*) when *a* and *h* are not very forceful. This is the origin of *ao, aer, aura, haugh, halare, haleine, atmos, athem, odem* (German). But since water is also a fluid and makes a noise, it seems to have come about that *Ah*, made coarser by being doubled to form *aha* or *ahha*, has come to stand for water. The Teutons and other Celts, in order to indicate motion better, prefixed their VV to both of them, so that *Wehen* and *Wind* (wind) indicate the movement of air, and *waten, vadum, Water* indicate movement of water or in water. But to return to *Aha*, it appears (as I have said) to be a kind of root, signifying water. The Icelanders, who have retained some features of ancient Scandinavian Teutonic, have reduced the aspiration and say *aa*; others who say *Aken* (meaning Aix, *Aquae grani*) have increased it, as have the Latins with their *aqua* and the Germans of certain regions who say *ach* in certain compounds to indicate water – for instance *Schwarzach*, signifying black water, and *Biberach*, beaver-water. And instead of *Wiser* or *Weser* they used to say *Wiseraha* in the old title-deeds; the former inhabitants called it *Wisurach*, which the Latins turned into *Visurgis*, just as they turned *Iler, Ilerach* into *Ilargus*. From *aqua, aigues, auue* the French have finally derived *eau*, which they pronounce *o*, so that nothing of its origin remains. Among the modern Germanic peoples *Auwe, Auge* is a place which is frequently flooded with water; it applies to pastures (*locus irriguus, pascuus*), but more especially it signifies an island, as in the name of the monastery of Reichenau (*Augia dives*) and many others. This must have occurred with many Teutonic and Celtic peoples, so that anything which stands isolated in a plain, so to speak, is called *Auge* or *Ooge* (*oculus*). This is what blobs of oil on water are called in German. For the Spaniards

284

---

[1] '*le loup*', the wolf.

ojo is a hole. But *Auge, ooge, oculus, occhio* etc. have been applied more especially to the eye, which makes that brilliant, isolated hole in the face; there is no doubt that the French *oeil* has the same ancestry, but its origin is quite unrecognizable unless one traces it through the successive steps which I have just set out. It appears that the Greek *omma* and *opsis* come from the same source. *Oe* or *oe-land* is an island among the Northern peoples, and there is some trace of it in Hebrew in which א (*Ai*) is an island. M. Bochart thought that this was the source of the name which he believed the Phoenicians gave to the Aegean Sea, which is full of islands. *Augere* (increase) also comes from *auue* or *auge*, i.e. from the overflowing of water; similarly in Old Saxon *ooken*, *auken* meant to increase, and *Augustus*, as applied to the Emperor, was translated as *ooker*. The river in Brunswick which rises in the Harz mountains and is consequently very subject to sudden spates is called the *Oocker*, and used to be called the *Ouacra*. I remark in passing that since the names of rivers ordinarily come from the earliest known times, they best indicate the old form of language and the ancient inhabitants; this is why they would be worth a special inquiry. Languages in general, being the oldest monuments of peoples, earlier than writing and the [practical] arts, best indicate their origins, kinships and migrations. This is why etymologies rightly understood would be interesting and important; but one must interrelate the languages of various peoples, and one should not make too many leaps from one nation to another remote one unless there is sound confirming evidence – especially evidence provided by intervening peoples. In general, one should put no trust in etymologies unless there is a great deal of concurrent evidence; to do otherwise is to goropize.

PHIL. Goropize? What does that mean?

THEO. The strange and often ridiculous etymologies of the learned sixteenth-century physician, *Goropius Becanus, have become proverbial; although, on the other hand, he was not far wrong in claiming that the Germanic language which he called Cimbric has even more marks of the primitive than Hebrew. I remember that that excellent philosopher the late M. Clauberg produced a short essay on the origins of the Germanic language which makes one regret losing what he had promised on this topic. I myself have presented some thoughts on this subject ['Unvorgreifliche Gedanken'], as well as having persuaded the late M. Gerhard *Meier, the Bremen theologian, to work on it – which he did, but was cut short by death. I hope, though, that the public will still profit from his work some day, as well as from the similar work of M. Schilter, the well-known Strasbourg jurist, who has also just died. It is certain at any rate that most inquiries into European origins, customs and antiquities have to do with the Teutonic language and antiquities. I wish that learned men would do as much with regard to Walloon, Biscayan, Slavonic, Finnish, Turkish, Persian, Armenian, Georgian, and others, the better to reveal their harmony – which, as I have said, would especially help to make clear the origin of nations.

PHIL. This proposal is important; but now the time has come to set aside *material* aspects of a word and return to *formal* ones, that is, to the signification which is common to different languages.[1] §2. Now you will grant me in the first place, sir, that when one man speaks to another, what he wants to give signs of are his own ideas, since he cannot apply words to things he does not know. 'Till he has some ideas of his own, he cannot suppose them to correspond with [the qualities of things or with][2] the conceptions of another man'.

THEO. Nevertheless, he very often professes to indicate what others think rather than what he thinks on his own account; this happens only too often with laymen who have an unquestioning faith. But I agree that the speaker, however *blind and vacuous his thought may be, always does mean something of a general sort by what he says. At least he takes care to put the words in the order that others customarily do, and contents himself with the thought that he could grasp their sense if the need arose. Thus a person is sometimes – oftener indeed than he thinks – a mere passer-on of thoughts, a carrier of someone else's message, as though it were a letter.

PHIL. You are right to add that a person always has something general in mind, however dense he may be. §3. 'A child having taken notice of nothing in the metal he hears called gold, but the bright shining yellow colour,' he gives the word *gold* to this same colour which he sees in a peacock's tail. Others will add great weight, fusibility and malleability. 287

THEO. I agree; but our idea of the object we speak of is often even more general than this child's. I have no doubt that a man born blind could speak aptly about colours and make a speech in praise of light, without being acquainted with it, just from having learned about its effects and about the conditions in which it occurs.

PHIL. This observation of yours is very true. 'It often happens that men ...do set their thoughts more on words than things. Nay, because words are [most][3] of them learned, before the ideas are known for which they stand: therefore some, not only children, but men, speak [often as] parrots do'.[4] §4. However, men usually think they are revealing their own thoughts, and in addition they attribute to their words 'a secret reference' to other people's ideas and to things themselves. For if the sounds were attached to another idea by the person with whom we are speaking, this

---

[1] Added by Leibniz. [2] Added by Leibniz.
[3] Locke: 'many'. Coste's change. [4] From Locke's §7.

would be 'to speak two languages.' It is true that men do not pause long to examine what the ideas of others are; it is assumed that our idea is the one which the majority and 'the understanding men of that country' attach to the same word. **§5.** This applies especially to 'simple ideas and modes'; but with regard to substances it is more especially believed that words 'stand also for the reality of things.'

THEO. Ideas represent substances and modes equally, and in each case words indicate the things as well as the ideas. So I do not see much difference, except that ideas of substantial things and of sensible qualities are more settled. Furthermore, it sometimes happens that our ideas and thoughts are the subject-matter[1] of our discourse and are the very things we wish to signify; and reflexive notions enter more than one might think into notions of things. Sometimes words themselves are spoken of materially,[2] and in such a context one cannot precisely replace the word by its signification, i.e. by its relation to ideas or to things. This happens not only when one speaks as a grammarian but also when one speaks as a lexicographer, giving the explanation of a name.

288

Chapter iii
'Of general terms.'

PHILALETHES. **§1.** Although nothing exists but particular things, 'the far greatest part of words [are nevertheless] general terms', because **§2.** 'it is impossible, that every particular thing should have a distinct peculiar name.' Furthermore, that would require a prodigious memory, compared with which that of certain generals who could call all their soldiers by name would be as nothing. The matter would even go to infinity[3] if every beast, every plant, indeed every leaf of a plant, every seed, and finally every grain of sand which one might need to designate had to have its own name. And how could we name the parts of sensibly uniform things like water and iron?[4] **§3.** Besides, these particular names would be useless, since the chief end of language is to excite in my hearer's mind an idea like my own, for which the similarity conveyed by general terms is sufficient.[5] **§4.** Nor would particular words by themselves be any use for extending our knowledge or for judging the future by the past or one individual by another.[6] However, since we often need to mention certain individuals, particularly of our own species, we make use of proper names; **§5.** which we give also to countries, cities, mountains, and other 'distinctions of

---

[1] 'la matière'. [2] 'matériellement'.
[3] Mention of infinity added by Leibniz.
[4] Sentence added by Leibniz.
[5] Clause added by Leibniz – Locke's point was quite different.
[6] Second half of sentence added by Leibniz.

place'. And jockeys give proper names to their horses, just as Alexander did to Bucephalus, in order to distinguish 'this or that particular horse, when he is out of sight.'

THEOPHILUS. These comments are good, and some of them agree with the ones I have just made. However, in keeping with what I said earlier, I will add that *proper names* such as Brutus, Caesar, Augustus, Capito, Lentulus, Piso, Cicero, Elbe, Rhine, Ruhr, Leine, Oker, Bucephalus, Alps, Brenner, or Pyrenees, have usually originated as *appellatives*, i.e. general terms. We know that the first Brutus was given this name because of his apparent stupidity, that Caesar was the name of a child delivered through an incision in his mother's abdomen,[1] that Augustus was a name expressing reverence, that Capito and Bucephalus both mean big-headed, that Lentulus, Piso and Cicero were names originally given to those who grew only certain kinds of vegetables. I have aready said what the names of the rivers Rhine, Ruhr, Leine, and Oker signify [pp. 282–5]. And we know that in Scandinavia all rivers are still called *Elbes*. Finally *Alps* are snow-covered mountains (compare *album*, white), and Brenner and Pyrenees signify great height, for *bren* in Celtic meant high or chief (compare *Brennus*), just as *brink* still means height in Low Saxon – there is a Brenner between Germany and Italy, and a Pyrenees between Gaul and Spain. In fact I would venture to say that almost all words were originally general terms, since it will very rarely happen that a name will be invented just for one given individual without any reason for it. So we can say that individual names used to be names of species which were given to some individual either as a prime example of the species or for some other reason: for instance, one might give the name 'Big-head' to the person with the biggest head in the whole town or to the most eminent big-head that one knew. Similarly, generic names are given to species; that is, we shall be satisfied with a vaguer or more general term to designate a more specific kind, if the differentiae are of no interest to us; for instance we are satisfied with the general term wormwood, even though there are so many species of it that one of the Bauhins has written a whole book on the subject.

289

PHIL. Your reflections on the origin of proper names are very sound. §6. But to move on to the origin of appellative names, or general terms, I am sure that you will agree, sir, that 'words become general, by being made the signs of general ideas: and ideas become general, by separating from them [by abstraction] time, and place, and any other [circumstances] that may determine them to this or that particular existence.'

THEO. I do not deny that abstractions are used in that way, but it involves an ascent from species to genera rather than from individuals to species. You see, paradoxical as it may seem, it is impossible for us to know

---

[1] The Latin *'caesus'* means 'cut'.

individuals or to find any way of precisely determining the individuality of any thing except by keeping hold of the thing itself.[1] For any set of circumstances could recur, with tiny differences which we would not take in; and place and time, far from being determinants by themselves, must themselves be determined by the things they contain. The most important point in this is that individuality involves infinity, and only someone who is capable of grasping the infinite could know the principle of individuation of a given thing. This arises from the influence – properly understood – that all the things in the universe have on one another. The case would be otherwise, it is true, if the atoms of Democritus existed, but then there would be no *difference* between two *different* individuals with the same shape and size.

PHIL. §7. Still 'there is nothing more evident, than that the ideas of the persons children converse with, (to instance in them alone,) are like the persons themselves, only particular. [Their] ideas of the nurse, and the mother, are well framed in their minds;...and the names of *Nurse* and *Mamma*, the child uses, [are related exclusively] to those persons. Afterwards, when time...has made them observe, that there are a great many other things [which] resemble their father and mother,...they frame an idea, which they find those many particulars do partake in; and to that they give, with others, the name *man*'. §8. In the same way they 'advance to more general names and notions.' For instance, the new idea of animal is made, not by any addition but only by leaving out the shape, and the properties which are special to man, and retaining 'a body, with life, sense, and spontaneous motion'.

THEO. Very good; but that only shows what I was just saying, for when the child proceeds by abstraction from observing the idea of man to observing that of animal, he has arrived at the idea of human nature from the more specific idea which he observed in his mother and father and other people. That he had no precise idea of the individual is shown by the fact that he could easily be deceived by a moderate resemblance into mistaking some other woman for his mother. You know the story of the false Martin Guerre who fooled even the wife and close relatives of the real one by his resemblance to him, combined with his cunning, and for a long time puzzled the judges even after the real one had turned up.

PHIL. §9. And so 'this whole mystery of *genera* and *species*, which make such a noise in the Schools, and are, with justice, so little regarded out of them, is nothing else but abstract ideas, more or less comprehensive, with names annexed to them.'

291 THEO. The art of ranking things in genera and species is of no small importance and very much assists our judgment as well as our memory.

---

[1] '*à moins que de la garder elle même*', which might mean 'except by keeping it unchanged'.

You know how much it matters in botany, not to mention animals and other substances, or again moral and notional entities as some call them [*Weigel]. Order largely depends on it, and many good authors write in such a way that their whole account could be divided and subdivided according to a procedure related to genera and species. This helps one not merely to retain things, but also to find them. And those who have laid out all sorts of notions under certain headings or categories have done something very useful.

PHIL. § 10. 'In the defining of words . . . we make use of the genus, or next general word[; and this is] to save the labour of enumerating the several simple ideas, which [this genus] stands for; or, perhaps, sometimes the shame of not being able to do it. But though defining by *genus* and *differentia* [as the logicians put it] be the shortest way; yet, I think, it may be doubted, whether it be the best.' At least it is not the only one. In the definition which says that man is a rational animal (a definition 'which though, perhaps, not the most exact, yet serves well enough to [the] present purpose'), the word *animal* could be replaced by its definition. This displays how little necessity there is for 'the rule, that a definition must consist of genus, and differentia', and how little advantage in strictly observing it. Also, 'languages are not always so made, according to the rules of logic, that every term can have its signification, exactly and clearly expressed by two others. [And] those who have made this rule, have done ill, that they have given us so few definitions conformable to it.'

THEO. I agree with your remarks. Yet there are many reasons why it would be useful if definitions could consist of two terms: that would certainly shorten them a great deal, and all divisions could be reduced to dichotomies, which are the best kind and are highly useful for *invention, judgment and memory. However, I do not believe that logicians require the genus or the differentia always to be expressed by a single word: for instance the term 'regular polygon' is acceptable as the genus of 'square', and in the case of the circle the genus could be 'curvilinear plane figure' and the differentia would consist in all the points on the circumference being equally distant from a certain central point. It is also worth mentioning that the genus can very often be turned into the differentia, and the differentia into the genus: for instance, a square is a 'regular quadrilateral', or equally well a 'quadrilateral regular-figure'; so that it seems that genus and differentia differ only as substantive and adjective. In place of saying that man is a 'reasonable animal' we could, if language permitted, say that man is an 'animable rational', that is a rational substance endowed with an animal nature, as contrasted with Spirits which are rational substances whose nature is not animal, i.e. not shared with the beasts. This interchange

292

of genera and differentiae depends on changing the order of the subdivisions.

PHIL. §11. From what I had just said it follows 'that *general* and *universal*, belong not to the...existence of things; but are the [workmanship]¹ of the understanding'. §12. And the essences of each species are only abstract ideas.

THEO. I cannot see that this follows: generality consists in the resemblance of singular things to one another, and this resemblance is a reality.

PHIL. §13. I was just going to tell you myself that these species are founded on resemblances.²

THEO. Then why not look for the essence of genera and species there too?

PHIL. §14. It will be found less surprising 'that I say these essences... are the workmanship of the understanding, [if it is borne in mind] that at least the complex ones are often, in [different] men, different collections of simple ideas: and therefore that is *covetousness* [in the mind of] one man, which is not so [in that of] another.'

THEO. I confess, sir, that I have seldom had so poor a grasp of the force of your argument as I do now, and this distresses me. If men disagree in the name, does that change the things themselves or their resemblances? If one person applies the name 'covetousness' to one resemblance, and another applies it to another, these will be two different species designated by the same name.

PHIL. 'In that species [of substances] which is most familiar to us, and with which we have the most intimate acquaintance: it [has] been more than once doubted, whether the foetus born of a woman were a *man*, even so far, as that it hath been debated, whether it were...to be nourished and baptized: which could not be, if the abstract idea or essence, to which the name *man* belonged, were of nature's making; and were not the uncertain and various collection of simple ideas, which the understanding puts together, and then [after rendering it general by means of abstraction],³ affixed a name to it. So that in truth every distinct [idea formed by abstraction] is a distinct essence'.

THEO. Forgive me for saying, sir, that I am puzzled by your manner of expressing yourself, because I do not find what you say coherent. If we cannot always judge inner similarities from the outside, does that make them any the less part of the inner nature? When it is doubted whether a monster is a man, it is because it is doubted whether it has reason. If we find that it has, the theologians will demand that it be baptized and the

293

---

¹ Locke: 'inventions and creatures'. Coste's change.
² Locke: 'similitude'. Coste: '*ressemblance*'.
³ Locke: 'and then abstracting it'. Coste's change.

jurists that it be fed. We can certainly disagree about lowest species, in the logical sense, since these depend upon differences in respect of accidental properties within a single *physical species or lineage. But there is no need for us to fix upon logically lowest species: we can indeed go on endlessly varying them, as is illustrated by the many varieties of oranges, limes and lemons which experts can name and tell apart. The same thing happened with tulips and carnations when these flowers were in fashion. In any case, man's combining or not combining such and such ideas – or indeed their being or not being actually combined in nature – has no bearing on essences, genera and species, since they depend only upon possibilities, and these are independent of our thinking.

PHIL. §15. 'There is ordinarily supposed a real constitution of the [species of each thing];[1] and 'tis past doubt, there must be [one] on which any collection of simple ideas [or qualities] coexisting [in that thing][2] must depend. But it being evident, that things are ranked under names into sorts or species, only as they agree to certain abstract ideas, to which we have annexed those names, the essence of each genus, or [species],[3] comes to be nothing but that abstract idea, which the general, or [specific][4] name stands for. And this we shall find to be that, which the word *essence* imports, in its most familiar use. These two sorts of essences, I suppose, may not unfitly be termed, the one the *real*, the other the *nominal* essence.'

THEO. It seems to me that your way of putting things constitutes a very novel mode of expression. People have certainly spoken of 'nominal' *definitions* and 'causal' or 'real' ones, but so far as I know they have not until now spoken of *essences* other than real ones, unless a 'nominal essence' is understood to be a false and impossible one – something that appeared to be one but really is not – as that of a regular decahedron, a regular solid bounded by ten planes or surfaces, would be. Essence is fundamentally nothing but the possibility of the thing under consideration. Something which is thought possible is expressed by a definition; but if this definition does not at the same time express this possibility then it is merely nominal, since in this case we can wonder whether the definition expresses anything real – that is, possible – until experience comes to our aid by acquainting us *a posteriori* with the reality (when the thing actually occurs in the world). This will do, when reason cannot acquaint us *a priori* with the reality of the thing defined by exhibiting its cause or the possibility of its being generated. So it is not within our discretion to put our ideas together as we see fit, unless the combination is justified either by reason, 294

---

[1] Locke: 'sorts of things'. Coste's change.
[2] Locke: 'simple ideas coexisting'.
[3] Locke: 'sort'. Coste's change.
[4] Locke: 'sortal (if I may have leave so to call it from *sort*, as I do *general* from *genus*,)'. Coste's change.

showing its possibility, or by experience, showing its actuality and hence its possibility. To reinforce the distinction between essence and definition, bear in mind that although a thing has only one essence, this can be expressed by several definitions, just as the same structure or the same town can be represented by different drawings in perspective depending on the direction from which it is viewed.

PHIL. §18. I think you will agree with me that the real and the nominal are always the same in 'simple ideas and [ideas of]¹ modes, . . . but in [ideas of]² substances, always quite different. . . . A figure including a space between three lines, is the real, as well as nominal essence of a triangle; it being not only the abstract idea to which the general name is annexed, but the very *essentia*, or being, of the thing it self, that foundation from which . . . its properties flow, and to which they are . . . annexed. But it is far otherwise concerning [gold].³ The real constitution of its . . . parts, on which depend [its] colour, weight, fusibility, fixedness, etc.', is unknown to us; and since we have no idea of it we have no name to be the sign of it. However, it is these qualities which make this matter be called gold; they are its nominal essence, i.e. they give it 'a right to that name'.⁴

THEO. I would sooner say, in keeping with accepted usage, that the essence of gold is what constitutes it and gives it the sensible qualities which let us recognize it and which make its *nominal* definition; whereas if we could explain this structure or inner constitution we would possess the *real*, *causal* definition. However, in our present case the nominal definition is also real, not in itself (since it does not show us *a priori* the possibility of this body, and its mode of origin) but through experience, in that we find that there is a body in which these qualities occur together. Otherwise we could doubt whether such a weight was compatible with so much malleability, just as we can still wonder whether glass which is malleable when cool is naturally possible. Nor do I agree, sir, with your view that in respect of this matter ideas of substances differ from ideas of predicates; that definitions of predicates (i.e. of modes and of objects of simple ideas) are always nominal and real at once, while those of substances are only nominal. I do agree that it is more difficult to have real definitions of bodies, which are substantial entities, because their structure is less sensible. But the same is not true of all substances: we have as intimate a knowledge of true substances or unities, like God and the soul, as we have with most modes. Besides, some predicates are no better known than is the structure of bodies: yellow and bitter, for instance, are objects of simple ideas or imaginings, and nevertheless we have only a confused knowledge of them;

295

¹ Added by Leibniz.   ² Added by Leibniz.
³ Locke: 'that parcel of matter, which makes the ring on my finger'.
⁴ Locke: '[It is this collection of qualities] which makes it to be gold, or gives it a right to that name, which is therefore its nominal essence.'

even in mathematics a single mode can have a nominal as well as a real definition. Not many people have properly explained the difference between these two definitions, a difference which also marks off essence from property. In my opinion, the difference is that the real definition displays the possibility of the definiendum and the nominal does not. For instance, the definition of two *parallel straight lines* as 'lines in the same plane which do not meet even if extended to infinity' is only nominal, for one could at first question whether that is possible. But once we understand that we can draw a straight line in a plane, parallel to a given straight line, by ensuring that the point of the stylus drawing the parallel line remains at the same distance from the given line, we can see at once that the thing is possible, and why the lines have the property of never meeting, which is their nominal definition (though this is a sign of parallelism only when both lines are straight: if at least one were curved they might be such that they could never meet, without thereby being parallel).

PHIL. §19. If essences were anything else but abstract ideas they would not be 'ingenerable, and incorruptible.' There are perhaps no unicorns, sirens or perfect circles in the world.

THEO. I have already said to you, sir, that essences are everlasting because   296
they only concern possibilities.

Chapter iv
'Of the names of simple ideas.'

PHILALETHES. §2. Although I have, I confess, always thought that the formation of modes was an arbitrary matter, it has been my conviction that simple ideas and ideas of substances must signify not just a possibility but a 'real existence'.

THEOPHILUS. I see no need for them to do so. God has ideas of substances before creating the objects of the ideas, and there is nothing to prevent him from passing such ideas on to intelligent creatures. There is not even a rigorous demonstration to prove that the objects of our senses, and of the simple ideas which the senses present us with, are outside us. This point holds especially for people who, like the *Cartesians and your famous author, believe that our simple ideas of sensible qualities in no way resemble anything which exists outside us and in objects; for then there would be no compelling reason why these ideas should be founded on any real existence.

PHIL. §§4–7. You will at least grant me this other difference between simple ideas and composite ones, that 'the names of simple ideas are not capable of any definitions [whereas] the names of [composite] ideas are.' For any definition should contain more than one term, each signifying an idea. Thus we can see what can and what cannot be defined, and why definitions cannot go on to infinity; which 'has not, that I know, hitherto been taken notice of by any body'.

THEO. In the little paper on ideas which appeared in the *Acta* of Leipzig about twenty years ago ['Meditations on knowledge, truth and ideas'], I also remarked that simple terms do not admit of nominal definition; but I also made the point there that terms which are simple only from our point of view because we have no way of *analysing them into the elementary perceptions which make them up – e.g. terms like hot, cold, yellow, green – do admit of real definitions which would explain what causes them. Thus the real definition of *green* is to be composed of a thorough mixture of blue and yellow; though green can no more be given a nominal definition, through which it could be recognized, than can blue or yellow. In contrast with this, if a term is simple in itself – i.e. if we have a vivid [*claire*], distinct conception of it – then it does not admit of any definition, nominal or real. In my little essay in the *Acta* of Leipzig you will find the groundwork of a good part of an account of the understanding, set out in summary fashion.

PHIL. §4. It was good to explain this matter, and to indicate what could and what could not be defined – 'the want whereof is (as I am apt to think) not seldom the occasion of great wrangling, and [much jargon] in men's discourses'. §8. Those famous triflings which have created such a stir in the Schools have arisen from neglect of this difference in our ideas. The greatest masters of the art have had perforce to leave most simple ideas undefined, and when they have undertaken definitions of them they have met with failure. 'What more exquisite jargon could the wit of man invent, than [is contained in] this definition [of Aristotle's: *Motion is*][1] *the act of a being in power, as far forth as in power*'. §9. And the modern philosophers 'who define motion to be a *passage from one place to another* [merely] put one synonymous word for another'.

THEO. I have already pointed out during one of our previous conversations that you treat as simple many ideas which are not so. *Motion* is one of them: I believe it to be definable, and the definition which says that it is *change of place* deserves respect. Aristotle's definition is not as absurd as it is thought to be by those who do not understand that for him the Greek *kinesis* did not signify what we call 'motion' but rather what we would express by the word 'change', which is why he gives it such an abstract and metaphysical definition [*Physics* III, 201^{a}10]; whereas what we call 'motion' – and he would call *phora* (carrying) – is one of the kinds of change (*hê kinesis*).

---

[1] Added by Leibniz.

297

PHIL. §10. But at least you will not defend the same author's definition of *light* as the act of the transparent.[1]

THEO. Like you, I find that utterly useless. Aristotle relies too much on his term 'act', which is not very informative. He takes 'the transparent' to be a medium through which vision is possible; and light, according to him, consists in the actual passage [of something through the medium. *De Anima* II, 418^{b}9]. Splendid!

PHIL. §11. We are in agreement, then, that our simple ideas cannot be nominally defined. We cannot know the taste of pineapple, for example, by listening to travellers' tales, unless we can taste things by the ears – like 'Sancho Panza, who had the faculty to see Dulcinea by hearsay', or like the blind man who, having often heard scarlet described as a blazing colour,[2] thought that it must be 'like the sound of a trumpet.'

THEO. You are right. All the travellers in the world could not have given us through their narratives what we have been given by a single one of our own countrymen – a gentleman who grows pineapples at a place near the banks of the Weser three leagues from Hanover. He has found out how to propagate them, so that some day we may have home-bred pineapples as plentifully as Portuguese oranges, though we could expect pineapples grown here to have lost some of the flavour.

PHIL. §12. 'The case is quite otherwise in complex ideas'. A blind man can understand what a statue is, §13. and someone can understand what a rainbow is without ever having seen one, so long as he has seen the colours that make it up. §15. Yet although simple ideas cannot be explained, they are nevertheless the least 'doubtful' ideas. This is because experience is more effective than definitions.

THEO. Still, there is something problematic about ideas which are simple only from our point of view. For example, it would be hard to mark precisely the boundary between blue and green, or in general to tell apart any pair of closely similar colours; whereas we can have precise notions of the terms which are employed in arithmetic and geometry.

PHIL. §16. Another special feature of simple ideas is that they involve very little subordination in what logicians call the line of predicates, from the lowest species to the highest genus. This is because 'the lowest species being but one simple idea, nothing can be left out of it'. For example, nothing can be left out of the ideas of white and of red while retaining the[3] common appearance in which they agree; and that is why they, along with

---

[1] Locke: 'the act of perspicuous, as far forth as perspicuous'. Coste: '*l'acte du transparent en tant que transparent*'. Leibniz: '*l'acte du transparent*'.

[2] This clause about hearing people speak of '*l'éclat d'écarlate*' is added by Leibniz. The French '*éclat*' can mean a flash (of light) or a burst (of noise).

[3] Locke: 'a'.

299   yellow and others, are 'comprehended under the genus or name *colour*'.[1] And when men wish to frame a still more general term, which comprehends also sounds, tastes and tactile qualities, they employ the general term *quality*, in its ordinary sense, to distinguish those qualities 'from extension, number, motion, pleasure, and pain, which [act] on the mind, and introduce their ideas by more senses than one.'

THEO. I have something to add regarding that remark; and I hope, sir, that here and elsewhere you will give me credit for being guided by what the subject-matter seems to demand, and not by a quarrelsome spirit. The fact that there is so little subordination among sensible qualities, and that they admit of so few subdivisions, is not one of their merits – it is merely a result of our having so little knowledge of them. At that, something can be 'left out of' our ideas of *colours: this is shown by the fact that all colours have in common being seen by the eyes, all passing through bodies which let the appearance of any of them through, and being reflected by polished surfaces of opaque bodies.[2] We even have a good ground for dividing colours into the *extreme* ones (of which one is positive, namely white, and the other is privative, namely black), and the *middle* ones which are called 'colours' in a narrower sense. These are obtained from light by refraction, and they in turn can be subdivided into those on the convex side of the refracted ray and those on its concave side. These divisions and subdivisions of colours are of considerable importance.

PHIL. But how can genera be found in these simple ideas?

THEO. They only appear to be simple. So when they occur there are other things going on which are connected with them, although the connection is not one that we understand; and these accompanying circumstances provide something that can be explained and subjected to analysis, which gives some hope that eventually we shall be able to discover the reasons for these phenomena. So there is a kind of redundancy in our perceptions of sensible qualities as well as of sensible portions of matter: it consists in the fact that we have more than one notion of a single subject. Gold can be nominally defined in various ways – it can be called the heaviest body we have, the most malleable, a fusible body which resists cupellation and aquafortis, etc. Each of these marks is sound, and suffices for the recognition of gold: provisionally, at least, and in the present state of the bodies around us, until the discovery of a still heavier one such as some alchemists claim their 'Philosopher's Stone' to be, or until we are shown

300   that 'fixed silver', a silver-coloured metal with nearly all the other

---

[1] Locke says that that is why, when men wish to comprehend them all under the name *colour*, they have 'to do it by a word, which denotes only the way they get into the mind.'

[2] This rendering implies that four of Leibniz's words – expressed by the second 'all', by 'any of them' and by 'reflected' – should have had feminine endings to agree with '*couleurs*'.

qualities of gold, which the Honourable Robert *Boyle seems to say that he has made. So one can say – and I think that I earlier did say [pp. 400f?] – that in matters where we have only the empiric's kind of knowledge our definitions are all merely provisional. Well, then, the fact is that we do not know demonstratively whether a colour could be generated by reflection alone, without refraction; or whether, through a hitherto unknown kind of refraction, colours which in ordinary refraction have always been observed on the concave side of the angle might occur on the convex side, and vice versa. The simple idea of blue would then no longer fall within the genus to which we have assigned it on the basis of our experiments. Still, there is nothing wrong with stopping at the blue which we have and at the concomitants which it has: at least they provide us with something out of which we can make genera and species.

PHIL. §17. But what do you say about the remark which has been made that 'simple ideas are...taken from the existence of things, and are not arbitrary at all', whereas ideas of mixed modes are 'perfectly arbitrary' and ideas of substances are somewhat so?

THEO. I think that the arbitrariness lies wholly in the words and not at all in the ideas. For an idea expresses only a possibility: so even if parricide had never occurred, and even if no lawmaker had any more thought of speaking of it than Solon had, it would still be a possible crime and the idea of it would be real.[1] For ideas are in God from all eternity, and they are in us, too, before we actually think of them, as I showed in our first discussions. If anyone wants to take ideas to be men's actual thoughts, he may; but he will be gratuitously going against accepted ways of speaking.

Chapter v
'Of the names of mixed modes and relations.'

PHILALETHES. §2. But does not the mind make ideas of mixed modes by combining simple ideas as it sees fit, without needing a real model, whereas simple ideas come to it without choice, 'by the real existence of things'? §3. Does not the mind often see a mixed idea before the thing itself exists?

THEOPHILUS. If you take ideas to be actual thoughts, you are right. But 301 I see no need to apply your distinction in connection with the very form or possibility of those thoughts; and that is what we are concerned with when we separate off the ideal world from the existent world. The real existence of beings which are not necessary is a matter of fact or of history, while the knowledge of possibilities and necessities (the *necessary* being that whose opposite is not *possible*) is what makes up the demonstrative sciences.

[1] This refers to Locke's II.xxii.4, 6.

PHIL. §6. But is there a greater connection between the ideas of killing and of man than between the ideas of killing and of sheep? Are the notions which make up parricide more connected than those which make up infanticide? And what the English call 'stabbing', that is murdering someone by thrusting the point of a weapon into him, which they regard as a worse offence than to kill someone by striking him with the edge of a sword:[1] is it more natural for this to have been granted a name and an idea, while not doing the same for the act of killing a sheep, say, or killing a man by slashing him with a sword?

THEO. If we are concerned only with possibilities, all these ideas are equally natural. Anyone who has seen a sheep killed has had an idea of that act in his thought, even if he has not deemed it worth his attention and has not given it a name. Why, then, should we restrict ourselves to names when our concern is with the ideas themselves, and why attend so much to the privileged position of ideas of mixed modes when our concern is with ideas in general?

PHIL. §8. Since men arbitrarily form various species of mixed modes, the result is that we find 'words in one language, which have not any that answer them in another.... The *Versura* of the Romans, or *Corban* of the Jews, have no words in other languages to answer them.... The Latin names *hora*, *pes*, *libra*, are, without difficulty, rendered by the...names, *hour*, *foot*, and *pound*'; but the Roman's ideas were very different from ours.

THEO. I see that many of the matters we discussed when we were concerned with ideas themselves, and their various kinds, are now being re-introduced by virtue of the names of those ideas. What you have said is true about names, and about human customs, but it makes no difference to the sciences or to the nature of things. It is true that someone who wanted to write a universal grammar would be well advised to move on from the essence of languages to their existence, and to compare the grammars of various languages; just as an author seeking to write a universal jurisprudence, derived from reason, would do well to bring in parallels from the laws and customs of the nations. This would be useful not only in a practical way but also theoretically, prompting the author himself to think of various considerations which would otherwise have escaped his notice. But in the science [of universal jurisprudence] itself, as distinct from its history and its [application to the realm of] existence, it does not matter whether or not the nations have actually conformed to the ordinances of reason.

PHIL. §9. 'The doubtful signification of the word *species* [makes] it sound harsh to some [when] the species of mixed modes are [said to be] made

[1] Clause added by Leibniz, on the authority of a footnote by Coste.

302

by the understanding; [but] I leave it to be considered, who makes the boundaries of [each] sort, or species; since with me, *species* and *sort'* are perfectly synonymous.

THEO. Ordinarily, these boundaries of species are fixed by the nature of things – for instance the line between man and beast, between stabbing and slashing. I do admit though that there are some notions which involve a truly arbitrary element: for example, determining a one-foot length, for since a straight line is uniform and indefinite[ly long] nature does not indicate any boundaries on it. There are also vague and imperfect essences, where individual opinion comes in – as in the question of how few hairs a man can have without being bald. This was one of the sophisms which the ancients used for putting pressure on an adversary, 'until he falls, tricked by the argument of the vanishing heap' [Horace]. But the right reply is that nature has not determined this notion, and that opinion plays a part; that there are people whose being bald or not bald is open to question; and that there are ambiguous cases whom some would regard as bald and others would not – as in your remark that a horse which counts as small in Holland will be deemed large in Wales [p. 229]. Something of the kind can occur even with simple ideas, for, as I have just remarked [p. 298], the outer limits of colours are doubtful. There are also essences which are truly *half-nominal*: these are ones where the name has a role in the definition of the thing; for instance, the rank or quality of Doctor, Knight, Ambassador, King is displayed through someone's acquiring the acknowledged right to use that name. A foreign emissary, no matter how great his power and how large his retinue, will not be accounted an 'Ambassador' unless his letter of credence so names him. But these essences and ideas are 'vague', 'doubtful', 'arbitrary', 'nominal' in slightly different senses from those you have mentioned.[1]

303

PHIL. §10. But it seems often to be the name that preserves the essences of mixed modes, which you believe not to be arbitrary. For example, without the name *triumph* we would have hardly any idea of what occurred in Rome on such occasions.

THEO. I agree that the name serves to bring one's attention onto things, and to preserve the memory and the present knowledge of them; but that does not affect the point which is at issue, and does not make essences nominal. I do not see the point of insisting with might and main, as your allies do, that essences themselves depend on choice and on names. One might have hoped that your illustrious author, instead of harping on that, would prefer to go in more detail into the nature of ideas and modes,

---

[1] Chapter v contains no basis, in Locke or Coste or Philalethes, for the allusion to 'vague'. Nor to 'doubtful', for the occurrence on p. 302 (v.9) is hardly relevant; but perhaps the reference is to p. 298 (iv.15).

ranking and further exploring their kinds. I would have followed him down that road with pleasure, and with profit, for he would certainly have given us a great many insights.

PHIL. §12. When we speak of a *horse*, or *iron*, we think of them as things 'which afford the original patterns of [our] ideas. But [when we speak of] mixed modes, at least the most considerable parts of them, which are moral beings, [– justice and gratitude, for example –] we consider the original patterns, as being in the mind'. That is why we speak of the *notion* of justice, or of temperance, but not of the notion of a horse, or of a stone.[1]

THEO. The patterns of one of these kinds of idea are just as real as the patterns of the other. The mind's qualities are no less real than the body's. True, one does not see justice as one sees a horse, but one understands it as well, or rather one understands it better. Whether or not one gives thought to it, justice inheres in actions as much as straightness and crookedness do in motions. To show you that my opinion is shared by others, even the ablest and most experienced in human affairs, I need only appeal to the authority of the Roman jurists, who have been followed by all the others. They speak of these 'mixed modes' or 'moral beings' of yours as *things*, specifically *incorporeal things*. For example, they speak of legal rights, such as a right of way over a neighbour's land, as incorporeal things which can be owned, can be acquired through long use, can be possessed, and can be claimed by legal action. As for the word 'notion': some very able people have used this in a sense as broad as that of 'idea'; Latin usage does not conflict with that, and I doubt if there is anything against it in English or French.

PHIL. §15. It should further be noted that men learn the names of mixed modes before learning the ideas of them, because it is the name which shows that this idea is worth attending to.

THEO. That is a good point. Though in fact these days, when children learn with the aid of vocabulary lists, this learning of names ahead of things occurs just as much with substances as with modes, and indeed even more. That is because those same vocabulary lists are defective in that they include only nouns, and no verbs; their makers ignore the fact that verbs, though they signify modes, are more needed in ordinary speech than are most of the nouns which indicate particular substances.

304

---

[1] Based mainly on a marginal note by Coste, which is presumably based on Locke's II.xxii.2 (see p. 213).

Chapter vi
'Of the names of substances.'

PHILALETHES. §1. The genera and *species of substances, as of other beings, are merely *sorts*. For example, suns are a sort of stars; specifically, they are fixed stars, for it is believed, with some reason, that each fixed star would present itself as a sun to a person who was placed at the right distance from it. §2. The 'boundary' of each sort is its 'essence'. It is known either by the inner structure or by the outer marks which make it known to us and make us give it a certain name. §3. In the same way, one may know the Strasbourg clock either in the manner of the clockmaker who built it or in the manner of a spectator who sees what it does.

THEOPHILUS. If you choose to express yourself thus, I have no objection.

PHIL. I am expressing myself in a way which should not start up our earlier disagreements. §4. And now I add that *essence* relates only to sorts, and that 'nothing [is] essential to individuals'.[1] 'An accident, or disease, may ...alter my colour, or shape; a fever, or fall, may take away my reason, or memory,...an apoplexy leave neither sense, nor understanding, no nor life....If it be asked, whether it be essential to me...to have reason? I say no'. 305

THEO. I believe that there is something essential to individuals, and more than there is thought to be. It is essential to substances to act, to created substances to be acted upon, to minds to think, to bodies to have extension and motion. That is, there are sorts or species such that if an individual has ever been of such a sort or species it cannot (naturally, at least) stop being of it, no matter what great events may occur in the natural realm. But I agree that some sorts or species are accidental to the individuals which are of them, and an individual can stop being of such a sort. Thus one can stop being healthy, handsome, wise, and even visible and tangible, but one does not stop having life and organs and perception. I have said enough earlier about why it appears to men that life and thought sometimes stop, although really they continue to exist and to have effects.

PHIL. §8. 'Many of the individuals that are ranked [under] one common name, and...received as being of one species, have yet qualities depending on their real [particular] constitutions,...far different from one another.... This, as it is easy to be observed by all, who have to do with natural bodies; so chemists...are often, by sad experience, convinced of it, when they,...in vain, seek for the same qualities in one parcel of sulphur, antimony, or vitriol, which they have found in others.'

---

[1] Locke's marginal summary of §§4–6.

THEO. You could not be more right. I could add some facts about this on my own account – e.g. that whole books have been devoted to 'the unsuccessfulness of experiments' in chemistry [Boyle]. The point is that people mistakenly take these bodies to be homogeneous or uniform, whereas really they are more mixed than they are thought to be. When dealing with heterogeneous bodies, one is not surprised to find differences between individual samples: physicians know only too well how much human bodies differ in their balance and their constitution. In short, as I have remarked earlier [p. 293], we shall never be able to find species which are logically the lowest; and two real, i.e. complete, individuals belonging to a single species will never be perfectly alike.

PHIL. §§9–10. We do not notice all these differences, because we do not know the minute parts or, therefore, the internal structures of things. So we cannot put things into sorts or species by means of them, and if we did try to fix species according to these essences, or according to what the Scholastics call 'substantial forms', we should be like a blind man trying to sort bodies by their colours. §11. We do not even know the essences of spirits. We cannot form different[1] specific ideas of angels, although we know quite well that there must be several species of spirits. Nor, it seems, do we distinguish God from spirits by any number of simple ideas, except that to God we attribute infinity.

306

THEO. In my system there is also another difference between God and created spirits, namely that I think that all created spirits must have bodies, just as our soul has one.

PHIL. §12. I believe that there is at least this analogy between bodies and spirits, that just as there are no gaps in the varieties of things the corporeal world contains, so there will be at least as much variety among thinking creatures. From us right down to the lowest things, 'the descent is by easy steps, and a continued series of things, that in each remove, differ very little one from the other. There are fishes that have wings, and are not strangers to the airy region: and there are some birds, that are inhabitants of the water; whose blood is cold as fishes, and their flesh so like in taste, that the scrupulous are allowed them on fish-days. There are animals so near of kin both to birds and beasts, that they are in the middle between both: amphibious animals link the terrestrial and aquatic together; seals live at land and at sea, and porpoises [whose French name *marsouin* means *sea-pig*][2] have the warm blood and entrails of a hog, not to mention what is... reported of... sea-men. There are some brutes, that seem to have as much knowledge and reason, as some [animals] that are called men: and the animal and vegetable kingdoms, are so nearly joined, that if you will take

[1] Locke: 'distinct'. Coste: '*diverses*'. Leibniz: '*différentes*'.
[2] Added by Leibniz.

the lowest of one, and the highest of the other, there will scarce be perceived any great difference between them; and so on till we come to the lowest and the most inorganical parts of matter, we shall find everywhere, that the several species are linked together, and differ but in almost insensible degrees. And when we consider the infinite power and wisdom of the [Author of all things], we have reason to think, that it is suitable to the magnificent harmony of the universe,[1] and the great design and infinite goodness of the Architect, that the species of creatures should also, by gentle degrees, ascend upward from us toward his infinite perfection[. So we have reason] to be persuaded, that there are far more species of creatures above us, than there are beneath; we being in degrees of perfection much more remote from the infinite being of God, than we are from . . . that which approaches nearest to nothing. And yet of all those [different] species . . . we have no clear distinct ideas.'

THEO. I had planned to say elsewhere something close to the line of thought you have just expounded, sir, but I am quite content to have been forestalled when I see things being said better than I could have hoped to do. Able philosophers have addressed themselves to this question of whether there is a *vacuum among forms, that is, whether there are possible species which do not actually exist, so that nature might seem to have overlooked them. I have reasons for believing that not all possible species are compossible in the universe, great as it is; not only with regard to things existing at the same time, but also with regard to the whole succession of things. My view, in other words, is that there must be species which never did and never will exist, since they are not compatible with that succession of creatures which God has chosen. But I believe that the universe contains everything that its perfect harmony could admit. It is agreeable to this harmony that between creatures which are far removed from one another there should be intermediate creatures, though not always on a single planet or in a single [planetary] system; and sometimes a thing is intermediate between two species in some respects and not in others. Birds, which are otherwise so different from man, approach him by virtue of their speech, but if monkeys could speak as parrots can they would approach him even more closely. The *Law of Continuity* states that nature leaves no gaps in the orderings which she follows, but not every form or species belongs to each ordering. As for Spirits: since I hold that every created intelligence has an organic body, whose level of perfection corresponds to that of the intelligence or mind which occupies the body by virtue of the *pre-established harmony, I hold that a very useful way to get some conception of the perfection of Spirits above ourselves is to think of perfections of bodily organs which surpass our own. To raise

307

---

[1] Leibniz emphasizes this phrase.

ourselves above ourselves in that manner, what we mostly need are the richest and liveliest imaginations – or, to use the untranslatable Italian phrase, *l'inventione la piu vaga*. And what I have said in defence of my theory of harmony [e.g. 'New system of the nature and communication of substances'], which exalts the divine perfections beyond what anyone had dreamed of, will also serve to give us ideas of incomparably greater creatures than any of which we have had ideas up to now.

PHIL. §13. To return to how little reality there is in species, even among substances, I ask you whether water and ice are of different species?

308 THEO. I reply with another question for you. Is gold melted in a crucible of the same species as gold which has been cooled into an ingot?

PHIL. One does not answer a question by putting a question, like someone who 'settles a controversy with a controversy'.[1] Still, judging from that, you will acknowledge that 'the ranking of things into species...is done ...according to the ideas that we have of them: which [is] sufficient to distinguish them by names'. But if we suppose that this distinguishing is founded on 'their real internal constitutions, and that things existing are distinguished by nature into species, by real essences, according as we [ourselves] distinguish them into species by [such and such] names, we shall be liable to great mistakes.'

THEO. All this trouble arises from a certain ambiguity in the term 'species' or 'of different species'. When that ambiguity is removed, there will be no further dispute except perhaps about the name. One can understand 'species' mathematically or else *physically. In mathematical strictness, the tiniest difference which stops two things from being alike in all respects makes them 'of different species'. It is in that sense that in geometry all circles are of a single species, because they are all perfectly alike, and for the same reason all parabolas are of a single species; but the same does not hold for ellipses and hyperbolas, for there is an infinity of sorts or species of these, each containing an infinity of members. A single species contains all the countless ellipses in which the distance between the foci has the same ratio to the distance between the vertices; but since there are countless different ratios between these distances, there are infinitely many species of ellipses. However, since the ratios of these distances vary only in magnitude, the result is that all these infinite species of ellipses make up but a single genus, and that there are no further subdivisions. In contrast with this, *trifocal ovals would comprise an infinity of such genera, the number of species being infinitely infinite, with a merely infinite number of them belonging to each genus. Two physical individuals will never be perfectly of the same species in this manner, because they will never be perfectly alike; and, furthermore, a single individual will move from

---

[1] Quotation from Horace, not in the *Essay*.

species to species, for it is never entirely similar to itself for more than a moment. But when men settle on physical species, they do not abide by 309 such rigorous standards; and it is for them to say whether stuff which they themselves are able to restore to its previous form continues to be of the same 'species' so far as they are concerned. And so we say that water, gold, quicksilver, and common salt remain such, and are merely disguised, in the ordinary changes they undergo; but in the case of organic bodies – i.e. the species of plants and animals – we define species by generation, so that two similar individuals belong to the same species if they did or could have come from the same origin or seed. In the case of man we demand not only human generation but also the quality of being a rational animal; and although some men remain like beasts all their lives, we presume that that is not for want of the faculty, i.e. of the fundamental capacity,[1] but rather because of impediments which hold it back. But we have not yet settled exactly what outer facts we are willing to take as sufficient to create this presumption. However, no matter what rules men make to govern how things are to be named and what entitlements go with names, provided that the system of rules is orderly (i.e. interconnected and intelligible) it will be founded in reality, and men will be able to imagine only such species as have already been made or distinguished by nature – nature which even encompasses possibilities. As for what is inner: although every outer appearance is grounded in the inner constitution, it can nevertheless happen that two different constitutions result in the same appearance; yet there will be something in common, and that is what philosophers call the 'immediate formal cause'. But even if that were not so, e.g. if M. *Mariotte were right (I think he is wrong) in saying that the blue of a rainbow has an entirely different cause from the blue of a turquoise, with no common formal cause; and even if we agreed that some of the apparent natures which lead us to name things had nothing in common internally; our definitions would nevertheless be grounded in real species, for *phenomena themselves are realities. It can be said, then, that whatever we truthfully distinguish or compare is also distinguished or made alike by nature, although nature has distinctions and comparisons which are unknown to us and which may be better than ours. So a great deal of care and experience is needed if one is to mark out genera and species in a manner which comes fairly close to nature. Modern botanists believe that distinctions drawn from the forms of flowers come closest to the natural order; but they have still encountered plenty of difficulties with that. It would be wise not to rest one's comparisons and rankings entirely on a single foundation, such 310 as the one drawn from flowers which I have just mentioned and which may be the best one so far devised for a system which is tolerable for and manageable by learners. It is better to be guided also by other foundations,

---

[1] 'faute de la faculté ou du principe'.

drawn from other parts and features of plants, with each ground of comparison being accorded its own separate chart. If this is not done, one may fail to capture many subordinate genera, and many useful comparisons, distinctions and observations. But the more deeply we study how species are generated, and the more thoroughly our rankings follow the necessary conditions of generation, the nearer we shall come to the natural order. That implies something about the conjecture which some sensible people have offered, that a plant contains not only the 'grain' or familiar seed which corresponds to the ovum of an animal, but also another seed which could fairly be called male; it is a powder (*pollen*)[1] which is quite often visible but sometimes invisible like the grain of certain plants; and it is spread around by the wind or by other contingencies, so that it combines with the grain – sometimes of the same plant and sometimes (as with cannabis) of a neighbouring plant of the same species. The [former] plant is thus analogous to the male, though perhaps there is always some of this same *pollen* in the female as well. My point was that if this theory proved to be true, and if we learned more about how plants are generated, I have no doubt that the differences we observed amongst them would provide a foundation for very natural divisions. And if we had the acuity of some of the higher Spirits, and knew things well enough, perhaps we would find for each species a fixed set of attributes which were common to all the individuals of that species and which a single living organism always retained no matter what changes or metamorphoses it might go through. (Reason is a fixed attribute of this kind, associated with the best-known physical species, namely that of humans; reason belongs inalienably to each individual member of the species, although one cannot always be aware of it.) But lacking such knowledge, we avail ourselves of the attributes which appear to us the most convenient for distinguishing and comparing things and, in short, for recognizing species or sorts; and those attributes always have their foundation in reality.

PHIL. §14. 'To distinguish substantial beings into species,[2] according to the usual supposition, [which has it] that there are certain precise essences or forms of things, whereby all the individuals existing, are, by nature, distinguished into species,' one would need to be assured: first, §15. 'that nature, in the production of things, always designs them to partake of certain regulated established essences,' serving as models; and secondly, §16. that nature always attains that goal. But monsters give us reason to doubt both of these. §17. 'Thirdly, it ought to be determined, whether those...monsters, be really a [new] distinct species,[3] [for] we find, that

311

---

[1] '*pollen*', which became a French word later in the century, here occurs as Latin for 'dust'.
[2] Taking the omission of Coste's '*en espèces*' to be a slip.
[3] Locke adds: 'according to the scholastic notion of the word *species*'.

some of these monstrous productions, have few or none of those qualities, which are supposed to result from...the essence of that species, from whence they derive their originals, and to which, by their descent, they seem to belong.'

THEO. In trying to determine whether a monster belongs to a given species, one is often reduced to conjectures. And that shows that one is not then restricting oneself to outer features; since one would like to guess whether the *inner nature* which is common to the individuals of a given species (for example reason, in man) is also present – as suggested by the facts of birth – in individuals lacking some of the *outer signs* which ordinarily occur in that species. But our uncertainty does not affect the nature of things: if there is such a common inner nature, the monster either has it or lacks it, whether or not we know which. And if the monster does not have the inner nature of any species, it can be of a species all of its own. But if the species we were interested in did not have such inner natures, and if we did not particularly dwell on the facts of birth either, then the boundaries of a species would be determined solely by outward signs. A monster would then not belong to the species from which it was deviant, unless the species was taken somewhat vaguely and loosely, and in that case it would be wasted labour to try to guess to what species the monster belonged. Perhaps that was what you meant in all your objections to species drawn from real inner essences. But then you would have to prove, sir, that there is nothing inner which is common to the whole of a species in cases where there are outer differences. But in the human species the contrary is the case, for sometimes children who have some gross abnormality eventually reach a stage at which they manifest reason. Why could there not be something similar with other species? It is true that we cannot define a species in terms of something which is unknown to us; but the outer features serve in place of it, though we recognize that they do not suffice for a *rigorous definition*, and that even *nominal definitions* in these cases are only conjectural and sometimes – as I have already pointed out [p. 300] – merely provisional. For example, a way might be found of counterfeiting 312 gold so that it would pass all the tests we have so far; but one might then also discover a new assaying method which would provide a way of distinguishing natural gold from this artificial gold. There are some old documents which attribute both of these discoveries to Augustus, Elector of Saxony, but I am not in a position to vouch for this. If it did happen, however, it could lead us to a more perfect definition of gold than we have at present; and if artificial gold could be made in large quantities at low cost, as the alchemists claim it could, this new test would be important, because it would enable mankind to retain the advantages which natural gold has in commerce, because of its rarity, in providing us with material which is durable, uniform, easy to divide and to recognize, and valuable in small quantities. I should like to take this opportunity to remove a difficulty (see §50 of the chapter on the names of substances of the author of the *Essay on Understanding*). The following objection is made: In the statement 'All gold is *fixed', either the word[1] 'gold' is taken to mean a collection of certain qualities of which fixedness is one, in which case one is uttering only a pointless identity, as though one said that whatever is fixed is fixed; or else it is taken to be a substantial entity endowed with a certain inner essence from which fixedness results, in which case what is being said is unintelligible, for this real essence is entirely unknown. I reply that the body which is endowed with that inner constitution is also indicated by other outward signs excluding fixedness: it is as though one were to say that the heaviest of all bodies is also one of the most fixed. But all of that is merely provisional, for we might some day find a volatile body – such as a new mercury might be – which was heavier than gold, so that gold would float upon it as lead does on the mercury we have.

PHIL. §19. The fact is that we can never, in this way, know precisely the[2] 'number of properties depending on the real essence of gold, . . . unless we knew the real essence of gold it self'. §21. However, if we restrict ourselves precisely to certain properties, that will suffice to let us have rigorous nominal definitions; and these will serve us in the meantime, though we may later change the significations of names if we hit upon some useful new way of distinguishing things.[3] But a nominal definition must at least conform to how the name is used, and must be able to be put in the place of the name. This serves to refute those who allege that extension is the essence of body; for when someone says that one body makes another move by impulse, obvious absurdity would result if we substituted 'extension' and said that one extension makes another extension move by impulse. For solidity[4] is also required. Similarly, one would not say that rationality, or what makes a man rational, conducts a conversation; for rationality is not the whole essence of man, and it is rational animals which have conversations with one another.

THEO. I believe that you are right, because the objects of abstract, incomplete ideas do not suffice to pick out the entities that are involved in all the actions of things. However, I think that 'conversation' pertains to all spirits which can communicate their thoughts to one another. The Scholastics are troubled about how the angels can do it; but if they allowed

313

---

[1] Taking '*l'idée*' as a slip for Coste's '*le mot*'. In Locke's §50 'idea' does not occur.
[2] Locke: 'know what are the precise'. Coste: '*connaître quel est précisément le*'. Leibniz: '*connaître précisément le*'.
[3] Added by Leibniz.
[4] Locke speaks not of 'solidity' but of 'an extended, solid thing'.

them to have rarefied bodies, as I follow the ancients in doing, they would have no further difficulty about that.

PHIL. §22. 'There are creatures...that have shapes like ours, but are hairy, and want language, and reason.[1] There are [imbeciles][2] amongst us, that have perfectly our shape, but want reason, and some of them language too. There are creatures, as 'tis said,...that with language, and reason,[3] and a shape in other things agreeing with ours, have hairy tails;' at least it is not at all impossible that there should be such creatures. There are 'others where the males have no beards, and others where the females have. If it be asked, whether these be all *men*, or no, all of human species: 'tis plain, the question refers only to the nominal [definition][4] or the complex idea' which we devise for ourselves in order to indicate it by that name.[5] For the internal essence is utterly unknown to us though 'we have reason to think, that where the faculties, or outward frame so much differs, the internal constitution is not exactly the same'.

THEO. In the case of man, I believe that we have a definition which is at once nominal and real. For reason is as internal to man as anything can be, and ordinarily it declares its presence. That is why beards and tails will not be treated on a level with it. A man of the forest, hairy though he is, will still be recognizable; and what disqualifies a baboon is not its fur. Imbeciles lack the use of reason; but we know from experience that reason is often held back so that it cannot be manifested, even in people who have exhibited it and will do so again. We plausibly make the same judgment about imbeciles on the strength of other signs, namely their bodily shape. 314 Those signs, together with the facts of birth, are our only basis when we assume that babies are human and will eventually manifest reason – and we are hardly wrong about that. But if there were rational animals whose outer form differed slightly from ours, we should be perplexed. This shows that when our definitions depend upon bodily exteriors, they are imperfect and provisional. If someone claimed to be an angel, and had knowledge or abilities far above our own, he could make himself believed. If someone else came from the *moon in some extraordinary machine, like Gonsales, and told us credible things about his homeland, we would take him to be a lunarian; and yet we might grant him the rights of a native and of a citizen in our society, as well as the title *man*, despite the fact that he was a stranger to our globe; but if he asked to be baptized, and to be regarded as a convert to our faith,[6] I believe that we would see great disputes arising among the

---

[1] Coste renders this phrase by '*l'usage de la parole, et de la raison*'.
[2] Locke uses the now obsolete 'naturals'.
[3] Coste: '*l'usage de la parole, et de la raison*'.
[4] Locke: 'essence'.
[5] This peculiar clause is Leibniz's rather than Locke's.
[6] Reading '*loi*' (law) as '*foi*'.

theologians. And if relations were opened up between ourselves and these planetary men – whom M. *Huygens says are not much different from men here – the problem would warrant calling an Ecumenical Council to determine whether we should undertake the propagation of the faith in regions beyond our globe. No doubt some would maintain that rational animals from those lands, not being descended from Adam, do not partake of redemption by Jesus Christ; but perhaps others would say that we do not know enough about all the places that Adam was ever in, or about what has become of all his descendants – for there have even been theologians who have thought that Paradise was located on the moön. Perhaps there would be a majority decision in favour of the safest course, which would be to baptize these suspect humans conditionally on their being baptizable. But I doubt if they would ever be found acceptable as priests of the Roman Church, because until there was some revelation their consecrations would always be suspect, and that, according to the doctrine of that Church, would expose people to the danger of unintentional idolatry. Fortunately we are spared these perplexities by the nature of things; but still these bizarre fictions have their uses in abstract studies, as aids to a better grasp of the nature of our ideas.

PHIL. §23. Not just in theological questions but in other matters too, some people might want to rely on descent,[1] and to say that 'propagation in animals by the mixture of male and female, and in plants by seeds, keeps the supposed real species distinct and entire.' But that would serve only to fix the species of animals and vegetables. 'What must we do for the rest?' And even in the case of the former, 'it is not sufficient: for if history lie not, women have conceived by' baboons.[2] And that is a new question – to what species should such a production belong? One often sees 'mules and jumarts' (see Ménage's *Dictionnaire étymologique*),[3] 'the one from the mixture of an ass and a mare, the other from the mixture of a bull and a mare.... I once saw a creature, that was the issue of a cat and a rat, and had the plain marks of both about it'. He who adds monstrous productions to all this will find it hard to determine species by generation. And if it cannot be done in any other way, must I go to the Indies to see the sire and dam of a tiger, and the seed of the tea plant, and have I no other way of judging whether individuals which come my way belong to these species?

THEO. Generation or pedigree does at least create a strong presumption (i.e. a provisional proof); I have already remarked that what we take as indications are very often conjectural. The pedigree is sometimes belied by the shape, when the child is unlike its father and mother, and a mixed

315

---

[1] Added by Leibniz.
[2] Locke uses the now obsolete 'drills'.   [3] Coste's reference.

shape is not always evidence of a mixed pedigree: a female can give birth to an animal which seems to belong to another species, this irregularity being caused simply by the mother's imagination – not to mention *'mola', as it is called. But if we judge provisionally as to species on the basis of pedigree, we also judge as to pedigree on the basis of species. The King of Poland, John Casimir, was presented with a forest child, captured in the company of bears; the child had many of their habits but eventually proved to be a rational animal. People had no hesitation in believing that he belonged to the race of Adam and baptizing him under the name of Joseph – although perhaps, following the practice of the Roman Church, with the condition 'If you are not already baptized', because he might have been carried off by a bear after his baptism. We still do not know enough about the results of crossing animals, and we often destroy monsters instead of raising them, although in any case they are seldom long-lived. It is believed that hybrid animals do not breed; yet Strabo claims that the mules of Cappadocia reproduce, and I am told in a letter from China that in neighbouring Tartary there are pure-bred mules. We find, too, that hybrid plants are able to perpetuate their new species. In any case, we do not know for sure with animals whether it is the male or the female, or both, or neither, which mainly determines the species. The theory of the female ovum, made famous by the late M. Kerckring, seemed to reduce males to a position like that of moist air in relation to plants, providing the seeds with what they need to sprout and to rise above the earth, as in the lines of Virgil which the *Priscillianists used to quote: 316

> Then, with fruitful showers, the almighty father Aether
> Descends into the bosom of his joyful spouse
> And, greatly mingling with her great body, nourishes all her offspring.

In short, on this hypothesis the male would hardly contribute more than does the rain. But M. *Leeuwenhoek has restored the male kind to its eminence, and the other sex has been lowered accordingly and regarded as having only the function which earth has with respect to seeds, namely providing them with lodging and nourishment. That could be the case even if we still accepted the theory of ova. But even if we were to suppose that the animal initially comes from the male, that would not prevent the female's imagination from having a great influence on the form of the foetus. For in the ordinary course of events it is bound to undergo great change while in this state, and will be so much the more prone to extraordinary changes as well. It is said that when a certain noble-woman's imagination was shocked by the sight of a cripple, it cut off a hand of her foetus, then very close to its term, and this hand was found later in the after-birth; though this story requires confirmation. Perhaps someone will come along and claim that although the soul can come from only one sex both sexes provide something organic, and that one body develops from two, just as we see that the silkworm is a sort of double animal which encloses a flying insect within the form of a caterpillar. This indicates how

317 much we are still in the dark about this important matter. Perhaps some day the analogy with plants will shed some light on it, but at present we do not even understand very well how plants are generated. The tentative view of the dust which has come to our attention, as something which could correspond to the male seed, is still not thoroughly elucidated. Besides, a slip from a plant is very often able to produce a new and complete plant, and no analogy to this has yet been observed among the animals; so the foot of an animal cannot be called an animal, in the way that it seems that each branch of a tree is a plant which is separately capable of bearing fruit. Furthermore the mixing of species, and even changes within a single species, often take place very successfully among plants. Perhaps at some time or in some place in the universe there are or were or will be species of animals more subject to change than those we have here now. Various cat-like animals, such as the lion, the tiger and the lynx, may once have been of the same race and may now amount to new subdivisions of the ancient cat species. Thus I keep returning to what I have already said several times: that our determinations of *physical species are provisional, and are adapted to what we know.

PHIL. §24. At least, when men made their divisions into species, 'substantial forms [were not] ever thought on by any, but those who have in this one part of the world [where we are][1] learned the language of the Schools'.

THEO. It seems that *'substantial forms' have recently acquired a bad name in certain quarters in which people are ashamed to speak of them. However, this is perhaps more a matter of fashion than of reason. When particular phenomena were to be explained, the Scholastics inappropriately used a general notion, but this misuse does not destroy the thing itself. The human soul somewhat shakes the confidence of some of our modern thinkers. Some of them acknowledge that it is the form of the man, but add that it is the only substantial form in the known part of nature. M. *Descartes speaks of it in this way; and he reproved M. *Regius for challenging the soul's quality of being a substantial form and for denying that man is *unum per se*, a being endowed with a genuine unity. Some believe that this distinguished man did so out of prudence. I rather doubt that, since I think that he was right about it. But the privilege should not be restricted to man alone, as though nature were put together higgledy-

318 piggledy. There is reason to think that there is an infinity of souls, or more generally of *primary entelechies, possessing something analogous to

[1] Added by Leibniz.

perception and appetite, and that all of them are and forever remain substantial forms of bodies. It is true that there appear to be species which are not really *unum per se* (i.e. bodies endowed with a genuine unity, or with an indivisible being which makes up their whole active principle), any more than a mill or a watch could be. Salts, minerals and metals could be of this nature, that is, simple compounds or masses which exhibit some regularity. But both kinds of bodies, animate bodies as well as lifeless compounds, will fall into species according to their inner structures; since even with the former – the animate ones – the soul and the machine is each sufficient by itself to determine [the species], since they agree perfectly. Though they have no immediate influence on each other, they mutually express each other, the one having concentrated into a perfect unity everything which the other has dispersed throughout its multiplicity. Thus, when things are to be ranked into species it is useless to dispute about substantial forms. Still, it is good for other reasons to know whether there are any, and how; for without that knowledge one will be a stranger in the intellectual realm. A final point: the Greeks and Arabs have spoken of these forms just as much as Europeans have; if the common man does not speak of them, he does not talk about algebra or incommensurables either.

PHIL. §25. Languages were established before sciences, and things were put into species by ignorant and illiterate people.

THEO. That is true, but the people who study a subject-matter correct popular notions. Assayers have found precise methods for identifying and separating metals, botanists have marvellously extended our knowledge of plants, and experiments that have been made on insects have given us new routes into the knowledge of animals. However, we are still far short of halfway along our journey.

PHIL. §26. If species[1] were nature's workmanship, they could not be conceived so differently[2] in different men. To one, *man* appears to be a *featherless biped with broad nails*; another, after a deeper examination, adds *reason*. Many men, however, 'determine of the [species] of animals, rather by their shape, than descent...; since it has been more than once debated, whether several human *foetus* should be...[3] received to baptism, or no, only because of the difference of their outward configuration, from the ordinary make of children, without knowing whether they were not as capable of reason, as infants cast in another mould: some whereof, though of an approved shape, are never capable of as much appearance of reason, all their lives, as is to be found in an ape, or an elephant; and never give any signs of being acted by a rational soul. Whereby it is evident, that the

319

---

[1] Locke: 'essences'.
[2] Locke: 'could not be so...different'.
[3] Locke: 'preserved, or'. Coste's omission.

outward figure, which only was found [defective],[1] and not the faculty of reason, which no body could know would be wanting in its due season, was made essential to the human species. The learned divine and lawyer, must, on such occasions, renounce his sacred definition of [rational animal],[2] and substitute some other essence of the human species. Monsieur Ménage furnishes us with an example worth [recounting] on this occasion. *When the Abbot of St Martin, says he, was born, he had so little of the figure of a man, that it bespake him rather a monster. 'Twas for some time under deliberation, whether he should be baptized or no. However, he was baptized and declared a man provisionally* (till time should show what he would prove.) *Nature had moulded him so untowardly, that he was called all his life the Abbot Malotru, i.e. ill-shaped. He was of Caen.* [*Menagiana*, vol. I, p. 278 in the Dutch edition of 1694.][3] This child we see was very near being excluded out of the species of man, barely by his shape. He escaped very narrowly as he was, and 'tis certain a figure a little more oddly turned had [deprived him of it for ever],[4] and he had been executed as a thing not to be allowed to pass for a man. And yet there can be no reason given, why if the lineaments of his face had been a little altered, a rational soul could not have been lodged in him; why a visage somewhat longer, or a nose flatter, or a wider mouth could not have consisted, as well as the rest of his ill figure, with such a soul, such parts, as made him, disfigured as he was, capable to be a dignitary in the Church.'

THEO. So far no rational animal has ever been discovered with an outer shape much different from our own. That is why, when there was some question of baptizing a child, its pedigree and its shape were never regarded as more than signs from which to judge whether or not it was a rational animal. So theologians and jurists had no need to give up their time-honoured definition on this account.

320   PHIL. §27. But if 'that monster...which is mentioned by Licetus [Bk. I, Ch. 3], with a man's head and hog's body [or other monsters] which to the bodies of men, had the heads of...dogs, horses, etc....had lived, and could have spoke, it would have increased the difficulty.'

THEO. I agree. A certain writer, a monk of the olden days named Hans Kalb (John Calf), portrayed himself in a book he wrote with a calf's head and pen in hand, so that some people foolishly believed that he really had a calf's head. Now if this actually happened and someone was made like that, from then on we would become more circumspect about getting rid of monsters. For it appears that reason would be decisive for the theologians

---

[1] Locke: 'found wanting', meaning 'found to be absent'. Coste's change.
[2] Locke: '*animal rationale*'. Coste replaces the Latin by French.
[3] Coste's version of the reference, but Locke's positioning of it.
[4] Locke: 'had cast him', i.e. condemned him. Coste's change.

and for the jurists, despite the shape and even the anatomical differences which could be found by the physicians; these would no more disqualify someone from being a man than did the reversal of internal organs in the man whose anatomy was seen by certain acquaintances of mine in Paris, where it created some stir. Nature

> In a mood of drunken spite
> Put the heart upon the right;
> And equally of wit bereft
> She put the liver on the left,

if I remember aright some of the lines which the late M. Alliot *père* wrote about this prodigy and showed to me; he was a famous physician, regarded as skilful in treating ulcers. That is obviously correct, provided that the variations in form among rational animals do not go too far. But if we found ourselves back in the age when beasts used to speak, we would lose the privilege of being the sole inheritors of reason; and we would thenceforth pay more attention to birth and to outward features in order to be able to distinguish members of the race of Adam from the descendants of some king or patriarch of a community of African monkeys. Our able author rightly points out (§29) that even if Balaam's she-ass had, all her life, discoursed as rationally as she did once with her master – assuming this was not a prophetic vision – she still would have had difficulty being accorded the status and dignity of a woman.[1]

PHIL. I can see that you are joking, and perhaps our author was too; but in all seriousness it is plain that species cannot always be assigned fixed boundaries. 321

THEO. I have already granted you that: when we are considering fictions and how things could be, there might be insensible transitions from one species to another, and telling them apart might sometimes be rather like the problem of deciding how much hair a man must have if he is not to be bald. This indeterminacy would hold even if we were perfectly acquainted with the inner natures of the creatures in question. But I do not see that this prevents things from having real essences independently of our understanding, or us from knowing them. It is true that the names and the boundaries of species would sometimes be like the names of measures and weights, where there are fixed boundaries only in so far as we choose them. However, in the ordinary course of events we have nothing like that to fear, because species which are too alike are seldom found together.

PHIL. We seem to be fundamentally in agreement on this point, although our terms differ a little. **§28.** I also grant you that there is less arbitrariness

---

[1] Locke: 'ass...man'. Coste: '*ânesse* [she-ass]...*homme*'. Leibniz: '*ânesse...femme*'.

in the denomination of substances than in the names of composite[1] modes. One would hardly think of joining 'the voice of a sheep, with the shape of a horse; nor the colour of lead, with the weight and fixedness of gold'; rather one prefers to copy nature.

THEO. It is not so much because with substances we are concerned only with what actually exists, as because with ideas of real things[2] (which are not very thoroughly understood) we are not sure whether the mixture is possible and useful unless we have its actual existence as a surety. But that holds for modes too: not only when their obscurity is impenetrable by us, as sometimes happens in natural science, but also when it is penetrable only with difficulty – and geometry provides plenty of examples of that. For in neither of these sciences is it in our power to make combinations just as we please, otherwise we would be entitled to speak of *regular decahedra*, and would explore the semicircle for a *centre of magnitude* like the *centre of gravity* which it actually has; for it is indeed surprising that the latter does exist while the former[3] cannot do so. With modes, then, combinations are not always arbitrary; and on the other side it turns out that they are sometimes arbitrary in the case of substances: we are often at liberty to combine qualities so as to define substantial entities in advance of experience, as long as we understand these qualities well enough to judge the possibility of their combining. In the same way gardeners who are expert in the greenhouse can purposefully and successfully undertake to produce some new species and to give it a name in advance.

322   PHIL. §29. You will agree with me, in any case, that when it comes to defining species, the number of ideas which are combined 'depends upon the various care, industry, or fancy of him that makes [this combination]. As in vegetables and animals 'tis the shape, so in most other [natural][4] bodies, not propagated by seed, 'tis the colour we most fix on, and are most led by.' §30. In fact, these are very often no more than gross, confused and inaccurate conceptions. 'Men are far enough from having agreed on the precise number of simple ideas, or qualities, belonging to any' species or name; since it requires much trouble, skill and time to find the simple ideas which are constantly united. However, the few qualities which make up these inaccurate definitions are usually sufficient for conversation. But despite the 'stir, about genus and species, . . . those forms, which there hath been so much noise made about [in the Schools],[5] are only chimeras; which give us no light into. . . specific natures'.

---

[1] Locke: 'mixed'. Coste: '*mixtes*'. Leibniz: '*composés*'. Similarly with every other use of 'composite modes' by Philalethes; they will not be noted separately.

[2] '*idées *physiques*', which could also mean 'ideas pertaining to natural science'.

[3] Reversing the order of '*le premier...l'autre*'.

[4] Added by Leibniz.   [5] Added by Coste.

THEO. Someone who makes a possible combination commits no error in doing that, or in giving it a name; but he does err if he believes that what he conceives is the whole of what others who are more expert conceive under the same name or in the same body. He may be conceiving too broad a genus in place of a more specific one. There is nothing in all this that goes against the Schools, and I do not see why you have returned to the attack on genera, species and forms, since you too have to recognize genera and species and even inner essences or forms – although we do not claim to use them to understand the 'specific nature' of a thing so long as we admit to still not knowing what they are.

PHIL. It is obvious, at least, that 'our boundaries of species, are not exactly conformable to those in nature.[1] For we, having need of general names for present use, stay not for a...discovery of [their] qualities, which would best show us their most [essential][2] differences and agreements; [and] we our selves divide them, by certain obvious appearances, into species, that we may the easier...communicate' with others.

THEO. If the ideas we combine are compatible, then the limits we assign to species are always 'exactly conformable' to nature; and if we are careful to combine ideas which actually occur together, our notions are also conformable to experience. If we regard them as only provisional with reference to actual bodies, and as subject to experiments which have been or will be made to discover more about them, and if we have recourse to the experts when fine points arise about whatever it is that the name is generally understood to stand for, then we shan't be doing anything wrong. Thus, although nature can furnish more perfect and more convenient ideas, it will not give the lie to any ideas we have which are sound and natural even if they are perhaps not the soundest and most natural.

PHIL. §32. Our generic ideas of substances – that of metal, for instance – 'follow not exactly the patterns set them by nature...; since there is no body to be found, which has barely malleableness and fusibility in it, without other qualities'.

THEO. No one is asking for patterns of that sort: it would be unreasonable to do so, as they do not exist even for the most distinct notions. We never find a number in which there is nothing to be seen but multiplicity in general, or something extended which has only extension, or a body which has only solidity and no other qualities. And when the specific differentiae are positive and mutually opposed, the genus is bound to select from amongst them.

---

[1] Locke: [If, which I do not believe,] nature sets the boundaries of the species of things..., our boundaries of species' etc.
[2] Locke: 'material'. Coste's change.

323

PHIL. 'If therefore any one will think, that a man, and a horse, and an animal, and a plant, etc. are distinguished by real essences made by nature, he must think nature to be very liberal of these real essences, making one for body, another for an animal, and another for a horse; and all these essences liberally bestowed upon Bucephalus. [Whereas really] all these genera and species [are] only more or less comprehensive signs'.

THEO. If you take real essences to be substantial patterns such as would be provided by a body which is nothing but a body, an animal with nothing more specific to it, a horse with no individual qualities, then you are right to regard them as chimeras. No one, I think – not even the most extreme of the old *realists – has claimed that there are as many substances with only a generic property as there are genera. But if general essences are not like that, it does not follow that they are merely 'signs': I have pointed out to you several times [pp. 292–4? 309?] that they are possibilities [inherent] in resemblances. Similarly, from the fact that colours are not always substances, i.e. extractible dyes, it does not follow that they are imaginary. Also, we could not exaggerate nature's 'liberality'; she goes beyond anything that we can devise, and all the dominant compatible possibilities are made real on her great Stage. Philosophers used to have two axioms: the *realist* one seemed to make nature profligate and the *nominalist* one seemed to declare her to be stingy. One says that nature permits no gaps, the other that she does nothing in vain. These are two good axioms, as long as they are understood: nature is like a good housekeeper who is sparing when necessary in order to be lavish at the right time and place. She is lavish in her effects and thrifty in the means she employs.

324

PHIL. We need not spend any more time arguing about real essences, as long as we achieve the purpose of language and word-use, which is to indicate our thoughts in a summary fashion.[1] §34. 'Were I to talk with any one, of a sort of birds...about three or four foot high, with a covering of something between feathers and hair, of a dark brown colour, without wings, but in the place thereof, two or three little branches, coming down [to the end of the body] like sprigs of Spanish broom; long great legs, with feet only of three claws, and without a tail; I must make this description of it, and so may make others understand me: but when I am told, that the name of [this animal] is *cassowary*, I may then use that word to stand in discourse for all [that composite] idea'.

THEO. Perhaps a very precise idea of that 'covering', or of some other part, would serve by itself to distinguish this animal from all known others, just as Hercules announced himself by the footprint he had made, and as the

---

[1] Remark about the 'purpose of language' based loosely on the opening of Locke's §33.

lion — according to the Latin proverb — is recognized by its claw. But the more features we accumulate the less provisional is the definition.

PHIL. In this case we can leave something out of the idea without prejudice to the thing; but if nature leaves something out of the thing, there is a question as to whether the species remains the same.[1] §35. For instance, if there were a body which had all the properties of gold except malleability, would it be gold? It is up to men to decide; so it is they who determine the species of things.

THEO. Not at all; they would only determine the name. But this discovery would teach us that malleability has no necessary connection with the other qualities of gold, taken together. So it would show us a new possibility and consequently a new species. As for gold which is 'eager' or brittle,[2] this property is merely the result of impurities, and does not stand alongside the other tests for gold, since the cupel and antimony remove this brittleness.

PHIL. §38. From our doctrine something follows which will seem very strange. It is 'that each abstract idea, with a name to it, makes a distinct species. But who can help it, if truth will have it so? . . . I would fain know, why a shock and a hound, are not as distinct species, as a spaniel and an elephant.'

THEO. I have distinguished earlier [pp. 308ff] between the various meanings of the word 'species'. In the logical, or rather the mathematical, sense, the least dissimilarity is enough, so that each different idea yields a new species, whether it has a name or not. However, in the *physical sense, we do not give weight to every variation; and we speak either unreservedly, when it is a question merely of appearances, or conjecturally, when it is a question of the inner truth of things, with the presumption that they have some essential and unchangeable nature, as man has reason. So the presumption is that things that differ only through accidental changes, such as water and ice or quicksilver in its liquid form and its sublimate, are of a single species. In organic bodies we ordinarily take generation or pedigree as a provisional indication of sameness of species, just as among bodies of a more homogeneous kind we go by how they can be produced. It is true that we cannot judge accurately, for lack of knowledge of the inner nature of things; but, as I have said more than once, we judge provisionally and often conjecturally. However, if we want to speak only of outward features, so as to say nothing[3] that isn't certain, then we have more freedom; and in that case to debate whether or not a difference is a specific one is to debate about a name. Taking this approach, there are such great differences amongst dogs that mastiffs and lap-dogs

[1] Added by Leibniz.   [2] Mentioned in Locke's §35.
[3] Taking 'rien de dire' as a slip for 'rien dire' (wrongly amended in the Academy edition).

325

can very well be said to be of different species. Yet it is not impossible that they are remote descendants of the same or similar breeds, which we would find if we could go back a long way, and that their ancestors were similar or the same, but that after much change some of their descendants became very large and others very small. In fact it would not be offending against reason to believe that they have in common an unchanging specific inner nature which is not further subdivided in our world,[1] i.e. which does not occur here as a component of various other such natures, and consequently which is further varied only by the addition of accidents; though nothing compels us to conclude that this is necessarily the situation with everything that we call a lowest species (*species infima*). But there is no *likelihood that a spaniel and an elephant come from a single ancestral line or that they have any such specific nature in common. So, when we talk about the different sorts of dogs in terms of appearances, we can distinguish their species, and when we talk in terms of inner essences we can remain uncertain; but when we compare a dog and an elephant we have no grounds for attributing to them, externally or internally, anything which would make us believe that they belonged to a single species. And so we have no grounds for hesitating to reject such a presumption. We could also distinguish species, logically speaking, among men; and if we laid stress on externals we should also find differences which, physically speaking, could count as specific. Thus there was an explorer who believed that Negroes, Chinese and American Indians had no ancestry in common with one another or with peoples resembling ourselves. But as we know the inner essence of man, namely reason, which resides in the individual man and is present in all men, and as we find among us no fixed inner feature which generates a subdivision, we have no grounds for thinking that the truth about their inner natures implies that there is any essential specific difference among men. Whereas such differences do obtain between man and beast – assuming that beasts are mere empirics, which they are according to the explanations I gave earlier [p. 271], and indeed experience gives us no grounds for any other judgment about them.

PHIL. Let us take the case of an artificial thing whose internal structure is known to us.[2] §39. 'A silent and a striking watch, are but one species, to those who have but one name for them: but he that has the name *watch* for one, and *clock* for the other,...[3] to him[4] they are different species.' It is the name and not the 'inward contrivance' which makes a new species; otherwise there would be too many species. 'There are some watches, that are made with four wheels, others with five.... Some have strings and fusees, and others none; some have the balance loose, and others regulated

326

---

[1] Taking '*ainsi*' to be a slip for '*ici*'. 　　　　[2] Added by Leibniz.
[3] Locke: 'and distinct complex ideas, to which those names belong'.
[4] Leibniz emphasizes the phrase translated by 'to him'.

by a spiral spring and others by hog's bristles: are any. . . [1] of these enough
to make a specific difference'? I say No, as long as these watches all agree
in bearing the name.

THEO. And I would say Yes; for, rather than attending much to the names,
I would prefer to consider the varieties of contrivance and in particular
how the balances differ; for now that the balance has been provided with
a spring that regulates its oscillations by means of its own, and thereby
makes them more equal, pocket-watches have changed in appearance and
have become incomparably more accurate. I once, myself, pointed out
another system of equalization which could be applied to watches ['Extract
from a letter concerning the principle of exactness in portable watches'].

PHIL. 'If any one will make. . .divisions from differences, that he knows
in the internal frame[, he can do so.] But yet they would be no distinct
species to men, ignorant of' how they are constructed.

THEO. I don't know why you and your associates always want to make
virtues, truths and species depend upon our opinion or knowledge. They
are present in nature, whether or not we know it or like it. To talk of them
in any other way is to change the names of things, and to change accepted
ways of speaking, without any cause. Until now men have probably
believed ˏthat there are several species of clocks or watches, without
learning how they are constructed or what they might be called.

PHIL. Still, you acknowledged not long ago [pp. 302, 321] that when we
try to distinguish physical species by appearances, we lay down arbitrary
limits for ourselves, whenever it seems appropriate – i.e. depending on
whether we find the difference more or less important, and on what our
purposes are. You yourself used the comparison with weights and measures,
which we organize and name according to our own good pleasure.

THEO. I have recently begun to understand you. [2] Between purely *logical*
specific differences, for which the slightest variation in definition is
sufficient, however accidental it may be, and purely *physical* specific
differences, which rest upon what is essential or unchangeable, we can
make room for an intermediate [kind of difference], but not one which we
can determine precisely. Our handling of it is governed by the weightiest
appearances, which are not entirely unchangeable but which do not change
readily, some coming closer than others to what is essential. And since some
connoisseurs make finer discriminations than others, the whole affair is
relative to men and appears to be arbitrary; which makes it appear
convenient that the use of names should be governed by these principal
differences. So we could speak of them as *civil* specific differences and as

327

---

[1] Locke: 'or all'.
[2] Reading *'depuis le temps'* as *'depuis quelque temps'*, as in the latest version in Leibniz's
own hand.

nominal species; but they must not be confused with what I earlier called *nominal definitions* [p. 295], which pertain to logical specific differences as well as to physical ones. Also, in addition to everyday usage, the laws themselves can authorize the significations of words, and then species would become *legal*, like the contracts which are called *nominati*, i.e. designated by a particular name. Or like Roman law making puberty begin at fourteen years of age. This whole line of thought deserves respect, but I do not see that it does very much here; for, apart from the fact that you have appeared to me to apply it in some cases where it does nothing, one will reach pretty much the same conclusion by recognizing that men are free to subdivide as far as they find appropriate and to abstract from additional differences without needing to deny that they exist, and that they are also free to choose the determinate in place of the indeterminate, so as to establish various notions and measures by giving them names.

328

PHIL. I am glad that we are no longer as far apart on this point as we appeared to be. §41. And so far as I can see, sir, you will also grant me that artificial things have species, as well as natural ones – contrary to the view of some philosophers.[1] §42. But before leaving the names of substances, I will add that of all our various ideas, only the ideas of substances have proper, i.e. individual, names. For it seldom happens that men need to make frequent references to any individual quality or to some other accidental individual.[2] Furthermore, individual actions perish straight away, and the concatenations of states of affairs which occur in them do not persist as in substances.

THEO. In certain cases, though, there has been a need to remember an individual accident, and it has been given a name. So your rule usually holds good but admits of exceptions. Religion provides us with some: for instance, the birth of Jesus Christ, the memory of which we celebrate every year; the Greeks called this event 'Theogony', and gave the name 'Epiphany' to the event of the adoration of the Magi. And the Hebrews applied the word 'Passah' especially to the passing over of the angel which caused the death of the Egyptians' first-born without harming those of the Hebrews; and this is the event whose memory they have been obliged to celebrate year after year. As for 'the species of artificial things', the scholastic philosophers raised objections to their being included under their categories. But their scruples were hardly necessary, since the tables of categories ought to provide a general survey of our ideas. Nevertheless, it is just as well to recognize the difference between perfect substances and the collections of substances (*aggregata*) which are substantial entities put together[3] by nature or by human artifice. For nature also contains such

---

[1] Phrase added by Leibniz.   [2] Locke adds: 'when it is absent.'
[3] '*composés*', which can also be an adjective meaning 'composite'.

aggregations: for instance, 'imperfectly mixed bodies' (*imperfecta mixta*), as our philosophers call them, which are not *unum per se* and do not have in themselves a perfect unity. I believe, however, that the four bodies they call elements, which they believe to be simple, as well as the salts, metals and other bodies which they believe to be perfectly mixed, with their ingredients in fixed proportions, are not *unum per se* either – particularly since we should regard them as only apparently uniform and homogeneous, and even a homogeneous body would still be an aggregation. In a word, perfect unity should be reserved for animate bodies, or bodies endowed with primary entelechies; for such entelechies bear some analogy to souls, and are as indivisible and imperishable as souls are. And I have shown elsewhere [e.g. 'New system of the nature and communication of substances' p. 456] that their organic bodies are really machines, although as much superior to the artificial ones which we design as is the Designer of those natural ones to us. For the machines of nature are as imperishable as souls themselves, and the animal together with its soul persists for ever. I can explain my meaning better with the help of a pleasant though very silly example: it is as if someone tried to strip Harlequin on the stage but could never finish the task because he had on so many costumes, one on top of the other; though the infinity of replications of its organic body which an animal contains are not as alike as suits of clothes, and nor are they arranged one on top of another, since nature's artifice is of an entirely different order of subtlety. This all shows that the philosophers were not utterly mistaken when they made so great a separation between artificial bodies and natural bodies endowed with true unity. But it fell to our age alone to unravel this mystery, and to demonstrate its importance and its consequences for the sound establishment of natural theology and of what is called *pneumatology, in a truly natural manner and in conformity with what we can experience and understand. It does not deprive us of any of the important considerations which should arise out of natural theology and pneumatology; rather, it enhances them, as does the system of pre-established harmony. And I believe that we cannot conclude this long discussion of the names of substances on a better note than that.

329

Chapter vii
'Of particles.'

PHILALETHES. §1. Besides words which name ideas, ones are needed which 'signify the connection [of] ideas, or propositions.... *Is*, and *is not*, are the general marks of' affirmation or negation. But as well as the parts of propositions, the mind connects whole sentences or propositions, §2. by means of words which express this connection[1] of various affirmations

---

[1] Locke: 'whereby [the mind] signifies what connection'. Coste's change.

and negations. These are 'called *particles*: and 'tis in the right use of these' that principally 'consists the art of well speaking.'[1] If reasonings are to be consecutive and methodical, we 'must have words to show... connection, restriction, distinction, opposition, emphasis, etc.'. When someone makes mistakes with these, he puzzles his hearer.

330

THEOPHILUS. I agree that the particles which connect propositions do valuable work, but I doubt that the art of speaking well consists principally in that. Suppose someone utters nothing but aphorisms or disconnected propositions. (This is often done in the universities and in what jurists cal' *articulated* pleadings, and it also occurs in the points which are put to witnesses.) As long as he arranges these propositions carefully, he will make himself almost as well understood as if he had connected them up and put in particles, since these are supplied by the reader. But I grant that the reader would be confused if the particles were put in wrongly, and much more so than if they were left out. If seems to me, too, that particles connect not only the component propositions of a discourse, and the component ideas of a proposition, but also the parts of an idea made up of other ideas variously combined. This last sort of connection is signified by *prepositions*, whereas *adverbs* govern affirmation, and negation when it occurs in the verb, and *conjunctions* govern the connections between various affirmations and negations. But no doubt you have noticed all this yourself, even though your words seem to say something different.

PHIL. §3. The part of grammar which deals with particles has been less cultivated than that which methodically sets forth 'cases and genders, moods and tenses, gerunds and supines[. It is true that] particles...in some languages, have been, with great show of exactness, ranked' under headings according to distinct subdivisions. But it is not enough to go through such lists.[2] A man must reflect on his own thoughts, and observe the 'postures of his mind in discoursing'; for particles are all marks of the action of the mind.[3]

THEO. It is quite true that the doctrine of particles is important, and I wish that it had been gone into in greater detail, for nothing would be more apt to reveal the various forms of the understanding. Genders are of no significance in philosophical grammar; but cases correspond to prepositions, and through them there is often a preposition contained in a noun, absorbed in it so to speak; and other particles are concealed in the inflections of verbs.

PHIL. §4. To explain particles properly, it is not enough 'to render them, as is usually in dictionaries, by words of another tongue which [come]

[1] From Locke's marginal summary.
[2] Sentence added by Coste.   [3] Clause based on Locke's §4.

nearest...: for what [precisely][1] is meant by them, is...as hard to be understood in one, as another language.' Besides, the significations of related words in two languages are not always exactly the same and even vary within a single language. I remember that in the Hebrew tongue there is a particle with only one letter, which is reckoned to have more than fifty significations.

THEO. Learned men have devoted themselves to writing whole books on Latin, Greek and Hebrew particles. The famous jurist *Strauch has written a book about the use of particles in jurisprudence, where the significations of words are of great importance. One usually finds, though, that people offer to explain them by means of examples and synonyms rather than by distinct notions. Nor can one always find a signification for them which is general – 'formal', as the late M. Bohl called it – and valid for every instance. But in spite of that, we could reduce all the uses of a word to a determinate number of significations; and that is what we ought to do.

PHIL. Indeed the number of significations greatly exceeds that of particles. §5. In English the particle *but* has very different significations. First, when I say '*BUT to say no more*: here it intimates a stop of the mind, in the course it was going, before it came to the end of it. Secondly [if I say] *I saw BUT two planets*: here it shows, that the mind limits the sense to what is expressed, with a negation of all other. Thirdly, [when I say] *You pray; BUT it is not that God would bring you to the true religion...*, *BUT that he would confirm you in your own*: the first of these *BUTS*, intimates a supposition in the mind, of something otherwise than it should be; the latter shows, that the mind makes a direct opposition between that, and what goes before it. [Fourthly] *All animals have sense; BUT a dog is an animal*: here it signifies...that the latter proposition is joined to the former'.[2]

THEO. The French *mais* could have been substituted in all these contexts except the second; but the German *allein*, used as a particle, signifies something combining 'but' with 'only', and it can certainly replace 'but' in all these examples except the last, where one might hesitate a little. 'But' is also sometimes expressed in German by *aber* and sometimes by *sondern* – which signifies separation or segregation and is not far from the particle *allein*. An abstract account of the kind we have just given here is not enough for a thorough explication of the particles: what we need is a paraphrase which can be substituted for the particle, just as a definition can be put in place of the defined expression. If we devote ourselves to

331

332

---

[1] Added by Coste.
[2] Coste replaces the examples in this section by French ones. Leibniz gives the English examples and explains them in French.

seeking and formulating these 'substitutable paraphrases' for all particles in so far as they admit of them, *then* we shall have dealt with the significations of particles. Let us try to do something like this with our four examples. In the first what is meant is: 'Let this much be said about it and no more' (*non piu*). In the second: 'I saw only two planets and no more.' In the third: 'You pray to God for one reason only, namely to be confirmed in your religion, and no more, etc.' In the fourth, it is as though one said: 'All animals have sense; we need to consider only this, no more being required. The dog is an animal. Therefore it has sense.' Thus, each of these examples indicates a limit, a *non plus ultra*, whether in things or in speech. In French *but* is an end, a finishing-post, as though the thought were 'Stop, we are there, we have arrived at our goal [*but*], why go further?' *But, Bute* is an old Teutonic word which signifies something fixed, a stopping-place. '*Beuten*' (an archaic word still to be found in some church hymns) means to abide. *Mais* comes from *magis*,[1] as if we meant: 'As for the remainder, we shall have to leave it', which amounts to saying: 'We need no more of it', 'That is enough of that', 'Let us turn to something else', or 'That is something else'. But since languages vary extraordinarily in their use of particles, we would have to look into examples in great detail if we were to deal adequately with the significations of particles. In French they avoid repeating *mais* with the aid of *cependant*. They would say 'You pray, but [*cependant*] not to learn the truth but [*mais*] to be confirmed in your opinion.' The Latin *sed* used often to be expressed by *ains*, which is the Italian *anzi*; when the French abolished *ains* they deprived their language of a useful expression. For instance: 'Nothing was certain, but [*cependant*] they were convinced of what I have told you, because people like to believe what they want to be the case; but [*mais*] it turned out that it was not so, but [*ains*] rather, etc.'

333 PHIL. §6. My intention has been to dwell only very briefly on this topic. I might add that often 'particles, some...constantly, and others in certain constructions, have the sense of a whole sentence contained in them.'

THEO. But when it is a 'complete sense', I believe that it is achieved through a sort of ellipsis. In my opinion, only interjections – like 'Ah!' or 'Alas!' – can stand on their own and say everything in a single word. When we say 'But', without adding anything further, it is an elliptical way of saying 'But let's wait and see – let's not applaud too soon'. The Latin *nisi* is somewhat similar: *si nisi non esset*, 'If it weren't for the *but*...'. In any case, sir, I would not have minded your going into a little more detail about the turns of thought that reveal themselves so wonderfully in our use of particles. But since we have reason to hurry, so as to complete this investigation of words and return to things, I don't want to hold you here

---

[1] Latin for 'more'.

any longer; although I really believe that languages are the best mirror of the human mind, and that a precise analysis of the significations of words would tell us more than anything else about the operations of the understanding.

Chapter viii
'Of abstract and concrete terms.'

PHILALETHES. §1. It remains to be noted that terms are either abstract or concrete. 'Each abstract idea [is] distinct, so that of any two the one can never be the other[:] the mind will,[1] by its intuitive knowledge, perceive their difference; and therefore...no two [of these][2] ideas can ever be affirmed one of another. [Everybody at once sees][3] the falsehood of these propositions; *Humanity is animality*, or *rationality*.... This is as evident, as any of the most allowed maxims.'

THEOPHILUS. There is something to be said about this, though. It is agreed that fairness is a virtue, a disposition (*habitus*), a quality, an accident, etc. Thus, two abstract terms can be asserted one of the other. Now, I always distinguish two sorts of abstract terms: *logical* and *real*. *Real abstract* terms, or at least those which are conceived as real, are either essences or parts of an essence, or else accidents – i.e. beings added to a substance. *Logical abstract* terms are predications reduced to single terms – as I might say 'to-be-man', 'to-be-animal' – and taken in this way we can assert one of the other: 'To be man is to be animal'. But with realities we cannot do this. We cannot say that *humanity*, or *manness* if you like, which is the whole essence of man, is *animality*, which is only a part of that essence. However, these abstract incomplete beings signified by real abstract terms also have their genera and species, and these are equally expressed by real abstract terms. So they can be predicated of one another, as I have shown by means of the example of fairness and virtue.

PHIL. §2. It can still be said that substances have only a few abstract names. A few – *humanity, animality, corporeity* – have been used in the Schools, but they have never obtained 'the licence of public approbation'.

THEO. The point is that only a few of these terms were needed to serve as examples and to illuminate the general notion, which it would have been wrong to ignore entirely. If the ancients did not use the word 'humanity' in the scholastic sense, they said 'human nature', which is the same thing. And they certainly also said 'divinity' or at least 'divine nature'. And when theologians needed to talk about these two natures, and about real

334

---

[1] Locke: 'each abstract idea being distinct..., the mind will', implying that the first clause explains the second.
[2] Locke: 'whole'. Coste's change.
[3] Locke: 'Every one, at first hearing, perceives'. Coste's change.

accidents, abstract entities took hold in the philosophical and theological schools – perhaps more than they should have.

Chapter ix
'Of the imperfection of words.'

PHILALETHES. §§ 1–2. We have already spoken of the double use of words. 'The first [is] for the recording our own thoughts for the help of our own memories, whereby...we talk to ourselves'. The other is 'for the communicating of our thoughts to others' by means of speech. It is in these two uses that we see 'the perfection, or imperfection of words'. When we are talking only to ourselves, it does not matter what words are used, provided that the meaning of each word is remembered and held constant. §3. Further, the communicative use of words is also of two sorts, civil and philosophical. The civil use consists in the conversation and practice of civil life. 'The philosophical use of words [is] such an use of them, as may serve to convey...precise notions', and to express certain truths in general propositions.

THEOPHILUS. Very good. Words are just as much reminders (*notae*) for oneself – in the way that numerals and algebraic symbols might be – as they are signs for others; and the use of words as signs occurs when general precepts are being applied in daily life, i.e. applied to individual cases, as well as when one is trying to discover or to verify these precepts. The former is a 'civil' and the latter a 'philosophical' use of signs.

PHIL. §5. Here are the principal cases where it is hard to learn and retain the idea which each word stands for. (1) Where the ideas are very composite; (2) where those ideas which make up a new one have no natural connection with one another,[1] 'and so no settled standard, any where in nature existing, to rectify and adjust them by'; (3) where the 'standard is not easy to be known'; (4) 'where the signification of the word, and the real essence...are not exactly the same.' The denominations of modes are more 'liable to doubtfulness and imperfection, for the two first of these reasons; and [those] of substances...for the two latter.' §6. When ideas of modes are highly complex, as are those of most moral words, they 'have seldom, in [the minds of] two different men, the same precise signification'. §7. The lack of 'standards' also makes these words ambiguous.[2] He who first invented the word *snub* understood it as he thought fit; and those who followed him in using it were not told precisely what he meant, nor did he show them any fixed pattern. §8. 'Common use regulates the meaning of words pretty well for common conversation;' but there is nothing

---

[1] Taking '*avec elles*' to be a slip for '*entre elles*'.
[2] Locke: 'various and doubtful'. Coste: '*équivoques*'.

335

precise about this, and there are daily disputes about which signification best fits the 'propriety of speech'. Many people speak of *glory*, but few of them agree in what they mean by it. **§9.** In many men's mouths they are 'little more than bare sounds', or at best they have very 'undetermined' significations. In a discourse or conversation about *honour, faith, grace, religion, church*, especially when there is controversy, it can be seen at once that men use the same terms to express different notions. And if it is hard to grasp the senses of terms used by one's contemporaries, it is even harder to understand the writings of antiquity. **§10.** It is just as well that we can do without the latter except when they contain something we are required to believe or to do.

THEO. Those are good remarks. With regard to ancient writings, though, we need to understand Holy Scripture above all things, and Roman law is still actively employed throughout a good part of Europe; and that in itself involves us in consulting many other ancient writings – rabbinical and patristic texts, and even secular histories. The ancient physicians are also worth understanding. The Greeks' way of practising medicine has come down to us from the Arabs: the spring-water was muddied in the Arab rivulets, and has had many impurities removed by recourse to the Greek originals. Nevertheless, these Arabs are useful all the same; it is said that *Ebenbitar, in his books about simples which were copied from Dioscorides, often makes him clearer. After religion and history, then, I find that it is principally in medicine – in its empirical aspects – that we can profit from what is passed on by the ancients and preserved in writing, and from other people's observations generally. That is why I have always had a great respect for physicians who are also steeped in the knowledge of ancient times; and it was most vexing to me that Reinesius, who excelled in both fields, preferred to work on explaining the rituals and the history of the ancients, rather than on recovering some part of their knowledge of nature – a task which he has shown that he could also have performed with marvellous success. When the day comes that the Romans, Greeks, Hebrews, and Arabs have been used up, the Chinese will come to the fore with their ancient books, and will furnish materials for the curiosity of occidental scholars. And then there are various old books by Persians, Armenians, Copts, and Brahmins; these will be dug up some day, so that we shall not neglect any light which antiquity might cast, through the transmission of its teachings and from the chronicles of events. And when there are no more ancient books to examine, their place will be taken by mankind's most ancient monument – languages. Eventually every language in the universe will be recorded, and contained in dictionaries and grammars; and comparisons will be made amongst them. This will be extremely useful for the knowledge of things, since their properties are

336

337 often reflected in their names (as can be seen from the names of plants among different nations), as well as for the knowledge of our mind and of the marvellous variety of its operations. Not to mention the origins of peoples, which will be discovered through well-grounded etymologies which can best be gained by comparing languages; but I have already spoken of this [p. 285]. All of that displays the usefulness and the extent of textual scholarship; yet some philosophers – able ones, too – hold it in low regard and feel free to speak slightingly of 'rabbinizing' and of philology generally. It is also evident that scholars will not run out of profitable materials for a long time to come, and that they ought not to while away the time with minutiae when there are so many more satisfying topics to work on; though I fully realize that sometimes the scholars must attend to minutiae as a means to more important discoveries. It is because textual scholarship rests largely on the significations of words and on the interpreting of authors, especially ancient ones, that our discussion of words together with your remark about the ancients led me to touch on this important topic. But to return now to your four defects in naming, let me tell you, sir, that they are all remediable, especially since the invention of writing, and that it is only because of our carelessness that they still occur. For we have the option of fixing significations, at least in some learned language, and of agreeing on them, so as to pull down this Tower of Babel. But there are two defects which are harder to remedy: one consists in the doubt which arises as to whether certain ideas are compatible, if experience has never provided us with all of them combined in a single subject; the other consists in the need for provisional definitions of sensible things, if one's experience of them has not sufficed for one to have more complete definitions of them; but I have already spoken more than once of each of these defects.

PHIL. What I am about to tell you will throw a certain amount of further light on the defects you have just pointed out. Also, of the defects which I indicated, the third one seems to imply that these definitions are provisional: it is when we have insufficient knowledge of our sensible standards, i.e. of substantial entities in corporeal nature. This defect also involves our not knowing whether it is permissible to combine sensible qualities which nature has not combined, because one's understanding of them is superficial.[1] §11. Well, then, if the signification of words standing for composite modes is doubtful because of the lack of standards which exhibit that same composition, the signification of the names of substantial entities[2] is doubtful for a quite opposite reason, namely that they have to signify something which is 'supposed conformable to the reality of things, and [have to be][3] referred to standards made by nature.'

---

[1] Added by Leibniz.   [2] Locke: 'substances'.   [3] Locke: 'are'.

THEO. I have already remarked more than once during our earlier conversations that that is not essential to ideas of substances; but I do concede that the most reliable and useful ideas are those which are modelled on nature.

PHIL. §12. When one does follow standards entirely made by nature, with the imagination being needed only to store representations of them,[1] the names of substantial entities[2] have, as has been shown, 'a double reference in their ordinary use.' The first is that they stand for 'the real [inner][3] constitution of things'. But this standard cannot be known, and so cannot govern significations.

THEO. That is not what we are concerned with now, since we are discussing ideas for which we do have standards. The thing has its inner essence, but it is not in dispute that it cannot serve as a pattern.

PHIL. §13. The second reference which the names of substantial entities[4] have is their immediate reference to the simple ideas that exist together in the substance. But as the number of such ideas that are united in the same subject is very large, those who speak of that one subject have very different ideas of it. This happens both through differences in the combinations of simple ideas that they make and also because most qualities of bodies consist in their powers to make changes in, or receive them from, other bodies. Look at the alterations that one of the baser metals can be put through by the operation of fire; and it can undergo more still at the hands of a chemist, by the application of other bodies. Again, one person is satisfied with colour and weight for the recognition of *gold*, another brings ductility and fixedness into it, a third believes that solubility in *aqua regia should be taken into account. §14. Also, as things often resemble one another, it is sometimes difficult to indicate exactly how they differ.

THEO. Indeed, since bodies are susceptible of being altered, disguised, falsified, counterfeited, it is very important to be able to distinguish and to recognize them. Gold is disguised in solution, but it can be recovered either by precipitating it or by distilling the water; and counterfeit or adulterated gold is recognized or purified by the assayers' art. Since this art is not known to everyone, it is no wonder that men do not all have the same idea of gold. As a rule, only the experts have sufficiently accurate ideas of a given material.

PHIL. §15. This variety, however, causes less trouble in everyday transactions than in philosophical inquiries.

---

[1] Added by Leibniz.
[3] Added by Leibniz.
[2] Locke: 'substances'.
[4] Locke: 'substances'.

THEO. It would be easier to bear if it made no practical difference. But in practice it often matters that one should not be fobbed off with a substitute, and thus that one should either know the signs of the thing or have access to people who know them. This is especially important in connection with drugs and costly substances which may be needed in important situations. It is with terms of a more general kind that the philosophical troubles become evident.

PHIL. §18. The names of simple ideas are less prone to ambiguity,[1] and mistakes are rarely made with the terms 'white', 'bitter', and so on.

THEO. Yet the fact is that these terms are not entirely free of uncertainty. I called attention earlier [p. 298] to the example of adjacent colours which lie within the confines of two genera, their own genus being 'doubtful'.[2]

PHIL. §19. 'The names of simple modes are next to those of simple ideas, least liable to doubt[, as for instance][3] those of figure and number'. §20. But all the trouble arises from composite modes and substances. §21. It will be said that rather than imputing these imperfections to words, we should lay the blame on our understanding; but I reply that words 'interpose themselves so much between our [mind] and the truth' of things that they are comparable with the medium through which rays from[4] visible objects pass, which 'does not seldom cast a mist before our eyes .... I am apt to imagine, that were the imperfections of language...more thoroughly weighed, [the majority of controversies] would of themselves cease; and the way to knowledge, and, perhaps, peace too, lie a great deal opener'.

THEO. I believe that controversies which are carried on in writing could be brought to an end right now if men would agree on certain rules and would take care to carry them out. But there would have to be changes in language if we were to conduct ourselves in a precise way in unprepared spoken discourse. I have explored that topic elsewhere [e.g. *On the Combinatorial Art* pp. 10f].

PHIL. §22. Until there is reform – and the time for it will not be soon[5] – this uncertainty of words should teach us moderation, especially with regard to imposing upon others our own interpretations of ancient authors; since one finds in the Greek authors that almost every one of them speaks a different language.

THEO. What has surprised me, on the contrary, is how much similarity one finds among Greek authors as distant from one another in time and place as Homer, Herodotus, Strabo, Plutarch, Lucian, Eusebius, Procopius, and

[1] Locke: 'mistakes'. Coste: '*équivoque*'.
[2] 'Doubtful' occurs in the marginal summary of Locke's §18.
[3] Locke: 'especially'.
[4] '*rayons des*' added by Coste.   [5] Added by Leibniz.

339

Photius; whereas the Latin writers changed so much, and the Germans, English and French even more. The fact is that right from the time of Homer, and even more when Athens was in its prime, the Greeks had good writers who were taken as models by subsequent generations – in writing, at least, for the everyday language of the Greeks must surely have been greatly changed even under Roman domination. That is also the reason 340 why Italian has changed less than French: the Italians, having had writers with lasting reputations, have imitated and still admire Dante, Petrarch, Boccaccio, and other authors from a period whose French writers are no longer read.

Chapter x
'Of the abuse of words.'

PHILALETHES. §1. Besides the natural imperfections of language, there are others which are 'wilful' and arise from 'neglect'. To make such poor use of words is to *abuse* them. §2. The first and most palpable abuse is the failure to associate a word with a clear idea. Words of this kind fall into two classes. One consists of the words which have never had any determinate idea, whether in their origin or in their ordinary use. Most of the sects of philosophy and religion have introduced some of these,[1] 'to support some strange opinions, or cover some weakness of their hypothesis'. Yet in the mouths of the members of sects they are 'distinguishing characters'. §3. There are other words which did at first have clear ideas in common usage, but which have since become associated with very important matters without any definite ideas being annexed to them.[2] This is how the words *wisdom, glory* and *grace* often occur in men's mouths.

THEOPHILUS. I believe there are fewer words lacking in signification than you think, and with a little care and the right attitude one could fill the gaps, i.e. remove the indeterminacies. *Wisdom* appears to be nothing but knowledge [*science*] of happiness. *Grace* is a benefit extended to those who have done nothing to deserve it but are in a condition where they need it. And *glory* is the renown of someone's excellence.

PHIL. I do not want to consider now whether there is anything to be said about those definitions. I am more concerned to point out the causes of the abuse of words. §4. Firstly, words are learned before the ideas which belong to them; and children, accustomed to this from their cradles, continue to do so all their lives; and all the more because they can still make themselves understood in conversation without ever having fixed their

---

[1] Locke: 'These, for the most part, the several sects of philosophy and religion have introduced'. Coste's change.

[2] Apparently based on a misunderstanding of Locke, who is not clear at this point.

ideas, by using a variety of different expressions to get others to grasp what they mean. Yet this 'fills their discourse with abundance of empty . . . noise . . . especially in moral matters. . . . Men take the words they find in use amongst their neighbours[, so] that they may not seem ignorant what they stand for, [and] use them confidently,[1] without [giving them] a certain

341 fixed meaning[. And] as in such discourses they seldom are in the right, so they are as seldom to be convinced, that they are in the wrong'. Trying to extricate them from their mistakes is like trying to dispossess a vagabond.

THEO. In fact, it is so unusual for anyone to take the trouble that would be needed for a good understanding of terms, or words, that I have sometimes been amazed that children can learn languages so early, and that they still speak so correctly when they are grown up; considering how little trouble is taken to instruct children in their native tongue, and how little thought adults give to getting sharp definitions (especially since the definitions taught in the schools are usually not of words which are in general use). Another point: I agree that men quite often fall into error, even when engaged in serious dispute and speaking from conviction. Yet I have also noticed that when people engage in disputes on theoretical questions which lie within their intellectual range, it also quite often happens that all the disputants on both sides of the issue are correct in everything except the mutual opposition arising from the misunderstanding of each others' opinions, which in turn arises from poor use of terms and sometimes also from contentiousness and a passion for getting the upper hand.

PHIL. §5. Secondly, the use of words is sometimes *inconstant*. This happens all too often among the learned; but ''tis plain cheat and abuse,' and if it is done wilfully it is 'folly, or . . . dishonesty.' If someone did this in numerical calculations – for instance taking an X to be a V – I wonder who would have anything to do with him?

THEO. This abuse is so common, not only among the learned but also in the world at large, that I think it arises from bad habits and carelessness rather than from dishonesty. Usually the different significations of a single word are akin to one another, so that one gets taken for another, and speakers do not pause to think as accurately as one would like them to about what they are saying. People are accustomed to figures of speech, and are easily carried away by elegant turns of phrase and spurious brilliancies.

342 This is because they are usually in pursuit less of the truth than of pleasure, entertainment and outward appearance; and an element of vanity comes into it too.

[1] Locke: 'Men take . . . ; and that they may not seem . . . , use them confidently'.

PHIL. **§6.** The third abuse is 'an *affected obscurity*, by either applying old words, to...unusual significations;' or introducing new terms without explaining them. The ancient Sophists, who were so justly ridiculed by Lucian, claimed to talk about everything, and hid their ignorance under the veil of verbal obscurity.[1] Among the philosophical sects, the *peripatetic one has made itself conspicuous by this fault, yet other sects, even among the modern ones, have not been wholly clear of it. For example, there are people who abuse the term 'extension' and find it necessary to confound it with 'body'. **§7.** Logic, i.e. the art of disputing, which has been so highly esteemed, has helped to maintain obscurity. **§8.** Those who are given to it have been useless, or rather harmful, to society at large. **§9.** Whereas craftsmen,[2] so despised by the learned, have been useful to human life. Yet these obscure doctors have been admired by the ignorant; and they have been believed to be invincible because they were armed with briars and thorns which it would have been painful to plunge into. For them 'there is no other defence left for absurdity, but obscurity.' **§12.** The mischief of it is that this art of making words obscure has 'perplexed...those two great rules [of human action], religion and justice.'

THEO. Your complaints are largely justified. Yet there are, though rarely, obscurities which are pardonable and even laudable – as when someone avowedly speaks in riddles when there is point in riddling. Pythagoras used them in that way, and so do the oriental philosophers, more or less. Alchemists who call themselves 'adepts' declare that they do not wish to be understood by any but the 'sons of the art', which would be well enough if the self-appointed sons of the art did have the key to the code. A certain obscurity might be permissible, but it must hide something which is worth trying to discover, and the riddle must be solvable. But *religion* and *justice* require perspicuous ideas. The tangled condition of religious and legal doctrines seems to be due to the unsystematic way they are taught, and they may have been harmed more by the indeterminateness of terms than by obscurity. As for *logic*: since it is the art which teaches us how to order 343 and connect our thoughts, I see no grounds for laying blame upon it. On the contrary, men's errors are due rather to their lack of logic.

PHIL. **§14.** The fourth abuse is when words are taken for things, that is, when terms are believed to correspond to the real essence of substances. 'Who is there, that has been bred up in the peripatetic philosophy, who does not think the ten names [which signify the categories][3] to be exactly conformable to the nature of things?...that *substantial forms, vegetative souls, abhorrence of a vacuum, intentional species,* etc. are something real?

[1] Sentence based on Locke's §8.
[2] Locke: 'the...mechanic'. Coste: '*la mécanique*'. Leibniz: '*les hommes mécaniques*'.
[3] Locke uses 'predicaments', in its now virtually obsolete sense of 'categories'.

...The Platonists have their *soul of the world*, and the Epicureans their *endeavour towards motion* in their atoms, when at rest.' If the 'aerial and aetherial vehicles' of Dr *More had prevailed anywhere in the world, they would equally have been believed to be real.

THEO. That is not, strictly speaking, a matter of taking words to be things, but rather of believing something to be true when it is not. It is an error which is too common among men in general; but it is not a matter of mere abuse of words, and consists of something else altogether. The scheme of the categories is a very useful one, and we should think of improving them rather than of rejecting them. It might be that all that is needed are five general headings for beings – namely substance, quantity, quality, action or passion, and relation – together with any which can be formed from those by composition; and in your own setting out of ideas weren't you trying to present them as categories? I have spoken above of 'substantial forms' [pp. 317f]. And I doubt that there are good enough grounds for rejecting 'vegetative souls', given that there are experienced and judicious people who recognize a strong analogy between plants and animals, and given that you yourself, sir, have appeared to admit that beasts have souls. The 'abhorrence of a vacuum' can be understood in a legitimate way, thus: on the assumption that all the spaces in nature have at some time been filled, and that bodies cannot interpenetrate and cannot shrink, nature cannot allow a vacuum; and I hold that those three assumptions are well founded. But the same cannot be said for the 'intentional species' which are supposed to let the soul interact with the body; though perhaps one might tolerate the 'sensible species' which travel from the object to the distant sense-organ, tacitly understanding this as the propagation of motion. I grant that Plato's 'soul of the world' does not exist, since God is above the world – an extramundane or rather supramundane Intelligence. When you speak of the 'endeavour towards motion' of the Epicureans' atoms, I am not sure whether you have in mind the weight which they attributed to atoms by claiming that all bodies move by themselves in a single direction – which is certainly a groundless doctrine. The late Mr Henry More, the Anglican theologian, brilliant as he was, was a little too quick to fabricate inscrutable and implausible hypotheses – for instance his 'hylarchic principle' which explains the weight and elasticity of matter as well as other wonders which are found in it. I have nothing to say to you about his 'aetherial vehicles', whose nature I have not investigated.

PHIL. §15. An example concerning the word 'matter' will give you a better grasp of my thought. Matter is taken to be a being really existing 'in nature,[1] distinct from body; as 'tis [utterly] evident, the word *matter* stands

---

[1] Locke: '[a] thing really in nature'. Coste's change.

for an idea distinct from' body;[1] otherwise these two ideas could 'indifferently...be put for one another.' For one can say 'There is one matter of all bodies' but not 'There is one body of all matters'. Nor, I think, will it be said that 'one matter is bigger than another.' *Matter* expresses 'the substance and solidity of body, [and so] we no more conceive...of different matters...than we do of different solidities'. Nevertheless, as soon as *matter* was taken to be 'the name of something ...existing under that precision', that thought produced unintelligible discourses and tangled disputes concerning prime matter.

THEO. This example appears to me to count more in favour of the peripatetic philosophy than against it. If all silver were shaped – or rather, *because* all silver *is* shaped, by nature or by art – does that make it any less correct to say that silver is 'a being really existing in nature', distinct (taking it in its 'precision') from the goblet and the coin? And although the silver manifests the weight, sound, colour, fusibility, and several other qualities of the coin, that will not lead us to say that silver is nothing but some qualities of the coin. So it is not as useless as you think to reason in general *natural science about prime matter and to determine its nature–whether it is always uniform, whether it has any essential properties other than impenetrability (in fact I have shown ['On nature itself' pp. 503f], following Kepler, that it also has what could be called 'inertia'), and so on – despite the fact that it never occurs naked and unadorned; just as it would be permissible to theorize about pure silver even if we never found any and had no methods for purifying silver. So I have nothing against Aristotle's speaking of prime matter [e.g. *Metap.* Z, 1029[a]]; but it is impossible to withhold some blame from those who have made too much of it, and have built illusions on the foundation of misunderstood words of this philosopher. Perhaps he has sometimes unduly laid himself open to these misconceptions and to high-sounding nonsense. Still, you should not so greatly exaggerate the faults of this famous writer, because it is known that several of his works were not completed or made public by him.

345

PHIL. §17. The fifth abuse is to put words 'in the place of things, which they do or can by no means signify.' This occurs when by the names of substances we would mean 'something more than this, that *what I call gold is malleable*' (though fundamentally *gold* then signifies nothing more than that which is malleable),[2] purporting to convey 'that malleableness depends on...the real essence of gold.' Thus we say that Aristotle's definition of 'man' as 'rational animal' is a good one, and that Plato's as 'two-legged animal with broad nails, and without feathers' is bad.

---

[1] Locke: 'the idea of body'.
[2] Locke is misrepresented in the sentence down to here.

§18. There is hardly anybody who does not suppose these words 'to stand for a thing having the real essence, on which those properties depend.' Yet this is a plain abuse, since the real essence is not included in the complex idea which the word signifies.

THEO. Well, I should have thought it was obviously wrong to criticize this common usage, since it is quite true that the complex idea of gold includes its being something which has a real essence whose detailed constitution is unknown to us, except for the fact that such qualities as malleability depend upon it. But to assert its malleability without [merely asserting an] identity and without the defect of pleonasm or redundancy (see vi.17), one must recognize this stuff by other qualities, such as colour and weight. And then it is as though one said that a certain fusible, yellow and very heavy body which is called 'gold' has a nature which endows it with the further quality of being very soft to the hammer and with the capacity for being made extremely thin. As for the 'definition of man' which is laid at Plato's door – which he appears to have devised only as an exercise, and which I do not think that you, sir, would want seriously to put alongside the received definition – it is obviously rather too external and too provisional. For if that cassowary of which you were speaking a little while ago (vi.34) were found to have broad nails, it would be a man! There would be no need to pluck its feathers, as Diogenes is said to have wanted to pluck a cock in order to turn it into a Platonic man.

346 PHIL. **§19.** In composite modes, the very moment that any of the ideas is 'changed, it is allowed to be another thing'. This appears plainly in the words 'murder', an English word which like the German *Mord* signifies homicide by premeditation; 'manslaughter', which is etymologically equivalent to *homicide*, but which signifies homicide which is voluntary though not premeditated; and 'chance-medley' – literally, affray which happens by chance – which signifies unintentional homicide.[1] For what is expressed by such names is identical with what I believe to be in the thing itself; or, in terms I used earlier, the nominal essence is identical with the real essence. But it is not like that with the names of substances. For if one man puts into the idea of gold something which another leaves out, for example fixedness and solubility in aqua regia, people do not believe that therefore the species has been changed; they merely believe that one of the men has a more perfect idea than the other of what constitutes the hidden real essence which they take the name *gold* to refer to; despite the fact that this 'tacit reference' is useless and serves only to make trouble for us.

---

[1] These definitions of the three English words are Coste's. The remarks about *Mord*, the etymology of 'manslaughter', and the literal meaning of 'chance-medley', are Leibniz's. On 'chance-medley', both are wrong (see *OED*).

THEO. I believe I have already said this [p. 321], but I shall here again make plain to you that what you have just said, sir, applies to modes as well as to substantial entities, and that there are no grounds for finding fault with this reference to an inner essence. Here is an example of what I mean. One can define a 'parabola', in the geometers' sense, as a figure in which all the rays parallel to a certain straight line are brought together by reflection at a particular point, the 'focus'. But what that idea or definition expresses is not so much the figure's inner essence, i.e. something which could let us straight away grasp its origin, but rather an external feature, a result. Wishing to construct a figure which has such a resulting property, one might even wonder initially whether it is something possible; and for me that is what shows whether a definition is a merely *nominal* one, drawn from properties, or whether instead it is *real*. If someone who names the parabola knows it only through the definition I have just given, he is nevertheless using the word to mean a figure which has a certain construction or constitution – he does not know what it is, but he hopes to find out, so as to be able to draw it. Another person who studies it more deeply will add some further property: he will discover, for instance, that in the figure in question the ordinate and the normal drawn from the same point of the curve always cut off a constant length along the axis, and that this is equal to the distance between its vertex and focus. He will thus have a more perfect idea than the first person had, and he will have less difficulty in drawing the figure, though he may not be able to yet. But it will be agreed that it is the same figure, but that its constitution is still hidden. You see then, sir, that everything which you find and partly criticize in the use of words signifying substantial things is also present, and is obviously beyond criticism, in the use of words signifying composite modes. What has led you to believe that substances differ from modes is your neglect of intellectual modes, which are difficult to dissect,[1] which turn out to be just like bodies in this respect, though bodies are even more difficult to know. 347

PHIL. In that case I fear that I ought to stifle what I wanted to tell you, sir, about the cause of what I had believed to be an abuse. **§20.** It seemed to be due to our wrongly believing 'that nature [always] works regularly ...and sets the boundaries to each...species', by means of that specific essence or internal constitution which we imply to be there and which 'goes always with the same specific name'.

THEO. Well, you can clearly see from the example of geometrical modes, sir, that there is nothing much wrong with referring to specific inner essences; though sensible things – whether substances or modes – of which we have only provisional nominal definitions, and for which we do

---

[1] '*de difficile discussion*', presumably derived from the Latin *discussere*, to break up, to scatter.

not expect easily to find real ones, differ considerably from the intellectual modes which are difficult to dissect, since we can eventually arrive at the inner constitutions of geometrical figures.

PHIL. Now I do see that I would have been wrong to condemn this reference to essences and inner constitutions on the pretext that it turns our words into signs of a nonentity or of an unknown. For what is unknown in certain aspects may reveal itself in some other way, and a thing's inner nature does reveal itself to some extent through the appearances to which it gives rise. As for the question 'whether...a monstrous foetus be a man or no?'[1] – I see that even if one cannot answer it straight away, the species may for all that be quite determinate in itself, as our ignorance does not affect the nature of things.

348

THEO. It has indeed happened that very able geometers, while knowing several properties of certain figures which seemed to exhaust the topic, did not properly understand what figures they were. For instance, there were the curves called *'pearls', whose quadratures had even been given, as had the dimensions of their surfaces and of their solids of revolution, before it was realized that all that was involved was a combination of certain cubic parabolas. Thus, prior to that insight, when these pearls were considered to be a distinct species, there was only a provisional knowledge of them. If that can happen in geometry, is it any wonder that we find it difficult to determine the incomparably more composite species in corporeal nature?

PHIL. §22. We now come to the sixth abuse (I stay with the original numbering, although I see very well that some should be omitted). This common though little noticed abuse is that men, having by long-standing usage attached certain ideas to certain words, imagine that the connection is an obvious one and that everyone accepts it. This makes them think it very strange when they are asked the meanings of their terms, even when it is absolutely necessary to do so. There are few people who would not be offended by being asked what they mean when they speak of *life*. Yet their idea of it may be a vague one which is not sufficient if it is a question of knowing 'whether a plant, that lies ready formed in the seed, have life; [or] the embryo in an egg before incubation, or a man in a swoon without sense or motion'. And though men will not wish to appear so dull or so importunate as to need to ask for explanations of the terms that are being used; 'nor so troublesomely critical, as to correct others [incessantly][2] in the use of the words they receive from them', yet when one is engaged in accurate inquiry, such explanations must be undertaken. Often 'learned men of different parties..., in their arguings one with another, [merely]

---

[1] Locke's question in §21; but this concessive speech is Leibniz's work.
[2] Added by Coste.

speak different languages....They think all the same: though perhaps [their interests] be different.'

THEO. I believe I have expounded my views about the notion of life fully enough already [pp. 318, 328f]. Life must always be accompanied by perception in the soul; otherwise it will be only an appearance, like the life which the savages in America attributed to watches and clocks, or the life which was attributed to puppets by those magistrates who thought the puppets were animated by demons and who wanted to punish for sorcery the man who first gave such a performance in their town.

PHIL. §23. To conclude: words serve (1) to make our thoughts understood,[1] (2) to do this with ease, and (3) to provide a way into the knowledge[2] of things. We fail in the first respect when we have no steady, determinate ideas for our words, or none which are accepted and understood by others. §24. We fail in respect of ease when we have very complex ideas without having distinct names. This is often the fault of the languages themselves, because they do not contain the names; but in many cases the fault lies with the man, who does not know the names. When this happens, long paraphrases are needed.[3] §25. There is a failure in the third respect when the ideas which words signify do not agree with what is real. §26 (1) Someone who has terms without ideas is like one who has nothing but a list of book-titles. §27. (2) Someone who has very complex ideas would be like a man who had a stock of books uncollated and untitled, so that he could not indicate any book except by producing its pages one by one. §28. (3) Someone who is inconstant in his use of signs would be like a merchant who sold different things by the same name. §29. (4) Someone who attaches his own special ideas to words in common use will not be able to give others the benefit of any insights he may have. §30. (5) Someone whose head is full of ideas of substances which have never existed will not be able to advance in real knowledge. §§32–3. The first will speak vainly of the 'tarantula' or of 'charity'. The second will see new animals without being easily able to make them known to others. The third will take 'body' sometimes to be whatever is solid and sometimes to be whatever is merely extended; and he will use 'frugality' sometimes to designate a virtue and sometimes to designate the neighbouring vice. The fourth will call a mule by the name *horse*, and will describe as *generous* what everyone else calls *spendthrift*; and the fifth, on the authority of Herodotus, will search in Tartary for a nation of one-eyed men.[4] I would point out that the first four defects are common to the names of substances and of modes, whereas the last one is special to substances.

[1] Locke: 'known'.
[2] Locke: 'convey the knowledge'. Coste: *'faire entrer dans l'esprit...la connaissance'*. Leibniz: *'donner entrée dans la connaissance'*.
[3] Sentence added by Leibniz.   [4] The last example is Leibniz's.

THEO. These are very instructive remarks. I will add only that there seems to me to be something chimerical also in people's ideas of accidents or ways of being, so that the fifth defect is also common to substances and to accidents. *The Fanciful Shepherd* deserved that name not only because he believed there were nymphs hiding among the trees but also because he was constantly expecting romantic adventures to come his way.

PHIL. §34. I had meant to stop, but I recall a seventh and last abuse, which is that of 'figurative speeches, and allusion'. Yet this will hardly be regarded as an abuse, because people are more receptive to what they call wit and imagination than they are to dry truth. That is acceptable in discourses where the aim is merely to give pleasure; but fundamentally 'all the art of rhetoric, besides order and clearness,' all these artificial and figurative applications of words, serve only 'to insinuate wrong ideas, move the passions, and . . . mislead the judgment; and so indeed are [nothing but] perfect cheat'. Yet it is this deceptive art which is rewarded and given the highest esteem. The fact is that men hardly care about truth, and they greatly love to deceive and be deceived. So true is this that what I have said against this art will no doubt be regarded as great boldness on my part; for 'eloquence, like the fair sex, has too prevailing beauties in it, to suffer it self ever to be' opposed.

THEO. Far from disapproving of your zeal for the truth, I find it very proper. And it is to be hoped that it may have some effect. I do not entirely despair of that; because, sir, you seem to be fighting eloquence with its own weapons, having at your command an eloquence which is superior to the deceptive kind you are attacking. In the same way there was a Venus, daughter of Uranus, the mother of divine love, in whose presence that other bastard Venus – the mother of a blind love – could not appear with her blindfolded child [Plato, *Symposium* 180ᶜ]. But that very fact proves that your thesis needs to be moderated and that certain devices of eloquence are like the Egyptian vases which could be used in the worship of the true God. Painting and music are similarly misused: the former is often used to depict fantasies which are grotesque and even harmful, the latter has an enervating effect, and the amusement which each provides is trivial; but they can be usefully employed, one to make the truth vivid and the other to make it affecting – which latter should also be the effect of poetry, which involves both rhetoric and music.

351

Chapter xi
'Of the remedies of the foregoing imperfections and abuses.'

PHILALETHES. This is not the place to turn our discussion into an exploration of the uses of a true eloquence, still less to reply to your kind compliment. **§1.** We must look for remedies for the imperfections we have noticed in words, thus bringing our whole treatment of words to a close. **§2.** It would be ridiculous to attempt to reform languages, or to want to make men confine their speech to what they know. **§3.** But it is not too much to demand that philosophers speak with exactness when they are seriously pursuing the truth, for otherwise everything will be full of errors, stubborn prejudices and pointless wrangles. **§8.** The first remedy is never to use any word without associating an idea with it. Whereas such words as 'instinct', 'sympathy' and 'antipathy' are often used without being given any sense.

THEOPHILUS. This is a good rule, but I am not sure that your examples are apt. It seems to me that everyone understands 'instinct' to be an inclination which an animal has – with no conception of the reason for it – towards something which is suitable to it. And even men ought to pay more attention to these instincts: they occur in humans as well, though our artificial way of life has almost wiped out most of them, as is well pointed out in *Physician to Oneself*. 'Sympathy' and 'antipathy' signify whatever it is in bodies devoid of sense which is analogous to the instinct of animals to come together or move apart. And although we do not understand the causes of these inclinations or endeavours as well as might be wished, still we have a notion of them which is sufficient for intelligible discourse about them.

PHIL. **§§9–10.** The second remedy is that the names of modes should have ideas which are determinate, at least, and that the names of substances should have ideas which are also in conformity with what exists. If someone says that 'justice' is law-abiding conduct which affects the well-being of others, this idea is not determinate enough when one has no distinct idea of what is being called 'law'.

THEO. It could be remarked at this point that the 'law' is a prescription imparted to us by wisdom, i.e. by the science of happiness.

PHIL. **§11.** The third remedy is to use words, as far as possible, in ways conforming to their common use. **§12.** The fourth is to declare what sense one takes a word to have, whether one is making words anew, or is employing old ones in new senses, or has found that usage has not adequately fixed the signification [of some word]. **§13.** But there is a distinction to be made. **§14.** Words which cannot be defined – ones with simple ideas – are explained either through better-known synonyms or else by showing the things themselves. In this way one can make a peasant understand what colour *feuillemorte* is by telling him it is the colour of withered leaves falling in autumn. **§15.** The names of composite modes should be explained by definition, for that can be done. **§16.** That is how morality is capable of demonstration. In that context one takes a *man* to

352

be 'a corporeal rational being', without troubling about his outward shape. §17. For it is through definitions that matters of morality can be treated clearly. To define justice it will be better to be guided by the idea of it in one's mind than to seek some external model, such as Aristides, and frame an idea which copies him. §18. And since most composite modes do not exist anywhere together, the only way they can be settled is by definitions in which the scattered elements are enumerated. §19. With substances there are usually several 'leading or characteristical' qualities 'which we take to be the most distinguishing idea of that species' and 'to which we suppose the other ideas, which make up [the] complex idea of [the] species, annexed'. In animals and vegetables it is shape, in inanimate bodies colour, and in some it is shape and colour together. §20. That is why Plato's definition of *man* is more characteristic than[1] Aristotle's, and if it were not one ought not to 'kill monstrous births'. §21. Often, sight alone is enough, with no further scrutiny; for people who are accustomed to examining gold 'will frequently distinguish true from counterfeit, pure from adulterate, by the sight'.

THEO. No doubt everything rests upon definitions which eventually go back to ideas from which all the others are derived. There may be several definitions for a single subject; but to know that they do all fit the same thing, one must either use reason to derive one definition from another or learn from experience that they constantly go together. As for morality: one part of it is wholly grounded in reasons, but there is another part which rests on experiences and has to do with [people's] temperaments. In our knowledge of substances our first ideas come from shape and colour, i.e. from what is visible, because that is how one knows things from a distance; but they are usually too provisional, and in cases which are important to us we try to know the substance from less far away. I am surprised that you return once more to that definition of 'man' which is attributed to Plato, just after saying (§16) that in morality one should 'take a man to be a corporeal rational being, without troubling about his outward shape'. Another point: It is true that long practice does much for one's ability to distinguish 'by the sight' something which another person might have trouble knowing by means of arduous tests. An experienced physician with good eyesight and memory often knows from one glance at the patient something which another would laboriously extract from him by dint of asking questions and feeling his pulse. But it is good to assemble all the clues one can get.

PHIL. §22. I acknowledge that someone who learns all the qualities of gold from a competent assayer will have a better knowledge of it than eyesight could give him. But if we could learn what the inner constitution of gold

353

---

[1] Locke: 'as good a definition [as]'.

is,[1] 'the signification of the word *gold* [would][2] as easily[3] be ascertained, as that of *triangle*.'

THEO. It would be just as determinate [*déterminée*], and there would no longer be anything provisional about it; but it would not be as easily ascertained [*déterminée*]. For I believe that it would take a rather wordy definition to explain the structure of gold, just as there are, even in geometry, some figures with lengthy definitions.

PHIL. §23. 'Spirits, separate from bodies,' no doubt have more perfect knowledge than we do, though we have no notion of how they might acquire it. Still, they could 'have as clear ideas of the radical constitution of [bodies][4] as we have of a triangle'.

THEO. I have already pointed out to you [p. 212], sir, that I have reasons for thinking that no created spirits are entirely separated from bodies. Still, there are doubtless some whose organs and whose understandings are incomparably more perfect than ours, and who surpass us in all sorts of conceptions, as much as and more than the common run of men are surpassed in mental arithmetic by M. *Frénicle and by that Swedish boy I told you about [p. 78].

PHIL. §24. We have already noted that although the definitions of substances can serve to explain the names, they are imperfect so far as the knowledge of the things is concerned. For usually we put the name in the place of the thing; hence the name says more than the definition does;[5] and so if substances are to be well defined, 'natural history is to be inquired into'.

THEO. So you do see, sir, that the name 'gold', for instance, signifies not merely what the speaker knows of gold, e.g. something yellow and very heavy, but also what he does not know, which may be known about gold by someone else, namely: a body endowed with an inner constitution from which flow its colour and weight, and which also generates other properties which he acknowledges to be better known by the experts. 354

PHIL. §25. 'It were [now] to be wished, that men, versed in physical inquiries..., would set down those simple ideas, wherein they observe the individuals of each [species][6] constantly to agree.... But a dictionary of this sort, containing, as it were, a natural history, requires too many hands, as well as too much time,...[7] pains, and sagacity, ever to be hoped for'. But it would be good if the words for things which are known by their outward shapes were to be accompanied by 'little draughts and prints' of the things.

---

[1] Locke: 'if the formal constitution of [gold] lay open to our senses'.
[2] Locke: 'might'.   [3] Leibniz emphasizes the word.
[4] Locke: 'substances'.   [5] Clause added by Leibniz.
[6] Locke: 'sort'. Coste's change.   [7] Locke: 'cost,'.

A dictionary made in this fashion would be most useful to posterity, and would spare the textual critics of the future a great deal of trouble. A little print of an *apium* or an *ibex* (a species of wild goat) would be more use than a long description of that plant or that animal. And anyone wanting to know what Latin-speakers meant by *strigilis, sistrum, toga, tunica,* or *pallium,* would be given incomparably more help by pictures in the margin than by being offered the supposed synonyms *currycomb, cymbal, gown, coat,* and *cloak,* which hardly enable us to identify them. §26. Finally: I shall not linger on the fifth[1] remedy for the abuse of words, which is to 'use the same word constantly in the same sense', or to give warning when the sense is being changed; for we have already said enough about this.

THEO. The Rev. Father *Grimaldi, President of the Mathematical Board in Peking, has told me that the Chinese have dictionaries in which pictures are used. There is a little word-list printed in Nuremberg in which there are such pictures – quite good ones – associated with each word. Such an illustrated Universal Dictionary is very desirable, and would not be very hard to construct. As for the 'description of species': that is exactly what natural history is, and it is being worked at gradually. Were it not for the wars which have disturbed Europe ever since the Royal Societies and *Academies were first founded, much progress would have been made, and people would already be in a position to derive benefit from our labours. But the great of this world are mostly ignorant of the importance of this work, and do not know what benefits they lose through neglecting the advancement of solid knowledge – not to mention the fact that they are usually too distracted by the pleasures of peace, or by the cares of war, to think about anything which does not at once catch their attention.

---

[1] Taking '7e' to be a slip for Coste's '*cinquième*'.

Chapter i
'Of knowledge in general.'

PHILALETHES. So far, we have spoken about ideas and about the words which represent them. §1. Let us now turn to the knowledge which is provided by our ideas, for it 'is only conversant about them.' §2. Knowledge is 'nothing but the perception of the connection and agreement, or disagreement and repugnancy of any [two][2] of our ideas.' Whether we 'fancy, guess, or believe,' that is always what it is. This is how we are aware, for instance, 'that white is not black', and that there is a necessary connection between the angles of a triangle and their equality with two right angles.

THEOPHILUS. Knowledge can be taken even more generally, so that it is involved in ideas and terms before we come to propositions and truths. If someone looks attentively at more pictures of plants and animals than another person, and at more diagrams of machines and descriptions and depictions of houses and fortresses, and if he reads more imaginative novels and listens to more strange stories, then he can be said to have more knowledge than the other, even if there is not a word of truth in all that he has seen and heard. That is because the practice he has had in portraying in his mind a great many actual, explicit conceptions and ideas makes him better able to conceive what is put to him. He will certainly be better educated, better trained, and more capable than someone who has seen and read and heard nothing – provided that he takes nothing in these stories and pictures to be true which really is not so, and that these impressions do not prevent him in other contexts from distinguishing the real from the imaginary, the existent from the possible. This is why it was not wrong for certain *Ramist-inclined logicians of the century of the Reformation to say that the *topics or places of invention (*argumenta*, as they called them) are as relevant to the explication and detailed description of an 'incomplex theme', i.e. a thing or idea, as to the proof of a 'complex theme', i.e. a thesis, proposition or truth. And for that matter a thesis can be explicated, so as to bring out better its sense and its force, without raising the question

356

---

[1] Locke: 'Of Knowledge and Opinion.' Coste's omission.
[2] Added by Coste.

of its truth or proof; we see this being done in sermons and homilies which elucidate particular passages in Holy Scripture, and in commentaries and lessons on texts in civil or canon law whose truth is taken for granted. There are indeed 'themes' which can be said to be midway between an idea and a proposition, namely *questions*. Some of these ask only for a Yes or a No, and these are the closest to propositions; but there are others which ask how, and ask for details, and so on, and more must be added to these if they are to become propositions. True, we can say that in descriptions, even of purely ideal things, there is a tacit assertion of possibility. But it is also true that just as we can undertake to explain and prove a falsehood, sometimes the better to refute it, so the art of description can also be brought to bear on the impossible. This is what we find in the tales of the Count of Scandiano, from whom Ariosto borrowed, and in *Amadis of Gaul* and other old novels, in the fairy stories which came back into fashion a few years ago, and in Lucian's *True Histories* and Cyrano de Bergerac's travels, not to mention the painters' grotesques. We also know that rhetoricians include fables among *progymnasmata* or preliminary exercises.

357 But taking 'knowledge' in the narrower sense of knowledge of the truth, as you do here, sir, I say that it is true indeed that truth is always grounded in the agreement or disagreement of ideas, but it is not generally the case that our knowledge of truth is a perception of this agreement and disagreement. For when we know the truth only in the manner of empirics, through having experienced it without knowing how things are connected or what principles are at work in what we have experienced, we have no 'perception' of that agreement or disagreement, unless you mean that we sense it confusedly without being aware of it. But your examples seem to indicate that you always demand knowledge in which one is aware of the connection or opposition, and that cannot be granted to you. Furthermore, one can deal with a 'complex theme' not only by looking for proofs of its truth, but also by explicating and otherwise elucidating it in accordance with its 'topical places', as I have already pointed out. I have just one more thing to say about your definition, namely that it appears to fit only categorical truths, in which there are two ideas, the subject and the predicate. But there is also knowledge of hypothetical truths and of what can be reduced to them – disjunctions and others – in which there is a connection between the antecedent and consequent propositions; and so more than two ideas may be involved.

PHIL. Let us restrict ourselves here to knowledge of the truth. And let us apply what will be said about the connections between ideas to the connections between propositions as well, so as to deal with both categoricals and hypotheticals together.[1] §3. Well, now, I think we may reduce

---

[1] Added by Leibniz.

'this agreement or disagreement...to these four sorts: 1. Identity, or diversity. 2. Relation. 3. Coexistence, or necessary connection. 4. Real existence.' **§4.** For the mind is immediately aware that one idea is not another, that white is not black. **§5.** Next, it is aware of their relation when it compares them together – for instance that 'two triangles upon equal basis, between two parallels are equal'.[1] **§6.** Then there is coexistence, or rather connectedness;[2] for instance, that fixedness always accompanies the other ideas of gold. **§7.** Finally there is real existence outside the mind, as when one says: 'God exists'.

THEO. I believe we can say that connection is nothing but relation taken in a general sense.[3] And I have already pointed out [p. 142] that all relation involves either *comparison* or *concurrence*. Relations of comparison yield identity and diversity, in all respects or in some only, which makes things the same or different, like or unlike. Concurrence includes what you call coexistence, i.e. connectedness of existence. But when it is said that something exists or possesses real existence, this existence itself is the predicate; i.e. the notion of existence is linked with the idea in question, and there is a connection[4] between these two notions. Or the existence of the object of an idea may be conceived as the concurrence of that object with myself. So I believe we can say that there is only comparison and concurrence; but that the comparison which indicates identity or diversity, and the concurrence of the thing with myself, are the relations which deserve to be singled out from all the others. One could perhaps carry out a more precise and searching investigation, but at present I confine myself to making comments.

358

PHIL. **§8.** 'There is *actual* knowledge, which is the present [perception][5] the mind has of the [relation of] ideas'; and there is *habitual* knowledge, when the mind is so clearly aware of the agreement or disagreement of ideas, and has it lodged in such a way in its memory, that whenever it has occasion to reflect on the proposition the mind is at once assured of the truth it contains, without the slightest doubt in the world. For, 'being able to think, clearly and distinctly, but on one thing at once, if men had no knowledge of any more than what they actually thought on, they would all be very ignorant: and he that knew most, would know but one truth'.

THEO. The fact is that our systematic knowledge [**science*], even of the most demonstrative sort, since it very often has to be gained through a long chain of reasoning, must involve the recollection of a past demonstration

---

[1] From Locke's §7.
[2] '*ou plutôt connexion*' added by Leibniz.
[3] '*le rapport, ou la relation prise généralement*'; a *rapport* is a way of referring or relating one thing to another.
[4] '*connexion*'; elsewhere in these two speeches 'connection' (Locke's word) translates **liaison*.   [5] Locke: 'view'. Coste's change.

which is no longer kept distinctly in mind once the conclusion is reached – otherwise we would be continually repeating the demonstration. Even while it is going on we cannot grasp the whole of it all at once, since all its parts cannot be simultaneously present to the mind; and if we continually called the preceding part back into view we would never reach the final one which yields the conclusion. This has the further implication that without writing it would be difficult to get the sciences properly established, since memory is not certain enough. But having written down a long demonstration, such as those of Apollonius, and having gone back over all its steps, as one might examine a chain link by link, men can become certain of their reasonings; checks are also useful for this purpose; and the final result justifies the whole procedure. However, it can be seen from this that since all belief consists in the memory of one's past grasp of proofs and reasons, it is not within our power or our free will to believe or not believe, since memory is not something which depends on our will.

359

PHIL. §9. Our habitual knowledge is of two sorts or degrees. In some cases, truths which are 'laid up in the memory' no sooner occur to the mind than it perceives the relation there is between the ideas which they involve.[1] But in other cases, the mind is satisfied with 'the memory of the conviction, without [retaining] the proofs', and often without even being able to recall them if it wished. One might take this to be belief in one's memory, rather than really knowing the truth in question; and it 'seemed formerly to me like something between opinion and knowledge, a sort of assurance which exceeds bare belief [relying] on[2] the testimony of another; yet upon a due examination I find it comes not short of perfect certainty'. I remember, i.e. I know (for memory is only the reviving of some past thing),[3] that I 'was once certain of the truth of this proposition, that the three angles of a triangle are equal to two right ones. The immutability of the same relations between the same immutable things' is now the intermediate idea which shows me that if they were once equal to two right angles they will be so still. 'Upon this ground it is, that particular demonstrations in mathematics afford general knowledge.' Without it, a geometer's knowledge 'would not reach beyond that particular diagram' which he had drawn in giving his demonstration.

360 THEO. The 'intermediate idea' you speak of, sir, presupposes the reliability of our memory;[4] but it sometimes happens that our memory is deceiving us and that we have not taken all necessary care although we believe that we have. This comes out clearly in the auditing of accounts. Sometimes

---

[1] Locke: 'between those ideas.'
[2] Locke: 'belief, for that relies on'. Coste: '*croyance qui est fondée sur*'. Leibniz: '*croyance fondée sur*'.
[3] Locke: 'of some past knowledge'. Coste's change.
[4] '*souvenir*', not '*mémoire*' as in preceding speech.

official auditors are appointed, like the ones for our mines in the *Harz mountains; and to make the accountants for the individual mines more careful, fines have been instituted for every error of calculation, despite which errors still occur. Still, the more care we take, the more trust we can put in past reasonings. I have devised a method of book-keeping in which the person who lists the column totals leaves on the page a record of his reasoning, in such a manner that no needless steps are taken. He can always look back over the page and correct his latest errors without their affecting his earlier [calculations]. And if someone else wants to carry out an audit, that is scarcely any trouble with this method, because that same record lies open to his inspection. Moreover, [it provides] the means of checking the posting of each entry, using a very convenient kind of checking procedure, without this survey adding much to the accountant's work. All of which plainly shows that men can have rigorous demonstrations on paper – and do have an endless number of them, no doubt. But unless we remember having employed perfect rigour, we cannot have this certainty in our minds. Now this rigour consists in a rule obedience to which at each step would provide an assurance regarding the whole. It is like inspecting a chain one link at a time: by examining each one to see that it is unbroken, and using one's hands to make sure not to miss any out, one becomes assured of the soundness of the chain. By this method we achieve all the certainty that human affairs are capable of. But I do not agree with what seems to be your view, that this kind of general certainty is provided in mathematics by 'particular demonstrations' concerning the diagram that has been drawn. You must understand that geometers do not derive their proofs from diagrams, although the expository approach makes it seem so. The cogency of the demonstration is independent of the diagram, whose only role is to make it easier to understand what is meant and to fix one's attention. It is universal propositions, i.e. definitions and axioms and theorems which have already been demonstrated, that make up the reasoning, and they would sustain it even if there were no diagram. This is why one learned geometer, named Scheubel, gave Euclid's diagrams without the letters which would link them with his accompanying demonstration, and another, named Herlin, reduced those same demonstrations to syllogisms and prosyllogisms.

361

Chapter ii
'Of the degrees of our knowledge.'

PHILALETHES. §1. Knowledge is *intuitive* when 'the mind perceives the agreement or disagreement of two ideas immediately by themselves, without the intervention of any other.... In this, the mind is at no pains of proving or examining...the truth[. As the eye sees light, so] the mind perceives, that white is not black, that a circle is not a triangle, that three [is] one and two. [This] knowledge is the clearest, and most certain, that human frailty is capable of.' It acts in an 'irresistible' manner, and leaves the mind 'no room for hesitation'. It is the knowledge that an idea in one's mind is[1] such as one perceives it to be. 'He that demands a greater certainty..., demands he knows not what'.

THEOPHILUS. The *primary truths which we know by 'intuition' are of two sorts, as are the derivative ones. They are either truths of reason or truths of fact. Truths of reason are necessary, and those of fact are contingent. The primary truths of reason are the ones to which I give the general name 'identities', because they seem to do nothing but repeat the same thing without telling us anything. They are either affirmative or negative. Examples of affirmative ones are: *What is, is*; *Each thing is what it is*, and as many others as you want: *A is A*; *B is B*; *I shall be what I shall be*; *I have written what I have written*. And say it in prose or say it in rhyme, *Nothing is nothing* – most of the time.[2] *An equilateral rectangle is an equilateral rectangle*; and by truncation: *An equilateral rectangle is a rectangle. A rational animal is still an animal.* And with hypotheticals: *If a regular four-sided figure is an equilateral rectangle then this figure is a rectangle.* Conjunctions, disjunctions and other propositions can likewise be identities. Furthermore, I take affirmatives to include even *Non-A is non-A.* Also these hypotheticals: *If A is non-B it follows that A is non-B*; *If non-A is BC it follows that non-A is B*; *If a figure with no obtuse angle can be a regular triangle then a figure with no obtuse angle can be regular.* I now turn to negative identities, which derive from either the principle of contradiction or from 'disparities'. Stated generally, the principle of contradiction is: *a proposition is either true or false*. This contains two assertions: first, that truth and falsity are incompatible in a single proposition, i.e. that *a proposition cannot be both true and false at once*; and second, that the contradictories or negations of the true and the false are not compatible, i.e. that there is nothing intermediate between the true and the false, or better that *it cannot happen that a proposition is neither true nor false*. Now, all of that holds true in application to every proposition one can imagine, such as *What is A cannot be non-A*, and *AB cannot be non-A*, and *An equilateral rectangle cannot be non-rectangular, It is true that every man is an animal so it is false that there is some man who is not an animal*. We can provide many variations on these assertions and apply them to hypotheticals, conjunctions, disjunctions, and others. As for 'disparities', these are propositions which say that the object of one idea is not the object of another idea; for instance *Warmth is not the same thing*

362

[1] Taking '*est dans l'esprit*' to be a slip for Coste's '*dans l'esprit est*'.
[2] '*Et rien en vers comme en prose, c'est être rien ou peu de chose.*'

as colour, Man and animal are not the same although every man is an animal. All these can be established with certainty, without any proof, i.e. without bringing them down to an opposition (i.e. down to the principle of contradiction), when the ideas are well enough understood not to need any analysis at this point. When that is not the case one is liable to error: someone who said *The triangle and the trilateral are not the same* would be wrong, since if we consider it carefully we find that three sides and three angles always go together. And if he said *The quadrilateral rectangle and the rectangle are not the same* he would be wrong again, since it turns out that only a four-sided figure can have all its angles right angles. However, one can still say in the abstract that *triangularity is not trilaterality*, or that the formal causes of the triangle and of the trilateral are not the same, as the philosophers put it. They are different aspects of one and the same thing.

363

Someone who has been listening patiently so far to what I have just been saying will finally lose patience and say that I am wasting time on trivial assertions and that identities are all useless. But this verdict would result from not having thought enough about these matters. The inferences of logic, for example, are demonstrated by means of identities, and geometers need the principle of contradiction for their demonstrations by *reductio ad absurdum*. At this point let me merely show how identities can be used in demonstrating [the soundness of] some inferences of reason. I maintain that the principle of contradiction alone is sufficient for demonstrating the second and third figures of the *syllogism by means of the first. For instance, the first figure in *Barbara* gives us:

> All B is C
> All A is B
> Therefore All A is C.

Now suppose that the conclusion is false, i.e. that it is true that some A is not C. Then one or other of the premisses will also be false. If we suppose that the second is true, the first, which says that all B is C, will have to be false, so its contradictory will be true, i.e. some B will not be C. And this will be the conclusion of a new argument, derived from the falsity of the conclusion and the truth of one of the premisses of the preceding argument. Here is the new argument:

364

> Some A is not C
> (contradictory of the previous conclusion assumed false)
> All A is B
> (previous premiss assumed true)
> Therefore Some B is not C
> (present true conclusion, contradicting previous false premiss).

This argument is in the mood *Disamis* of the third figure, which can thus be demonstrated quickly and obviously from the mood *Barbara* of the first figure, using only the principle of contradiction. In my youth, when I looked carefully into these questions, I noticed that all the moods of the second and third figures could be derived from the first by this single procedure [*On the Combinatorial Art* p. 184]: assume that the first-figure mood is sound, so that if its conclusion is taken to be false – or its contradictory to be true – and one of the premisses is also taken to be true, the contradictory of the other premiss must be true. It is true that in logic classes they prefer to use conversion to derive the 'subsidiary' figures from the first figure which is the 'principal' one, because that appears easier for the students. But those who seek demonstrative reasons, in which one should make as few assumptions as possible, will not assume conversion for a demonstration which can be carried out purely by the primary principle, namely the principle of contradiction which assumes nothing. I have also observed – and it appears to be worth noting – that only the so-called 'direct' subsidiary figures, namely the second and the third, can be demonstrated by the principle of contradiction alone, but that the 'indirect' subsidiary figure, the fourth, has the drawback that it cannot be derived from the first or principal figure simply by this procedure, but also requires the further assumption of conversion. (The discovery of the fourth figure is attributed by the Arabs to Galen, although we find nothing about it in those of his writings which we still possess, nor in the other Greek writers.) Thus the fourth figure is one step further removed than the second and the third are, they being on a level with one another, at an equal distance from the first; whereas the fourth figure can be demonstrated only with the help of the second and third as well, for it turns out very opportunely that the very conversions which the fourth figure needs can be demonstrated by the second or third figure, which are themselves demonstrable, as I have just shown, without conversion. It was Petrus *Ramus who pointed out that conversion can be demonstrated by means of these figures; and, if I am not wrong, he brought a charge of circularity against logicians who demonstrate these figures with the aid of conversion; though they ought to be accused not so much of circularity – since they did not use these figures in turn to justify conversion – as of *hysteron proteron*, or doing things backwards, since conversion ought to be demonstrated from these figures rather than these figures from conversion. But as this demonstration of conversion further displays the usefulness of affirmative identities, which some regard as utterly trivial, it will be all the more appropriate to present it here. I intend to treat only of conversion without contraposition, which is all I need here, including both 'simple conversion' and 'conversion *per accidens*', as they are called. Simple conversion is of two kinds: that of universal negatives, for instance: *No square is obtuse-angled*, therefore *No obtuse-angled figure is square*; and that of particular affirmatives, for instance: *Some triangle is obtuse-angled*,

365

therefore *Some obtuse-angled figure is a triangle*. However, what is called conversion *per accidens* applies to the universal affirmative, as in: *Every square is a rectangle*, therefore *Some rectangle is a square* (still taking 'rectangle' to mean a figure all of whose angles are right angles, and taking 'square' to mean a regular quadrilateral). We must now prove these three kinds of conversion, namely:

1.   No A is B, therefore No B is A.
2.   Some A is B, therefore Some B is A.
3.   All A is B, therefore Some B is A.

Here are the demonstrations, presented formally:

Demonstration of the first conversion in *Cesare*, which is in the second figure:

> No A is B
> All B is B
> Therefore No B is A.

Demonstration of the second conversion in *Datisi*, which is in the third figure:

> All A is A
> Some A is B
> Therefore Some B is A.

Demonstration of the third conversion in *Darapti*, which is in the third figure:

> All A is A
> All A is B
> Therefore Some B is A

This shows that the purest identities, which appear entirely useless, are really of considerable use in abstract and general matters; and that can teach us that no truth should be scorned.

As for the proposition that *Three is equal to two and one*, which you also adduce, sir, as an example of intuitive knowledge, I will tell you that this is nothing but the definition of the term *three*. The simplest definitions of numbers are constructed like this: *Two* is one and one; *Three* is two and one; *Four* is three and one; and so on. It is true that a hidden assertion is involved, as I have already noted [pp. 321f], namely that these ideas are possible – which in these present cases we know 'intuitively'. Thus definitions can be said to include intuitive knowledge in cases where their possibility is straight away apparent. In this fashion all 'adequate' definitions contain primary truths of reason, and hence intuitive knowledge. Finally we can say in general that all the primary truths of reason are immediate with the *immediacy of ideas*.

As for primary truths of fact, these are inner experiences which are immediate with the *immediacy of feeling*. This is where the first truth of the *Cartesians and St Augustine belongs: *I think, therefore I am*. That

366

367

is, *I am a thing which thinks*. But we must realize that just as identities can be general or particular, and that they are equally evident[1] in either case (since *A is A* is just as evident as *A thing is what it is*), so it is with the first[2] truths of fact. For not only is it immediately evident to me that *I think*, but it is just as evident that *I think various thoughts*: at one time *I think about A* and at another *about B* and so on. Thus the Cartesian principle is sound, but it is not the only one of its kind. This shows that all of the primary truths of reason and of fact have in common that we cannot prove them by anything more certain.

PHIL. I am very glad, sir, that you have further developed this topic of intuitive knowledge, which I had merely touched on. Now, *demonstrative* knowledge is just a chain of items of intuitive knowledge bearing on 'all the connections of the intermediate ideas'. §2. For frequently the mind cannot immediately join, compare or apply its ideas one to another, and it has to avail itself of one or more intermediate ideas to discover the agreement or disagreement which is sought; and this is what we call *reasoning*. For instance, in demonstrating that the three angles of a triangle are equal to two right angles, one finds other angles which can be seen to be equal both to the three angles of the triangle and to two right angles. §3. 'Those intervening ideas...are called *proofs*', and the mind's disposition to find[3] them is called *sagacity*. §4. And even when they are found, this knowledge cannot be gained 'without pains and attention [or by means of] one transient view[. One must engage in] a progression [of ideas] by steps and degrees'; §5. and 'before the demonstration there [is] a doubt'. §6. It is less clear than intuitive knowledge, just as the image 'reflected by several mirrors one to another [grows feebler each time it is reflected,] and is not at first sight so knowable, especially to weak eyes. Thus it is with knowledge, made out by a long train of proofs.' §7. Although every step that reason makes in demonstrating is intuitively known or directly seen, nevertheless because the memory does not always 'exactly retain' these connections of ideas in this long sequence of proofs, 'men embrace often falsehoods for demonstrations.'

THEO. As well as natural 'sagacity' and that acquired by training, there is an *art of finding intermediate ideas (the 'middle term') – and this is the art of *'analysis'. It should be borne in mind that sometimes it is a matter of finding the truth or falsity of a given proposition, which is the same as answering a 'whether' question, i.e. whether it is or isn't so; while sometimes the question to be answered is (other things being equal) more difficult – when it is asked for instance 'By whom and how?', in which

---

[1] '*claires*'.

[2] Or 'primary', if '*premières*' is a slip for '*primitives*'.

[3] Locke: 'a quickness in the mind to find out'. Coste: '*la disposition que l'esprit a à trouver promptement*'. Leibniz: '*la disposition de l'esprit à...trouver*'.

368

case something more has to be added. It is only questions like this, which leave part of the proposition blank, that the mathematicians call 'problems'. An example would be someone who wants to find a *mirror which will bring all the sun's rays together at a point, that is, wants to know its shape or how it is constructed. In the case of questions of the first kind, where truth or falsity alone is at issue and there is nothing to be added, in the subject or the predicate, less *invention* is involved; some is, however, and *judgment* alone is not enough. A man of good judgment, that is, who can exercise care and restraint, and who has the necessary leisure, patience and openness of mind, can indeed understand the most difficult demonstration if it is properly presented. But the most judicious man on earth will not, without other aids, always be able to find this demonstration. So invention is involved here too. Among geometers there used to be more of it than there is now; for when analysis was less developed, more sagacity was needed to carry it out. This is why some geometers of the old school, and others who are not yet really at home in the new methods, still believe they are working wonders when they find the demonstration of some theorem which was the invention of others. But those who are versed in the art of invention know whether or not it deserves praise: for instance, if someone publishes the *quadrature of an area bounded by a curve and a straight line, which applies to all its segments and which is of the sort I call general, it is always in our power, if we care to take the trouble, to find the demonstration of it according to our methods. But there are special cases – quadratures of certain portions – where the matter can be so tangled that in some cases it is not yet in our power to untangle it. It can also happen that induction presents us with numerical and geometrical truths for which we have still not discovered general reasons. For we are far from having perfected geometrical and numerical analysis, as some have been led to think we have by the bragging of some otherwise excellent men who are just a little too hasty or too ambitious.

369

But it is much harder to find important truths, and still more to find ways of doing what one wants exactly when one wants it, than to find demonstrations for truths which someone else has discovered. Fine truths are often reached by 'synthesis', going from the simple to the composite, but when it is a matter of finding exactly the right way of doing what is required, synthesis is not usually sufficient – to try to make all the necessary combinations would often be like drinking the ocean. However the 'method of exclusions' can often help with this by eliminating a good proportion of the useless combinations, and often nature permits no other method. But means are sometimes lacking to follow it properly. Then it is for analysis to give us a thread through the labyrinth – if there is one, for there are cases where the very nature of the question requires us to explore every avenue, since short-cuts are not always possible.

PHIL. **§8.** Now, when demonstrating we always presuppose intuitive knowledge, and that, I think, is what has given occasion[1] to the axiom that all reasoning is from things already known and conceded (*ex praecognitis et praeconcessis*). But we shall have occasion to discuss how far that axiom is mistaken, when we discuss maxims, which are mistakenly 'supposed to be the foundations of all our...reasonings.'

THEO. I shall be interested to see what you can find wrong in such an apparently reasonable axiom. If we had always to reduce everything to what is intuitively known, demonstrations would often be intolerably wordy; and that is why the mathematicians have adroitly broken up difficult questions and demonstrated intervening propositions separately. There is art in this too: since ancillary truths (which are called 'lemmas' when they appear extraneous) can be given in various ways, it is helpful to both understanding and memory if we choose ones which greatly shorten the proof and which appear memorable and worth demonstrating for their own sakes. But there is another obstacle, namely that it is not easy to demonstrate all the axioms, or to break the demonstrations right down into what is intuitively known. And if people had been willing to wait until that could be done, we might still have no science of geometry. But we spoke of that in our earliest conversations [pp. 74ff?], and we shall later have occasion to say more about it.

370

PHIL. **§9.** We shall come to it shortly [pp. 415, 450–3]. Now I shall repeat what I have already mentioned more than once, that 'it has been generally taken for granted, that [the mathematical sciences][2] alone are capable of demonstrative certainty: but to have such an agreement or disagreement, as may intuitively be [known],[3] being...not the privilege of the ideas of number...and figure alone, it may possibly be [from] the want of... application in us' that only the mathematicians have achieved demonstrations. **§10.** This has come from several causes working together: the 'general usefulness' of the mathematical sciences; the fact that in them the least difference is very easy to recognize.[4] **§11.** There are no 'exact measures of the different degrees' of 'those other simple ideas [which are] appearances or sensations, produced in us'. **§13.** But where, as for instance with these visible qualities,[5] 'the difference is so great as to produce in the mind clearly' distinguished[6] ideas such as those of blue and red, they 'are as capable of demonstration, as ideas of number and extension.'

THEO. There are some rather notable examples of demonstration outside mathematics, and it can be said that Aristotle gave some in his *Prior*

---

[1] Locke: 'The necessity of this intuitive knowledge, in...demonstrative reasoning, gave occasion'. Coste's change. [2] Locke: 'mathematics'.

[3] Locke: 'perceived'. Coste uses '*connaître*'.

[4] Locke: 'very...perceivable'. Coste uses '*reconnaître*'.

[5] Phrase added by Leibniz. [6] Locke: 'distinct'.

Analytics. Indeed, logic admits of demonstration as much as geometry does, and geometers' logic – that is, the methods of argument which *Euclid explained and established through his treatment of proportions – can be regarded as an extension or particular application of general logic. Archimedes is the first man whose works we possess who practised the art of demonstration in a context involving physical matters, as he did in his book *On Equilibrium*. What is more, jurists can be credited with some sound demonstrative arguments, particularly the ancient Roman jurists, fragments of whose writings have been preserved for us in the *Pandects*. I entirely agree with Lorenzo Valla, whose admiration for these authors is boundless, in part because they always speak so plainly and exactly and, indeed, reason in a way which comes very close to being demonstration, and often is just that. I know of no other science, apart from law and warfare, where the Romans have substantially added to what they had received from the Greeks.

371

> O Roman, remember to rule the nations by your command;
> These shall be your arts: to impose the way of peace,
> To spare the submissive and to subdue the proud. [Virgil]

Because of their precise way of expressing themselves, all the jurists in the *Pandects* read like a single author, even though some of them are very distant from others in time, and one would have great difficulty telling them apart if their names did not head the selections; just as it would be hard to distinguish Euclid, Archimedes and Apollonius by reading their demonstrations about matters with which they all dealt. It must be acknowledged that in mathematics the Greeks reasoned with the greatest possible accuracy, and that they have bequeathed to mankind models of the art of demonstration; for even if the Babylonians and Egyptians had a geometry that went a little beyond the empiric level, nothing remains of it. But it is surprising how far these same Greeks fell away from that standard the moment they moved away, however little, from numbers and figures in order to do philosophy. Strangely enough, one does not find a trace of demonstration in Plato or in Aristotle (except in his *Prior Analytics*) or in the other ancient philosophers. Proclus was a fine geometer, but he seems to be a different man when he treats of philosophy. What has made it easier to reason demonstratively in mathematics is largely that experience[1] can vouch for each step in the reasoning, as also happens with the figures of the syllogism. But in metaphysics and ethics there is no longer this parallel between reasoning and experience,[2] and in *natural science experiments[3] require labour and expense. Now, the moment men are deprived of that faithful guide, experience, which aids and sustains their steps like the little wheeled device which keeps toddlers

---

[1] '*expérience*'.　　　　[2] '*expériences*'.　　　　[3] '*expériences*'.

from falling down, they at once allow their attention to waver and as a result they go astray. There has been an alternative [method of keeping them from straying],[1] but it is one which has not been and still is not sufficiently taken into account. I shall speak of it at the proper time. As for your last point, blue and red can hardly provide material for demonstrations through the ideas we have of them, since these ideas are confused. These colours provide material for reasoning only to the extent that we find them through experience to be accompanied by distinct ideas, but without their connection with their accompanying ideas being an apparent one.

372

PHIL. §14. Apart from intuition and demonstration, which are the two 'degrees of our knowledge', everything else 'is but faith, or opinion, but not knowledge, at least in all general truths. [But there is] another perception of the mind, employed about the particular existence of finite beings without us;' and this is *sensitive* knowledge.

THEO. Perhaps *opinion*, based on likelihood, also deserves the name of knowledge; otherwise nearly all historical knowledge will collapse, and a good deal more. But, without arguing about names, I maintain that *the study of the degrees of *probability* would be very valuable and is still lacking, and that this is a serious shortcoming in our treatises on logic. For when one cannot absolutely settle a question one could still establish the degree of likelihood on the evidence, and so one can judge rationally which side is the most plausible. And when our moralists – I mean the wisest of them, such as the present General of the Jesuits – bring in the question of what is safest as well as of what is most probable, and even put safety ahead of probability, they do not really abandon the most probable [*probabilism]. For here the question of *safety* is the question of the *improbability of an impending evil*. Moralists who are lax about this have gone wrong largely because they have had an inadequate and over-narrow notion of probability, which they have confused with Aristotle's *endoxon* or *acceptability*: in his *Topics* Aristotle aimed only to conform to the opinions of other people, as did the orators and the Sophists. *Endoxon*, for him, is whatever is accepted by the greatest number or by the most authoritative; he was wrong to restrict his *Topics* to that, and this approach meant that he only concerned himself there with accepted maxims, most of them vague – as though wanting to reason by means of nothing but old jokes and proverbs. But probability or likelihood is broader: it must be drawn from the nature of things; and the opinion of weighty authorities is one of the things which can contribute to the likelihood of an opinion, but it does not produce the entire likelihood by itself. And at the time when Copernicus was almost alone in his opinion, it was still incomparably more *likely* than that of all the rest of the human race. I suspect that establishment

373

---

[1] '*Il y avait quelque* succedaneum'.

of an *art of estimating likelihoods* would be more useful than a good proportion of our demonstrative sciences, and I have more than once contemplated it.

PHIL. Sensitive knowledge – i.e. knowledge which establishes the existence of particular beings outside us – goes 'beyond bare probability [without] reaching perfectly to either of the foregoing degrees of certainty[. There is] nothing more certain, than that the idea we receive from an external object is in our minds; this is intuitive knowledge. But. . .whether we can thence certainly infer the existence of any thing without us, which corresponds to that idea, is that, whereof some men think there may be a question made, because men may have such ideas in their minds, when no such thing exists. . . . But yet here, I think, we are provided with [a degree of] evidence, that puts us past doubting'. Anyone is invincibly persuaded that there is a great difference between the perceptions he has 'when he looks on the sun by day, and thinks on it by night'. And the idea which is revived by memory is quite different from that which actually comes to us by the senses. Someone will say that a dream may do the same thing. I reply, firstly, that it is 'no great matter, whether I remove [this doubt]: where all is but dream, reasoning [is] of no use, truth and knowledge nothing.' Secondly, I believe he will acknowledge the 'difference between dreaming of being in the fire, and being actually in it.' And if he persists in appearing sceptical, I shall tell him that it is enough 'that we certainly [find] that pleasure or pain follows upon the application of certain objects to us, [be they real or dreamt; and that] this certainty is as great[1] as our happiness, or misery, beyond which, we have no concernment'. So I think we can count three sorts[2] 'of knowledge, viz. intuitive, demonstrative, and sensitive'.

THEO. I believe you are right, sir, and I even think that to these three kinds of certainty or *certain knowledge* you could add *knowledge of likelihood*. So there will be two sorts of knowledge, just as there are two sorts of proof: one results in certainty and the other leads only to probability. But let us turn to the sceptics' dispute with the dogmatists regarding the existence of things outside us. We have already mentioned it [p. 296] but must now come back 374 to it. I used to argue strenuously about it, orally and in writing, with the late Abbé *Foucher, Canon of Dijon; he was a learned and shrewd man, but a little too taken with his Academics, whose sect he would have liked to revive, just as M. *Gassendi had brought Epicurus's back onto the stage. His *Critique of the Search after Truth*, and the other little treatises he subsequently had published, gave him a good reputation. When I informed the public about my system of *pre-established harmony ['New system

---

[1] Locke says: *because* 'pleasure or pain follows' etc., *therefore* 'this certainty is as great' etc.   [2] Locke: 'degrees'. Coste's change.

of the nature and communication of substances'], after turning it over in my mind for several years, he brought out objections to it in the *Journal des savants*; but death prevented him from answering my reply ['Explanation of the new system of the communication of substances']. He was always urging that one should beware of preconceptions and cultivate great accuracy; but besides not taking trouble to practise what he preached – for which he can largely be excused – he seemed to me not to notice when someone else practised it, no doubt taking it for granted that no one ever would. Well, I showed him that the truth about sensible things consists only in the linking together of *phenomena, this linking (for which there must be a reason) being what distinguishes sensible things from dreams; but that the truth about our existence and about the cause of phenomena is of a different order, since it establishes [the existence of] substances; and that the sceptics were spoiling their good case by pushing it too far, wanting to extend their doubts to immediate experience and the truths of geometry (not that M. Foucher did so, however), and to the other truths of reason (and here he was a little guilty). But to come back to you, sir: you are right when you say that there is usually a difference between *sensations and imaginings, but the sceptics will say that a difference in degree does not create a difference in kind. And anyway, although *sensations are ordinarily livelier than imaginings, still we know that sometimes imaginative people are as much impressed by their imaginings as others are by the truth of things, and perhaps more so. Consequently I believe that where objects of the senses are concerned the true criterion is the linking together of phenomena, i.e. the connectedness of what happens at different times and places and in the experience of different men – with men themselves being phenomena to one another, and very important ones so far as this present matter is concerned. And the linking of phenomena which warrants the
375 *truths of fact* about sensible things outside us is itself verified by means of *truths of reason*, just as optical appearances are explained by geometry. It must be acknowledged, though, as you have clearly recognized, that none of this certainty is of the highest degree. For it is not impossible, metaphysically speaking, for a dream to be as coherent and prolonged as a man's life. But this would be as contrary to reason as the fiction of a book's resulting by chance from jumbling the printer's type together. Besides, so long as the phenomena are linked together it doesn't matter whether we call them dreams or not, since experience shows that we do not go wrong in the practical steps we take on the basis of phenomena, so long as we take them in accordance with the truths of reason.

PHIL. §15. Moreover, knowledge is not always clear, even when our ideas are. 'A man that has as clear ideas of the angles of a triangle, and of equality to two right ones, as any mathematician in the world, may yet have but a very obscure perception of their agreement'.

THEO. Ordinarily, when ideas are thoroughly understood, their agreements and disagreements are apparent. Yet I admit that some of them are so composite that great care is needed to bring out what is concealed in them, and consequently certain agreements and disagreements may remain obscure. Regarding your example, I would point out that one can have the angles of a triangle in one's imagination without thereby having clear ideas of them. Imagination cannot provide us with an image common to acute-angled and obtuse-angled triangles, yet the idea of triangle is common to them; so this idea does not consist in images, and it is not as easy as one might think to understand the angles of a triangle thoroughly.

Chapter iii
'Of the extent of human knowledge.'

PHILALETHES. §1. Our knowledge does not extend further than our ideas, §2. or further than our perception of their agreement or disagreement. §3. It cannot always be intuitive, because we cannot always make an 'immediate 376 comparison' between things, for instance the sizes of two equal but very dissimilar triangles on the same base. §4. Nor can our knowledge always be demonstrative, because we cannot always find the intervening ideas. §5. Finally, our sensitive knowledge concerns only 'the existence of things actually [affecting][1] our senses'. §6. So not only are our ideas very limited, but our knowledge is even more so. 'Nevertheless, I do not question, but that human knowledge...may be carried much farther...if men would sincerely, and with freedom of mind, [devote themselves to] improving the means of discovering[2] truth', with all that assiduity and all that industry which they employ 'for the colouring or support of falsehood, to maintain a system [which they have espoused, or indeed some] interest, or party, they are once engaged in. But yet after all...our knowledge [could][3] never reach to all we might desire to know concerning those ideas we have'. For instance, we shall perhaps 'never be able to find a circle equal to a square, and certainly know' whether there is such a thing.[4]

THEOPHILUS. There are confused ideas where we cannot expect complete knowledge, such as the ideas of some sensible qualities. But with distinct ideas there is reason to hope for everything. As for the matter of the square equal to a circle: Archimedes has already shown that 'there is such a thing'. It is the square whose side is the mean proportional between the radius and the semi-circumference of the circle. He even determined a straight line equal to the circumference of a circle, by means of a straight line

---

[1] Locke: 'present to'. Coste: '*qui frappent*'.
[2] Taking '*trouver les moyens de perfectionner*' to be a slip for Coste's '*perfectionner les moyens de découvrir*'.   [3] Locke: 'would'. Coste's change.
[4] Locke: 'know that it is so'. Coste's change.

tangent to the spiral, as others did by means of the tangent to the quadratrix (a technique of quadrature with which Clavius was perfectly satisfied); not to mention a thread laid around the circumference and then straightened out, or the rolling circumference which describes a cycloid and thus becomes a straight line. There are those who require that the construction be done with nothing but ruler and compass, but there are few geometrical problems in which the construction can be done in that way. So what is needed, rather, is to find the proportion between the square and the circle. But since this proportion cannot be expressed in finitely many rational numbers, it has been necessary, so as to use nothing but rationals, to express this proportion by an infinite series of those numbers – a series which I have specified in a quite simple way [*quadrature]. What one would now like to know is whether there is not some finite quantity, even if only a surd or *super-surd one, which might express this infinite series; that is, whether a precise abbreviated form of the series can be found. But finite expressions – and especially the irrationals, if one goes out to the super-surds – can vary in so many ways that one cannot enumerate them and easily determine all the possibilities. There might be a way of doing it if the required surd number were representable by means of an ordinary equation (or even indeed an extraordinary one which introduced irrationals or the unknown itself into the exponent); but it would need a tremendous calculation to carry that out, and we shall not find it easy to complete the task unless some day an abbreviated form is discovered which gets us out of it. But one cannot exclude all finite expressions, for I do know some myself; to discover precisely which of them is the best is an immense task. What all this shows is that the human mind raises questions which are so strange, especially when infinity is involved, that it is not surprising that it is hard to get to the bottom of them. Especially since often in these geometrical matters everything depends upon having a short formula; and that is something we cannot always expect, just as we cannot always reduce fractions to least terms or find the divisors of a given number. It is true that one can always discover the divisors if this is made possible by their enumeration's being finite. But when one has to cope with something which is infinitely variable, ascending by degrees, one is not the master of it as one would like to be; and to do everything that is needed for an attempt to arrive methodically at a short formula or at a rule of progression which makes it unnecessary to go any further – that is too laborious. And since the benefits are not commensurate with the labour, one leaves it to posterity to succeed in the task: they may meet with success when the additional groundwork and new approaches, which time may bring, have made the task shorter and less onerous. If the people who occasionally address themselves to these studies were willing to do precisely what is needed for further progress to be made, one could hope for a large advance in a short time. It should not be supposed that everything is done, since even in ordinary geometry we have as yet no method for determining the best constructions in problems which have a modicum of complexity. If we are to have better success with that, our analysis should be mingled with some measure of synthesis. I remember hearing it said that Pensionary *De Witt had some thoughts on that subject.

PHIL. A further problem is 'to know, whether any [purely]¹ material being thinks, or no'. Perhaps we shall never be capable of knowing this, despite the fact that 'we have the ideas of matter and thinking, [because it is] impossible for us, by the contemplation of our own ideas, without revelation, to discover, whether Omnipotency has not given to some systems of matter fitly disposed, a power to perceive and think, or else joined and fixed to matter so disposed, a thinking immaterial substance: it being, in respect of our notions, not much more remote from our comprehension to conceive, that God can, if he pleases, superadd to [our idea of]² matter a faculty of thinking, than that he should superadd to it another substance, with a faculty of thinking; since we know not wherein thinking consists, nor to what sort of substances the Almighty has been pleased to [grant]³ that power, which cannot be in any created being, but merely by the good pleasure and bounty of the Creator.'   378

THEO. There is no doubt that this question is incomparably more important than the preceding one. But I venture to say to you, sir, that I wish we could affect souls for their own good, and cure bodies of their ills, with an ease which matched the power which I believe we have to settle this question. I hope you will at least admit that I can make some progress with the problem, without 'offending against modesty', and without 'pronouncing magisterially'⁴ as a substitute for having good reasons; for what I say will agree with commonly accepted views, and furthermore I think that I have brought to the question an uncommon amount of attention. For a start, I grant you, sir, that when people have only confused ideas of *thought* and of *matter*, which is usually all they do have, it is no wonder that they cannot see how to resolve such questions. Similarly, as I remarked a little while back [p. 375], if someone has ideas of the angles of a triangle only in the way in which these ideas are commonly had, he will never come upon the discovery that they are always equal to two right angles. It should be borne in mind that matter, understood as a complete being (i.e. 'secondary matter', in contrast with 'prime matter' which is something purely passive and therefore incomplete), is nothing but an aggregate or the result of one; and that any real aggregate presupposes simple substances or *real unities*. If one also bears in mind what constitutes

¹ Locke: 'mere'. Coste's change.   ² Added by Coste.
³ Locke: 'give'. Coste: '*accorder*'.   ⁴ Quoted phrases echo Locke's §6.

the nature of those real unities, namely perception and its consequences, one is transported into another world, so to speak: from having existed entirely amongst the phenomena of the senses, one comes to occupy the intelligible world of substances. And this knowledge of the inner nature of matter shows well enough what it is naturally capable of. And it shows that whenever God gives matter organs suitable for the expression of reasoning, 379 it will also be given an immaterial substance which reasons; this is because of that harmony which is yet another consequence of the nature of substances.[1] There cannot be matter without immaterial substances, i.e. without unities: that should put an end to the question of whether God is free to give or not to give immaterial substances to matter; and if the correspondence or harmony which I have just spoken of did not obtain amongst these substances, God would not be acting according to the natural order. To speak of sheerly 'giving' or 'granting' powers is to return to the bare faculties of the Scholastics, and to entertain a picture of little subsistent beings which can fly in and out like pigeons with a dovecote. It is unwittingly to turn them into substances. Primary powers are what make up the substances themselves; derivative powers, or 'faculties' if you like, are merely 'ways of being' – and they must be derived from substances, and are not derivable from matter considered as wholly mechanical, i.e. abstractly considered as merely that incomplete being which is prime matter or the purely passive. I believe you agree, sir, that it is not within the power of a bare machine to give rise to perception, sensation, reason. So these must stem from some other substantial thing. To maintain that God acts in any other way, and gives things accidents which are not 'ways of being' or modifications arising from substances, is to have recourse to miracles and to what the Scholastics used to call 'obediential power'. It would involve a kind of supernatural elevating of things, as in the claim of some theologians that hell-fire burns separated souls; which leaves open the question of whether it would be the fire which was acting, rather than God acting in place of the fire and producing the same effect.

PHIL. These explanations of yours have rather taken me by surprise; and you are anticipating a number of things I was going to tell you about the limits of our knowledge. I would have told you that we are not in a 'state ...of vision', as the theologians say;[2] that 'we must, in many things, content our selves with faith and probability', especially with regard to 'the immateriality of the soul'; that 'all the great ends of morality and religion, are well enough secured, without philosophical proofs of [that] immateriality; [and that] it is evident, that he who made us at first begin

---

[1] '*encore une suite naturelle des substances*'.
[2] Phrase added by Coste.

to subsist here, sensible intelligent beings, and for several years continued
us in such a state, can and will restore us to the like state of sensibility in   380
[the after-life],[1] and make us capable there to receive the retribution he
has designed to men, according to their doings in this life'; and, finally,
that one can see from this that the question of whether the soul is
immaterial is 'not of such mighty necessity to determine one way or
t'other' as some people, over-zealous for their own view, have tried to
make us[2] believe. I had been going to say all that, and still more to the
same effect; but now I see what a great difference there is between saying
that we are naturally sensible, thinking and immortal, and saying that we
are so only through a miracle. I acknowledge that such a miracle will indeed
have to be admitted if the soul is not immaterial; but this belief in miracles,
as well as being groundless, will not have a very good effect on many
people's minds. Your approach also shows me that we can rationally settle
the present question, without needing to enjoy a 'state of vision' which
would put us in the company of those superior *Spirits who can see right
into the 'inward constitution of things' – Spirits whose quick and
'penetrating sight' and large 'field of knowledge' enables us to guess at
how happy they must be. I had believed that it is 'out of the reach of our
knowledge' to join[3] 'sensation...to extended matter; or existence to
any thing that hath no extension at all'. That is why I had become
convinced that those who took sides on this question were following the
'unfair way [of] some men...who, because of the unconceivableness of
something they find in one, throw themselves violently into the contrary
hypothesis, though altogether as unintelligible'. I thought that this arose
from the fact that some, their minds being too immersed (so to speak) in
matter, 'can allow no existence to what is not material: [while others,]
finding not *cogitation* within the natural powers of matter,' conclude that
even God cannot give life and perception[4] to a solid substance except by
adding some immaterial substance to it. Whereas now I see that if he did
so it would be by a miracle, and that the union of soul with body, or the
joining of sensation with matter, no longer seems incomprehensible in the
light of your hypothesis of the pre-established agreement between different
substances.

THEO. Indeed, there is nothing unintelligible in this new hypothesis, since
all it attributes to the soul and to bodies are modifications which we
experience in ourselves and in bodies; only it establishes these modifications
as being more regular and connected than they have so far been thought
to be. The residual problem exists only for those who want to *imagine*   381

---

[1] Locke: 'another world'. Coste: '*l'autre monde*'. Leibniz: '*l'autre vie*'.
[2] Coste's '*le*' (him), copied by Leibniz, is presumably a slip.
[3] Locke: 'reconcil[e]'. Coste: '*allier*'.
[4] Locke: 'cannot give perception and thought'. Coste's change.

something which can only be *thought*, like wanting to see sounds or hear colours. These are the people who 'deny existence to whatever is not extended', which commits them to denying it to God himself, i.e. to relinquishing causes, and to relinquishing reasons for changes in general and for these changes in particular.[1] That is because these reasons cannot come from extension and from purely passive natures, nor even in their entirety from particular lower active natures without the pure and universal activity of the supreme substance.

PHIL. On the subject of the natural capacities of matter, I still have one objection. 'Body as far as we can conceive [is] able only to strike and affect body; and motion [is] able to produce nothing but motion, so that when we allow it to produce pleasure or pain, or the idea of a colour, or sound, [it seems that][2] we are fain to quit our reason, go beyond our [own] ideas, and attribute it wholly to the good pleasure of our Maker.' What reason shall we find, then, to conclude that perception does not occur in matter in that same way? I can see pretty well what reply this is open to. You have already said a certain amount about this on several occasions, but I have never understood you as well as I do now, sir. Still, I shall be glad to hear your reply to this again in this important context.

THEO. You are correct in predicting, sir, that I will deny that matter can produce pleasure, pain or *sensation in us. It is the soul that produces these in itself, in conformity with what happens in matter. And among our contemporaries, some able people [e.g. *Bayle, *Lamy] are starting to declare that they understand *occasional causes only in my way. Now, given my view, nothing unintelligible happens, except that we cannot sort out everything which has a part in our confused perceptions; they are expressions of the details of what happens in bodies, and even have about them something infinite. As for 'the good pleasure of our Maker', it should be said that he conducts himself in accordance with the natures of things, in such a way that he produces and conserves in them only what is suitable to them and can be explained through their natures; explained in a general way, at least, for often the details are beyond us, just as we lack the diligence and the power to arrange the grains in a mountain of sand according to their shapes, although apart from their sheer multiplicity there is nothing difficult to understand about that. If on the other hand that knowledge were inherently beyond us, and if we could not even conceive of a general explanation for the relations between soul and body, and if, finally, God gave things *accidental powers which were not rooted in their natures* and were therefore out of reach of reason in general; that would be a back door through which to re-admit 'over-occult qualities' which no mind can

---

[1] '*raisons des changements et de tels changements*'.
[2] Added by Leibniz.

understand, along with inexplicable 'faculties' (those little goblins), 'and whatever the idle School dreamed of' – helpful goblins which come forward like gods on the stage, or like the fairies in *Amadis*, to do on demand anything that a philosopher wants of them, without ways or means. But to attribute their origin to God's 'good pleasure' – that appears hardly worthy of him who is the supreme reason, and with whom everything is orderly, everything is connected. This good pleasure would indeed be neither good nor pleasure if God's power did not perpetually run parallel to his wisdom.

PHIL. §8. Our knowledge of identity and diversity stretches as far as our ideas. §§9–10. But we have very poor knowledge – indeed almost none – of how our ideas are connected by coexistence in a single subject. §11. This holds especially for secondary qualities such as colours, sounds and tastes, §12. because we do not know how they are connected with primary qualities, that is, §13. how they depend upon size, figure and motion. §15. We know a little more about incompatibilities amongst those secondary qualities: for instance, a subject cannot have two colours at once; and when one seems to see two colours at once in 'an opal, or in the infusion of *lignum nephriticum*,' the colours are in different parts of the object. §16. The same holds true for the active and passive powers of bodies. Our inquiries into this matter must depend upon experience.

THEO. Ideas of sensible qualities are confused; and so they must be produced by powers which are a source only of ideas that have something confused about them. So if we are to know other than through experience how these ideas are linked, it can only be by resolving them into distinct ideas which accompany them, as has been done for instance with the colours of the rainbow and of prisms. This method provides a starting point for analysis, which is very useful in natural science; and I have no doubt that it will enable the study of medicine eventually to make considerable advances, especially if society takes rather more interest in it than it has done up until now.

PHIL. §18. As for our knowledge of relations: this 'is the largest field of our knowledge, [and] it is hard to determine how far it may extend[. Advances depend on] sagacity, in finding intermediate ideas.... They that are ignorant of algebra cannot imagine the wonders in this kind [which] are to be done by it: and what farther improvements and helps, advantageous to other parts of knowledge, the sagacious mind of man may yet find out, 'tis not easy to determine....At least...the ideas of quantity are not those alone that are capable of demonstration'.[1] Other, and perhaps the most important,[2] 'parts of contemplation, would afford us certainty,

383

---

[1] Locke: 'demonstration and knowledge'. Coste's omission.
[2] Locke: 'more useful'. Coste's change.

if vices, passions, and domineering interest did not [directly oppose][1] such endeavours.'

THEO. You could not be more right in what you have just said, sir. Consider the things that I believe we have established about the nature of substances, about unities and multiplicities, about identity and diversity, the constitution of individuals, the impossibility of vacuum and atoms, the source of cohesion, the law of continuity and the other laws of nature; and above all about the harmony amongst things, the immateriality of souls, the union of soul with body, and the preservation after death of souls and even of animals. What is more important than all this, if it is true? And I believe that it all has been or can be demonstrated.

PHIL. Indeed, your theory appears to hold together extremely well and to be very simple: one able man in France who tried to refute it admits publicly that he has been impressed by it [*Lamy]. And its simplicity strikes me as being extremely fruitful. It will be good to make this doctrine more and more widely known. But when I spoke of things 'which are of the most import to us', what I had in mind was morality. I grant that your 384 metaphysics provides wonderful foundations for that; but morality can be firmly enough grounded without digging so deeply. Although, as I remember your remarking [p. 201], the foundations of morality may not extend so far if they do not have a natural theology like yours as their base, still, merely by considering the goods of this life we can establish inferences which are important for the ordering of human societies. One can judge concerning *just* and *unjust* as incontestably as one can judge in mathematics. For example, '*Where there is no property, there is no injustice*, is a proposition as certain as any demonstration in Euclid'; because property is a right to a certain thing, and injustice[2] is the violation of a right.[3] Similarly with '*No government allows absolute liberty*'; for government is the establishment of certain laws to which it requires conformity, and absolute liberty is the power of each person to do whatever he pleases.

THEO. The ordinary use of the word 'property' is slightly different from that, for it is taken to mean a person's *exclusive* right to a thing. So even if there were no property, e.g. because everything was held in common, there could nevertheless be injustice. Also, in your definition of 'property' you must take 'things' to include actions as well; for otherwise, even if there were no rights over 'things' it would still be unjust to prevent men from acting as they need to. But that explanation makes it impossible that there should be no 'property'. As for the proposition about the

[1] Locke: 'oppose, or menace'. Coste's change.
[2] Locke refers to *the idea of* property, of injustice, and – in the next example – of government and of absolute liberty.
[3] Locke: 'that right'. Coste's change.

incompatibility of government with absolute liberty: it belongs among the corollaries, i.e. the propositions which have only to be brought to one's attention [for their truth to be recognized]. In jurisprudence there are more complex ones, such as those having to do with the so-called *Jus accrescendi*, with conditions, and with various other matters. I showed this when as a young man I published my theses *De conditionibus* in which I proved several corollaries. I should revise that work if I could spare the time to do so.

PHIL. That would please those who are interested in such matters, and would let you forestall anyone who might reprint it in its unrevised form.

THEO. That is what happened with my *Art of Combinations*, as I have already complained. It was a product of my adolescence, and yet they re-issued it many years later, without consulting me or so much as indicating that it was a second printing; which hurt my reputation by leading some people to believe that I was capable of publishing such a work in my maturity. For although it contains some important thoughts which I still approve, it also contains some which would not befit anyone but a young student.

385

PHIL. §19. The uncertainty of words can be substantially remedied, I find, by the use of 'diagrams'; but 'this cannot be thus done in moral ideas'. Furthermore, moral ideas are more composite than 'the figures ordinarily considered in mathematics'; and so the mind cannot easily retain the 'precise combinations' of constituents of moral ideas as 'perfectly, as is necessary in...long deductions'. And if in arithmetic the various stages were not indicated 'by marks, whose precise significations are known, and [which] last and remain in view..., it would be almost impossible' to perform long reckonings. §20. Definitions afford some remedy in moral discourse, provided they are adhered to steadily. 'And what methods algebra, or something of that kind, may hereafter suggest, to remove the other difficulties, is not easy to foretell.'

THEO. The late M. Erhard *Weigel, a mathematician of Jena in Thuringia, devised ingenious diagrams to represent moral entities. And when his disciple the late M. Samuel *Pufendorf issued his own *Elements of Universal Jurisprudence*, a work which is pretty much in accordance with M. Weigel's thought, that mathematician's 'Moral Sphere' was included in the Jena edition of the work. But these diagrams are a kind of allegory – rather like the *Picture* of Cebes, though less *popular – and they help the memory to retain and organize ideas rather than helping the judgment to gain demonstrative knowledge. They are nevertheless of some use in arousing the mind. Geometrical figures appear simpler than moral entities; but they are not so, because anything which is continuous involves an infinity, from which selections must be made. For instance, the problem of dividing a triangle into four equal parts by means of two straight lines at right angles to each other – it appears simple, and is quite hard. It is not like that with questions of morality, in cases where they can be settled by reason alone. As for your last point: this is not the place to discuss extending the boundaries of the science of demonstration, or to suggest the right means for taking the art of demonstration beyond its age-old limits which until now have almost coincided with those of the realm of mathematics. I hope that if God gives me the needed time I shall one day present some work in which I actually make use of these means and do not limit myself to the accepted rules.

PHIL. If you do carry out that plan, sir, and do it properly, you will put infinitely into your debt those who are Philalethes as I am, that is, people who sincerely wish to know the truth. Truth is naturally beautiful to minds, and there is 'nothing so deformed and irreconcilable to the understanding, as a lie.' Yet men cannot be expected to apply themselves assiduously to such discoveries 'whilst the desire of esteem, riches, or power, makes men espouse the well endowed opinions in fashion, and then seek arguments, either to make good their beauty, or varnish over, and cover their deformity....Whilst the parties of men, cram their tenets down all men's throats, whom they can get into their power, without [examining]¹ their truth or falsehood;...what [new]² light can be hoped for in the moral sciences? The subject part of mankind, in most places, might, instead thereof,' expect a darkness as thick as Egypt's if it were not that 'the candle of the Lord' is itself present in men's minds, a sacred light 'which it is impossible for the...power of man wholly to extinguish.'

THEO. I am not without hope that at some quieter time or in some quieter land men will avail themselves of reason more than they have done. For indeed one should not despair of anything; and I believe that mankind is destined to undergo great changes for better and for worse, but ultimately more for better than for worse. Suppose it happens that some day a great Prince has a long and thoroughly peaceful reign, like the ancient kings of Assyria and of Egypt, or like another Solomon; and suppose that this Prince, being a lover of virtue and truth, and endowed with a firmness and breadth of mind, resolves to make men happier and less quarrelsome, and to increase their command over nature; what marvels will he not achieve within a few years? Certainly, under those circumstances more would be achieved in ten years than would come about in a hundred, or perhaps a thousand, if events were left to take their ordinary course. But even without that, if the way could just once be opened up, many people would start along it – as the geometers did along theirs – if only for the pleasure of it, or as a means to fame. As society becomes more civilized, it will eventually

¹ Locke: 'permitting them to examine'. ² Locke: 'greater'. Coste's change.

give more attention to the advancement of medicine than it has done so far: in every country journals of natural history will be issued like almanacs or the *Mercure galant*; no sound observations will be left unrecorded; those who are engaged in this work will be helped; the art of making such observations will be highly developed, as will also the art of using them as bases for *aphorisms. The time will come when there are more good physicians, and correspondingly fewer members of certain other professions for which there will then be less need; so that society will be in a position to give more encouragement to the exploration of nature, and especially to the advancement of medicine; and then that important science will grow visibly, and will very soon reach a level far above its present one. Indeed, I believe that this aspect of public policy will become almost the chief concern of those who govern, second only to the concern for virtue; and that one of the greatest results of sound morality and sound politics will be our getting an improved medical science – when men start being wiser than they are now, and when people of high station have learned better ways of using their wealth and power in the interests of their own happiness.

PHIL. §21. With regard to the knowledge of real existence (which is the fourth sort of knowledge), it should be said that we have an *intuitive* knowledge of our own existence, a *demonstrative* one of the existence of God,[1] and a *sensitive* one of other things. We shall discuss this more fully later on [pp. 434–47].

THEO. You could not be more right.

PHIL. §22. If we want to discover more about 'the present state of our minds,' it would be a good idea, now that we have spoken of *knowledge*, to 'look a little into the dark side, and take a view of our *ignorance*: [since it is] infinitely larger than our knowledge'. Here are the causes of this ignorance. 'First, want of ideas. Secondly, want of a discoverable connection between the ideas we have. Thirdly, [neglect] of tracing, and [precisely][2] examining our ideas.' §23. Concerning the 'want of ideas': we have no simple ideas except what come to us from our inner and outer senses;[3] and so, with regard to the existence and qualities of an infinity of created things in the universe, we are like blind men in relation to colours, not even having the faculties that would be needed to know them. And man 'in all probability, is [on the lowest level][4] of all intellectual beings.'

THEO. I am not sure that there are not also some below us – why should we want needlessly to denigrate ourselves? We may occupy a quite honourable level amongst rational animals, for it could be that the higher

388

---

[1] Locke: 'of a God'. Coste's change.   [2] Added by Coste.
[3] The content of this is in Locke's §23, but the phrase '*sens internes ou externes*' is Leibniz's.   [4] Locke: 'one of the lowest'. Coste's change.

Spirits have bodies of a different sort such that the name 'animal' could not be applied to them. There is no telling whether, of the great multitude of suns, more are superior to our sun than are inferior to it; and we are well placed within its system, for Earth holds a middle position among the planets, and its distance appears well chosen for a contemplative animal who has to inhabit it. Furthermore, we have immeasurably more reason to congratulate ourselves than to complain of our lot, since for most of our hardships we have only ourselves to blame. It would be especially wrong to complain of the deficiencies in our knowledge, when we make so little use of the knowledge which kindly nature does give to us.

PHIL. §24. However, the vast distance of nearly all of the visible parts of the world hides them from our knowledge;[1] and apparently the visible world is only a small part of this immense universe. We are enclosed in a little corner of space, i.e. the 'system of our sun', yet we do not even know what goes on on the other planets which, like our globe, revolve around it. §25. Such knowledge eludes us for reasons of largeness and[2] of distance; but other bodies are hidden from us by their smallness, and these are the ones which it would matter most to us to know about.[3] For from the structures they make we could infer the uses and the modes of operation of visible bodies, and could know why rhubarb purges, hemlock kills, and opium makes one sleep. §26. So 'I am apt to doubt that, how far soever human industry may advance...experimental philosophy in physical things, [scientific knowledge] will still be out of our reach'.

THEO. I do believe that we shall never advance as far as one might wish; yet it seems to me that considerable progress will eventually be made in explaining various phenomena. That is because the great number of experiments which are within our reach can supply us with more than sufficient data, so that all we lack is the art of employing them; and I am not without hope that the small beginnings of that will be extended, now that the *infinitesimal calculus has given us the means for allying geometry with natural science and now that dynamics has supplied us with the general laws of nature.

PHIL. §27. 'Spirits...are yet more remote from our knowledge[. We cannot] frame to our selves any...[4] ideas of their several ranks[; and yet the] intellectual world [is] a greater certainly, and more beautiful world, than the material.'

THEO. Those worlds are always perfectly parallel so far as efficient causes go, but not final causes. For to the extent that spirits hold sway within matter, they produce wonderful arrangements in it. That is apparent in the changes which men have made so as to embellish the earth's surface,

389

---

[1] This clause misrepresents Locke.   [2] 'de la grandeur et' added by Leibniz.
[3] Clause added by Leibniz.   [4] Locke: 'distinct'.

like little gods imitating the great Architect of the universe, although only by using bodies and the laws of bodies. What may we not conjecture about that immeasurable multitude of spirits which surpass ourselves? And as spirits all together form a kind of State under God, one which is perfectly governed, we are a long way from understanding the system of this intellectual world; from conceiving of the punishments and rewards which are laid up within it for those, who, according to the strictest reason, deserve them; and from imagining that which eye has not seen nor ear heard and which has never entered into the heart of man. Yet all of this shows that we do have all the distinct ideas that are needed for a knowledge of bodies and spirits, but not sufficiently detailed [knowledge of] particular facts, and that we also lack senses which are sharp enough to sort out the confused ideas and comprehensive enough to perceive them all.

PHIL. §28. With regard to the undiscovered connections between the ideas which we have, I was going to tell you that 'the mechanical affections of bodies [have] no affinity at all' with the ideas of colours, sounds, smells, and tastes, or of pleasure and pain; and that their connection depends only on the good pleasure and arbitrary will of God. But I remember that you hold that there is a perfect *correspondence* even though it is not always a complete *resemblance*. You recognize, however, that ideas involve too much minute detail for us to be able to disentangle what is concealed in them; but you still hope that we shall come much closer to doing so. So you would not want anyone to say, as my distinguished author does, that it is 'lost labour' to engage in such an inquiry;[1] for fear that that belief might impede the growth of science. I would have spoken to you also of the difficulty which we have had until now in explaining the connection between the soul and the body, since one cannot conceive that a 'thought should produce a motion in body' or that a motion 'should produce [a] thought in the mind.' But now that I grasp your theory of the pre-established harmony, that difficulty – which we had despaired of solving – appears to me to have suddenly vanished as though by magic. §30. There remains, then, the third cause of our ignorance. It is our 'want of tracing those ideas which we have, or may have', and our not applying ourselves to 'finding... intermediate ideas'. That is how one can be 'ignorant of mathematical truths, not out of any imperfection of [our] faculties, or uncertainty in the things themselves'. The 'ill use of words' has been the greatest hindrance to our finding out the agreements and disagreements of ideas; and mathematicians, forming their thoughts independently of names,[2] 'and accustoming themselves to set before their minds, the ideas themselves ... and not sounds...,[3] have avoided thereby a great part of [the] perplexity....

390

---

[1] Clause based on Locke's §29.

[2] Locke: 'abstracting their thoughts from names'. Coste's change.

[3] Locke: 'instead of them'.

Had men, in the discoveries of the material, done, as they have in those of the intellectual world,' confused everything in a chaos of terms with uncertain significations, they would have disputed endlessly about zones, tides, the building of ships, and the routes to be followed; they would never have ventured 'beyond the line: and the Antipodes would be still as much unknown, as when it was declared heresy to hold there were any.'

THEO. This third 'cause of our ignorance' is the only one which is blameworthy. And you do see, sir, that it includes despair about making any progress. This despondency does great harm; and some able and eminent people have hindered the progress of medicine by their mistaken view that work on it is wasted labour. When you read the Aristotelian philosophers of bygone days treating of atmospheric phenomena – of the rainbow, for instance – you will find that they believed that one should not even think of distinctly explaining this phenomenon; and the undertakings of Maurolyco, and later of Marco Antonio de Dominis, struck them as being like a flight of Icarus. Yet what has happened since has shown everyone that that was wrong. It is true that the misuse of terms has caused much of the disarray which occurs in our knowledge – not only in the moral and metaphysical sphere which you call 'the intellectual world', but also in medicine, where this abuse of terms is increasing more and more. We cannot always summon diagrams to our aid, as we can in geometry, but algebra shows that one can make great discoveries without constantly having recourse to the actual ideas of things. With regard to the alleged heresy of the Antipodes, I will remark in passing that it is true that Boniface, Archbishop of Mainz, wrote a letter to the Pope in which he made an accusation against *Virgilius of Salzburg on this topic, and that the Pope's reply showed that he was pretty much of Boniface's opinion; but nothing seems to have resulted from this accusation. Virgilius has not lost his standing. Both antagonists are regarded as saints; and Bavarian scholars, who regard Virgilius as 'the Apostle of Carinthia' and of the neighbouring regions, have vindicated his memory.

Chapter iv
'Of the reality of our knowledge.'

PHILALETHES. §1. Someone who does not grasp the importance of having good ideas and of understanding their agreements and disagreements will think that in reasoning so carefully on this topic we are building a castle in the air, and that our whole system contains nothing but what is ideal and imaginary. An extravagant man with a heated imagination will have the advantage, 'as having the more ideas, and the more lively. And so ...he will be the more knowing.... The visions of an enthusiast, and the reasonings of a sober man, will be equally certain', provided that the enthusiast talks 'conformably'. It will be as true to say 'that an harpy is not a centaur' as to say 'that a square is not a circle.' **§3.** I answer that our 'ideas agree with things.' But it will be asked what the criterion for this is. **§4.** And I answer *firstly*, that there is obviously such an agreement in the case of the simple ideas in our mind, for since the latter cannot make these of its own accord they must be produced by things' acting upon the mind. And *secondly* that **§5.** 'all our complex ideas, except those of substances, being archetypes of the mind's own making, not intended to be the copies of any thing, nor referred to the existence of any thing, as to their originals, cannot want any conformity [to things]¹ necessary to real knowledge.'

THEOPHILUS. Our certainty would be small, or rather non-existent, if it had no foundation of simple ideas except the one deriving from the senses. Have you forgotten, sir, how I have shown that ideas are inherently² in our mind, and that even our thoughts come to us from our own depths without any other created things' being capable of any immediate influence on the soul? Also, our certainty regarding universal and eternal truths is grounded in the ideas themselves, independently of the senses, just as pure ideas, ideas of the intellect – e.g. those of *being, one, same* etc. – are also independent of the senses. But the ideas of sensible qualities such as colour, flavour etc. (which are really only illusory images³) do come to us through the senses, i.e. from our confused perceptions. And the truth about contingent singular things is grounded in success, whereby⁴ sensory phenomena are linked together in just the way required by truths of the intellect. That is the distinction which ought to be drawn; whereas the one you draw here between simple ideas and composite ones, and within the latter between ideas of substances and those of accidents, appears to me to be without foundation, since all ideas of the intellect have their archetypes in the eternal possibility of things.

PHIL. Indeed, our composite ideas have no need of archetypes outside the mind unless there is a question of whether those complex ideas, and the simple ones of which they are composed, are actually united outside us in an existent substance. **§6.** Knowledge of mathematical truths is real: although it is based entirely on our ideas, and although exact circles are not found anywhere, still we can be certain that in so far as what we postulate in our archetypes turns out to exist, those real things will conform to the archetypes. **§7.** The reality of moral knowledge⁵ is established in the same way. **§8.** 'Tully's *Offices* [are not] less true, because there is no body in the world that exactly . . . lives up to that pattern of a virtuous man,

---

¹ Added by Leibniz.   ² '*originairement*'.
³ '*ne sont que des fantômes*'; cf. pp. 403f.   ⁴ '*le succès, qui fait que*'.
⁵ Taking '*choses*' to be a slip for Coste's '*connaissances*'.

which he has given us'. **§9.** 'But it will here be said, that if...moral ideas ...be of our own making, what strange notions will there be of *justice* and *temperance?*' **§10.** I answer that the uncertainty will lie only in the language, because speakers are not always understood, or not always in the same way.

THEO. Another reply you could make, sir, and in my view a better one, is that the ideas of justice and of temperance are not 'of our own making', any more than the ideas of circle and square. I think I have shown this well enough [pp. 251f].

PHIL. **§11.** With regard to ideas of substances which exist outside us, our knowledge is real in so far as it conforms to those archetypes; and **§12.** here the mind must not combine ideas arbitrarily, especially as 'there are very few [simple ideas] that we can be sure are, or are not inconsistent in nature, any farther than...sensible observation reaches.'

THEO. As I have more than once said, that is because those ideas whose compatibility or connection cannot be judged by reason are confused ones, such as those of particular sensory qualities.

PHIL. **§13.** With regard to existing substances it is advisable not to confine ourselves to names or to species which are thought to be fixed by names. That brings me back to something we have already discussed quite often, regarding the definition of man. Of a changeling which has lived for forty years 'without any appearance of reason,' could it not be said that it is 'something between a man and a beast'? That 'would possibly be thought a bold paradox, if not a very dangerous falsehood'. Yet there was a time when it seemed to me – as it still does to some of my friends whom I have not yet been able to cure of their error – that that results merely from a 'prejudice...founded upon...a false supposition, that these two names, *man* and *beast*, stand for distinct species so set out by real essences [in nature], that there can come no other species between them: [as though] there were a certain number of these essences, wherein all things, as in moulds, were cast and formed'.[1] **§14.** When asked what species of animal these changelings do belong to, if they are neither man nor beast, these friends of mind reply that they are changelings and that that is enough. When it is further asked what will become of them in the other world, my friends reply that it does not concern them to know or to inquire. 'To their own master they stand or fall' (*Romans* 14:4), say my friends; and he is bountiful and faithful and 'disposes not of his creatures according to our narrow thoughts or [private] opinions, nor distinguishes them according to names and species of our contrivance.' It is enough for us, they say, that 'those, who are capable of instruction...shall come to an account, and

394

---

[1] Leibniz: '*comme si toutes les choses étaient jetées au moule suivant le nombre précis de ces essences*'. Since this is hardly intelligible, we revert to Locke's formulation.

receive [their due] according to what they have done in this body' (2 *Corinthians* 5:10). **§15.** I shall go on to give you the rest of their reasoning. The question (they say) of whether imbeciles should be deprived of a future state 'is founded on...[1] two suppositions, which are both false. The first is, that all things that have the outward shape and appearance of a man [are] designed to an immortal future being, after this life'; and the second is[2] that whatever is of human birth must have this privilege. 'Take away these imaginations, and such questions will be [seen to be][3] groundless and ridiculous.' And really I think that the former supposition will be disowned, and that no one's mind is so 'immersed in matter' that he thinks that eternal life is due to any shape of a mass of matter, so that the mass is to be everlastingly sentient 'because it was moulded into this or that figure'. **§16.** But the second supposition comes to the rescue:[4] it will be said that the changeling 'is the issue of rational parents, and must therefore be concluded to have a rational soul. I know not by what logic' this inference can be secured; nor do I see how, after such a conclusion, anyone would dare 'to destroy ill-formed and mis-shaped productions. Aye, but these are monsters', it will be said. Well, so be it. But 'what will your [always] intractable changeling be? Shall a defect in the body make a monster; a defect in the mind...not?' That is to return to the first supposition, which has already been refuted, that the externals are decisive. The well-shaped changeling is believed to be a man, and to have a rational soul though it does not appear. But 'make the ears a little longer, and more pointed, and the nose a little flatter than ordinary, and then you begin to boggle: make the face yet narrower, flatter, and longer, and then you are at a stand:[5] [and if] the head be perfectly that of some...animal, then [without doubt] 'tis a monster; and 'tis demonstration with you, that it hath no rational soul, and must be destroyed. Where now (I ask) shall be the just measure, [where shall be the utmost bounds that carry with them][6] a rational soul?...There has been human foetuses produced, half beast, and half man; and others three parts one, and one part t'other'. How are we to determine what are 'those precise lineaments' which indicate reason? Furthermore, would not this monster be a species intermediate between man and beast? 'And just so is the changeling before-mentioned.'

THEO. We have already given enough attention to this matter, more than once indeed [pp. 234f, 311, 313f, 317–20, 326]. I am surprised that you should return to it, and that you have not done better in catechizing your friends. If we distinguish man from beast by the faculty of reason, there is no intermediate case: the animal in question must either have it or not

---

[1] Locke: 'one of'.   [2] Locke: 'or, secondly'.
[3] Added by Coste.   [4] Added by Leibniz.
[5] Taking *'déterminé'* to be a slip for Coste's *'indéterminé'*.
[6] Locke: 'which [shall be] the utmost bounds of that shape, that carries with it'.

395   have it. But as this faculty is sometimes not manifested, we judge of it from indications – ones which are not conclusive as to the truth – until such time as reason makes its appearance; for we know, from our experience of those who have lost their reason and those who have acquired the use of it late, that its operation can be suspended for a while. Birth and outward form create presumptions about what is hidden within. But the presumption created by birth is erased (*eliditur*) if the shape is extremely different from the human one, as was that of an animal born to a Zeeland woman, according to Levinus Lemnius (Bk I, ch. 8): it had a hooked beak, a long, curved neck, gleaming eyes, and a pointed tail; and it immediately ran about the room with great agility. But it will be said that there are monsters – or 'Lombard brothers', as the physicians used to call them, because the women of Lombardy were said to be subject to such births – which come closer to human shape. Well, so be it! Then how (you will ask) can we determine the precise limits of the shape which should count as human? I answer that one cannot be precise in conjectural matters. And that's the end of the matter. It is objected that the changeling does not display reason and yet is counted as a man, but would not be so counted if he had a monstrous shape, so that more attention is being paid to shape than to reason. But does this monster manifest reason? – certainly not. So, you see, it lacks more than the changeling does. A lack of the use of reason is often temporary, but in those who also have heads like dogs' it is permanent. Furthermore, if this human-shaped animal is not a man, no great harm will come from caring for it while we are uncertain about its fate. And whether it has a rational soul or one which is not rational, God will not have created that soul for no purpose. As for the souls of men who remain always in a state like that of earliest infancy: one would think that they might have the same fate as the souls of infants who die in the cradle.

396

Chapter v
'Of truth in general.'

PHILALETHES. §1. 'What is truth, was an inquiry many ages since'. §2. My friends believe that it is 'the joining or separating of signs, as the things signified by them, do agree or disagree one with another. The joining or separating of signs here meant is what by another name, we call proposition.'

THEOPHILUS. But a phrase, e.g. 'the wise man', does not make a proposition; yet it involves a joining of two terms.[1] Nor is negation the same as separation; for saying 'the man' and then after a pause uttering 'wise' is not making a denial. Furthermore, what is expressed by a

---

[1] The French for 'the wise man' has the same word order as the French for 'The man is wise'.

proposition is not strictly 'agreement' or 'disagreement'. Agreement obtains between two eggs, disagreement between two enemies. What we are dealing with here is a quite special way of agreeing or disagreeing, and I do not think that your definition explains it. But what is least to my liking in your definition of truth is that it looks for truth among words, so that if the same sense is expressed in Latin, German, English, and French it will not be the same truth; and we shall have to say with Mr *Hobbes that truth depends upon the good pleasure of men. That is a very strange way of speaking. Truth is attributed even to God, and I think you will agree that he has no need for signs. In short, this is not the first time that I have been surprised by the attitude of these friends of yours who are pleased to make essences, species and truths *nominal*.

PHIL. Do not go too fast. They take signs to include ideas; and so truths will be either mental or nominal, according to the kind of signs.

THEO. If distinctions are to be made among truths on the basis of signs, 397 we shall also have *written* truths, which can be divided into paper truths and parchment ones, and into ordinary-ink truths and printer's-ink ones. It would be better to assign truth to the relationships amongst the objects of the ideas, by virtue of which one idea is or is not included within another. That does not depend on languages, and is something we have in common with God and the angels. And when God displays a truth to us, we come to possess the truth which is in his understanding, for although his ideas are infinitely more perfect and extensive than ours they still have the same relationships that ours do. So it is to these relationships that truth should be assigned; and we can distinguish *truths*, which are independent of our good pleasure, from *expressions*, which we invent as we see fit.

PHIL. §4. It is only too true that even in their minds men put words in place of ideas,[1] especially when the ideas are complex and indeterminate. But it is true also, as you have observed [p. 286], that in such a case the mind contents itself with merely taking note of the truth without yet understanding it, being convinced that it can understand it whenever it wishes to. §6. Furthermore, the action one performs when affirming or denying 'is easier to be conceived by reflecting on what passes in us..., than to be explained by words'; so do not take it amiss that I have spoken of 'putting together and separating', for lack of something better. §8. You will also acknowledge that propositions, at least, can be called verbal, and that true propositions are both verbal and real.[2] This is because §9. falsehood consists in combining names otherwise than as their ideas agree or disagree. At any rate, §10. 'words are...the great conduits of truth'.

---

[1] Taking '*choses*' to be a slip for Coste's '*idées*'.

[2] This misrepresents Locke's §8, which distinguishes 'real truth' from what is 'only verbal truth'.

§11. There is also '*moral truth*, which is speaking things according to the persuasion of our own minds[; and finally there is] *metaphysical truth*, which is...the real existence of things, conformable to the ideas' which we have of them.[1]

THEO. Moral truth is called 'veracity' by some; and 'metaphysical truth' is commonly taken by the metaphysicians to be an attribute of Being, but it is a thoroughly useless and almost senseless attribute. Let us be content with looking for truth in the correspondence between the propositions which are in the mind and the things which they are about. It is true that I have also attributed truth to ideas, by saying that ideas are either true or false [p. 269]; but what I mean by that is the truth of the proposition which affirms that the object of the idea is possible. And in that sense one could also say that an entity is true, i.e. [attribute truth to] the proposition which affirms its actual or at least possible existence.

Chapter vi
'Of universal propositions, their truth and certainty.'

PHILALETHES. §2. All our knowledge is of general or of particular truths. The former, which are the most important, 'can never be well made known, and [are] very seldom apprehended, but as conceived and expressed in words.'

THEOPHILUS. I believe that other marks could also produce the same result – the characters[2] of the Chinese show this. And we could introduce a Universal *Symbolism – a very *popular one, better than theirs – if in place of words we used little diagrams which represented visible things pictorially and invisible things by means of the visible ones which go with them, also bringing in certain additional marks suitable for conveying inflections and particles. This would at once enable us to communicate easily with remote peoples; but if we adopted it among ourselves (though without abandoning ordinary writing), the use of this way of writing would be of great service in enriching our imaginations and giving us thoughts which were less blind and less verbal than our present ones are. Of course not everyone knows how to draw, so that apart from books printed in this manner, which everyone would soon learn to read, some people would only be able to make use of this system by printing of a sort – by having engravings ready to use for printing the pictures on paper and then adding the marks for the inflections and particles by pen. But in time everyone would learn to draw during childhood, so as to be able to take advantage of this pictorial symbolism; it would literally *speak to the eyes*, and would be much liked by the populace. In fact peasants already have almanacs

[1] Locke: 'the ideas to which we have annexed their names.'
[2] '*caractères*' – rendered by 'symbols' except in reference to Chinese.

398

399

which wordlessly tell them much of what they want to know. And I remember seeing satirical broadsheets, in copperplate, which were somewhat of the nature of puzzles, containing inherently significant pictures mixed with words; our letters and Chinese characters, on the other hand, are significant only through the will of men (*ex *instituto*).

PHIL. That sort of writing strikes me as so satisfactory and natural that I believe that your scheme will some day be put into operation; and it promises to contribute in no small measure to perfecting our minds and making our thoughts more real. **§3.** But to return to general knowledge and its certainty, it is appropriate to point out that there is 'certainty of *truth*, and [also] certainty of *knowledge*. Certainty of truth is, when words are so put together in propositions, as exactly to express the agreement or disagreement...[1] as really it is. Certainty of knowledge is, to perceive the agreement or disagreement of ideas, as expressed in any proposition. This we usually call' being certain of a proposition.[2]

THEO. Really in the latter case the *certainty* is enough, without the use of words. It is nothing but a perfect knowledge of the truth, whereas the former kind of certainty appears to be just the truth itself.

PHIL. **§4.** 'Now because we cannot be certain of the truth of any general proposition, unless we know the precise bounds [of what] its terms stand for, it is necessary we should know the essence of each species, [which in] simple ideas and modes, is not hard to do....But in substances, wherein a real essence, distinct from the nominal, is supposed to...determine... the species, the extent of the general word is very uncertain', because we do not know this real essence; and, consequently, on this view we cannot be certain about any general proposition concerning such substances. But where it is supposed that the species of substances are nothing but the sorting of substantial individuals[3] 'under general names, according as they agree to several abstract ideas, of which we make those names the signs,' we can be in no doubt, with regard to a proposition which is thoroughly known as it should be,[4] whether it is true or not.

THEO. I fail to see, sir, why you return yet again to a topic which we have argued about a good deal, and which I believed to be exhausted. But after all I am pleased that you have done so, because you are giving me what seems to be an excellent opportunity to set you right once again. So let me tell you that there are, for example, hundreds of truths that we can be certain of concerning gold, i.e. that body whose inner essence reveals itself through the greatest weight known here on earth, or through the greatest

400

---

[1] Locke: 'of the ideas they stand for'. Coste's omission.
[2] Locke: 'knowing, or being certain of the truth of any proposition.'
[3] Locke: 'species of things are [nothing] but the sorting of them'. Coste puts '*substances*' for 'things' and for 'them'.
[4] '*bien connue comme il faut*'; not based on anything in Locke or Coste.

ductility or by other marks. For we can say that the body with the greatest known ductility is also the heaviest of all known bodies. Of course, it is not impossible that everything that we have so far observed in gold will some day be found to characterize two bodies which can be told apart by means of other new qualities; in which case gold would no longer be the lowest species, as we have provisionally taken it to be up to now. It could also happen that one sort was still rare while the other was common, and that we saw fit to restrict the name of true gold to the rare species, so as to set it aside – with the aid of new assays which were specific to it – for use in coinage. If that happens, there will then be no doubt that these two species have different inner essences. Even if the definition of an actually existing substance was not fully determinate in all respects (as in fact that of man is not, with respect to outer shape), one could still have an infinity of general propositions about him which followed from the rationality and other qualities that were recognized in him. All that can be said about these general propositions is that if we regard man as a lowest species, restricted to the race of Adam, then we shall not have any properties of man which are *in quarto modo, as they say, i.e. which can be affirmed of him in a reciprocal or simply convertible proposition, unless it is affirmed provisionally, as in saying that *man is the only rational animal*. If 'man' is being understood as those who belong to our race, then what makes this provisional is its reliance on his being the only rational one among the animals which are known to us. For there may some day come to be animals which have – in common with all the descendants of men who are alive now – everything we have so far observed in men, but who have had a different origin from us. Suppose for instance that the imaginary 'Austra-
401   lians' swarmed into our latitudes: it is likely that some way would be found of distinguishing them from us; but if not, and if God had forbidden the mingling of these races, and if Jesus Christ had redeemed only our own, then we should have to try to introduce artificial marks to distinguish the races from one another. No doubt there would be an inner difference, but since we should be unable to detect it we should have to rely solely on the 'extrinsic *denomination' of birth, and try to associate it with an indelible artificial mark which would provide an 'intrinsic denomination' and a permanent means of telling our race apart from theirs. This is all fiction; since we are the only rational animals on this globe, we have no need to resort to this kind of differentiation. Still, such fictions help us to know the nature of ideas of substances, and of general truths about them. But if 'man' were not regarded as a lowest species, nor as the species of rational animals of the race of Adam; and if instead the word signified a genus shared by several species, with only one known race belonging to it now but with the possibility of its also containing others, these being distinguishable – like those pretended 'Australians' – either by birth alone

or by other natural marks; then there would be reciprocal propositions about this genus, and the present definition of *man* would not be provisional. It is the same with *gold*. Suppose that some day we were to have two discernible sorts of it – a rare one which we already know, and a common one, perhaps artificial, which is to be discovered in the future; and suppose further that the name 'gold' were to be kept for the present species, i.e. for natural, rare gold, so as to use it to preserve the convenience of gold coinage, which depends on the rarity of that metal; in that case the definition of gold which we have known up to now, in terms of intrinsic denominations, would have been merely provisional and will have to be supplemented by new marks which will be discovered, so as to distinguish rare gold (i.e. gold of the old species) from the new, artificial gold. But if by 'gold' were meant a genus for which we do not yet know any subdivision, and which we now treat as a lowest species (but only provisionally, until a subdivision is found); so that if a new species – an artificial gold which was easy to make and which might become common – were found, the name of gold ought to go on being shared by the two species; then the definition of the genus, taken in that sense, should be regarded not as provisional but as permanent. Indeed, without troubling ourselves over the names 'man' and 'gold', whatever name we give to a genus or a lowest known species, and even if we give them no name at all, what has just been said would always be true of the ideas of genera and species, and species will be only provisionally defined – sometimes by the definitions of genera. Still, it will always be permissible and reasonable to take it that there is – whether with the genus or with the species – a real inner essence which is ascribable by a reciprocal proposition and which ordinarily reveals its presence by external marks. So far I have been assuming that a race will not degenerate or change; but if the same race were to develop into another species, there would be all the more need to fall back on other marks and intrinsic or extrinsic denominations, without relying on race.

PHIL. §7. 'The complex ideas, that our names of the species of substances properly stand for,[1] are collections [of the ideas][2] of such qualities, as have been observed to coexist in an unknown *substratum* which we call *substance*; but what other qualities necessarily coexist with such combinations, we cannot certainly know, unless we can discover' how they depend upon their primary qualities.

THEO. I have already pointed out [p. 346] that the same thing obtains with ideas of accidents, if their nature is a little hard to fathom, as in the case of geometrical shapes. For instance, if we wanted to find the shape of a

---

[1] Taking '*justifient*' to be a slip for Coste's '*signifient*'.
[2] Added by Leibniz.

402

*mirror which would bring all the parallel rays of light together at a point, the focus; we may find various properties of such a mirror without knowing how to construct it, but we shall remain unsure about many other possible features of it until we find the fact about it which corresponds to the inner constitution of a substance – namely, how to construct the figure that defines the mirror's shape, this being like a key to further knowledge.

PHIL. But if we did know the internal constitution of such a body, we would only find such primary (or, as you call them, manifest) qualities as might depend upon it – i.e. come to know what sizes, shapes and moving forces depend on it. But we would never know what connection they might have with the secondary or confused[1] qualities, i.e. sensible qualities such as colours, tastes and so on.

403

THEO. So you are again assuming that these sensible qualities, or rather our ideas of them, do not depend naturally on shapes or motion, but only on the good pleasure of God who gives us these ideas. You thus appear to have forgotten, sir, my repeated objections to this view, in which I have tried to convince you [pp. 131–3] that these 'sensory ideas' depend on detail in the shapes and motions, which they precisely express, though the mechanical processes which act on our senses are too small and too great in number for us to sort out this detail within the confusion. But if we had arrived at the inner constitutions of certain bodies, these [sensible] qualities would be traced back to their intelligible causes and we should see under what circumstances they were bound to be present; even though it would never be in our power to recognize their causes sensorily, in our sensory ideas which are the confused effects of bodies acting on us. For instance, we now have a complete analysis of green into blue and yellow, and almost all our remaining questions about it concern these ingredients; yet we are quite unable to discern the ideas of blue and yellow within our sensory idea of green, simply because it is a confused idea. Somewhat similarly, when the swift rotation of a cog-wheel makes us perceive an artificial transparency, as I have noticed on visits to clock-makers, we are not able to discern the idea of the cause of this, i.e. the idea of the teeth on the wheel. The wheel's rotation makes the teeth disappear and an imaginary continuous transparent [ring] appear in their place; it is made up of successive appearances of teeth and of gaps between them, but in such rapid succession that our imagination[2] cannot distinguish them. So the teeth are encountered in the distinct notion of this transparency, but not in that confused sensory perception of it. It is the latter's nature to be confused and to remain so; for if the confusion ceased (e.g. if the motion slowed down enough for us to be able to observe the parts in succession)

---

[1] 'ou confuses' added by Leibniz.
[2] 'fantaisie', not 'imagination' as elsewhere.

it would no longer be this same perception, i.e. it would no longer be this image[1] of transparency. Now, there is no need to suppose that God bestows this image upon us through his good pleasure, and that it is independent of the motion of the teeth on the wheel and of the gaps between them. On the contrary, we grasp that it is only a confused expression of what is occurring in this motion – an expression, I say, which consists in the blurring together of successive things into an apparent simultaneity. And so we can readily conclude that the situation will be the same with regard to those other 'sensory images', like *colours and tastes and so on, of which we do not yet have such a perfect analysis. (For the truth is that these ought to be called 'images' rather than 'qualities' or even 'ideas'.) It would be enough for all our purposes if we understood them as well as we do that artificial transparency: it would be neither reasonable nor possible to profess to know more; for it is self-contradictory to want these confused images to persist while wanting their components to be discerned by the imagination[2] itself. It is like wanting to enjoy being deceived by some charming perspective and wanting to see through the deception at the same time – which would spoil the effect. In short, this is a point where 'you will get no further ahead than if you set out to rave rationally' [Terence]. But men often look for 'a knot in a bulrush' [Plautus] and give themselves problems where none exist, by asking for the impossible and then bewailing their helplessness and the limits of their insight.

404

PHIL. §8. '*All gold is fixed*, is a proposition whose truth we cannot be certain of'. For if *gold* stands for a species of things distinguished by a real essence which nature has given it, we do not know 'what particular substances are of that species; and so cannot, with certainty, affirm any thing...of gold.' And if we take *gold* to stand for a body endowed with 'a certain yellow colour, malleable, fusible, and heavier than any[3] other known..., there is no difficulty to know what is, or is not gold. But yet no other quality can with certainty be...affirmed or denied of gold, but what hath a discoverable connection, or inconsistency with that' idea. Now fixedness, having no known necessary connection[4] with the colour, weight, or the other simple ideas which I have supposed constitute the complex idea that we have of gold,[5] 'it is impossible that we should certainly know the truth of this proposition, that *all gold is fixed*.'

THEO. We know almost as certainly that the heaviest of all bodies known on earth is *fixed, as that the sun will rise tomorrow. This is because it

---

[1] In this paragraph, 'image' always renders '*fantôme*', not '*image*' as elsewhere. '*Fantôme*' has connotations of illusoriness which '*image*' lacks.
[2] '*fantaisie*'.   [3] Taking '*un*' to be a slip for Coste's '*aucun*'.
[4] Locke: 'no necessary connection, that we can discover'. Coste: '*aucune connexion nécessaire*'. Leibniz: '*aucune connexion nécessaire connue*'.
[5] Locke: 'or any other simple idea of our complex one'. Coste's expansion, except for '*que j'ai supposé*' which is Leibniz's.

405 has been experienced a hundred thousand times. It is a certainty of experience and of fact, even though we do not know how fixity is linked with the other qualities that this body has. Besides, we should not contrast two things which agree and which amount to the same thing. When I think of a body which is at once yellow, fusible and resistant to *cupellation, I am thinking of a body whose specific essence, though hidden from me within it, gives rise to these qualities and reveals itself, at least confusedly, through them. I see nothing wrong with this, nor anything deserving of such often-repeated hostile accusations.

PHIL. All I need for present purposes is that §9. our knowledge that the heaviest of bodies is fixed does not rest on the agreement or disagreement of ideas. §10. 'I imagine, amongst all the secondary qualities of [bodies],[1] and the powers relating to them, there cannot any two be named, whose necessary coexistence, or repugnance to coexist, can certainly be known, unless in those of the same sense, which necessarily exclude one another,' enabling it to be said, for instance, that what is white is not black.

THEO. I believe, though, that some might be found. For example: every body which is tangible (i.e. can be sensed by touch) is visible; every hard body makes a sound when struck in air; a string or thread produces a note which is in subduplicate ratio to the weight causing the tension in it. The fact is that what you are asking for can be attained only in so far as we conceive distinct ideas combined with the confused sensory ones.

PHIL. §11. It should never be supposed that a body has 'all its qualities in it self, and independent of other things....A piece of gold..., separate from the reach and influence of all other bodies, [would] immediately lose all its [yellow] colour and weight, and perhaps malleableness too', becoming friable. We know how much the vegetables and animals depend on earth, air and sun; and who knows but that even the most remote fixed stars have some influence on us?

THEO. This is a very good point. Even if we did know the structure of various bodies, we should still be unable to judge very much about what their effects would be unless we knew the inner nature of the other bodies which touch or penetrate them.

PHIL. §13. Yet our judgment can outreach our knowledge. For 'observing men may...penetrate farther, and on probabilities taken[2] from wary
406 observation, and hints well laid together, often guess right at what experience has not yet discovered to them. But this is but guessing still'.

THEO. But if experience supports these conclusions in a regular way, do you not think that we can arrive in this way at propositions which are

---

[1] Locke: 'substances'.
[2] Taking the omission of Coste's 'déduites' to be a slip.

certain? – as certain, at least, as those which affirm that the heaviest body we possess is fixed, and that the next heaviest is volatile. For it seems to me that, in the case of propositions which we have learned from experience alone and not by the analysis and connection of ideas, we rightly attain to *certainty* (moral or *physical, that is) but not to *necessity* (metaphysical certainty).

Chapter vii
Of the propositions which are named maxims or axioms.[1]

PHILALETHES. §1. 'There are a sort of propositions, which under the name of *maxims* and *axioms*, [pass] for principles of science: and because they are self-evident, [people are prepared to call them] *innate*, without that any body (that I know)[2] ever went about to show the reason and foundation' of their extreme clearness, which forces us, as it were, to give our consent.[3] It is worthwhile, however, to pursue this inquiry and to see whether this great evidence is peculiar to these propositions alone, 'and also to examine how far they [contribute to][4] our other knowledge.'

THEOPHILUS. Such an inquiry is very useful and even important. But you should not imagine, sir, that it has been entirely neglected. You will find a hundred passages in which scholastic philosophers have said that such propositions are evident *ex terminis* – from the terms – as soon as they are understood. That is, they were satisfied that the 'force' of their convincingness is grounded in the understanding of the terms, i.e. in the connections of the associated ideas. But the geometers have gone further still: they have often undertaken to demonstrate such propositions. Proclus says that one of the earliest known geometers, Thales of Miletus, had 407 sought to demonstrate propositions which *Euclid later assumed as evident. Apollonius is reported to have demonstrated other axioms, as did Proclus. The late M. *Roberval, when he was eighty or so, was planning to publish new *Elements of Geometry*, which I believe I have already mentioned to you [pp. 107f]. Perhaps M. *Arnauld's *New Elements*, which were making a stir at that time, had something to do with it. He presented a sample of it in the Royal *Academy of Sciences, and some people objected to his assuming the axiom that 'If equal magnitudes are added to equals, the wholes are equal' in order to prove this other axiom, which is judged to be similarly evident, 'If equal magnitudes are subtracted from equals, the remainders are equal'. They said that he ought to either assume them both or demonstrate them both. But this was not my opinion; I believed that to reduce the number of axioms was always something gained. And

---

1 Locke: 'Of maxims.' Coste's change.
2 This clause is emphasized by Leibniz.
3 Locke: 'foundation of their clearness or cogency.' Coste's expansion.
4 Locke: 'influence and govern'. Coste's change.

addition is unquestionably prior to and simpler than subtraction, because in addition both terms are dealt with in the same way while in subtraction they are not. M. Arnauld did just the opposite to M. Roberval: he assumed even more than Euclid. This can be helpful to beginners, who are hindered by rigour, but it is a different matter when the foundations of a science are at issue. So Arnauld and Roberval may both have been right. As for 'maxims': sometimes established propositions, whether evident or not, are taken to be such. That is what maxims are often taken to be in moral philosophy, and even by the logicians with their *Topics: the latter contain a generous supply of 'maxims', though some of them are rather vague and obscure. Anyway, I have for a long time been urging, both publicly [e.g. 'Meditations on knowledge, truth and ideas' pp. 293f] and in private, the importance of demonstrating all the secondary axioms which we ordinarily use, by bringing them back to axioms which are primary, i.e. immediate and indemonstrable; they are the ones which, recently [p. 361] and in other places, I have been calling 'identities'.

408

PHIL. §2. 'Knowledge is *self-evident*' when 'the agreement or disagreement of ideas... is perceived immediately'. §3. But there are 'other truths, not allowed to be axioms,' which are no less self-evident. Let us see whether they are provided by the four sorts of agreement which we discussed a little while ago (i.3 and iii.7), namely identity, connection,[1] relation, and real existence. §4. As regards identity and diversity, we have as many evident propositions as we have distinct ideas. For we can deny one of the other, e.g. in saying '*A man is not a horse*; *Red is not blue.*' Also, it is as evident to say that '*Whatsoever is, is*' as to say that '*A man is a man*'.

THEO. That is true, and I have already pointed out [p. 367] that it is just as evident to say with reference to one illustrative example that *A is A*, as to say in general that *a thing is what it is*. But I have also pointed out [p. 363] that it is not always safe, with the subjects of two different ideas, to deny one of the other – like someone thinking that a trilateral (i.e. a three-sided thing) is not a triangle, on the grounds that trilateralness is not triangularity. Similarly, if someone had said that M. de Sluse's *pearls*, which I mentioned to you a little while ago [p. 348], are not lines of a cubic parabola, he would have been mistaken; yet that would have appeared obviously right to many people. The late M. *Hardy, who was a magistrate at the Châtelet in *Paris, an excellent geometer, an orientalist, well read in the ancient geometers, and the editor of Marinus's commentary on the *Data* of Euclid, was so convinced that the section of a cone which is called an ellipse is different from the oblique section of a cylinder that Serenus's demonstration appeared to him to be fallacious. I remonstrated with him

---

[1] Locke: 'coexistence'.

to no avail. Of course he was almost as old as M. Roberval when I encountered him, and I was a very young man, and that difference between us cannot have inclined him to take me very seriously, although in other respects I was on very good terms with him. This example illustrates, by the way, the power of prejudice even over clever men, for M. Hardy certainly was that, and is spoken of with respect in M. *Descartes's letters. But I mentioned him only to indicate how far wrong one can go in denying one idea of another, if the case is one where the ideas need to be explored in depth and this has not been done.

PHIL. §5. As to connection or coexistence, we have very few 'propositions   409 that are self-evident, though some there are[: it appears to be] a self-evident proposition, *that two bodies cannot be in the same place.'*

THEO. Many Christians disagree with you, as I have already pointed out [p. 82]; and you ought not to get agreement from Aristotle either, or from those who follow him in accepting real, literal condensation – the reduction of an entire body into a smaller space than it previously occupied – and who claim (as did the late M. *Comenius in a little book he devoted to this topic) to have overturned modern science by an experiment with an air-gun. If you take a body to be an impenetrable mass then your statement will be true, since it will be an identity or very close to one; but it won't be conceded [by your opponents] that that is what a real body is. At the least they will say that God could make a body differently, so that they will accept this impenetrability only as following from the natural order which God has established among things and which experience has vouchsafed to us, although it would have to be admitted that it is also very consonant with reason.

PHIL. §6. 'As to the relations of modes, mathematicians have framed many axioms concerning that one relation of equality', for example the one which you have just discussed: '*Equals taken from equals, the remainder will be equals*'. But I find it no less evident 'that *One and one, are equal to two*; [and] that *If you take from the five fingers of one hand two, and from the five fingers of the other hand two, the remaining numbers will be equal.'*

THEO. That one and one make two is not strictly speaking a truth, but rather the definition of *two*; though it partakes of the true and the evident, in that it is the definition of a possible thing. As for applying Euclid's axiom to the fingers of the hand, I am ready to agree that we can grasp what you say about fingers just as easily as we can see it for As and Bs; but to avoid frequent repetitions of the same thing we indicate it generally, and then we need only make substitutions. Otherwise it would be like dispensing with general rules in favour of calculating with particular numbers, which would mean achieving less than one might. For it is better to resolve this general problem: 'Find two numbers whose sum is one given number and

whose difference is another given number', than merely to look for two
numbers whose sum is 10 and whose difference is 6. If I use a mixture of
arithmetic and algebra to solve the second problem the calculation will go
like this:

$$\text{Let } a+b = 10 \quad \text{and let} \quad a-b = 6;$$

then I add the two right sides and the two left sides together, which gives
me:

$$a+b+a-b = 10+6,$$

and, since $+b$ and $-b$ cancel out, this yields:

$$2a = 16, \quad \text{or} \quad a = 8.$$

Then by subtracting right side from right side and left from left, and seeing
that taking away $a-b$ is adding $-a+b$, I derive:

$$a+b-a+b = 10-6,$$

that is:

$$2b = 4, \quad \text{or} \quad b = 2.$$

In this way I shall indeed get the numbers a and b that I am looking for,
namely 8 and 2; they answer the problem, since their sum is 10 and their
difference is 6. But that does not give me the general method for any other
numbers which one might want or be able to put in place of 10 and 6,
although this method is as easy to find as the numbers 8 and 2, simply by
putting x and y in place of 10 and 6. For if we proceed just as before, we
shall have:

$$a+b+a-b = x+y; \quad \text{that is} \quad 2a = x+y; \quad \text{that is} \quad a = \tfrac{1}{2}(x+y),$$

and we shall also have:

$$a+b-a+b = x-y; \quad \text{that is} \quad 2b = x-y; \quad \text{that is} \quad b = \tfrac{1}{2}(x-y).$$

This calculation yields the theorem or general rule that when seeking two
numbers whose sum and difference are given, one has only to take the larger
sought number to be half the *sum* of the given sum and difference, and the
smaller sought number to be half the *difference* of the given sum and
difference. You might notice that I could have dispensed with letters, by
treating numbers like letters: instead of putting $2a = 16$ and $2b = 4$, I could
have written $2a = 10+6$ and $2b = 10-6$; this would have given me
$a = \tfrac{1}{2}(10+6)$ and $b = \tfrac{1}{2}(10-6)$. Thus the particular calculation would in
itself have contained the general one, through my taking these marks 10
and 6 for general numbers like the letters x and y, so as to get a more general
truth or method; and by taking these same symbols 10 and 6 also for the

numbers which they ordinarily signify, I shall have an example which can be grasped by the senses and which can even serve as a check. Whereas Viète substituted letters for numbers to achieve greater generality, I have wanted to reintroduce numerical symbols since they are more suitable than letters, even in algebra. I have found it very helpful to use numbers in place of letters in extended calculations, for avoiding mistakes and even for carrying out checks (e.g. by *casting out nines) in mid-calculation without waiting for the final result; which is often possible if one selects the numbers shrewdly, so that the assumptions turn out true in the particular case. It is also useful in displaying connections and patterns which the mind would not be made to sort out so well by letters alone. I have shown this elsewhere [e.g. 'Responsio ad Dn. Nic. Fatii Duillierii imputationes'], having found that a good *symbolism is one of the greatest aids to the human mind.

PHIL. §7. As to real existence, which I listed as the fourth kind of agreement to be found among ideas, it cannot provide us with any axioms, since we do not even have demonstrative knowledge of any being outside ourselves, with the sole exception of God.

THEO. One can always say that the proposition *I exist* is evident in the highest degree, since it cannot be proved by anyone else – indeed, that it is an 'immediate truth'. To say *I think therefore I am* is not really to prove existence from thought, since *to think* and *to be thinking* are one and the same, and to say *I am thinking*[1] is already to say *I am*. Still, there is some reason for your not including this proposition among the axioms: it is a proposition of fact, founded on immediate experience, and is not a necessary proposition whose necessity is seen in the immediate agreement of ideas. On the contrary, only God can see how these two terms, *I* and *existence*, are connected – that is, why I exist. But if you take axioms, in a more general manner, to be immediate or non-provable truths, then the proposition *I am* can be called an axiom. In any case we can be confident that it is a primary truth, and indeed *unum ex primis cognitis inter terminos complexos*, i.e. one of the first known statements – in the natural order of our knowledge, that is, since it may never have occurred to a man to form this proposition explicitly, even though it is innate in him.

PHIL. I had always believed that axioms do not have much influence on the other parts of our knowledge. But you have disabused me by actually showing me an important use for identities. But bear with me, sir, if I still tell you what I had in mind on this point, since your explanations may serve to set others right as well.§8. It is a famous rule in the Schools that all reasonings are from things already known and agreed to – *ex praecognitis et praeconcessis*. This rule seems to take these maxims to be truths known

---

[1] '*Je suis pensant*'.

411

412 to the mind before the rest, and the other parts of our knowledge as truths which depend upon the axioms. §9. I thought I had shown (1.i.) that axioms are not the first things known, on the grounds that the child knows that the switch I show him is not the sugar he has tasted, long before knowing any axiom you please. But you have distinguished knowledge of particulars or experience of facts, on the one hand, from the principles of universal and necessary knowledge on the other – and I acknowledge that with the latter we must resort to axioms. And you have also distinguished between the accidental and natural orders.

THEO. And I added, furthermore, that in the natural order the statement that a thing is what it is, is prior to the statement that it is not something else [p. 82]; for we are not concerned here with the sequence of our discoveries, which differs from one man to another, but with the connection and natural order of truths, which is always the same. But your remark that what the child sees is only a fact, calls for yet further consideration. For, as you yourself pointed out not long ago [p. 373], sir, sense-experience does not provide absolutely certain truths, free from all risk of illusion: if I may make up a story which is metaphysically possible, the sugar could change into a switch in some undetectable manner, to punish the child when he had been naughty – just as in our country the water changes into wine on Christmas Eve to reward him if he has been well behaved. But you will say that all the same the pain inflicted by the switch will never turn into the pleasure which the sugar provides. I reply that the child will be as late in explicitly forming that proposition as he will in noticing the axiom that one cannot truthfully say that what is, at the same time is not; even though he is thoroughly aware of the difference between pleasure and pain, as well as of that between awareness and unawareness.

PHIL. §10. Yet there are a great many other truths which have as much self-evidence as these maxims. For instance, that '*One and two are equal to three*' is as evident a proposition as the axiom that '*The whole is equal to all its parts taken together*'.

THEO. You appear to have forgotten, sir, how I have called to your attention more than once [e.g. p. 409] that 'one and two is three' is the definition of the term 'three', so that saying that one and two is 'equal to three' is just saying that something is equal to itself. As for the axiom 413 that 'The whole is equal to all its parts taken together', Euclid does not use precisely that. Furthermore, this axiom needs to be qualified, for it must be added that the parts should not themselves contain parts in common: 7 and 8 are parts of 12, but they add up to more than 12; the upper half of a man and his trunk add up to more than the man, since they have his chest in common. But Euclid does say that 'The whole is greater than its part', and this needs no qualification. The statement that the body is greater than the trunk differs from Euclid's axiom only in that the axiom restricts itself to precisely what needs to be said; but by exemplifying it – giving it a body – we turn something which can be thought into something which can also be grasped by the senses. You see, the statement that *this* whole is greater than *that* part of it is actually the proposition that a whole is greater than its part, but with its features coloured in or augmented – just as one who says AB says A. So we shouldn't here be contrasting the axiom with the example, as though they were different truths in this respect [sc. of how evident they are], but rather regarding the axiom as embodied in the example and as making the example true. It is another matter when the example is not itself evident, and is affirmed as a deduction from the universal proposition and not merely as an instance of it; and this can happen with axioms too.

PHIL. Our capable author says at this point: 'I think, I may ask these men, who will needs have all knowledge [which is not of fact][1] to depend on general, innate, and self-evident principles, what principle [they need] to prove, that...*two and two are four*'? For, according to him, the truth of such propositions is 'known without any proof'. What do you say to this, sir?

THEO. I say that I was ready and waiting for you. That *two and two are four* is not quite an immediate truth. Assume that 'four' signifies 'three and one'. Then we can demonstrate it, and here is how.

Definitions. (1) *Two* is one and one.

(2) *Three* is two and one.

(3) *Four* is three and one.

Axiom. If equals be substituted for equals, the equality remains.

Demonstration. 2 and 2 is 2 and 1 and 1 (def. 1) $2+2$ 414

2 and 1 and 1 is 3 and 1 (def. 2) $2+\overbrace{1+1}$

3 and 1 is 4   (def. 3) $\overbrace{3+1}$

$\underbrace{}$
4

Therefore (by the Axiom)

2 and 2 is 4. Which is what was to be demonstrated.

Instead of saying that 2 and 2 *is* 2 and 1 and 1, I could say that 2 and 2 *is equal to* 2 and 1 and 1, and similarly with the others. But we can assume that this has already been done throughout, on the strength of another axiom which maintains that a thing is equal to itself, or that whatever is the same is equal.

PHIL. The demonstration of such a thoroughly known conclusion is hardly necessary, but it does show how truths depend on axioms and definitions. So I can foresee how you will deal with various objections that are brought

[1] Added by Leibniz.

against the use of axioms. It is objected that there will be a countless multitude of principles. But this comes from including among principles the corollaries which follow from the definitions with the help of some axiom: since there are countless definitions or ideas, there will on this view be countless principles too – even if we follow you in supposing that indemonstrable principles are axiomatic identities. Exemplification also gives rise to innumerable principles, but we can really count *A is A* and *B is B* as a single principle variously garbed.

THEO. Furthermore, in view of the differences in degrees of evidence, I disagree with your distinguished author when he holds that all these truths – which he calls principles, and regards as self-evident because they are so close to the first indemonstrable axioms – are entirely independent of each other and incapable of deriving proof or illumination one from another. For we can always bring them right back to axioms or to other truths closer than they are to the axioms, as you were shown by the truth that two and two make four. And I have just told you how M. Roberval reduced the number of Euclid's axioms by deriving some of them from others.

415 PHIL. §11. This judicious writer who has provided the occasion for our discussions agrees that maxims have their use, but he believes that it is rather to silence the obstinate than to provide foundations for the sciences. 'I would be glad to be shown', he says, 'any such science erected upon these...general axioms..., that could not be shown to stand as firm without' axioms.

THEO. Geometry is certainly one such science. *Euclid uses axioms explicitly in his demonstrations, and both he and Archimedes use the axiom that 'If two magnitudes are commensurable, and neither is larger than the other, then they are equal', as the foundation of their demonstrations concerning the magnitudes of curvilinear figures. Archimedes used axioms not needed by Euclid, for instance: 'Given two lines each of which is everywhere convex the same way, that which encloses the other is the greater'. Nor can we do without axiomatic identities in geometry, such as the principle of contradiction, i.e. the principle of arguments *ad absurdum*. As for the other axioms which can be demonstrated from these, strictly speaking we can dispense with them and derive our conclusions immediately from identities and definitions; but if we had always to start again from the beginning, our demonstrations would be so wordy and would involve us in such endless repetition that there would be horrible confusion; whereas by assuming intermediate principles which have already been demonstrated we can readily push ahead. This assumption of already-known truths is particularly useful with respect to axioms, since they come up so often that geometers are obliged to employ them constantly without citing them. So that it would be a mistake to believe that they are not involved just because they may not always be seen cited in the margin.

PHIL. But he proposes theology as an example to the contrary. It is from revelation that we have received the knowledge of our holy religion, says our author, and if we had lacked that aid maxims could never have given us the knowledge. Light comes to us, then, either from things themselves or immediately from God's unerring veracity.

THEO. That is as if I were to say that since medicine is founded on experience, reason has nothing to contribute to it. Christian theology – the true medicine of souls – is founded on revelation, which corresponds to experience; but to make it into a completed system we have also to bring in natural theology, which is derived from the axioms of eternal Reason. You acknowledge that the certainty of revelation is founded on God's 416 veracity; but is not the very principle that *veracity is an attribute of God* a maxim drawn from natural theology?

PHIL. Our author wants the method of acquiring knowledge to be distinguished from that of teaching it, or rather that of teaching and communicating it. 'When schools were erected, and sciences had their professors to teach what others had found out, they often made use of maxims' to imprint these sciences on the minds of their scholars, and to convince them, by means of axioms, of certain particular truths. Whereas particular truths enabled 'the first discoverers' to find out the truth, without general maxims.

THEO. I wish he had offered support for this supposed procedure by giving us some examples of particular truths. But if we look carefully into the matter, we will not find this procedure employed in the founding of the sciences. If a discoverer finds only a particular truth, he is only a half-discoverer. If Pythagoras had merely noticed that a triangle whose sides are 3, 4, 5 has the property that the square on its hypotenuse equals those on its sides (i.e. that $9 + 16$ makes 25), would this have made him the discoverer of that great truth which holds for all right-angled triangles and has become a maxim among the geometers? It is true that an example hit on by chance will often prompt an intelligent man to look for the general truth involved; but finding it is usually a very different matter. In any case, this way of discovering things is not the best, nor is it the one most used by those who proceed in an orderly and methodical way – they make use of it only in situations where better methods fall short. Some people have believed that Archimedes found the quadrature of the parabola by weighing a piece of wood which was carved into the shape of a parabola – that he found the general truth by means of this particular experiment; but those who know that great man's acuteness of mind see clearly that he had no need for this sort of aid. And this empiric's way of particular truths, even if it had been the *occasion* of all discoveries, would not have been sufficient to *provide* them. Discoverers have been delighted to catch sight of maxims and general truths when they have succeeded in arriving at them, since otherwise their discoveries would have remained quite incomplete. So the only thing we can impute to 'schools' and 'professors' is having collected and ordered these maxims and other general truths. And would to God it had been done even more, and with greater care and discrimination – the sciences would not be so fragmentary and chaotic. Another point: I grant that there is often a difference between the method used to teach the sciences and that by which they have been found, but that is not the point at issue. Sometimes, as I have already remarked, a chance happening provides the occasion for a discovery. If note had been taken of these occasions and a record of them kept for posterity (which would have been very useful), these facts would have constituted a very substantial part of the history of the [practical] *arts, but would not have been suitable for rendering them systematic; sometimes discoverers have proceeded by rational means, but very circuitously, towards the truth. I think that the authors of major achievements would have performed a public service if they had candidly undertaken, in their writings, to sketch their various attempts. But if a scientific system had to be constructed on that principle, it would be like wanting to retain in a finished house all the scaffolding which the builders had needed for putting it up. Sound methods of *teaching* a science are all of such a kind that it could reliably have been *found* by means of them. And if they are not the empiric's methods, i.e. if the truths are taught through reasons or by proofs derived from ideas, this will always be by means of axioms, theorems, rules, and other such general propositions. It is a different matter when the truths are 'aphorisms' such as those of Hippocrates, i.e. statements of fact which are always or at least usually true, which are learned by observation or grounded in experiments, and for which there are no wholly convincing reasons. But these truths are beside the point here, since they are not known through the connection of ideas.

PHIL. This is how our gifted author believes that the need for maxims arose. 'The Schools having made disputation the touchstone of men's abilities,...adjudged victory to him that kept the field' and spoke last.[1] But as a means of winning over the obstinate, maxims had to be established.

THEO. No doubt the philosophy schools would have done better to combine theory with practice, as do the schools of medicine, chemistry and mathematics, and to give the prize, especially in moral philosophy, to the one who did best rather than to the one who spoke best. However, there are subjects, such as metaphysics, where discourse itself is a product of

---

[1] Locke: 'had the last word'. Coste: '*parlait le dernier*'.

skill – and sometimes the only one, the one formal proof of a man's mastery. So in some cases it has been right to judge people's skill by their success in discussion. We even know that at the start of the Reformation the Protestants challenged their adversaries to conferences and debates, and that sometimes their success in these debates led the people to decide in favour of reform. And we also know how much the art of speaking and of producing and marshalling reasons – what might be called the art of debate – can achieve in councils of state and of war, in law courts, in medical consultations, even in conversations. In these situations we are compelled to resort to this procedure, being satisfied with words in place of deeds, simply because what is in question is some future event and we cannot wait to learn the truth from what ensues. So the art of debate, or of combat with reasons (which I here take to include the citing of instances and authorities), is very great and very important; but unfortunately it is most disorderly, which is why so often no decision – or a bad decision – is reached. For this reason, I have more than once thought of commenting on theologians' disputations of which we have some account, to point out the defects which can be found in them and to suggest remedies which could be applied. In conferences about practical matters, unless those who have the greatest power are very firm of mind they will usually be swayed by authority and by eloquence when these two join forces against the truth. In short, the art of discussion and debate needs to be totally reorganized. As for the advantage of being the last to speak, this is hardly a factor except in informal conversation, for in councils voting takes place in order of rank, from highest to lowest or the reverse. Ordinarily, it is true, the President begins and ends, i.e. puts the question and decides it, but he decides according to the plurality of votes. And in academic debates the 'respondent', who maintains the thesis, speaks last and by established custom is usually left in possession of the field. The point is to test him, not to defeat him; otherwise one is treating him as an adversary. The fact is that in these encounters truth is pretty much beside the point, and contradictory theses are maintained at different times from the same rostrum. When Casaubon was shown the hall of the Sorbonne and told: In this room they have debated for many centuries, he replied: And what conclusions have they reached?

PHIL. In order to prevent the debate running on into an endless train of syllogisms, however, and to provide a means of deciding between two equally skilful combatants, 'certain general propositions, most of them ...self-evident, were introduced..., which being such as all men allowed and agreed in, were looked on as general measures of truth, and served instead of principles, (where the disputants had not laid down any other ...) beyond which there was no going, and which must not be receded from by either side. And thus these maxims getting the name of *principles*,' which could not be denied in the course of the dispute, and which settled the question, were taken – wrongly, according to my author – to be the source of all knowledge and the foundations of the sciences.

THEO. If only they had used them in this way in their debates! There would have been nothing to complain about, for then they would have decided something. And what could be better than to reduce the controversy – i.e. the truths in contention – to evident and incontestable truths? Would not this be to establish them demonstratively? And who can doubt that those principles which ended debates by establishing the truth would at the same time be sources of knowledge? For as long as one's reasoning is sound, it hardly matters whether it is done quietly in one's study or displayed on a public platform. And even if these principles were postulates rather than axioms (with postulates understood not in Euclid's way but in Aristotle's, namely as assumptions which we are willing to agree on while awaiting an opportunity to prove them [*Post. An.* 1, 76^{b}23f]), they would still be useful, in that by means of them all the other questions would be reduced to a small number of propositions. So I am really astonished to see something so praiseworthy attacked, because of who knows what prejudice. The example of your author shows clearly that the cleverest men are liable to prejudice when off their guard. Unfortunately academic debates are conducted quite differently. Instead of establishing general axioms, everything possible is done to weaken them by means of vague and poorly thought out distinctions. There are certain philosophical rules – big books crammed with them – which people like to use, but these are quite unreliable and imprecise, and anyway debaters take delight in evading their force by splitting hairs. This is not the way to settle debates, but rather to make them endless and finally to wear one's opponent down. It is as though he were led into a dark room and subjected to blows from all directions, with no one being able to judge them. This is an excellent arrangement for 'respondents' who have undertaken to maintain certain theses: Vulcan's shield to make them invulnerable, and *Orci galea*, Pluto's helmet, to make them invisible. They have to be very unskilled or very unlucky to get caught under these conditions. It is true that some rules have exceptions, particularly those that bear on complex situations, as in jurisprudence. But for such rules to be reliable the exceptions must, so far as possible, be determinate as to their number and their sense; and it can then happen that there are sub-exceptions to the exceptions – i.e. that an exception has its *'replication' and the replication its 'duplication', and so on – but taking everything into account, when all these exceptions and sub-exceptions are precisely determined and added to the rule, the result must be universally true. Jurisprudence provides some very remarkable

420

examples of this. But if rules like this, with all their exceptions and sub-exceptions, should be brought into academic debates, one would have to debate pen in hand and keep minutes of what is said on each side. And that would also be necessary in a debate which was formal throughout, using various syllogisms, prosyllogisms and proprosyllogisms, interspersed from time to time with distinctions; this would defeat the best of memories. But people come nowhere near to taking the kind of trouble that would be involved in pursuing the truth by elaborating and recording formal syllogisms, if there is no benefit to be got from it;[1] not that they would ever reach any conclusion, even if they wanted to, unless distinctions were either avoided or handled in a more orderly way.

PHIL. Nevertheless, it is true, as our author points out, that the method of the Schools, having been introduced into conversation outside the Schools, to stop the mouths of cavillers, has had an unfortunate effect there. For as long as we have 'intermediate ideas', their connection can be seen without the help of maxims and before they have been produced; and that would be enough for sincere and reasonable people. 'But the method of the Schools, having allowed and encouraged men to oppose and resist evident truth, till they are...reduced to contradict themselves, or some established principle; 'tis no wonder that they should not in civil conversation be ashamed of that, which in the Schools is counted a virtue and a glory'. The author adds that rational people spread throughout the rest of the world, who have not been 'corrupted by education,[2] could scarce believe [that such a method] should ever be admitted amongst the [professed] lovers of truth [who spend their lives as] students of religion or nature.... How much such a way of learning is likely to turn young men's minds from the sincere search and love of truth; nay, and to make them doubt whether there is any such thing, or at least worth the adhering to, I shall not now inquire', he says. And he adds: 'This, I think, 421 that bating those places, which brought the peripatetic philosophy into their Schools, where it continued many ages, without teaching the world any thing but the art of wrangling; these maxims were no where thought the foundations on which the sciences were built, nor the great helps to the advancement of knowledge.'

THEO. Your gifted author holds that it is only the Schools that are prone to form maxims; but this is a general and very reasonable human instinct. You can see this from the proverbs which are current in every nation, and which are usually nothing but maxims accepted by the whole populace. However, when men of good judgment say things which appear to us to conflict with the truth, we should in fairness to them suspect that there

---

[1] 'elle', which may refer to the trouble or to the truth.
[2] Locke: 'the rational part of mankind not corrupted by education'. Coste's change.

is more wrong with their wording than with their beliefs. Our author is an example of this, and I begin to perceive the cause of his opposition to maxims: namely, that in ordinary conversation, which is not concerned with training as in the Schools, it really is cavilling to insist on being convinced before one will yield; and besides, it is there usually more graceful to suppress obvious major premises and to be satisfied with *enthymemes. Often, indeed, one has only to supply the 'middle term' or intermediate idea for the mind to grasp the link between the premises, without its being expressed and without the premises' even being formed. That is well enough when the link is indisputable; but you will also concede to me, sir, that we are often too quick in taking it for granted, and that this engenders fallacies, so that very often it would be better to have a care for the certainty of what one says rather than preferring brevity and elegance. Yet your author's prejudice against maxims has made him dismiss out of hand their contribution to the establishing of truth, and go so far as to hold them partly to blame for the confusions of conversation. It is true that young people who are habituated to academic training – in which there is a little too much concern with training and not enough with the gathering of its finest fruit, namely knowledge – have difficulty getting free of it in the world. And one of their 'cavils' is never being willing to yield to the truth until it has been made utterly obvious to them, although candour and even politeness ought to prevent them from expecting such extremes and thus making themselves a nuisance and giving themselves a bad reputation. It has to be admitted that men of letters are often found to be tainted with this vice. But the fault does not consist in wanting to reduce truths to maxims, but in wanting to do so needlessly and inopportunely. For the human mind takes in a great deal at a glance, and we hobble it when we try to make it halt at every step it takes and express everything that it is thinking. It is exactly like someone settling accounts with a merchant or innkeeper and insisting that he count everything up on his fingers, so as to be more certain. To require that, one would have to be either stupid or capricious. In fact one sometimes finds that Petronius was right in saying 'Schools turn children into utter blockheads' – that young people become stupid and sometimes even hare-brained in the very places that ought to be schools of wisdom: the corruption of the best is the worst. But more often still they become conceited, blundering, muddle-headed, capricious, a nuisance – often depending on the temperament of their masters. Even so, I find far worse sins in conversation than excessive desire for clarity; for people usually succumb to the opposite vice, and neither provide nor require enough clarity. And if the one is vexatious, the other is harmful and dangerous.

PHIL. §12. The use of maxims is also harmful sometimes, when they are associated with notions which are 'wrong, loose, or unsteady'. For then

422

maxims 'serve to confirm us in mistakes; and [even] to prove contradictions: v.g. he that with Descartes, shall frame. . .an idea of what he calls
body, to be nothing but extension, may easily demonstrate, that there is
no vacuum; i.e. no space void of body, by this maxim, *What is, is.* . . . For
he knows his own idea. . ., and knows that it is what it is, and not another
idea'. Since for him 'extension, body, space' are three words standing for
the same thing, it is for him just as true to say that *space is body* as to say
that *body is body*. **§13.** But someone else for whom 'body' stands for an
extended solid will be led by a similar argument to conclude that '*space
is not body*' is as sure as 'this maxim, *It is impossible for the same thing to
be, and not to be* [*at the same time*], can make any proposition.'

THEO. The misuse of maxims ought not to bring discredit on all use of
them: every truth is subject to this disadvantage, that in combining it with
falsehoods one can draw false or even contradictory conclusions. And in
your example there is hardly any need for those axiomatic identities which
you take to be the source of the error and of the contradiction. That would
emerge if the arguments of those who infer from their definitions that space
is body, or that space is not body, were laid out formally. Indeed the
inference 'Body is extended and solid, so extension (i.e. that which is
extended) is not body, and extendedness is not corporeal-thinghood'
overreaches itself; for I have remarked earlier [pp. 363, 408] that there
are redundant ways of expressing *ideas*, which add nothing to *things*. It is
as though someone were to say 'By *Triquetrum* I mean a trilateral triangle',
and to infer from that that some trilaterals are not triangular. Thus, a
Cartesian can say that the idea of an extended solid is of this same nature,
i.e. that it contains a redundancy; since indeed if what is extended[1] is
understood to be something substantial, it will be the case that everything
extended is solid, i.e. that everything extended is corporeal. As for the void,
a Cartesian will be right to infer from his idea – or his so-called idea – that
there is no void, assuming that his idea is sound; but someone else will
not be right to infer straight away from *his* idea that a void is possible. I,
for instance, do not favour the Cartesian view, but I believe that there is
no void. Your example strikes me as involving a misuse of ideas rather than
of maxims.

PHIL. **§15.** It seems, at least, that whatever use one may make of maxims
in verbal propositions, they cannot yield us the slightest knowledge of
substances which exist outside us.

THEO. I am of an entirely different opinion. For example, the maxim that
nature acts by the shortest way, or at least by the most determinate way,
is sufficient by itself to explain almost the whole of optics, including the

423

---

[1] Reading '*l'étendue*' (extendedness) as '*l'étendu*' (extended thing); and twice more in
this sentence.

optics of reflection and refraction, i.e. the whole of what goes on 'outside us' in the actions of light. I once showed this [' *Unicum opticae, catoptricae et dioptricae principium* '], and Mr *Molyneux strongly commended it in his *Dioptrica*, which is a very fine book.

PHIL. It is maintained, however, that 'when these principles [– these identities –]¹ are made use of in the probation of propositions, wherein are words standing for [composite] ideas, v.g. *man* [or] *virtue*', their use is extremely dangerous, and forces men into regarding and receiving false-hood as manifest truth. And it is maintained that this is because men think that 'where the same terms are preserved, the propositions are about the same things, though the ideas they stand for are in truth different....So that [since] men take words for things, as usually they do, these maxims ...commonly serve to prove contradictory propositions.'

424 THEO. How unfair to blame the poor maxims for what ought to be charged against the misuse and the ambiguity of terms! By that argument, syllogisms will be criticized because people argue badly when the terms are ambiguous. But that is not the syllogism's fault, because in such cases there are really four terms, which breaks the syllogistic rules. That same argument would also have one criticizing arithmetical or algebraical methods of calculation because they can lead one to draw false or contradictory conclusions if one puts X instead of V or inadvertently takes an a to be a b.

PHIL. §19. I should think, at least, that maxims are not much use when one has clear and distinct ideas; and others even contend that maxims are then utterly useless,² claiming that anyone who in such cases cannot discern truth and falsehood without such maxims cannot do so with their aid either. Our author even shows (§§16, 17) that they do not serve to settle whether such-and-such is a man or not.

THEO. When the truths are very simple and evident, and are very near to identities or definitions, one hardly needs to make explicit use of maxims in order to derive these truths from them [sc. from the identities or definitions], for the mind employs the maxims implicitly, and reaches its conclusion all at once without any stops along the way. But mathematicians would find it very difficult to get anywhere if they did not have axioms and theorems which were already known. For in a long deduction it is good to stop from time to time and, as it were, set up a milestone for oneself in the middle of the road; this will also help to mark out the route to others. If that is not done, these long roads will be too hard to follow, and may even seem rambling and dark, preventing one from picking out and taking

---

¹ Added by Leibniz.
² Locke asserts that 'there is little need, or no use at all of these maxims' when etc., with no mention of what 'others' say.

a bearing on anything apart from the place one is in. It is like travelling by sea without a compass, on a dark night when one cannot see the sea-bed or the shore or the stars; or tramping over vast plains where there are no trees or hills or streams. It is also like a chain for measuring lengths, one containing several hundred links, all perfectly alike, with no beads, or larger seeds or links, or other dividers to mark off the feet, fathoms, perches etc. Now, the mind, which likes unity in multiplicity,[1] puts together several inferences to get intermediate conclusions from them, and that is where maxims and theorems come in. This procedure increases pleasure, illumination, memorability, and applicability, and reduces the amount of repetition. If some analyst wanted to do his calculations without assuming these two geometrical maxims: 'The square on the hypotenuse is equal to the squares on the two sides of the right angle', and 'The corresponding sides of similar triangles are proportional to one another', because he thought that, since there is a demonstration of these two theorems through the connection of the ideas which they involve, he could easily dispense 425 with them by putting the ideas themselves in their place, he would discover that he was very far from the mark. But lest you should think, sir, that maxims are serviceable only within the confines of the mathematical sciences, you will find them just as useful in jurisprudence. One of the chief ways of making jurisprudence more manageable, and of surveying its vast ocean, as though in a geographical chart, is by tracing a large number of particular decisions back to more general principles; for instance, it will be found that many laws in the *Digest*, many actions or defences, and even actions which are called *in factum*, depend upon the maxim *ne quis alterius damno fiat locupletior*, that is, that no one should be enriched as a result of harm which befalls another. Though that ought to be expressed a little more precisely. The fact is that there is a big distinction to be drawn within legal rules. I am speaking of sound ones, and not of certain vague and obscure adages (*brocardia*) which the teachers [of law] have introduced; though some of these rules could be reformed so as also to be sound and useful, whereas at present they achieve nothing, with their endless distinctions (*cum suis fallentiis*), except to cause confusion. Well, then, sound rules divide into Aphorisms and Maxims, taking Maxims to include axioms as well as theorems. Aphorisms are based not on the *a priori* use of reason, but rather on induction and observation: they are rules which able people have framed after a review of established law. Something which the jurist Paul said, in the part of the *Digest* dealing with rules of law, applies to them, namely: *non ex regula jus sumi, sed ex jure quod est, regulam fieri*, which means that rules are drawn from already known law, to make it easier to remember, and that law is not built upon them. But there

---

[1] '*l'Esprit qui aime l'unité dans la multitude*', which could mean 'a mind which likes unity in multiplicity'.

are *fundamental Maxims* which constitute the very law itself; they make up the actions, defences, replications etc. which, when they are taught by pure reason and do not come from the arbitrary power of the state, constitute natural law; and the rule I have just mentioned, forbidding profit from harm, is of this kind. There are also rules which admit of only rare exceptions and which are therefore regarded as universal. An example of this is the rule in the *Institutes* of the Emperor Justinian (in §2 of the part entitled 'Of Actions'), which says that a legal action concerning a material thing cannot be brought by the person who has possession of it – except in just one case which the Emperor says is indicated in the *Digest*, but they are still looking for it. In fact some have adopted the reading *sane non uno* for *sane uno casu* ['not a single one' for 'one case, however']. Also, one can sometimes make several cases out of a single one. Among physicians the late M. Barner, who by giving us his work *Prodromus* gave us hope of a 'new Sennert' – i.e. a system of medicine adapted to the latest discoveries and opinions – contends that the physicians' usual way of presenting their systems of medical practice is this: they set out the art of healing by taking illnesses one at a time, following the order of the parts of the human body or some other order, without having given any universal practical precepts which would apply equally to many illnesses and symptoms. This involves them in endless repetitions, he says, so that one could eliminate three quarters of Sennert, and could infinitely abbreviate medical science by the use of general propositions, especially those to which Aristotle's 'primary universal' conforms [*Post. An.* II, 99ᵃ34–5], i.e. which are reciprocal or very close to being so. I believe that Barner is right to advise the use of this method (especially with regard to precepts) in the theoretical areas of medicine, but in so far as medicine is empirical it is harder and more hazardous to form universal propositions. Furthermore, there are usually complications in particular illnesses. Illnesses imitate substances, so to speak, in such a way that an illness resembles a plant or animal which requires a description all of its own. That is, illnesses are 'modes' or ways of being which fit what we have said about bodies or substantial things, a quartan fever being as hard to understand thoroughly as is gold or quicksilver. So it is good – universal precepts notwithstanding – to search among the kinds of illnesses for healing methods and remedies which will deal with several symptoms and conjunctions of causes at once, and above all to collect the cures which are warranted by experience. Sennert was not thorough enough about this, for able people have noticed that many of the prescriptions which he proposes are made up in ways which owe less to the authority of experience – which is what he needed if he was to be sure of what he was saying – than to ingenious guesswork. So I believe that it will be best to combine the two methods, and not to complain of repetitions in such a delicate and important matter as medicine is. What medicine lacks, I find, is what we have too much of in jurisprudence, in my opinion, namely books full of particular cases and catalogues of previously observed facts. For I believe that a thousandth part of the books of the jurists would suffice, whereas we would not have too much in medicine if we had a thousand times as many well-documented observations. The point is that jurisprudence, when dealing with matters which are not explicitly treated by laws or by customs, is entirely grounded in reasons; for that part of it can always be derived by reason from the law of the land or, if not from that, from natural law. And the laws of each land are finite, and they are determinate or can become so. In medicine, on the other hand, there could not be too many observations – those first principles of experience – giving reason more chance to decipher things which nature has only half-revealed to us. My final point is that I know of no one who employs axioms in the way alleged by the able author of whom you are speaking (§§16, 17). It would be like someone who used the principle that 'Whatever is, is' as an aid to demonstrating to a child that a negro is a man, by saying: A negro has a rational soul; but a rational soul is the same thing as a man; and therefore if he had a rational soul but were not a man, it would be false that 'Whatever is, is', or rather a single thing would both be and not be at the same time. Without using these maxims – which are quite out of place here, have no active role in the reasoning, and do nothing to help it forward – everyone will be satisfied to argue like this: A negro has a rational soul; whoever has a rational soul is a man; so a negro is a man. And if someone who holds the prejudice that there is no rational soul where none appears to us were to conclude that newly born babies and imbeciles are not of the human species (and indeed our author reports having talked with very reasonable people who made that denial), I do not believe that it would be the misuse of the maxim 'It is impossible that a single thing should both be and not be' which led him astray, or that he would so much as think of it when coming to his conclusion. The source of his error would be an extension of a principle of our author's: *he* denies that there is anything in the soul of which it is not aware, whereas these other gentlemen go so far as to deny the soul itself on the grounds that others do not perceive it.

Chapter viii
'Of trifling propositions.'

PHILALETHES. I am sure that reasonable people would never use axiomatic identities in the way we have been discussing.[1] **§2.** So it seems that these purely identical maxims are merely trifling – or *nugatoriae*, as even the Scholastics call them.[2] And I would not be satisfied with just saying that

[1] Added by Leibniz.
[2] Remark introducing '*nugatoriae*' added by Leibniz.

that *seems* to be so, had not your surprising example of the demonstration of conversion by the interposition of identities made me step with care when it comes to being scornful of anything. Still, I shall report to you the reason which is adduced for saying that they are utterly trifling. It is that these can be seen 'at first blush...to contain no instruction in them [except] sometimes to show a man the absurdity he is guilty of'.

THEOPHILUS. Do you count that as nothing, sir? Do you not recognize that to reduce a proposition to absurdity is to demonstrate its contradictory? I quite agree that one will not teach a man anything by telling him that he ought not to deny and affirm the same thing at the same time; but one does teach him something when one shows him, by force of inference, that he is doing so without thinking about it. In my opinion it is hard always to forgo these 'apagogical' demonstrations, i.e. ones by *reductio ad absurdum*, and to prove everything by 'ostensive' [direct] demonstrations, as they are called. This is a fact of which geometers, who are very interested in the question, have had plenty of experience. Proclus takes note, from time to time, when he sees that certain ancient geometers, later than Euclid, have found demonstrations which are more direct (so it is believed) than Euclid's own. But the silences of this ancient commentator show well enough that this was not always done.

PHIL. §3. You will at least grant me, sir, that one can make a million propositions, at small expense but also with very little profit; for is it not trifling to remark that *Oyster is oyster*, and that it is wrong to deny this or to say that oyster is not oyster? Our author has an amusing remark about this. He says that a man who treated this oyster now as subject and now as attribute or predicate would be 'like a monkey shifting his oyster from one hand to the other,' which would have as much power to satisfy the monkey's hunger as these propositions have to satisfy the man's understanding.

THEO. I find this author as witty as he is judicious, and I think that he is absolutely right to speak out against those who would behave in such a way. But you can see quite well how identities should be used if they are to be useful – namely by showing that other truths which one wishes to establish can be reduced to them by means of deductions and definitions.

PHIL. §4. I acknowledge that, and I can see that there is an even better case for saying it about propositions – which appear trifling and often are so[1] – in which a part of the complex idea is predicated of the object of that idea,[2] as when one says *Lead is a metal*. The only good it does, in the mind of someone who knows what these terms stand for, and knows that 'lead' signifies a body which is very heavy, fusible and malleable, is that in saying

429

---

[1] Locke implies that all such propositions are trifling.
[2] Locke: 'is predicated of the name of the whole'.

'metal' one indicates to him several of the simple ideas all at once instead of going through them one by one. §§5–7. The same holds when a part of a definition is affirmed of the term defined: as in saying *All gold is fusible* (assuming that 'gold' has been defined as a body which is yellow, heavy, fusible, and malleable), or *A triangle has three sides*, or *Man is an animal*, or *A palfrey* ([from] old French) *is a neighing animal* – which define the words but do not teach one anything beyond the definitions. But we are taught something by being told that man has a notion of God and that he is cast into sleep by opium.

THEO. In addition to what I have said about completely identical propositions, these semi-identicals will be found also to be useful in their own special way. For example: *A wise man is still a man* lets one know that he is not infallible, that he is mortal, and so on. Someone in a situation of danger needs a pistol-bullet, he has a mould for making bullets but has no lead to use in it; and a friend says to him 'Remember that the *silver* you have in your purse *is fusible*'. This friend will not teach him a quality of the silver, but he will make him think of a use he can make of it, as a source of bullets in this emergency. A good proportion of moral truths and of the finest literary aphorisms are of that nature: quite often they teach one nothing, but they do make one think at the right time about what one knows already. This iambic hexameter from Latin tragedy: *Cuivis potest accidere, quod cuiquam potest* [Publilius Syrus], which is a more elegant way of saying 'What can happen to one can happen to any', merely serves to remind us of the human condition, 'that we ought not to regard anything human as alien to us' [Terence]. The jurists' rule which says: *qui jure suo utitur, nemini facit injuriam* (he who exercises his rights does wrong to nobody) appears trifling. Yet it has an excellent use in certain cases, where it makes one have the very thought that is needed. For example, if someone built his house up to the greatest height allowed by the statutes and usages, thus depriving a neighbour of part of his view, if the neighbour ventured to complain he would at once be rebuffed with this rule of law. I would add that propositions of fact, i.e. experiences,[1] such as that opium is a narcotic, lead us on further than do truths of reason, which can never make us go beyond what is in our distinct ideas. As for the proposition that every man has a notion of God, if 'notion' signifies *idea* then that is a proposition of reason, because in my view the idea of God is innate in all men. But if 'notion' signifies an idea which involves actual thinking, then it is a proposition of fact, belonging to the natural history of mankind. One last point: the proposition that a triangle has three sides is not as much of an identity as it seems, for it takes a little attention to see that a polygon must have as many angles as sides; and if

430

---

[1] '*expériences*'; cf. p. 434.

the polygon were not assumed to be closed, the sides would outnumber the angles by one.

PHIL. **§9.** It seems that 'the general propositions that are made about substances, if they are certain, are for the most part but trifling'. And anyone who knows the significations of the words '*substance, man, animal, form, soul, vegetative, sensitive, rational,* may make several undoubted' but useless propositions – especially about the soul, which people often talk about without knowing what it really is. 'A man may find an infinite number of propositions, reasonings, and conclusions [of this nature], in books of metaphysics, School-divinity, and some sort of *natural philosophy; and after all, know as little of God, spirits, or bodies, as he did before he' had skimmed through those books.

THEO. It is true that the general run of surveys of metaphysics, and of other books of that stamp, teach nothing but words. For instance, to say that metaphysics is the 'Science of Being' in general, which explains the principles of Being and the affections to which it gives rise; and to say that the principles of Being are Essence and Existence, and that its affections divide into the primary ones (one, true, good) and the derivative ones (same and different, simple and composite, etc.); and to use each of these terms in association only with vague notions and verbal distinctions – that is just to abuse the name 'science'. But to be fair to the deeper Scholastics, such as Suarez (of whom Grotius made so much), it should be acknowledged that their works sometimes contain substantial discussions – for instance of the continuum, of the infinite, of contingency, of the reality of what is abstract, of the principle of individuation, of the origin of forms and of a *vacuum among forms, of the soul and its faculties, of God's communion with created things etc., and even, in moral philosophy, of the nature of the will and the principles of justice. In short, it must be admitted that there is still gold in that dross. But only enlightened people can profit from it; and to burden the young with a great jumble of useless stuff, just because it contains good things here and there, is to waste the most precious of all things, namely time. I would add that we are not entirely lacking in general propositions about substances which are certainly true and also worth knowing: our able author's doctrines include – whether as original to him or partly following others – some great and beautiful truths about God and about the soul; and perhaps we too have been able to add something to them. As for knowledge of general truths about bodies: many significant ones have been added to those which Aristotle bequeathed to us, and it ought to be said that natural science – even the general part of it – is much more real than it used to be. As for real metaphysics, we are all but beginning to get it established, and are discovering important general truths, based on reason and confirmed by experience, which hold for substances in general. I hope that I too have contributed a little to what is known of the soul, and of spirits, in general. That is the sort of metaphysics which Aristotle asked for – it is the science which he called *zetoumenon* meaning 'the desire' or what he was looking for [*Metap*. A, 982^{a}15]. It was to relate to the other theoretical sciences as the science of happiness does to the [practical] arts upon which it relies, and as the architect does to the builders. That is why Aristotle said that the other sciences depend upon metaphysics as the most general science, and should borrow their principles from metaphysics which is where they are demonstrated. It should also be understood that metaphysics relates to true moral philosophy as theory to practice. That is because of the dependence on the doctrine of substances in general of that knowledge about spirits – and especially about God and the soul – which gives to justice and to virtue their proper extent. For, as I have remarked elsewhere [Preface to *Codex juris gentium* p. 423], if there were neither providence nor an after-life, the wise man's practice of virtue would be more restricted, since he would refer everything only to his present satisfaction; and even that satisfaction – which has already been exemplified in Socrates, the Emperor Marcus Aurelius, Epictetus, and other ancients – would not always be as well grounded, in the absence of those broad and beautiful perspectives which are opened up to us by the order and harmony of the universe, extending to an unlimited future; for without them the soul's tranquillity would amount merely to resignation. So it can be said that natural theology – with its two divisions, theoretical and practical – contains both real metaphysics and the most perfect moral philosophy. 432

PHIL. Those are cases of knowledge which are certainly very far from being trifling or merely verbal. **§12.** But it seems that 'barely verbal propositions [are ones] wherein two abstract terms are affirmed one of another, [for example] that *Parsimony is frugality*, [or] that *Gratitude is justice*.... However specious[1] these and [other] propositions may [sometimes][2] at first sight seem,' yet if we squeeze out their content[3] 'we shall find that it all amounts to nothing, but the signification of...terms.'

THEO. But the principles of all demonstrations are expressed by significations of terms (i.e. definitions) together with axiomatic identities; and since these definitions can show what the ideas are and, at the same time, that they are possible, it is evident that not everything that depends on them is purely verbal. Take the example 'Gratitude is justice', or rather 'a part of justice': that should not be held in contempt, for it conveys the knowledge that the *actio ingrati* as they call it, i.e. the accusation which

---

[1] In the now obsolete sense of 'plausible' or 'attractive'.
[2] Added by Leibniz.
[3] Locke: 'press them'. Coste: '*presser la signification*'. Leibniz: '*press*[*er*] *la force*'.

can be brought against someone who is ungrateful, should receive more attention in the law courts. The Romans entertained this kind of legal action against freedmen, i.e. those who had been released from slavery, and even today it ought to be valid in connection with the revocation of gifts. Finally: I have already remarked elsewhere [p. 333] that abstract ideas can also be attributed to one another as genus to species,[1] as when one says that *duration is a continuous quantity*, or that *virtue is a disposition*; but *universal justice* is not merely *a virtue* – rather, it is the whole of moral virtue.

433

Chapter ix
'Of our knowledge of [our][2] existence.'

PHILALETHES. §1. 'Hitherto we have only considered the essences of things'; and since our mind knows these only by abstraction, separating them from all 'particular existence' except what is in our understanding, they give us 'no knowledge of real existence at all. [And] universal propositions, of [which] we can have certain knowledge, concern not existence'. Furthermore, whenever something is attributed to an individual belonging to a given genus or species, by a proposition which would not be certain if it made the same attribution to the genus or species as a whole, the proposition only concerns existence, and only declares an accidental relationship in particular existing things – as when it is said that a certain man is learned.

THEOPHILUS. Yes, indeed! And that is how the matter is viewed by philosophers, too, when in their often-repeated distinction between what pertains to essence and what to existence they associate with existence everything which is accidental or contingent. Very often one does not even know that a universal proposition which is known only through experience may not be accidental too, for our experience is limited. For example, in a country where water never freezes, they would arrive at the proposition that water is always in a fluid state; but this is not essential, as is discovered by coming to colder lands. However, we can take the *accidental* in a narrower way, so that there is a kind of middle ground between it and the *essential*: this middle ground is the *natural*, meaning that which does not necessarily belong to the thing but which nevertheless is inherently appropriate to it if there is nothing which prevents it. Thus someone could

434 maintain that fluidity is not really essential to water but is at least natural to it. One could maintain this, I repeat, but still it is not something which has been demonstrated, and perhaps the inhabitants of the moon, if there were any, would have grounds for believing that they were just as entitled

---

[1] Locke implies in §12 that any proposition linking two abstract terms is an identity. The genus-to-species attributions mentioned in §13 do not involve abstract terms.

[2] Added by Coste.

to say that it is natural for water to be frozen. There are other cases, though, where naturalness is less problematic: for example, a light-ray always travels in a straight line while in the same medium unless it happens to meet a surface which reflects it. I would add that Aristotle always treats matter as the source of accidental things [e.g. *Metap.* E, 1027ª8–15]; but that requires that 'matter' be taken as secondary matter, i.e. as the accumulation or mass of bodies.

PHIL. §2. I have already remarked, following the excellent English author of the *Essay Concerning Understanding*, that we know our own existence by intuition, that of God by demonstration, and that of other things by sensation; and I recall that you heartily applauded [p. 387]. §3. Now, this intuition which makes our own existence known to us does so in a wholly evident manner which neither admits of proof nor needs it; with the result that even when I undertake to doubt everything, this very doubt will not allow me to doubt my existence. In short, on this topic we have the highest imaginable degree of certainty.

THEO. I am wholly in agreement with all this. And I add that the immediate awareness of our existence and of our thoughts provides us with the first *a posteriori* truths or truths of fact, i.e. *the first experiences*; while identical propositions embody the first *a priori* truths or truths of reason, i.e. *the first illuminations*. Neither kind admits of proof, and each can be called 'immediate' – the former because nothing comes between[1] the understanding and its object, the latter because nothing comes between the subject and the predicate.

Chapter x
'Of our knowledge of the existence of...[2] God.'

PHILALETHES. §1. 'God..., having furnished [our soul] with those faculties [it is] endowed with, he hath not left himself without witness: [for] sense, [understanding],[3] and reason' provide us with clear proofs of his existence.

THEOPHILUS. Not only has God endowed the soul with the faculties it needs to know him, but it has also imprinted upon it characters which delineate him, though faculties are needed if the soul is to be aware of these characters. But I don't want to revive our earlier discussions of innate ideas and truths, amongst which I count the idea of God and the truth of his existence. Let us instead come to the point.

435

---

[1] '*il y a immédiation*'; cf. p. 367.
[2] Locke standardly speaks of the existence or being 'of a God', and Coste always drops the article. Future occurrences will not be noted separately.
[3] Locke: 'perception'. Coste: '*intelligence*'.

PHIL. Well, although the existence of God 'be the most obvious truth that reason discovers; and though its evidence be (if I mistake not) equal to mathematical certainty: yet it requires...attention'. All that is needed for a start is to reflect upon ourselves and upon our own indubitable existence. **§2.** Accordingly, I take it that everyone knows 'that he is something that actually exists', and thus that he is a real being. If there is anyone who can doubt his own existence, I declare that it is not him to whom I am speaking. **§3.** Next, we know 'by an intuitive certainty, that bare nothing [cannot] produce any real being'. Whence it follows with mathematical evidence that something has existed from all eternity;[1] since whatever 'had a beginning must be produced by something else.' **§4.** Now, any being which draws its existence from something else also draws everything it has, including all its faculties, from the same source. So this eternal source of all beings is also the origin of all their powers; and so this eternal being must be also omnipotent.[2] **§5.** Further, 'a man finds in himself... knowledge.' So there exists 'some knowing intelligent being[. But it is] impossible, that things wholly void of knowledge [and] perception, should produce a knowing being, [and it is] repugnant to the idea of senseless matter, that it should put [sense] into itself'. So things have their source in a knowing being, and 'there has been...a knowing being from eternity.' **§6.** 'An eternal, most powerful, and most knowing being [is what is called *God*.] If nevertheless any one should be found so [unreasonable] as to suppose man alone knowing and wise, but yet the product of mere... chance; and that all the rest of the universe acted only by that blind haphazard: I shall [advise him to study at his leisure] that very rational and emphatical rebuke of Tully (*De legibus*, Bk. II).... "What can be more sillily arrogant...than for a man to think that he has [reason] and understanding in him, but [that there is no intelligence which governs this whole vast universe][3]?" From what has been said, it is plain...we have a more certain knowledge of the existence of...God, than of...any thing else without us.'

THEO. I assure you perfectly sincerely, sir, that I am most distressed to
436 have to find fault with this demonstration; but I do so only in order to prompt you to fill the gap in it. It is mainly at the place (§3) where you infer that something has existed from all eternity. I find an ambiguity there. If it means that *there has never been a time when nothing existed*, then I agree with it, and it really does follow with entirely mathematical rigour from the preceding propositions. For if there had ever been nothing, there would always have been nothing, since a being cannot be produced by

[1] Locke: 'it is an evident demonstration, that from eternity there has been something'. Coste's change.
[2] Locke: 'the most powerful'. Coste: '*Toutpuissant*'.
[3] Locke: 'but yet in all the universe beside, there is no such thing'. Coste's change.

nothing; and in that case we ourselves would not have existed, which conflicts with the first truth of experience. But you go straight on in a way which shows that when you say that something has existed from all eternity you mean an eternal thing. But from what you have asserted so far it does not follow that if there has always been something then one certain thing has always been, i.e. that there is an eternal being. For some opponents will say that I was produced by other things, and these by yet others. Furthermore, there are those who, if they do admit eternal beings (as the Epicureans do with their atoms), will not regard themselves as committed to granting that there is an eternal being which is the sole source of all the others. For though they would acknowledge that whatever confers existence also confers the thing's other qualities and powers, they will deny that a single thing gives existence to the others, and will even say that for each thing the joint action of several others is required. Thus, we shan't be brought by that argument, unaided, to one source of all powers. However, it is highly reasonable to believe that there is such a source, and indeed that wisdom rules over the universe. But those who believe that matter can have sense will not be inclined to accept that matter cannot possibly produce sense; at least, it will be hard to adduce a proof of this which does not also show that matter is entirely incapable of sense. Also, supposing that our thought does come from a thinking being, can we take it for granted, without harming the demonstration, that this being must be God?

PHIL. I have no doubt that the excellent man from whom I have borrowed this demonstration is capable of rendering it flawless; and I shall try to induce him to do so, as there is hardly a greater service that he could render to the world at large. You wish for this too, which leads me to believe that you do not believe §7. that to silence the atheists we should make everything turn on the existence of the idea of God within us; like those who, 'out of an overfondness of that darling invention,' reject all other demonstrations of God's existence or at least endeavour to weaken them, 'and forbid us to hearken to those proofs, as being weak, or fallacious, which our own existence, and the sensible parts of the universe, offer so clearly, and cogently to our thoughts, that I deem it impossible for a considering man to withstand them.'   437

THEO. Although I support innate ideas, and especially that of God, I do not believe that the Cartesians' demonstrations from the idea of God are complete. I have shown fully elsewhere – in the *Acta* of Leipzig ['Meditations on knowledge, truth and ideas' pp. 292f] and in the *Mémoires de Trévoux* ['Extrait d'une lettre touchant la démonstration cartésienne de l'existence de Dieu'] – that the demonstration which M. Descartes borrowed from Anselm, Archbishop of Canterbury, is truly most elegant and ingenious but that there is still a gap to be filled. That famous

Archbishop, who was certainly one of the ablest men of his time, was proud – not without reason – of having found a way of proving God's existence *a priori*, from the notion of God and without recourse to his effects [*Proslogion* ch. 2]. His argument runs more or less as follows. God is the greatest or (as Descartes says) the most perfect of beings; which is to say that he is a being whose greatness or perfection is supreme, containing within himself every degree of it. That is the notion of God. Now here is how existence follows from that notion. Existing is something more than not existing, i.e. existence adds a degree to the greatness or to the perfection – as M. Descartes puts it, existence is itself a perfection. So this degree of greatness and perfection (or rather this perfection) which consists in existence is in that wholly great and wholly perfect supreme being; for otherwise he[1] would be lacking in some degree, which is contrary to his definition. And so it follows that this supreme being exists. The Scholastics, including even their Angelic Doctor, held this argument in low esteem, regarding it as fallacious [Thomas Aquinas, *S.T.* 1a.ii.1 ad 2um]; but this was a great mistake on their part, and M. Descartes, having studied scholastic philosophy for a good while at the Jesuit College of La Flèche, was quite right to revive the argument. It is not fallacious, but it is an incomplete demonstration which assumes something which should also be proved in order to render the argument mathematically evident. The point is that it is tacitly assumed that this idea of a wholly great or wholly perfect being is possible and does not imply a contradiction. Even that remark enables us to prove something, namely that *If God is possible he exists* – a privilege which only the Divinity possesses. We are entitled to assume the possibility of any being, and above all of God, until someone proves the contrary; and so the foregoing metaphysical argument does yield a demonstrated moral conclusion, namely that in the present state of our knowledge we ought to judge that God exists and to act accordingly. But it is desirable that able people should fill the demonstration out, so as to achieve strict mathematical evidence, and I have said something elsewhere which I believe may contribute to that end ['Extrait d'une lettre touchant la démonstration cartésienne de l'existence de Dieu']. M. Descartes's other argument, which undertakes to prove the existence of God on the grounds that the idea of him is in our souls and that it must have come from that of which it is an idea, is even less conclusive. For, firstly, this argument shares with the preceding one the defect of assuming that there is such an idea in us, i.e. that God is possible. M. Descartes argues that when we speak of God we know what we are saying and therefore have the relevant idea; but that is a misleading sign; for when we speak of perpetual mechanical motion, for example, we know what we are saying,

438

---

[1] Or 'it'.

and yet such motion is an impossibility and so we can only appear to have an idea of it. And, secondly, this argument does not adequately prove that the idea of God, if we do have it, must come from that of which it is an idea; but I don't want to dwell on that now. You will tell me, sir, that since I acknowledge the idea of God to be innate in us I ought not to say that one can entertain doubts about whether there is such an idea? But I allow such doubts only with reference to a rigorous demonstration founded wholly on the idea; for we have from other sources enough assurance of the idea and of the existence of God. You will remember, too, that I have shown how ideas are in us [pp. 76–80] – not always so that we are aware of them, but always in such a way that we can draw them from our own depths and bring them within reach of our awareness. I think it is like that with the idea of God, whose possibility and existence I hold to have been demonstrated in more than one way – the pre-established harmony itself provides a new and unassailable method. I believe indeed that almost all the methods which have been used to prove the existence of God are sound, and could serve the purpose if they were rendered complete; and I am not at all of the opinion that we should ignore the proof based on the order of things.

PHIL. §§8–9. It may be to the purpose to dwell a little on the question 439 of whether a thinking being can come from a non-thinking being, one devoid of sense and knowledge, such as matter might be. §10. It is pretty obvious that a 'parcel of matter [is], in it self, able to produce nothing', and cannot put itself into motion; and so 'the motion it has, must also be from eternity, or else be...[1] added to matter' by some more powerful being. If this motion were eternal, it could never produce knowledge. 'Divide matter into as minute parts as you will [– as though to spiritualize it –][2] vary the figure and motion of it, as much as you please, [make of it] a globe, cube, cone, prism, cylinder, etc. whose diameters are but 1 000 000th part of a *gry*' – which is a tenth of a line, which is a tenth of an inch, which is a tenth of a philosophical foot, which is a third of a pendulum which oscillates once per second at the 45-degree latitude. This particle of matter, however small it is, 'will operate no otherwise upon other bodies of proportionable bulk, than those of an inch or foot diameter [act upon one another; and one] may as rationally expect to produce sense, thought, and knowledge, by putting together in a certain figure and motion, gross particles of matter, as by those that are the very minutest, that do any where exist. They knock, impel, and resist one another, just as the greater do, and that is all they can do.' But if matter could draw 'sense, perception, and knowledge' from within itself (immediately and without

[1] Locke: 'produced, and'. Coste's omission.
[2] Locke: '(which we are apt to imagine a sort of spiritualizing, or making a thinking thing of it,)'.

any mechanism, i.e. without the aid of figures and motions)[1] then these 'must be a property...inseparable from matter and every particle of it. Not to add, that though our general or specific conception of matter makes us speak of it as one thing, yet really all matter is not one individual thing [which exists as][2] one material being or one single body that we know or can conceive. And therefore if matter were the eternal first cogitative being, there would not be one eternal infinite cogitative being, but an infinite number of eternal [infinite][3] cogitative beings, independent one of another, of limited force, and distinct thoughts, which could never produce that order, harmony, and beauty which is to be found in nature. [Whence] it necessarily follows, that the first eternal being cannot be matter.' I hope, sir, that you will be better satisfied with this reasoning than you were with the preceding demonstration by the same celebrated author.

440 THEO. This present reasoning strikes me as perfectly sound, and as being not only rigorous but also deep and worthy of its author. I utterly agree with him that material particles, however small they might be, could not be combined or modified so as to produce perception; seeing that large particles could not do so (as is obvious), and that in small particles everything is proportional to what can occur in large ones [*mill]. The author makes here another important point about matter when he says that it should not be regarded as 'one thing', or (in my way of putting it) as a true and perfect *'monad' or 'unity', because it is only a mass containing an infinite number of beings. At this point our excellent author was only one step away from my system. For what I do is to attribute perception to all this infinity of beings: each of them is like an animal, endowed with a soul (or some comparable active principle which makes it a true unity), along with whatever the being needs in order to be passive, and endowed with an organic body. Now, these beings have received their nature which is active as well as passive (i.e. have received both their immaterial and their material features) from a universal and supreme cause; for otherwise, as our author has so well said, their mutual independence would have made it impossible for them ever to have produced this order, this harmony, this beauty that we find in nature. But this argument, which appears to have only moral certainty, is brought to a state of absolute metaphysical necessity by the new kind of harmony which I have introduced, namely the pre-established harmony. Here is how: each of these souls expresses in its own manner what occurs outside itself, and it cannot do so through any influence of other particular beings (or, to put it a better way, it has to draw up this expression from the depths of its own nature); and so necessarily each soul must have received this

[1] Parenthetical passage added by Leibniz.
[2] Locke: 'neither is there any such thing existing as'. Coste's change.
[3] Locke: 'finite'.

nature – this inner source of the expressions of what lies without – from a universal cause, upon which all of these beings depend and which brings it about that each of them perfectly agrees with and corresponds to the others. That could not occur without infinite knowledge and power. And great ingenuity would be needed, especially, to bring about the spontaneous agreement of the machine with the actions of the rational soul; so great, indeed, that a distinguished writer [*Bayle] who offered some objections in his wonderful *Dictionary* came close to doubting whether *all possible* wisdom would suffice for the task – for he said that the wisdom of God   441 did not appear to him to be more than was needed for such a result. He acknowledged, at least, that the feeble conceptions of divine perfection which are all we can achieve have never been placed in such sharp relief.

PHIL. What pleasure I get from this agreement between your thoughts and those of my author! I hope that you will not be vexed, sir, if I recount to you the rest of his reasoning on this topic. §12. First, he considers whether the thinking being upon which all other knowing beings (and *a fortiori* all other beings) depend is material or not. §13. He considers the objection that a thinking being could be material. But he replies that even if that were so, it is enough that this should be an eternal being, with infinite knowledge and power. Furthermore, 'if thinking and matter may be separated, the eternal existence of matter, will not follow from the eternal existence of a cogitative being'. §14. Those who make God material are further asked whether they believe that 'every particle of matter, thinks?' In that case, it would follow that there were as many Gods as particles of matter. But if the individual particles of matter do not think, then once more we have a thinking being made up of unthinking parts – which has already been refuted. §15. To say that just one atom of matter thinks and that the other parts, though equally eternal, do not think – this is to say, quite gratuitously, that non-eternal thinking beings are produced by one part of matter which is infinitely above the rest. §16. If it be maintained that the eternal and material thinking being is a certain particular mass of matter[1] whose parts are unthinking, we are back with something which has already been refuted; for nothing is achieved by combining the parts of matter – all they acquire is 'a new relation of position, which 'tis impossible should [communicate][2] knowledge to them.' §17. It makes no difference whether this mass is at rest or in motion. 'If it be...at rest, it is but one [inactive] lump, and so can have no privileges above one atom.' If it is in motion, this motion which distinguishes it from other parts[3] must be what produces the thought; and so 'all the thoughts [will be] accidental, and limited', since each part by itself is without thoughts and has nothing which

[1] Locke: 'some certain system of matter'. Coste's change.
[2] Locke: 'give'. Coste's change.
[3] '*qui le distingue d'autres parties*' added by Leibniz.

regulates its movements. There will thus be neither freedom nor choice nor wisdom, any more than there is in 'pure blind matter'. **§ 18.** Some people may well believe that matter is at least co-eternal with God. But they do not say why; and the bringing into existence of a thinking being, which they do allow, is much harder than the production of matter, which is less perfect. 'Nay possibly,' says the author, 'if we would emancipate our selves from vulgar [ideas], and raise our thoughts, as far as they would reach, to a closer contemplation of things, we might be able to aim at some dim and seeming conception how matter might at first be made, and begin to exist by the power of that eternal first being: but to give beginning and being to a spirit, would be found a more inconceivable effect of omnipotent power. But this being what would perhaps lead us too far from the notions, on which the philosophy now in the world is [established, he adds,] it would not be pardonable to deviate so far from them; or to inquire, so far as grammar . . . would authorize, if the common settled opinion opposes [this personal view]: especially in this place [on the earth],[1] where the received doctrine serves well enough to our present purpose, and leaves this past doubt, that the creation or beginning of any one SUBSTANCE out of nothing, being once admitted, the creation of all other, but the CREATOR himself, may, with the same ease, be supposed.'

THEO. You have given me real pleasure, sir, by recounting something of a profound thought of your able author, which his over-scrupulous caution has stopped him from offering in its entirety. It would be a great pity if he suppressed it and, having brought us to a certain point with our mouths watering, left us standing there. I assure you, sir, that I believe there is something fine and important hidden under this rather *enigmatic passage. The word 'substance' in capital letters might make one suspect that he conceives the production of matter in the manner of the production of accidents; there is not thought to be any problem about *their* being derived from nothing. And when he distinguishes his personal thought from 'the philosophy which is now established in the world' or in 'this place on the earth', I suspect that he has the Platonists in mind: they took matter to be something fleeting and transitory, in the way accidents are, and had an entirely different idea of minds and souls.

PHIL. **§ 19.** Finally, if any should deny the Creation by which things are made out of nothing, on the grounds that they cannot conceive it, our author (writing without knowledge of your discovery concerning the explanation of the soul's union with the body) objects that they do not understand, either, how voluntary movements are produced in bodies by the will of the soul, and yet they still believe that this happens, being convinced of it by experience. And to those who reply that the soul, being

---

[1] Added by Coste. Locke evidently means 'in this place in my book'.

unable to produce a new movement, merely produces a new determination of the animal spirits, he rightly says that one is as inconceivable as the other. And there could not be a finer remark than the one he adds at this point: 'This is to make our comprehension infinite, or God finite, when what he can do, is limited to what we can conceive of it.'

THEO. Although in my opinion the difficulty about the union of soul and body has now been removed, other difficulties remain. I have shown *a posteriori*, through the pre-established harmony, that all monads were created by God and depend on him; yet we cannot understand in detail *how* this was done; and fundamentally the preservation of monads is nothing but a continual creation, as the Scholastics knew very well.

443

Chapter xi
'Of our knowledge of the existence of other things.'

PHILALETHES. §1. Since it is only the existence of God that has a necessary connection with our own, the idea we may have of a thing 'no more proves the existence of that thing, than the picture of a man evidences[1] his being in the world'. §2. However, I am as certain, by means of sensations, of the white and black on this paper, as I am of the movement of my hand, and this is surpassed only by our knowledge of our own existence and of God's. §3. This certainty 'deserves the name of knowledge. ... For I think no body can, in earnest, be so sceptical, as to be uncertain of the existence of those things which he sees and feels. At least, he that can doubt so far...will never have any controversy with me; since he can never be sure I say any thing contrary to his own opinion.' §4. The perceptions of sensible things are produced 'by exterior causes affecting our senses'; for we do not acquire these perceptions without the organs, and if the organs alone were enough they would produce them constantly. §5. Furthermore, 'sometimes I find, that I cannot avoid the having those ideas produced in my mind': light, for instance, when I am open-eyed in a place where the daylight can enter; whereas I can 'lay by' the ideas which are in my memory. 'And therefore it must...be some exterior cause [of this lively impression],[2] whose efficacy I cannot resist'. §6. Some of those perceptions[3] 'are produced in us with pain, which afterwards we remember without the least offence.... Though mathematical demonstrations depend not upon sense, yet the examining them by diagrams, gives great credit to the evidence of our sight, and seems to give it a certainty approaching to that of the demonstration it self.'

444

---

[1] Coste: '*démontre*'. Leibniz: '*prouve*'.
[2] Locke: 'and the brisk acting of some objects without me'. Coste: '*et l'impression vive de quelques objets hors de moi*'. Leibniz: '*de cette impression vive*'.
[3] Locke: 'many of those ideas'.

§7. Also, 'our senses, in many cases bear witness to...each other.... He that sees a fire, may, if he doubt [about it], feel it too; [and] I see, whilst I write this, I can change the appearance of the paper; and...tell beforehand what new idea it shall' present to the mind. But when those characters have been written, I cannot 'choose afterwards but see them as they are'. In addition, the sight of those characters will draw the same sounds from another man. §8. If anyone believes that all this is but a long dream, 'if he pleases, he may dream that I make him this answer,' that our certainty, founded on the testimony of our senses, is 'as great as our frame can attain to [and] as our condition needs.' He that sees a candle burning, and experiences the heat of its flame, which does him harm if he does not withdraw his finger, will not require 'greater certainty to govern his actions'. And if this dreamer did not do so, he would wake up. Thus, such assurance is enough for us, 'being as certain to us, as our pleasure or pain...; beyond which we have no concernment' with the knowledge or existence of things. §9. But beyond our 'actual sensation'[1] there is no knowledge but only 'likelihood', as when I believe that there are men in the world, for which there is a very high probability, although being now alone in my study I do not see any of them. §10. So it would be folly to expect demonstration in everything, and not to act in accordance with very clear and evident[2] truths when they are not demonstrable. And a man who was willing to conduct himself in that way would be sure of nothing but of perishing quickly.

THEOPHILUS. I have already pointed out during our earlier discussions, that the truth of sensible things is established[3] by the links amongst them [pp. 374f, 392]; these depend upon intellectual truths, grounded in reason, and upon observations of regularities among sensible things themselves, even when the reasons are not apparent. Since these reasons and observations provide us with means to make judgments about the future as it bears upon our interests, and since these judgments, when they are reasonable, meet with success, we can neither ask for nor, indeed, attain any greater certainty about such objects. Furthermore, we can even explain dreams and how little they are linked with other phenomena. Still, I believe that the terms 'knowledge' and 'certainty' could be extended beyond 'actual sensations', since clarity and *evidence which I regard as a kind of certainty, go beyond them, and it would certainly be insane to doubt in earnest that there are men in the world when we do not see any. To 'doubt in earnest' is to doubt in a practical way. *Certainty* might be taken to be knowledge of a truth such that to doubt it in a practical way would be insane; and sometimes it is taken even more broadly, to cover cases where

445

---

[1] From Locke's marginal summary.
[2] Locke: 'very plain and clear'. Coste's change.   [3] 'se justifie'.

doubt would be very blameworthy. (Whereas *evidence* is luminous certainty, where we have no doubt because of the way we can see the ideas to be linked together.) On this definition of certainty, we are certain that Constantinople is in the world, and that Constantine, Alexander the Great and Julius Caesar have lived. Of course some peasant from the Ardennes could justifiably doubt this, for lack of information; but a man of letters or of the world could not do so unless his mind was unhinged.

PHIL. §11. We are reliably assured of many past things by our memory, but we cannot certainly judge whether they still exist. I saw water yesterday, and a certain number of very fine colours on the bubbles on that water. I am now certain that the bubbles existed as well as the water, but 'it is no more certainly known to me, that the water doth now exist, than that the bubbles...do so; [though the former is infinitely[1]] more probable, because water hath been observed to' be lasting, and bubbles to disappear. §12. Finally, apart from ourselves and God, we know of other Spirits only by revelation, and have only the certainty of faith regarding them.

THEO. It has already been pointed out [p. 360] that our memory sometimes deceives us. Whether or not we put our faith in it depends on how vivid it is and how closely linked with things that we know. And even when we are sure of the main point, we can often be in doubt about the details. I remember having known a certain man, because I sense that his image is familiar to me, and his voice too, and this double indication is a better warrant than just one of them; but I cannot remember where I have seen him. However, it does happen, though rarely, that we see a person in a dream before seeing him in flesh and blood. I have been assured that a lady at a well-known court saw in a dream the man she later married and the room where the betrothal took place, and she described these to her friends, all before she had seen or known either the man or the place. This was attributed to some secret presentiment or other; but chance could produce such a result since it happens rather rarely; and in any case the images in dreams are a little hazy, which gives one more freedom in subsequently relating them[2] with others [sc. other images].

PHIL. §13. We can conclude that there are two sorts of propositions: the one, *particular* and concerning existence – for instance, that an elephant exists; the other, *general* and concerning the dependence of ideas – for instance, that men ought to obey God. §14. Most[3] of these 'general certain propositions' are called 'eternal truths', 'and all of them indeed are so; ...not because they are eternal propositions actually formed' somewhere from all eternity, nor because they are engraved on the mind from any

446

---

[1] Locke: 'exceedingly much'. Coste's change.
[2] Taking '*le*' to be a slip for '*les*'.　　　　[3] Locke: 'many'. Coste's change.

patterns that always existed,[1] but because we can be sure, with regard to any creature endowed with the required faculties and means, that he will,[2] 'when he applies his thoughts to the consideration of his ideas, know the truth of [these] propositions'.

THEO. The distinction you draw appears to amount to mine, between 'propositions of fact' and 'propositions of reason'. Propositions of fact can also become general, in a way; but that is by induction or observation, so that what we have is only a multitude of similar facts, such as the observation that all quicksilver is evaporated by the action of fire. This is not perfect generality, since we cannot see its necessity. General propositions of reason are necessary, although reason also yields propositions which are not absolutely general, and are only likely – for instance, when we assume that an idea is possible until a more accurate inquiry reveals that it is not. Finally there are 'mixed propositions' which derive from premisses some of which come from facts and observations while others are necessary propositions. These include a great many of the findings of geography and astronomy about the sphere of the earth and the paths of the stars, arrived at by combining the observations of travellers and astronomers with the theorems of geometry and arithmetic. But according to a principle of the logicians, a conclusion depends upon and cannot be more certain than the weakest of the premisses; so these mixed propositions have only the degree of certainty and generality which observations have. As for 'eternal truths', it must be understood that fundamentally they are all conditional; they say, in effect: given so and so, such and such is the case. For instance, when I say: *Any figure which has three sides will also have three angles*, I am saying nothing more than that given that there is a figure with three sides that same figure will have three angles. I say 'that same', which is the respect in which categorical propositions, which can be stated unconditionally although they are fundamentally conditional, differ from those we call 'hypothetical'. An example of the latter would be the proposition: *If a figure has three sides, its angles are equal to two right angles*; we can see that here the 'antecedent' (i.e. *The figure is three-sided*) and the 'consequent' (i.e. *The angles of the three-sided figure are equal to two right angles*) do not have the same subject. Whereas in the former case, in which the antecedent was *This figure is three-sided* and the consequent was *The figure in question has three angles*, they did have the same subject. Though hypotheticals too can often be transformed into categoricals, by modifying their terms a little. For instance, in place of the foregoing hypothetical I could say: *The angles of every three-sided figure are equal to two right angles*. The Scholastics hotly debated *de constantia*

447

---

[1] Locke has 'imprinted', not 'engraved'. The change is Coste's, as is the addition of the 'eternity' phrase and of 'always'.
[2] Locke: 'he must needs'.

subjecti, as they put it, i.e. how a proposition about a subject can have a real truth if the subject does not exist. The answer is that its truth is a merely conditional one which says that if the subject ever does exist it will be found to be thus and so. But it will be further asked what the ground is for this connection, since there is a reality in it which does not mislead. The reply is that it is grounded in the linking together of ideas. In response to this it will be asked where these ideas would be if there were no mind, and what would then become of the real foundation of this certainty of eternal truths. This question brings us at last to the ultimate foundation of truth, namely to that Supreme and Universal Mind who cannot fail to exist and whose understanding is indeed the domain of eternal truths. St Augustine knew this and expresses it pretty forcefully [e.g. *Free Choice* II.12]. And lest you should think that it is unnecessary to have recourse to this Mind, it should be borne in mind that these necessary truths contain the determining reason and regulating principle of existent things – the laws of the universe, in short. Therefore, since these necessary truths are prior to the existence of contingent beings, they must be grounded in the existence of a necessary substance. That is where I find the pattern for the ideas and truths which are engraved in our souls. They are engraved there not in the form of propositions, but rather as sources which, by being employed in particular circumstances, will give rise to actual assertions.

Chapter xii
Of ways of increasing our knowledge.[1]

PHILALETHES. We have discussed the kinds of knowledge we possess. Let us turn now to the ways of increasing knowledge, i.e. of finding out the truth. §1. It is 'the common received opinion amongst men of letters, that maxims [are] the foundations of all knowledge; and that the sciences [are] each of them built upon certain *praecognita*' or things already known. §2. I admit that the great success of mathematics seems to favour this method, and you have relied a good deal upon that. §3. But there is still a question as to whether it is not the connection of ideas which has served this purpose, rather than 'two or three general maxims laid down in the beginning[. A young lad knows that his] body is bigger than his little finger, but [not] by virtue of this axiom, that *The whole is bigger than a part*'. Knowledge began with particular propositions, but then there was a desire to 'disburden the memory of the cumbersome load of particular' ideas, by means of general notions. If the language were so imperfect that it did not include the relative terms *whole* and *part*, could one not know that the body is larger than the finger? That is my author's reasoning, at least, but

---

[1] Locke: 'Of the improvement of our knowledge', using 'improve' in its now obsolete sense of 'increase'. The insertion of 'ways of' (*moyens de*) is Coste's.

from what you have already said I believe that I foresee how you will be able to reply.

THEOPHILUS. I don't know why he dislikes maxims so much that he has to attack them all over again. If they serve to 'disburden the memory' of 'a great many particular ideas', as he acknowledges, they must be very useful even if they are good for nothing else. But let me add that that is not what gives rise to them, since we do not discover them by induction from instances. He who knows that ten is more than nine, that his body is larger than his finger, and that the house is too large to be able to escape through the door, knows each of these particular propositions by means of a single general principle. The principle is embodied in and coloured by them, as it were – just like looking at coloured lines in circumstances where the shape and proportion are determined by the lines, irrespective of their colour. Now, this common principle is the axiom itself, which is known implicitly, so to speak, though not at first in an abstract and isolated way. The instances derive their truth from the embodied axiom, and the axiom is not grounded in the instances. And since this principle which is common to these particular truths is in the minds of all men, you can readily see that someone can be imbued with it without having the words 'whole' and 'part' in his vocabulary.

PHIL. §4. But is it not dangerous to give authority to assumptions, in the guise of axioms? One person will assume, following some of the ancients, that 'all is matter'; another, with Polemo, that the world is God; and a third will lay it down as a fact that the sun is the chief divinity. Think what a religion we should have if that were permitted. 'Nothing can be so dangerous, as principles thus taken up without questioning...; especially if they be such as concern morality'. For some will expect a different life, similar rather to that of Aristippus, who placed blessedness in bodily pleasure, than to that of 'Antisthenes, who made virtue sufficient to felicity'.[1] And Archelaus, who will lay 'it down as a principle, that right and wrong, honest and dishonest, are defined only by laws, and not by nature, will have other measures of moral rectitude and pravity, than those who [recognize] obligations antecedent to...human constitutions.' §5. Principles must therefore be certain. §6. But this certainty comes only from the comparison of ideas, and so we have no need for other principles; and by following 'this one rule' we shall get further than by 'putting our minds into the disposal of others.'

THEO. I am surprised, sir, that you bring against maxims, i.e. against evident principles, the charge which could and should be levelled at principles assumed gratuitously. When we ask for *praecognita* in the

[1] Locke: We can 'justly expect another kind of life in Aristippus...and in Antisthenes...'.

sciences, i.e. for antecedent knowledge to serve as the foundation for a science, we are asking for *known principles*, and not for arbitrary positings [of propositions] whose truth is unknown. Aristotle himself understood that the lower and subordinate sciences borrow their principles from other higher sciences within which these principles have been demonstrated [e.g. *Metap.* Γ, 1005ᵃ18–36]. The only exception is the first of the sciences, which we call metaphysics: according to him, this asks for nothing from the other sciences, and provides them with the principles they need. And when he says *dei pisteuein ton manthanonta*, that the apprentice ought to believe his master, he means that he should do so only for the time being, until he has been instructed in the higher sciences; so that the belief is only provisional [*Soph. Refut.* 165ᵇ3]. This is very far from being receptive to 'gratuitous principles'.[1] I should add that even principles which are not completely certain can have their uses, if we build upon them purely demonstratively. You see, even though all our conclusions from them would then be merely conditional, and would be worth having only if the principle in question were true, nevertheless the very fact that this connection holds would have been demonstrated, as would those conditional assertions. So that it would be very desirable for us to have many books written in this way: the reader or student, having been warned about the condition [to which the book is subject], would be in no danger of error. And conduct would be governed by these conclusions only to the extent that the initial assumption was independently verified. This same method has another use, namely to verify assumptions or hypotheses, in cases where many conclusions flow from them which are known on other grounds to be true; sometimes the process can work perfectly in reverse, yielding a demonstration of the truth of the hypothesis. M. *Conring, who was a physician by profession but was accomplished in every branch of learning except perhaps mathematics, wrote to a friend at Helmstedt who was engaged in having the book reprinted in which the distinguished peripatetic philosopher Viotti tries to explain demonstrative reasoning and Aristotle's *Posterior Analytics*; and this letter was appended to the book. In it M. Conring reproved Pappus for saying that *analysis* undertakes to discover the unknown by assuming it and then proceeding by inference from it to known truths. This, he said, is contrary to logic, which teaches that truths can be inferred from falsehoods. But I subsequently showed him that analysis makes use of definitions and other reciprocal propositions, which provide a way of reversing the process and finding synthetic demonstrations. And even when this reverse process is not demonstrative – in natural science, for instance – it still sometimes yields great likelihood, when the hypothesis easily explains many phenomena which would be

450

---

[1] In the marginal summary of §4 Coste uses *'principes gratuits'* to render Locke's 'precarious principles'.

otherwise puzzling and which are quite independent of one another. I maintain, sir, that the principle of principles really amounts to making good use of ideas and of experiments; but if we take this a little deeper we will find that what it involves, so far as ideas are concerned, is nothing but the

451 connecting of definitions by means of axiomatic identities. Still, it is not always easy to attain to such an ultimate analysis, and much as the geometers (or at least the ancient ones) have evidently wanted to achieve this, they have not yet been able to do so. If the distinguished author of the *Essay Concerning Human Understanding* were to complete this undertaking, which is a little more difficult than it is thought to be, he would make them very happy. *Euclid, for instance, has included in his axioms what amounts to the statement that two straight lines can meet only once. Imagination, drawing on sense-experience, does not allow us to depict two straight lines meeting more than once, but this is not the right foundation for a science. And if anyone believes that his imagination presents him with connections between *distinct ideas, then he is inadequately informed as to the source of truths, and would count as immediate a great many propositions which really are demonstrable from prior ones. This is something which has not been properly thought out by many people who have found fault with Euclid: images of this sort are merely confused ideas, and someone who knows a straight line only by means of them will be incapable of demonstrating anything about it. Euclid had no distinctly expressed idea of a straight line, i.e. no definition of it (for the one he offers provisionally is unclear, and useless to him in his demonstrations), and so he was obliged to have recourse to two axioms which served him in place of a definition and which he uses in his demonstrations: the one, that two straight lines do not have any parts in common, and the other, that they do not enclose a space. Archimedes gave a sort of definition of 'straight line' when he said that it is the shortest line between two points. But in his demonstrations, when he uses elements such as Euclid's, founded on the two axioms I have just referred to, he tacitly assumes that the properties spoken of in those axioms are possessed by the line which he has defined. So if you and your friends appeal to the agreement and disagreement of ideas to justify your belief that it was and still is permissible to admit into geometry what images tell us, without seeking the rigorous demonstration from definitions and axioms on which the ancients insisted in this science (and I believe that many people will in their ignorance believe this), then I must tell you, sir, that this may be good enough for those who are only

452 concerned with unpolished practical geometry, but it will not do for those who want a science of geometry – a science by which even the practical [kind of geometry] is improved. And if the ancients had taken that view, and had been lax about this matter, I believe that they would have made hardly any progress and would have left us only an empiric geometry such

as the Egyptians apparently had and the Chinese seem to have still. This would have deprived us of the most beautiful discoveries of *natural science and mechanics, which geometry has enabled us to make, and which are unknown wherever our geometry is unknown. It is likely, too, that by allowing our senses and their images to guide us we would be led into errors; we see something of the sort in the fact that people who have not been taught strict geometry believe, on the authority of their imaginations, that it is beyond doubt that two lines which continually approach each other must eventually meet. Whereas geometers offer as examples to the contrary certain lines which they call asymptotes. But apart from that, we would be deprived of what I value most in geometry, considered as a contemplative study, namely its letting us glimpse the true source of eternal truths and of the way in which we can come to grasp their necessity, which is something that the confused ideas of sensory images can never distinctly reveal. You will tell me that Euclid was nevertheless obliged to rest content with certain axioms whose *evidence can be seen only confusedly, by means of images. I admit that he contented himself with those axioms; but it was better to content himself with a small number of truths of that nature, which appeared to him the simplest, and to deduce from them the other truths which someone less rigorous would have taken as certain without demonstration, than to leave a great deal undemonstrated and – worse still – to leave people free to relax their rigour as the mood takes them. So you see, sir, that what you and your friends have said about the connection of ideas as the genuine source of truths needs elucidation. If you are willing to be satisfied with seeing such connections confusedly, you will weaken the rigour of demonstrations; Euclid did incomparably better by reducing everything to definitions and a small number of axioms. But if you want this connection of ideas to be exhibited and expressed distinctly, you will have to avail yourselves of definitions and axiomatic identities, as I require. Sometimes, when you are having trouble in carrying out a complete analysis, you will have to rest content with some axioms which are less primary, as Euclid and Archimedes did; but it is better to do this than to miss or postpone some fine discovery which you could make straight away with their help. Indeed, as I have said before, sir, I believe that we would have almost no geometry at all (as a 453 demonstrative science, I mean), if the ancients had not been willing to push ahead before having demonstrated the axioms which they were compelled to use.

PHIL. I am beginning to understand what a distinctly known connection of ideas is, and I plainly see that in this case axioms are required. §7. I also see plainly why the method we follow in our inquiries into ideas must be modelled on that of 'the mathematicians, who from very plain and easy beginnings' – which are nothing other than axioms and definitions[1] – 'by gentle degrees, and a continued chain of reasonings, proceed to the discovery and demonstration of truths, that appear at first sight beyond human capacity. The art of finding proofs, and the admirable methods they have invented for the singling out, and laying in order...intermediate ideas...is that which has...produced such wonderful and unexpected discoveries: but whether something like this, in respect of other ideas, as well as those of magnitude, may not in time be found out, I will not determine. [At least,] if other ideas...were pursued in the way familiar to mathematicians, they would carry our thoughts farther...than possibly we are apt to imagine.' **§8.** And that could be done in morality in particular, as I have several times said.

THEO. I believe that you are right, sir, and I have long been inclined to set about fulfilling your predictions.

PHIL. **§9.** With regard to the knowledge of bodies,[2] 'we are to take a quite contrary course, [for] the want of ideas of their real essences sends us [to] experience'. **§10.** However, 'I deny not, but a man accustomed to rational and regular experiments shall be able to...guess righter [than another] at their yet unknown properties, [but] this is but judgment and opinion, not knowledge and certainty. This...makes me suspect, that *natural philosophy is not capable of being made a *science [by us. However,] experiments and historical observations we may have, from which we may draw advantages of...health, and...conveniences for this life'.

THEO. I agree that the whole of natural philosophy will never be perfectly a science for us; but still we shall be able to have some science of nature, and indeed we have some samples of it already. For instance, magnetology can be regarded as such a science: from a few assumptions grounded in experience we can demonstrate by rigorous inference a large number of phenomena which do in fact occur in the way we see to be implied by reason. We cannot hope to account for every experiment; even the geometers have still not proved all their axioms. But just as they have been satisfied with deducing a great number of theorems from a small number of rational principles, similarly it will be enough if practitioners of natural science can, by means of certain principles of experience, account for a great many phenomena and even predict them in practice.

PHIL. **§11.** So 'since our faculties are not fitted to penetrate into the internal fabric...of bodies[, we should consider it enough that they] discover to us the being of...God, and the knowledge of our selves, enough to lead us into a full and clear discovery of our duty, and great concernment, [above all in regard to eternity. And] I think I may conclude, that morality

454

---

[1] Added by Leibniz.　　　　　[2] Locke: 'substantial beings'.

is the proper science, and business of mankind in general;...as [the] several arts, conversant about several parts of nature, are the lot...of particular men'. For instance, ignorance of the use of iron can be said to be the reason why the country of America, which abounds with all sorts of natural plenty, lacks the greatest part of the conveniences of life. §12. Far from disesteeming the science of nature, then, I hold that this study, 'if rightly directed, may be of greater benefit to mankind' than everything that has been done up to now. And 'he that first invented printing; discovered the use of the compass; or made public the virtue...of quinquina, did more for the propagation of knowledge; for the supply and increase of useful commodities; and saved more from the grave,' than the founders of colleges and hospitals and other 'monuments of exemplary charity, that have at so great charge been raised'.

THEO. You could not have said anything more to my liking, sir. True morality or piety, far from supporting the idleness of certain lazy *Quietists, ought to incite us to cultivate the [practical] arts. And as I said not long ago [pp. 426f], better policies would be able to provide us some day with far better medical knowledge than we have now. That is something which, second only to concern for virtue, cannot be urged strongly enough.

PHIL. §13. Although I recommend experimentation, I do not lack respect for probable hypotheses; they can lead us to new discoveries and are at least great helps to the memory. But our mind is very apt to go too hastily, and to be content with flimsy conjectures, rather than taking the time and trouble needed to test them against a multitude of phenomena.

THEO. The art of discovering the causes of phenomena, or genuine hypotheses, is like that of deciphering: an inspired guess often provides a generous short-cut. Lord *Bacon started putting the art of experimenting 455 into the form of rules, and the Honourable Robert *Boyle was a gifted practitioner of it. But unless we add to that the art of *using* experiments and of drawing conclusions from them, we can lay out a king's ransom and still achieve less than an acute thinker could discover in a moment. M. Descartes, who certainly fits that description, said something to the same effect in one of his letters, referring to the English Chancellor's method. And *Spinoza (whom I am quite prepared to quote when he says something good) offered a similar reflection in one of his letters to the Secretary of the Royal Society of England, the late Mr *Oldenburg; it was published among the posthumous works of that discerning Jew. He was commenting on a work of Mr Boyle's, who, it must be said, does spend rather too long on drawing from countless fine experiments no conclusion except one which he could have adopted as a principle, namely that everything in nature takes place mechanically – a principle which can be made certain by reason alone, and never by experiments, however many of them one conducts.

PHIL. §14. Once we have established clear and distinct ideas with settled names, the great way to enlarge our knowledge 'is the art of finding out those intermediate ideas, which may show us the agreement, or repugnancy' of the extreme ideas. §15. Maxims, at least, will not furnish them. 'Suppose...a man, not to have [an] exact idea of a right angle,...he will in vain' struggle to demonstrate something about a right-angled triangle. And whatever maxims one employs, one will have trouble proving with their help that the squares on the sides which contain the right angle are equal to the square on the hypotenuse. 'A man may...pore long enough on those axioms, without ever seeing [more clearly into][1] mathematical truths.'

THEO. It is useless to 'pore on' axioms unless you have something to apply them to. Axioms often serve to connect ideas; for instance, the maxim that similar magnitudes of two and three dimensions are in the doubled and tripled ratio of the corresponding magnitudes of one dimension, is extremely useful. For example, the quadrature of the lunule of Hippocrates follows directly from it in the case of circles, on combining the maxim with the application of the one figure to the other, when their given position permits it – for their known comparison [i.e. that of their corresponding linear magnitudes] promises to throw light on the quadrature.

456
Chapter xiii
'Some farther considerations concerning our knowledge.'

PHILALETHES. §1. It should perhaps be added that 'our knowledge, as in other things, so in this, has a great conformity with...sight, that it is neither wholly necessary, nor wholly voluntary.... A man with his eyes open in the light, cannot but see; yet there be certain objects, which he may...turn his eyes to'. §2. And he may survey them more or less intently. Thus, as long as the faculty is employed, 'our will hath no power to determine...knowledge', any more than a man can prevent himself from seeing what he does see. §3. But one must employ one's faculties in the right way to be informed.

THEOPHILUS. We discussed this point earlier, and established that a man is not responsible for having this or that opinion at the present time, but that he is responsible for taking steps to have it or not have it later on [p. 182]. So that opinions are voluntary only in an indirect way.

---

[1] Locke: 'one jot more of'. Coste's change.

Chapter xiv
'Of judgment.'

PHILALETHES. §1. Man would find himself 'in most of the actions of his life, perfectly at a stand, had he nothing to guide him in the absence of ...certain knowledge.' §2. He must often content himself with 'only the twilight...of probability'. §3. The faculty by which we avail ourselves of this is *judgment*. Often we rest content with this out of necessity, but often 'out of laziness, unskilfulness, or haste'. It is 'called *assent* or *dissent*'; and §4. it is exercised when something is '*presumed* to be so;' that is, when it is taken to be true before it is proved. And if that occurs in conformity with how 'in reality things are, it is *right* judgment.'

THEOPHILUS. There are people for whom 'judging' is the action which is performed whenever one pronounces in accordance with some knowledge of the case, and some of them may even distinguish judgment from opinion, as not having to be so uncertain. But I do not want to join issue   457 with anyone over the use of words; and it is permissible, sir, for you to take a judgment to be a probable belief. As for 'presumption', which is a jurists' term, good usage in legal circles distinguishes it from 'conjecture'. It is something more than that, and should be accepted provisionally as true until there is proof to the contrary; whereas an indication, a conjecture, often has to be weighed against another conjecture. For instance, someone who admits having borrowed money from someone else is *presumed* to be obliged to repay it unless he shows that he has already done so, or that the debt has been cancelled for some other reason. In this sense, therefore, to *presume* something is not to accept it *before*[1] it has been proved, which is never permissible, but to accept it *provisionally*[2] but not groundlessly, while waiting for a proof to the contrary.

Chapter xv
'Of probability.'

PHILALETHES. §1. If demonstration exhibits the connection of ideas, probability is nothing but the appearance of such connections, resting on[3] proofs in which no immutable connection is seen. §2. There are several 'degrees of assent from...assurance...quite down to conjecture, doubt, and distrust.' §3. When there is certainty, each part of the reasoning which marks one of its connections contains intuition. But 'that which makes me believe, is something extraneous'. §4. And probability is grounded either in conformity with something we know or in the testimony of those who know it.

[1] '*avant*'.   [2] '*par avance*'.
[3] Locke: 'by the intervention of'.

THEOPHILUS. I would rather maintain that it is always grounded in likelihood or in conformity to truth; the testimony of others is something else that the truth customarily has on its side when it concerns facts which are within reach. So we can say that the resemblance between the probable and the true comes either from the thing itself or from 'something extraneous'. Rhetoricians distinguish two kinds of arguments: *'artful' ones which are developed from things by means of reasoning, and 'artless' ones which simply rest on the explicit testimony either of some man or even, perhaps, of the thing itself. But there are also 'mixed' ones, since testimony can itself provide a fact which serves in the construction of an 'artful' argument.

458

PHIL. §5. We do not readily believe what is remote from everything we know, because of its lack of resemblance to the true. Thus when an ambassador told the King of Siam that in our country the water turned so hard in winter that an elephant could walk on it without breaking through, the King said to him: Hitherto I have believed you to be a man of honour, but now I see that you lie. §6. But if the *testimony* of others can make a fact probable, the *opinion* of others should not count by itself as a true ground of probability, since there is more error than knowledge amongst men. And if the 'persuasions of others, whom we know and think well of, be a [legitimate] ground of assent, men have reason to be Heathens in Japan, Mahommedans in Turkey, Papists in Spain, [Calvinists in Holland],[1] and Lutherans in Sweden.'

THEO. Men's testimony doubtless carries more weight than their opinions do, and we give it greater consideration in the courts. However, we know that judges sometimes require an oath of 'credulity', as it is called, to be taken; during an examination witnesses are often asked not only what they saw, but what they judge and at the same time the reasons for their judgment; and what they say receives appropriate consideration. Furthermore, judges show great deference to the views and opinions of experts in every field; private individuals are no less obliged to do the same, in so far as the matter is not one for them to investigate for themselves. So a child, or an inexpert adult, whose position in this respect is hardly better than a child's, is obliged – even if he is quite highly placed – to follow the religion of his country so long as he sees nothing wrong with it and is not in a position to inquire into whether there is a better one. A supervisor of page-boys, whatever his own sect, will make each of his charges attend the church which is frequented by the lad's co-religionists. I refer you to the debates between M. *Nicole and others over 'the argument from *large numbers' in matters of faith; some people have had too much respect for it, and others have not given it enough weight. There are other

---

[1] Locke: 'Protestants in England'.

presumptions[1] like this, by which men would be very glad to escape from controversy. These are what Tertullian, in a treatise devoted to the subject, calls *'prescriptions'. This is a term by which the ancient jurists, with 459 whose language he was familiar, denoted all sorts of defences or extraneous prior objections to a claim; nowadays, however, it is almost always used in the sense of a temporal prescription, in which someone purports to rebut someone else's claim on the ground that it was not made within the period set by law. This is why it was possible to publish 'legitimate presumptions' on both the Roman Catholic and the Protestant sides. Ways have been found, for example, of bringing a charge of *innovation* against certain aspects of each of them: when the Protestants mostly abandoned the old form of ordination of clergy, for instance, and when the Roman Catholics altered the old canon of the books of the Old Testament. (I have established the latter point clearly enough in the debate which I intermittently carried on in writing with the Bishop of Meaux [*Bossuet], news of whose recent death came just a few days ago.) Thus, since these accusations flow in both directions, innovation is not a clear proof of error in these matters, even though it arouses suspicion of it.

Chapter xvi
'Of the degrees of assent.'

PHILALETHES. §1. Concerning the degrees of assent, it should be noticed that our grounds of probability operate no further in this matter[2] than the degree of *likelihood that we find in them. Or *did* find when we looked into them: for it must be admitted that assent cannot be 'always from an actual view of the reasons that [have prevailed on the mind; and it would be] very hard, even for those who have very admirable memories, [always] to retain all the proofs, which...made them embrace that side of the 460 question' – 'which sometimes [are] enough to fill a...volume upon one single question'.[3] 'It suffices, that they have once with care and fairness, sifted the matter [and] cast up the account', so to speak. §2. 'Without this,...men must be either very sceptics, or change [their opinions] every moment, and yield themselves up to whoever, having lately studied the question, offers them arguments; which for want of memory [or of leisured study],[4] they are not able presently to answer' in their entirety. §3. It must be admitted that this often makes men obstinate in error. 'But the fault is not that they rely on their memories,...but because they judged [badly] before'. For often, noting that 'they never thought otherwise' serves men as a substitute for investigation and reason. But usually those who have least examined their opinions are the firmest in holding to them. It is

---

[1] '*préjugés*', not '*présomption(s)*' as on p. 457.
[2] '*en cela*'; Locke has 'operate no farther on the mind'.
[3] Clause transferred from Locke's §2. [4] Added by Leibniz.

commendable to hold to what we have seen, however, but not always to what we have believed,[1] since we may have overlooked something which could overturn it all. And there may be no one in the world 'that hath the leisure, patience, and means, to collect together all the proofs' on each side of the questions on which he has opinions, and to compare these proofs so as safely to conclude that there is nothing more for him to know for his better information. However, 'the conduct of our lives, and the management of our great concerns, will not bear delay: [and] the determination of our judgment [is absolutely necessary] in points, wherein we are not capable of certain...knowledge'.

THEOPHILUS. What you have just said, sir, is thoroughly sound and good. In certain cases, though, one could wish that men did keep written summaries, in the form of memoranda, of the reasons which have led them to some important view which they will often have to justify later on, to themselves or others. Let me add that although it is not usually permitted in the courts to rescind a judgment after it has been delivered, or to do a revision after having 'cast up the account' (otherwise we would have to be in perpetual disquiet, which would be all the more intolerable because we cannot always keep records of past events), nevertheless we are sometimes allowed to appeal to the courts on new evidence, and even to obtain what is called 'restitution *in integrum*' against a previous ruling. It is like that also in our personal affairs and especially in the most important matters, in cases where it is still open to us to plunge in or to draw back, and is not harmful to postpone action or to edge cautiously ahead: the pronouncements that our minds make on the grounds of probabilities should never be taken *in rem judicatam*, as the jurists say – i.e. as settled – to such an extent that we shall be unwilling to revise our reasoning in the light of substantial new reasons to the contrary. But when there is no time left for deliberation, we must abide by the judgment we have made as resolutely as if it were infallible, although not always as inflexibly.

461

PHIL. §4. Since, therefore, men cannot avoid exposing themselves to error when they judge, or avoid having differing opinions when they cannot see matters from the same point of view, they ought 'to maintain peace, and the...offices of humanity,...in the diversity of opinions,' and not expect that anyone should readily give up a deep-rooted opinion just because we object to it – especially if he has reason to suspect his opponent of interest or ambition or other personal motive. And usually those who would force others to yield to their opinions have hardly examined things well. For those who have explored an issue deeply enough to be past doubt are so

---

[1] Where Philalethes contrasts 'seen' (*vu*) with 'believed' (*cru*), Locke contrasts 'knowledge' with 'probability'.

few in number, and find so little reason to condemn others, 'that nothing [violent][1] is to be expected from them'.

THEO. Really, what we are most justified in censuring is not men's opinions, but their immoderate condemnation of the opinions of others, as if only a fool or a knave could judge otherwise than they do. This attitude, on the part of those who foment these passions and hatreds among the people, results from a haughty and partisan mind which loves to dominate and cannot bear to be contradicted. Not that there is not often good reason to censure the opinions of others; but this should be done fair-mindedly and with compassion for human frailty. We certainly have the right to protect ourselves against evil doctrines which influence morality and pious observances, but we should not malign people by ascribing these to them without good evidence. Impartiality counsels mercy, but piety commands that when people's dogmas are harmful their $\quad$ 462 bad effects be pointed out, where it is appropriate to do so: for example, beliefs which go against the providence of a perfectly good, wise and just God, or against that immortality of souls which lays them open to the operations of his justice; not to mention other opinions which are dangerous to morality and public order. I know that some excellent and well-meaning people maintain that these theoretical opinions have less practical effect than is generally thought. I know too that there are people with fine characters who would never be induced by doctrines to do anything unworthy of themselves; moreover, those who reach these erroneous opinions through speculation are not only inclined by nature to be aloof from the vices to which ordinary men are prone, but also are concerned for the good name of the sect of which they are, as it were, the leaders. One can acknowledge that Epicurus and Spinoza, for instance, led exemplary lives. But these considerations usually fail to apply to their disciples and imitators; believing themselves to be relieved of the inhibiting fear of an overseeing Providence and of a threatening future, they give their brutish passions free rein and apply their thoughts to seducing and corrupting others. If they are ambitious and by nature rather callous, they are capable of setting fire to the four corners of the earth, for their pleasure or advancement – I knew men of this stamp whom death has carried off. I even find that somewhat similar opinions, by stealing gradually into the minds of men of high station who rule the rest and on whom affairs depend, and by slithering into fashionable books, are inclining everything towards the universal revolution with which Europe is threatened, and are completing the destruction of what still remains in the world of the generous sentiments of the ancient Greeks and Romans, who placed love of country and of the public good, and the welfare of future generations, before

---

[1] Locke: 'insolent and imperious'.

fortune and even before life. This 'public spirit',[1] as the English call it, is dwindling away and is no longer in fashion; it will die away all the more when it ceases being sustained by the good morality and true religion which natural reason itself teaches us. Among those of the contrary character, which is beginning to prevail, the best have no other principle but what they call 'honour'. But for them the mark of an honest man or a man of honour is merely that he will do nothing that they consider base. And if, to display his power or on a whim, someone spilled a sea of blood or turned everything upside down, they would think nothing of it; a Herostratus from the ancient world or indeed a Don Juan in [Molière's] *Festin de Pierre*

463   would count as a hero. They sneer openly at love of country, and they ridicule those who are concerned for the public good. And when some well-meaning man speaks of the prospects for posterity, they say 'Let the future look after itself.' But these people may come to experience for themselves the evils that they believe will only befall others. If they cure themselves of this spiritual epidemic whose bad effects are starting to show, those evils will perhaps be prevented; but if the disease continues to spread, it will engender a revolution, and providence will cure men by means of that; for although that may happen, in the final account things will always turn out for the best over all. That, however, should not and cannot come about without the punishment of those whose evil actions have actually helped good to triumph. But let me get back to my main point; thinking about harmful beliefs and our right to criticize them has led me to digress. In theology censure is carried even further than in other areas. Those who prize their orthodoxy often condemn their adversaries; and are in turn opposed, even within their own sect, by those who are called *'syncretists' by *their* adversaries. The result of this opposition is civil war between the rigid and the yielding within a single sect. However, it is an encroachment on God's prerogative to deny eternal salvation to those who hold different opinions; and so the wisest of the condemners confine themselves to the peril in which, in their view, these erring souls stand; they leave to the peculiar mercy of God those who are not so wicked that they cannot profit from it, and they believe themselves obliged to make every imaginable effort to remove these people from their perilous position. If these people who think in this way about the peril of others have reached their opinion after an appropriate investigation, and if there is no way of undeceiving them, we cannot find fault with their conduct as long as they employ only lenient measures. But as soon as they go beyond this they violate the laws of impartiality. For they should bear in mind that other people, who are just as convinced as they are, have just as much right to maintain their own views and even to propagate them if they believe them important. An

---

[1] '*ces* publiks spirits': the phrase could be used in the plural in Leibniz's day, though not with a plural adjective.

exception should be made of opinions which advocate crimes which ought not to be tolerated; we have the right to stamp these out by stern measures – even if the person who holds them cannot shake himself free of them – just as we have the right to destroy a venomous beast, innocent as it is. But I am speaking of stamping out the sect, not the men, since we can prevent them from doing harm and from preaching their dogmas.

PHIL. §5. To return to the grounds and degrees of assent, we should notice that propositions[1] are of two sorts: those of 'matter of fact', which because they fall under observation can rest upon human testimony; and those of 'speculation',[2] which are not open to such testimony because they concern things which our senses cannot reveal to us. §6. When a particular fact is 'consonant to the constant observation of our selves' and to the uniform reports of others, we rely 'as firmly upon it, as if it were certain knowledge'. And when it conforms with the testimony 'of all men, in all ages, as far as it can be known,' this is 'the first...and highest degree of probability'. For example, that fire warms, that iron sinks in water.[3] 'Our belief thus grounded, rises to *assurance*.' §7. Secondly, the historians all report that so-and-so preferred his private advantage to the public. Since it has always been observed that this is the practice of most men, the assent which I give to these histories is a case of '*confidence*'. §8. Thirdly, when there is nothing in the nature of things for or against a fact, and it is vouched for by the testimony of people who are not suspect – for instance, that Julius Caesar lived – it is accepted with 'confident belief'.[4] §9. But 'when testimonies....clash with the ordinary course of nature, or with one another', the degrees of probability can 'infinitely vary'.[5] Hence arise the degrees which 'we call *belief, conjecture,...*[6] *doubt, wavering, distrust*'. 'There it is, where...exactness is required, to form a right judgment, and to proportion the assent' to the degrees of probability.

THEO. When jurists discuss proofs, presumptions, conjectures, and evidence, they have a great many good things to say on the subject and go into considerable detail. They begin with *common knowledge*, where there is no need for proof. They deal next with *complete *proofs*, or what pass for them: judgments are delivered on the strength of these, at least in civil actions. In some places they are more cautious in criminal actions; in these there is nothing wrong with insisting on *more-than-full* proofs, and above all for the so-called *corpus delicti* if it is that sort of case. So there are more-than-full proofs, and also ordinary *full* ones. Then there are *presumptions*, which are accepted provisionally as complete proofs – that is, for

464

---

[1] Locke: 'propositions we receive upon inducements of probability'.
[2] From Locke's marginal summary.
[3] Locke: 'fire warmed a man...iron sunk in water'.
[4] From Locke's marginal summary.   [5] From Locke's marginal summary.
[6] Locke: 'guess,'; omitted by Coste, as is 'disbelief' at the end of the list.

as long as the contrary is not proved. There are proofs which are, strictly speaking, *more than half full*; a person who founds his case on such a proof is allowed to take an oath to make up its deficiency (*juramentum suppletorium*). And there are others that are *less than half full*; with these, on the contrary, the oath is administered to the one who denies the charge, to clear him (*juramentum purgationis*). Apart from these, there are many degrees of conjecture and of evidence. And in criminal proceedings, in

465 particular, there is evidence (*ad torturam*) for applying torture (which itself has varying degrees, depending on what the charge is); there is evidence (*ad terrendum*) sufficient for displaying the instruments of torture and making preparations as though one intended to use them. There is evidence (*ad capturam*) for arresting the suspect, and (*ad inquirendum*) for gathering evidence surreptitiously. These differences are also serviceable in other analogous situations. The entire form of judicial procedures is, in fact, nothing but a kind of logic, applied to legal questions. Physicians, too, can be observed to recognize many differences of degree[1] among their signs and symptoms. Mathematicians have begun, in our own day, to calculate the chances in games. It was the Chevalier de *Méré – a man of acute mind, a gambler and philosopher, whose *Agréments* and other works have been published – who prompted them by raising questions about the division of the stakes, wanting to know how much [a given player's part in] a game would be worth if the game were interrupted at such and such a point. Accordingly he enlisted his friend M. Pascal to take a brief look at the problem. The question caused a stir and prompted M. Huygens to write his treatise on chance. Other learned men joined in. Certain principles were established, and were also employed by Pensionary De Witt in a little discourse, published in Dutch, on annuities. The foundation they built on involved *prosthaphaeresis*, i.e. arriving at an arithmetic mean between several equally admissible hypotheses. Our peasants have used this method for a long time, guided by their natural mathematics. For instance, when some inheritance or piece of land is to be sold, they appoint three teams of assessors – these teams are called *Schurzen* in Low Saxon – and each team assesses the commodity in question. Now suppose that the first estimates its value at 1000 crowns, the second at 1400 and the third at 1500; they take the total of these three, which is 3900, and because there were three teams they take a third of this, 1300, as the mean value sought. Or, what comes to the same thing, they take the sum of one third of each estimate. This is the axiom: *aequalibus aequalia* – like hypotheses must receive like consideration. But when the hypotheses are unlike, we compare them with one another. Suppose, for instance, that with two dice one player will win if he throws a 7 and the other if he throws a 9. We want to know

466 their relative *likelihoods of winning. I say that the second player is only

---

[1] '*de degrés et de différences*', literally 'degrees and differences'.

two thirds as likely to win as the first player, since there are three ways in which the first can throw a 7 with two dice – 1 and 6, or 2 and 5, or 3 and 4 – whereas there are only two ways in which the second can throw a 9, namely by throwing 3 and 6, or 4 and 5. And all these ways are equally possible. So that the likelihoods, which match the numbers of equal possibilities, will be as 3 to 2, or 1 to $^2/_3$. I have said more than once [pp. 206, 372] that we need a new kind of logic, concerned with degrees of probability, since Aristotle in his *Topics* could not have been further from it: he was content to set out certain familiar rules, arranged according to the commonplaces – rules which may be useful in some contexts where a discourse has to be developed and given some likelihood – without taking the trouble to provide us with balances which are needed to weigh likelihoods and to arrive at sound judgments regarding them. Anyone wanting to deal with this question would do well to pursue the investigation of *games of chance. In general, I wish that some able mathematician were interested in producing a detailed study of all kinds of games, carefully reasoned and with full particulars. This would be of great value in improving the art of *invention, since the human mind appears to better advantage in games than in the most serious pursuits.

PHIL. § 10. The law of England observes this rule, that the copy of a record is a good proof if it is acknowledged to be authentic by witnesses, but 'the copy of a copy never so well attested, and by never so credible witnesses, will not be admitted as a proof in judicature....I never yet heard of any one that blamed [this wise precaution. It at least] carries this observation along with it, viz. that any testimony, the farther off it is from the original truth [that lies in the thing itself], the less force...it has. [In contrast with this,] amongst some men, the quite contrary [is] practised, who look on opinions to gain force by growing older; and what a thousand years since would not, to a rational man, contemporary with the first voucher, have appeared at all probable, is now urged as certain' because various people have related it upon the strength of his testimony.

THEO. Scholars in the field of history have great respect for contemporary witnesses to things; though the principal claim to credence, even of a contemporary, is restricted to public events. Still, when he speaks of motives, secrets, hidden machinations, and such uncertain matters as poisonings and assassinations, one does at least learn what various people have believed. When Procopius addresses himself to Belisarius's war against the Vandals and the Goths, he is highly credible; but when in his *Anecdotes* he spreads abroad dreadful slurs on the Empress Theodora, believe them if you will! In general, one should treat satirical writings with a good deal of scepticism: in our own time we have seen the publication of satires which, although against all likelihood, have been greedily

467

gobbled up by ignorant people. The day may come when it is said: Could anyone have dared to publish those things at that time if there was not some likely foundation for them? But if that *is* said some day, it will be very bad judgment. Yet people are drawn towards satire, and I shall give just one example. The late M. du Maurier *fils* was led by heaven knows what flaw in his character to publish in his memoirs, which were printed a few years ago, certain totally unfounded allegations against the incomparable Hugo Grotius, the Swedish Ambassador in France; it seems that something – I don't know what – had made him hostile to the memory of that distinguished friend of his father; and I have noticed that many authors have vied with one another to repeat the allegations, despite the fact that their falsehood is clearly enough shown by the great man's negotiations and his letters. People even feel free to put fiction into the writing of history: the author of the latest *Life of Cromwell* believed that it was permissible for him, in dealing with the still-private life of that able usurper, to enliven the material by taking him on a journey to France and following him, like a private tutor, into the inns of Paris. And yet from the *History of Cromwell* which the well-informed Carrington wrote and dedicated to Cromwell's son Richard while the latter was still acting as Protector, it appears that Cromwell never left the British Isles. It is especially hard to be sure about details. We have hardly any good accounts of battles: most of Livy's appear to be imaginary, as do those of Quintus Curtius. What would be needed are accounts, from both sides, by intelligent and careful people who would even draw up battle-maps like the ones which Count Dahlberg had engraved to illustrate the military actions and battles of King Charles of Sweden (Dahlberg had earlier served with distinction under this monarch, and recently as Governor-General of Latvia he conducted the defence of Riga). Still, one should not be too quick to denigrate a good historian on the strength of what is said by some monarch or minister exclaiming against him because of some episode or theme which is not to their liking – in which indeed he may be somewhat at fault. It is said that Charles the Fifth, when he wanted to have something of Sleidan's read to him, used to say 'Bring me my book of lies', and that Carlowitz, a Saxon nobleman who was very active in the events of that period, used to say that Sleidan's history was destroying in his mind all his former good opinion of histories of ancient times. That, I maintain, will be powerless to overturn the authority of Sleidan's history in the minds of informed people; it is a history which is largely woven out of public Acts of Parliaments and Assemblies and out of writings authorized by the monarchs. If there had remained the least doubt about that, it has just been removed by the excellent history written by my distinguished friend the late M. von *Seckendorf (though I cannot refrain from deploring the occurrence in its title of the word 'Lutheranism', which bad common usage has sanctioned

468

in Saxony). Most of the things in it are confirmed by extracts from countless pieces taken from the Saxon Archives, to which the author had access. The Bishop of Meaux [*Bossuet], who is attacked in the book and to whom I sent a copy, replied to me only that it is horribly long-winded; but I should have liked it to be twice as large, though on the same scale. The fuller it was, the more open to criticism it must have been, since the critic would merely have had to pick out his passages. And, besides, some admired works of history are much larger. Lastly, authors who write about times earlier than their own are sometimes respected, when what they relate is likely on other grounds. And it sometimes happens that they preserve fragments from earlier writers. For example, there was a question about what family Bishop Suibert of Bamberg belonged to (he was later Pope, under the name of Clement II). An anonymous fourteenth-century author of a history of *Brunswick had identified the family, but people well versed in our history had been unwilling to pay attention to what he said. However, I acquired a much older chronicle, still unpublished, where the same thing is said with more supporting detail; from this it appears that the family was that of the former independent lords of Hornburg (not very far from Wolfenbüttel) whose lands were donated to the cathedral church of Halberstadt by their last owner.

PHIL. §11. 'I would not be thought here to lessen the credit and use of history [by my remark.] We receive from it a great part of the useful truths we have, with a convincing evidence. I think nothing more valuable than the records of antiquity: I wish we had more of them, and more uncorrupted.' But it remains the case that no copy can rise above the certainty of its first original.[1]

THEO. When we have just one writer of antiquity to attest to some fact,   469 then certainly none of those who have copied what he said have added any weight to it – indeed they should all be entirely disregarded. What they say should be treated exactly as though it belonged to the *hapax legomena*, the 'things which have been said only once', of which M. Ménage wanted to make a book. Even today, when a hundred thousand scribblers repeat the calumnies of Bolsec (for instance), a judicious man will give no more heed to this than to the noise of goslings. Jurists have written about *historical credibility, but the topic would be worth a more painstaking inquiry, and some of these gentlemen have not been demanding enough. As for remote antiquity, some of the most resounding 'facts' are dubious. Competent people have doubted, and not without reason, whether Romulus was the first founder of the city of Rome. There is disagreement about the death of Cyrus, and the discrepancies between Herodotus and Ctesias have also cast the history of the Assyrians, Babylonians and Persians into doubt.

---

[1] Locke: 'that no probability can arise higher than its first original'.

Great difficulties beset the story of Nebuchadnezzar, of Judith, and indeed of Ahasuerus in the Book of Esther. The Romans in speaking of 'the *gold of Toulouse' go against their own account of the defeat of the Gauls by Camillus. Above all, no trust should be put in a nation's own private history of itself if it is not drawn from really old documents and does not conform pretty well to the histories of other nations. That is why what we are told about ancient kings – German, Gaulish, British, Scottish, Polish, and others – are rightly taken to be freely invented fables. The Trebeta, son of Ninus, who founded Trèves, and the Brutus who fathered the Britons (or Brittains), are as real as Amadis. The tales taken from certain story-tellers, tales which Trithemius, Aventinus, and even Albinus and Suffridus Petri have allowed themselves to tell regarding ancient princes of the Franks, the Boii, the Saxons, and the Frisians; and what we are told by Saxo Grammaticus and by the *Edda* about the northern lands in times of remote antiquity; all this can have no more authority than can the amusing acount – passed on to us by Kadlubek, the first Polish historian – of one of the Polish kings being a son-in-law of Julius Caesar. But when the histories of different nations converge, in matters where it is not likely that one has been copied from the other, that is powerful evidence of truth.

470 The agreement in many things between Herodotus and the history of the Old Testament is like that; for instance his account of the battle at Megiddo between the King of Egypt and the Syrians of Palestine (i.e. the Jews), at which, according to the account in the Holy Scripture which we have from the Hebrews, King Josiah was mortally wounded. Again, those who are trying to establish the facts get satisfaction from the agreement between Arabic, Persian and Turkish historians on the one hand, and Greek, Roman and other western ones on the other; as also from the way books which have come down to us from the ancients, and which are indeed copies of copies, are attested to by the medals and inscriptions which have survived from ancient times. It remains to be seen what more the history of China will teach us when we are better equipped to make judgments about it so that it comes to have an inherent credibility. History is useful mainly for the satisfaction one gets from knowing about origins, for the justice that is done to men who have deserved well of others, for the establishment of historical scholarship, especially in sacred history which contains the foundations of revelation, and (setting aside the genealogies and entitlements of princes and powers) for the useful lessons we can learn through examples. I am not scornful of the sifting of the materials of antiquity right down to the tiniest trifles, for sometimes the knowledge scholars infer from these can be helpful in more important matters. I am willing, for instance, that the entire history of clothing and tailoring should be written, from the vestments of the Hebrew priests, or if you like from the coats of skins which God gave to the first couple when they left

Paradise, right through to the wigs and flounces of our own times; introducing also whatever can be inferred from ancient sculptures and from paintings several centuries old. I shall even provide, if anyone so desires, the memoirs of a man of Augsburg of the previous century who made paintings showing himself in every suit he had worn from his infancy to the age of sixty-three. And someone – I forget who – told me that the late Duke d'Aumont, who was a great connoisseur of fine antiquities, owned a rarity of a similar kind. Such knowledge might help us to tell monuments which are genuine from ones which are not, not to mention various other uses. And since it is permissible for men to play games, it is even more permissible for them to amuse themselves with this sort of work so long as essential tasks do not suffer by it. But I could wish that there were people who would devote themselves rather to the task of deriving the most useful things from history – such as unusual examples of virtue, remarks about the conveniences of life, and political and military stratagems. And I wish that someone would write a sort of universal history which was expressly restricted to things like that and some others of the most significant kind; for sometimes one will read a big history-book, one which is learned, well written, just right for its author's purpose, and excellent of its kind, but containing almost nothing in the way of useful lessons. By that I do not mean simple moralizings, of which the *Systematic Conspectus of Human Life* and other such anthologies are filled, but rather skills and items of knowledge which not everyone would think of just when they were needed. I wish further that books of travel were used as a source for endless profitable things of this nature and that they were organized according to their subject matters. But it is astonishing that with so many useful things still to be done, men nearly always spend their time on what has been done already, or on what is utterly useless, or anyway on the least important things; and I can see virtually no remedy for this until, in calmer times, society at large takes more of a hand in these matters.

471

PHIL. Your digressions are enjoyable and instructive. §12. But let us turn from the probabilities of matters of fact to those of opinions concerning 'things...such, that falling not under the reach of our senses, they are not capable of testimony.' For example, concerning the existence and nature of 'Spirits, angels, devils, etc.', and concerning the corporeal substances which exist 'in the planets, and other mansions of the vast universe. [Finally,] concerning the manner of operation in most...of the works of nature'. In all these things we can only conjecture, with analogy being the great rule of probability. For since these matters cannot be attested to, 'they can appear...probable, only as they more or less agree to truths that are established[. Since the] rubbing of two bodies violently one upon another, produces heat, and...fire it self,' and since the refractions of transparent bodies make colours appear, we judge that 'fire, consists in a violent agitation of...imperceptible...parts', and that colours whose origins we do not see also come from a similar kind of refraction.[1] And, 'finding in all parts of the creation, that fall under human observation, that there is a gradual connection..., without any great...gaps between,... we have reason to be persuaded, that by such gentle steps things ascend upwards in degrees of perfection. 'Tis an hard matter to say where sensible and rational begin, and...which is the lowest species of living things'. It is like the way quantity augments or lessens 'in a regular cone.... The difference is exceeding great between some men, and some [brute] animals: but if we will compare the understanding and abilities of some men, and some brutes, we shall find so little difference, that 'twill be hard to say, that that of [those men] is either clearer or larger [than that of those brutes].

472   Observing, I say, such gradual and gentle descents downwards in those parts of the creation, that are beneath man, [right down to the lowest,] the rule of analogy [leads us to regard it as] probable, that it is so also in things above us, and our observation'. This sort of probability is the great foundation of rational hypotheses.

THEO. It is on this *analogy* that M. Huygens judges, in his *Cosmotheoros*, that the other principal planets are in a condition much like our own, except for differences which are bound to arise from their different distances from the sun; and M. de *Fontenelle, who had already contributed his very witty and well-informed *Conversations on the Plurality of Worlds*, has had some pretty things to say about this, and has found the art of enlivening difficult material. One could say, more or less, that as in *Harlequin's lunar empire it is 'just like here'. It is true that moons (which are merely satellites) are thought of quite differently from principal planets. Kepler left a little book containing an ingenious fictional account of the state of things on the *moon; and an imaginative Englishman has given us an amusing description of the travels of a Spaniard, invented by him, who was carried to the moon by migrating birds; and then there is Cyrano, who went later in search of that Spaniard. Some imaginative writers, wanting to depict the after-life in attractive terms, conduct the blessed souls from world to world: we may imagine that that makes up some part of the fine pastimes that can be assigned to Spirits; but however hard our imagination strains, I doubt if it can ever be equal to the task, because these Spirits are so varied and separated by such a chasm from ourselves. Until we discover telescopes like those of which M. Descartes held out hope [*Optics* IX], which would let us pick out things no bigger than our houses on the lunar surface, we shall be unable to settle what there is on any globe other than ours. Our

[1] Locke: 'that the colour and shining of bodies, is in them nothing but the different arrangement and refraction of their minute and insensible parts.'

conjectures about the inner parts of terrestrial bodies will be more useful and more open to confirmation: I hope that on many matters we shall get beyond mere conjecture; and I believe that at least the violent agitation of the parts of fire, of which you have just spoken, should not be counted amongst the merely probable things. It is a pity that M. Descartes's hypothesis about the structure of the parts of the visible universe has had so little confirmation from subsequent research and discovery, or that M. Descartes did not live fifty years later so that he could give us as ingenious an hypothesis for our present knowledge as he gave for what was known in his time. As for the 'gradual connection' of species: we have already had something to say about that in a previous discussion [p. 307], when I commented that philosophers have in the past reasoned about a *'vacuum among forms' or among species. In nature everything happens by degrees, and nothing by jumps; and this rule about change is one part of my law of continuity. But the beauty of nature, which insists upon perceptions which stand out from one another, asks for the appearance of jumps and for musical cadences (so to speak) amongst phenomena, and takes pleasure in mingling species. Thus, although in some other world there may be species intermediate between man and beast (depending upon what senses these words are taken in), and although in all likelihood there are rational animals, somewhere, which surpass us, nature has seen fit to keep these at a distance from us so that there will be no challenge to our superiority on our own globe. I speak of intermediate *species*, and I would not want to handle this matter in terms of human *individuals* who resemble brutes, because it is likely that what they suffer from is not a lack of the faculty [of reason] but an impediment to its being exercised. So I believe that the stupidest man (if he is not in a condition which is contrary to nature, through illness or some other permanent defect which plays the part of an illness) is incomparably more rational and teachable than the most intellectual of all the beasts; although the opposite is sometimes said as a joke. I would add that I strongly favour inquiry into analogies: more and more of them are going to be yielded by plants, insects and the comparative anatomy of animals, especially as the microscope continues to be used more than it has been. And in regard to more general matters, my views about monads will be found manifested everywhere – views about their endless duration, about the preservation of the animal along with the soul, about the occurrence of indistinct perceptions in a certain state such as that of death in simple animals, about the bodies which can reasonably be attributed to Spirits, and about the harmony between souls and bodies, such that each perfectly follows its own laws without being disturbed by the other and with no need for a distinction between voluntary and involuntary. It will be found, I claim, that all these views are in complete conformity with the analogies amongst things which come to our notice;

473

474

that I am merely going on beyond our observations, not restricting them to certain portions of matter or to certain kinds of action; and that the only difference is that between large and small, between sensible and insensible.

PHIL. §13. Nevertheless, there is one case where we give weight not so much to the analogy with natural things which we have encountered in experience as to the contrary testimony of a strange fact which is remote from our experience. 'For where...supernatural events are suitable to [the] ends [of] him, who has the power to change the course of nature,' we have no grounds for refusing to believe them when they are well attested. 'This is the...case of miracles, which...do not only find credit themselves; but give it also to other truths, which need such confirmation.' §14. Finally, there is a testimony that is superior to[1] every other kind of assent. It is *revelation*, that is, the testimony of God, who can neither deceive nor be deceived; and our assent to it is called *faith*, which 'as perfectly excludes all wavering' as does the most certain knowledge. But it is important to 'be sure, that it be a divine revelation, and that we understand it right'; otherwise one will be exposed to fanaticism and to the errors of a wrong interpretation. And in a case where the existence and the sense of the revelation are only probable, our assent cannot have a higher probability than that of the proofs. But we shall say more about this later on.

THEO. The theologians distinguish *rational grounds for belief, along with the natural assent which can arise only from such grounds and which cannot have a higher probability than they have, from the supernatural assent which is brought about by divine grace. Whole books have been devoted to 'the analysis of faith': they somewhat disagree amongst themselves, but since we are going to treat of the topic later [pp. 518f], I do not want to anticipate now what we shall have to say in the proper place.

475

Chapter xvii
'Of reason.'

PHILALETHES. §1. Before separately discussing the topic of faith, we shall deal with reason. 'Sometimes it is taken for true, and clear principles: sometimes for...deductions from those principles: and sometimes for the cause, and particularly the final cause. [But here it is to be considered as] that faculty, whereby man is supposed to be distinguished from beasts, and wherein it is evident he much surpasses them.' §2. We need it 'both for the enlargement of our knowledge, and regulating our' opinion.[2] Properly understood, it consists of two faculties, namely *sagacity* in the finding of 'intermediate ideas', and the faculty for drawing conclusions or *inferring*.

---

[1] Locke: 'challenges'. Coste's change.   [2] Locke: 'assent'.

§3. And 'we may in reason consider these four degrees; [1] the discovering ...of proofs; [2] the...laying them in [an] order, to make their connection' be seen; (3) the being aware of the connection in each part of the deduction; (4) drawing a conclusion from it.[1] These degrees may be observed in mathematical demonstrations.

THEOPHILUS. A reason is a known truth whose connection with some less well-known truth leads us to give our assent to the latter. But it is called a 'reason', especially and *par excellence*, if it is the cause not only of our judgment but also of the truth itself – which makes it what is known as an '*a priori* reason'. A *cause* in the realm of things corresponds to a *reason* in the realm of truths, which is why causes themselves – and especially final ones – are often called 'reasons'. And, lastly, the faculty which is aware of this connection amongst truths, i.e. the faculty for reasoning, is also called 'reason', and it is in that sense that you are using the word. Now, here on earth this faculty really is exclusive to man alone and does not appear in any other animals on earth; for I showed earlier [pp. 5of, 271] that the shadow of reason which can be seen in beasts is merely an expectation of a similar issue in a case which appears to resemble the past, with no knowledge of whether the same reason obtains. And that is just how men behave too, in cases where they are merely empirics. But they rise above the beasts in so far as they see the connections between truths – connections which themselves constitute necessary and universal truths. These connections may be necessary even when all they lead to is an opinion: this happens when after precise inquiries one can demonstrate on which side the greatest probability lies, in so far as that can be judged from the given facts; these being cases where there is a demonstration not of the truth of the matter but of which side prudence would have one take. In dividing up this faculty of reason, I believe that one does well to recognize two parts in it, in accordance with the quite common view which distinguishes 'invention' from 'judgment' [*Ramus]. As for the 'four degrees' which you find in the demonstrations of mathematicians: in my experience the first of them, namely the discovery of the proof, is usually not presented, as one would like it to be; one is offered a synthesis which has been found without analysis or with the analysis being suppressed. Geometers start their demonstrations with the 'proposition' which is to be proved, and then prepare the way for demonstration of it by offering the 'exposition', as it is called, in which whatever is *given* is displayed in a diagram; after which they proceed to the 'preparation', drawing in further lines which they need for the reasoning – the finding of this preparation often being the most skilful part of the task. When that has

476

[1] Locke: 'to make their connection...perceived; the third is the perceiving their connection; and the fourth, the making a right conclusion.' Coste's changes.

been done, they conduct the 'reasoning' itself, drawing conclusions from what has been given in the exposition and what has been added to it in the preparation; and, with the aid of truths already known or demonstrated, they arrive at the 'conclusion'. But there are cases where the exposition and the preparation are dispensed with.

PHIL. §4. *'Syllogism...is generally thought, [to] be the proper instrument of [reason], and the usefullest way of exercising this faculty. [I doubt this, because it serves only] to show the connection of the proofs in any one instance, and no more'; but the mind sees this just as easily, and perhaps better, without that aid. Those who know how to make use of Figures and Moods mostly take that use for granted, through 'an implicit faith in their teachers', and without understanding the reasons for it. If the syllogism is necessary, nobody knew anything at all by reason before it was invented; and we must say that God, having made men two-legged, 'left it to Aristotle to make them rational, i.e. those few of them that he could get...to examine the grounds of syllogisms [in which,][1] in above threescore ways, that three propositions may be laid together, there are but about fourteen [trustworthy ones]. God has been more bountiful to mankind than so. He has given them a mind that can reason.... I say not this...to lessen Aristotle, whom I look on as one of the greatest men amongst the ancients; whose large views, acuteness and penetration of thought, and strength of judgment, few have equalled: and who in this very invention of [this little system of][2] forms of argumentation..., did great service against those, who were not ashamed to deny any thing. [But these forms] are not the only, nor the best way of reasoning[; and Aristotle discovered them] not by the forms themselves but by the original way of ...[3] the visible agreement of ideas.' And the knowledge of them gained through the natural order[4] in mathematical demonstrations appears better without the aid of any syllogism. To infer is to derive a proposition as true from another already laid down as true, relying on a certain connection of intermediate ideas. For example, from the proposition that *Men shall be punished in another world* it will be inferred that *They can determine themselves in this world*,[5] these being connected as follows. *Men shall be punished* and *God is the punisher*, so *The punishment is just*; so *The punished is guilty*, so *He could have done otherwise*; so *He possesses freedom* and so, finally, *He has the power to determine himself*. This shows the connection better than would a 'jumble of five or six syllogisms [in which the ideas were] transposed and repeated,' and enshrined in 'artificial forms'. What matters is to know 'what connection the intermediate [idea] has with...

477

---

[1] Locke: 'could get so to examine the grounds of syllogisms, as to see, that'.
[2] Added by Coste.   [3] Locke: 'knowledge, i.e. by'.
[4] Locke: 'knowledge gained thereby'. Mainly Coste's change. Locke uses 'the natural order' later in §4.   [5] '*ici*', added by Leibniz.

the extremes in [the] syllogism, [but] that no syllogism...can show.' It is the mind that can perceive those ideas as they 'stand there in that juxtaposition', purely by inspection. 'Of what use then are syllogisms? [They are of use] in the schools, where men are allowed without shame to deny the agreement of ideas, that do manifestly agree. ... Hence it is, that men in their own inquiries after truth never use syllogisms to convince themselves, (or in teaching...[1] willing learners].' It is quite clear, too, that this order:

$$man—animal—living$$

i.e. man is an animal, animals are living, so man is living, is more natural than the syllogistic order:

$$animal—living \qquad man–animal[2]$$
$$man—living$$

i.e. animals are living, man is an animal, so man is living. It is true that syllogisms can serve to expose a falsehood hidden under a brilliant rhetorical display, and I used to believe that syllogisms were necessary, if only to guard one against fallacies concealed in florid discourses; but upon a strict examination I have found that in order to show the incoherence of an argument one has only to separate out the ideas which the inference depends upon from the superfluous ones, and arrange them in a natural order. I have known a man to whom the rules of syllogism were entirely unknown,[3] 'who at first hearing could perceive the weakness and inconclusiveness of a long artificial and plausible discourse, wherewith others [skilled in all the niceties of logic][4] have been misled. And I believe there are few of my readers who do not know such. And...if it were not so, ...princes in matters that concern their crowns and dignities [would not fail] to bring syllogism into the debates of moment' – where in fact everyone would think it ridiculous to use them. They have almost never been heard of in Asia, Africa or America, among peoples who are not under European influence. Finally, 'those scholastic forms of discourse' are after all 'not less liable to fallacies'; and men are seldom 'silenced in this scholastic way' and still more rarely convinced and won over. At most, they will 'acknowledge their adversary to be the more skilful...; but rest nevertheless persuaded of the truth on their side.... And if...fallacy can be couched in syllogisms,...it must be something else, and not syllogism that must discover them.' I am not, however, in favour of rejecting syllogisms or of doing without anything which can aid the understanding.

478

[1] Locke: 'others to instruct'. Coste's omission.
[2] Locke: '*animal—vivens—homo—animal.*' The change of layout is Leibniz's as is the addition of the next line.
[3] Locke: 'a man unskilful in syllogism'. Coste's change.
[4] Locke: 'better skilled in syllogism'. Coste's change.

'Some eyes want spectacles...; but let not those that use them...say, no body can see clearly without them:' that would be too much to discredit nature in favour of art. Perhaps *they* are somewhat indebted to art – unless the situation is the other way around, and they have suffered the fate of the person who has used spectacles too much or too early, namely that these have so dimmed his sight that he can no longer see without their aid.

THEO. Your reasoning about how little use syllogisms are is full of many sound, fine remarks. It must be admitted that the scholastic syllogistic form is not much employed in the world, and that if anyone tried to use it seriously the result would be prolixity and confusion. And yet – would you believe it? – I hold that the invention of the syllogistic form is one of the finest, and indeed one of the most important, to have been made by the human mind. It is a kind of universal mathematics whose importance is too little known. It can be said to include an *art of infallibility, provided that one knows how to use it and gets the chance to do so – which sometimes one does not. But it must be grasped that by 'formal arguments' I mean not only the scholastic manner of arguing which they use in the colleges, but also any reasoning in which the conclusion is reached by virtue of the form, with no need for anything to be added. So: a *sorites, some other sequence of syllogisms in which repetition is avoided, even a well drawn-up statement of accounts, an algebraic calculation, an infinitesimal analysis – I shall count all of these as formal arguments, more or less, because in each of them the form of reasoning has been demonstrated in advance so that one is sure of not going wrong with it. Most of Euclid's demonstrations, too, are close to being formal arguments. For when he constructs what appears to be an enthymeme, the proposition which is suppressed and which seems to be missing is supplied by a citation in the margin which enables one to find the earlier proof of it – a procedure which greatly shortens the argument without any loss of cogency. Euclid's invertings, compoundings and dividings of ratios are merely particular kinds of argument-form which are special to the mathematicians and to their subject matter; and they demonstrate [the soundness of] these forms with the aid of the universal forms of general logic. It should also be realized that there are *valid non-syllogistic inferences* which cannot be rigorously demonstrated in any syllogism unless the terms are changed a little, and this altering of the terms is the non-syllogistic inference. There are several of these, including arguments from the direct to the indirect – e.g. 'If Jesus Christ is God, then the mother of Jesus Christ is the mother of God'. And again, the argument-form which some good logicians have called relation-conversion, as illustrated by the inference: 'If David is the father of Solomon, then certainly Solomon is the son of David'. These inferences are nevertheless demonstrable through truths on which ordinary

479

syllogisms themselves depend. Also, syllogisms are not all categorical, for there are also hypothetical ones (which include disjunctive syllogisms). Categoricals can be divided into simple and composite. Simple categoricals are those which are ordinarily counted [as syllogisms], i.e. according to the system of moods and figures; and I have found that the four figures have six moods each, making twenty-four moods in all [*On the Combinatorial Art* pp. 184f]. The four ordinary moods of the first figure result merely from the significations of the signs 'All', 'No', 'Some'. And the two which I add for completeness' sake are just the subalterns of universal propositions. For from these two ordinary moods:

All B is C, and all A is B, so all A is C; and

No B is C, all A is B, so no A is C,

we can form these two additional moods:

All B is C, all A is B, so some A is C; and

No B is C, all A is B, so some A is not C.

For there is no need to demonstrate [the soundness of] subalternation, or to prove its inferences:

All A is C, so some A is C; and

No A is C, so some A is not C;

though they can be demonstrated by means of identities combined with already accepted first-figure moods, thus:

All A is C, some A is A, so some A is C; and

No A is C, some A is A, so some A is not C.

So the two additional moods of the first figure are demonstrated from the first two ordinary moods of that figure with the aid of subalternation, which is itself demonstrable through the remaining two moods of the same figure. And the second figure also acquires two new moods in the same way. Thus the first and second figures have six moods; the third has had six all along; the fourth has been assigned five, but we find that the same procedure can be used to add a sixth to it as well. It must not be thought, however, that logical form obliges us to use the customary order of propositions, and I share your opinion, sir, that it would be better to use this arrangement instead:

All A is B, all B is C, so all A is C.

That is especially evident with sorites, which are sequences of such syllogisms. For if one had a further syllogism:

All A is C, all C is D, so all A is D,

one could construct out of these two syllogisms a sequence which avoids repetition by saying:

All A is B, all B is C, all C is D, so all A is D.

In this, as you can see, the useless proposition 'All A is C' is dropped, and the useless repetition of it which the two syllogisms require is avoided. For that proposition is no longer any use: the sequence is a complete, well-formed argument without it, now that the validity of the sequence has been demonstrated, once for all, by means of those two syllogisms. There are countless other sequences which are more composite, not only because they contain a greater number of simple syllogisms, but also because their constituent syllogisms are more varied. For one can bring into them not only simple categoricals but also conjunctions, not merely categoricals but also hypotheticals, and not merely complete syllogisms but also enthymemes in which propositions which are believed to be evident are suppressed. Add to that non-syllogistic inferences, changes in the order of propositions, and numerous phrases and constructions which have propositions concealed in them (sometimes through the mind's natural tendency to abbreviate, sometimes through properties[1] of language – some of which can be seen in the use of particles); and you can make a chain of reasoning which will represent all the argumentation even of an orator. It will have been stripped of its ornamentation and reduced to the bare bones of 'logical form', not in the scholastic manner but still sufficiently to show its validity according to the laws of logic. The latter are nothing but the laws of good sense, set into order in writing, which makes no more change in them than the customs of a region would undergo if they were written down for the first time. The only difference is that their being put in writing and made easier to take in all at once enables one to see them more clearly with a view to developing and applying them. For when natural good sense undertakes to analyse a piece of reasoning without help from the art [of logic], it will sometimes be in a little difficulty about the validity of the inferences – finding for example that the reasoning involves some [syllogistic] mood which is indeed sound but which is not in common use.

481

But a logician who was opposed to the use of such sequences, or who was not willing to use them himself, on the grounds that all composite arguments should always be reduced to the simple syllogisms on which they do in fact depend – such a person would be, according to what I have already said to you, like a man making a purchase and wanting to make the shopkeeper count out the numbers one by one, like counting on one's fingers or counting out the hours struck by the town clock. That would show his stupidity, if he could count in no other way and could only learn on his finger-tips that 5 and 3 make 8; or it would show his capriciousness, if he did know these abbreviations and was unwilling to use them or let others do so. It would also be like someone who was opposed to the use of previously demonstrated axioms and theorems, claiming that reasoning should always be taken back to the first principles in which the immediate connections of ideas can be seen, principles on which those intermediate theorems do indeed depend.

[1] '*propriétés*', which could mean 'proprieties' or 'correctnesses'.

Having explained the correct use – as I believe it to be – of logical forms, I turn now to the points you were making. I do not see how you can maintain, sir, that syllogism serves only to show the connection of proofs in 'one instance'. It is by no means always the case that 'the mind can see easily' whether something follows: in the reasonings of other people, at least, one sometimes finds inferences which one has reason to view initially with scepticism, until a demonstration is given. The normal use of 'instances' is to confirm inferences, but sometimes that is not a very reliable procedure, though there is a way of choosing instances which would not come out true if the inference were not valid. I had not thought that in well-conducted schools it was permitted to 'deny without shame' the obvious agreements of ideas, nor does it seem to me that the syllogism is used to show those agreements. At any rate, that is not its single principal use. It happens oftener than you might think that in examining writers' fallacies one finds that they have sinned against the rule of logic; and I have had personal experience of controversies – even ones in writing, with people of good faith – where mutual understanding began only after we had resorted to formal arguments to sort out our tangle of reasonings. To want to argue in the scholastic manner in important deliberations would of course be ridiculous, because of the troublesome and awkward prolixities of that form of reasoning, and because it would be like counting on one's fingers. Still, it is only too true that in the most important deliberations – the ones concerning life, the state, salvation – men often let themselves be over-impressed by the weight of authority, by the glow of eloquence, by inapt examples, by enthymemes which wrongly assume that the propositions they suppress are evident, and even by faulty inferences. It is therefore only too necessary that they should have a strict logic, though of a different type from the scholastic one – among other things for determining on which side the greatest likelihood lies. As for the further point that the common run of men know nothing about logic as an *art, and that they nevertheless reason as well as – and sometimes better than – people who are practised in logic: the uselessness of logic is no more proved by that than is the uselessness of arithmetic as an art by the fact that some people who have never learned to read or write, and who do not know how to handle a pen or counters, are seen to count satisfactorily in everyday situations, to the point where they even correct the mistakes made by someone else who has learned to calculate but may have been careless or have become muddled about the characters or marks. It is true that syllogisms also can become sophistical, but their own laws enable us to recognize such cases. Again, syllogisms make no converts, and sometimes they are not even convincing; but that is because the misuse of distinctions and of poorly understood terms makes the syllogistic reasoning so prolix that it would be unbearable if one had to follow it through to the end.

482

All that remains for me to do here is to discuss and to fill out the argument which you adduce as an example of clear reasoning which is not in logicians' form: *God punishes man* (assumed to be given as a fact), *God justly punishes whomever he punishes* (truth of reason which can be taken as demonstrated), so *God punishes man justly* (syllogistic inference, augmented by the non-syllogistic inference from direct to indirect), so *Man is punished justly* (relation-conversion, suppressed because it is evident), so *Man is guilty* (by an enthymeme which suppresses the proposition, which is really just a definition, that whoever is punished justly is 'guilty'), so *Man could have done otherwise* (the proposition that whoever is guilty could have done otherwise is suppressed), so *Man was free* (another suppression: whoever could have done otherwise was free), so *He had the power to determine himself* (by the definition of 'free'). Which is what was to be proved. I would add that this [last] 'so' can be said really to include within itself the tacitly understood proposition (that whoever is 'free' has the power to determine himself) and to have the function of avoiding repetition of terms. Viewed in that way, the argument would have nothing missing from it and could be regarded as, in that respect, complete. You can see that this reasoning is a sequence of syllogisms which is wholly in conformity with logic. I do not want now to go into its content, about which there are perhaps some things to be said or clarifications to be asked for. For example, there are cases where a man cannot do otherwise and yet could be guilty before God – e.g. where he is very pleased to have the excuse that he cannot help his neighbour. In conclusion, I acknowledge that the scholastic form of argument is usually inconvenient, inadequate and poorly handled, but I also say that nothing could be more important than the art of conducting arguments formally, in accordance with true logic. That requires completeness of content, and also perspicuity with regard to the validity of the inferences (whether previously demonstrated or self-evident) and with regard to the order in which they occur.

PHIL. **§5.** I used to believe[1] that the syllogism 'is of far less, or no use at all in *probabilities*', on the grounds that it pursues only 'one *topical argument'. But I now see that there is always a need for a sound proof of whatever is certain in the topical argument itself, namely the likelihood that is involved, and that the cogency of the inference depends on its form. **§6.** Still, even if syllogisms are useful for judgment, I doubt if they can be useful for invention,[2] 'that is the finding out of proofs, and making new discoveries. [For example, the discovery of] the 47th proposition of the First Book of Euclid is..., I think, not owing to any rules of common logic. A man knows first, and then he is able to prove syllogistically.'

[1] Locke: 'I think I may truly say'.
[2] Locke: '[Even if it] convinc[es] men of their errors[,] it fails our reason in...its hardest task'. Regarding Leibniz's version, cf. p. 476.

483

THEO. Taking 'syllogisms' to cover also sequences of syllogisms and everything that I have called formal argument, it can be said that any knowledge which is not self-evident is acquired by inferences and that the latter are not sound unless they have their proper form. In the demonstration of the proposition you have mentioned, which makes the square on the hypotenuse equal to the two squares on the sides, the large square is divided into parts, as are also the two small ones, and we find that the parts of the two small squares can be found in the large one with nothing left over. That formally proves the equality; and the equalities amongst the parts can also be shown by sound formal arguments. According to Pappus, analysis as practised by the ancients was the procedure of taking the proposition which is to be proved and deriving consequences from it until something given or known is reached. I have noted [p. 450] that for this to be effective the propositions must be reciprocal ones, so that a synthetic demonstration can move backwards along the path which the analysis has followed; but it is still a matter of drawing inferences. It is worth noting here, though, that in the hypotheses of astronomy and natural science the return journey cannot occur; but neither does a success[ful prediction] demonstrate the truth of the hypothesis. It does indeed make it probable; but as this probability appears to sin against the rule of logic which tells us that truths can be derived from falsehoods, it may be thought that logical rules are not entirely applicable to matters of probability. My reply to this is that although it is possible that a truth should follow from a falsehood, it is not always probable, especially when a single hypothesis explains many truths – something which is rare and not easily encountered. One might say, as Cardano does, that the logic of probables involves different inferences from the logic of necessary truths. But the probability of these inferences must be demonstrated through inferences belonging to the logic of necessary propositions.

PHIL. You give an appearance of defending common logic, but I see clearly that what you are presenting belongs to a much higher logic which relates to the common sort as erudition does to the learning of the alphabet. **§7.** This brings to mind a passage by 'the judicious Hooker', who says in his *Ecclesiastical Polity* (i.vi.3): 'If there might be added the right helps of true art and learning, (which helps...this age of the world carrying the name of a learned age, doth neither much know, nor...regard,) there would ...be...as much difference in maturity of judgment between men therewith inured, and that which now men are, as between men that are now' and imbeciles. I hope that our discussion may give some people an opportunity to find some 'of those *right helps of art*, this great man of deep thought mentions'. They will not be imitators, who follow the beaten track as cattle do (*Imitators, you slavish herd!*).[1] 'But I can be bold to say, that this age

---

[1] A phrase of Horace's, mentioned by Locke and quoted in Coste's margin.

is adorned with...men of that strength of judgment, and largeness of comprehension, that if they would employ their thoughts on this subject, could [find] new...ways to the advancement of knowledge.'

THEO. You do well to remark with the late Mr Hooker, sir, that people make very little effort in this direction; if they did, I believe that there are and have been some capable of succeeding at it. It must be granted, though, that we now have a great deal of help, not only from mathematics but also from philosophy – and not least from your excellent friend's *Essay Concerning Human Understanding*. We shall see whether anyone can profit by it.

PHIL. **§8.** I ought to tell you also, sir, that I used to believe that there is 'one manifest mistake in the rules of syllogism', but what you have said in our discussion has given me pause. Still, I shall lay my difficulty before you. It is said 'that no syllogistical reasoning can be...conclusive, but what has, at least, one [universal][1] proposition in it. [But it seems that] the immediate object of all our reasoning and knowledge, is nothing but particulars.' Knowledge rests wholly on the agreement and disagreement of our ideas, each of which is only a particular existence which represents only an individual thing.[2]

THEO. In so far as you conceive the similarities amongst things, you are conceiving something in addition [to the things themselves], and that is all that universality is. You will never clearly present any of our arguments without making use of universal truths. But it is as well to notice that singular propositions are counted, so far as their form goes, among universal ones. For although there is indeed only a single Apostle Peter, it can still be said that anyone who was the Apostle Peter denied his Master. Thus the syllogism: 'St Peter denied his Master, St Peter was a disciple, so some disciple denied his Master', although it has only singular premisses, is deemed to have universal affirmative ones, which puts it into the third-figure mood Darapti.

PHIL. I was also going to tell you that it appeared to me preferable to reverse the order of the premisses of syllogisms, and to say: *All A is B, all B is C, so all A is C*, rather than saying *All B is C, all A is B, so all A is C*. But from what you have said it seems that something close to this is accepted and that those two would be counted as a single mood. It remains true, as you remarked, that the arrangement which differs from the common one is better for constructing a sequence of several syllogisms.

486

---

[1] Locke: 'general'.
[2] The last six words reflect a misunderstanding, perhaps abetted by Coste's rendering, of Locke's 'and our knowledge...about other things, is only as they correspond with those our particular ideas.'

THEO. I entirely agree with you. It seems to have been believed, though, that for teaching purposes it was better to begin with a universal proposition, such as the major premiss in the first and second figures. There are still orators who adopt this practice. But the connection can be seen better in the way you suggest. I have remarked on a previous occasion [*On the Combinatorial Art* p. 183] that Aristotle may have had a special reason for adopting [what is now] the common arrangement. For rather than saying 'A is B' he usually says 'B is in A' [e.g. *Prior An.* 1, 25^{b}32]. And with that way of stating it he achieves, through the accepted arrangement, the very connection which you insist upon. For instead of saying 'B is C, A is B, so A is C', Aristotle will express it thus: 'C is in B, B is in A, so C is in A'. For instance, instead of saying 'Rectangles are isogons (i.e. have equal angles), squares are rectangles, so squares are isogons', Aristotle will put the 'middle term' in the middle position without changing the order of the propositions, by stating each of them in a manner which reverses the order of the terms, thus: 'Isogon is in rectangle, rectangle is in square, so isogon is in square'. This manner of statement deserves respect; for indeed the predicate is in the subject, or rather the idea of the predicate is included in the idea of the subject. Isogon is in rectangle, for instance, because a rectangle is a figure all of whose angles are right angles; but all right angles are equal to one another; and so the idea of a rectangle is the idea of a figure all of whose angles are equal to one another, which is the idea of an isogon. The common manner of statement concerns individuals, whereas Aristotle's refers rather to ideas or universals. For when I say *Every man is an animal* I mean that all the men are included amongst all the animals; but at the same time I mean that the idea of animal is included in the idea of man. 'Animal' comprises more individuals than 'man' does, but 'man' comprises more ideas or more attributes: one has more instances, the other more degrees of reality; one has the greater extension, the other the greater intension. So it can truthfully be said that the whole theory of syllogism could be demonstrated from the theory *de continente et contento*, of container and contained. The latter is different from that of whole and part, for the whole is always greater than the part, but the container and the contained are sometimes equal, as happens with reciprocal propositions.

PHIL.[1] I am beginning to form an entirely different idea of logic from my former one. I took it to be a game for schoolboys, but I now see that, in your conception of it, it involves a sort of universal mathematics. God grant that it may be developed beyond its present state, to become that *true help of reason* of which Hooker spoke, which would raise men well above their present condition. And reason is a faculty which has all the more need of

487

---

[1] Everything down to '§9' is added by Leibniz.

it, since **§9.** its extent is quite limited and 'there are many instances wherein it fails us'. This is (1) because we often lack the ideas themselves. **§10.** And then (2) they are often 'obscure and imperfect';[1] whereas when they are clear and distinct, as in the case of numbers, we meet with none of those 'inextricable difficulties' and fall into no contradictions. **§11.** (3) We are often in difficulty also through 'want of intermediate ideas'.[2] It is known that before 'algebra, that great instrument and [remarkable proof][3] of human sagacity, was discovered, men, with amazement, looked on several of the demonstrations of ancient mathematicians'. **§12.** (4) It also happens that we proceed upon false principles, which can engage us in difficulties; and reason, so far from clearing these away, entangles us the more. **§13.** (5) Lastly, words whose signification is uncertain puzzle the reason.

THEO. I am not convinced that ideas – *distinct* ideas, that is – are as lacking to us as you believe. As for confused ideas or rather images – or 'impressions' if you prefer – such as colours, tastes and so on, resulting from various minute ideas which are distinct in themselves though we are not distinctly aware of them: we lack an infinity of these which befit other creatures more than they do ourselves. But the role of these impressions is to provide us with natural inclinations, and to provide a grounding for observations of experience, rather than to furnish materials for reasoning – except in so far as distinct perceptions come with them. So what holds us back is primarily the inadequacy of our knowledge of these distinct ideas concealed within the confused ones; and even when everything is revealed distinctly to our senses or our minds, the multiplicity of things which must be taken into account sometimes confuses us. For instance, if we had a thousand cannon-balls heaped up in front of us, and wanted to take in the number and the [mathematical] properties of this assemblage, it would obviously be a great help to arrange them in patterns, as they do in arsenals, so as to have distinct ideas of them and to fix them in our minds so that we need not trouble to count them more than once. In the science of numbers themselves, great difficulties arise because so many things have to be taken into account: what we are looking for are short formulae, but we do not always know in a given case whether what we are seeking is there in nature to be found. For instance, what is simpler in appearance than the notion of a *prime number*? That is, a whole number divisible only by 488 itself and unity. And yet we are still hunting for an easy, positive criterion by which they can be identified with certainty, without having to try out all the prime divisors less than the square root of the prime in question. There are plenty of criteria which show without much calculation that a given number is not prime; but we want one which is easy and which shows

[1] From Locke's marginal summary.   [2] From Locke's marginal summary.
[3] Locke: 'instance'. Coste's change.

decisively, for any prime number, that it is prime. That is also why algebra is still so imperfect, even though nothing is better known than the ideas which it employs, since they merely signify numbers in general; but people still lack the means of extracting the irrational roots of any equation higher than the fourth degree (except in very restricted cases). The methods used by Diophantus, Scipione del Ferro and Ludovico Ferrari respectively to reduce *equations of the second, third and fourth degree to ones of the first, and to reduce adfected equations to pure ones, all differ from one another. That is, what serves for one degree is different from what serves for another. The second degree, i.e. that of quadratic equations, is reduced to the first merely by eliminating the second term. The third degree – the degree of cubic equations – has been solved because, fortunately, by dividing the unknown into parts we produce an equation of the second degree. And with the fourth degree – that of biquadratic equations – we add something to both sides of the equation in order to make it extractable on both sides; and it happens, fortunately, that we need only a cubic equation to bring this about. But all this is merely a matter of good luck or chance, mixed with art or method. When the attempt was being made to solve the two last-mentioned degrees, it was not known whether it would succeed. So if we are to deal with the fifth and sixth degrees – those of the sursolid and the bicubic – we need an entirely different stratagem. M. Descartes believed that the method he used on the fourth, treating these equations as the product of two quadratic equations (a method which fundamentally has no more power than Ferrari's), would also succeed with the sixth; but that was not found to be the case. This difficulty shows that even the clearest and most distinct ideas do not always yield us all that we seek for and all that could be derived from them. And this leads to the conclusion that algebra falls far short of being the art of *invention, since even it needs the assistance of a more general art. Indeed, we can say that generalized algebra or the art of *symbols is a marvellous aid, in that it unburdens the imagination. If we look at Diophantus's *Arithmetic* and the geometrical treatises of Apollonius and Pappus, we shall not doubt that the ancients had something of it. Viète gave it wider scope by expressing not only what was sought, but also the given numbers, by general symbols, thereby doing in calculation what Euclid had already done in reasoning. And Descartes extended the application of this calculus to geometry by representing lines by equations. However, even after the discovery of our modern algebra, M. Ismael *Boulliau, an unquestionably excellent geometer whom I knew in Paris, still looked with amazement at Archimedes's demonstrations concerning the spiral, and could not understand how it had occurred to that great man to use the tangent to this curve for the mensuration of the circle [*quadrature]. Father Grégoire de Saint-Vincent appears to have found the right answer, namely that he

489

arrived at it by way of the correspondence of the spiral with the parabola. But this method is merely a particular one, whereas the new *infinitesimal calculus, proceeding by the method of differences, which I have discovered and made public with good results, provides a general procedure in terms of which this discovery about spirals is mere child's play and the simplest of exercises, like almost everything that had previously been found out about the mensuration of curves. This new calculus is better, also, because it unburdens the imagination in the case of those problems which M. Descartes had excluded from his *Geometry*, on the pretext that they usually led to *mechanical considerations but really because they did not suit his mode of calculation. As for the errors that arise from ambiguous terms and false principles, it lies with us to avoid them.

PHIL. §14. There is also a case where reason cannot be applied, but where we also have no need of it and where vision is better than reason. This is in *intuitive knowledge*, where the connection of ideas and of truths is immediately seen. Knowledge of indubitable maxims consists in this, and I am apt to think that this is the 'degree of evidence... that angels have now, and the spirits of just men made perfect, shall have, in a future state, of thousands of things, which now... escape our apprehensions'. §15. But demonstration founded on intermediate ideas yields *rational knowledge*. This is because between the intermediate idea and the extremes there is a necessary connection, which is seen by laying evident truths side by side,[1] like applying a yard-stick first to one piece of cloth and then to another, to show that they are equal. §16. But if the connection is only probable, the judgment yields only an *opinion*.[2]

THEO. Only God has the privilege of having nothing but intuitive knowledge. The souls of the blessed, and Spirits, have knowledge which is incomparably more intuitive than ours; they often see at a glance what we can only discover by dint of inference and at the cost of time and effort. But the former, however detached they are from gross bodies like ours, and even the latter, however sublime they are, must also encounter difficulties in their path; otherwise they would not enjoy the pleasure of discovery, which is one of the greatest pleasures. And it must be acknowledged that there will always be an infinity of truths which are hidden from them, either entirely or for a while, which they must arrive at through inference and demonstration or even by conjecture in many cases.

PHIL. So these Spirits are just animals like ourselves, only more perfect. It is as though you were to say, like Harlequin, the Emperor of the Moon: *It is just like here.*

490

---

[1] '*une juxtaposition d'évidence*', which does not match any phrase of Locke's. This sentence is mainly based on Locke's §18.
[2] Locke: 'never amounts to knowledge'.

THEO. I do say that; not in every respect, since the kinds and degrees of perfection vary infinitely, but as regards the *foundations* of things. The foundations are everywhere the same; this is a fundamental maxim for me, which governs my whole philosophy. And I conceive unknown and confusedly known things always in the manner of things that are distinctly known to us. This makes philosophy very easy, and I really believe that this is how it should be carried on. But if this philosophy is the simplest in resources it is also the richest in kinds [of effects], because nature can vary these infinitely – and so it does, with the greatest imaginable abundance, order and adornment. This is why I believe that there is no Spirit, however exalted, who does not have an infinite number of others superior to him. However, although we are much inferior to so many intelligent beings, we have the privilege of not being visibly over-mastered on this planet, on which we hold unchallenged supremacy; for all the ignorance in which we are plunged, we still have the satisfaction of not seeing anything that outdoes us. And if we were vain we could adopt Caesar's opinion that it is better to hold first place in a village than second place in Rome. Of course, I am speaking here only about the natural knowledge of these Spirits, and not about the 'beatific vision' or about the supernatural insights which it is God's will to grant them.

PHIL. **§19.** Since everyone employs reason either on his own account or in dealing with others, 'it may be worth our while a little to reflect on four sorts of arguments, that men...do ordinarily make use of, to prevail on [others'] assent; or at least so to awe them, as to silence their opposition.' The first argument may be called *argumentum ad verecundiam*, which 'is, to allege the opinions of men, whose...learning, eminency, power, or some other cause has gained [them] authority.' For when a man does not readily yield to these opinions, he is apt to be censured as being full of vanity, and is even charged with insolence. **§20.** Secondly, there is *argumentum ad ignorantiam*, which is 'to require the adversary to admit [the] proof, or to assign a better.' **§21.** Thirdly, there is *argumentum ad hominem*, in which a man is pressed with what he has himself said. **§22.** Finally, there is *argumentum ad judicium*, which consists in 'the using of proofs drawn from any of the foundations of knowledge, or probability.' This is the only one of them all which advances and instructs us. For if, out of respect, I dare not contradict you, or if I have nothing better to say, or if I contradict myself, it does not at all follow that you are right. I may be modest, ignorant, in error, and still you may be in error too.

THEO. We must certainly distinguish what it is good to say from what it is correct to believe; but since most truths can be boldly upheld, there is some presumption against an opinion which must be concealed. The argument *ad ignorantiam* is sound in cases where there is a presumption, such that it is reasonable to hold to one opinion until its contrary is proved. What the argument *ad hominem* achieves is to show that one or other assertion is false and that one's adversary is mistaken however one takes him. Other arguments which people use could be mentioned, for instance what might be called the argument *ad vertiginem*, when one reasons thus: 'If this proof is not accepted, we have no way to attain certainty about the matter in question', this being taken to be absurd. This argument is sound in certain cases – for instance, if someone wanted to deny primary, immediate truths, such as that nothing can both be and not be at the same time, or that we ourselves exist; for if he were right there would be no way of knowing anything whatever. But when someone has devised certain principles and wants to uphold them on the grounds that without them some accepted doctrine would collapse, the argument is not conclusive. Because what is necessary to uphold our knowledge must be distinguished from what serves as a foundation for our accepted doctrines or for our

492   practices. Jurists have sometimes used a similar line of reasoning in defence of condemning or torturing alleged sorcerers on the testimony of others accused of the same crime. If this argument is rejected, they have said, how shall we convict them? And some writers maintain that in the criminal cases where it is harder to obtain conviction, weaker evidence can be accepted as adequate. But that is no reason. All that follows is that we must employ greater care, not that we ought to believe more readily; except with extremely dangerous crimes – such as high treason, for example – where this consideration does carry weight, not in condemning a man but in preventing him from doing harm. So there can be a middle course, not between *guilt* and *innocence*, but between *condemnation* and *acquittal*, where law and custom permit such judgments. A similar argument was used in Germany some time ago to justify the *coining of bad money. For (they said) if the existing laws must be obeyed, money cannot be minted except at a loss. Therefore it must be permissible to debase the alloy. But, quite apart from the fact that, to make counterfeiting more difficult, they ought to have reduced the weight merely and not the proportion of silver in the alloy, they were assuming a practice to be necessary which is not so. For there is no edict, human or divine, that requires people to mint money when they have neither mines nor access to silver bullion. Coining money from money is a bad practice and leads naturally to its debasement. But how (they ask) shall we exercise our prerogative to mint coins? The answer is simple: if you believe that it matters to you to have your face on the coinage, then content yourself with minting a small amount of good silver, even at some loss; but you have neither need nor right to flood the world with bad coinage.

PHIL. §23. Having said a little about the relation of our reason to other men, let us add something about its relation to God.[1] This requires that we distinguish what is *contrary to* reason from what is *above* reason. Of the former sort is everything which is 'inconsistent with...our clear and distinct ideas.' Of the latter, every view whose truth or probability we do not see to be derivable[2] by reason from sensation or from reflection. 'Thus the existence...of more than one God [is] contrary to reason; the resurrection of the dead, above reason.'

THEO. I have a comment to make about your definition of what is 'above reason', at least if you are relating it to the accepted use of this phrase. It seems to me that your way of putting this definition makes it go too far in one direction and not far enough in the other. According to it, everything we do not know and lack the capacity to know in our present state would be above reason. For instance, whether such-and-such a fixed star is larger or smaller than the sun, or whether Vesuvius will erupt in such-and-such a year – knowledge of these facts is beyond us, not because they are above reason but because they are above the senses. After all, we could judge very soundly about these matters if we had more perfect organs and more information as to the facts. There are also problems which are above our present faculty but not above all reason. For instance, there is no astronomer on earth who could calculate the particulars of an eclipse in his head, in the time it takes to recite the Lord's prayer; yet there may be Spirits for whom that would be merely child's play. Thus all these things could become known or achievable with the help of reason if we had fuller information as to the facts, more perfect organs and more exalted minds. 493

PHIL. If I take my definition to include not only our sensation and reflection but also that of any other possible created mind, then that objection fails.

THEO. If you take it in that way, you are right. But then there will be the other difficulty, namely that by your definition nothing will be 'above reason', because God can always bestow the means of finding out any truth whatever through sensation and reflection. Indeed, the greatest mysteries are made known to us by God's testimony, which we recognize through those rational grounds for belief on which our religion rests – grounds which unquestionably depend on sensation and reflection. The question, then, seems to be not whether the existence of a fact or the truth of a proposition can be deduced from the sources which reason employs (from sensation and reflection, that is, or rather from the outer and inner senses),

[1] Added by Leibniz.
[2] Locke: 'we cannot...derive'. Coste's change.

but whether a created mind is capable of knowing the wherefore of this fact or the *a priori* 'reason' for this truth. Thus we can say that what is 'above reason' can indeed be *learned* but cannot be *understood*[1] by the methods and powers of created reason, of however great and exalted a kind. It is God's unique privilege to understand it, as it is his sole prerogative to proclaim it.

494 PHIL. That view of the matter appears sound to me, and that is how I want my definitions to be understood. This same approach also confirms me in my opinion that §24. the way of speaking in which reason is opposed to faith, though authorized by common use, is improper. For it is by reason that we establish what we ought to believe. 'Faith is...a firm assent'; and assent, if it is regulated as it should be, 'cannot be afforded...but upon good reason[. Thus,] he that believes, without having any reason for believing, may be in love with his own fancies; but neither seeks truth ...nor pays the obedience due to his [divine Master], who would have him use those...faculties he has given him, to keep him out of...error.' Otherwise, if he is in the right, it is by chance; and if he is in the wrong, it is by his own fault, for which he is accountable to God.

THEO. I heartily commend you, sir, for maintaining that faith is grounded in reason; otherwise why would we prefer the Bible to the Koran or to the ancient writings of the Brahmins? Our theologians and other learned men have also thoroughly recognized this: that is why we come to have such fine works on the truth of the Christian religion, and so many fine proofs which have been advanced against the pagans and other unbelievers, ancient and modern. Furthermore, wise men have always looked askance at those who have maintained that there is no need to trouble with reasons and proofs when it is a question of belief – which is indeed impossible unless 'believe' signifies recite, or repeat and acquiesce in without taking any trouble over it. A good many people do just this, and it is even characteristic of some nations more than of others. That is why the last Lateran Council under Leo X was right (as I believe I have already remarked) to oppose certain Aristotelian philosophers of the fifteenth and sixteenth centuries who maintained that there are two opposed truths, one philosophical and the other theological. Traces of their thought have lingered on long after that period, as can be seen from the letters of the late M. Naudé and the *Naudeana*. A very similar dispute broke out some time ago in Helmstedt, between the theologian Daniel Hofmann and the philosopher Cornelius Martini, but with this difference that the philosopher was seeking to harmonize philosophy with revelation, whereas the theologian abjured the use of it. But Duke Julius, who founded the university there, pronounced in favour of the philosopher. It is true that in our own day a person of the most exalted rank [*Christina] has said that

---

[1] The contrast 'learned'/'understood' translates '*appris*'/'*compris*'.

in questions of faith we have to put out our eyes in order to see clearly, 495
and Tertullian said somewhere: 'This is true because it is impossible; we
must believe it because it is absurd.' But even if people who express
themselves like this have good intentions, what they say is still extravagant
and apt to do harm. St Paul speaks more correctly when he says that the
wisdom of God is foolishness to men. This is because men judge things
only in accordance with their experience, which is extremely limited, and
whatever does not conform with it appears to them absurd. But such a
judgment is very rash: there is in fact an infinity of natural things which,
if we were told about them, would seem just as absurd to us as the ice which
was said to cover our rivers seemed to the King of Siam. But the order
of nature itself, being without metaphysical necessity, is grounded solely
in God's good pleasure, so that he may depart from it for higher reasons
of grace. But we should not infer that he has done so except on good
evidence, which can come only from the testimony of God himself,
testimony to which we must utterly defer once it has been duly confirmed.

Chapter xviii
'Of faith and reason, and their distinct provinces.'

PHILALETHES. §1. Let us adapt ourselves to the accepted way of speaking,
however, and allow faith to be distinguished from reason in a certain way.
But it is fitting that this way should be explained very clearly, and the
boundaries between the two established; for the unsettled nature of these
boundaries has certainly[1] 'been the cause, if not of great disorders, yet at
least of great disputes...in the world.' In any case, it is obvious that until
they are settled we shall dispute in vain, since reason must be used in
disputing about faith.[2] §2. 'I find every sect, as far as [they think that]³
reason will help them, make use of it gladly: [yet] where it fails them, they
cry out, *'Tis matter of faith, and above reason.*' But when they are engaged
in reasoning with an opponent, he can make use of the same plea, unless 496
they can show why he is not permitted to use it in what seems to be a
parallel case. '*Reason*...here...I take to be the discovery of the certainty
or probability of such propositions [as are deduced from knowledge⁴] got
by the use of [our] natural faculties, viz. by sensation or reflection.' And
I take *faith* to be 'the assent to any proposition' on the basis of revelation,
that is, as having been made known to men by God in an 'extraordinary
way of communication'. §3. But 'no man inspired by God, can...
communicate to others any new simple ideas', because he can only use
words or other signs that revive in us the simple ideas – or combinations
thereof – that custom has attached to them. Thus, whatever new ideas St

---

¹ Locke: 'may possibly have'. Coste's change.　　² Clause added by Leibniz.
³ Added by Leibniz.　　⁴ Locke: 'from...ideas'.

Paul received when he was rapt up into the third heaven, all he could say about them was that they 'are such things, *as eye hath not seen, nor ear heard, nor hath it entered into the heart of man to conceive.*' Suppose that on the planet Jupiter there were creatures endowed with six senses, and that God supernaturally gave the ideas of that sixth sense to a man among us: 'he could [not] by words, produce [them] in the minds of other men'. So a distinction is needed between *original* and *traditional* revelation. The former is an 'impression, which is made immediately by God, on the mind..., to which we cannot set any bounds;' the other comes only by the ordinary ways of communication, and cannot provide any new simple ideas. §4. Indeed, the truths which are discoverable by reason may also be communicated to us by a traditional revelation;[1] as would have been the case if God had willed to communicate the theorems of geometry to men, but that would not have been with as much certainty as if we had demonstrated them from the connections of ideas. Likewise, Noah had a more certain knowledge of the flood than we have from Moses' book; just as the certainty of someone who saw that Moses actually wrote it, and that he performed the miracles which show that he was inspired,[2] was greater than our own. §5. This is why 'revelation cannot [go] against the clear evidence of reason';[3] since, even when the revelation is immediate and original, this requires evident knowledge 'that we deceive not our selves in ascribing it to God [and] that we understand it'; and the evidentness of this can never be greater than[4] that of our intuitive knowledge. 'And therefore, no proposition can be received for divine revelation...if it be contradictory to [this immediate knowledge. Otherwise,] there would be left no difference between truth and falsehood, no measures of credible and incredible in the world[. And it is inconceivable that something should] come from God, the bountiful Author of our being, which if received for true, must overturn all the...foundations of [our] knowledge [and] render all our faculties useless'. §6. And those who do not receive revelation immediately, but only through transmission by word of mouth or by writing, have all the more need of reason to assure them of it. §7. It remains true, however, that the things which are 'beyond the discovery of our natural faculties [are] the proper matter of faith.' For instance, the fall of the rebellious angels and the resurrection of the dead. §9. In these matters, 'revelation [alone] ought to be hearkened to.'[5] And in 'probable propositions...an evident revelation [will] determine [us] even against probability.'[6]

497

---

[1] Locke: 'may be discovered, and conveyed down from revelation'. Coste's changes.
[2] Clause added by Leibniz.   [3] From Locke's marginal summary.
[4] Locke: 'so great, as'.   [5] From Locke's marginal summary.
[6] Taking the placing of '*même*' ('*même à l'égard des propositions probables*', as against Coste's '*même contre la probabilité*') to be a slip.

THEOPHILUS. If you take faith to be only what rests on *rational grounds for belief*, and separate it from the inward grace which immediately endows the mind with faith, everything you say, sir, is beyond dispute. For it must be acknowledged that many judgments are more evident than the ones which depend on these rational grounds. Some people have advanced further towards the latter than others have; and indeed plenty of people, far from having weighed up such reasons, have never known them and consequently do not even have what could count as *grounds for probability*. But the inward grace of the Holy Spirit makes up for this immediately and supernaturally, and it is this that creates what theologians strictly call 'divine faith'. God, it is true, never bestows this faith unless what he is making one believe is grounded in reason – otherwise he would subvert our capacity to recognize truth, and open the door to enthusiasm – but it is not necessary that all who possess this divine faith should know those reasons, and still less that they should have them perpetually before their eyes. Otherwise none of the unsophisticated or of the feeble-minded – now at least – would have the true faith, and the most enlightened people might not have it when they most needed it, since no one can always remember his reasons for believing. The question of the use of reason in theology has been one of the liveliest issues, between *Socinians and those who may be called 'Catholics' in a broad sense of the term, as well as between *Reformed and Evangelicals – the latter being the preferable name which is given in Germany to those whom some people inappropriately call 'Lutherans'. I remember once reading a metaphysical treatise by a Socinian named Stegmann (not to be confused with Josua Stegmann, who actually wrote against the Socinians); it has still not been published, so far as I know. And on the other side a Saxon theologian, Kesler, wrote a treatise on logic and several other philosophical studies devoted to attacking the Socinians. In general one can say that the Socinians are too quick to reject everything that fails to conform to the order of nature, even when they cannot conclusively prove its impossibility. But sometimes their adversaries also go too far and push mystery to the verge of contradiction, thereby wronging the truth they seek to defend. I was surprised one day to find in the *Summa of Theology* of Father Honoré *Fabri – who nevertheless was one of the ablest members of his order – that he denied the validity in divine matters of the great principle that *things that are the same as a third thing are the same as each other*. Some other theologians still do so. This is unwittingly to hand the victory to one's opponents, and to deprive all reasoning of any certainty. What ought to be said rather is that in divine matters the principle has been misapplied. In his *Philosophy* the same author rejects the 'virtual distinctions' which the *Scotists apply to created things, because, he says, they would violate the principle of contradiction; and when it is brought against him that we must acknowledge

498

such distinctions in God, he replies that that is ordained by faith. But how can faith ordain anything that violates a principle in whose absence all belief, and affirmation and negation, would be pointless? So it is necessarily the case that two propositions which are both true at the same time do not wholly contradict one another; and if A and C are not the same thing, then B which is the same as A must be regarded as different from B which is the same as C. Nicholaus Vedelius, who was Professor at Geneva and then at Deventer, some time ago published a book entitled *Theological Knowledge*, and Johann Musaeus, Professor at Jena (an Evangelical university in Thuringia), countered with another book on the same subject, entitled *On the Use of Reason in Theology*. I remember studying them at one time, and noticing that the main controversy was tangled up with side issues, such as the question as to what a theological conclusion is, and whether this should be decided by the terms which make it up or by the method of proving it, and consequently whether Ockham was right or not in saying that the knowledge of a given conclusion is the same whatever method is used to prove it [*Quodlibeta* v, Q.1]. They dwell on all kinds of other even more trivial details, which merely concern terms. However, for his part, Musaeus agreed that principles of reason which are necessary because they have logical necessity – i.e. ones whose negations imply contradictions – should and can be safely employed in theology. But he had grounds for his denial that anything which is necessary merely through physical necessity (i.e. necessity founded on induction from what takes place in nature, or on natural laws which result from divine *institution, so to speak) is sufficient to rule out belief in a mystery or a miracle, since God is free to change the ordinary course of things. Thus, going by the order of nature one can be confident that the same person cannot be at once a mother and a virgin, and that a human body cannot be inaccessible to the senses; though the contrary of each of them is possible for God. Vedelius seemed to accept this distinction too. But there is sometimes disagreement as to whether certain principles are logically, or merely physically, necessary. Of this kind is the dispute with the Socinians over whether there can be a plurality of subsistences when there is only one individual essence, and the dispute with the *Zwinglians over whether a body can be in more than one place. Now, we must realize that if a proposition's logical necessity is not demonstrated, we cannot presume it to have any necessity except the physical sort. But it seems to me that a question remains which the authors I have just mentioned did not investigate thoroughly enough, namely: suppose that on the one hand we have the literal sense of a text from Holy Scripture, and that on the other we have a strong appearance of a logical impossibility or at least a recognized physical impossibility; then is it more reasonable to give up the literal sense or to give up the philosophical principle? There are certainly passages where there is no objection to abandoning the literal sense – for instance, where Scripture gives God hands, or attributes to him anger, repentance and other human affects. Otherwise we would have to side with the Anthropomorphites, or with certain English fanatics who believed that when Jesus called Herod a fox he was actually turned into one. This is where the rules of interpretation come into play; but if they provide nothing which goes against the literal sense in deference to the philosophical maxim, and if furthermore the literal sense contains nothing imputing some imperfection to God or involving a threat to pious observances, it is safer and indeed more reasonable to keep to the letter. The two authors whom I have just mentioned also wrangle over Keckermann's attempt (like the earlier one by Raymond Lull) to provide a demonstration, through reason, of the Trinity. But Musaeus is impartial enough to acknowledge that if the Reformed author's demonstration had been sound, there would have been no more to say, and he [sc. Vedelius] would have been right to maintain that this is an article of faith in regard to which the light of the Holy Spirit could be kindled by philosophy. They also debated the famous question whether those who have died in a state of natural piety, but in ignorance of the Old and New Testament revelations, could be saved through their piety and granted remission of sins. Clement of Alexandria, Justin Martyr and St Chrysostom are known to have been more or less inclined to take this view. Indeed, I once showed M. *Pellisson that many eminent doctors of the Roman Church, far from damning lax Protestants, have been willing to save even pagans and to maintain that the people in question may have been saved by an act of contrition, i.e. of penitence resting on a *love of benevolence* – leading to a love of God above all other things, since his perfections make him supremely worthy of love. This leads one to a whole-hearted endeavour to conform to God's will and to imitate his perfections, the better to be united with him, since it appears just that God should not withhold his grace from those who are in this state of mind. Without mentioning Erasmus and Ludovicus Vives, I adduced the view of a Portuguese teacher, Diego Payva de Andrada, who was very famous in his day and had been one of the theologians at the Council of Trent. He went so far as to say that those who took the opposite view of the matter were making God supremely cruel – 'For,' he said, 'there can be no worse cruelty.' M. Pellisson had trouble finding this book in Paris, which indicates that authors who are highly thought of in their own day are often disregarded afterwards. This is what led M. Bayle to conclude that some people quote Andrada only on the authority of his opponent, Chemnitz. That may well be so, but in my case I had read him before I cited him. His dispute with Chemnitz made him famous in Germany, for he attacked that author on behalf of the Jesuits, and his book is a source of many facts about the origins of that renowned Society. I have noticed

500

501

that some Protestants even gave the name 'Andradians' to those who shared his opinion on the matter I was just speaking about. There have been authors who, with the approval of the censors, have addressed themselves to the question of Aristotle's salvation, invoking these same principles. Collio's book in Latin, and La Mothe le Vayer's in French, about the salvation of the pagans, are well known. But a certain Francesco Pucci went too far. And St Augustine, in spite of his intelligence and insight, rushed to the other extreme and damned children who die unbaptized [e.g. *De gratia Christi* ch. 19]. The Scholastics appear to have been right to part company with him; though there are people – able ones, indeed, and some of them very worthy but of a rather misanthropic disposition regarding this matter – who have sought to revive this Father's doctrine and have perhaps exaggerated it. This attitude may have influenced the dispute which a number of over-zealous teachers had with the *Jesuit missionaries in China: the latter had suggested that the ancient Chinese had had the true religion of their time, and true saints, and that there was nothing idolatrous or atheistic in the teachings of Confucius. Rome seems to have been more reasonable in not wanting to condemn a very large nation without a hearing. We are fortunate that God is more charitable than men. I know people who, thinking they can show their zeal by the harshness of their views, suppose that one could not believe in original sin without holding their opinion – but in that they are wrong. Nor are those who accord salvation to pagans, or to others who lack the ordinary aids, thereby obliged to rely for this on natural processes alone (although some of the Fathers may have held that view). One can, after all, maintain that when God gives them grace sufficient to call forth an act of contrition he also gives them before their death, even if only in the final moments, all the light of faith and all the fervour of love which they need for salvation; this being given to them either explicitly or dispositionally, but in any case supernaturally. Some Reformed churchmen, following Vedelius, expound Zwingli's view in this way; he had been as outspoken on this matter of the salvation of virtuous pagans as the teachers in the Roman Church could have been. Let me add that none of this gives this doctrine anything in common with the special views of the *Pelagians and Semipelagians, with whom Zwingli is known to have differed entirely. Contrary to the Pelagians, all three of the accepted religions (excluding perhaps M. Pajon's followers) agree in teaching that there is a supernatural grace in all who possess faith, and they even attribute faith, or at least movements towards it, to children who receive baptism. So it is not very out of the way to grant as much, at least at the point of death, to persons of good will who have not had the advantage of being instructed in Christianity in the ordinary way. But the wisest course is to take no position regarding things of which so little is known, and to be satisfied with the general belief that God can

502

do nothing which is not entirely good and just: 'It is better to doubt concerning what is hidden than to argue over what is uncertain' (Augustine, *De genesi ad litteram* VIII.5).

Chapter xix
'Of enthusiasm.'

503

PHILALETHES. If only all theologians, including St Augustine himself, had always acted on the maxim expressed in that passage! **§1.** But men believe that a spirit of dogmatism is a sign of their zeal for the truth; when it is just the opposite – we truly love truth only in so far as we love to examine the proofs which make it known for what it is. And when someone jumps to a conclusion he is always impelled by less high-minded reasons. **§2.** A domineering disposition is not among the least common of these; **§3.** and another, which gives rise to enthusiasm, is a certain complacent satisfaction with our own day-dreams. *Enthusiasm* is the name given to the defect possessed by those who take to be an immediate revelation something which is not grounded in reason. **§4.** As we can say that 'reason is natural revelation', of which God is the author just as he is of nature, so we can say also that revelation is supernatural reason, that is,[1] 'reason enlarged by a new set of discoveries communicated by God immediately'. But these discoveries are possible only if we have the means to recognize them, which is just what reason is. And a readiness to take away reason so as to make way for revelation would be like putting out one's eyes so as the better to see the moons of Jupiter[2] through a telescope. **§5.** What gives rise to enthusiasm is the greater ease and brevity of an immediate revelation, as compared with a long and tedious and not always successful labour of reasoning. In all ages, men are seen whose melancholy, mixed with devotion and combined with their conceit of themselves, has raised in them the opinion that their familiarity with God is different from other men's. Taking this to be something he has promised to his own, they believe that they – in preference to others – are his people. **§6.** Their fancy becomes 'an illumination' and a 'divine authority', and their plans are an infallible 'direction from heaven, and must be obeyed'. **§7.** This belief has had great consequences and has caused great evils, for a man acts more vigorously when he obeys his own impulses and when his belief in a divine authority is sustained by his own inclination. **§8.** Because this professed 'certainty without proof' flatters men's vanity and their love of the extraordinary, ''tis a hard matter to get them out of it.' Fanatics liken their opinions to matters of seeing and feeling. They see the divine light 'as we do that of the sun at noon, and need not the twilight of reason to show it' to them.

504

---

[1] '*une raison surnaturelle, c'est à dire*', added by Leibniz.
[2] Locke: 'to receive the remote light of an invisible star'.

§9. 'They are sure, because they are sure: and their persuasion' is right because it is strong; for this is all that their metaphorical language amounts to. **§10.** But as there are two perceptions – of the proposition and of the revelation – they can be asked where the clear light is to be found. If it is in the seeing of the truth of[1] the proposition, then revelation is needless. So it must be in the 'feeling' of revelation; but how can they see that it is God who reveals it, and that it is not 'an *ignis fatuus* that leads them continually round in this circle. It is a revelation, because they firmly believe it, and they believe it, because it is a revelation.' **§11.** Is there anything more apt to run us into error than to take imagination as our guide? **§12.** St Paul had great zeal when he persecuted the Christians, and yet he was mistaken. **§13.** The devil is known to have had his martyrs;[2] and if all that is needed is to be strongly persuaded, it will be impossible to 'distinguish between the delusions of Satan, and the inspirations of the Holy Ghost'. **§14.** So it is reason that makes the truth of revelation known. **§15.** If it were our belief that provided the warrant, we should be in the circle I have just spoken of. 'The holy men...who had revelations from God,...had outward signs to convince them' of the truth of 'that internal light'. 'Moses saw the bush burn without being consumed, and heard a voice' from the middle of the bush. And when God sent him into Egypt to free his brethren, he employed the miracle of the rod turned into a serpent to assure him further of his mission. Gideon was sent by an angel to deliver the people of Israel from the yoke of the Midianites, 'and yet he desired a sign to convince him, that this commission was from God.' **§16.** However, I do not deny that God 'doth sometimes enlighten men's minds in the apprehending of certain [important][3] truths, or excite them to good actions by the immediate influence and assistance of the Holy Spirit, without any extraordinary signs accompanying it. But in such cases too we have reason and the Scripture, [two] unerring rules' for judging these illuminations. For if they conform to these rules we at least[4] run no risk in viewing them as inspired by God, 'though perhaps...not an immediate revelation'.

THEOPHILUS. 'Enthusiasm' was at first a favourable name. Just as 'sophism' indicates literally an exercise of wisdom, so 'enthusiasm' signifies that there is a divinity inside us. 'There is a God within us' [Ovid]. And Socrates claimed that a God or Daemon gave him inner warnings, so that 'enthusiasm' [in his case] would be a divine instinct. But men sanctified their passions, and took their fancies and dreams and even their ravings to be something divine, and as a result 'enthusiasm' began to signify a disorder of the mind ascribed to the action of some divinity,

505

---

[1] Taking the omission of Coste's '*la vérité de*' to be a slip.   [2] Added by Leibniz.
[3] Added by Leibniz.   [4] '*au moins*', added by Leibniz.

supposedly inside those who were seized by it. For prophets and prophe-
tesses, such as Virgil's Cumean Sybil, did manifest mental derangement
while their God had possession of them. More recently the term has been
applied to people who believe groundlessly that their impulses come from
God. That same poet's Nisus, when he felt himself being impelled by
something or other which was driving him towards a dangerous undertaking,
in which eventually he and his friend died, put it to his friend in words
full of reasonable doubt, thus: 'Is it the Gods, Euryalus, who impart this
ardour to our minds? Or does his own fierce desire become a God to each
of us?' [Virgil]. He nevertheless followed this instinct, without knowing
whether it came from God or from an ill-fated craving for fame. But had
he succeeded he would certainly have allowed himself to do the same thing
on another occasion and have believed himself impelled by some divine
power. Today's 'enthusiasts' believe that they also receive doctrinal
instruction from God. The Quakers are convinced of this, and their first
systematic writer, Barclay, claims that they find within themselves a certain
light which itself announces what it is. But why call something 'light' if
it doesn't cause anything to be seen? I know that there are people with
that cast of mind, who see sparks and even something brighter; but this
image of corporeal light, aroused when their minds become over-heated,
brings no light to the mind. Some half-wits, when their imaginations
become worked up, form conceptions which they did not previously have;
they become capable of saying things which strike them as very fine, or
at least very lively; they astonish themselves and others with this fecundity
which is taken to be inspired. They possess this ability mainly in virtue 506
of a powerful imagination aroused by passion, and a fortunate memory
which has copiously stored the turns of phrase of prophetic books which
they are familiar with through reading or through hearing them talked
about. Antoinette de *Bourignon adduced her gift for speaking and writing
as proof of her divine mission. And I know a visionary who rests his claims
on his capacity to speak and pray aloud almost all day long without tiring
or running out of words. There are people who, after practising austerities
or after a period of sorrow, experience a peace and consolation in the soul;
this delights them, and they find such sweetness in it that they believe it
to be the work of the Holy Spirit. It is certainly true that the contentment
we find in contemplating God's greatness and goodness, and in carrying
out his will and practising the virtues, is a blessing from God, and one of
the greatest. But it is not always a blessing which needs renewed supernatural assistance, as many of these good people claim. A certain young
lady attracted attention not long ago [*Asseburg] – she was in every other
respect a very sober-minded person – who believed from her childhood
that she spoke to Jesus Christ and that she was his wife in a quite special
way. Her mother was said to be a little 'enthusiastic' herself, but the

daughter, having started early, went a great deal further. Her joy and satisfaction were inexpressible, and her good sense was evident from her conduct, as was her liveliness of mind from her conversation. Yet things went so far that she was accepting letters addressed to Our Lord and returning them sealed as she had received them, with answers which appeared sometimes to be to the point and always to be reasonable. But she finally stopped accepting them for fear of creating too much commotion. In Spain she would have been another St Teresa. But not everyone who has had similar fantasies has behaved like this. Some of them – as England has confirmed in a curious way – attempt to form sects and even to stir up trouble. When these people are sincere in their behaviour they are hard to bring around; sometimes having all their schemes go to ruin sets them straight, but often this comes too late. There was a visionary, who died not long ago, who believed that because he was very old and in good health he was immortal. It was not that he had read a recently published book by an Englishman [*Asgill] who tried to convince us that Jesus Christ had come again to exempt true believers from bodily death; his views had been pretty much the same for many years. But when he sensed that he was dying he went as far as to doubt all religion, because it did not fit in with his delusion. A Silesian, Quirin Kuhlmann, was a learned and intelligent man, but latterly he went in for two sorts of equally dangerous fantasies: 'enthusiastic' ones and alchemical ones, and made a stir in England and Holland and all the way to Constantinople. Having eventually taken it into his head to go to Muscovy and get himself mixed up in certain plots against the administration, during Princess Sophia's rule, he was condemned to be burned, and did not die like a man who believed in his own preaching. The way these people clash with one another should further convince them that their alleged 'inner witness' is not divine, and that other signs are required to confirm it. The *Labadists, for instance, disagree with Mlle Antoinette; and although William Penn travelled to Germany for the purpose, apparently, of bringing about some kind of mutual understanding among those who rely on this 'witness', he does not appear to have succeeded. (An account has been published of his travels.) It is indeed desirable that good people should agree with one another and should work in unison; nothing could contribute more to making the human race better and happier. But they must themselves be truly numbered among the people of good will, that is, people who do good and are reasonable and ready to learn. Whereas all too many of those who are called religious nowadays are accused of being dour and arrogant and unyielding. Their disputes show, at the least, that their inner witness needs outer verification if it is to be believed, and they would have to work miracles before they would deserve to be accepted as inspired prophets. Still, such inspired utterances could bring their *proofs

507

with them; this would be the case if they truly enlightened the mind through the important revelation of some surprising truth which was beyond the powers of the person who had discovered it, unless he had help from outside. For instance, Jacob Boehme, the famous shoemaker from Lusatia, whose writings have been translated from German into other languages as 'Teutonic Philosophy' and, for a man in his station, actually do have something fine and grand about them; if he had been able to make gold, as some people believed (like St John the Evangelist who, if we can believe the hymn in praise of him, 'possesses an inexhaustible treasure and made gold from twigs, and gems from pebbles' [Adam of St-Victor]), then we would have some reason to give more credence to this remarkable shoemaker. And if the French engineer in Hamburg, Bertrand de La Coste, had really received from Mlle Antoinette Bourignon the scientific insight which he believed she had bestowed on him – as he reveals in dedicating to her his book *On the Quadrature of the Circle* (where he calls her the A of theology and himself the B of mathematics, referring to 'Antoinette' and 'Bertrand') – then we would not have known what to say. But we find no cases of notable achievements of this nature, any more than we do of successful detailed predictions by such people. The prophecies of Ponia-tovia, Drabicius and others, which the good Comenius published in his *Light in Darkness*, helped to foment disturbances in the Emperor's hereditary domains; but they turned out to be false, which was unfortunate for those who had given them credence. Rakoczy, Prince of Transylvania, was incited by Drabicius to his adventure in Poland; he lost his army there, which eventually led to the loss of his lands and his life. And poor Drabicius, years later when he was over 80, finally had his head chopped off by order of the Emperor. But I have no doubt that people are inopportunely reviving these same predictions during the present accumu-lation of troubles in Hungary, ignoring the fact that those alleged prophets were talking about events of their own day. That would be to behave a little like the man who, after the bombardment of Brussels, published a handbill containing a passage from one of Mlle Antoinette's books, about how she did not want to go to Brussels because (if I remember rightly) she had dreamt of seeing it in flames; but in fact the bombardment took place long after her death. I knew a man who went to France during the war which was brought to an end by the Treaty of Nijmegen, to urge on M. de Montausier and M. de *Pomponne how well-grounded were the prophecies published by Comenius; if he had happened to make his pronouncements during a period like our own, I think he would have believed that he himself was inspired; which shows not only how ill-grounded such obsessions are, but also how dangerous. The histories are full of the bad results of false or misunderstood prophecies; this can be seen from the learned and judicious treatise, *On Good Men's Duty with*

508

509

Regard to Future Contingencies, published some time ago by a famous Leipzig professor, the late Jacob *Thomasius. It is true, however, that such beliefs sometimes have good results and lead to great things, for God can make use of error to establish and preserve the truth. But I do not believe that we are entitled glibly to employ pious frauds for good purposes. And as for the dogmas of religion, we have no need for new revelations: if we are presented with rules which are conducive to salvation we are bound to obey them, even if the person who presents them performs no miracles. And although Jesus Christ had the power, he nevertheless refused sometimes to exercise it for the gratification of 'this...evil generation' which 'seek a sign', when he was preaching only virtue and what had already been taught by natural reason and the prophets.

Chapter xx
Of error.[1]

PHILALETHES. **§1.** Having spoken sufficiently of all our ways of knowing or guessing the truth, let us now say something about our errors and wrong judgments. Men must often be in error, since there are so many disagreements amongst them. 'The reasons whereof...may all be reduced to these four. 1. Want of proofs. 2. Want of ability to use them. 3. Want of will to use them. 4. Wrong measures of probability.' **§2.** When I speak of *want of proofs*, I include also the ones which might be procured if one had the requisite means and opportunity – which in most cases are lacking. 'In this state are [men] whose lives are [passed] in the provisions for living.' They are no more informed about what goes on in the world 'than a packhorse, who is driven constantly [on the same road can] be skilled in the geography of the country.' They would need languages, reading, conversation, observations of nature, and experience of the [practical] arts. **§3.** Since none of that is suitable to their condition, 'shall we say then [that] the bulk of mankind [has] no other guide, but...blind chance, to conduct them to their happiness, or misery?' Must they give themselves over to 'the current opinions, and licensed guides' of the country, even with regard to everlasting happiness or unhappiness? Or shall someone be eternally unhappy because he was born in one country rather than another? It must be acknowledged, though, that 'no man is so wholly taken up with the attendance on the means of living, as to have no spare time at all to think of his soul, and inform himself in matters of religion[, if he were] as intent upon this, as...on things of lower concernment'.

THEOPHILUS. Let us take it that men are not always in a position to instruct themselves, and that since they cannot prudently give up providing

510

---

[1] Locke: 'Of wrong assent, or error.' Coste's omission.

for their families in order to search after elusive truths, they are compelled to abide by the views which are given authority in their societies; still, we ought to judge that in those who have the true religion without having proofs of it, inward grace will be making up for the absence of rational grounds for belief. And charity leads us to judge further, as I have already remarked to you [p. 502], that when people of good will are brought up amongst the deep shadows of the most dangerous errors, God will do for them everything that his goodness and justice require, even though we may not know how. One hears stories, which are acclaimed in the Roman Church, of people who have been brought back to life just so that they should not be without aids to salvation. But God can save souls by the inward working of the Holy Spirit, with no need of such a great miracle. What is so good and comforting for mankind is the fact that to be in the state of God's grace one needs only to have, sincerely and seriously, a good will. I acknowledge that this good will itself does not occur without the grace of God, in that every good – natural or supernatural – comes from him; but, still, all that matters is that one only needs such a will, and that it is impossible that God should have set an easier or more reasonable condition.

PHIL. §4. 'There are [those] whose largeness of fortune would plentifully enough supply [the] requisites for clearing of doubts'. But they are deterred from doing so by elaborately contrived obstacles: it is quite easy to see what these are, without needing to put them on display here.[1] §5. I would rather speak of 'those who want skill to use those evidences they have' – right at hand, so to speak – and 'who cannot carry a [long] train of consequences', or weigh all the circumstances. 'There are some men of one, some but of two syllogisms, and no more'. This is not the place to decide whether this imperfection arises from natural differences in the souls themselves or in the organs, or whether it depends upon a lack of the use which refines the natural faculties. All that matters here is that it visibly exists, and that one has only to go from Westminster Hall or the Exchange to Bedlam and the almshouses in order to be aware of it.[2]

511

THEO. It is not only the poor who are in need. There are some rich people who lack more than the poor do, because they want too much and thus voluntarily put themselves into a kind of indigence which stops them from giving their attention to important matters. Example is very important here. People assiduously follow the example of their peers, and they have to do this without appearing reluctant, which easily leads to their becoming like them. It is very difficult to satisfy reason and custom both at once. As

---

[1] This sentence is Coste's substitute for a longer passage about 'places...where men are forced...to be of the religion of the country; and must therefore swallow down opinions, as silly people do empirics' pills, without knowing what they are made of'.

[2] Using Locke's London examples rather than Coste's Parisian substitutes.

for those who lack capacity: there may be fewer of these than you think, for I believe that good sense together with diligence can achieve any task for which speed is not required. I stipulate good sense because I don't believe that you would require the inmates of Bedlam to engage in the pursuit of truth. The fact is that most of them could recover, if only we knew how to bring this about. Whatever inherent differences there are between our souls (and I believe there are indeed some), there is no doubt that any soul could achieve as much as any other, though perhaps not so quickly, if it were given proper guidance.

PHIL. §6. There is another sort of person whose only lack is in the will. 'Their hot pursuit of pleasure, or constant drudgery [in connection with their fortune, or] laziness and oscitancy in general, or a particular aversion for...study, and meditation keep [them] from any serious thoughts' about the truth. There are even some who fear that a wholly 'impartial inquiry would not favour those opinions, which best suit their prejudices...and designs.... We know some men will not read a letter, which is supposed to bring ill news; and many men forbear to cast up their accounts,' or to inquire into the state of their affairs, for fear of learning something which they would prefer to go on not knowing. There are some who have great incomes which they spend wholly on 'provisions for the body', without thinking about how to improve their understandings. They 'take great care to appear always in a neat and splendid outside..., and yet contentedly suffer their minds' to be dressed in miserable rags of prejudice and error, and allow their nakedness – i.e. their ignorance – to show through. Leaving aside the concern they should have with a future state, they are no less neglectful of the things which it concerns them to know in their life in this world. And it is a strange thing that very often those who regard power and authority as 'concomitants of their birth [or] fortune' negligently abandon them to men whose condition is lower than theirs but 'who surpass them in knowledge. [For] they who are blind, [must] be led by those that see, or else fall into the ditch'; and there is no worse slavery than that of the understanding.

THEO. Men's carelessness regarding their real interests is proved by nothing more clearly than by how little they care to know or do what is conducive to health, which is one of our greatest blessings. And although the harmful effects of this bear at least as heavily on people of high station as on others, they do not mend their ways. And as for matters regarding the faith, some people look on the sort of thought which might bring them to an examination of that as a temptation of the Devil which is best overcome, they believe, by turning the mind to something quite different. Men who love nothing but pleasure, or who are engrossed in some occupation, are apt to neglect other matters. A gambler, a hunter, a drinker,

512

a rake, even a collector of trifles, will sacrifice his fortune and his well-being because he will not take the trouble to institute a lawsuit or to speak to people in high positions. Some of them are like the Emperor Honorius who, when he was brought the news of the loss of Rome, thought they meant his hen which was also called 'Rome'; and that distressed him more than the truth did when he learned it. One wishes that the men who have power had knowledge in proportion: even if it did not include detailed knowledge of the sciences, the [practical] arts, history, and languages, it might suffice if they had sound, practised judgment and knowledge of broad and general matters – in brief, of the most important points. And just as the Emperor Augustus had a summary of the powers and requirements of the state, which he called *Report on the Empire*, one could – if men were willing to have a care for what is most important to them – have a summary of the requirements of man, which could rightly be called *Manual of Wisdom*.

PHIL. §7. Finally, most of our errors come from wrong measures of probability which are adopted, whether through suspending judgment despite 'manifest reasons', or through giving assent in the face of contrary probabilities. These wrong measures consist in 1. 'doubtful propositions taken for principles.'[1] '2. Received hypotheses. 3. Predominant passions or inclinations. 4. Authority.' §8. We usually judge of the truth by its conformity with what we look upon as unchallengeable principles; and that leads us to dismiss the testimony of others, and even that of our senses, when they appear to be contrary to those principles. But before putting such confident trust in the latter, we should examine them with the utmost strictness. §9. Children have propositions insinuated into them by their father and mother, nurses, tutors, and others around them; and once these propositions have taken root they are treated as sacred, like a '*Urim* and *Thummim* set up in their minds...by God himself'. §10. Anything which offends against 'these internal oracles' can hardly be tolerated, whereas the greatest absurdities which conform to them are 'digested'. This is shown by 'the great obstinacy, that is to be found in [different] men firmly believing quite contrary opinions,' as though they were articles of faith, though in many cases they are 'equally absurd'. Take a man who, though intelligent, is convinced of the maxim that one should believe what is believed in one's communion, as it is taught at Wittenberg or in Sweden: will he not find it easy to accept the doctrine of consubstantiation and to believe that a single thing is at once flesh and bread?[2]

THEO. It is quite obvious, sir, that you are not properly informed about the views of the Evangelicals who accept the real presence of the body of

513

---

[1] Locke's marginal summary of §8.
[2] This person whose theology emanates from Wittenberg or Sweden is a creature of Coste's: he puts '*luthérien*' and '*consubstantiation*' for Locke's 'Romanist' and 'transubstantiation'.

Our Lord in the Eucharist. They have explained hundreds of times that they do not hold that the bread and wine are consubstantiated with the body and blood of Jesus Christ, still less that a single thing is both flesh and blood at once. Their doctrine is merely that in receiving the visible symbols one invisibly and supernaturally receives the body of the Saviour, without its being contained within the bread. And the 'presence' which they mean is not one of location – not spatial, so to speak[1] – i.e. it is not determined by the dimensions of the body which is 'present'; so that they need not be concerned with any contrary evidence which the senses may provide. And to show that they are unaffected also by the difficulties which could be derived from reason, they insist that what they mean by the substance of a body does not consist in extension or dimension; and they freely admit that the glorified body of Jesus Christ retains a certain ordinary presence of location, though of a kind suitable to its condition in the sublime place it now occupies; but they regard that as quite different from the sacramental presence we are now concerned with, or from Christ's miraculous presence through which he governs the Church. This means that he is not everywhere, as God, but only where he wishes to be – that being the view of those who are the most moderate. So one could not show that their whole doctrine is absurd without demonstrating that extension, together with anything which is measured purely in terms of it, makes up the whole essence of body; and no one has yet shown that, so far as I know. Also, this whole difficulty arises just as much for Reformed churchmen who adhere to the Gallican and Belgian Confessions; to the declaration of the assembly of Sandomir, which was composed of members of the Augsburg and Helvetic Confessions (their declaration was modelled on the Saxon Confession which was intended for the Council of Trent); to the profession of faith of the Reformed churchmen who came to the conference at Torun, which was convened under the authority of King Ladislas of Poland; or to the unwavering doctrine of Calvin and of Beza, who declared with all possible clarity and emphasis that what the symbols represent is actually provided by them, and that we come to partake of the very substance of the body and blood of Jesus Christ. And Calvin, having refuted those who are satisfied with a metaphorical participation, in thought or symbol only, and with a union of faith, adds that no statement of the reality of the participation can be too strong for him to be prepared to sign his name to it, so long as it is free of anything to do with confinement within a limited place or with being spread out through all places. So it appears that his doctrine was fundamentally the same as Melanchthon's, and even – as Calvin himself takes for granted in one of his letters – the same as Luther's. The only difference is that whereas Luther is satisfied with the single condition that the symbols be perceived, Calvin requires

[1] Leibniz uses 'spatiale', which became standard French only in the nineteenth century.

also that there be faith: this is so as to prevent the unworthy from participating. I have found Calvin so emphatic about this real communion, in dozens of places in his works, and even in personal correspondence where there was no need for it, that I see no grounds for suspecting that he was insincere about it.

PHIL. I apologize if I have followed the common view about these gentlemen. And I do now recall noticing that this *real participation* has been supported by some highly capable Anglican theologians. §11. But let us move on from established principles to 'received hypotheses'. Those who recognize that these are only hypotheses nevertheless often defend them warmly, almost like assured principles, and depreciate the contrary probabilities. It would be insufferable for a learned professor to have his authority of thirty or forty years' standing, acquired with no small expense of time, supported by much Greek and Latin,[1] 'and confirmed by general tradition, and a reverend beard, in an instant overturned by an upstart novelist' who rejected his hypotheses. All the arguments that can be used to convince him of the falsity of his hypothesis 'will be as little able to prevail [on his mind], as the wind did with the traveller, to part with his cloak, which he held only the faster' as the wind blew more violently.

515

THEO. Indeed, the Copernicans have learned from their experience of their adversaries that hypotheses which are recognized as such are still upheld with ardent zeal. And Cartesians are as emphatic in defence of their *striated particles and little spheres of the *second element as if they were theorems of Euclid. Our zeal in defence of our hypotheses seems to be merely a result of our passionate desire for personal respect. It is true that those who condemned Galileo believed that the earth's state of rest was more than an hypothesis, for they held it to be in conformity with Scripture and with reason. But since then people have become aware that reason, at least, no longer supports it; and as for Scripture, Father Fabri, who was the Penitentiary of St Peter's and an excellent theologian and philosopher, took this matter up in the course of his defence of the observations of the famous student of optics Eustachio Divini, published in Rome itself. He said openly that the understanding of the sacred text as referring to a true movement of the sun was only a provisional one, and that if Copernicus's view came to be verified there would be no objection to expounding the passage in the same way as Virgil's 'The lands and the cities recede'. Yet they still go on suppressing the Copernican doctrine in Italy and Spain, and even in the hereditary domains of the Emperor. This is greatly to the discredit of those nations: if only they had a reasonable amount of freedom

---

[1] The sentence down to here reflects Coste's muting of Locke's rhetoric, by omission, addition, and alteration.

in philosophizing,[1] their minds could be raised to the most splendid discoveries.

PHIL. §12. It does appear, as you say, that 'prevailing passions' are indeed the source of men's love of hypotheses; but passions extend much further than that. The greatest probability in the world will be powerless to make a covetous or ambitious man see that he is unjust; and nothing could be easier than for a lover to let himself be deceived by his mistress, so great is the truth in the saying that 'what suits our wishes, is forwardly believed,' and, as Virgil says, *those who love contrive dreams for themselves*. This leads to our having 'two ways…of evading the most apparent probabilities' when they threaten our passions and our prejudices. §13. The first is to think that 'there may be a fallacy latent in' the argument which is brought against us. §14. And the second is to suppose that we could advance equally good or even better arguments to defeat our adversary, if we had the opportunity or the cleverness or the help that would be needed to find them. §15. These ways of holding conviction at bay are sometimes sound; but it is sophistical to use them in a case where the issue has been set out quite clearly and everything has been taken account of; for once that is done there are ways of determining which side has the greater over-all probability. Thus, there are no grounds for doubting that animals were formed through motions 'guided by an understanding agent,' rather than through a 'fortuitous concourse of atoms'. Just as no one has the slightest doubt about whether the printer's letters which make an intelligible discourse have been put together through human care or by random jumbling. These are not cases, I should think, where it is open to us to suspend judgment; but we can do so when the probability is less clear, and can even rest content with weaker proofs which suit our inclination better. 'That a man should [lean] to that side, on which the less probability appears to him, seems to me [indeed] impracticable': §16. perception, knowledge and assent are not arbitrary; just as it is not open to me to see or not see the agreement of two ideas when my mind is directed towards them. Yet we can voluntarily halt the progress of our inquiries; and if we could not, 'ignorance [and] error…could not in any case be a fault.' That is where we exercise our freedom. In cases where one's interests are not involved, indeed, one accepts 'the common opinion, or [that of] the first comer'; but in matters which concern our happiness or unhappiness, 'the mind sets it self [more] seriously to [weigh] the probability: there, [i.e. when we are attending,][2] I think, it is not in our choice, to take which side we please, if [there are manifest differences between the two.] The greater probability, I think,…will determine the assent'.

---

[1] Following Leibniz's first draft ('*raisonnable en philosophant*') rather than the corrector's revised version ('*raisonnable et philosophique*') which appears in the Academy text.
[2] Added by Leibniz.

THEO. Fundamentally I share your view; and we have already said enough
about this when we treated of freedom in our earlier discussions. I showed
then [p. 182] that what we believe is never just what we want to believe
but rather what we see as most likely; and that nevertheless we can bring
it about indirectly that we believe what we want to believe. We can do this
by turning our attention away from a disagreeable object so as to apply
ourselves to something else which we find pleasing; so that by thinking
further about the reasons for the side which we favour, we end up by
believing it to be the most likely. As for opinions which we hardly care
about at all, and which we embrace for feeble reasons: that happens
because when an opinion has been put to us in a favourable light and we
can see almost nothing against it, we find it superior to the opposing view,
which has no support that we can see, by at least as much as if there were
many reasons on both sides; for the difference between 0 and 1, or between
2 and 3, is just as great as that between 9 and 10. We are aware of that
superiority, and we give no thought to – and are not encouraged to engage
in – the kind of scrutiny which would be needed for a sound judgment to
be made.

PHIL. §17. The last wrong measure of probability I shall take notice of
is *misunderstood authority*,[1] 'which keeps in ignorance, or error, more
people than all the other together'. How many men can be seen who have
no other ground for their belief than the opinions that are received among
our friends or the members of our profession, or within our party or our
country? The doctrine has had the approval 'of reverend antiquity, it
comes to me with the passport of former ages, [other men submit to it,][2]
and therefore I am secure [from error] in the reception I give it'. One
would be as justified in arriving at one's opinions by tossing a coin as in
getting them by such measures. Apart from the fact that 'all men are liable
to error, [I think that] if we could but see the secret motives, that influenced
the men of...learning..., and the leaders of parties,' we should often find
something totally other than the sheer love of truth. At least there is surely
'not an opinion so absurd, which a man may not receive upon this ground',
since there is almost no error[3] 'which has not had its professors'.

THEO. It must be admitted, though, that in many cases one cannot help
yielding to authority. St Augustine wrote a rather good book, *On the
Usefulness of Belief*, which is worth reading on this subject. As for 'received
opinions': they have in their favour something close to what creates a
'presumption', as the jurists call it; and although one is not obliged always
to adopt them without proof, neither is one permitted to destroy them in
the minds of others unless one has proofs against them. The point is that

---

[1] 'Authority' occurs in Locke's marginal summary; 'misunderstood' is Leibniz's.
[2] Added by Leibniz. [3] Locke: 'there is no error to be named'.

it is wrong to alter anything without reason. Since the late M. Nicole published his book on the Church, there has been much controversy over the 'argument drawn from large numbers' – the large numbers of people holding a given view – but all that can be derived from that argument, when what is at issue is approval of a reason rather than testimony to a fact, is something which amounts to what I have just been saying. Just as a hundred horses run no faster than one, although they can haul a greater load, so with a hundred men as compared with a single man: they cannot walk any straighter, but they will work more effectively; they cannot judge better, but they will be able to provide more of the materials on which judgment may be exercised. That is the meaning of the proverb 'Two eyes see more than one'. This can be observed in assemblies, where vast numbers of considerations are presented which one or two people might never have thought of; though there is often a risk that the best decision will not be reached through these considerations, because no competent people have been given the task of thinking them over and weighing them up. That is why some judicious theologians of the Roman sect, seeing that the authority of the Church – i.e. of its highest-ranking dignitaries, and those with the most popular support – could not be infallible in matters concerned with reasoning, have restricted it to the mere certification of facts under the name of 'tradition'. That was the view of Henry Holden, an Englishman who taught at the Sorbonne and wrote a book called *Analysis of the Faith*. In that, following the principles of the *Commonitorium* of Vincent of Lerins, he maintains that new decisions cannot be made in the Church, and that all that the Bishops assembled in Council can do is to bear witness that the [Church's] doctrine is accepted in their dioceses. The principle is plausible when looked at in the abstract; but in trying to put it into practice one finds that for a long time different opinions have been accepted in different countries; and also within single countries opinion has shifted from white to black, notwithstanding M. *Arnauld's arguments against drifting; furthermore, instead of confining themselves to testifying, the Bishops often involve themselves in passing judgment. The learned Bavarian Jesuit Gretser, who wrote another *Analysis of the Faith* which was approved by the theologians of his order, was also fundamentally of the opinion that the Church, relying on the promised aid of the Holy Spirit, can pass judgment on controversial matters by developing new articles of faith. But mostly they try to disguise this view, especially in France, pretending that the Church merely clarifies doctrines which are already established. But the 'clarification' is either a pronouncement[1] which is accepted already or a new one which is believed to be derived from accepted doctrine: the former case seldom occurs in practice, and as for the latter – the establishment of some new

519

[1] '*énonciation*'.

pronouncement – what can that be but a new article of faith? However, I don't favour contempt towards antiquity in religious matters. And I am even inclined to think that God has until now protected the truly ecumenical councils from any error which is contrary to saving doctrine. But what a strange thing sectarian prejudice is! I have seen people ardently embrace an opinion merely because it is accepted in their order, or even just because it conflicts with the opinions of someone whose religion or nationality they dislike, even though the question has almost nothing to do with religion or with national interests. They may not have known that their zeal really arose from that source; but I have noticed that upon first hearing that a certain person has written such and such a thing, they have rummaged through libraries and boiled up their animal spirits in the search for something with which to refute him. The same thing is often done, too, by people defending theses in universities and trying to shine against their adversaries. But what are we to say of the doctrines which are laid down in the *symbolic books of the various sects, even among the Protestants, which people are often obliged to accept upon their oath? (Some believe that in our case this signifies only an obligation to profess whatever these books or formularies contain which is also in Holy Scripture, while others deny this.) And in the religious orders of the Roman sect, not satisfied with the doctrines established in their Church, they lay down still stricter limits for their teachers: witness the propositions which, if I am not mistaken, the General of the Jesuits, Claudio Acquaviva, forbade to be taught in their schools. I remark in passing that it would be good to make a systematic list of the propositions which have been judged and condemned by Councils, Popes, Bishops, Superiors, Faculties; they would be useful for ecclesiastical history. There is a distinction between teaching a view and accepting it: no oath in the world, and no prohibition, can compel a man to stay with an opinion, because beliefs are inherently involuntary; but he 520 can and should abstain from teaching a doctrine which is thought to be dangerous, unless he finds that his conscience compels him to it. And in the latter case he should, if he is an appointed teacher, frankly declare where he stands and resign from his post – provided he can do so without putting himself into great danger, for that might compel him to leave quietly. That seems to be almost the only way of reconciling the rights of society with those of the individual, where the former has to prevent something it judges to be bad, while the latter cannot excuse himself from the duties laid upon him by his conscience.

PHIL. §18. This conflict between public and private, and even between the public opinions of different sects, is an unavoidable evil.[1] Often, though, these conflicts are illusory, and there is nothing to them but

---

[1] Added by Leibniz.

differences of wording. 'I must [also] do mankind that right, as to say, there are not so many men in errors...as is commonly supposed. Not that I think they embrace the truth; but indeed, because, concerning those doctrines they keep such a stir about, they have...no [positive] opinion[1] at all.' Without any examination, and without having in their minds even the most superficial ideas about the matter at issue, 'they are resolved to stick to [their] party,' like soldiers who do not examine the cause they are fighting for. 'If a man's life shows, that he has no serious regard to religion', all he needs if he is to 'approve himself to those, who can give him... protection', is 'to have his hand and his tongue ready for the support of the common' opinion.

THEO. In 'doing mankind that right' you are not praising them: it is more pardonable to stand sincerely by one's opinions than to counterfeit them out of self-interest. Perhaps, though, there is more sincerity in men's actions than you seem to intimate. For they may, without having any knowledge of the case, have arrived at an *implicit faith* by submitting themselves – totally, sometimes blindly, but often sincerely – to the judgment of others whose authority they have at some time acknowledged. It is true that their submission may be due partly to self-interest, but that does not alter the fact that the opinion eventually comes to be held. In the Church of Rome they are satisfied with something approximating to this implicit faith, perhaps because they have no revealed articles of faith which they judge to be absolutely fundamental and which they regard as necessary *necessitate medii*, i.e. as absolutely having to be believed if one is to be saved. Their articles of faith are all necessary *necessitate praecepti*, i.e. through the so-called 'necessity' that (according to Roman doctrine) one should obey the Church and give all due attention to what it says, speaking as though on God's behalf; this being required under penalty of mortal sin. But according to the most learned doctors of that Church, this necessity requires only that one be reasonably teachable, and does not absolutely oblige one to assent. Cardinal Bellarmine even believed that there is nothing superior to that childlike faith in which one submits to an established authority, and he reports with approval the words of a dying man who kept the Devil at bay by means of this circle which he was heard to recite over and over: 'I believe whatever the Church believes. The Church believes what I believe.'

Chapter xxi
'Of the division of the *sciences.'

PHILALETHES. Here we are at the end of our journey, with all the operations of the understanding made clear. We are not planning to explore

---

[1] Locke: 'no thought, no opinion'. Coste: '*point d'opinion ni aucune pensée positive*'. Leibniz: '*point d'opinion positive*'.

521

the detail of what we know; but still it may be appropriate, before we finish, to look over it in a general way by considering the divisions of the sciences.[1] **§1.** 'All that can fall within the compass of human understanding [is] either...the nature of things...in themselves'; or, secondly, man considered as an agent who is inclined towards goals, especially his happiness; or, thirdly, the 'means, whereby...knowledge [is] attained and communicated'. So there you have science divided into three sorts. **§2.** The first is '*physica*' or *'natural philosophy'', which embraces not only bodies and their affections such as number and figure, but also spirits, God himself, and the angels. **§3.** The second is practical philosophy, or ethics,[2] which teaches the means for 'the attainment of things good and useful', and which aims not only at the knowledge of truth but also at the doing of what is right. **§4.** Finally, the third is *logic* or the doctrine of signs (*logos* means *word*). 'To communicate our thoughts to one another, as well as record them for our own use, signs of our ideas are...necessary.' Perhaps if we 'distinctly weighed, and [with all possible care][3] considered' this last kind of science which turns upon ideas and words, we should have 'another sort of logic and critique, than what we have been hitherto acquainted with.' **§5.** And these three sorts – natural philosophy, ethics, and logic – are 'the three great provinces of the intellectual world, wholly separate and distinct one from another.'

THEOPHILUS. That division was a famous one even among the ancients. Like you, they took 'logic' to include everything having to do with words and with making our thoughts known – 'the art of speaking'. But there is a problem about this, namely that the science of reasoning, of judgment and of *invention, appears quite different from the knowledge – which is neither determinate nor principled[4] – of etymologies and language use. Furthermore, one cannot explain words without making incursions into the sciences themselves, as is evident from dictionaries; and, conversely, one cannot present a science without at the same time defining its terms. But the chief problem about that division of the sciences is that each of the branches appears to engulf the others. Firstly, ethics and logic fall under 'natural philosophy' when that is taken as broadly as you have just done. For in treating of 'spirits', i.e. substances which have understanding and will, and giving a thorough account of their understanding, you will bring in the whole of logic; and if your doctrine about these spirits includes an account of matters pertaining to the will, you will have to talk about good and evil, happiness and misery, and it depends entirely on you

---

[1] Added by Leibniz.
[2] '*la morale*', rendered by 'morality' or 'moral philosophy' except in this chapter where it corresponds to Locke's 'ethics'.
[3] Locke: 'duly'. Coste's change.
[4] '*qui est quelque chose d'indéfini et d'arbitraire*'.

522

whether you develop that topic far enough to bring in the whole of practical philosophy. On the other hand, everything is relevant to our happiness, and so could be included within practical philosophy. As you know, theology is rightly regarded as a practical science; and jurisprudence, and medicine too, are not less so. So that the study of human happiness or of our well- and ill-being, if it deals adequately with all the ways of reaching the goal which reason sets before itself, will take in everything we know. So it is that Zwinger included everything in his *Systematic Conspectus of Human Life*, which Beyerlinck mangled by putting it into alphabetical order. And the study of languages, which you and the ancients take to belong to logic, i.e. to what is deductive, will in turn annex the territories of the other two – by treating every topic in alphabetically arranged dictionaries. So there are your three great provinces of the realm of knowledge,[1] perpetually at war with one another because each of them keeps encroaching on the rights of the others. The nominalists believed that there were as many particular sciences as there are truths, with the latter falling into groups only in so far as someone has organized them in that way. Others compare the totality of our knowledge with an uninterrupted ocean which is divided into the North Sea, the Atlantic Ocean, the Indian Ocean and the Red Sea only by arbitrary lines. A single truth can usually be put in different places, according to the various terms it contains, and even according to the middle terms or causes which it depends on, and the consequences and effects which it may have. A simple categorical proposition has only two terms, but a hypothetical may have four; not to mention composite statements. A memorable anecdote may be placed in the annals of general history, or in the history of the particular country where it happened, or in the biography of some man who was concerned in it. And suppose that it has to do with some fine moral precept, some military stratagem, or some discovery which is useful for the *arts which serve the convenience of life or the health of men: then it will be useful to assign this same anecdote to the science or art to which it is relevant. And within that science it might even be mentioned twice: once in the history of the discipline concerned, telling how it actually developed; and again in the statement of its rules, confirming or elucidating them through examples. For instance, the very apt story that is told in the biography of Cardinal Ximénez, of how a Moorish woman cured him of an almost hopeless bout of hectic fever merely by rubbing, is worth a place in a medical treatise, both in the chapter on hectic fever and also in the part dealing with medical regimens, taking these to include [physical] exercises. And that same episode would have a further use in helping to

523

---

[1] '*provinces de l'Encyclopédie*', not meaning 'encyclopedia' in the twentieth-century sense.

reveal the causes of that illness. It might also be mentioned in the logic of medicine, which is concerned with the art of finding methods of cure, and also in the history of medicine to illustrate how remedies have come to men's knowledge – quite often with the aid of simple lay-healers or even of charlatans. Beverwijck's agreeable work *On Ancient Medicine*, which draws only upon authors who were not physicians, would have been even finer if it had gone on to include modern ones. It can be seen from this that a single truth can have many places according to different matters to 524 which it is relevant. Those who are organizing a *library are very often unsure about where to place certain books, being unable to decide between two or three equally suitable places for them. But now let us speak only of general doctrines, setting aside particular facts, history, and languages. I know of two main ways of organizing the totality of doctrinal truths. Each has its merits, and is worth bringing in. One is *synthetic* and *theoretical*: it involves setting out truths according to the order in which they are proved, as the mathematicians do, so that each proposition comes after those on which it depends. The other arrangement is *analytic* and *practical*: it starts with the goal of mankind, namely with the goods whose sum total is happiness, and conducts an orderly search for means which will achieve those goods and avoid the corresponding ills. These two methods are applicable to the realm of knowledge in general, and some people have also used them within particular sciences. Even geometry, which Euclid treated synthetically as a science, has been treated by others as an *art; but in this latter form it could still be handled demonstratively, and that would even show how the art is discovered. It is like someone who sets out to measure all kinds of plane figures, starting with the rectilinear ones, and realizes that such figures can be divided into triangles each of which is half of a parallelogram, and that parallelograms can be reduced to rectangles which are easy to measure. If one were writing an encyclopedic account of the whole of knowledge, employing both methods at once, one could use a system of references so as to avoid repetition. To these two kinds of arrangement we must add a third. It is *classification by terms*, and really all it produces is a kind of Inventory. The latter could be systematic, with the terms being ordered according to certain categories shared by all peoples, or it could have an alphabetical order within the accepted language of the learned world. This Inventory is needed if one is to assemble all the propositions in which a given term occurs in a significant enough way. For in the other two procedures, where truths are set out according to their origins or according to their use, the truths which concern some one term cannot all occur together. For example, when Euclid was explaining how to bisect an angle, it would not have been permissible for him to go straight on with the method for trisecting angles, because that would have required reference to conic sections, which could not yet be taken account of at that stage in the work. But the Inventory could and should indicate the locations of the important propositions concerning a given subject. We still

525 have no such Inventory for geometry. It would be a very useful thing to have, and could even be a help to discovery and to the growth of that science, for it would relieve the memory and would often save us the trouble of searching out anew something which has already been completely found. And there is even more reason why these Inventories should be useful in the other sciences, where the art of reasoning has less power, and they are utterly necessary in medicine above all. The constructing of them would require no little skill. Well, now, it strikes me as curious that these three kinds of arrangement correspond to the ancient division, revived by you, which divides science or philosophy into theoretical, practical and deductive, or into natural philosophy, ethics and logic. The synthetic arrangement corresponds to the theoretical, the analytic to the practical, and the one with an Inventory according to terms corresponds to logic. So that the ancient division serves very well, just so long as it is understood in the same way as the above three arrangements, on the account I have just given of them – namely, not as distinct sciences but rather as different ways in which one can organize the same truths, if one sees fit to express them more than once. There is also an administrative[1] way of dividing the sciences, according to the faculties and the professions. This is employed in the universities and in organizing libraries. The fullest though not the best catalogue of books has been bequeathed to us by Draud, together with Lipen who carried on his work. Rather than following the entirely systematic method of Gesner's *Pandects*, they were content – almost like booksellers – to employ a grand division of subjects according to the four so-called 'faculties' of Theology, Jurisprudence, Medicine, and Philosophy; then within each faculty they grouped the books according to the principal terms occurring in the material on their title-pages, with these words being taken alphabetically. This made things easy for those two authors, because they had no need to see a book or to understand its subject-matter, but – quite apart from the numerous mistakes they made – their method is much less useful to other people, unless each heading is accompanied by references to others with a similar signification. For clearly a single thing may be called by different names, as for example: 'legal observations', 'miscellanies', 'conjectures', 'selections', 'semi-annual law-reports', 'sound judgments', 'good resolutions', and many other similar sub-titles; a law-book's being labelled in any of those ways merely indicates that it is a miscellany of Roman law. That is why the systematic arrangement of topics is undoubtedly the best, and to it one can

526 add very full alphabetical indexes of terms and of authors. The accepted

---

[1] '*civile*'.

administrative division, according to the four faculties, deserves respect. Theology treats of eternal happiness, and of everything that bears upon that in so far as it depends upon the soul and the conscience. It is a sort of jurisprudence which has to do with the matters which are said to concern the *'inner tribunal', and which brings in invisible substances and minds. Jurisprudence is concerned with government and with laws, whose goal is the happiness of men in so far as it can be furthered by what is outer and sensible. Its chief concern, though, is only with matters that depend on the nature of the mind, and it doesn't go far into the detail of corporeal things, taking their nature for granted in order to use them as means. This at once relieves it of one large matter, namely the health, strength and improvement of the human body – the care of that being assigned to the faculty of Medicine. Some people have believed, not without reason, that along with the others there should be an *Economic* faculty: this would include the mathematical and mechanical arts, and everything having to do with the fine points of human survival and the conveniences of life; and it would include agriculture and architecture. But the faculty of Philosophy is left to pick up everything which is not contained in the three faculties which are deemed to be superior. That was not a very good thing to do, for it has left those in this fourth faculty with no way of improving their skills by exercising them, as can those who teach in the other faculties. And so the faculty of Philosophy, except perhaps for mathematics, is regarded as merely an introduction to the others. That is why it is expected to teach young people history and the arts of speaking, and also to teach – under the titles of metaphysics or *pneumatology, ethics and politics – some of the rudiments of natural theology and jurisprudence, which are independent of divine and human laws; with a little natural science as well, for the benefit of the young physicians. There, then, is the administrative division of the sciences, in accordance with the professional bodies of learned men who teach them. And then there are the professions whose members serve society other than by what they say, and who ought to be guided by those who are truly learned – if only learning were valued as it ought to be. Even in the higher manual arts there has been an alliance of practice with learning, and it could go further. As indeed they are allied in medicine, not only in ancient times when physicians were also surgeons and apothecaries, but even today, especially among the *chemists. This alliance between practice and theory can also be seen in war, and among those who teach manoeuvres, among painters, sculptors and musicians, and among certain other kinds of *virtuosi*. If the principles of all these professions, arts and even trades were taught in a practical way by the philosophers – or it might be in some other faculty of learned men – the latter would truly be the teachers of mankind. But this would require many changes in the present state of things in literature, in the education of the

527

young, and thus in public policies. When I reflect on how greatly human knowledge has increased in the past century or two, and how easy it would be for men to go incomparably further along the road to happiness, I am not in despair of the achievement of considerable improvements, in a more peaceful time under some great Prince whom God may raise up for the good of mankind.

NOTES

The Notes provide information relevant to certain words and phrases which occur in the text; a word which is preceded by an asterisk, anywhere in this work, occurs as the title, or the first word of the title, of a note, or is a suitably close cognate of a word which so occurs. The Notes provide information about people and events and schools of thought alluded to in the text and significant in Leibniz's career; they explain certain technical or unusual terms and certain philosophical conceptions; they deal with certain recurrent translation problems. With regard to this last category, anything said in a note about our policy for translating a given French word can, unless we say otherwise, be taken to apply *mutatis mutandis* to its close relatives – in saying that we render *'preuve'* by 'proof', we mean to imply that we also render *'prouver'* by 'prove'. Unadorned page numbers in the Notes always refer to our text of the *New Essays*, as do all references to 'the text'. Other references can be unravelled with the help of the Key to Abbreviations, which immediately follows the Table of Contents, and the Bibliography, which follows these Notes; in particular, the Key to Abbreviations explains the method used to refer to Leibniz's *Sämtliche Schriften und Briefe*.

Academies of science. Public institutions to promote scientific research and the communication of its findings were a creation of the later seventeenth century. The Royal Society of London, 'for the improving of Natural Knowledge', grew out of informal meetings of scientists in Oxford and London and was chartered in 1660, with provision for fifty-five members. Leibniz took note of its activities and, in 1668, saw in them the prospect of 'philosophy reformed for the benefit of the human race' (II.1, p. 10). In 1673 he visited London and attended meetings of the Society, of which he was subsequently made a Fellow (*Paris). The Académie des Sciences, in Paris, originated in a similar way out of informal gatherings, initially at the house of Marin Mersenne – unlike the Royal Society, which came into existence through the decision of its members, the Académie had existence thrust upon it, in 1666, by Colbert, the chief minister of Louis XIV. Its nucleus consisted of about a dozen distinguished scientists, including *Huygens, who received salaries and research funds from the Crown. While in Paris, Leibniz became acquainted with members of the Académie and attended its meetings. On *Roberval's death, in 1675, he hoped to succeed to his place in the nucleus but was disappointed; according to *Fontenelle, in his *Éloge de Monsieur Leibniz* (1717), Leibniz could have had the post had he agreed to convert to Catholicism. The *Index biographique* of the Académie indicates that he became a member in 1675. The idea of founding scientific societies in Germany was much in Leibniz's mind from his earliest maturity, usually in connection with his projects for a universal *symbolism. Some of his early proposals envisage a new sort of religious order, modelled on the Jesuits but dedicated to the discovery and propagation of scientific truth (1.2, pp. 76f; cf.

Couturat pp. 3ff). With the cooperation of the Duke of *Brunswick, he actually embarked on a scheme to fund an academy by increasing the yield of the *Harz silver mines, but was incapable of carrying it through. When his pupil Sophie Charlotte of Brunswick married the Elector of Brandenburg, Leibniz's hopes were renewed. With her help the Elector was persuaded to found, in 1700, a Royal Society of Science at Berlin, with Leibniz as its president. It was supported by a monopoly on the production and sale of reformed calendars (*Weigel). The first volume of its transactions, most of it written by Leibniz, appeared in 1710. In spite of Leibniz's incessant efforts, the Society did not officially open until 1711. Shortly thereafter, on the accession of the unsympathetic Frederick William I, it went into a decline from which it was eventually rescued, and reorganized as the Berlin Academy of Sciences, by Frederick the Great. (The documents pertaining to the establishment of the Berlin Academy are in A. Harnack, *Geschichte der Königlich Preussischen Akademie der Wissenschaften zu Berlin* (1900)). Leibniz was involved with three other academies, actual or possible. In 1704 he took to Dresden a proposal for a Saxon Academy of Sciences, to be funded by a monopoly on the silk industry. In 1711, while attending the wedding of a Brunswick princess to the son of Peter the Great, he seized the opportunity to urge the Tsar to establish a network of academies, libraries, museums, and universities throughout his vast realm (*Wiener* pp. 594ff). Peter favoured the project, appointed Leibniz a privy councillor with responsibility for science and mathematics, and drew up plans for what became, in 1725, the St Petersburg Academy of Science. During this same period Leibniz spent two years, 1712–14, in Vienna advising the Hapsburg Emperor on founding an academy to pursue the study, not only of science and mathematics, but of history and philosophy as well. The Emperor was enthusiastic, but the Jesuits were implacably opposed to the idea of an academy under Protestant management – in the event Leibniz went back to Hanover and his project lay dormant until 1846. (Additional documents relating to Leibniz's activities as a founder of academies are in *Foucher de Careil* VII and *Klopp* X.) See p. 354.

Albert the Great (c. 1200–80). German philosopher, theologian, scientist, and churchman; the teacher of Thomas Aquinas. See *Edwards*. An interest in experimentation brought Albert a reputation as a magician. The story about flowers in winter, to which Leibniz alludes on p. 266, is in *Bayle's *Dictionary* (article 'Albert-le-Grand', note G): Albert is said to have entertained a guest by turning a day in mid-winter into a summer one 'full of flowers and fruit'.

Amadis of Gaul. A romance of chivalry of great popularity and influence in the sixteenth and early seventeenth centuries, and of great length. It was through much reading of *Amadis* and its imitators that Don Quixote addled his wits. Stories of Amadis's knight errantry began to appear in Spain and Portugal in the fourteenth century, grew by accretion, and were put into print, in Spanish, in the sixteenth century. French, Italian, English, and German versions followed rapidly. See pp. 356, 382, 469.

Analysis. The notion of analysis is pervasive and many-sided in Leibniz's writings. It includes calling for definitions for 'all terms which admit of them, ...and demonstrations...for all axioms which are not primary' (pp. 74f). Leibniz held that 'always, in every true affirmative proposition, necessary or contingent, universal or particular, the concept of the predicate is in a sense included in that of the subject' (*Leibniz–Arnauld* p. 63), and was for a time inclined to believe that all true propositions could be reduced to identities (*Loemker* p. 283); in about 1686 he came to hold that, for contingent truths, 'the reduction proceeds to infinity and is never terminated' (*Morris and Parkinson* p. 75) – so that what certainty we may have of them must rest on something other than 'the analysis and connection of ideas' (p. 406 of the text). Leibniz speaks of defining *terms*, but by 'term' he means 'not a name, but a concept, i.e. that which is signified by a name; . . . a notion, an idea' (*Parkinson* p. 39). Definitions, whether nominal or real (p. 346), are analyses of ideas into those which are 'thoroughly original and primary' (p. 212; cf. p. 120) and, closely linked with these, of things and their properties in terms of their inner natures and underlying causes (pp. 297, 299). To understand inner natures and underlying causes requires a delicate interplay of reasoning and observation (pp. 80, 267, 293f, 453ff; cf. *Loemker* pp. 280ff). Developments in mathematics – the invention of the *infinitesimal calculus in particular – greatly increase our power to decipher nature (pp. 368, 478); but Leibniz regards the calculus as only a part of a more comprehensive analytical instrument: his intention is to elaborate a 'general science' or 'art of invention' (p. 488), incorporating a logic of *probability. Like Descartes, he was spurred on by the belief that something of this art was already known to the mathematicians of ancient Greece (pp. 488f; cf. Descartes, *Regulae* IV), namely the linked methods of 'analysis' and 'synthesis'. The fullest description of these ancient methods occurs in Pappus's commentary on Euclid's *Elements* (see Heath's edition of the *Elements* (1926) I, pp. 137ff): analysis consists in assuming the proposition which is to be proved and deducing conclusions from it until one is arrived at which is independently known to be true (*reductio ad absurdum* is a variant form); synthesis consists in starting from known truths and deducing a series of previously unknown conclusions. Leibniz points out (pp. 450f, 484; cf. *Loemker* pp. 187f), with regard to analysis, that deducing a known truth from a proposition will establish the truth of that proposition only if each step in the deduction conforms to a true biconditional; when this condition is satisfied the process can be reversed and the proposition in question arrived at, by synthesis, from the known truth. Leibniz believed that more was involved in the ancient method of analysis than Pappus reveals (*LPG* I, p. 395). He adverts repeatedly to the need for 'a much higher logic' (p. 484), embodying both analysis and synthesis (pp. 368f) – an 'art of using the understanding not only to judge proposed truth but also to discover [*erfinden* = *invent] hidden truth' (*Loemker* p. 463).

'animal'. This translates '*animal*', a word which, though Leibniz will not apply it to all embodied minds (see p. 388), is usually taken to cover humans. It is confined to sub-human animals on p. 72 and in a few other places, but mostly the lower animals are '*bêtes*' and '*brutes*', beasts and brutes. When we quote a passage in which Locke uses any of these three words, we follow his choice of word even where Coste has not translated it according to our principles.

'aphorism'. 'From the "Aphorisms of Hippocrates", transferred to other sententious statements of the principles of physical science' (*OED*). We use it to translate '*aphorisme*', although according to dictionaries and to Leibniz (pp. 417, 425) the French word seems to mean a rule of thumb rather than a 'principle' properly so-called. See also pp. 330, 387.

Aqua regia. 'A mixture of nitric and hydrochloric acids, so called because it can dissolve the "noble" metals, gold and platinum' (*OED*). See pp. 338, 346.

Archei. J. B. van *Helmont (1577–1644) popularized the idea that vital functions depend upon the activity of resident spiritual agents, i.e. archei, one for the organism as a whole and a subsidiary one for each particular organ – a notion which he shared with Paracelsus, *Fludd and Henry *More. Leibniz contended that all natural phenomena can be explained mechanistically, but he nevertheless attributed an essential role in metaphysics to the notions of *entelechy and *substantial form (see *Loemker* pp. 308f, 587ff). See p. 72.

Arminius. Jacob Harmens (1560–1609), Dutch Protestant who founded the Arminian or Remonstrant sect in opposition to the Calvinist doctrine of predestination. See *Edwards*. Locke associated with Arminians during his exile in Holland. See pp. 75f.

Arnauld, Antoine (1612–94). French theologian, philosopher and mathematician. See *Edwards*. In the 1640s he became the leader of the Jansenist faction, in subsequent association with Pascal and *Nicole; its emphasis was on the Augustinian doctrine of grace, in particular opposition to the Jesuits and to *probabilism. He wrote the 'Fourth set of objections' (1641) to *Descartes's *Meditations* and, with Nicole, the very influential 'Port Royal Logic': *Logique, ou l'art de penser* (1642). Arnauld's writings also include *Nouveaux éléments de géométrie* (1667), referred to on p. 407, and, again with Nicole, *La perpétuité de la foi de l'Église catholique* (1669–74), referred to on p. 518. Leibniz wrote to Arnauld in 1671 (II.1, pp. 169ff; tr. in part *Loemker* pp. 148ff) before visiting *Paris, and came to know him there (*Theodicy* pp. 67, 260). Their correspondence during 1686–90 was of great importance in the development of Leibniz's philosophy (see *Leibniz–Arnauld*) and Leibniz himself considered publishing it (*Loemker* p. 460).

'art'. This renders '*art*' throughout, and no other rendering is used except for a few places where 'skill' is preferred. In French, as in English at the time Leibniz wrote, an 'art' is essentially an assemblage of techniques or disciplined skills. We would often have rendered 'the art of X' by 'techniques for X-ing' if 'technique' were not anachronistic. Where 'art' is contrasted with *'science', the contrast is between practical and theoretical (e.g. p. 386 which speaks of the science and the art of demonstration). Sometimes '*les arts*' seem to be thought of as earthily practical, e.g. as including carpentry and agriculture, and in those contexts we have put 'the [practical] arts'. In some other contexts, the basic contrast is not between practical and theoretical (arts and sciences) but rather between what is technical and rule-governed on the one hand and what is natural or intuitive or unschooled on the other: for instance, the remarks on p. 482 about those who can spot a bad argument or do a good calculation while knowing nothing of logic or arithmetic 'as an art' (see also p. 369). When Leibniz says that syllogism includes an 'art of infallibility' (p. 478), he must mean that it embodies techniques which guarantee one against making (introducing?) errors.

Artful, artless. Cf. Aristotle: 'Of the modes of persuasion some belong strictly to the art of rhetoric and some do not. By the latter I mean such things as are not supplied by the speaker but are there at the outset – witnesses, evidence given under torture, written contracts, and so on. By the former I mean such as we can ourselves construct by means of the principles of rhetoric. The one kind has merely to be used, the other has to be invented.' (*Rhetoric* I, 1355^{b}36, tr. Roberts). Cf. *Ramus. See pp. 457f.

Asgill, John (1659–1738). English lawyer and pamphleteer. On p. 506 Leibniz refers to Asgill's *Argument Proving, that According to the Covenant of Eternal Life Revealed in the Scriptures, Man may be Translated from Hence into that Eternal Life, without Passing through Death*...(1700); in large part it is an interpretation of the doctrine of Redemption, by means of the principles of English law, but by way of preamble Asgill argues that 'as the life or death of one man is no cause of the life or death of another, so the multitude of examples don't alter the case'. Writing to Queen Sophie Charlotte in 1702, Leibniz describes this argument of Asgill's as based on the 'uncertainty of induction' but as pushing it 'a little too far' (*Loemker* pp. 550f).

Asseburg, Rosamunde von der (c. 1672–1712), a noblewoman from Luneburg. Princess *Sophie first heard of her from Rosamunde's sister, who was at the Hanoverian court, and later met her and was delighted by her. In 1691 Sophie consulted Leibniz about Rosamunde's visions and mysterious powers, and there ensued a lively correspondence about prophecy, imagination and pre-natal influences (1.7, pp. 30ff). Leibniz concluded that the phenomena had a natural explanation; he advised that she should not be punished, as the local theologians were urging, but cherished like some rare curio (1.7, p. 190). See p. 506.

Averroists. Followers of the Islamic philosopher Ibn Rushd (1126–98), known to Christendom as 'Averroes'. See *Edwards*. They were accused of believing in the eternity of matter, the participation of all mankind in a single intellect and the possibility of a proposition's being philosophically true but theologically false, and of denying personal immortality and free will. The 'Averroistic heresy' was a recurrent bogy and enticement from the thirteenth to the seventeenth century. Leibniz purported to detect Averroism in Naudé and *Spinoza and among the *Quietists (cf. *Loemker* p. 554; *Theodicy* pp. 77ff). See pp. 59, 494.

'aware'. In Leibniz's French, to perceive is '*apercevoir*', and to be aware of is '*s'apercevoir de*'. The noun for the former is '*perception*', while for the latter Leibniz coins '*aperception*' (as it is spelled today in French). For the latter, we use 'aware' and its cognates, rather than – as some English writers do – borrowing 'apperception' and 'apperceive' from French, complete with seventeenth-century spelling. We pay a price, though, for thus staying with the English language: certain contrasts lose their dramatic sharpness in our rendering, as when Leibniz says (p. 162) that we are never without *perceptions* but are often without *aperceptions*. See also p. 134.

Bacon, Francis (1561–1626). English statesman and philosopher. See *Edwards*. He became Lord Chancellor under James I. His greatest influence came from his proposals for the conduct of scientific research, e.g. in his *Novum organum* (1620). Leibniz's references on p. 455 to *Descartes and *Spinoza are misleading. What Descartes says (letter to Mersenne, 10 May 1632) is that he is seeking 'the cause of the position of each fixed star', that this would be the key to 'the highest and most perfect science of material things which men can ever attain', that it would help him greatly in this endeavour if someone would write 'the history of celestial phenomena in accordance with the Baconian method...without any arguments or hypotheses', but that he has no real hope that anyone will do so, and that in any case the desired science 'is beyond the reach of the human mind' (tr. Kenny). And what Spinoza says (letter to *Oldenburg, April 1662) is that

*Boyle's attempts to prove by experiment that 'all tactile qualities depend only on motion, shape, and the remaining mechanical states' are superfluous, since 'this has already been proved sufficiently and more than sufficiently by [Bacon] and afterwards by Descartes' (tr. Wolf).

Bayle, Pierre (1647–1706). French Protestant; fideist, sceptic and philosophical critic. He became professor of philosophy and history at Rotterdam in 1681 but was deprived of his chair in 1693 because of his zeal for religious toleration. See *Edwards*. In 1684 he founded the *Nouvelles de la république des lettres*, in which Leibniz published, and edited it for three years. Bayle's *Dictionnaire historique et critique* (1695–7, 2nd edn 1702; English tr. 1734–41) appends discussion of major issues of seventeenth-century thought to articles of the utmost obscurity: notes H and L to the article 'Rorarius' criticize Leibniz's philosophical system. Leibniz repeatedly misreports (e.g. p. 55) Bayle's remark that the system of *pre-established harmony 'raises the power and intelligence of divine art above what we can conceive' (note L). Bayle's remark about Payva de Andrada (p. 501) occurs in the *Dictionary* article 'Andrada'. Leibniz corresponded with Bayle, on physics and philosophy, between 1687 and 1702 (*LPG* III, pp. 21ff) and published a series of replies to his criticisms: 'Clarification of the difficulties which M. Bayle has found in the new system of the union of soul and body', 'Reply to the thoughts on the system of pre-established harmony', and ultimately the *Theodicy*; he gives a short history of their controversies in his preface to the *Theodicy*. See also pp. 71, 440.

'blind thoughts'. This phrase is commonly used to translate Leibniz's '*pensées sourdes*' – literally thoughts which are 'deaf' or 'muffled', but 'blind' is sanctioned by Leibniz's equating this phrase with the Latin '*cogitationes caecae*' (p. 185). It may be worth noting that '*sourd*' is also a mathematical term meaning 'irrational', and connects etymologically with the English 'absurd'.

Bossuet, Jacques Bénigne (1627–1704). French Roman Catholic preacher and religious writer; Bishop of Meaux. He was a vigorous controversialist, particularly against the Protestants. See *Edwards*. He and Leibniz corresponded, off and on, from 1679 to 1702, principally on the issue of reuniting the Lutheran and Roman Catholic churches (their letters are published in *CB*). Leibniz had imbibed ideas of reunion from his first employers, Boineburg and the Elector of Mainz (*Paris), both converts to Roman Catholicism; in Hanover, as adviser to the Roman Catholic ruler of a Lutheran populace, the topic was constantly before his mind. In the early 1690s discussion with Roman Catholics created hopes for the recognition of a semi-autonomous German Catholic Church (*Pellisson); Leibniz put the question to Bossuet: 'Would the churches united with Rome be permitted in good conscience to enter into ecclesiastical union with churches submissive to the opinions of the Catholic Church and even prepared to be incorporated into the Roman hierarchy, but which do not agree with certain decisions...and which, furthermore, insist on effective reformation of certain abuses which Rome itself cannot condone?' (I.7, p. 271; *CB* V, p. 42). The stumbling block was the Council of Trent, with its anathemas against Protestant doctrines: if it could be agreed that Trent was not ecumenical or, at least, if the German Church could be dispensed from a few of its decisions, then there would be no serious obstacle to German Protestants participating with the Roman Church in a general council to resolve all outstanding differences. But Bossuet could not consent to such an accommodation: 'If the least particle of the

Church's decisions is relaxed [Christ's] promise is annulled and with it the whole body of revelation' (1.9, p. 159; *CB* v, p. 436); if Protestants want to be reunited with Rome they must confess their errors and submit to her authority. Very quickly they found themselves at loggerheads; the correspondence limped through a few more letters and then died. Bossuet became occupied with the *Quietists in his own church, and Leibniz turned his hand to reuniting the Calvinists and Lutherans of Germany. Then, in 1699, Bossuet revived the correspondence. The time was inopportune: Hanover and Leibniz were nego- tiating with Protestant England concerning the royal succession (*Sophie) and with Protestant Brandenburg. Leibniz had been dissatisfied from the start with the tone of the earlier discussion: 'I sometimes object to eloquence and, in important matters, prefer reasoning which is entirely plain and bare, without ornaments or charm, designed to lead us to the truth by the kind of route followed by accountants and surveyors when they deal with numbers and lines. This route is rough but straight. I admire everything that I see from the Bishop of Meaux and M. Pellisson; the beauty and vigour of their style, as much as that of their thoughts, charms me so greatly that my understanding is, so to speak, held captive as long as I am in its presence. But when the force of the spell has abated and I begin to take stock of their reasoning in my own way – when I strip off this borrowed finery, which comes from the author rather than from the subject matter – when, in short, I begin to function as logician and reckoner, then I cannot get my bearings and it seems that their reasons, which had so impressed me, have slipped through my fingers' (letter to Brinon, 1.8, pp. 124f). When he again found Bossuet employing the same tactics to defend the same position he dressed him down roundly, urging him to 'distinguish between what is suitable *ad populum* and what is suitable among persons who profess precision', and to adopt a method of discussion which does not beg questions, which proceeds by precise reasoning and which 'eliminates all unpleasantness, dispels the mists of oratory and deprives great men of the advantages of eloquence and authority, so that the only winner is truth' (*CB* xii, pp. 326f). The correspondence persisted, somewhat strained in tone, for another year; its final phase was given over to discussion of the canonical books of the Old Testament (p. 459 of the text). In 1705 Leibniz summed it up for Thomas Burnett: 'M. Pellisson and I debated the subject with the greatest civility and loved to discuss points on which we could agree. But after M. Pellisson's death the Bishop of Meaux wanted to continue the correspondence, took too decisive a tone and attempted to push matters too far, putting forward doctrines which I could not accept without betraying my conscience and the truth. As a result I replied to him firmly and forcefully and assumed a tone as lofty as his own, to show him, great controversialist that he was, that I saw through his tricks too well to be caught out by them. Our disputations could make up a whole book' (*LPG* iii, pp. 303f). See pp. 459, 468.

Bouhours, Dominique (1628–1702). French Jesuit literary critic and religious writer. He alternated so regularly between these two genres that it was said of him that 'he served heaven and earth by the semester' (*Encyc. Brit.*). *La manière de bien penser sur les ouvrages d'esprit* (1687) was influential in the development of neo-classical literary criticism; Leibniz discusses it at length, with special emphasis on Bouhours's treatment of Lucan's epigram, in a letter to Queen Sophie Charlotte of Prussia written in August 1702 (*LPG* vi, pp. 522ff). See p. 141.

Boulliau (Boulliaud, Bouillaud, Bullialdus), Ismael (1605–94). French mathematician and astronomer; author of a treatise on spirals. Although a Roman Catholic priest, he wrote in defence of the motion of the earth after the condemnation of Galileo, to *Descartes's astonishment (letter to Mersenne, April 1634). Leibniz found him 'very obstinate and, as is typical of old people, wedded to the opinions of the ancients and unwilling to listen to the moderns' (*Dutens* VI.1, p. 333). In a letter to Johann Bernoulli in 1705 Leibniz says that when *Huygens found the area of the surface of a spheroid 'few understood it, and Bullialdus would not believe it' (*LMG* III, p. 772). See p. 489.

Bourignon, Antoinette de (1616–80). Flemish visionary. She left her birth-place, Lille, after being acquitted of witchcraft, and eventually settled in Amsterdam where she enjoyed a great vogue, captivated the aged *Comenius and founded a sect. Her writings, which were published in nineteen volumes (1679–86), suggest that 'she was a visionary of the ordinary type, distinguished only by the audacity and persistency of her pretensions' (*Encyc. Brit.*). Leibniz followed her later career with sympathetic curiosity (see 1.3, pp. 355ff, 462f; *Grua* pp. 75ff). See pp. 506ff.

Boyle, Robert (1627–91). Anglo-Irish scientist, philosopher and theologian; one of the founders of the Royal Society (*academies). See *Edwards*. A convinced *Baconian, he compiled 'histories' of natural qualities and, by precept and example, promoted the idea of systematic and precisely recorded experimentation. He was also an alchemist and the advocate of a version of mechanistic atomism allegedly consistent with Christian theism. His account of making 'fixed silver' (p. 300) occurs in 'An historical account of a degradation of gold, made by an anti-elixir: a strange chemical narrative' (*Works*, ed. T. Birch (1772), IV) and is plainly science fiction, featuring a traveller from the East with a mysterious powder capable of degrading gold into a *fixed silvery metal. Other references in the text are to 'An essay of the intestine motions of the particles of quiescent solids: where the absolute rest of bodies is called in question' (*Works* I), on p. 53; to 'Two essays concerning the unsuccessfulness of experiments...' (*Works* I), on p. 305; and to 'A physico-chemical essay, containing an experiment, with some considerations touching the differing parts and redintegration of salt-petre' (*Works* I), on p. 455. Leibniz visited Boyle in London, and was considerably influenced by him (see *Loemker* pp. 165f, 715).

Brunswick. In 1676, having abandoned hope of a salaried position in *Paris, Leibniz entered the service of the Dukes of Brunswick-Lüneburg and Brunswick-Wolfenbüttel – as *librarian, legal counsel, mining engineer, tutor, poet-laureate, envoy, political propagandist, theologian etc. In 1680, in a prospectus addressed to the new head of the family, Duke Ernst August, he proposed writing 'a short but solid history of this princely house, supported throughout by appropriate documents' (1.3, p. 200). In 1685 the Duke terminated the *Harz fiasco, relieved Leibniz of his regular legal duties, promised him a life pension, an expense account and a secretary, and commissioned him to write the history of the Guelph family of Brunswick (1.4, pp. 205f). After ransacking the ducal libraries and archives Leibniz embarked, in 1687, on two and a half years of research in southern Germany, Austria and Italy; he amassed a collection of historical documents and established the link between the houses of Guelph and Este (1.5, pp. 662ff). In 1691 he took charge of Duke Anton Ulrich's great library at Wolfenbüttel, assuring Ernst August that this would, if anything, facilitate his writing the history, which he undertook to complete within two years (1.6, p. 21); at the same time he proposed expanding it to encompass the history of Lower Saxony from 'the remotest antiquity of this country', beginning with its geological formation and with the provenance of its 'most ancient inhabitants' as revealed by the root elements of their language (1.6, pp. 23ff). In c. 1694 he proposed presenting the early part of the history proper in the form of annals, embodying 'material drawn from the old authors and from state papers, arranged chronologically', this to be followed shortly by a more popular version containing their quintessence (1.9, pp. 57ff). In 1695 he acknowledged that he had taken on too much: that in attempting to finish the history without allowing his correspondence to fall behind or losing track of the new developments in mathematics, philosophy and literature, he often did not know which way to turn (*Müller* p. 134); in 1696 he wrote that 'if Death will only allow me time to carry out the projects that I have already undertaken, I will promise to take on no others.... But Death cares not a whit for all our projects or for the advancement of knowledge' (*LPG* III, pp. 174f). That same year he was appointed a Privy Councillor of Justice; two years later, Ernst August having been succeeded by his less patient son Georg Ludwig and nothing of the history having yet appeared, the appointment was revoked (*Müller* p. 155; Leibniz protested that in basing his account entirely on primary sources he was doing something unprecedented in German and Italian historiography, and added: 'I have never allowed myself to be confined to a single sort of work; what sustains me is change, rather than rest', *Müller*, p. 157). The eighteen years between Georg Ludwig's accession and Leibniz's death was a battle: on Georg Ludwig's side to urge, cajole, compel Leibniz to finish the history; on Leibniz's, to keep up his other interests and undertakings (and, on occasion, to augment them), to collect his pension and reimbursement for his expenses, to follow the Court to London and there become historiographer of England (*Müller* p. 251; Georg Ludwig's reaction to *this* suggestion: 'First he must show me that he can write history; I've heard that he is hard-working.' *Müller* p.253). Relations reached their nadir when, after spending a decade founding the Berlin *Academy and assisting Tsar Peter to enlighten Russia, Leibniz settled down in Vienna to advise the Hapsburg Emperor on setting up his own academy of science. His report, in January 1713, that the Emperor agreed that writing a history of Brunswick really required writing a history of the whole Empire did not reassure his employers in Hanover (*Müller* p. 234). In September 1714, after a crescendo of summonses, he returned at last to Hanover, having been absent for twenty-two months; his closest friends, Ernst August's widow *Sophie and Duke Anton Ulrich, had died during his absence and he had just missed Georg Ludwig's departure, for London, to ascend the British throne as George I. Leibniz was now forbidden to leave the vicinity of Hanover. In the hope of regaining his freedom and of returning to Vienna or London or Paris, he at last concentrated his efforts on the history: 'I now devote to this work all the time that my daily responsibilities and the preservation of my health will permit; I have had to set aside all the mathematical, philosophical and legal inquiries to which I feel inclined. For the same reason my correspondence has also come to a halt' (*Bodemann* p. 185). In 1698 the historian J. G. Eckhart had been appointed to assist Leibniz (and, apparently, to keep the Court informed as to his diligence); in 1716 Georg Ludwig instructed his Council in Hanover to give Eckhart responsibility for the later part of the history, after 1024, 'but to say nothing to Leibniz about this' (*Müller* p. 256). Leibniz's historical researches produced, in addition to several volumes of collected documents – political, legal and historical – and various dissertations on the geology and primordial settlement of Lower Saxony, the *Annales imperii occidentis Brunsvicenses* covering the period 768–1005. In November 1716 the gout or arthritis, which had long troubled Leibniz's feet, moved into his hands, preventing him from writing. In mid-November, on the penultimate day of Leibniz's life, Eckhart reported that 'Herr Leibniz lies bound hand and foot, with his shoulders so pulled in by the gout that I have never seen anything like it before. He cannot hear of work now and when I ask him about some problem he answers that I must deal with it as I see fit, that I can handle it perfectly well, that in his condition he cannot concern himself with anything any more. The only thing that could bring him around now would be the Tsar or a dozen great gentlemen promising him a pension – that would soon get him back on his feet again.' He adds that Leibniz will never finish the history; that 'he is too easily distracted and because he wants to do everything and mix himself up in everything he can never finish anything, even if he had angels for helpers' (*Müller* pp. 261f).

Cartesians. *Descartes attracted a great following, especially in France and Holland; its members proceeded to expound, winnow and revise his doctrines. In the seventeenth and early eighteenth centuries the 'Cartesians' were most particularly those who sought to carry out Descartes's project for a universal science (Leibniz explains his own use of the term at *Loemker* p. 94). Jacques Rohault (1620–75) was the most distinguished of these: his *Traité de physique* (1671) became the standard text of Cartesianism and in its English translation by John Clarke (*System of Natural Philosophy* (1723)), with Samuel Clarke's notes, became the definitive confrontation between Descartes and Newton. Other scientific Cartesians included Descartes's Dutch pupil *Regius and Johann Clauberg (1622–65), who carried the word from Holland to Germany. E. W. von Tschirnhaus (*Paris), the friend of Leibniz and *Spinoza, and Christiaan *Huygens were both products of scientific Cartesianism. Descartes's most notable continuators in philosophy included *Arnauld, *Malebranche and the Occasionalists (*occasional causes). The statement (pp. 72, 224) that the Cartesians believed that the soul could change the direction, although not the force, of motion of a body does not seem to be true of any know Cartesian; it is, in fact, something that Leibniz often says of Descartes himself – tentatively at first (*Leibniz–Arnauld* p. 117) and confidently later (*Morris and Parkinson* pp. 129f) – but without textual substantiation. See also pp. 56, 67, 125ff, 131, 171, 296, 423.

Casting out nines. A method of checking calculations which depends on the fact (i) that if two numbers are divided by any given number, yielding remainders a and b, and if the product of the two numbers and the product of a and b are each divided by the given number, the remainders will be the same, and on the fact (ii) that if both a number and a sum of the digits of that number are divided by nine, the remainders (if any) will be the same. See p. 410.

Centre. That the centre of gravity of a (flat) object cannot be found by bisecting its area two or more times was one of the first things that Leibniz learned from *Huygens (*Child* p. 215). As Leibniz explains in more detail in a letter written in 1692 (1.8, pp. 196f), if a flat object is balanced in several different ways on a knife edge all the lines of balance will pass through some one point on the surface of the object; on the other hand it is not necessarily the case that all the lines bisecting the area of a flat object will pass through a single point. See p. 321.

Centripetal force. 'A force which draws or impels a body toward some point as a centre, and thus acts as a counterpoise to the centrifugal tendency in circular motion' (*OED*). *Roberval, in his *Aristarchus* (1644), had advanced the 'very absurd suggestion that all the particles of matter making up the universe possess a certain property by virtue of which they are all drawn towards one another and mutually attract each other' (Descartes to Mersenne, 20 April 1646; see *Loemker* p. 663). Newton introduced the notion of centripetal force into his system in the fifth definition of his *Principia* (1687). In *Opticks* (Query 31, 1706 edn) he says that 'what I call Attraction may be perform'd by *impulse, or by some other means unknown to me. I use that Word here to signify only in general any Force by which Bodies tend towards one another, whatsoever be the Cause', but in the General Scholium (1713) to the *Principia*, in words reminiscent of Henry *More, he speaks of 'a certain most subtle spirit which pervades and lies hid in all gross bodies: by the force and action of which spirit the particles of bodies attract one another at near distances, and *cohere, if contiguous'. Leibniz was prepared to say that bodies attract one another; that they do so in accordance with the law of inverse squares was something that he claimed to have demonstrated, independently of Newton, from Cartesian premisses (*Loemker* pp. 417f, 513). But he denies 'that attraction is a primary property essential to matter' and asserts that it 'can happen only in a way that has an explanation, namely, by the impact of more subtle bodies' (*Loemker* p. 663), since 'a body is never moved naturally, except by another body which touches it and pushes it. . . . Any other kind of operation on bodies is either miraculous or imaginary' (*Leibniz–Clarke* v, §35; cf. §§118–23). See pp. 6off, 131.

Chemist. The reference is to those medical practitioners who believed, following Paracelsus, that 'the conditions and functions of the body in health and in disease were explained by the chemical doctrines of the time; morbid conditions being referred to disturbances of fermentations, effervescence of humours, and such like, and being treated accordingly' (*OED*, 'chemiatric'). See p. 527.

Christina (1626–89). Queen of Sweden. In the early years of her reign she was a great patron of learning and brought to Stockholm *Descartes (whose health endured the rigours of Swedish Court life for barely three months), Hugo Grotius, Isaac Voss (*Codex argenteus), *Comenius, and *Pufendorf among others. In 1654 she abdicated the throne, in order to take up Roman Catholicism, and settled in Rome. She fell seriously ill in February 1689, much to Leibniz's dismay: he was on his way to Rome with a letter to her admirer, Cardinal Azzolini (1.5, p. 682). At Venice 'they believed that Queen Christina was dead, but she is out of danger and I shall be able to see her. My vows undoubtedly contributed to it, for I was distressed to see her die just when I was going to Rome' (1.5, p. 410). In fact she did die, on 19 April, and Azzolini not long after her, so that Leibniz met neither of them. The opinion that we must blind ourselves to see clearly is explicitly attributed to Christina in *Theodicy*, p. 96. See p. 494.

'*clair*', 'clear'. The basic meaning of '*clair*' is 'vivid, bright', etc., which explains how ideas can be at once '*claires*' and confused (see pp. 137, 255). Cf. *'*distinct*'. Sometimes, mainly in ii.xxix, Locke's 'clear' is rendered by Coste as '*clair*' and so we put it back into 'clear' again. Similarly, we render '*obscur*' by 'obscure' in those passages, although sometimes 'dark' seems closer to the meaning. At p. 254 '*clair*' does mean more than 'vivid'; an idea or image is said to be '*claire*' if it makes possible some kind of recognition or identification.

Codex argenteus. Manuscript of the fourth-century translation of the Gospels into Gothic, by the Arian bishop Ulfilas, for the Black Sea Goths. The manuscript probably comes from sixth-century Ostrogoth Italy; it is written in silver and gold ink on purple vellum in characters based upon Greek, Runic and Latin letters and said to have been invented by Ulfilas. According to their own legends the Black Sea Goths came via the Vistula from the vicinity of Sweden. The *Codex* probably reached Werden in the late eighth century and lay forgotten there until the mid sixteenth century. By 1600 it was in Prague in the possession of the Hapsburg Emperor. When the Swedes took Prague in 1648 they sent it to Queen *Christina. In 1652 the Dutch classical scholar Isaac Voss took it with him to Holland on leaving Christina's employ – according to Leibniz he 'fished it out of her library' (1.7, p. 397. Not his only fishing trip, apparently: see *Dutens* VI.1, p. 330). In 1662 the Swedish Chancellor, Magnus de la Gardie, bought it back from Voss, encased it in silver and returned it to the Queen, who deposited it in the library of Uppsala University, where it remains. See p. 280.

Cohesion. How can we explain the firmness of bodies and the cohesion of their parts? 'Why does not the wind carry off our heads like balloons? Why does not a stone hurled to the Earth penetrate it to its centre...?' These questions, ridiculous as they are, are difficult to answer' (II.1, p. 63; tr. *OC* VII, p. 167). Leibniz rejects *Descartes's theory that firmness consists in parts being at rest relative to one another (*Principles* II, §54), since it fails to account for the difference between contiguous parts and cohering parts (*Loemker* pp. 403ff). He rejects *Gassendi's theory that cohesion results from atoms hooking together, and the theory that it results from the pressure of surrounding material – as in the case of two slabs of polished marble – since both theories presuppose the firmness of the cohering parts (*Loemker* pp. 407f). He rejects *Huygens's theory that firm atoms are an ultimate fact, both because he rejects atoms and because he rejects ultimate, unexplainable facts (*Loemker* pp. 415f). On similar grounds he rejects the theory that there are ultimate forces of attraction between particles of matter (*centripetal force). Leibniz entertained these questions very early in his career and by July 1670 believed he had found 'the true theory of motion ..., in which I seem to myself to have disclosed the cause of the cohesion, bending, and hardness of bodies' (II.1, p. 59; tr. *OC* VII, p. 66): in short 'whatever things so move that one seeks to enter into the place of another, these cohere, so long as that endeavor lasts.... If a whole body be so moved that one part expels another from its place and succeeds it there, those parts cohere, not indeed absolutely but until a stronger motion impinges' (II.1, p. 64; tr. *OC* VII, p. 168) – he instances the firmness of a jet of water (*Loemker* p. 407). Given this basic cause of firmness and cohesion, cohesion and 'traction' can in special circumstances result from the hooking together of firm particles or from the pressure of surrounding material (*Loemker* p. 416). See pp. 59f, 123ff, 130f, 222f.

Coining. Leibniz's responsibilities as both mining engineer and statesman underlie his interest in coinage. Apparently Brunswick, with its silver mines in the *Harz mountains, issued coins of greater intrinsic value than those of the same denomination issued elsewhere. Leibniz foresaw a general tendency towards debasement of coinage and for several years, beginning about 1688, waged a campaign in Germany for monetary reform (e.g. 1.5, pp. 47ff, 103f, 126ff, 598; 1.6, pp. 261ff. Cf. *LPG* III, p. 201). See p. 492.

Colour. When he wrote the *New Essays* Leibniz knew about the finite velocity of light (p. 135; Römer, whom he had known in *Paris, had succeeded in measuring the velocity of light in 1676) and agreed with *Huygens that light consists in the transmission of waves of motion, generated by motion in the source, through a continuous material medium (pp. 131f, 165; cf. *LBG* p. 607). Huygens refused to commit himself as to the nature of colours (*LBG* p. 597), but Leibniz tentatively accepted the fairly general view that in its fundamental state light appears white to us and that it comes to appear coloured as a result of being refracted, the particular colour depending on the angle of refraction (p. 299). He was inclined to reject *Mariotte's more complex account (p. 309) and to maintain that the colours of 'liquids and surfaces. . .which are called opaque [? *fixes*] come from refractions no less than do those which are called transparent' (*LBG* p. 595). Given his belief that the colour of a beam of light is, so to speak, accidental to it, and that any beam can come to assume any colour, it is understandable that he should say that every colour 'can pass through bodies which let the appearance of any of them through' (p. 299), although he could have expressed his point more felicitously. This belief was contradicted by Newton's *Opticks* (1704), a work which Leibniz awaited eagerly (*LPG* III, pp. 261f, 268) and obtained from England (*Gerland* p. 106), presumably as soon as it was published. According to Newton, the colour of a beam of light is, so to speak, intrinsic to it; for it to appear to change colour it must consist in a mixture of light-rays of different colours and some of these must be removed from it by refraction or absorption. In a letter dated December 1706 Leibniz writes: 'Mr Newton holds that coloured rays, separated out of the mixture, are fundamental and are susceptible of no further change, whereas M. Mariotte claims to have observed that the red ray, for instance, which Mr Newton regards as simple, can again change colour and yield blue or white. But since Mr Newton has carried out a very great number of experiments, his opinion appears to be the best' (*LPG* III, pp. 488f). See also pp. 219, 300, 383, 403f.

Comenius (i.e. Komensky), Jan Amos (1592–1670). Bohemian educational reformer and Bishop of the Moravian Brethren. See *Edwards*. In his later years he wandered the length and breadth of Europe, coming finally to rest in Amsterdam where, according to *Bayle, 'the shower of gold which fell upon him...obliged him to stay for the remainder of his days' (*Dictionary*, 'Comenius'). He had become increasingly sure that the millennium was at hand, to be introduced by the overthrow of the Papacy and the Hapsburg Empire; to invigorate the Protestant cause he published, in *Lux in tenebris* (1657), the prophetic revelations of Christopher Kotter, Christina Poniatowska and Nicholas Drabik (p. 508). The anonymous *Cartesius cum sua naturali philosophia a mechanicis eversus* (1659), which is attributed to him, describes an air-gun constructed by two Amsterdam craftsmen and argues that it refutes the Cartesian principle that matter cannot be condensed or rarefied, thereby overthrowing the whole Cartesian system of science (p. 409). In 1671 Leibniz wrote an appreciation of Comenius's writings – mostly with regard to his proposals for an 'encyclopedia' – and obituary verses (II.1, pp. 199ff and 201).

Conring, Hermann (1610–81). German physician, jurist, theologian, historian, and philosopher. He was at various times professor of natural science, medicine and politics at Helmstedt, privy councillor to the Duke of Brunswick and private physician to the King of Sweden. In philosophy he was an Aristotelian (*Peripatetics). He was the teacher and friend of Leibniz's first patron, Johann Christian von Boineburg (1622–72). In 1668 Boineburg sent Conring a copy of Leibniz's *New Method for Learning and Teaching Jurisprudence*. This led to a correspondence between Leibniz and Conring, on law, philosophy and mathematics, which went on intermittently until 1679 (see II.1, passim; one of Leibniz's letters to Conring is translated in *Loemker* pp. 186ff). Conring's misconceptions about *analysis are corrected in Leibniz's letter of February 1679 (II. 1, pp. 457f). Leibniz attributes to Conring the idea that a deterrent/reformative, or 'medicinal', theory of punishment does not presuppose free will (*Theodicy* pp. 422f). See p. 450.

'conscious'. Locke makes personal identity depend upon 'consciousness', which Coste translates by '*con-science*'. Philalethes adopts this word, nearly always dropping the hyphen. Theophilus uses it sometimes, but more often uses Leibniz's coined word '*consciosité*'. We use 'conscious' only in rendering those two words, and the only times when we use anything else for them are: 'conscience' at pp. 243 and 526, and 'self-consciousness' at pp. 65 and 241. (Apart from pp. 65 and 526, neither '*conscience*' nor '*consciosité*' occurs outside the personal identity discussion on pp. 235–47.) When Coste translates Locke's 'consciousness' by '*sentiment*', we render the latter by 'sense' rather than reverting to Locke's word, so as to show clearly which word-occurrences will have been taken by Leibniz – working mainly from Coste's version – as occurrences of Locke's technical term. That he did regard '*conscience*' and '*consciosité*' as alternative words for a single concept is shown by the last footnote on p. 235.

Conway, Anne (1631–79). English metaphysician: 'her ruling passion was for the most abstruse treatises on theosophy and mysticism' (*DNB*). She was the pupil and friend of Henry *More; to his great dismay she eventually became a Quaker. Of her many writings only one was published, after her death: *The Principles of the Most Ancient and Modern Philosophy concerning God, Christ, and the Creatures, viz. of Spirit and Matter in General; whereby may be resolved all those problems or difficulties, which neither by the school nor common modern philosophy, nor by the Cartesian, Hobbesian, or Spinosian could be discussed* (Latin tr. 1690; re-tr. into English 1692). *Helmont, who had treated her incessant headaches by means of 'occult medicine', saw her book through the press and drew it to Leibniz's attention. See p. 72.

Cupellation. A process for separating out gold and silver from lead and other base metals. When heated in a *cupel* – a container moulded out of wood- and bone-ash – the base metals oxidize, the lead oxide absorbs the oxides of the other base metals and is in turn absorbed by the bone-ash. A button of gold or silver or their alloy is left in the cupel. In the process of *parting*, the silver is separated off by being dissolved in aquafortis – usually nitric acid. See p. 267.

Denominations, intrinsic and extrinsic. An intrinsic denomination of a thing is a characterization of it which involves only the thing itself, whereas an extrinsic denomination relates it to something else. If two minds were exactly alike in their instrinsic natures, but were minds *of* two different people, they would differ purely extrinsically. Leibniz declares this to be impossible: to every extrinsic denomination there corresponds an intrinsic denomination which is its basis

(p. 231; *Loemker* pp. 526f); 'no one becomes a widower in India by the death of his wife in Europe unless a real change occurs in him' (*Loemker* p. 365). This impossibility constitutes what Leibniz calls the principle of the 'identity of indiscernibles' ('Monadology' §9). The main ground of his doctrine that every extrinsic denomination rests on an intrinsic one seems to be his view that a *monad *is*, in some way, just the sum total of its intrinsic properties (p. 110), or at any rate that it can be properly identified only through them (pp. 289ff; *Leibniz–Arnauld* pp. 29f), so that one could not conceivably distinguish two monads each answering to the same complete intrinsic description. Leibniz also maintains the identity of indiscernibles with regard to *phenomena such as material things, contending that two particles of matter in different places will also differ in some other way. That rules out classical atoms (pp. 230f). He says, though, that the existence of two material things which are dissimilar only in their location is not absolutely impossible but merely contrary to God's wisdom (*Leibniz–Clarke* v, §§23ff). See also pp. 227, 401f.

Desargues, Girard (1591–1661). French engineer, architect and self-taught mathematician. He was associated with the group around Mersenne in Paris. His work on perspective, to which Leibniz refers on p. 135, laid the foundations of projective geometry – although this was not recognized until the nineteenth century. Leibniz probably knew Desargues's work through A. Bosse: *La manière universelle de M. Desargues pour pratiquer la perspective* (1648), since by Leibniz's time Desargues's own publications were virtually unobtainable.

Descartes, René (1596–1650). French philosopher, mathematician and scientist; the founder of the *Cartesian school. See *Edwards*. He attempted to establish a new system of knowledge from first principles, founded on his certainty of his own existence as a thinking being (*Meditations* II; cf. p. 367 of the text) and of the existence of God. He deduces God's existence from the fact that he has an idea of God (*Meditations* III; cf. p. 438 of the text), and to be doubly sure he proposes a revised version of Anselm's ontological argument (*Meditations* V; cf. p. 437 of the text). His system of physics was immensely influential – Newton, *Huygens and Leibniz all cut their teeth on it – and radically incoherent. Matter is identical with extension, i.e. three-dimensional space (*Principles* II, §4; cf. pp. 72, 127f of the text). It follows that vacuum is inconceivable and that the rarefaction and condensation of matter are only apparent (*Principles* II, §§5ff, 16f; cf. pp. 151, 409 of the text). It also follows that outer limits to the material universe are inconceivable (cf. pp. 150f); the world, although not strictly infinite, is indefinite in extent (letter to More, 5 Feb. 1649, §4). Into extension God injects a certain quantity of motion which stirs itself in and, by differences of motion, marks off one portion of matter from another (*Principles* II, §23). Three elements, i.e. distinct kinds of particles, are the result: earthy, opaque lumps constitute the third element; tiny transparent spheres, the *second element; and luminous dust – 'scrapings' – the first (*Principles* III, §52). Particles of these three kinds tend to be sorted out and re-arranged by the cosmic vortices which their motion generates (*Principles* III, §65). Since matter *is* extension, the physical sciences reduce in principle to geometry (*Principles* II, §64), which science Descartes did much to make accessible to algebraic procedures (*Geometry*). The laws of motion, in his view, depend on the theological certainty that God maintains a constant quantity of motion in the universe (*Principles* II, §36); from this he infers (*Principles* II, §40) that the quantity of motion remains constant throughout each particular physical interaction (cf. p. 224). The laws of physics account fully for the behaviour of plants and non-human animals, which are all natural automata (*Discourse on Method* v); animals probably have neither thoughts nor feelings, any more than clocks do (letter to More, 5 Feb. 1649, §5; cf. p. 67 of the text). Man is unique in being a machine with a rational soul – a soul capable, apparently, of outliving its body (*Discourse on Method* v). Since thinking is the essence of the soul, souls think all the time (*Reply to Objections V*, re *Meditations* II; cf. pp. 53, 113ff of the text). The soul is not in the body like a pilot in a ship, but forms a single whole with it (letter to *Regius, Jan. 1642; cf. p. 317 of the text); nevertheless, it is particularly associated with the pineal gland (cf. p. 221) and by controlling its position controls the flow of the animal spirits and, thereby, the movements of the body (*Passions of the Soul* I, §34). When the sense organs of a human body are stimulated its soul perceives (*Passions of the Soul* I, §35), but there is no reason to suppose that physical objects resemble our perceptions of them (*Meditations* VI; cf. pp. 56, 131ff of the text). Leibniz subjected various aspects of Descartes's system to detailed criticism in 'Meditations on knowledge, truth and ideas', 'Brief demonstration of a notable error of Descartes', and 'Critical thoughts on the general part of the *Principles* of Descartes', among others.

De Witt, Jan (1625–72). Dutch statesman and mathematician. He was Grand Pensionary of the province of Holland from the age of twenty-eight until two weeks before his death; in this position he dominated the affairs of the Dutch Republic during the period of its greatest ascendancy. He had studied mathematics under Descartes's friend Isaac Beeckman and, as a young man, wrote a notable treatise applying Cartesian principles to conic sections: *De elementis curvarum linearum* (1659) – this presumably contains the 'thoughts' referred to on p. 377. De Witt was a pioneer in what he called 'social mathematics'; for the guidance of Dutch governments in selling annuities, he produced the work to which Leibniz refers on p. 465: *Waerdije van Lijf-renten naar proportie van Los-renten* (1671). In August 1672 De Witt was forced out of office by William of Orange; two weeks later, in the Hague, he and his brother were murdered by the street mob. *Spinoza, who was probably personally acquainted with the De Witts and was certainly of their party, told Leibniz in 1676 'that on the day of the De Witts' murder he had intended to go out at night and put up a notice, somewhere near the spot, with the words "*ultimi barbarorum* [lowest savages]"'. But his landlord locked him in the house to prevent him going out, since he would have risked being torn to pieces' (*Freudenthal* p. 201).

'*distinct*'. It would usually produce better English and clearer philosophy if this were rendered by 'clear'. Descartes's '*idées claires et distinctes*' are ideas which are vivid and clear, in that order. Cf. *'clair'. But the standard practice of putting the English 'distinct' for the French '*distinct*' is now undislodgeable, and anyway it leads to infelicity rather than error or nonsense; so we have reluctantly adopted it ourselves, except for a few places where '*distinctement*' could not tolerably be rendered except by 'clearly', and places (e.g. p. 210) where Coste renders 'clear' by '*distinct*' and we reverse the process. We also sometimes (e.g. pp. 113, 117) use 'distinct' to render '*distingué*' – literally 'distinguished' – a word for which we have been unable to find a uniform rendering.

Ebenbitar. Ibn al-Baitar (c. 1195–1248). Hispano-Moslem botanist and pharmacologist. His main work is his 'collection of simple drugs and foodstuffs' –

Kitab al-jami – in Arabic; it incorporates the work of Dioscorides and Galen, but it also draws on the author's own plant-collecting throughout the Islamic Mediterranean. An abridged translation into French was made in the seventeenth century but was never published. See p. 336.

'endeavour'. Leibniz uses '*tendance*' to stand for some kind of active force or thrust or pressure, something which always 'results in action unless it is prevented' (p. 172). Every one of his uses of the term shows that 'tendency' would be a quite wrong translation (and when the latter occurs in this work it translates '*habitude*'). Except for the phrase 'comes closer to' on p. 211, we always translate '*tendance*' and the verb '*tendre*' by 'endeavour'. This rendering could be questioned. Leibniz says that there is an infinity of *tendances* in any subject at any time (p. 110), that true power always involves not only the possibility of doing something but also a *tendance* to do it (pp. 112, 169, 216, 226), that a stone falling to the earth manifests a *tendance* (p. 189), and that people have *tendances* of which they are not aware (p. 192): all of which might suggest that a less psychological term than 'endeavour' would be more appropriate. But on the other side there is the fact that Leibniz certainly does use psychological terms generously, as in his doctrine that every state of every monad is a 'perception'. Certain anthropomorphic flavours are noted in a footnote on p. 122, and the falling stone mentioned above is credited with having a 'goal'. Also, with regard to '*tendance*' in particular: Leibniz equates it with 'effort' and with '*conatus*', the latter being the Latin for 'endeavour' (p. 172). It is also noteworthy that in one place where Locke uses 'endeavour', Coste translates it by '*tendance*' (p. 343). The only occurrence of 'endeavour' not translating '*tendre*' is on p. 210, where 'an endeavour towards' renders '*un exercice de*'.

Enigmatic passage. Locke's hint, quoted on pp. 441f, that he had a theory about how matter might originally have been created, really did make Leibniz's mouth water. In 1704 he wrote to Lady *Masham (*LPG* III, p. 364) with an urgent request that she ask Locke to elucidate – but Locke was dead by the time she received the letter and Lady Masham could not recall ever having heard him discuss the topic. Fortunately (although too late to satisfy Leibniz's curiosity), Coste found out what Locke had had in mind and gave an account of it in a footnote to IV.x.18 in the second edition of his translation of Locke's *Essay* (1729): he had had it from Newton himself that Locke was alluding to a suggestion of Newton's that God might have created matter simply by making certain regions of space impenetrable to one another. For a more detailed discussion see J. Bennett and P. Remnant: 'How matter might at first be made', *Canadian Journal of Philosophy*, Supplementary Volume IV (1978), pp. 1ff.

Entelechy. In *De anima* II Aristotle says that the soul is 'the first actuality [*entelecheia*] of a natural body potentially possessing life' (412^a28, tr. Hett). By '*first* actuality', or 'first entelechy', he is referring to the possession of a capacity, as opposed to its exercise. The soul is a first entelechy since 'both sleeping and waking depend upon the presence of soul' (412^a23, tr. Hett). In his 'New system of the nature and the communication of substances' Leibniz describes how he rejected the atomism of Democritus and *Gassendi and discovered 'genuine unities', helped by the old notion of *substantial forms. He came to conceive of these unitary substances as centres of force or active power (pp. 169, 172, 216 of the text), not only indivisible in themselves but capable of unifying aggregations of substances and thereby constituting them organisms (pp. 328f). He argues that, from the fact that their nature consists of force, it follows that they have 'something analogous to sense and appetition'; hence, that they resemble souls and what Aristotle calls 'first entelechies' (*Loemker* pp. 454ff). Since 'soul' suggests consciousness, he later restricted this term to entelechies which possess awareness ('Monadology' §§ 18f); the passage on pp. 169f, and in particular the preliminary drafts for it (VI.6, p. 169n), indicate that he was still in process of settling his terminology when he wrote the *New Essays* (cf. p. 210). In his later writings he uses 'entelechy' interchangeably with *'monad'.

Enthymeme. 'A *syllogism in which one premiss is suppressed' (*OED*). See pp. 83, 479.

Equations. An *adfected* equation (p. 488) is one whose terms possess two or more different powers of the unknown, e.g. $x^2 + ax + b = 0$, as contrasted with a *pure* equation, such as $x^2 + b = c$. A general method for solving quadratic equations is given in Euclid's *Elements* and in the *Arithmetica* of Diophantus of Alexandria (third century A.D.). A method for solving certain cubic equations was discovered by Scipione del Ferro (c. 1465–1526) and was either communicated to or re-discovered by Nicolo Tartaglia. He in turn passed it on, under an oath of secrecy according to his own account, to Girolamo Cardano (1501–76) who generalized it and published it in his *Ars magna* (1545), together with the method for solving biquadratics discovered by his pupil Ludovico Ferrari (1522–65). Ferrari's method involved finding a quantity such that, when the terms of the equation have been suitably arranged on either side of the equal sign and the quantity in question is added to both sides, each side becomes a perfect square. The whole subject was greatly advanced by François Viète (1540–1603), who, in addition to contributing to the solution of equations, introduced the convention of using letters to represent quantities (see pp. 410, 489); he called the resulting expressions *logistica speciosa*, and regarded them as constituting a system of generalized arithmetic. *Descartes laid the foundations for analytical geometry by submitting the whole of classical geometry to algebraic treatment. With regard to equations he claimed, incorrectly, to have developed a general procedure applicable to equations of the fifth and sixth and, indeed, any degree (*Geometry* III). Leibniz rejected this claim and criticized Descartes's boastfulness (*Child* p. 187; *Loemker* p. 223) – presumably the remarks about braggarts on p. 369 are directed at Descartes and his associates. Leibniz himself became interested in the solution of higher equations in 1675, while in *Paris, and designed an instrument by means of which 'the roots of all equations may be had in numbers...without any calculation' (III.1, p. 255; tr. *OC* XI, pp. 332f. See also III.1, pp. 272, 280, 333f; the first and last of these tr. *OC* XI, p. 395 and *NC* I, p. 402 respectively).

Euclid. Leibniz's references on pp. 415 and 451f are to the definitions, axioms and postulates of Book 1 of Euclid's *Elements of Geometry*, for which he seems to have relied largely on the revised edition of C. Clavius (1574). As Leibniz seems to have been aware, not everything in Clavius – and not everything he cites – can be found in the original text of the *Elements* (e.g. as tr. by T. L. Heath, 1926). Heath's edition of Archimedes (1912) contains translations of all his extant works; Leibniz refers (on pp. 370, 376, 415, and 451 respectively) to *On the Equilibrium of Planes, Measurement of a Circle* and *On Spirals* (props. 18, 19),

On the Sphere and the Cylinder (assump. 2), and *On the Sphere and the Cylinder* (assump. 1).

'evidence'. Sometimes this word – translating *'évidence'* – means 'degree of evidentness', as it does in Locke. An argument which has 'mathematical evidence' is one which is evident in the way mathematical arguments are, not one for which there is support from mathematics.

Fabri, Honoré (c. 1606–88). French Jesuit scientist, philosopher and theologian. After a teaching career in French universities he went to Rome as Penitentiary – i.e. priest in charge of administering penance – of St Peter's. He discovered the circulation of the blood independently of Harvey, and wrote in opposition to *Descartes's laws of motion. According to Leibniz he was 'one of the most brilliant, scholarly and universal minds of his order, but he lacked the true method of analysis. He proceeded very cavalierly in his proofs' (*Wiener* p. 54). Leibniz studied Fabri's *Physica* (1669) and related writings in the early 1670s and commented on them (VI.2, pp. 186ff); they seem to have exchanged letters at that time and there is a 1676 draft of a long letter to him by Leibniz, containing an anti-Cartesian theory of motion (II.1, pp. 185ff, 286ff). See pp. 498, 515.

Fabricius, Johann Ludwig (1632–96). German philosopher and theologian; professor at Heidelberg. Leibniz visited him there (*Theodicy* p. 67), apparently in the winter of 1670–1 (I.1, p. 125). Fabricius's *Apologeticus pro genere humano contra atheismi calumniam* is said to have been published in 1682, but Leibniz knew of it in Feb. 1670 (I.1, p. 85). It was Fabricius who, in 1673, at the behest of the Elector Palatine, offered *Spinoza the chair of philosophy at Heidelberg. In 1674 French troops ravaged Heidelberg and closed the University; Fabricius fled and spent the rest of his life on the move. After his death Leibniz wrote that 'he was a man of sound learning and judgment and dear to his Elector' (*Foucher de Careil* II, p. 132). See p. 103.

'feel'. This, when it occurs, translates *'sentir'*. Usually the cluster including *'sens'*, *'sensible'*, *'sentant'* etc. are rendered by 'sense', 'sensible', 'sentient' etc.; but sometimes it seems better to use 'feel', and in one passage 'conscious', instead. The first use of 'feel' in any such passage is marked with an asterisk. We regret having to use 'immediacy of feeling' for *'immédiation de sentiment'* on p. 367. Leibniz is there contrasting logical truths, in which one idea is immediately juxtaposed with another (immediacy of ideas), with truths concerning one's own present inner state – truths in which a mind comes hard up against a *'sentiment'*, i.e. something sensed or felt or given, a datum, perhaps, or a Kantian intuition. See also p. 434 regarding this.

Fixed. 'Not easily volatilized; not losing weight under the influence of fire' (*OED*).

Fludd, Robert (1574–1637). English physician, philosopher and self-styled Rosicrucian. See *Edwards*. In his *Philosophia Moysaica* (1638), which reappeared in 1659 in his own English translation, he maintained that the true philosophy had been revealed to Moses and could be extracted from the Scriptures. Leibniz considered him to be, among other things, a precursor of the Occasionalists (*occasional causes; see *Loemker* p. 502). See p. 68.

Fontenelle, Bernard le Bovier de (1657–1757). French scientist and writer; one of the precursors of the Enlightenment. See *Edwards*. In 1697 he became permanent secretary of the Académie des Sciences, of which he wrote a history (1708–22). Leibniz's personal association with Fontenelle, and his correspondence with him, dates from 1699. Fontenelle's duties included pronouncing eulogies to the Académie on its deceased members – during a period of forty-two years he delivered sixty-nine of these. His eulogy on Leibniz, delivered in 1717, fixed the picture of Leibniz's character and achievement for the eighteenth century; it is included in Fontenelle's *Éloges des académiciens morts depuis 1699 jusqu'en 1717* and in *Dutens* I. See p. 472.

Foucher, Simon (1644–96). French philosopher and churchman. He was a moderate sceptic, in the tradition of the later Platonic Academy, and a vigorous opponent of *Cartesianism. His sceptical arguments found their way into the main stream via *Bayle's *Dictionary*. His *Critique de la recherche de la vérité* (1675), directed against Descartes and Malebranche, was his principal work. See *Edwards*. Leibniz knew him in *Paris and wrote a brief account of their first meeting (E. Bodemann, *Die Leibniz-Handschriften* (1895), p. 339). Their correspondence, on physics and philosophy, ran from 1675 until Foucher's death (*LPG* I, pp. 363ff; cf. *Loemker* pp. 151ff). In 1695 Leibniz published an account of his system of *pre-established harmony for the first time ('New system of the nature and communication of substances'), in the *Journal des savants*. Foucher published a criticism of it in the same journal later that year and Leibniz replied with an 'Explanation of the new system' early in 1696. See p. 374.

Frénicle de Bessy, Bernard (1605–75). French mathematician; his best work was on number theory and magic squares. He enjoyed the unusual distinction of having his work praised by Descartes (letter to Frénicle, 9 Jan. 1639). He was a founding member of the Académie des Sciences. In 1676 *Mariotte edited Frénicle's treatise on rational right-angled triangles with the help of Leibniz who was then in *Paris. See p. 353.

Fromondus. Libert Froidmont (1587–1653). Belgian philosopher and theologian; he wrote objections to Descartes's *Discourse on Method* on its first appearance. The book referred to on p. 225 was entitled *Labyrinthus, sive de compositione continui* (1631). Leibniz appropriated these words – he speaks of 'the labyrinth of the composition of the continuum' in a letter to Oldenburg of March 1671 (II.1, p. 90) – and built on them: 'There are two labyrinths of the human mind: one concerns the composition of the continuum, and the other the nature of freedom, and both spring from the same source – the infinite' (*Morris and Parkinson* p. 107; see also *Theodicy* pp. 53f, 89; *Loemker* pp. 159, 343). Ariadne's thread through this labyrinth is *analysis (p. 369).

Games. Leibniz speaks of the human mind as '*paraissant mieux dans les jeux*' than in more serious pursuits (p. 466). This could mean that the mind *is more thoroughly displayed* in games, or that it *appears to perform more creditably* in games. The latter reading, which we opt for in the translation, expresses an opinion which Leibniz certainly held (*LPG* III, pp. 621, 667 and IV, p. 570). He envisaged 'a comprehensive study of games, dealt with mathematically': first 'all the games which rely on numbers'; next, 'the games which also involve position, such as backgammon, checkers and especially chess'; and after them 'the games which involve motion, such as billiards and tennis'. '"What would be the point of this?" you ask. I reply: to perfect the art of discovery' (*LPG* III, pp. 667ff). Leibniz himself sketched out analyses of the different types of games (see *Couturat* pp. 568ff and *Dutens* V, pp. 203ff).

Gassendi, Pierre (1592–1655). French philosopher. He was the most influential seventeenth-century exponent of the theory of Democritus and Epicurus, that observable events can be fully explained in terms of the motions and groupings of variously shaped small material particles in empty space. See *Edwards*. His doctrines were summarized for his contemporaries in F. Bernier's seven-volume *Abrégé de la philosophie de M. Gassendi* (1674–78), but he is now perhaps best known as the author of the 'Fifth set of objections' (1641) to Descartes's *Meditations*. Leibniz rejected atomism out of hand but remained respectful of Gassendi (see *Loemker* pp. 454, 657). See pp. 67, 70, 374.,

Gold of Toulouse. Leibniz's remark on p. 469 about the Romans' inconsistent attitude to gold is explained by two things: (i) 'In 106 B.C. the pillage of its [sc. Toulouse's] temple by Q. S. Cepio...gave rise to the famous Latin proverb *habet aurum Tolosanum* [he has the gold of Toulouse], in allusion to ill-gotten gains' (*Encyc. Brit.*, 'Toulouse'), and (ii) 'Camillus...lifted the gold out of the scales and gave it to his attendants, and then ordered the Gauls to take their scales and weights and to be off, saying that it was the custom of the Romans to deliver their city with iron and not with gold' (Plutarch's *Lives*, 'Camillus').

Goropius Becanus. Johan van Gorp (1518–72). Dutch physician and philologist. In his *Origines Antverpianae* (1569) he established that the Antwerp dialect was the original language of mankind, spoken in Paradise by Adam and Eve. See p. 285.

Grimaldi, Claudio Filippo (1639–1712). Italian Jesuit scientist and missionary. He joined the *Jesuit mission in Peking in 1671; in 1685 he became President of the (Chinese) Imperial Mathematical Board and, a year later, was sent by the Emperor of China to open communications between Peking and Rome and to deliver a letter to Peter the Great. Leibniz talked to him in Rome, in 1689, in the hope of learning about China, but complained that Grimaldi was only interested in 'plundering Europe to enrich China' (I.7, p. 357). Grimaldi planned to take back with him to China thirty or forty Jesuit scientists, doctors and artisans, and samples of Western technology, including one of Leibniz's calculating machines (I.7, p. 622; *LBG* p. 492). He proposed to send most of his company by sea but himself to travel overland with half a dozen companions, via Moscow. Leibniz, who hoped to see Protestant missionaries follow the same route (*Grua* pp. 204f), was greatly interested. In the event Grimaldi was refused permission to go through Russia and, after travelling through Persia, sailed from Goa for the Far East (I.7, p. 398; I.8, pp. 276f). Leibniz sent a letter after him, full of questions about the countries he was travelling through (I.7, pp. 617ff), which Grimaldi acknowledged tersely from Goa (I.9, pp. 628f). Grimaldi's letter was published with other documents bearing on China in Leibniz's *Novissima Sinica*. See p. 354.

Guericke, Otto von (1602–86). German engineer and natural scientist; as burgomaster of Magdeburg he pursued his researches in his spare time. In 1650 he invented the air-pump. He believed that there was vacuum outside the earth's atmosphere and that, with his air-pump, it was possible to produce a near-vacuum within it (for Leibniz's comments see *Leibniz–Clarke* V, §34). In 1654 he demonstrated that a pair of hemispheres, fitted together and emptied of air, could not be pulled apart by teams of horses. An account of these achievements, at second hand, published in 1657, led *Boyle to investigate the properties of air. Guericke did not publish his own account of his work, in his *Experimenta nova*, until 1672. Leibniz wrote to him in 1671 and they corresponded briefly (II.1, pp. 100ff). See pp. 126, 149.

'habitude'. This can mean 'habit', 'custom', 'character-trait', 'tendency', 'general disposition'. In most occurrences 'disposition' seems right; but where '*disposition*' is also present we render '*habitude*' by 'tendency' instead. Sometimes, notably in II.xxi, '*habitude*' is used to contrast not dispositional with actual, but rather general with particular, within the realm of actual behaviour. In these contexts we use 'habit' or 'practice' or, once, 'regularity of conduct'. On p. 250 we render '*habitude*' by 'general disposition' because Leibniz may there be using the word to embody both the dispositional/actual and general/particular contrasts.

Hardy, Claude (c. 1605–78). French mathematician, linguist and lawyer – the Châtelet housed the law-courts for the city of Paris. He belonged to Mersenne's group in Paris, which became the nucleus of the *Académie des Sciences; Descartes was acquainted with him, mentioned him frequently in his letters and had a high opinion of his abilities. He published a Latin version of Euclid's *Data* (1625) together with Marinus's commentary (fifth century A.D.). Leibniz knew Hardy in Paris; the disagreement between them which is reported on p. 408 concerns the demonstration by Serenus of Antinoeia (c. fourth century A.D.) that the oblique sections of cones and cylinders are both ellipses.

Harlequin. The principal character in Fatouville's *Arlequin, Empereur dans la lune* (1683); the repeated refrain of the final scene is that, on the *moon, everyone behaves 'just like here'. Leibniz adopts this as a fundamental maxim: 'My great principle, as regards natural things, is that of Harlequin, Emperor of the Moon,...*that it is always and everywhere in all things just like here.* That is, that nature is fundamentally uniform, although it varies as to more and less and in degrees of perfection. This results in the simplest and most intelligible philosophy in the world' (*LPG* III, p. 343; see also *Loemker* p. 590). See pp. 71f, 472, 490.

Harz. In 1679 Leibniz undertook to find a more efficient way of pumping water out of the Duke of *Brunswick's silver mines in the Harz mountains, his hope being to apply some of the increased profits to supporting a scientific *academy which he proposed to found in Hanover. In place of water-power, which became insufficient in dry weather, he planned to drive the pumps with wind-power generated by windmills of his own design (see *Gerland* pp. 181ff). He struggled for years with the design and construction of pumps and windmills – one of his projects involved transmitting energy from windmill to pump by means of compressed air (1.3, p. 211; cf. *Gerland* pp. 169f) – perpetually frustrated by bad luck, inadequate materials and the growing hostility of the miners, until finally called off in 1685 by the new Duke (1.4, pp. 189, 205f). During this period Leibniz familiarized himself with every aspect of mining and smelting, from geology to *coining to book-keeping (pp. 206f, 360). His geological findings are presented in his *Protogaea* (1691) and many of his notes and sketches for pumps and windmills are given in *Gerland* (pp. 146ff); F. Klemm, *A History of Western*

Technology (1959, pp. 208ff) quotes Leibniz and an eighteenth-century writer concerning the Harz windmills. See p. 360.

Helmont, Franciscus Mercurius van (1614–98). Flemish scientist, physician, occultist, and theosophist; son of J. B. van Helmont (*archei), whose works he edited. Leibniz seems to have first met him in 1671, at which time he had several 'pretty intimate' conversations with him (*Gerland* p. 10; 1.3, p. 260). In 1680 rumours reached Leibniz, who discounted them, that Helmont was having some success at alchemy and that he had become so 'completely Quakerized' that he refused to doff his hat to princes (1.3, pp. 260, 440, 442). In 1696 Helmont was in Hanover in March and again in August: he conducted morning seminars attended by Princess *Sophie (who was an old friend) and by Leibniz, in which he expounded his own views and those of *More and *Conway (*LPG* III, p. 176). He believed (p. 233) in 'the transmigration of souls, but confined them always within a single species and believed that there was always the same number of men, and likewise of dogs and cats and other sorts of animals and that the soul of a dead animal returned soon after in one newly-born' (*LPG* III, pp. 252f) – Leibniz suggested to him that he could test his theory by seeing whether the birth-rate rose after a massacre (*Stein* p. 335). In particular, Helmont believed that Jesus was Adam reincarnated (p. 240), come back to mend the damage he had done (*LPG* III, p. 306). Helmont's influence on Leibniz's thought was substantial: not only had Leibniz always been fascinated by the alchemical, occultist, theosophical undercurrents (from at least as early as 1667, when he belonged to an alchemists' society in Nuremburg), but he believed that they embodied, in distorted shapes, an important element of truth missing from (but compatible with) mechanism (p. 72). He studied Helmont's writings and kept notes on them (*Grua* pp. 94ff); he is thought to have taken from Helmont the term *'monad' and something of the associated doctrine; though rejecting metempsychosis he seems to have borrowed Helmont's example of the caterpillar and the butterfly (*SB* p. 150) to illustrate his own doctrine of metamorphosis (p. 58; cf. 'Monadology' §§72–4); and his belief that metamorphosis tends towards a higher perfection (p. 139; cf. *Loemker* pp. 490f, 638) apparently owed much to Helmont (*SB* p. 391; *Grua* p. 95).

Hercules. Leibniz's metaphor on p. 52, to which he adverts on pp. 80 and 86f, is not an entirely happy one for what he clearly regards as dispositional properties. He may have acquired the idea of a human form in a block of stone from Pliny, who tells of the stone-breakers in the Parian quarries splitting a stone and finding a likeness of Silenus inside it (*Natural History* XXXVI.iv), or from Albert the Great, who says that he was actually present, in Venice, when a block of marble was sawn in two revealing 'a most beautiful picture of a king's head with a crown and a long beard' (*Book of Minerals* II.iii.1, tr. Wyckoff).

Hippocrates. Compare with Leibniz's remark on p. 55: 'And it can be known, from the nature of things, that as Hippocrates says about the bodies of animals, so in the whole universe *sympnoia panta*; and everything harmonizes with everything in a certain fixed way' (*Couturat* pp. 14f; see also 1.9, pp. 229f). The French and Latin words '*conspirer*/*conspirare*', which we translate 'harmonize', mean literally 'breathe together' – as does the Greek '*sympnoia*'.

Historical credibility. We translate Leibniz's '*de fide historica*' (p. 469) by 'about historical credibility'. This is probably a reference to *De fide historica* *commentarius* (1679) by Johannes Eisenhart (1643–1707), professor of law at Helmstedt. Eisenhart initiated a correspondence with Leibniz in 1677 (1.2, pp. 262ff) which limped on until 1702; Leibniz's letter of Feb. (?) 1679 (1.2, pp. 426ff) is devoted to the question of historical credibility.

Hobbes, Thomas (1588–1679). English philosopher. See *Edwards*. By his own account Leibniz was strongly influenced by Hobbes in his early years – by his political philosophy, his mechanistic account of natural processes and his doctrine that all thinking is computation (*symbolism). He wrote to Hobbes in 1670 (*Loemker* pp. 105ff) – when he was twenty-four and Hobbes eighty-two – but does not seem to have received a reply. Hobbes's doctrine that truth is arbitrarily determined by the imposition of names (cf. p. 396 and *Loemker* pp. 182ff) is presented in *De corpore* 1.iii, §8. Hobbes had useful things to say about mathematics, but his claim to have squared the circle (cf. pp. 95f and *quadrature) embroiled him in protracted and humiliating squabbles with John Wallis and other mathematicians. He was frank about his timidity, but the story (p. 270) that he was afraid of ghosts was, according to his friend John Aubrey, a lie put about by his enemies: 'I have often heard him say that he was not afrayd of *Sprights*, but afrayd of being knockt on the head for five or ten pounds, which rogues might think he had in his chamber' (*Brief Lives*). See *positive. See also p. 273.

Huygens, Christiaan (1629–95). Dutch scientist and mathematician; next to Newton the greatest physicist of the period. His earliest achievements were in geometrical *quadratures. In 1655 he and his brother constructed an improved telescope by means of which he was able to give a correct account of Saturn's rings. In 1656 he designed the first practicable pendulum clock. He continued throughout his career to work on clocks and marine chronometers and in 1675 invented the balance spring (p. 326). His *Ratiociniis in aleae ludo* (1657; English tr. 1692) makes an important early contribution to probability theory (p. 465). In 1665 he received a salaried post at the newly founded *Académie des Sciences in Paris, where he lived until 1681 and where he met and worked with Leibniz. Huygens's study of the dynamics of pendulums (p. 147), *Horologium oscillatorium* (1673), a copy of which he gave to Leibniz in the spring of 1673, was beyond Leibniz's capacities at that time and helped stimulate his serious study of mathematics (*Child* p. 36). Huygens's greatest contributions to optics are in his *Traité de la lumière* (1690; English tr. 1912), in which he propounds the wave theory of light and describes the phenomenon of polarization (*colour). A posthumously published work *Cosmotheoros* (1698; English tr. as *The Celestial Worlds Discovered*, 1698), consists of 'conjectures concerning the inhabitants, plants and productions of the worlds in the planets', in the words of the subtitle (*moon). Huygens grew up in the *Cartesian system and always retained certain of its fundamental principles: e.g. that scientific explanation consists in finding 'the causes of all natural effects in terms of mechanical motions' (*Traité de la lumière*, ch. 1) and that gravitation, light and magnetism are to be explained in terms of the motion of matter in a plenum (*centripetal force). During and after their association in Paris, Leibniz and Huygens carried on an active correspondence, mainly about science and mathematics, until Huygens's death (*LBG* pp. 525ff; also in *HOC, passim*; selections tr. *Loemker* pp. 248ff, 413ff). See also p. 472.

Impulse. 'The act of impelling; an application of sudden force causing motion; a thrust, a push' (*OED*); cf. David Hume: 'The impulse of one billiard-ball is attended with motion in the second' (quoted in *OED*). Leibniz was 'of the opinion that bodies act only by impulse' (p. 130) and sought to introduce the same notion into psychological explanations (see pp. 166, 192). Cf. *centripetal force and *cohesion.

Incline without necessitating. Leibniz is committed in at least two ways to determinism about human action: (i) everything in the material world is rigorously governed by mechanistic principles (*Loemker* pp. 715f) and (ii) every particular fact about any *monad follows inevitably from its inner nature ('Monadology' §22). Faced with the problem of reconciling this with moral accountability, he invokes the notion of factors which 'incline without necessitating' (*Loemker* pp. 226f). The phrase, as he notes (*Theodicy* p. 147), echoes the astrologers' maxim that 'the stars incline but do not necessitate' – in consequence, he adds, it is misleading: the astrologers mean that 'the event towards which the stars tend . . . does not always come to pass, whereas the course towards which the will is more inclined never fails to be adopted' (cf. p. 199 of the text). Leibniz wishes to distinguish his position both from *Spinoza's *necessitarianism* and from *indeterminism* or 'the liberty of indifference' (pp. 116, 188; cf. *Theodicy* pp. 143ff). To do so he differentiates between necessity and determinism – or, as he sometimes confusingly puts it, between *absolute* necessity and *hypothetical* necessity (e.g. *Leibniz–Arnauld* p. 13). It is not (absolutely) necessary – though morally inevitable – that God always acts for the best; so the *pre-established harmony among monads, which arises from God's will, is not necessary, and thus the laws which govern the material world, in expression of that harmony, are not necessary either (pp. 178f; *Leibniz–Clarke* v, §§2ff). When Leibniz also says that within an individual soul or monad the earlier states can lead to a later one – or that reasons can lead to a movement of the will – by 'inclining without necessitating' (p. 175; 'Discourse on metaphysics' §13) this seems not to square with the claim that it is of the nature of each monad to have 'a concept so complete' that 'the individual concept of Adam contains everything that will ever happen to him' (*Leibniz–Arnauld* p. 47). Nor is it clear that the accountability problem is solved by a plea that the determining relation is not absolutely necessary since it is admittedly 'certain and infallible' (p. 175). Leibniz struggles with both difficulties in 'Discourse on metaphysics' §30 and in *Leibniz–Arnauld*.

Infinitesimal calculus. Leibniz was almost entirely ignorant of the advances in mathematics made in his own century until the spring of 1673; by the autumn of 1675 he had discovered the fundamental principles of the integral and differential calculus. Contrary to later allegations he did so without any clear awareness of the work of Barrow and Newton in the same area. Shortly after his arrival in *Paris, he was encouraged by *Huygens to pursue his interest in number series, with the result that he succeeded almost immediately in summing certain infinite series of fractions (*Child* pp. 49f). The discovery that others had already reached the same results, and his inability to understand Huygens's *Horologium oscillatorium* (1673), induced him to study recent developments in mathematics (*Child* p. 215). He made rapid progress in geometry during 1673, to which he applied the notion of an infinitesimal element of a curve. (The notion of infinitesimal quantities, which is basic to Leibniz's formulation of the calculus, has been regarded as a weak point in his account; it has recently been argued, by A. Robinson, *Non-standard Analysis* (1966), 'that Leibniz' ideas can be fully vindicated and that they lead to a novel and fruitful approach to classical Analysis and to many other branches of mathematics', p. 2.) At the end of 1673 or early in the next year he found the rational *quadrature of a segment of the cycloid and the 'arithmetical tetragonism' of the circle (p. 85). These discoveries are described in his letter of 15 July 1674 to *Oldenburg (III.1, pp. 119f; tr. *OC* XI, pp. 45f; see also *Child* pp. 42ff). In October 1674 he recognized that 'the quadratures of all figures follow from the inverse method of tangents, and thus the whole science of sums and quadratures can be reduced to analysis, a thing that nobody even had any hopes of before' (*Child* pp. 60f). A year later, after an excursion into clock design and the solution of higher *equations, he returned to inverse-tangent problems: he now introduced the symbols ∫ and d to represent the operations of summation (or integration) and differentiation and proceeded to express his discoveries about tangents and quadratures in this new notation. There is a detailed account of Leibniz's mathematical work during this period in J. E. Hofmann, *Leibniz in Paris 1672–1676* (1974). In mid-1676 Newton and Leibniz began a correspondence, via Oldenburg, and in June 1677 Leibniz wrote Newton a full and clear account of the differential calculus (*NC* II, pp. 212ff; all the Newton–Leibniz letters of this period are in *NC* II; see also III.1). In 1684 Leibniz published a summary account of the differential calculus in the *Acta eruditorum*: 'A new method for maxima and minima'. Two years later, in the same journal, he gave details of the integral calculus: 'On a deeply hidden geometry'. Thereafter the calculus developed rapidly; Leibniz left much of the work for other, younger mathematicians – 'I cannot spare the time for long calculations. I proceed like the tiger, of which it is said that what he cannot catch in one, two, three bounds he lets run away' (*LMG* VII, pp. 377f) – most notably the brothers Jakob and Johann Bernoulli. Mathematicians in England had never entirely revised their initial negative impression of Leibniz, formed during his London visit in 1673, and their suspicions increased with the magnitude of his achievements. In 1699 an associate of Newton's hinted that Leibniz had acquired the essential ideas for the calculus from Newton; in the preface to the first edition of the *Opticks* (1704) Newton revealed a similar suspicion – and Leibniz, in 1705, in an anonymous review of the mathematical essays appended to the *Opticks*, hinted that Newton had borrowed from *him*. In 1708 another of Newton's associates, John Keill, openly accused Leibniz of plagiarism. In response to Leibniz's protest the Royal Society appointed a committee, in March 1712, to examine and publish the relevant documents and to report as to Keill's accusation. The committee, which worked in close touch with Newton, reported in April 1712; its findings were published as *Commercium epistolicum* (1712) and were, predictably, derogatory of Leibniz. Leibniz wrote his own account of the discovery of the calculus – 'History and origin of the differential calculus' – but did not publish it; its veracity has been substantiated by Hofmann's inquiries. There is a full and fair-minded account of the Newton–Leibniz controversy in A. R. Hall, *Philosophers at War* (1980); much of the primary material is published, with English translations in *NC* v and vi. See pp. 389, 489.

Inner tribunal. I.e. *'forum internum'* (see p. 526). Medieval writers speak interchangeably of the *forum internum* and the *forum conscientiae* – the tribunal of conscience – in contrast to the *forum externum* – the outer tribunal of Church or State. Cf. Hobbes: 'The laws of nature oblige *in foro interno*; that is to say, they bind to a desire they should take place; but *in foro externo*; that is, to the putting them in act, not always' (*Leviathan* 1.15).

In quarto modo. Literally, 'in the fourth manner'. Porphyry's *Isagoge* (third century A.D.), revising Aristotle, lists five *predicables*, i.e. 'classes or kinds of predicates viewed relatively to their subjects' (*OED*), namely: genus, species, difference, property, accident. The fourth of these, property, comprises any predicate 'which is not the essence of the subject, yet belongs to that species alone and is predicated convertibly of it' (W. and M. Kneale, *The Development of Logic* (1962), p. 35). See p. 400.

'institution'. This is used to translate '*institution*', which carries a special emphasis on something's being instituted voluntarily, by fiat. There is thus a strong contrast between *institution* and *nature*. When Leibniz says (p. 499) that the laws of nature result from God's institution, 'so to speak', he is offering a small logical joke. At p. 278, Locke's 'imposition' is Coste's '*institution*'.

'invent'. The French '*inventer*' is sometimes rendered by 'discover' (so is '*découvrir*', though sometimes it is rendered by 'reveal'). Occasionally 'invent' is used because it is Locke's word (on p. 453 we adopt Locke's 'invent' and 'find out', though Coste uses '*inventer*' for both). On about ten occasions, all in Book IV, 'invent' is used because Leibniz is invoking a distinction between '*jugement*' and '*invention*' belonging to a certain theory about logical activity (cf. *Ramus, *topics), and English formulations of that theory standardly use 'invention'. There are borderline cases: on pp. 416f, for instance, four occurrences of 'discover' ought perhaps to be 'invent'; and similarly with 'discovered' and 'discovery' on pp. 524f. On p. 483 'invention' occurs because, as the footnote shows, Leibniz has crammed the judgment/invention distinction into Philalethes' mouth with little basis in Locke's text. In that passage, 'discovery' renders '*découverte*'.

'item'. The French '*être*', the verb 'to be', is also a noun which we usually render by 'being'; though on stylistic grounds we employ 'entity' on pp. 217, 398, and in rendering Leibniz's frequently repeated phrase '*être substantiel*'. On p. 216, where '*être*' seems to be maximally non-committal, we have recourse to 'item'. None of the three English words mentioned above is used for anything but '*être*', except that 'item of knowledge' always translates '*une connaissance*', and on p. 385 '*choses morales*' is translated as 'moral entities' (*Weigel).

Jesuit missionaries in China. Following in the path of St Francis Xavier the Jesuits founded a mission in China in 1582, from 1601 located in Peking. From the start they wooed the Chinese with Western science and mathematics. They also took a tolerant attitude towards Confucianism and ancestor worship. Criticism by missionaries from other orders led to the Chinese Rites Controversy. A papal commission in Rome studied the problem in 1697–1704 and took a conciliatory position, but the final resolution in 1742 was unfavourable to the Jesuits. Cf. *Grimaldi. See pp. 501f.

Journals. Leibniz published extensively in most of the scholarly journals of his day, beginning with the *Journal des savants* (Paris 1665– ; from 1684 a pirated edition also appeared in Amsterdam). Most of his articles appeared in Mencke's *Acta eruditorum* (Leipzig 1682–1731) of which he himself was one of the founders (1.3, pp. 502ff). He also published in *Bayle's short-lived *Nouvelles de la* *république des lettres* (Rotterdam 1684–7) and in its successor, the *Histoire des ouvrages des savants* (Rotterdam 1687–1709), and in *Oldenburg's *Philosophical Transactions* of the Royal Society (London 1665–). After 1701 he published frequently in the Jesuits' *Mémoires pour servir à l'histoire des sciences et des beaux arts* (Trévoux 1701–67), known as the *Mémoires de Trévoux*. Cf. *Mercure galant. See p. 71.

Koerbagh, Adriaan (?–1669). Dutch lawyer and physician. He was a friend of *Spinoza's and the author of *Een bloemhof van allerley lieflijkheyd* (1668), 'a flower-garden of assorted delights'; this was a philosophical dictionary with extensive digressions, rather like *Bayle's, and inspired by Spinozism. Its publication led to Koerbagh's arrest and trial; the cross-examination persistently, but unsuccessfully, attempted to implicate Spinoza. Koerbagh's book was suppressed and he was fined 4000 florins, plus 2000 florins costs, and sentenced to ten years imprisonment followed by ten years banishment (see *Freudenthal* pp. 119ff). He died in prison eighteen months later. See p. 277.

Labadists. Followers of Jean de Labadie (1610–74); a French Jesuit, he converted to Protestantism about 1650 and taught an extreme form of pietism according to which the Bible can be understood only by means of direct spiritual inspiration. See p. 507.

La Loubère, Simon de (1642–1729). French lawyer and diplomat. He visited Hanover in 1680, in connection with settling the estate of Duke Johann Friedrich, and talked to Leibniz about mathematics. They carried on a desultory correspondence thereafter (1.3, pp. 366ff). During 1687–8 La Loubère was 'envoy extraordinary' from Louis XIV to the King of Siam (the King wanted French protection from Dutch rapacity, and the French wanted a trade agreement and garrisons in Bangkok and Mergui); on his return to France he published his *Du royaume de Siam* (1691; English tr. 1693), 'wherein a full and curious account is given of the Chinese way of arithmetick, and mathematical learning'. In 1691 he sent Leibniz a copy of his book (1.6, pp. 504f) and they resumed their correspondence – on mathematics and oriental languages – which went on until 1705 (1.7, pp. 384ff). It was La Loubère who informed *Bossuet that Leibniz, in addition to being a theologian, was also a philosopher (1.7, p. 289). See p. 65.

Lamy, François (1636–1711). French Benedictine and philosopher. In the 'Analysis' which concludes the second treatise of his *De la connaissance de soi-même* (1694–8), Lamy says that, when he examined Leibniz's account of the union of the mind and the body, 'he found himself at first very pleasantly struck by it and so delighted that he was on the point of accepting it...since it seemed to him both simpler and wiser' than its rivals, interactionism and *occasionalism. But more careful reflection dispelled the charm – and he proceeds to make a series of objections. Leibniz's replies to these are in *LPG* IV, pp. 572–95. See p. 383.

Lannion, Pierre de (1644–?). French mathematician and philosopher. He published his *Méditations sur la métaphysique* (1678) under the pseudonymn 'Guillaume Wander' and ostensibly at Cologne – actually at Paris. Leibniz attributed it to *Malebranche whom he congratulated accordingly; Malebranche identified the author as the 'Abbé de Lanion' (II.1, pp. 477, 480; tr. *Loemker* pp. 210, 212. See also *Theodicy* p. 169). In 1679 Lannion was made a member of the *Académie des Sciences; he became its president in 1684 but was expelled in 1686. *Bayle re-issued the *Méditations* in his *Recueil de quelques pièces curieuses* *concernant la philosophie de M. Descartes* (1684) – see his *Oeuvres diverses* (1727–31) III, p. 547. Lannion and *Huygens were acquainted – see *HOC* IX, pp. 250ff. See p. 233.

Large numbers. Leibniz is presumably referring, on pp. 458 and 518, to the argument advanced by Pierre Jurieu in his *Vrai système de l'Église* (1686) and attacked by *Nicole (in his *De l'unité de l'Église*, 1687), *Pellisson (*Réflexions sur les différends de la religion* II, 1687) and *Bayle (*Dictionary*, 'Arius' and 'Nicole'). According to Jurieu (*Vrai système* p. 236), the major Christian communities – 'Greeks, Latins, Protestants, Abyssinians, Armenians, Nestorians, Russians etc.' – constitute the Universal Church and those doctrines on which they agree represent the essential and infallible truths of the Christian faith: 'For God could not allow large Christian societies to fall into mortal errors and to persist in them for long; at least, if we are guided by experience we ought not to believe this to be possible, since it has not happened.' Nicole replied that of all doctrines the one most universally and persistently accepted is 'that the Catholic Church is one unique community, from which all heretical sects are excluded'; every community 'has claimed to be the Catholic Church...but at the same time they have agreed that there is only one such'; Jurieu is guilty of 'prodigious temerity' in proposing 'his new system which compiles the Catholic Church out of all those sects which, in his opinion, have preserved their trust' (*De l'unité* pp. 236–7).

Leeuwenhoek, Antoni van (1632–1723). Dutch scientist and instrument maker. He produced the finest lenses and the most powerful microscopes of his day and used them to observe, among other things, the union of ova and spermatozoa. He believed that life and the inherited traits of the new organism come from the male parent via the spermatozoon – he attempted to prove this by mating grey male rabbits with white females, thereby producing grey offspring. The controversy between the proponents of this 'animalculist' theory and 'ovists' like Theodor Kerckring (1640–93), who championed the ovum as the source of life and inherent nature, raged on for a century. Leibniz greeted Leeuwenhoek's discovery of microscopic life as evidence that 'the birth of every animal is merely a transformation of an animal already alive' and as confirming his own system (*Leibniz–Arnauld* pp. 98, 156f; *Theodicy* pp. 172f). Although Leibniz visited Leeuwenhoek in Delft in 1676, on his way from *Paris to Hanover, their existing correspondence dates from 1715–16: Leibniz apprised Leeuwenhoek of his theory of animal transformation and urged him to publish more of his findings and to consider setting up a school of microscopy, 'to swell the hoard of human knowledge' (*Bodemann* p. 133). See p. 316.

Le Gobien, Charles (1653–1708). French Jesuit historian; secretary, in Paris, of the *Jesuit mission in China. He was the author of an *Histoire des îles Mariannes* (1700). Leibniz corresponded with him between 1698 and 1703, mostly about China and the Far East. In November 1701 Le Gobien wrote to Leibniz at length 'on the ceremonies which the Chinese perform in honour of Confucius; [that] the Emperor of China is the head of the state religion; [and] on the early missionaries' (*Dutens* IV.1, pp. 145ff). See p. 105.

'liaison'. This means 'connection', and is often so used by Coste and by us. Where we use 'link', this translates '*liaison*' in a context where '*connexion*' is also present and/or Leibniz seems to have in mind a less-than-necessary connection. The cases satisfying the latter condition are not deeply or sharply demarcated; and we are sure that Leibniz often made no considered distinction between '*liaison*' and '*connexion*' – a fact which is reflected in our using 'connection' sometimes for the former and always for the latter.

'*liberté*'. Coste uses this for both 'freedom' and 'liberty'. We follow Locke in rendering Philalethes, but for Theophilus we put 'freedom' throughout.

Library. Leibniz was, in the words of Christian Thomasius, 'a living library' (*Bodemann* p. 336); he was also for forty years a working librarian. He went to Hanover, in 1676, as, among other things, Librarian to Duke Johann Friedrich of *Brunswick, and he continued to occupy this post until his death. Had he been willing to convert to Roman Catholicism, in 1689, he would, it seems, have been given charge of the Vatican Library, 'from which one moves on often enough to the cardinalate'; the same condition caused him to decline the post of Royal Librarian in Paris a few years later (*Bodemann* pp. 4, 143). In 1690, while retaining his post at Hanover, he also became Director of the Bibliotheca Augusta in Wolfenbüttel (1.6, pp. 17f), one of the finest libraries in Germany; not only did he see to the production of a comprehensive author catalogue – the first ever compiled for a major German library, and the only one before the nineteenth century – for the Bibliotheca Augusta (1.6, pp. 52, 55ff), but, between 1705 and 1713, he supervised the planning and construction of a new building to house the collection, the first free-standing library building built in the modern era. Leibniz's career as a librarian is described in L. M. Newman, *Leibniz (1646–1716) and the German Library Scene* (1966); it contains translations of two papers on library management by Leibniz. See p. 524.

Lignum nephriticum. The wood of the horse-radish tree. The infusion was used in treating kidney disease. According to Isaac Newton, 'there are some liquors, as the tincture of *lignum nephriticum*...which transmit one sort of light most copiously, and reflect another sort, and thereby look of several colours, according to the position of the eye to the light'; in daylight the infusion 'looks blue by the reflected part of the light, and red by the transmitted part of it' (*Opticks* 1.2, Props. 10–11). See p. 382.

'*likely*'. This translates '*vraisemblable*', except for a few places where it translates '*apparent*'. The latter usually means 'apparent', but clearly means 'likely' in some passages, e.g. pp. 138, 153, 459–517. Its uses on pp. 325 and 459 seem to combine both meanings. On p. 459 Locke has said that the scope of certain items is restricted to how 'they appear', faithfully rendered by Coste as '*ils paraissent*'; but Leibniz says that the scope is restricted by the '*degré de l'Apparence*' which is found in them, which has to mean 'degree of likelihood'. We do not know what governed Leibniz's choice between '*vraisemblance*' and '*apparence*', but it seems not to have been a difference of meaning: his use first of one and then the other near the start of p. 517 suggests that for him they are synonymous. We render '*probable*' by 'probable' throughout, and use the latter for no other purpose except for a few occurrences of the confident-conjecture use of the future tense ('*Il sera à la maison*', 'He's probably at home').

Love. In the Preface to his *Codex juris gentium* (1693) Leibniz proposed a solution to 'the knotty question of how there can be a disinterested love which is free from hope and fear, and from every consideration of utility' (*Loemker* p. 421); he thereby anticipated the bitter dispute over the nature of disinterested love that broke out a few years later between *Bossuet, on the one side, and François Fénelon and the *Quietists on the other. Fénelon's *Explications des maximes des saints* (1697) advocated a disinterested love of God so free from desire for personal happiness as to be indifferent to salvation. In consequence he was attacked by Bossuet, exiled to his diocese by Louis XIV and, in 1699, condemned by the Pope (see *Loemker* p. 424), who remarked that Fénelon had erred by loving God too much and Bossuet by loving his neighbour too little (*Encyc. Brit.*, 'Fénelon'). Leibniz distinguishes between *mercenary* love, which is straightforwardly self-interested, and *disinterested* love, which occurs in those cases in which 'we find that not only our own advantage but even our pleasure is in the good of someone else' (*Loemker* p. 630; cf. *Loemker* pp. 594f). See p. 163.

Malebranche, Nicolas (1638–1715). French philosopher. See *Edwards*. In the main he accepted the *Cartesian account of man and nature, but with two major modifications: that we do not perceive the physical world directly but see everything, particulars and universals, 'in God'; and that there is no causal nexus between minds and bodies or even between one physical event and another, but that God acts directly on each individual thing in a way generally consistent with the laws of nature (*occasional causes). These doctrines were first put forward in his *Recherche de la vérité* (1674–5). Leibniz became acquainted with him in *Paris and they carried on a desultory correspondence for the rest of their lives (*LPG* I, pp. 315ff; selections tr. in *Loemker* pp. 209–12). Leibniz's criticisms, e.g. in his 'Letter on a general principle useful in explaining the laws of nature', induced Malebranche, in his *Traité des lois de la communication des mouvements* (1692), to abandon the Cartesian laws of motion (see *Loemker* p. 448). See pp. 70, 171.

Mariotte, Edmé (1620–84). French scientist and mathematician. In addition to his independent discovery of *Boyle's Law, he discovered the blind spot in the eye, caused by the fovea – *Nouvelle découverte touchant la vue* (1668); and he formulated a theory as to the nature of *colours – 'De la nature des couleurs', in his *Essais de physique* (1679–81). He was one of the founding members of the *Académie des Sciences. Leibniz knew him well in *Paris and they corresponded on scientific and mathematical topics (II.1 and III.1). See *Frénicle. See pp. 121, 309.

Masham, Damaris (1658–1708). Daughter of the Cambridge Platonist Ralph Cudworth (1617–88), the author of *The True Intellectual System of the Universe* (1678). She linked her father's circle with Locke's. Among the frequent visitors at her home, Oates, were Newton, Shaftesbury, Samuel Clarke, John Norris; Locke lived there for the last dozen years of his life; Coste was her son's tutor. In 1703 she sent a copy of her father's book to Leibniz, and a philosophical correspondence ensued which continued until her death (see *LPG* III, pp. 331–75). On Cudworth see *Edwards* and *Loemker* p. 589. See p. 70.

Mechanical. In mathematics, 'applied to curves not expressible by equations of finite and rational algebraical form; = Transcendental'(*OED*). In *Geometry* II *Descartes distinguishes between 'geometry' as 'that which is precise and exact' and 'mechanics...which is not; the spiral, the quadratrix, and similar curves...truly belong only to mechanics and are not among the number that I think should be included here; for we can conceive them as being described by two separate movements which have no precisely measurable relation to each other' (tr. Olscamp). Leibniz discovered that problems of *quadrature 'might be reduced to equations, in which the exponents of the powers were unknowns'; he called the resulting analysis *transcendental 'because it employed equations beyond all degrees', and he called 'algebraical' those lines 'that Descartes calls geometrical' (*LBG* p. 409; tr. *Child* p. 219). Describing his invention of the *infinitesimal calculus, Leibniz (speaking in the third person) says that the more advanced, or Archimedean, parts of geometry were called 'mechanical' by Descartes and excluded from his system, 'but now by the calculus of Leibniz the whole of geometry is subjected to analytical computation, and those transcendent lines that Descartes called mechanical are also reduced to equations chosen to suit them, by considering the differences dx, ddx etc., and the sums that are the inverses of these differences, as functions of the x's; and this, by merely introducing the calculus, whereas before this no other functions were admissible but x, xx, x^3, $\sqrt{x}$ etc., that is to say, powers and roots' (*LMG* v, p. 394; tr. *Child* p. 26. See *Leibniz–Arnauld* pp. 70f). See p. 489.

Meier, Gerhard (1646–1703). Mathematician, historian, linguist, theologian; church pastor in Bremen. He met Leibniz in 1690, while visiting Hanover, and thereafter they corresponded regularly until Meier's death; during the early part of this period Meier also served as the intermediary for the correspondence between Leibniz and *Huygens. The Leibniz–Meier correspondence ranges over *Cartesian philosophy, theology, German history, and, most especially, the history of German dialects (1.6ff). Leibniz included a selection from it in his *Collectanea etymologica* (together with, among other things, his own 'Unvorgreifliche Gedanken', selected correspondence with *Witsen, and Clauberg's *Ars etymologica Teutonum* which is referred to on p. 285). Meier left an unfinished *Glossarium linguae Saxonicae*, which is presumably the work referred to on p. 286.

'memory'. This translates '*souvenir*' and, less often, '*mémoire*'. On p. 77 both words occur in a manner suggesting that for Leibniz they are synonymous, though he may have some tendency to use the former for the activity and the latter for the faculty (pp. 140, 206). Throughout the work, 'recollection' translates '*réminiscence*', though at pp. 106f the latter is rendered by 'remembering', in fidelity to Locke's text.

Mercure galant. French popular newspaper, founded in 1672; under its later name, *Mercure de France*, it survived until the mid nineteenth century. The *Journal des savants* of 4 March 1686 testifies to the *Mercure*'s success in popularizing scientific ideas: it has enabled the mathematicians and their jargon to find their way into ladies' sitting-rooms and bedrooms 'to such an extent that no one talks of anything but problems, corollaries, theorems, right angles, obtuse angles, rhomboids, and the like'; things have gone so far that in Paris one young lady has refused to listen to proposals of marriage until her suitor has learned how to make one of the telescopes 'so often described in the *Mercure galant*', and another 'has turned down a perfectly respectable man because he failed, in the time she gave him, to make an original contribution to squaring the circle.' See p. 387.

Méré, Antoine Gombault, Chevalier de (1607–84). Parisian wit, gambler, free-thinker, and authority on questions of decorum; he wrote several volumes of *Discours*, including *Des agréments* (1677). He was acquainted with Blaise Pascal and, in about 1654, asked him about calculating the relative chances of each of the players in an unfinished game, as a basis for dividing the stake; according to Leibniz, 'being a great gambler, [Méré] made the first ventures into the calculation of divisions [*partis*], and it was this that led to the beautiful studies on chance by MM. Fermat, Pascal and *Huygens, of which M. *Roberval could or would understand nothing' (*LPG* IV, p. 570; tr. *Loemker* p. 584. Gerhardt misreads '*partis*' as '*paris*' and Loemker accordingly translates it 'wagers'). Two kinds of cases are discussed. In the first, which Méré was able to solve, a player has to obtain, say, a pair of sixes in a given number of throws of two dice, in order to win: what are his chances? In the second, for any game which is won by the player who first accumulates a certain number of points, what are each player's chances of winning at any given stage of the game? Pascal and Fermat gave solutions for several cases, in letters written to each other in 1654. Huygens's *De ratiociniis in ludo aleae* (1657) gives solutions for various other cases. Leibniz had heard something of Méré and of the problem of the division of the stake when he was in *Paris (*Couturat* p. 575) but he seems not to have got the whole story until 1696 (see *Loemker* p. 472). See *games and *probability. See p. 465.

Mill. Leibniz's remark on pp. 66f, that 'a sentient or thinking being is not a mechanical thing like a watch or a mill' and that 'one cannot conceive of sizes and shapes and motions combining mechanically to produce something which thinks, and senses too', represents a preliminary draft of an argument presented more fully in 'Monadology' §17: 'Furthermore, we must admit that *perception*, and whatever depends on it, *cannot be explained on mechanical principles*, i.e. by shapes and movements. If we pretend that there is a machine whose structure makes it think, sense and have perception, then we can conceive it enlarged, but keeping to the same proportions, so that we might go inside it as into a mill. Suppose that we do: then if we inspect the interior we shall find there nothing but parts which push one another, and never anything which could explain a perception. Thus, perception must be sought in simple substances, not in what is composite or in machines.' See also p. 440.

Minute perceptions. This expression is used to translate Leibniz's '*petites perceptions*'. Leibniz holds that each person's mind reflects everything that is happening in the universe ('Discourse on metaphysics' §9), that every change in a mind or *monad is a 'perception' and that we have countless perceptions of which we have no *awareness – we can be unaware of a perception either because it is too unvarying or because it is too '*petite*' (p. 53). When Leibniz speaks of a perception as '*petite*', he implies that it lacks at least some sort of magnitude which perceptions can have, but he seems never to explain what magnitudes he has in mind. There seem to be only two candidates: a perception may be '*petite*' because it lacks intensive magnitude, i.e. is *weak*; or because it lacks temporal extensive magnitude, i.e. is *brief*. It cannot lack spatial extensive magnitude by being literally *small*, since for Leibniz perceptions are not spatial (e.g. p. 145). The existence of minute perceptions accounts for the confused perceptions of which we are aware: for example, Leibniz says that one's perception of the roaring of the sea contains as many minute perceptions as there are waves breaking on the beach at any moment; each wave alters the mind of the hearer and their totality alters it enough for him to be aware of a confused roaring noise (p. 54; see also pp. 120, 134). And minute perceptions are essential for explaining human actions (pp. 115f, 194). See also pp. 164f.

Mirror. This example seems to derive from a controversy between Leibniz and Tschirnhaus, about 1682, over the design of concave mirrors – Tschirnhaus was attempting to construct a solar furnace (*LBG* pp. 414ff). The controversy is alluded to in the Leibniz–*Huygens correspondence of 1691–2 (*LBG* pp. 603, 647, 651f). See pp. 368, 402.

Mnemonics. Leibniz's writings contain repeated references to the possibility of an art of mnemonics, 'that is, an art of retaining and recalling to mind those things that we have learned'; and he adds that 'that part ought especially to be cultivated, namely the art of recollection, by means of which we recall the things we need that lurk in our memory but do not come to mind – for retention is one thing and recall is another' (*Couturat* p. 37. See also *Morris and Parkinson* p. 5, *Wiener* pp. 77ff, *Loemker* p. 464). There are various devices by which memory is assisted: diagrams, humorous verses, lists of items associated with the terms of some familiar ordered series; he illustrates the last of these, using the names of the successive Emperors of Rome as his familiar series (*Couturat* p. 281). In his *New Method for Learning and Teaching Jurisprudence*, and in extensive revisions carried out thirty years later, Leibniz puts forward memory and reason – the latter in turn comprising invention and judgment (cf. pp. 291, 476 of the text) – as mental capacities proper to man; to these two capacities correspond mnemonics and logic (*analysis, *topics). Mnemonics depends upon perceptible *marks* which stand in some definite relationship to the things to be remembered – hence the invention of words, which 'are not merely signs of my present thoughts to others but are also marks of my past thoughts to myself'. Those marks 'are most mnemonic, moreover, which are most perceptible', and hence the efficacy of diagrams, verses and pictographic languages like Chinese and ancient Egyptian. 'But what pertains most of all to mnemonics and the theory of marks is the understanding of language whence its foundation derives' (VI.1, pp. 277ff; tr. in part *Loemker* p. 88). Leibniz's ideas about mnemonics and 'the theory of marks' presumably connect with his plans for a universal *symbolism which, among other things, will have the notable feature that 'he who has once learned this language will be unable to forget it, or if he does forget it will easily by himself recover all the necessary terms' (*LPG* VII, p. 13). The relationship between Leibniz's thoughts on mnemonics and those of his predecessors is explored in F. A. Yates, *The Art of Memory* (1966). See pp. 77, 206.

Mola. 'A fleshy mass occurring in the womb; a false conception' (*OED*).

Molyneux, William (1656–98). Irish scientist, philosopher and politician. His *Dioptrica Nova, a Treatise of Dioptrics* (1692) summarized and commended Leibniz's theory of the refraction of light, as expounded in his 'Unicum opticae, catoptricae et dioptricae principium' (see *Loemker* pp. 442, 479ff). Locke and Molyneux were close friends; their correspondence, from 1692–8, was published in *Some Familiar Letters between Mr Locke and Several of his Friends* (1708). Molyneux communicated his 'jocose problem' to Locke in his letter of 2 March 1693. In April 1697 Locke sent to Molyneux a copy of 'Quelques remarques sur le livre de M. Locke intitulé *Essay of Understanding*'; Leibniz had sent it some time earlier to his friend Thomas Burnett (*LPG* III, p. 176), adding in his next letter that Burnett might show it to whomsoever he wished and that if it fell into

Locke's hands 'so much the better, for that will give him the opportunity to instruct us and to illuminate the matter' (*LPG* III, p. 180). Locke sent back fulsome comments on Leibniz's erudition but professed himself too busy to provide illumination (*LPG* III, p. 197); however, his remark to Burnett that 'we get on very amicably with German gentlemen because they don't understand our books and we don't read theirs' (*LPG* III, p. 208) is more revealing. In their next few letters Locke and Molyneux outdid each other in denigrating Leibniz – all of which came eventually to his notice when the *Familiar Letters* were published (see *Loemker* pp. 656ff). See pp. 135f, 423.

Monad. Leibniz's word for what he took to be the ultimate constituents of reality, the simple substances out of which the universe is made up; since monads have no parts they are indivisible and unextended ('Monadology' §§ 1–3; cf. *Leibniz–Arnauld* pp. 93ff). Minds are monads, and even monads which are not minds are on a continuum with those which are. Leibniz is therefore willing to call each episodic state of a monad a 'perception', though possibly only a *minute one, an individual monad's history being just the sequence of its 'perceptions' of the states of all the other monads from its own point of view. These perceptions are not caused by the other monads, but come about through the *pre-established harmony. The extended world does not have monads as parts, but is a 'result' of them (*Loemker* p. 536). When Leibniz calls monads *substantial forms (*Loemker* pp. 503f), he is thinking not of their *being* individuals but of their role in conferring a kind of individuality on organisms (p. 231). Leibniz can maintain that every monad is a substantial form because he holds not merely that the entire material realm is organic (p. 72) but, even more strongly, that every monad has an organic body (p. 68). Matter comes and goes in this body, but the body is never annihilated: Leibniz defends the immortality not just of the 'soul' but of the 'animal' (p. 329). The doctrine that *every monad dominates a body* sits uneasily with the doctrine that *every body is a colony of monads*, but contradiction is presumably avoided because Leibniz can invoke an infinite regress (*Loemker* p. 590). However, since no monad can really act on any other, the sense in which one monad can *confer* unity on an organic body must be a very attenuated one. Yet Leibniz attached great significance to their role as substantial forms and freely spoke of them in terms of 'activity', 'motive force' and *'entelechy' ('Monadology' §§61–82). Cf. *phenomenon. See also pp. 440, 443, 473.

Moon. Increasing acceptance of the Copernican theory and, more particularly, Galileo's description, in his *Sidereus nuncius* (1610), of the moon as seen through a telescope created a new fashion in science fiction (pp. 314, 472). The medieval idea that the moon and the other heavenly bodies are the aetherial abode of departed spirits was giving way to the idea that they are earthy spheres, much like our own, perhaps inhabited by living beings and in principle accessible to explorers from our planet. The *Somnium* (1634; English tr. 1967) of Johannes Kepler (1571–1630) is the first of these seventeenth-century accounts of moon travel; its hero is transported to the moon by sorcery, but what he finds there is pretty consistent with the best scientific knowledge of the time. *Huygens's *Cosmotheoros* (1698) and *Fontenelle's *Entretiens sur la pluralité des mondes* (1686; English tr. 1688) are similarly constrained: although both are much concerned with questions about the inhabitation of the sun, moon and planets, and both draw on the notion of space travel to the extent of urging their readers to imagine themselves voyaging through the heavens, still they are both primarily popular accounts of the latest discoveries in astronomy and of their philosophical implications. *The Man in the Moone: or a Discourse of a Voyage Thither* (1638) by Bishop Francis Godwin (1562–1633) shows little concern for scientific fact or possibility: its hero, Domingo Gonsales, tells how he has been carried to the moon by a flock of migrating swans harnessed to an ingenious contraption in which he rides; he finds a lunarian utopia there which he leaves with regret when it is time for his swans to migrate back to earth. These same lunarians reappear in Fatouville's *Arlequin* (*Harlequin) and in the *États et empires de la lune* (1657) and *du soleil* (1662) of Cyrano de Bergerac (1619–55). Cyrano's voyages satirize accounts of space travel and much else: he sets out for the moon, borne up by vials of dew which is drawn towards the sun; to control his flight and guide it towards the moon he breaks some of the vials – too many, and he crash-lands in Canada. His second, inadvertent, voyage is by rocket; this time he does reach the moon, where he meets Gonsales amongst others. His last voyage, in a space vehicle powered by solar energy, takes him to the sun and to the 'great plains of day'.

More, Henry (1614–87). English philosopher and theologian; Cambridge Platonist. His uncle, who saw to his education, threatened to flog him 'for his immature forwardness in philosophising' (*DNB*). See *Edwards*. During 1648–9 he initiated and pursued an important correspondence with *Descartes; in spite of his initial enthusiasm he later became a vigorous opponent of what he saw as the atheistic tendencies of *Cartesian mechanism. In his *Immortality of the Soul* (1659), 1.3, §1, he distinguishes two kinds of substances, *spirit* and *matter*, both extended; a spirit is capable of self-penetration, and thereby of genuine condensation and rarefaction (p. 82), and of penetrating matter (*penetration of dimensions) and animating it (*Immortality* 1.7; see also *Leibniz–Clarke* v, §48). The various species of spirits animate appropriate kinds of material bodies, or *vehicles*; in particular, 'the Soul of an *Angel* may vitally actuate an *Aerial* or *Aetherial* Body, but cannot be born into this world in a *Terrestrial* one' (*Immortality* 1.8. §6; see p. 343 of the text). In *Immortality* 11.12 he maintains that 'the Hypothesis of Praeexistence [of Souls] is more agreeable to Reason than any other Hypothesis' (cf. p. 240 of the text; see also *Theodicy* p. 169). In *Immortality* 111.12. §1 he postulates an incorporeal spirit of nature 'pervading the whole matter of the universe, and . . . raising such phaenomena in the world, by directing the parts of the matter and their motion, as cannot be resolved into mere mechanical powers'. This spirit's most impressive achievement is universal gravitation (*centripetal force). In his *Enchiridion metaphysicum* (1671) More proposes the name 'hylarchic principle' as appropriate for this being (see p. 344 of the text). Leibniz consistently rejected the claim that mechanism needs to be supplemented by *archei or other vitalistic agents (see 'Discourse on metaphysics' §10 and 'Considerations on vital principles and plastic natures'; see also *Loemker* pp. 441f), but he was sympathetic to contemporary neo-platonism (*Conway, *Helmont) and had studied More's writings carefully (*Grua* pp. 509ff). See also p. 72.

Motus primo primi. Literally, 'the very first motions' – i.e. 'the movement of the appetites which is so fundamental as to be involuntary' (R. J. Deferrari and I. Barry, *A Lexicon of St Thomas Aquinas* (1948), p. 708). See p. 189.

'natural science', 'natural philosophy'. Leibniz's noun '*physique*' belongs to a trichotomy – running back to Aristotle, and presented by Philalethes on

p. 521 – of logic (what must be), ethics (what should be), physics (what is). So *physique* is the study of reality; and if the meaning is sometimes narrower than that, it is never as narrow as that of 'physics' today. We translate it by 'natural science' except at pp. 81, 430, 453, and 521 where 'natural philosophy' is used in fidelity to Locke's text. Our phrase 'natural science', though conveying the right idea, should not be thought of as containing *'science' as a detachable term carrying the full load it carried for Locke and Leibniz – as witness Philalethes' view (p. 453) that we can never turn '*la Physique*' into '*science*'. At p. 78, 'natural sciences' translates '*sciences naturelles*'.

Niceron, Jean-François (1613–46). Author of *La perspective curieuse* (1638). The pictures referred to on pp. 258f are *anamorphoses*, an anamorphosis being 'a distorted projection or drawing of anything, so made that when viewed from a particular point, or by reflection from a suitable mirror, it appears regular and properly proportioned' (*OED*).

Nicole, Pierre (1625–95). French theologian and philosopher; a leader of the Jansenist sect and closely associated with *Arnauld and Blaise Pascal. His *Préjugés légitimes contre les Calvinistes* (1671) evoked, in due course, *Préjugés légitimes contre le Papisme* (1685) from the French Calvinist Pierre Jurieu (1637–1713) – see the references to 'legitimate presumptions' on p. 459 of the text. When Jurieu published his *Vrai système de l'Église* (1686), Nicole replied (p. 518) with *De l'unité de l'Église* (1687). During his stay in *Paris, Leibniz 'had the honour of several conversations with M. Nicole at M. Arnauld's, but we never spoke of religious matters, any more than I did with M. Arnauld' (1.4, p. 352). See *large numbers.

Occasional causes. In consequence of *Descartes's difficulties with the problem of mind–body interaction (*Regius), several *Cartesians developed the doctrine of 'occasional causes', which resembles, and influenced, Leibniz's theory of *pre-established harmony. They argued that there can be no interaction between minds and bodies, or even between bodies and bodies, but that when the circumstances are appropriate God brings about interaction-like results: e.g. when a moving particle reaches a point adjacent to another particle, God sets the second particle in motion with a velocity consistent with the laws of mechanics – the behaviour of the first particle may be called the *occasional* cause of the motion of the second particle, but God is its true cause. Similarly, mental events are merely occasional causes of bodily actions, and neural processes of sense impressions. See *Malebranche. For Leibniz's comments on occasionalism, see *Loemker* pp. 444f, 457f. See p. 381.

Oldenburg, Henry (c. 1620–77). German diplomat and, latterly, scientific correspondent. In 1653, after a decade of wandering about Europe, he went to England as Bremen's consular representative, and settled there. He became acquainted with *Boyle and with his scientific associates and, in the late 1650s, became a founding member of the Royal Society and one of its two secretaries (*academies). In this latter capacity he maintained a voluminous correspondence with scholars and scientists throughout Europe; like Mersenne in Paris he served the scientific community as a clearing-house for ideas and information. The Royal Society's *Philosophical Transactions* (1665–), which Oldenburg founded, edited and, in large part, wrote, were begun by him as a private venture (see *OC* II, pp. 209f, 405); at about the same time he also agreed to serve as English correspondent for the *Journal des savants* (*OC* II, p. 320; see *journals). Leibniz, who had plans of his own for becoming a clearing-house (1.2, pp. 16f), wrote to Oldenburg in 1670 – they met during Leibniz's visit to England in 1673 (*Paris) – and they continued to correspond until Oldenburg's death (II.1 and III.1; English tr. *OC* VIIff). See p. 455.

Paris. After completing his formal education, in law and scholastic philosophy, Leibniz was employed as a legal adviser, in 1667, by the Elector of Mainz, probably on the recommendation of the diplomat Baron Boineburg (*Conring). In March 1672, at the age of twenty-five, Leibniz set out for Paris on the invitation of the French Foreign Minister, Arnauld de *Pomponne. He had two assignments, both secret: to see to the payment of a pension granted to Boineburg for diplomatic services to the French Crown, and to persuade Louis XIV to direct his forces against the Turks in Egypt rather than towards North Germany and the Low Countries. Leibniz seems never to have seen Pomponne, but during the summer of 1672 he met Antoine *Arnauld, with whom he had corresponded before coming to Paris, and through him *Nicole; he also began to meet the scientists and mathematicians connected with the *Académie des Sciences, *Huygens in particular. Before coming to Paris he had conceived of a calculating machine on the principle of the pedometer (*Couturat* p. 573): 'I call it an automatic calculating-table...it adds, subtracts, multiplies, divides, and even extracts square and cube roots, without requiring any mental exertion. One merely sets the given numbers on the machine, which takes no more time than writing them down, and the result is arrived at by the action of the machine itself. The advantage of this is that the machine cannot miscalculate unless it breaks' (II.1, p. 160). Now, while he waited for his audience with Pomponne, he worked on his machine with the intention of exhibiting it and selling facsimiles (1.1, pp. 488f). In November 1672 he joined a diplomatic delegation from Mainz, led by the Elector's nephew; by January the delegation had despaired of influencing Louis directly, and it moved on to London, Leibniz with it, to seek an alliance against the French. Here Leibniz met *Oldenburg, at whose invitation he attended meetings of the Royal Society and demonstrated a rough model of his calculating machine. Boineburg had died in December 1672; the Elector of Mainz died in February 1673, just before Leibniz returned to Paris. Boineburg's seventeen year old son had come to Paris, and Leibniz applied for and was given responsibility for tutoring him (1.1, p. 338); but he found the boy lazy and immature and the boy evidently found him tiresome (1.1, pp. 370ff). The appointment was terminated abruptly in September 1674 (1.1, p. 396). Although he was still nominally in the employ of Mainz, Leibniz had no official duties; in March 1673 he began an intensive study of mathematics and science, largely under Huygens's guidance (*Child* pp. 11ff, 36ff). He also met *Mariotte, with whom he discussed questions in mechanics (III.1, pp. 101ff). In April 1673 he was elected a Fellow of the Royal Society (III.1, p. 79; tr. *OC* IX, p. 583). A letter to Oldenburg in July 1674 (III.1, pp. 118ff; tr. *OC* XI, pp. 44ff) reports on a series of major discoveries in mathematics, including 'certain analytical methods, extremely general and far-reaching' (*infinitesimal calculus), and on the successful construction of a working model of the calculating machine. In January 1675 Leibniz demonstrated the calculating machine to the Académie des Sciences (III.1, p. 180) and received an order for three of them: 'One is to be presented to the King, another is to be placed in the Royal Observatory for mathematical use and the third M. Colbert [chief minister of Louis XIV] will keep at his own disposal' (1.1, p. 495). He had begun to cast about for a more assured position – in Paris, Vienna, Copenhagen; he now informed Duke Johann Friedrich of *Brunswick that his work in Paris was nearly completed and that he was willing to accept the offer (made two years earlier: 1.1, pp. 490f) of a position in Hanover (1.1, pp. 491ff). Nevertheless he lingered on in Paris. He met *Malebranche, and *Roberval with whom he discussed Descartes's *Geometry*. He also became interested in Huygens's work on clock mechanisms: in March 1675 he sent a paper, 'Extract from a letter concerning the principle of exactness in portable watches', to the *Journal des savants*, and in April he demonstrated a chronometer of his own design to the Académie des Sciences (III.1, pp. 181ff, 245; see p. 326 of the text). In the autumn of 1675 he succeeded in laying the foundations of the infinitesimal calculus. At about this same time he met *Spinoza's friend E. W. von Tschirnhaus (1651–1708), a Cartesian and an able mathematician, who quickly became Leibniz's friend and co-worker; their correspondence continued for thirty years (*LBG* pp. 30ff). Leibniz had still not resigned himself to leaving Paris and he explored the possibility of a salaried post in the Académie des Sciences (III.1, pp. 276, 303ff). Roberval's death, in October 1675, seemed to improve his chances but, when he thought that the position was within his grasp, 'M. the Duke de Chevreuse (M. Colbert's son-in-law) told me bluntly that I must not take it ill if a Frenchman were preferred over me...since the Académie already had M. Huygens and M. Cassini, one a Dutchman and the other an Italian, and there was sufficient resentment of them' (1.2, p. 124; but according to *Fontenelle, Leibniz could have had the position by converting to Roman Catholicism). Roberval's death had also left vacant the *Ramus professorship at the Collège de France, for which there was to be a contest in March 1676, but Leibniz did not wait: in January of that year he accepted a position as Councillor to the Dukes of Brunswick in Hanover (1.1, pp. 504ff) – hope was expressed that he would set out without delay (1.1, p. 508). In February, still in Paris, he and Tschirnhaus visited Clerselier and inspected Descartes's unpublished papers; at about this time he also studied unpublished papers of Pascal's (III.1, p. 253). Throughout this period, in spite of his absorption in mathematics and science, his philosophical ideas had been developing, partly through discussion with such as Arnauld, Malebranche, *Foucher, and Pierre Huet, partly in connection with his scientific discoveries, partly through study of the classics, ancient and modern; philosophical notes which he made in 1676 have been published by I. Jagodinski, *Leibnitiana* (1913) and excerpts are translated in *Loemker* pp. 157ff. In April he was told that he might postpone his arrival in Hanover until 14 May, but no later (1.1, p. 515); at the end of June he was offered an additional appointment as Ducal Librarian and was asked to say positively whether or not he intended to accept (1.1, pp. 515f). These urgings were repeated in July and September (1.1, pp. 516f). At the beginning of October he took ship for Dover; in spite of his belief that his new appointment would be short-lived and that he would be 'an amphibian, sometimes in Germany, sometimes in France...until I find occasion to settle down advantageously' (1.1, p. 445), he was in fact leaving France for ever, to remain in the service of the Dukes of Brunswick for the remaining forty years of his life. In London he saw Oldenburg and gave him a calculating machine for presentation to the Royal Society. He embarked for Holland at the end of the month but for several days contrary winds confined his ship in the mouth of the Thames: 'Not knowing what to do during this time and with no one in the vessel except the sailors... I thought about my old plan of a rational language or writing: its giving the different nations something in common and enabling them to communicate with one another would be the least of its effects. Its true purpose would be to depict not speech... but thoughts, and to speak to the understanding rather than to the eyes. For if we had the sort of thing I envisage we could reason in metaphysics and ethics more or less as we do in geometry and analysis' (II.I, p. 380; see *symbolism). He reached Amsterdam, via Rotterdam, in mid-November, spent a few days with the scientific community there, 'and then took another little tour through Holland, to Haarlem, Leyden, Delft, and The Hague, and then back again to Amsterdam' (I.2, p. 4). In Delft he visited *Leeuwenhoek and in The Hague, Spinoza. He finally left Amsterdam at the end of November and, after a leisurely journey, arrived at Hanover in mid-December 1676. See pp. 85, 107f, 408.

Pearls. Curves with the general Cartesian equation $x^p (ax + b)^q = y^r$. They were discussed in the years 1657–9 in correspondence between R. F. de Sluse (1622–85), Pascal and *Huygens. Pascal named them 'pearls' (see Sluse's letter to Huygens, July 1659; *HOC* II, p. 438). We have retained Leibniz's word 'paraboloid', in its seventeenth-century sense of a parabola-like curve. See pp. 348, 408.

Pelagians. Followers of Pelagius (fifth century A.D.), who 'denied the Catholic doctrine of original sin, asserting that Adam's fall did not involve his posterity, and maintained that the human will is of itself capable of good without the assistance of divine grace' (*OED*). 'The Semipelagians think that an assisting Grace is necessary, but that the first turn of the will to God is the effect of a man's own choice' (Tindal, quoted in *OED*). Claude Pajon (1626–85), a French Protestant theologian, founded a sect which denied any immediate and special divine intervention in the course of nature or the spiritual life of human beings (see *Grua* pp. 232f). See p. 502.

Pellisson-Fontanier, Paul (1624–93). French historian and religious polemicist; from 1666 he was court historian to Louis XIV. In 1670 he converted from Calvinism to Roman Catholicism and began writing against Protestantism; his *Réflexions sur les différends de la religion* (1686–92) is the most important of his polemical writings. In 1690 Louise Hollandine, Abbess of Maubuisson – herself a convert – sent a volume of the *Réflexions* to her sister, Princess *Sophie, in the course of a persistent attempt to convert her, and the Hanoverian court, to Catholicism. Sophie passed the book on to Leibniz for his appraisal and forwarded his comments to Pellisson (I.6, pp. 75ff). Pellisson replied through the Abbess's secretary, Marie de Brinon (I.6, pp. 83ff). The ensuing correspondence (published in I.6–9) was devoted chiefly to the project of church reunion, was voluminous, important and friendly, and continued until Pellisson's death. In 1690 Leibniz drew Pellisson's attention to Payva's *Explicationes orthodoxae* (1564) and Pellisson finally located a copy in the library of the Sorbonne (I.6, pp. 82, 124). In 1691 Brinon succeeded in drawing *Bossuet into their discussion (I.7, pp. 132, 156ff, 176). See *Scudéry. See p. 500.

Penetration of dimensions, according to John Harris (*Lexicon technicum,* 1704), 'is a philosophical way of expressing, that two bodies are in the same place, so that the parts of one do every where penetrate into, and adequately fill up the dimensions or places of the parts of the other; which is manifestly impossible, and contradictory to reason.' Nevertheless, Christians (p. 82) who believe in consubstantiation are thereby committed to believing that two bodies can occupy the same space (cf. *Wiener* p. 65). See *More. See also p. 230.

Peripatetic. A term first applied to Aristotle and his pupils, probably because they used to meet at a house with a covered walking place, or *peripatos*. See *Edwards*. The term has also been used for Aristotelians more generally: especially for ones living before about 200 A.D. but also, sometimes, without restriction as to time. Leibniz uses it unrestrictedly, in reference to medieval 'Peripatetics' (*Loemker* p. 554) and also to 'Peripatetics' of his own time (p. 70). Prominent among the latter was his own teacher Jacob *Thomasius. See also pp. 82, 124, 342.

Phenomenon. When Leibniz uses this word in a deliberate manner, it expresses the idea of something which belongs to the realm of appearance rather than of fundamental reality, but which nevertheless is not merely illusory, because it has a systematic and reliable relationship to what is fundamentally real. This double idea is sometimes expressed in the phrase 'real phenomenon' (*Loemker* pp. 363, 614) or 'well-founded phenomenon'. The rainbow example (pp. 146, 219) is supposed to illustrate this: the rainbow pertains to appearance because it misleadingly looks as though it might be touched, viewed from close up, blown away; but it is not illusory, because it is interpersonally perceptible and has a dependable relationship to the world of things which can be touched and blown away. Ultimately, Leibniz thinks that the whole extended world is a phenomenon (hence motion is a phenomenon, p. 210), since he thinks that basic reality consists of non-extended *monads. Still, the relationship of a rainbow to ordinary physical objects is analogous to that between a phenomenon and basic reality. See also pp. 309, 374f, 444.

'physical', '*physique*'. Had it been stylistically permissible, we would have translated the adjective '*physique*' throughout by 'grounded in the natures of real things': for the source of its meaning, see *'natural science', in which the role of '*physique*' as a noun is discussed (the present note is concerned with it only as an adjective). Sometimes we render the adjective by 'real' (see below), and sometimes by 'natural' or a phrase containing it (pp. 250, 281). Mostly, though, we use 'physical', reserving 'natural' and 'real' for '*naturel*' and '*réel*' respectively. Leibniz may have viewed '*physique*' and '*réel*' as virtually synonymous (see p. 63, and pp. 236–47 where both words are used often and apparently interchangeably); but, not being sure about that, we have cautiously rendered the two French words by two English ones. The need for this use of 'physical' is regrettable, because, despite what seems to be indicated by Leibniz's chart on p. 64, he does not use '*physique*' to imply a restriction to what is 'physical' in our sense, e.g. to what exists in space. He uses it in four distinct ways. (i) To characterize a kind of influence or dependence – a kind which does not in fact obtain between any two substances, and is contrasted with the seeming influence which does obtain because of the *pre-established harmony. Our renderings of '*physique*' by 'real' pertain to this use of it (pp. 135, 177). (ii) To contrast 'physical' with merely 'personal or moral' identity, the former depending on sameness of substance while the latter is just a matter of memory-links (pp. 236–47). The distribution of '*physique*' in those pages is curious. Throughout pp. 236–45 there are eight occurrences of '*réel*', and only three of '*physique*', each of them on the same line as '*réel*'; and then when the entire discussion is being summed up on pp. 246f there are four uses of '*physique*' and none of '*réel*'. (iii) To contrast 'physical' with 'mathematical' (or 'logical') approaches to classification: any consistent description marks off a 'mathematical' species, but a 'physical' one must have a boundary laid down in the nature of things (pp. 63f, 293, 308ff, 317, 325ff). (iv) In a contrast between kinds of determination or necessity or certainty: on one side there is 'metaphysical' and on the other 'physical and moral' (p. 178) or 'moral or physical' (p. 406). When *contrasted* with '*morale*' on p. 179, '*physique*' seems to mean something close to 'physical' in the twentieth-century sense.

Physician to Oneself. This expression translates Leibniz's '*le médecin de soi-même*'. The reference is probably to *Le médecin de soi-même, ou l'art de conserver la santé par l'instinct* (1682) by the Paris surgeon Jean Devaux. See p. 351.

Picture of Cebes. An ancient Greek philosophical dialogue which purports to comment on an allegorical picture of a soul prior to its union with a body. It is traditionally, although improbably, attributed to Cebes of Thebes, the pupil of Socrates. See p. 385.

Pneumatology. 'The science, doctrine, or theory of spirits or spiritual beings: in the 17th c. considered as forming a department of metaphysics called *Special Metaphysics* as opposed to *General Metaphysics* or ontology, and comprehending the doctrine of God as known by natural reason, of angels and demons, and of the human soul' (*OED*). See pp. 56ff.

Pomponne, Simon Arnauld de (1616–99). French foreign minister under Louis XIV; nephew of Antoine *Arnauld. In 1672 Leibniz went to *Paris at Pomponne's invitation in the hope of engaging in secret diplomacy intended to dissuade Louis from his aggressive designs on north-west Europe (much of the relevant material is in I.1 and IV.1). Leibniz did not succeed and it is doubtful whether he ever met Pomponne, despite having a letter of introduction to him from Arnauld (*Klopp* II, p. 139). The Treaty of Nijmegen, which terminated the war in north-west Europe and was Pomponne's masterpiece, preceded his downfall by a few weeks (1.2, pp. 525f). See p. 509.

'popular'. This translates '*populaire*'. It means: 'accessible to ordinary, unskilled people'. We would have used 'popularized' if that, in the intended sense, had not been anachronistic.

Positive. Cf. *Hobbes: 'Another division of laws, is into *natural* and *positive*. *Natural* are those which have been laws from all eternity; and are called not only *natural*, but also *moral* laws.... *Positive*, are those which...have been made laws by the will of those that have had the sovereign power over others.... *Divine positive laws*...are...the commandments of God, not from all eternity, nor universally addressed to all men, but only to a certain people, or to certain persons' (*Leviathan* II.26). See p. 250.

Pre-established harmony. Leibniz denied that substances can really act upon one another ('Discourse on metaphysics' §14). He apparently thought that 'a substance' properly so-called must have a kind of self-sufficiency which is incompatible with causal dependence; and he may also have assumed that the notion of causal interaction involves the absurd notion of a property's being literally transferred from one item to another (see pp. 171f and *Loemker* pp. 269,

457f). In Leibniz's view, the cause of any fact about a substance or *monad lies within itself: God in creating each monad endows it with an inner nature from which its entire history inevitably flows. But he so chooses the histories that the states of each monad correspond in a regular way to the states of all the others ('Monadology' §§51f). This divinely 'pre-established harmony' among the monads enables Leibniz to describe the correspondence between body and mind without having to allow that they really interact (*Loemker* pp. 457f). The laws of the material world also manifest the harmony, and are not the results of substances acting upon one another. Leibniz considered that the pre-established harmony 'provides a new and unassailable method' of demonstrating the existence of God (pp. 438, 440; cf. *Leibniz–Clarke* v, §87). Cf. *occasional causes. See also pp. 55, 220ff, 374, 473f.

Prescriptions. In Roman law a prescription 'meant the cutting short of a question by the refusal to hear the adversary's arguments, on the ground of an anterior point which must cut away the ground under his feet. So Tertullian deals with heresies' in his *De praescriptione haereticorum* (*Catholic Encyclopedia*, 'Tertullian'). See p. 458.

'primary'. This is used only to translate '*primitif*'. An item which is '*primitif*' is one which is basic, fundamental, an underived source of other things. (At p. 211 Coste calls certain ideas '*primitives*' where Locke says that 'all the others are derived' from them, and at p. 352 we use this translation in reverse for one use of '*idées primitives*' by Theophilus.) We did not use 'basic' because it is anachronistic; or 'primitive', because it has too much unwanted meaning. On a few occasions 'primitive' is used in fidelity to Locke's text; and it is used to characterize certain features of language on pp. 281 and 285, though even there it should be realized that those features are being described as foundational rather than as crude or uncivilized. With those exceptions, and the one on p. 352, '*primitif*' is always translated as 'primary'.

Priscillianists. Followers of Priscillian (c. 340–85), heretical bishop of Avila. His tenets were austere and smacked of Manichæism. His followers eschewed marriage but were thought to practise free love. According to St Jerome they chanted the lines from Virgil during their orgies (Migne, *Patrologia Latina* XXII, col. 1150). See p. 316.

Probabilism. The doctrine, in the seventeenth century particularly associated with the Jesuits, that when there is doubt as to the permissibility of an action of a kind prohibited by the moral law, its performance is permissible if there is a *solidly probable* opinion in support of it, even if the opposing opinion is *more probable*. An opinion is solidly probable if it is held by several prudent and learned theologians, or even by one theologian of exceptional authority. An opinion is more probable if it has weightier support. An opinion in favour of conformity to the moral law is a *safe opinion*. Thyrsus Gonzales (1624–1705), the Jesuit General to whom Leibniz refers on p. 372, defended *probabiliorism* in his *Fundamentum theologiae moralis* (1694), according to which it is permissible to act contrary to the moral law only if the supporting opinion is more probable than the safe opinion. Jansenists adhered to a *rigorist* position, according to which the safe opinion must be followed however probable the opposing opinion, and accused probabilists of *laxism*, i.e. of permitting violations of the moral law on the strength of any supporting opinion, however slight. See *Arnauld. See also p. 206.

Probability. The idea 'that we need a new kind of logic, concerned with degrees of probability' (p. 466), occurred to Leibniz early in his career – in connection both with his legal studies (pp. 464ff) and with his attempts to demonstrate the fundamental tenets of Christianity (letter to Duke Johann Friedrich, 1679 (?), II.1, p. 489; tr. *Loemker* p. 260). Leibniz rejects the view that probability is connected with the universality or intensity or authority of a belief (pp. 372f): 'I am not talking here of the casuists' probability [*probabilism], which depends on the number and reputation of the Doctors [of the Church], but of the kind which derives from the nature of things in proportion to what we know about them, and which can be called "likelihood"' (*LPG* VII, p. 167). 'Likelihood' is connected with what Leibniz calls 'feasibility': 'The art of guessing depends on what is more or less easy, that is, more or less feasible [*faisable*, literally 'do-able']. . . . For instance, with two dice it is as feasible to throw a 12 as to throw an 11. . .but it is three times more feasible to throw a 7. . . . We also estimate likelihoods *a posteriori*, from experience, to which we ought to resort when we lack reasons *a priori*. For instance, it is equally likely for a child who is about to be born to be a boy or a girl, since the number of boys and girls in the world is roughly equal. One could say that what happens more or less often is also more or less feasible in the present state of affairs, putting together all the considerations which must concur in bringing about a fact' (*LPG* III, pp. 569f). A logic of probability would form an integral part of the universal *symbolism, making it possible, in the absence of decisive reasons for one or another alternative, to calculate where the preponderance lay (see *Wiener* p. 24; *Leibniz–Arnauld* p. 168; *Loemker* p. 655). The fullest account of the place of probability in Leibniz's system occurs in a letter to Thomas Burnett, written in February 1697: 'Philosophy has two parts, theoretical and practical. Theoretical philosophy depends on genuine analysis: mathematics provides examples of it, but it should also be used in metaphysics and natural theology, through the provision of good definitions and sound axioms. But practical philosophy depends on genuine *topics or dialectic, that is, on the art of estimating degrees of proof [*probation*]. This is still not to be found in the writers on logic, and only the jurists have provided worthwhile examples of it – ones which can serve as the starting point for creating a science of *proofs [*preuves*] which would be suitable for confirming historical events and for interpreting texts. . . . It is often said, rightly, that reasons should not be counted, but weighed; however, no one has as yet provided us with scales on which to weigh the cogency of reasons. This is one of the greatest defects of our logic, and we ourselves feel its consequences in the most important and serious affairs of life, concerning justice, and the peace and welfare of states, the health of mankind, and even religion. I said this publicly almost thirty years ago' (*LPG* III, pp. 193f). Leibniz watched with great interest the application of mathematics to *games of chance and to the design of annuity schemes (p. 466); but although he encouraged these developments (*LPG* III, pp. 570, 667ff), he did not contribute substantially to them. For an account of the development of the theory of probability and of Leibniz's share in the process, see Ian Hacking, *The Emergence of Probability* (1975). See also pp. 206, 450, 457, 472ff, 483f.

'proof'. This is used only to translate '*preuve*'. Usually what is meant is weaker than strict 'proof' in the modern sense, and sometimes we render '*preuve*' by 'evidence'. When stressing that he is speaking of a rigorous and conclusive proof, Leibniz uses '*démonstration*', which we always translate by 'demonstration', in line with Locke's usage.

Prosyllogism. 'A *syllogism of which the conclusion forms the major or minor premiss of another syllogism' (*OED*).

Pufendorf, Samuel (1632–94). Professor of law at Heidelberg – where the chair of 'natural and international law', the first of its kind in Germany, was created for him – and at Lund; historiographer to the Swedish court and to the Elector of Brandenburg, whom he also served as privy councillor. His principal work was his *De jure naturae et gentium* (1672; English tr. 1710). Like Leibniz, but earlier, he was a student of Erhard *Weigel's at Jena. In 1658 he was imprisoned for political reasons at Copenhagen, and spent the eight months of his imprisonment meditating on the ideas of Weigel, Grotius and *Hobbes. After his release he set down his conclusions in *Elementorum jurisprudentiae universalis* (1660; English tr. 1931). In this work, the exposition of Definition 17 employs Weigel's 'moral sphere' in an attempt – not very successful – to elucidate various ethical notions. Leibniz corresponded with Pufendorf occasionally and without enthusiasm, between 1690 and 1693 (1.5 and 1.9); their political convictions were fundamentally opposed and Leibniz held him in low esteem (see *Theodicy* p. 241; *Grua* pp. 374ff, 593ff). Leibniz wrote an 'Opinion on the principles of Pufendorf', in which he reviewed Pufendorf's *De officio hominis* (1673). See p. 385.

Quadrature. 'The expression of an area bounded by a curve...by means of an equivalent square' (*OED*). According to Proclus, Hippocrates of Chios (fifth century B.C.) was the first to square a particular set of lunules, a lunule being the area contained by two or more circular arcs (see p. 455). Archimedes proved that 'the area of any circle is equal to a right-angled triangle in which one of the sides about the right angle is equal to the radius, and the other to the circumference, of the circle' (*Measurement of a Circle*); from which follows Leibniz's statement on p. 376 that the area of a circle is equal to 'the square whose side is the mean proportional between the radius and the semi-circumference of the circle.' Archimedes also proved that a line drawn from the origin of a spiral, perpendicular to the line connecting the origin to the end point of the first turn of the spiral, will meet the tangent to that end point at a distance from the point of origin equal to the circumference of the 'first circle' of the spiral (*On Spirals*, props. 18 and 19); he thereby provided a measure for the arc length of a circle. However, the ultimate goal of circle-squarers, namely the construction, using ruler and compass alone, of a square equal in area to a given circle, remained unachieved. *Hobbes and Joseph Scaliger (1540–1609) both claimed success in this endeavour (pp. 95f). Scaliger also claimed to have shown in the process that the perimeter of a polygon inscribed in a circle is greater than that of the circle, and increasingly so the more sides it has – which led him to announce that a theorem could be false in geometry although true in arithmetic. A new goal came into view in the seventeenth century: to express the area of a circle by means of a rational number, or failing that by an ordinary irrational. The first fruits of Leibniz's mathematical studies in *Paris included discovery of a 'transmutation theorem' by means of which he found the quadratures of a segment of the cycloid and of the circle – his 'arithmetical tetragonism' of the circle (*infinitesimal calculus). In the latter case he showed that the ratio of the area of a quadrant of a circle to the square of its radius can be expressed by the infinite series of rational numbers $\frac{1}{1} - \frac{1}{3} + \frac{1}{5} - \frac{1}{7} + \frac{1}{9}$ etc. (p. 376). He announced these two discoveries in July 1674 (III.1, pp. 118ff; tr. *OC* XI, pp. 44ff) but did not send *Huygens the proof of the circle quadrature until October (III.1, pp. 141ff); it was presumably Huygens who, between summer and autumn, tested the tetragonism by means of 'Ludolph's numbers' (p. 85) – i.e. the value of π to thirty-five places, as worked out by Ludolph van Ceulen (1540–1610). In the face of Huygens's hope that the tetragonism series might have a rational sum (III.1, pp. 170f), Leibniz denied that it could (*Loemker* p. 274) but remained unsure what order of irrational was involved (p. 377). See *super-surd. See also p. 368.

Quietists. A movement within the Roman Catholic church, during the seventeenth century, which stressed passive contemplation and complete resignation to the will of God – 'like a feather blown about by all the winds of grace' in Fénelon's phrase (*Encyc. Brit.*). When this state of 'holy indifference' has been achieved, overt behaviour ceases to be morally significant. The chief exponents of Quietism were Miguel de Molinos (c. 1640–97) in Spain and Italy and Jeanne Marie Guyon (1648–1717) and François Fénelon (1651–1715) in France. *Bossuet attacked Quietism during the 1690s and by bringing about the condemnation of Fénelon's *Maximes* (*love) effectively terminated the movement. Leibniz, who suspected the Quietists of *Averroism (p. 59; cf. *Loemker* p. 554) if not outright nihilism (*Theodicy* p. 79), had no sympathy for the movement (*Grua* pp. 73ff). He is wrong, however, when he accuses Quietists of idleness (p. 454) – they were, if anything, too industrious: 'The chief complaint made against the Quietists by their adversaries was that they would not keep quiet' (R. A. Knox, *Enthusiasm* (1950), p. 262).

Ramus, Petrus (1515–72). French philosopher and logician. See *Edwards*. He attempted to establish a new logic to replace the Aristotelian: he rejects the distinction between logic and dialectic in favour of a single discipline devoted to the art of sound disputation and of reasoning about any subject whatever. It consists of two parts, which correspond to the two basic activities of the mind, *invention and judgment (cf. pp. 368, 476): invention deals with the possible relations of pairs of terms (cf. p. 488), in conformity with the *topics, and judgment deals with the construction of arguments – *artful ones since dialectic is unconcerned with artless persuasion, which depends on authority. Ramus discusses demonstrating conversion by the figures of the *syllogism (cf. p. 365) in his *Scholae dialecticae* (1569), VII.4. Although Leibniz appears to have drawn upon the Ramist tradition he had little good to say of its constructive side (cf. *LPG* VII, p. 67). Ramus was a professor at the Collège de France and endowed a chair of mathematics there. In Leibniz's words, Ramus 'left a testamentary injunction that it should be filled by the most deserving candidate, and that a competition should be authorized, as though to win a prize.... Ramus added that in case the diligence of the professor once installed should grow cold, every three years opportunity would be given to anyone to compete with him. This arrangement seems to me rather delightful' (III.1, p. 329; tr. *NC* I, p. 400). *Roberval, who had occupied the chair continuously since 1634, died in 1675, and for a time Leibniz considered competing for it (*Paris). Ramus, who was a Protestant convert, died in the St Bartholemew massacre. See also p. 356.

Rational grounds for belief. Leibniz's phrase '*motifs de credibilité*' (literally 'motives of credibility') and our rendering of it by 'rational grounds for belief' are explained by his distinction between *explicable* and *inexplicable* reasons for belief: 'Explicable reasons can be propounded to others by plain reasoning; but inexplicable reasons consist uniquely in our experience of inner feeling which we cannot bring others to share unless we can find a way of bringing them to sense the same things in the same manner. For instance, we cannot always explain to others what we find pleasant or unpleasant in a person, or a painting, or a sonnet, or a stew.... Now those who claim to find an inner divine light inside themselves, or an illumination which makes them sense some truth, build upon inexplicable reasons. And I find that not only Protestants, but also Roman Catholics appeal to this illumination: for, in addition to motives of belief or credibility (as they call them), that is, in addition to the explicable reasons for our faith,...they ask for a light of grace from heaven which brings about complete conviction and produces what we call divine faith' (1.6, p. 76). See pp. 474, 493, 497, 510.

Realists and nominalists. Leibniz refers on pp. 174 and 323f to a series of debates, beginning in the eleventh century, on a wide range of topics of which the debate over universals was central and typical. Realists thought that universals such as humanity and greenness are fundamental constituents of reality, whereas nominalists took them rather to be creatures of the mind or of language. More generally, realists tended to assume that every noun denotes something which belongs in the inventory of the thing-like items of which reality is composed, while nominalists were prepared to treat many nouns as standing for aspects, properties, functions of things which belong in that inventory. See *Edwards*, 'Universals'. See also p. 523.

Reformed and Evangelical. What, in spite of Leibniz's objections, have come to be generally known as Calvinists and Lutherans. He disapproved of these names as smacking too much of sectarianism (see *Grua* p. 460). See pp. 468, 497.

Regius. Henrik van Roy (1598–1679). Dutch physician and sometime *Cartesian. On the strength of Descartes's assertion that the human soul is 'expressly created' and 'of a nature entirely independent of the body', and thus able to exist apart from it (*Discourse on Method* v), Regius taught that a man, being a union of soul and body, is an accidental entity and not a true substance of which the soul is the form. This indiscretion stirred up a theological storm and embarrassed Descartes, who counselled Regius on philosophy and tactics in a series of letters beginning in December 1641, but finally felt obliged to disown him. See p. 317.

Replication, duplication. In legal terminology *replication* consists in 'the reply of the plaintiff to the plea or answer of the defendant, being the third step in common pleadings' (*OED*); *duplication*, in civil and canon law, is 'a pleading on the part of the defendant in reply to the replication, corresponding to the rejoinder at common law' (*OED*). See p. 420.

Roberval, Gilles Personne de (1602–75). French mathematician and scientist; he was a founding member of the *Académie des Sciences and, for forty-one years, holder of the *Ramus chair at the Collège de France. Leibniz knew him in *Paris, and hoped to succeed to one or other of the posts vacated by his death – but in the event he did not. Leibniz and Tschirnhaus examined Roberval's papers and decided that the *Elements of Geometry* was not worth publishing (III.1, p. 328; tr. *NC* I, p. 400). For Leibniz's further comments on the significance, to him, of Roberval's attempt to demonstrate Euclid's axioms, see his letter of July 1676 to Mariotte (II.1, pp. 270f). See *centripetal force. See pp. 107f, 407f, 414.

'science', '*science*'. Leibniz's '*science*' means something like 'systematic knowledge', and on p. 358 it is so rendered (see also p. 50). Usually we use 'science', as the only tolerable uniform treatment; but it must be remembered that '*science*' for Leibniz, like 'science' for Locke, sometimes implies an extremely high level of rigour and theoretical organization – see for instance pp. 389, 453, and cf. *'art'. Also, the word sometimes implies an especially high level of certainty – see p. 78. Most uses of '*science*' in IV.xxi could have been rendered by 'branch of knowledge', but we have stayed with 'science' both for uniformity and for fidelity to Locke's text. Cf. *'natural science'.

Scotists. Followers of John Duns Scotus (c. 1265–1308). See *Edwards*. During the seventeenth century, with the support of the Franciscan Order, the Scotists became the most powerful philosophical school in the European universities. Duns Scotus introduces the notion of a virtual distinction with the explanation that a thing 'which has such a distinction in itself does not have thing and thing, but is one thing having virtually or eminently, as it were, two realities, for to either reality, as it is in that thing, belongs the property which is in such reality as though it were a distinct thing' (*Opus oxoniense* I.ii.7, tr. Peirce); this distinction – which seems to be identical with the Scotists' 'formal distinction' – holds between the persons of the Trinity, but it is also invoked to resolve a great many more mundane philosophical problems. See p. 498.

Scudéry, Madeleine de (1607–1701). French novelist: author of several mammoth romances – including *Clelia* (1654–61; English tr. 1678), whose characters were thinly disguised portraits of herself and her contemporaries – leader of a salon, and close friend of Paul *Pellisson. The country of Tenderness was their creation and *Clelia* reveals its geography: lovers who set out from the village of New-Friendship may find their way to Tenderness-on-Inclination or Tenderness-on-Respect or, if they stray from the path, may fall into the Lake of Indifference, and so on. In 1697, when Scudéry was ninety, Leibniz sent her French verses in praise of Louis XIV (*Pertz* IV, pp. 316ff) and during the next two years they exchanged several letters. In his last letter to Clarke he offers as evidence that men have grown 'out of conceit with reason itself, and...weary of light' the fact that popular taste has drifted away from 'rational romances' such as *Clelia* towards 'the tales of fairies' (*Leibniz–Clarke* v, §114; cf. p. 356 of the text). Shortly after her death he published a 'brief biography' of her. See p. 215.

Seckendorf, Veit Ludwig von (1626–92). German scholar and statesman; author of several works on law, history and church reform, of which the most important is his *Commentarius historicus et apologeticus de Lutheranismo* (1688) – the work to which Leibniz refers on p. 468. Leibniz first wrote to him in 1682 and they corresponded regularly until von Seckendorf's death – mainly about politics, history and church reform (1.3–9; II.1; *Loemker* p. 275). On Leibniz's objection to the term 'Lutheran', see *Reformed.

Second element. According to *Descartes (*Principles* III, §46), the various forms of matter can be supposed to have originated by God's dividing extension into precisely equal small bits – perfect cubes, presumably (cf. p. 57) – and setting them in motion. The outcome of this, he supposed (*Principles* III, §52), is three basic forms of matter, the second of these consisting in minute spheres (see p. 515) and constituting the material of the heavens. See *striated particles.

'sensation'. The eight occurrences of this which are marked with an asterisk translate '*sentiment*'; all the others translate '*sensation*'. There is some evidence that Leibniz was uncomfortable with the latter word, and used it mainly in deference to Locke (his definition of it on p. 161 may be a suggestion for Locke rather than something Leibniz thought important). Twice he takes the trouble to change Coste's '*sensation*', once to '*sentiment*' (p. 131) and once to '*les sens*' (p. 140); and on p. 493 he expresses a preference for 'the outer and inner senses' over 'sensation and reflection' (see also p. 53). And so, although we have found no consistent pattern in Leibniz's selections of the two words, we have not wanted to smudge the difference between them. Since in these contexts 'sense' was impossible and 'feeling' intolerable, we had to use 'sensation' and asterisks. See pp. 54, 82, 113, 121, 165, 263, 374, 381.

'signify'. This translates '*signifier*'. A word's '*signification*' is sometimes clearly its meaning, and sometimes clearly the item it stands for; but Leibniz does not deploy that distinction or anything like it, and to avoid forcing it upon him we have had to reconcile ourselves to the ugly 'signification'. When Coste uses '*signifier*' for Locke's 'mean' or 'stand for', we follow Locke.

Socinians. Followers of Fausto Sozzini or Socinus (1539–1604) and forerunners of the Deists and Unitarians. See *Edwards*. Socinians denied the doctrines of the Trinity and of the divinity of Christ; furthermore, according to Leibniz, they 'have a very low conception of God: apparently they tie him to a particular place and deny him foreknowledge, as inconsistent with human free will, and as for the soul, they believe that it would die naturally with the body but is preserved through grace' (1.6, p. 160). He derived these opinions in particular from a manuscript, *Metaphysica repurgata*, by the Socinian Christoph Stegmann (c. 1598–1646), which he had found in Baron Boineburg's library in about 1670 (1.6, pp. 159f). The Stegmann manuscript seems to have come into his hands again some time between 1704 and 1710 (cf. *Theodicy* p. 84), when he wrote a refutation of it (see N. Jolley, 'An unpublished Leibniz MS on metaphysics', *Studia Leibnitiana* VII (1975), pp. 161ff). Socinianism was particularly influential in seventeenth-century Poland, Holland and Britain – not least on certain of Locke's associates, including Isaac Newton and the *Arminians. See pp. 497f.

Sophie. The 'great princess, of lofty intelligence' (p. 231) is the Princess Sophie (1630–1714), the wife of Leibniz's employer, Ernst August, Elector of *Brunswick. Her mother was the daughter of James I of England and her father was the Elector Palatine Frederick, the unfortunate Winter King of Bohemia. Her twelve siblings included the Elector Karl Ludwig who offered *Spinoza the chair of philosophy at Heidelberg, Descartes's Princess Elizabeth, the Abbess Louise Hollandine (*Pellisson), and the notorious Prince Rupert who led the cavalry of his uncle Charles I against Cromwell's forces. In the Act of Settlement she was named heir to the British crown; in the event she died two months before Queen Anne and the crown passed to her eldest son, the Elector Georg Ludwig, who thereby became George I. Her daughter Sophie Charlotte (1668–1705) – Leibniz's able pupil (*academies) – married the Elector of Brandenburg and in due course became the first Queen of Prussia. Through her intermediacy and that of Georg Ludwig, Sophie became the great-grandmother, twice over, of Frederick the Great. Sophie lacked the philosophical grasp of her sister Elizabeth and of her daughter, but she possessed abundant common sense, wit and strength of character; for over thirty years she and Leibniz provided each other with a degree of intellectual companionship otherwise unavailable to them in Hanover. In Leibniz's words (to Thomas Burnett, 17 March 1696): 'My problem is that I am not in a great city like Paris or London, abounding with learned men whom one can avail oneself of and profit from. But here it is difficult to find anyone to talk to – or rather, as a courtier one can't talk about learned matters, and without Madam the Electress one would talk about them even less' (*LPG* III, p. 175). When they were apart from each other they wrote regularly – 'I write to you simply to receive letters back from you' (Sophie to Leibniz, 5 Nov. 1701; *Müller* p. 72). Their correspondence is published in 1.4ff and in *Klopp* VIII and IX. The leaf hunt took place in the gardens of Herrenhausen, the Electoral palace, probably in about 1685; the 'clever gentleman' was Carl August von Alvensleben, an official at the Hanoverian Court, and the great principle at stake was the identity of indiscernibles (see *Leibniz–Clarke* IV, §4; *LPG* VII, p. 563).

Sorites. 'A series of propositions, in which the predicate of each is the subject of the next, the conclusion being formed of the first subject and the last predicate' (Mansel, quoted in *OED*).

'soul'. This is used always and only to translate '*âme*'. When Coste renders 'mind' by '*âme*', as he does about twenty times, mostly in Book II, we follow him rather than Locke. That explains each occurrence of 'soul' under square brackets; and on pp. 167–208 there are eight further cases which are not so indicated. On p. 75 Coste uses '*esprits*' – minds – for Locke's 'souls'.

'species'. We translate '*espèce*' by 'species' where Locke has used the latter, and in passages dominated by Locke's use of 'species'; also where 'species' is being opposed to 'genus'. Most other occurrences of '*espèce*' are translated by 'kind'. Where in a Lockean passage 'species' occurs in square brackets or just outside quotation marks, Locke has used 'sort' and Coste has put '*espèce*'.

Spinoza, Baruch or Benedict (1632–77). Dutch Jewish philosopher; his system, most fully expounded in his *Ethics* (1677), is the boldest of all ventures in rationalist metaphysics. See *Edwards*. Leibniz wrote to him in 1671 (II.1, p. 155) with a question about lens-making, on which Spinoza was an expert; Spinoza replied (II.1, pp. 184f) and offered Leibniz a copy of his *Tractatus theologico-politicus* (1670) – their letters are translated in Wolf, *Correspondence of Spinoza* (1928). In *Paris Leibniz met Tschirnhaus and heard from him about Spinoza's metaphysical theories (see Wolf, *Correspondence* pp. 338f, 341). On his way to Hanover, in November 1676, he visited Spinoza in The Hague: 'The famous Jew Spinoza was olive complexioned with a somewhat Spanish face: in fact his origins are in that country. He was a philosopher by vocation and lived a calm and detached life, which he spent polishing lenses for telescopes and microscopes'

(*Dutens* VI.1, p. 329). 'I saw him on my way through Holland and I talked to him several times and at great length. He has a strange metaphysics, full of paradoxes. Among other things he believes that the world and God are one and the same thing in substance, that God is the substance of all things and that creatures are only modes or accidents. But I could see that some of the alleged demonstrations that he showed me were unsound. It is not as easy as people think to give genuine demonstrations in metaphysics' (II.1, pp. 379f). What he failed to find out from the master he found out 'from some of his disciples whom I knew pretty well' (II.1, p. 535). In February 1677 one of these disciples, G. H. Schuller, wrote to tell Leibniz that Spinoza had died a few days before and that the autograph manuscript of the still unpublished *Ethics* could be purchased for 150 florins; a month later he wrote that the disciples had decided, on second thoughts, to publish the *Ethics* themselves, together with a selection of letters and other writings of Spinoza's (II.1, pp. 304f). The *Opera posthuma* came out towards the end of 1677 and Leibniz was quick to obtain a copy (see II.1, p. 393; tr. *Loemker* p. 195). Leibniz's writings from this period show that he studied Spinoza's system carefully (e.g. *Loemker* pp. 196ff) – he acknowledged later that he came 'very close to the opinions of those who hold everything to be absolutely necessary', i.e. the Spinozists, but that he was 'pulled back from the precipice by considering those possible things which neither are nor will be nor have been' (*Loemker* p. 263). He was subsequently at pains to distinguish his own system from Spinoza's (e.g. *Wiener* pp. 485ff; *Theodicy* pp. 67f, 234ff). See *De Witt. See pp. 73, 455, 462.

'Spirit'. When this word occurs with an initial capital, it translates Leibniz's '*génie*' (or an occurrence of his '*esprits*' in a context which clearly equates this with '*génie*'). Whereas an ordinary '*esprit*' is just a mind, a '*génie*' is a higher spiritual being which Leibniz concedes to be only lightly embodied and which would generally be regarded as disembodied, i.e. as purely spiritual. In a few places '*esprit*' is rendered by 'spirit' without a capital, in conformity either with Locke's text or with the literary convention that the endless war is waged between flesh and spirit, not flesh and mind (p. 186).

Stillingfleet, Edward (1635–99), Bishop of Worcester. Suspecting Locke's *Essay* of *Socinian tendencies, Stillingfleet attacked it in his *Discourse in Vindication of the Doctrine of the Trinity* (1696). Locke defended himself in *A Letter to the Right Reverend Ld Bishop of Worcester* (1697), thereby eliciting *The Bishop of Worcester's Answer to Mr Locke's Letter* (1697). There followed *Mr Locke's Reply to the...Bishop of Worcester's Answer to his Letter* (1697), *The Bishop of Worcester's Answer to Mr Locke's Second Letter* (1698) and *Mr Locke's Reply to the...Bishop of Worcester's Answer to his Second Letter* (1699). At this point Stillingfleet died, leaving Locke with the last word. Leibniz wrote two accounts of their dispute, just before beginning work on the *New Essays* (VI.6, pp. 16ff). See pp. 60ff.

Strauch, Johann (1614–79). German professor of law, at Jena and Giessen. He married Leibniz's mother's sister. In 1664, shortly after his mother's death, Leibniz – who was still a minor – visited Strauch in the hope of getting a share of the inheritance, but apparently without success (G. E. Guhrauer, *Leibniz. Eine Biographie* (1846), I, note to p. 35). He sent Strauch a copy of his dissertation *De conditionibus* in 1665 and received a gracious acknowledgment (II.1, p. 4), but beyond that there was not much contact between them. The work referred to on p. 331 is Strauch's *Lexicon particularum juris* (1671).

Striated particles. In *Descartes's account of the world, empty space is impossible: every region of space must be filled with matter of some sort – just because extension *is* matter. The little spaces between spheres of the *second element are occupied by *striated particles*, composed of the luminous dust which constitutes the first element. Descartes says that these particles are elongated and of indeterminate length, triangular and fluted in cross-section (corresponding to the shape of the area enclosed by three contiguous circles) and 'twisted like the shells of snails' (*Principles* III, §90) – he seems to have been as confused about the shape of snails' shells as about that of the spaces between contiguous spheres. The first occurrences in English of 'striate' and 'striated' are in descriptions of Descartes's particles (see *OED*). See p. 515.

Substantial form. 'The nature or distinctive character in virtue of possessing which a thing is what it (specifically or individually) is' (*OED*). For Locke the appeal to substantial forms is a prime example of philosophical nonsense (pp. 269, 343). Leibniz acknowledges that substantial forms have no place in the explanation of particular events (p. 317) and that all organic phenomena can be explained mechanistically (p. 139), but nevertheless maintains that 'the general principles of corporeal nature and of mechanics itself' are metaphysical and require 'certain indivisible forms or natures' ('Discourse on metaphysics' §18). He had, for a time, followed the atomists and the *Cartesians in rejecting substantial forms, but had found himself constrained to re-introduce them: they were needed to provide a primary source of the activity of bodies (pp. 169f) and to account for the sort of genuine unity which organisms possess (pp. 317f) – as well as to account for the possibility of transubstantiation and of a body's capacity to be in more than one place at a single time (see *Loemker* pp. 117f, 261, 271, 309f, 454; cf. *Zwinglians). No material thing as such is a substance, but organisms are substantial in that they have a deeper sort of unity than that of an accidental assemblage such as a heap of sand. The substantial form is to any organism as the soul is to an organism endowed with *awareness; Leibniz holds that the entire material realm is organic (p. 72) and, at his most rhapsodic, proclaims that 'everything is full of souls' (*Dutens* VI.1, p. 332), but for the most part he confines souls to conscious beings. A major part of the correspondence with *Arnauld consists in a debate about substantial forms (*Leibniz–Arnauld* pp. 79ff). In the late 1690s Leibniz adopted the term *'monad', which he may have acquired from *Helmont, in place of 'substantial form': the deeper unity which characterizes organisms consists in their possessing a dominant monad. The reappearance of 'substantial form' in the *New Essays* was probably provoked by Locke's jibes. See *entelechy. See also pp. 306, 322.

'suffering'. In translating '*douleur*', the choice between 'suffering' and 'pain' – which are equally good renderings of the word – has been guided only by a sense of appropriateness in the given context.

Super-surd. Leibniz speaks of quantities which are '*plus que sourdes*' – which we translate by 'super-surd' – but he does not explain what he means. There is a hint on p. 377, where he distinguishes between surds which are 'representable by means of an ordinary equation' and those which require 'an extraordinary one which introduces irrationals or the unknown itself into the exponent'. In a letter to Wallis in 1697 he speaks of '*Geometrice-irrationalia . . .* which Descartes does not admit into his geometry', and distinguishes two species of these: 'Some are of a definite degree, but irrational, whose exponent is a surd, e.g. $\sqrt{2}\sqrt{2} . . .$

and these I call *Intercedentia*, since their degree falls between rational degrees
.... The others are truly of indefinite degree, e.g. x^y, and these I call more
precisely *Transcendentia*' (*LMG* IV, pp. 27f; see *transcendental). It would seem
that super-surds are *transcendentia* – this surmise is encouraged by the fact that,
in an early draft of the *New Essays*, Leibniz wrote '*plus que sourdes, que j'appelle*
transcen' and then crossed out the final clause (VI.6, p. 377n). Cf. *mechanical.

Syllogism. Leibniz's impeccable lecture on the syllogistic moods and figures
(pp. 363ff) presupposes the following information. A syllogism is an argument
in which one proposition is derived from two others, each being of the form (A)
'All...is...', (I) 'Some...is...', (E) 'No...is...', and (O) 'Some...is not
...'. Using 'S' and 'P' respectively for the subject and predicate of the
conclusion, and 'M' for the 'middle' term – i.e. the term which occurs in both
premisses but not in the conclusion – the four *figures* can be represented thus:

I	II	III	IV
M P	P M	M P	P M
S M	S M	M S	M S
S P	S P	S P	S P

Each figure comprises several *moods*, a mood being defined not just by the above
patterns but also by the facts about which of the constituent propositions are of
the form A, which are I, which are E, and which are O. These facts are embodied
in the Latin names for the moods: for instance, the first mood-name on p. 366,
'Cesare', has the vowels E–A–E, and so it designates a form of syllogism in which
the premiss which is conventionally put first (i.e. the one which contains the
predicate of the conclusion) is of the form (E) 'No...is...', the second premiss
is (A) 'All...is...' and the conclusion is E. Given the further fact that *Cesare*
is a second-figure mood, it follows that any syllogism in *Cesare* has the form

> No P is M
> All S is M
> ———
> No S is P

and what Leibniz gives on p. 366 is just the special case of this where S = M.
For the Latin names of all the syllogistic moods, and facts about the significance
of some of the consonants in them, see *Edwards*, 'Traditional Logic'. See also
pp. 476ff.

Symbolic books. '*Symbolic Books*, in the language of the church, is a phrase
that signifies the same as Creeds and Confessions' (*Chambers's Encyclopædia*,
quoted in *OED*).

Symbolism, symbols. Leibniz asserts that 'created minds and souls...cannot
reason without symbols' (p. 212; cf. p. 77); an argument intended to support
a similar conclusion occurs in the 'Paris notes' of 1676 (*Loemker* p. 160). In a
paper written in the following year he maintains that symbols can be used
effectively for reasoning because 'there is in them a kind of complex mutual
relation or order which fits the things' which they represent (*Loemker* p. 184);
and again, in a letter of 1678, that the contemplation of symbols 'does not lead
us away from the things themselves; on the contrary, it leads us into the interior
of things. For we often have confused notions today because the characters we
use are badly arranged', but given appropriate symbols 'we will easily have the
most distinct notions, for we will have at hand a mechanical thread of meditation,
as it were, with whose aid we can very easily resolve any idea whatever into those

of which it is composed' (*Loemker* p. 193). Given his conviction that 'good symbolism is one of the greatest aids to the human mind' (p. 411), it is not surprising to find that he was constantly concerned with devising and promulgating the most appropriate symbols for the topics on which he was engaged. (His contributions to mathematical notation are summarized in F. Cajori, *A History of Mathematical Notations* (1928–9), II, pp. 180ff.) But Leibniz had more ambitious plans than merely rationalizing the notation of mathematics: throughout his career he believed passionately in the possibility of setting out all existing knowledge systematically in a perspicuous symbolism which would not only facilitate the retrieval of known truths when needed (*mnemonics), but would at the same time embody the method by which knowledge might be extended. This project, which drew inspiration from *Descartes's reflections on method (see *Wiener* pp. 21f, *Couturat* pp. 27f), from *Hobbes's conviction 'that everything done by our mind is a computation' (*Parkinson* p. 3) and from the proposals for a universal language advanced by John Wilkins (1614–72) and George Dalgarno (c. 1626–87), he usually refers to as his 'universal symbolism'. In a letter of 1714 he describes it as a sort of general algebra 'in which all truths of reason would be reduced to a kind of calculus. At the same time this could be a kind of universal language or writing, though infinitely different from all such languages which have thus far been proposed, for the characters and the words themselves would give directions to reason, and the errors – except those of fact – would be only mistakes in calculation.... When we lack sufficient data to arrive at certainty in our truths, it would also serve to estimate degrees of *probability and to see what is needed to provide this certainty' (*Loemker* p. 654). According to his own account, he was eighteen when he first conceived of the possibility of a symbolism 'appropriate for expressing all our thoughts as definitely and as exactly as arithmetic expresses numbers' (*Wiener* pp. 15, 17); in the last year of his life he complained that his historical studies were preventing him 'following out my idea of putting philosophy into deductive form' through 'the invention of a general symbolism which could do, for every inquiry in which certainty is attainable, what algebra has done for mathematics' (*Bodemann* pp. 15f). The first fruits of this project were published as *On the Combinatorial Art* (1666) – the work which inaugurates the history of symbolic logic – in which he explored the possible permutations and combinations of subject and predicate terms of propositions. He arrived at the following conclusions: that definable concepts can be analysed into undefinable 'first terms', that the signs which designate those terms will constitute an 'alphabet' of human thoughts, and that by choosing suitable signs for first terms we can create 'a universal writing, i.e. one which is intelligible to anyone who reads it, whatever language he knows' (*Parkinson* pp. 4, 10f). This writing would be pictorial, like ancient Egyptian or Chinese, but based on a fixed alphabet and such that each word would display the structure of the concept which it represented. His invention of the *infinitesimal calculus in 1675 involved the development of a new symbolism by means of which it became possible to reason precisely about previously inaccessible questions; this seems to have re-awakened his hopes of establishing a general 'science of forms' by means of which appropriate symbols could 'be devised for algebra, for music, and even for logic itself' (*Loemker* p. 192). Writing to *Oldenburg in 1676 he speaks of a 'combinatorial art' which does not differ 'from that supreme analysis to the heart of which, so far as I can judge, Descartes did not penetrate; for in order to set it up we need an alphabet of human thoughts, and for finding this alphabet we need an analysis of axioms' (III.1, p. 503; tr. *NC* II, p. 70). Once established, it would enable philosophers to settle their disagreements as conclusively and dispassionately as do accountants: 'for they will need only take up their pens and sit down at their desks and...say to one another, "Let us work it out"' (*LPG* VII, p. 200; cf. *Wiener* p. 15). Furthermore, 'being independent of any particular language, this new philosophical calculus would be a marvellous aid in making even the most remote peoples – the Chinese and others like them – whose languages are so different from ours, appreciate the most important and most abstract truths of natural religion, on which revealed truth is, so to speak, grafted' (*Bodemann* p. 358). The project of a universal symbolism was very much on Leibniz's mind when he took up his post in Hanover (*Brunswick) at the end of 1676: he recognized that its achievement would require the compilation of an 'encyclopedia' or 'general inventory of all knowledge already existing among men', practical as well as theoretical (*Wiener* p. 48), and that this task transcended even his capacities. Accordingly for the next few years his letters are full of proposals for collaborative research; it was, as much as anything, his project for a universal symbolism that motivated his persistent efforts to found properly staffed, equipped and funded research establishments (*academies). While he waited for these schemes to bear fruit, he continued to draft accounts of his new science of symbols (e.g. *Loemker* pp. 221–46, *Parkinson* pp. 17–87). See also pp. 398f, 488f.

Syncretists. Followers of Georg Calixtus (1586–1656) of Helmstedt, who elaborated a theological system intended to make possible a reconciliation between Lutherans, Calvinists and Roman Catholics. In this respect Calixtus was a precursor of Leibniz – see *Bossuet. See p. 463.

Thomasius, Jacob (1622–84). Professor of rhetoric and law at Leipzig, and the father of Christian Thomasius. He taught Leibniz and supervised his bachelor's dissertation, *De principio individui*. Leibniz thought highly of Thomasius and kept up an active correspondence with him until 1672, largely on philosophical topics (II.1; *Loemker* pp. 93ff), the work referred to on p. 509 is *Disputatio de officio hominis circa notitiam futurorum contingentium* (1664).

Topics, topical. The term goes back to the ancient Greek rhetoricians, for whom topics were 'places' to which a speaker could direct his thoughts when seeking for things to say about his subject matter – e.g. to its definition, its causes and effects, its similarities to and differences from other things. Aristotle's *Topics* is a handbook of informal argumentation for public speakers and dialecticians (cf. pp. 372, 466), whereas his studies of formal logic are for philosophers. Dialectical reasoning proceeds from generally accepted opinions, i.e. from opinions 'which commend themselves to all or to the majority or to the wise – that is to all of the wise or to the majority or to the most famous and distinguished of them' (*Topics* I, 100ª30–100ᵇ22, tr. Forster). The *Topics* sets out a great number of *topoi*, or maxims of argument: some of these are rules for valid non-syllogistic inference, some hold good only for certain kinds of case, some are thoroughly sophistical. (*Topical arguments* are ones which depend on maxims which are not invariably true; they are therefore not invariably valid and yield conclusions which can be expected to be true in, at best, most cases – see p. 483.) Later writers, beginning with Cicero and Boethius, identified the *topoi* or *loci communes*, not with the maxims, but with the general headings, or 'commonplaces', under which the maxims had come to be classified (p. 466); commonplaces, or 'places of *invention' (p. 356), came to be thought of as, in W. D. Ross's phrase, 'the pigeon-holes from which dialectical reasoning is to draw its arguments' (*Aristotle* (1930), p. 59). Leibniz's outlines of a new logic consisting of a topics and an analytics – the former comprising the 'art of invention' and the latter the 'art of judging' (VI.1, pp. 277ff; tr. *Loemker* p. 88; see also *Couturat* p. 37) – appear to owe something to *Ramus and his followers.

Torricellian tube. An experiment performed in 1643 under instructions from Evangelista Torricelli (1608–47) showed that if a glass ~~tube is~~ sealed at one end, filled with mercury and inverted in a bowl of mercury, the height of the resulting column of mercury in the tube is never more than approximately 76 cm, however long the tube. This experiment generated vigorous debate on two issues: whether or not the column of mercury is supported by the weight of the atmosphere, and whether the space at the top of a tube longer than 76 cm is a true vacuum. Various ingenious theories were propounded by antivacuists: by *Descartes, that an appropriate quantity of 'subtle matter' passes through the walls of the tube; by the Aristotelians, that inevitably and invariably at least one atom of air remains in the tube when it is being filled with mercury, and that this expands to fill the top of the tube – the limit on how far this air can expand sets the limit on how far it permits the mercury to drop. Leibniz himself inclined to the subtle matter theory – that only gross matter is evacuated from the tube (*Leibniz–Clarke* v, §34). See p. 126.

Transcendental. Leibniz seems to have been the first to use this term in mathematical contexts, although not in its modern sense. Writing to Oldenburg in 1675 (III.1, pp. 203f), he says that quadrature of the circle may require irrationals 'or even an expression of the kind I call transcendental.' Writing to Tschirnhaus three years later he says that 'transcendental quantities can be expressed by equations – but transcendental ones in which an unknown enters the exponent' (*LBG* p. 376), and to Wallis in 1697, that 'I call those [equations] transcendental which transcend all algebraical degrees' (*LMG* IV, p. 26). Cf. *mechanical and *super-surd. See p. 156.

Trifocal oval. The Cartesian oval, which has a bipolar equation, with respect to any two of its three collinear foci, of the form $x \pm ny = k$ (where x and y are distances to the two foci) – an account is given in the latter half of Descartes's *Geometry* II. See p. 308 of the text.

Trotter, Catharine (1679–1749), dramatist and philosopher. See *DNB*, under 'Cockburn'. Her first play was performed at the Theatre Royal, London, when she was sixteen. Leibniz heard of her *Defence of the Essay of Human Understanding* (1702) from his correspondent Thomas Burnett in 1704 (*LPG* III, p. 297), but did not actually see and read it until 1706 (*LPG* III, pp. 305, 307). They communicated with each other through Burnett (*LPG* III, p. 311) – in 1710 we find Leibniz wondering whether she can read French, in order to give him an assessment of the *Theodicy* (*LPG* III, p. 322). In 1708 she married Patrick Cockburn. See p. 70.

Tulp, Nicolaas (1593–1674). Dutch anatomist. He commissioned Rembrandt's 'Anatomy Lesson', in which he himself is the demonstrator. Leibniz's reference on p. 234 is to Tulp's *Observationes medicae* (1652).

Vacuum among forms. Are there vacuums among forms? That is, are there 'possible species which do not actually exist' (p. 307)? Leibniz's acceptance of the Law of Continuity, which tolerates no jumps in nature, seems to imply that there are no vacuums among forms (see p. 473; see also *Morris and Parkinson* p. 84, *Leibniz–Arnauld* p. 160, *Loemker* p. 588). On the other hand, he also accepts the Principle of Contingency, according to which there are unrealized possibilities (e.g. *Loemker* pp. 263f), and this implies that 'there must be species which never did and never will exist' (p. 307 of the text). Leibniz seeks to satisfy both these constraints on his position by arguing in effect that the original question is ambiguous. The species of things which exist constitute a continuous series, 'like so many ordinates of the same curve, whose unity does not allow us to place some other ordinates between two of them' (*Wiener* pp. 186f); so if a 'vacuum among forms' is an uninstantiated species which could be fitted into that series, then there are no vacuums among forms. But there are, nevertheless, uninstantiated species, for some things which are internally possible are not 'compossible' with the existing series of species or forms. 'Not all possible species are compossible in the universe'; each species belongs to some series or ordering, but 'not every form or species belongs to each ordering' (p. 307), and, in particular, no species which is in fact uninstantiated could have been fitted into the ordering which the actual world manifests. That is why their absence from it does not create vacuums or discontinuities. God chose this series, rather than some other, Leibniz says, because this is 'the greatest of all possible series' (*Morris and Parkinson* p. 146; cf. pp. 323f of the text). This is the famous Leibnizian 'optimism', but it harbours a problem: why doesn't God instantiate further species which don't belong in this series? That is, how can Leibniz explain possible species' being non-compossible with a given world? His answer might be that if any more species were instantiated, there would be a loss in the simplicity of general laws which was not compensated for by the gain in the richness of particular facts; which is to say that the world would be a worse one in consequence.

Virgilius of Salzburg (c. 700–84). Irish churchman and scholar. St Boniface took exception not only to his scientific theories but to his governing the diocese of Salzburg without having been consecrated bishop; in 748 he wrote to the Pope to accuse Virgilius of heretical opinions about the sphericity of the earth and the existence of the antipodes (see *The Letters of Saint Boniface* (1940), p. 147). Boniface notwithstanding, Virgilius was eventually consecrated. He converted the Carinthian Slavs in 772, and was canonized in 1233. See p. 391.

Weigel, Erhard (1625–99). Professor of mathematics and jack of all trades at Jena – his colleagues protested his tendency to trespass into their disciplines, as they did his practice of lecturing in German. He valued the study of mathematics particularly for its morally improving influence. Leibniz and *Pufendorf were both students of his (Leibniz in the summer of 1663), and he seems to have had a powerful influence on them both. In 1679 Leibniz began a correspondence with Weigel (II.1, pp. 485ff), on mathematics and educational reform, which went on intermittently until 1697 – but, in Leibniz's words, 'I could see that he took me for an exoteric; indeed, he who knows me only from my published works does not really know me at all' (*Dutens* VI.1, pp. 64f). Weigel produced a demonstration of God on which Leibniz commented several times (e.g. *Theodicy* p. 355; *Grua* pp. 329ff), and his project for a number system to the base four may have inspired

Leibniz's invention of the binary number system (see Couturat, *La logique de Leibniz* (1901), app. III). According to Leibniz (VI.1, p. 94), Weigel 'established three highest genera of entities: natural, moral and notional'; hence Leibniz's reference (p. 385) to '*choses morales*', which we have translated 'moral entities'. On his 'moral sphere', see *Pufendorf (see also *Couturat* pp. 179f). Weigel's most important contribution may have been his part in persuading Protestant Germany to adopt the reformed calendar, which it did the year after his death, and his suggestion – taken up by Leibniz – that funds for an observatory or scientific society in Germany be provided by a state monopoly on the production of reformed calendars (*academies).

Witsen, Nicolaas (1641–1717). Dutch merchant, geographer and politician. As a young man he studied under the versatile Jacob Gool or Golius (1596–1667) who, in addition to being Professor of Oriental Languages at Leyden (p. 274), was the founder and *de facto* director of the Leyden astronomical observatory. Witsen's business ventures interested him in remote countries; as a Regent of the Dutch East India Company he founded the coffee trade with Java. At the age of twenty-three he had gone on a diplomatic mission to Moscow; in addition to writing about Russia he made a map of North and East Tartary – Russia and Siberia – 'as big as a house door' (*Grua* p. 116). Leibniz heard of the map in 1690, wanted especially to know whether it showed if there was a land-bridge between Asia and America (*LBG* pp. 606, 616) and moved mountains to obtain a copy – which he finally did in 1694. Witsen was burgomaster of Amsterdam from 1682–1705. His book on ship-building attracted Tsar Peter the Great to Amsterdam in 1697 where Witsen was his host. Leibniz corresponded with Witsen from 1694 until 1712: in addition to wanting information about distant countries and their languages he wanted access to the Tsar (*Grua* p. 125). Leibniz published selections from their correspondence, and samples of the Lord's Prayer in exotic languages, in his *Collectanea etymologica* (see p. 103 of the text).

Zwinglians. Followers of the Swiss Protestant Ulrich Zwingli (1484–1531). He broke with Luther by denying all versions of the real presence, maintaining that Christ's body is a real human body, that it is in Heaven at the right hand of the Father and that a human body cannot be in more than one place at any one time.

BIBLIOGRAPHY

The Bibliography lists works by Leibniz alluded to in the text or in the Notes. Works for which there is an English translation, in whole or significant part, are identified by a title in English. This is followed, in the Bibliography, by abbreviated reference to accessible locations of the translated text. The original title, if any, is given next, followed by the place and date of publication if Leibniz published the work, and otherwise by the date of its completion. Finally, abbreviated reference is given to a good accessible edition of the original text. The abbreviations are explained in the Key to Abbreviations on pp. viii–ix. For further bibliographical information see E. Ravier, *Bibliographie des oeuvres de Leibniz* (1937) and P. Schrecker's corrections and additions in *Revue philosophique de la France et de l'étranger* CXXVI (1938).

Annales imperii occidentis Brunsvicenses, unfinished at Leibniz's death (*Pertz* I–III).
Art of combinations: *see* On the combinatorial art.
Brief demonstration of a notable error of Descartes (*Loemker* pp. 296–8): 'Brevis demonstratio erroris memorabilis Cartesii et aliorum circa legem naturae, secundum quam volunt a Deo eandem semper quantitatem motus conservari; qua et in re mechanica abutuntur', *Acta eruditorum* (March 1686), pp. 161–3 (*LMG* VI, pp. 117–19).
Clarification of the difficulties which M. Bayle has found in the new system of the union of soul and body (*Loemker* pp. 492–7): 'Lettre de M. Leibniz à l'auteur, contenant un éclaircissement des difficultés que Monsieur Bayle a trouvées dans le système nouveau de l'union de l'âme et du corps', *Histoire des ouvrages des savants* (July 1698), pp. 332–42 (*LPG* IV, pp. 517–24).
Codex juris gentium: *see* Preface to *Codex juris gentium*.
Collectanea etymologica, illustrationi linguarum, veteris Celticae, Germanicae, Gallicae, aliarumque inservientia, ed. J. G. Eckhart, Hanover, 1717 (*Dutens* VI.2, pp. 6–232 – selection).
Confession of nature against atheists (*Loemker* pp. 109–13): 'Confessio naturae contra atheistas', c. 1668 (VI.1, pp. 489–93).
Considerations on vital principles and plastic natures (*Loemker* pp. 586–90; *Wiener* pp. 190–9): 'Considérations sur les principes de vie, et sur les natures plastiques, par l'auteur du système de l'harmonie préétablie', *Histoire des ouvrages des savants* (May 1705), pp. 222–36 (*LPG* VI, pp. 539–46).
Critical thoughts on the general part of the *Principles* of Descartes (*Loemker* pp. 383–410; *Schrecker* pp. 22–80): 'Animadversiones in partem generalem Principiorum Cartesianorum', 1692 (*LPG* IV, pp. 354–92).
De conditionibus: *Disputatio juridica de conditionibus, Disputatio juridica posterior de conditionibus*, Leipzig, 1665 (VI.1, pp. 99–150).

De principio individui: *Disputatio metaphysica de principio individui*, Leipzig, 1663 (VI.I, pp. 9–19).

Discourse on metaphysics (tr. Peter G. Lucas and Leslie Grint, Manchester, 1953; *Loemker* pp. 303–28; *Wiener* pp. 290–345): French original untitled, 1686 (Leibniz, *Discours de métaphysique*, ed. Henri Lestienne, Paris, 1929).

Dynamics: a summary (*Loemker* pp. 435–44; *Wiener* pp. 119–37): 'Specimen dynamicum, pro admirandi naturae legibus circa corporum vires et mutuas actiones detegendis, et ad suas causas revocandis', *Acta eruditorum* (April 1695), pp. 145–57 (*LMG* VI, pp. 234–46).

Explanation of the new system of the communication of substances (*Morris and Parkinson* pp. 125–30): 'Éclaircissement du nouveau système de la communication des substances, pour servir de réponse à ce qui en a été dit dans le *Journal* du 12 septembre 1695', *Journal des savants*, Paris (2 April and 9 April 1696), pp. 166–71 (*LPG* IV, pp. 493–8).

Extract from a letter concerning the principle of exactness in portable watches (III.I, pp. 193–201): 'Extrait d'une lettre de Monsieur Leibniz à l'auteur du *Journal*, touchant le principe de justesse des horloges portatives de son invention', *Journal des savants*, Paris (25 March 1675), pp. 93–6 (III.I, pp. 193–201).

Extrait d'une lettre touchant la démonstration cartésienne de l'existence de Dieu: 'Extrait d'une lettre de M. de Leibniz sur ce qu'il y a dans les *Mémoires* de janvier et de février, touchant la génération de la glace, et touchant la démonstration cartésienne de l'existence de Dieu, par le R. P. Lamy Bénédictin', *Mémoires de Trévoux* (September 1701), pp. 200–7 (*LPG* IV, pp. 405–6).

History and origin of the differential calculus (*Child* pp. 22–57): 'Historia et origo calculi differentialis', 1714 (*LMG* V, pp. 392–410).

'Kurze Lebens-Beschreibung der Fräulein von Scudéry', *Monatlicher Auszug* (December 1701), pp. 34–48 (Leibniz, *Deutsche Schriften*, ed. G. E. Guhrauer, Berlin, 1840, II, pp. 416–20).

Leibniz–Arnauld: *see* Key to Abbreviations.

Leibniz–Clarke: *see* Key to Abbreviations.

Letter on a general principle useful in explaining the laws of nature (*Loemker* pp. 351–3): 'Extrait d'un lettre de M. L. sur un principe général, utile à l'explication des lois de la nature, par la considération de la sagesse divine; pour servir de réplique à la réponse du R. P. M.', *Nouvelles de la république des lettres* (July 1687), pp. 744–53 (*LPG* III, pp. 51–5).

Meditations on knowledge, truth and ideas (*Loemker* pp. 291–4; *Schrecker* pp. 3–10; *Wiener* pp. 283–90): 'Meditationes de cognitione, veritate et ideis', *Acta eruditorum* (November 1684), pp. 537–42 (*LPG* IV, pp. 422–6).

Monadology (*Loemker* pp. 643–52; *Morris and Parkinson* pp. 179–94; *Schrecker* pp. 148–63; *Wiener* pp. 533–52): 'Les principes de la philosophie', 1714 (Leibniz, *Principes de la nature et de la grace fondés en raison et principes de la philosophie ou monadologie*, ed. André Robinet, Paris, 1954).

New essays: *Nouveaux essais sur l'entendement humain*, 1705 (VI.6, pp. 43–527).

New method for learning and teaching jurisprudence (*Loemker* pp. 85–90 – selection): *Nova methodus discendae docendaeque jurisprudentiae*, Frankfurt, 1667 (VI.I, pp. 261–364).

New method for maxima and minima (*Struik* pp. 272–80): 'Nova methodus pro maximis et minimis, itemque tangentibus, quae nec fractas, irrationales quantitates moratum, et singulare pro illis calculi genus', *Acta eruditorum* (October 1684), pp. 467–73 (*LMG* v, pp. 220–6).

New system of the nature and communication of substances (*Loemker* pp. 453–9; *Morris and Parkinson* pp. 115–25; *Wiener* pp. 106–17): 'Système nouveau de la nature et de la communication des substances, aussi bien que de l'union qu'il y a entre l'âme et le corps', *Journal des savants*, Paris (27 June and 4 July 1695), pp. 294–306 (Leibniz, *Ausgewählte philosophische Schriften*, ed. Hermann Schmalenbach, Leipzig, 1914, I, pp. 119–31).

Novissima Sinica historiam nostri temporis illustratura, [Hanover], 1697.

On a deeply hidden geometry (*Struik* pp. 281–2 – selection): 'De geometria recondita et analysi indivisibilium et infinitorum', *Acta eruditorum* (July 1686), pp. 292–300 (*LMG* v, pp. 226–33).

On nature itself (*Loemker* pp. 498–507; *Schrecker* pp. 95–113; *Wiener* pp. 137–56): 'De ipsa natura, sive de vi insita, actionibusque creaturarum; pro dynamicis suis confirmandis illustrandisque', *Acta eruditorum* (September 1698), pp. 427–40 (*LPG* IV, pp. 504–16).

On the combinatorial art (*Loemker* pp. 73–83 – selection; *Parkinson* pp. 1–11 – selection): *Dissertatio de arte combinatoria, in qua ex arithmeticae fundamentis complicationum ac transpositionum doctrina novis praeceptis exstruitur, et usus ambarum per universum scientiarum orbem ostenditur; nova etiam artis meditandi, seu logicae inventionis semina sparguntur*, Leipzig, 1666 (VI.1, pp. 165–230).

Opinion on the principles of Pufendorf (*Riley* pp. 64–75): 'Epistola ad amicum, qua monita quaedam ad principia Pufendorfiani operis de officio hominis et civis continentur', 1706 (*Dutens* IV.3, pp. 275–83).

Preface to *Codex juris gentium* (*Loemker* pp. 421–4 – selection; *Riley* pp. 165–76 – selection; *Wiener* pp. 559–63 – selection): *Codex juris gentium diplomaticus*, Hanover, 1693, 'Praefatio ad lectorem', pp. i–xviii (*LPG* III, pp. 386–9 – selection).

Protogaea, 1715 (ed. W. v. Engelhardt, Stuttgart, 1949 – Latin with German tr.).

'Quelques remarques sur le livre de M. Locke intitulé *Essay of Understanding*', 1697 (VI.1, pp. 4–9).

Reply to the thoughts on the system of pre-established harmony (*Loemker* pp. 574–85): 'Réponse de M. Leibniz aux réflexions contenues dans la seconde édition du *Dictionnaire critique* de M. Bayle, article Rorarius, sur le système de l'harmonie préétablie', *Histoire critique de la république des lettres* (1716), pp. 78–115 (*LPG* IV, pp. 554–71).

'Responsio ad Dn. Nic. Fatii Duillierii imputationes. Accessit nova artis analyticae promotio specimine indicata; cum designatione per numeros assumtitios loco literarum. Algebra ex combinatoria arte lucem capit', *Acta eruditorum* (May 1700), pp. 198–208 (*LMG* v, pp. 340–9).

Review of the mathematical essays appended to the *Opticks*: 'Isaaci Newtoni tractatus duo, de speciebus et magnitudine figuram curvilinearum...1704', *Acta eruditorum* (January 1705), pp. 30–6.

Theodicy (ed. Austin Farrer and tr. E. M. Huggard, London, 1952): *Essais de théodicée sur la bonté de Dieu, la liberté de l'homme et l'origine du mal*, Amsterdam, 1710 (*LPG* VI, pp. 21–462).

'Unicum opticae, catoptricae et dioptricae principium', *Acta eruditorum* (June 1682), pp. 185–90 (*Dutens* III, pp. 145–51).

'Unvorgreifliche Gedanken, betreffend die Ausübung und Verbesserung der deutschen Sprache', c. 1697 (Leibniz, *Collectanea etymologica*, pp. 255ff; *Dutens* VI.2, pp. 6–51).

INDEX OF NAMES

This lists the most significant occurrences of references – usually though not always by name – to identifiable individual people, in the text and in the Notes. For a virtually complete index of proper names occurring in the text, the reader is referred to the Academy edition.

Acquaviva, Claudio, 519
Adam, 240, 257, 314, 320, 400f, xlv
Albert the Great, 266, *xxiv, xlv
Alexander the Great, 201, 256
Alliot, Pierre, 320
Andrada, see Payva de Andrada
Anselm of Canterbury, 437
Apollonius of Perga, 107f, 371, 407, 489
Aquinas, see Thomas Aquinas
Archimedes, 95f, 370f, 376, 415f, 451f, 489, xlf, lxvii
Aristotle 47f, 59, 71, 98, 153, 169, 175f, 201, 297f, 344f, 370-2, 409, 419, 426, 431, 434, 449f, 466, 476f, 486, xxvi, xxxixf, xlix, lxiii, lxxvii; see also Peripatetics
Arminius (Jacob Harmens), 75, *xxvi
Arnauld, Antoine, 407, 518, *xxvi, lix, lxiv,
Asgill, John, 506f, *xxvii
Asseburg, Rosamunde von der, 506, *xxvii
Augustine of Hippo, 367, 447, 501-3, 517
Averroes (Ibn Rushd), 59, *xxvii

Bacon, Francis, 455, *xxviif
Barclay, Robert, 505
Barner, Jakob, 426
Bayle, Pierre, 55, 71, 440f, 501, *xxviii, xxxv, li
Bellarmine, Robert, 521
Bernier, François, 70
Bernoulli, Jakob, xlviii
Bernoulli, Johann, xlviii
Beverwijck, Jan van, 523
Beza, Theodor, 514
Boccaccio, Giovanni, 340
Boehme, Jacob, 281, 507f
Boethius, lxxviif

Boineburg, Johann Christian von, xxviii, xxxvi, lx
Boniface of Mainz, 391, lxxix
Borgia, Francisco, 187
Bossuet, Jacques Bénigne, 459, 468, *xxviiif, liii, lxviii
Bouhours, Dominique, 141, *xxix
Boulliau, Ismael, 489, *xxx
Bourignon, Antoinette de, 506-8, *xxx
Boyle, Robert, 53, 300, 455, *xxx, xliv
Buratini, Giovanni Michele, 147
Burnett, Thomas, lvif, lxxviii

Calixtus, Georg, lxxvii
Calvin, Jean, 514
Campanella, Tommaso, 72
Cardano, Girolamo, 72, 484, xl
Casati, Paolo, 171f
Casaubon, Isaac, 418
Charles V, Emperor, 467f
Chemnitz, Martin, 501
Christina, Queen of Sweden, 494f, *xxxiii, xxxiv
Cicero, M. Tullius, 186, 252, 435, lxxviif
Clarke, Samuel, xxxii
Clauberg, Johann, 285f, xxxii, liv
Clavius, Christoph, 376, xl
Comenius, Jan Amos, 409, 508f, *xxxv
Confucius, 501
Conring, Hermann, 450, *xxxvf
Conway, Anne, 72, *xxxvi
Copernicus, Nicolaus, 74, 373, 515
Coste, Pierre, xii, xviiif, 164, xxxix, liii
Cromwell, Oliver, 467
Cudworth, Ralph, 70, liii
Cyrano de Bergerac, 220, 356, 472, lviii

Dahlberg, Erik Jönsson, 467
Dalgarno, George, 278, lxxvi

Dante Alighieri, 340
Democritus, 67, 70f, 265, 290
Desargues, Girard, 135, *xxxvii
Descartes, René, 70–2, 74, 123, 132, 150, 221, 255, 270, 317, 408, 422, 437f, 455, 472f, 488f, xxviif, xxxiii, xxxiv, *xxxviif, xl, liiif, lviii, lix, lxi, lxix, lxxi, lxxiv, lxxvi, lxxviii; see also Cartesians
De Witt, Jan, 377, 465, *xxxviii
Digby, Kenelm, 82
Diogenes of Sinope, 345
Diophantus of Alexandria, 488f, xl
Dioscorides, 336, xxxix
Dominis, Marco Antonio de, 390f
Drabik, Nicholas, 508, xxxv
Draud, Georg, 525
Duns Scotus, John, 377, 498, *lxx

Ebenbitar (Ibn al-Baitar), 336, *xxxviiif
Eckhart, J. G., xxxif
Eisenhart, Johannes, xlvf
Epictetus, 432
Epicurus, 60, 125, 130f, 374, 462
Episcopius (Bisschop), Simon, 174
Ernst August, Elector of Brunswick, xxxf, lxxi
Euclid, 50, 95, 101, 107, 361, 370f, 407, 413, 415, 419, 428, 451f, 479, 489, 524, *xlf

Fabri, Honoré, 498, 515, *xli
Fabricius, Johann Ludwig, 103, *xli
Fénelon, François, liii, lxviii
Fermat, Pierre de, lv
Ferrari, Ludovico, 488, xl
Ferro, Scipione del, 488, xl
Fludd, Robert, 68, *xli
Fontenelle, Bernard le Bovier de, 472, *xlii, lviif
Foucher, Simon, 374, *xlii
Frénicle de Bessy, Bernard, 353, *xlii
Fromondus (Libert Froidmont), 225, *xlii

Galen, 364f, xxxix
Galilei, Galileo, 229, 515, lvii
Gassendi, Pierre, 67, 70f, 374, xxxiv, *xliii
Georg Ludwig, Elector of Brunswick (King George I of England), xxxi, lxxii
Gesner, Conrad, 525
Golius (Gool), Jacob, 274, lxxx
Gonzales, Thyrsus, 372, lxv
Goropius Becanus (Jan van Gorp), 285, *xliii

Greaves, John, 147
Gretser, Jakob, 518
Grimaldi, Claudio Filippo, 354, *xliii
Grotius, Hugo, 431, 467, xxxiii, lxvii
Guericke, Otto von, 126, 149, *xliiif

Hardy, Claude, 408, *xliv
Helmont, Franciscus Mercurius van, 72, 233, 240, xxxvi, *xlv, lxxiv
Helmont, J. B. van, xxvi, xlv
Herbert of Cherbury, Edward, 97
Hippocrates of Chios, 455, lxvii
Hippocrates of Cos, 55, 417, *xlv
Hobbes, Thomas, 95, 270, 273, 396, *xlvi, xlviiif, lxiv, lxvii, lxxvi
Hofmann, Daniel, 494
Holden, Henry, 518
Hooker, Richard, 484f
Huygens, Christiaan, 147, 314, 465, 472, xxxii, xxxiv, xxxv, *xlvi, xlvii, lv, lviif, lxf, lxviii

Jesus of Nazareth, 58, 240, 314, 401, 506, 509, 513f, xlv
Johann Friedrich, Duke of Brunswick, lii, lxi
Jurieu, Pierre, li, lix
Justinian, Emperor, 425f

Kant, Immanuel, xiii
Keckermann, Bartholomaeus, 500
Kepler, Johannes, 123, 344, 472, lvii
Kerckring, Theodor, 316, li
Kesler, Andreas, 498
Koerbagh, Adriaan, 277, *l
Kuhlmann, Quirin, 507

Labadie, Jean de, 507, *l
Labbé, Philippe, 279
La Coste, Bertrand de, 508
La Loubère, Simon de, 65, *l
Lamy, François, 278, 383, *l
Lannion, Pierre de, *l
Leeuwenhoek, Antoni van, 316, *li, lxii
Le Gobien, Charles, 105, *li
Leo X, Pope, 494
Lessius (Leys), Leonhard, 149
Lipen, Martin, 525
Locke, John, xi–xiii, xvf, 70, xxvi, xxxix, liii, lvif, lxxiii, lxxiv
Ludolph van Ceulen, 85, lxviii
Lull, Raymond, 500
Luther, Martin, 514

Malebranche, Nicolas, 70, 171, l, *liii, lxi
Marcus Aurelius, Emperor, 432

Mariotte, Edmé, 121, 309, xxxv, *liii, lx
Martini, Cornelius, 494
Masham, Damaris, 70, xxxix, *liii
Maurier, Louis Aubery du, 467
Maurolyco, Francesco, 390f
Meier, Gerhard, 286, *liv
Melanchthon, Philipp, 514
Ménage, Gilles, 315, 319, 469
Méré, Antoine Gombault, Chevalier de, 465, *livf
Mersenne, Marin, xxiii
Molyneux, William, 135f, 423, *lvif
More, Henry, 72, 240, 343f, xxxiii, xxvi, *lviii
Mouton, Gabriel, 147
Musaeus, Johannes, 498–500

Naudé, Gabriel, 494, xxvii
Newton, Isaac, 60, 64f, xxxii, xxxiii, xxxv, xxxix, xlviif, lii, lxxi
Niceron, Jean-François, 258, *lix
Nicole, Pierre, 458, 518, xxvi, li, *lix, lx

Ockham, see William of Ockham
Oldenburg, Henry, 455, *lixf, lxf

Pajon, Claude, 502, lxii
Pappus, 450, 484, 489, xxv
Pascal, Blaise, 465, xxvi, lv, lxi, lxii
Paul, the Apostle, 48f, 92, 150, 495f
Paul, the Roman jurist, 425
Payva de Andrada, Diego, 501, xxviii, lxii
Pellisson-Fontanier, Paul, 500f, xxix, li, *lxii, lxx
Penn, William, 507
Petrarch, Francesco, 340
Petronius Arbiter, 422
Philip of Macedonia, 196
Pisani, Ottavio, 270f
Plato, 47f, 71, 77, 94, 165, 343, 345, 352f 371; see also Platonists
Pomponne, Simon Arnauld de, 508f, lx, *lxiv
Poniatowska, Christina, 508, xxxv
Priscillian of Avila, 316, *lxv
Proclus, 107f, 371, 406f, 428
Procopius of Caesarea, 466
Pufendorf, Samuel, 385, *lxvii, lxxixf
Pythagoras, 342, 416

Rakoczy, Georg, 508
Ramus, Petrus, 356, 365, *lxviiif, lxxviii
Regius (Henrik van Roy), 317, *lxix
Reinesius, Thomas, 336
Roberval, Gilles Personne de, 107, 407f, 414, xxxiii, lv, lxi, lxviii, *lxixf

Rohault, Jacques, 224, xxxii

Saint-Vincent, Grégoire de, 489
Scaliger, Joseph Justus, 95, 106f, lxvii
Scaliger, Julius Caesar, 49, 106f
Schilter, Johann, 280, 286
Schönberg, Ulrich, 106
Scotus, see Duns Scotus
Scudéry, Madeleine de, *lxx
Seckendorf, Veit Ludwig von, 468, *lxxf
Sennert, Daniel, 426
Serenus of Antinoeia, 408, xliv
Sleidan, Johan Philippson, 114, 467f
Sluse, René François de, 408, lxii
Socinus (Fausto Sozzini), 497f, *lxxi
Socrates, 77, 165, 432, 505
Solomon, 154
Sophie, Princess, Electress of Brunswick, 231, xxvii, xlv, lxii, *lxxif
Sophie Charlotte, Queen of Prussia, xxiv, lxxii
Spinoza, Baruch or Benedict, 73, 455, 462, xxviif, xxxviii, l, lxii, *lxxiif
Stegmann, Christoph, 497, lxxi
Stillingfleet, Edward, xi, 60, 62–4, *lxxiii
Strauch, Johann, 331, *lxxiii
Suarez, Francisco, 431

Tertullian, Quintus Septimius, 458, 495, lxv
Thales of Miletus, 406f
Theodora, Empress, 466
Thomas Aquinas, 222, 437
Thomasius, Jacob, 509, lxiii, *lxxvii
Torricelli, Evangelista, 126, *lxxviii
Trotter, Catharine, 70, *lxxviii
Tschirnhaus, E. W. von, xxxii, lvi, lxi, lxx, lxxii
Tulp, Nicolaas, 234, *lxxviii

Vedelius (Wedel), Nicholaus, 498–500, 502
Viète, François, 410, 489, xl
Vincent of Lerins, 518
Virgilius of Salzburg, 391, *lxxix
Voss, Isaak, xxxiv

Weigel, Erhard, 385, lxvii, *lxxixf
Wilkins, John, 278, lxxvi
William of Ockham, 499
Witsen, Nicolaas, 103, *lxxx

Zwinger, Theodor, 522
Zwingli, Ulrich, 499, 502, *lxxx

absolute, 65f, 154, 157–9, 228; *see also* necessity

abstract idea, entity, 57, 110, 127, 145, 150, 174, 213, 217f, 312f, 323, 333f, 432

abstraction (process), 57, 142, 218, 289–91

academies of science, *xxiiif, xxxi, xliv, lixf, lx

accident, *see* essence/accident; mode/substance

reification of, 62, 150, 171f, 217, 224, 231, 303f, 334, 379

accountability, *see* identity, moral; punishment

accountancy, 206f, 360, 478, xxix

action at a distance, 60f, 64–6, 130f, xxxiii, lviii

metaphorically speaking, 182f, 193

action/disposition, 52, 87, 98, 106, 169, 250, 358, xxxix, xliv; *see also* disposition; potentially

active/passive, 114, 119, 144f, 169–71, 210f, 213, 216, 225, 264; *see also* passion

advancement of knowledge, hopes and plans for, 354, 383, 386f, 389–91, 416f, 454, 471, 515, 527; *see also* academies of science

affinity (alliance), 249

after-life, 190f, 200f, 208f, 379f, 432, 462, 472, 489f, xxvii, xlv; *see also* immortality; punishment and reward

aggregates, 146, 226, 328, 378, xxxixf, lxxiv; *see also* unity; substance, simple

alchemy, 299f, 342, xxx, xlv

algebra, 158, 186, 391, 410f, 488f, xl, lxxvi

analogy, *see* uniformity

analysis, 73–5, 120, 186, 212, 228, 255f, 297–9, 368f, 377, 383, 403f, 450f, 476, 478, 484, *xxivf, lxxv–lxxvii

angels, 58f, 220–2, 306, 313, 397, 489f, lviii

anger, 167f, 499f

animal, 388, 440, *xxv, lvii; *see also* beasts; embodiment; life; plants

appetition, 173, 189, lviii; *see also* disquiet; 'volition'

Arabs, 248, 318, 336

arbitrariness, 56, 66, 85, 131–3, 165f, 264, 268, 302f, 381f, 403f, 522n; *see also* archetypes; language, arbitrariness in; miracles; sufficient reason

archetypes of ideas, 264–8, 287, 294–6, 300–3, 321–3, 337f, 349f, 392f

argument, kinds of, 491

arithmetic, 50, 77f, 85f, 385, xxxii

and definition, 366f, 409, 412–14

Arminians, 75f, *xxvi

atoms, 57, 59f, 70, 72, 125f, 130f, 219, 230f, 290, 343f, 436, xxx, xxxvii, xliii

attention, 50, 54, 80, 84, 86f, 96, 100, 102, 113, 115, 160f

attraction, *see* traction

attribute, 63–6, 213, 310; *see also* substance, idea of

authority, 206, 372f, 418, 458f, 517–20

Averroists, 59, *xxvii

awareness ('*aperception*'), 53–9, 76–8, 83f, 113, 115–18, 134, 139, 161f, 173, 188f, 192, 194, 239, 263, 357, 412, 438, *xxvii; *see also* attention; confusion; idea, distinct; minute

axioms, 73, 75, 101, 107, 170, 406–27, 448–53, 455, lxx, lxxvif; *see also* truths, identical

beasts, 51, 65, 67, 72, 86, 93, 98f, 113f, 134, 142f, 167f, 173, 180, 232, 234f, 325f, 471–3; *see also* humanity

and language, 142, 273–5, 307, 320

death of, 55, 59, 236, 473

pseudo-reasonings of, 50f, 73, 143, 271, 475

being, 51, 85f, 101f, 104, 218, 430f

Bible, 469f, 499f, 515, xxix, l

'blind' thoughts, 185f, 188f, 191, 202, 254, 259f, 275, 286, *xxviii

body, *see* embodiment; division; impenetrability; matter; harmony, soul with body

brain, 116f, 144f
Brunswick, House of, *xxx–xxxii, xliv, lii, lxif, lxxif
'but', 331f

Cartesians, 53, 56, 67, 70–2, 113f, 125–8, 131, 150f, 224, 296, 367, 423, 437, 515, *xxxii, xxxv, xxxviif, xlvi, liii, lxix
categories, 328, 343, 524
cause, 216, 228, liii, lix, lxivf; see also interaction
  final, 73, 216, 389
  /reason, 475
certainty, 68, 85, 238, 359–75, 399f, 404–6; see also demonstrative; intuition; sensible things
  moral/metaphysical, 68, 406
children, 86f, 304, 314, 341, 412, 421f
Chinese language, 84, 274, 354, 398f
  mathematics, 452
  people, 336, xliii
  religion, 501f, xlix, li
Christianity, threats to, 58, 62, 212, 277, 416f
church reunion, xxviiif, lxii, lxxvii
coexistence, 149, 357f, 382f
'Cogito', 367, 411
cohesion, 59f 123–6, 223, *xxxiv; see also extension; fluid/rigid
colour, 219, 298–300, 323, *xxxv, lii; see also qualities, secondary, sensible
common notions, 49, 75, 97
common sense, the, 128
compossibility, 265, 307, 323f, lxxix
conatus, see endeavour
condensation and rarefaction, 82, 124, 126, 409, xxxv, lviii; see also impenetrability
confusion, 53–5, 81, 84, 88, 91, 113, 117, 120, 132f, 137, 139, 159, 165f, 186f, 194f, 200, 210, 228, 254–63, 295, 357, 381f, 403f, 451f; see also idea/image; idea, distinct; quality, sensible; sensible/intelligible
conscience, duties and rights of, 519f
consciousness, 235–46, *xxxvi
conservatism, 100, 458f, 517f
constraint, physical/moral, 179
contingency, 175f, 178, 433, xxivf, lxxix; see also truths of reason/fact
contingent things, 392, 447
continuity, mathematical, 149, 152, 156, 225, 385

of change, 54, 56–8, 60, 117, 473
  taxonomic, see vacuum among forms
contradiction, principle of, 75f, 82f, 101f, 362, 498
conversion (logical), 364–6
Copernicans, 74, 515
creation, 216, 441f
  continual, 67, 443

death, see after-life; beasts, death of; immortality; transmigration
debate, conduct of, 259, 339, 390, 417–22, 477f, 481f
definition, 101, 137, 162, 266f, 291–300, 311, 313, 332, 351–3, 432, 451f; see also analysis; arithmetic and definition; axioms; essence; idea, distinct; truths, identical
  causal, 194, 298
  provisional, 300, 311f, 317, 322, 324, 347
  real/nominal, difference explained, 295, 346
demonstration, benefits of, 424f, 449–53
  methods of, 358–61, 367–72, 428, 475f; see also intuition; logic; syllogism
  scope of, 260f, 383–6, 425
demonstrative knowledge, 50, 85, 301, 373, 411, 524; see also innate theoretical principles; intuition; sensible/ intelligible; truths of reason
design in nature, 104f, 516f
desire, 56, 163–5, 183f, 191f, 195–9; see also appetition; disquiet; taste; will to will
despair, 167
determined/forced, 178f
dignity and propriety, 93f
disability, intellectual, 143f, 207, 309, 395, 473, 493, 510f; see also madness
  sensory, 76, 106, 127, 132, 136–8, 287, 493
disparities, 362f, 408
disposition, active/passive, 79f, 84, 106, 110, 112, 169f; see also endeavour; power, active/inactive
disquiet, 56, 115f, 164–8, 183–5, 188–93
distance, 146f, 202
  epistemic, 352
division of the extended, 57, 59f, 151, 219, 225
dreams, 106f, 213, 374f, 445
duration, 51, 151–4, 211f

embodiment of souls, 58, 67f, 72, 113f,

embodiment (*cont.*)
117f, 155, 212, 220f, 307, 317f, 328f, 388, 490; *see also* rarefied body; transmigration
empiric, 50, 271, 300, 357, 416f, 475f; *see also* beasts, pseudo-reasonings of; induction
endeavour, 110, 112, 165, 167, 169f, 172f, 186, 192f, 216, 226, *xxxix
entelechy, 71, 169f, 172, 210, 216, 225, 318, 328f, *xxxixf
enthusiasm, *see* fanaticism
enthymeme, 76, 83, 421, 482, *xl
envy, 168
error, 202f, 205f, 509–21
esotericism, 260f, 342
essence/accident, 161, 180, 325, 433f
  as possibility, 293–6, 323
  /existence, *see* contingency
  individual, 304f, 310
  nominal, 293–5, 302, 346
  of modes, 346–8, 402, 426
  real, 292–6, 310–29, 338, 345f, 399–402, 404f; *see also* gold; humanity; species
etymologies, 104, 276–8, 346; *see also* particles; prepositions; sounds
evidence, weighing of, 456–61, 466–71, lxvi; *see also* probability; testimony
existence, 129, 211f, 411; *see also* contingency
  as coexistence, 358, 411
experience, *see* senses
experiences (propositions), 367, 430, 434
experiment, 50, 85, 371, 389, 454f, xxviif, xxx
experiments, mentioned individually, 121, 126, 133, 147, 409, 416
extension, 149, 158, 211f, 223; *see also* cohesion; division; matter; space
  and matter or body, 72, 102f, 126–8, 150f, 422f, xxxvii
extrinsic denomination, 227, 230f, 401f, *xxxvif; *see also* identity of indiscernibles; relations

faculties, reified, 174, 179f, 379
  unexplained, 61, 67f, 110, 140, 196, 379, 381f; *see also* qualities, occult
faith and reason, 379f, 494–502, 520f, lxix; *see also* revelation
fanaticism, 503–9
fear, 167, 274
fiction, 245, 314, 355f, 401
fire, 471, 473
fluid/rigid, 59f, 111f, 123–6, 151, 222; *see also* cohesion

'free will', 175f, 180f, 195
freedom, 174–82, 195–9, 207f, 477, 482f; *see also* indifference
  of mind, 181, 195–7; *see also* passions
future development of souls, 79, 139, 194, 219, 242, 246, xlv

games, 465f, 470, *xliif, livf
generality, not mind-dependent, 292f; *see also* essence, real
genus/differentia, 291f
  real/logical, 63–6
geometry, 50, 77, 86, 267, 308, 346–8, 385, 389, 479, 489, xxxiif, xxxvii, xliv, liiif, lxii, lxxviii; *see also* quadrature
  and the senses, 77, 137
  methods of, 158, 261f, 360f, 368–70, 406f, 415f, 428, 451f, 476, 524f
  practical/scientific, 371, 451–3, 524, lvi
God, arguments for existence of, 68, 104f, 434–41, xxxvii, lxv; *see also* faith; revelation
  as ground for eternal truth, 145, 149, 155, 158, 227, 300, 397, 447
  men's idea of, 75f, 96f, 103f, 109, 225
  nature of, 73, 114, 158, 306, 343, 502, 510; *see also* morality and religion
  powers and actions of, 57, 60–2, 64f, 67, 82, 179, 181, 198f, 381f, 440f, 493; *see also* arbitrariness; harmony
gold, criteria for, 267, 294, 299f, 312, 324, 338, 346, 400–2
golden rule, 91f
good/evil, 162, 165, 185f, 193–5, 522; *see also* moral
grammar, 301f, 330, 336
gravitation, *see* traction
Greeks, 318, 336, 339, 371, 462, xxv

happiness, 90f, 163, 189, 193f, 199f, 207, 522, 524, 526; *see also* joy
hard/soft, *see* fluid/rigid
harmony, cosmic, 55, 71, 227, 306f, 329, 389, 440f, *lxivf
  soul with body, 54, 71f, 77, 116f, 172f, 177, 220–2, 224, 240–2, 307, 380f, 390, 442f, 473f, l, lix; *see also* interaction
Hebrews, 246, 336
history, 466–71, xxx–xxxii, xlvf
homogeneity, 53, 57, 72f, 110, 230, 302, 305, 328
hope, 167
horology, 326, xlvi, lxi
humanity, criteria for, 234f, 246f, 292f,

humanity (*cont.*)
    309–11, 313–15, 318–20, 393–5, 400f, 473, 475f
    one species?, 326
hunger, 118, 164, 189
hypothetico-deductive method, 450, 453f, 484

idea, adequate, 266–8
  clear ('*claire*'), 96, 219, 254f, 297, *xxxiiif
  complex, 142
  confused, *see* confusion
  distinct, 73, 84, 96, 109, 111, 119, 137, 219, 255f, 261–3, 297, 382f, 389, 405, 487f, *xxxviii; *see also* confusion
  /image, 77, 137, 261–3, 375, 392, 404, 451f, 487
  intellectual, 51, 81, 85f, 392
  obscure, 254–9, 261, 321
  /quality, 217, 228, 404
  real, *see* archetypes
  /signification, 173
  simple, 120, 128f, 170, 211f, 217, 254, 263f, 296–300, 339, 392
  /thought, 109, 119, 140, 300f
  true, 73, 128, 268f, 398
  vivid ('*claire*'), 73, 137, 297, xxxiiif
ideas and possibility, 438
  association of, 269–71
  (dis)agreement of, 355, 357, 375, 396
  Locke's taxonomy of, 213
identity, 55, 102, 229–47, 357f
  and substance, 218
  moral or personal, 58, 114, 233–47
  of man, 102, 232–5, 246
  real or physical, 236–47
identity of indiscernibles, 57f, 110, 230f, 245f, 290, 305, 499, xxxvif, lxxii
ignorance, 206, 388–91
imagination, *see* idea/image
immediate knowledge, 51f, 109, 135, 236–8, 367, 374, 434, 491; *see also* inner/outer; truths, primary
immortality, 58f, 67, 72, 89, 113f, 139, 162, 236; *see also* after-life
impenetrability, 81f, 122–4, 126, 170, 230, 343f, 409, lviii, lxiif
impetus, 63, 123f, 216
impulse (mechanical), 60f, 130f, 223f, xxxiii, *xlvii
incline without necessitating, 116, 175, 178f, 199, *xlvii
indifference of equilibrium, 56, 116, 166, 180, 188, 196–8
individuation, 230f, 289f; *see also* identity of indiscernibles

induction, 49, 80, 85, 158, 368f, 417, 425, 446, xxvii; *see also* empiric; regularity
inertia, 123f, 170, 344
infinite/indefinite, 151, 154, xxxvii
infinitesimal, 158, xlviif
  calculus, 389, 489, xxv, *xlviif, lxi, lxxvi
infinity, concept of, 150f, 154, 157–9, 225, 262f, xlii
  in contingent world, 55, 57, 289f, 308, 329, 381; *see also* division
  in mathematics, 308, 376f, 385; *see also* continuity, mathematical
innate, 48–53, 57, 70, 109–11, 140f, 447; *see also* interaction
  ideas, 48–53, 81–6, 101–11, 158, 225, 430
  practical principles, 88–101, 103
  theoretical principles, 74–88, 90, 101–8
inner/outer, 237f, 292f, 309, 311, 314, 388, 493; *see also* essence, real
insensible, 52–9, 112f, 115–17, 183, 188, 192–4, 197, 239f, 245; *see also* awareness; confusion; minute
instant, 152
instinct, 76, 84, 89–94, 97f, 101, 107, 165, 351
instituted/natural, 249f, 278, 399, 499, *xlix; *see also* arbitrariness
intension/extension, inversely correlated, 275, 486
intensity, 159, lv
intentional species, 61, 343
interaction between substances, 55, 74, 135, 177, 195, 210, 222, 392, lix; *see also* accident, reification of; active/passive; harmony
intuition, 361, 366f, 369f, 372, 434f, 489f; *see also* axioms; truths, identical
invention, 291, 356, 368f, 466, 476, 483, 488, 522, *xlix, lvi, lxviii
involuntary, *see* constraint; 'volition'; will to believe, to will
  thoughts, 177

journals, 71, *xlixf, liv, lixf
joy and sorrow, 88, 90f, 166f, 189, 204
judgment, 134f, 141, 456f, 476, 522; *see also* invention
jurisprudence, *see* law
  natural and universal, 50, 93, 302
justice, 89f, 93, 243f, 246, 384

knowledge, *see* certainty; demonstrative knowledge; truths of reason; reason
  non-propositional, 355f

language, *see* beasts; Chinese; etymologies; definition; grammar; humanity; nominalism; sounds
  and communication, 138, 273–5, 287, 334f, 339, 398f
  and logic, 522f
  and migration of peoples, 279–81, 285, 337, xxxi
  and mind, 274, 330, 333, 336f
  and reasoning, 275, 335, lxii, lxxv–lxxvii
  arbitrariness in, 278f, 281–5
  changes in, 339f
  deep structure in, 330, 480
  ellipsis in, 333
  iconic, 354, 398f, lvi, lxxvi
  learning of, 341
  misuse of, 260f, 340–50
  musical, 274
  written, 337, 359
large/small, 439f, 474
law, 331, 351, 370f, 384, 419f, 425–7, 430, 432, 457–61, 464f, 491f, lxiv, lxv, lxvii, lxix
libraries, 524f, *lii
life, 113f, 231f, 305f, 318, 328f, 348f, 380; *see also* animal; plant
light, 137, 287, 298, 423, 434, 505, xxxv, xlvi, lii
  finite speed of, 135, xxxv
  of nature, 84, 89, 91f, 94, 98, 100
logic and mathematics, 370, 478f, 486f
  natural, 77f, 91, 477f, 482
  nature of, 91, 342f, 363–6, 482, 521–5, lxviii; *see also* syllogism
  of probability, 206, 372, 466
logical form, 478–84
  necessity, *see* necessity, absolute; truths of reason
love, 73, 89, 93, 162f, 215, *liif
lowest species, 255, 275, 293, 325, 400–2

madness, 143f, 242, 505
magnetism, 125
mass, 130, 210f, 222
material mode, 287
mathematics, 50, 85f, 91, 295, 368, 370f, 386, 408, 424f, 453, 487f, xl, xliv, liiif, lxf; *see also* algebra; arithmetic; continuity, mathematical; demonstration; geometry; infinitesimal calculus; logic and mathematics; number; quadrature
  compared with morality, 92, 95f, 98, 260f, 385f
matter, 59–68, 71, 122–8, 344f; *see also* action at a distance; cohesion;

division; extension; motion; quality, primary
  creation of, 441f, xxxix
  physical/metaphysical, 63f
  prime, 110, 222, 344f, 378f
  producing thought, 65–7, 379, 381, 436, 439–41, lv
  secondary, 130, 222, 378, 434
  unthinking, 62–8, 70, 378–82, 436, 441f; *see also* soul, immaterial
maxims, *see* axioms
measure, 49f, 147, 152f, 155, 302, 321
mechanism, 66f, 72, 92, 139, 220, 329, 455, xliii, xlvi, xlvii, lviii; *see also* matter
medicine, 336, 353, 378, 383, 387, 390, 426f, 454, 465, 523, 525–7, lxiv
memory, 52, 54, 77f, 106f, 114f, 140, 156, 160f, 206, 233f, 236–46, 359, 445, lvi; *see also* demonstration and memory
  and induction, 51, 271
  and present experience, 54, 238
metaphysics, 50, 209, 371, 430–2, 449f, lxxiii
meteorology, 390f
microscope, 219f, 473, li
mind, *see* harmony, soul with body; innate; perception; soul
mining and metallurgy, 360, xxv, xxxvi, xlivf
minute perceptions, 53–8, 113, 115f, 133f, 161f, 164f, 188, 194, 239, *lvf; *see also* awareness; confusion; sensible
miracles, 65–8, 379f, 474, 499, 507–9
mode, intellectual, 347
  simple, 145f, 148, 156f, 159f
  /substance, 145, 304, 442; *see also* accident; archetypes; attribute; essence, real
monad, 55, 102, 145, 223, 231, 440, 443, 473f, xxxix, *lvii, lxivf, lxxiv; *see also* soul; substance, simple; unity
monsters, *see* humanity
moral deterioration, 98f, 350, 461–3, 511f
  relativism, 97f, 249–53, 303f, 393
  science (ethics), 50, 88f, 92f, 372, 383f, 432, 521f; *see also* reason, practical
  training, 177, 186–91, 195f, 202, 204, 207, 378
morality and religion, 89f, 96–8, 200f, 237, 240, 389, 432, 462, lxvf, lxviii
Moslems, 190
motion, 53f, 123f, 129f, 151, 171f, 210f, 297; *see also* impulse; quality, primary; rest
  laws of, 56, 72, 152, 171, 224, xxxii, xxxviif, liii

myself, 235–8, 241, 358, 411

name, *see* language; nominalism
   personal, 247f
   proper, 275f, 288f, 328
natural religion, *see* design in nature;
   God; revelation
   science, 56f, 78, 116, 321, 344, 371, 383,
     389, 453f, 484, 521f, *lviiif
necessary, *see* axioms; demonstrative
   knowledge; truths, identical
   /certain, 406
   /contingent, *see* truths of reason/fact
   /determined, 178f, xlvii
necessity, absolute/relative, 176, 178f,
   406, 495, 499, xlvii
   and innateness, 49, 79f, 86, 96f, 158
negation, 396; *see also* privative
nominalism, 84f, 213f, 246f, 256–9, 292–5,
   301–4, 323f, 396f, *lxix; *see also*
   essence, real; possibilities, reality of
non-existent subject, truth about, 447
'notion', 213, 303f, 430
notions, three levels of, 209
number, 81, 85, 127, 132, 142, 145, 155–7,
   159, 211f, 261, 266, 368f, 487f,
   lxxivf, lxxviii

open-mindedness, 460f, 502f, 514f; *see
   also* fanaticism
opinion, 372; *see also* evidence; moral
   relativism; probability; testimony
optics, *see* light
order, natural/epistemic, 81, 83f, 154,
   212, 276, 411f
Origenists, 246

pain, 131–3, 183f; *see also* pleasure
Paris, 85, 107f, 408, xl, *lx–lxii
part, *see* whole
particles (language), 329–33
particular/general, 82f, 142, 275, 288–90,
   359–61, 409–11, 416f, 445f, 448f, 485
passion, 94f, 98, 115, 166–8, 175, 188,
   191f, 194–6; *see also* active/passive
   and belief, 167
Pelagians, 502, *lxii
perception, 51, 139, 222f; *see also* representation; soul
   /awareness ('*aperception*'), 134; *see
     also* awareness; confusion; minute
   /thought, 133f, 210
Peripatetics, 70, 82, 124, 342–4, 390, 494,
   *lxiii
perspective, 135, 257f, xxxvii, lix
phenomenon, 145, 210, 309, 374f, *lxiii

'Philalethes', 73, 386
place, 148f, 221f, 230, 289; *see also*
   space
plants, 64, 138f, 231f, 309f, 314f, 317,
   473; *see also* soul, vegetative
Platonists, 52, 78, 246, 343, 442; *see also*
   recollection
pleasure (and pain), 51, 129, 162–8, 183–5,
   187–9, 194
pneumatology, 56f, 329, 526f, *lxiv
point, 152
possibilities, reality of, 155, 227, 300f,
   309, 323; *see also* essence
postulates, 419
potentially in mind, 52, 83f, 86f; *see also*
   action/disposition; idea/thought
power, 129, 168–72, 210–12, 216, 225f,
   379, 382
   active/inactive, 110, 112, 169–72, 216;
     see also active/passive; disposition;
     endeavour
practical arts and skills, 417, 431, 451f,
   454, 523–7, xxvi
prejudice, 74, 100, 408, 419
prepositions, 277f, 330
present/future good, 90, 94f, 187, 190–2,
   202–6
preservation, *see* creation, continuous;
   immortality
Priscillianists, 316, lxv
privative/positive, 129f, 276
probability, 68, 205–7, 372f, 444, 457–9,
   465f, 483f, 516f, lv, *lxvi; *see also*
   evidence
property (legal), 384
property (metaphysical), *see* attribute;
   mode; quality
prophecy, 161, 507–9, xxxv
propositions, complex, 357, 446f
   formation of, 396f; *see also* truths
Protestants, 418, 459, 500–2, 513f, 519,
   lxix; *see also* church reunion
punishment and reward, 96, 236, 241–6,
   250, 252f, 389, 477, 482f; *see also*
   after-life; identity, moral
   /remedy, 243, xxxvi

quadrature, 85, 96, 368f, 376f, 455, xlvi,
   xlviii, *lxviif
quality and power, 225f
   fundamental, 159
   occult, 65f, 68, 196, 382; *see also*
     faculties, unexplained
   original, 222f
   primary/secondary, 130–3, 382, 402f,
     405

quality and power (*cont.*)
  sensible, 54, 56, 120, 132, 165f, 170, 219, 298f, 372, 382f, 392, 403f
questions, 356, 368
Quietists, 59, 454, *lxviii

rarefied body, 58f, 233, 240, 313
real/possible, 301
reality, 145f, 263–6, 296, 447; *see also* archetypes; nominalism; sensible things
reason, 50f, 89f, 98f, 129, 136–8, 143, 196, 275, 378f, 394f, 475f; *see also* argument; faith; humanity; revelation; sensible/intelligible; sufficient reason; truths of reason
  /cause, 475
  contrary to/above, 492f
  parallel with experience, 371, 374f, 392, 444
  practical, 89, 94, 186–90, 194, 199f, 352
recollection, Platonic, 52, 78f, 87
reductio ad absurdum, 415, 428, xxv
reflection, 51–3, 81, 85f, 105, 111, 118f, 128f, 133f, 139, 160, 171–3, 213, 238; *see also* consciousness; innate; self-consciousness
regularity, assumption of, 49–51, 176, 404f; *see also* beasts; empiric; induction; reason, parallel
relations, 141f, 145f, 180, 213, 216, 226–8, 264f, 358
  moral, 247–54
representation, 109, 132f, 144f, 155, 177, 238
rest, 53, 109–12, 129f, 222; *see also* motion; substance, inactive
retrieval, mental, 52, 55, 77, 114f, 206, 291, lvi
revelation, 68, 76, 415f, 474, 494–7, 509, l; *see also* faith; fanaticism
rhetoric, 260, 341f, 350f, 482, xxvi, lxxviif
Roman Catholic, 234, 314, 459, 500–2, 518–21, xlix, li, lxviii; *see also* church reunion
Romans, 100, 370f, 462, 469f

salvation, requirements for, 314, 401, 463, 500–2, 510, 520f; *see also* humanity
savages, 76, 87, 89, 92f, 98f
scepticism, *see* sensible things
Scholastics (schoolmen), 48, 58, 67, 71, 189, 221f, 224, 278, 317, 322, 328, 406, 420f, 428, 430f, 437, 443, 447, 501; *see also* abstract...entity; faculties, unexplained

Scotists, 498, *lxx
second element, Descartes's, 57, 515, *lxxi
self, *see* myself
self-consciousness, 65, 241; *see also* awareness; consciousness; reflection
self-interest, 89f, 163, 276
senses, 77f, 110f, 113, 117, 121, 124f, 128f, 154, 160f, 200, 211f, 220, 371–3, 388f, 392; *see also* confusion; innate; quality, sensible; reason; sensible
sensible/intelligible, 61, 124, 128, 130, 378, 381, 392
  species, 144, 343
  things, existence of, 135, 296, 373–5, 412, 443–5, xlii
separated souls, *see* embodiment
sex, 310, 316f
shame, 168
shape (figure), 66, 128, 136–8, 147f, 156f, 230f
sight, *see* geometry and the senses; light; touch
signification, *see* idea/signification; language; particles; prepositions; sounds
similarity, mathematical, 156f
size, 263
sleep, 53f, 58, 112f, 115f, 161; *see also* dreams
Socinians, 497–9, *lxxi
solidity, *see* cohesion; fluid/rigid; impenetrability
sorrow, 167
soul, *see* entelechy; innate; monad; substance
  always thinks, 53, 57, 111–14, 119, 221; *see also* sleep; substance, inactive
  and entelechy, 170, 225
  immaterial, 110f, 116; *see also* matter, producing thought, unthinking
  vegetative, 139, 343
sounds, meanings of, 281–5
space, 64, 110, 127, 146, 149, 154f, 221, 422f; *see also* extension; place; vacuum
  one-dimensional, 155
space-travel, 314, 472, lviif
species, borderlines of, 308–21; *see also* gold; humanity
  nominal, 327, 396
  real/logical, 308f, 325–8; *see also* essence; genus, real/logical; vacuum among forms
specious present, 238

Spirits, suprahuman, 220, 246, 307, 310, 380, 388f, 472, 490, *lxxiii
Stoics, 49, 167, 175, 201
subject/predicate, 277f, 357, 486
substance, idea of, 51, 62, 105, 145, 150, 217–19; see also mode/substance
inactive, 53, 57, 65, 109–12
simple, 57, 73, 149, 211, 231f, 318, 328f, 378; see also aggregate; identity, real; monad; unity
substance's traces of past, future, other substances, 55, 58, 72f, 109, 114f, 228, 239, 440, lv
substantial form, 269, 306, 317f, 343, xxxixf, lvii, lxix, *lxxiv
substantial unity, see monad; substance, simple; unity
suffering, see pain
sufficient reason, principle of, 56, 179; see also arbitrariness
sun, 49f, 388
syllogism, 363–6, 371, 420, 424, 476–86, xl, lxvii, lxxii, *lxxv
symbols, 77, 185–7, 204, 275, 335, 410f, 488f, lvi, lxii, *lxxv–lxxvii
synthesis, 369, 377, 450, 476, 484, xxivf

tastes, 200f, 208
testimony, evidential value of, 236f, 457f, 466–70; see also revelation
textual scholarship, 336f; see also history
theology, 50, 329, 415f, 432, 498, 522, 526, xxviiif, l, li, lix
'Theophilus', 73
thought, 86f, 133f, 173, 210; see also idea/thought; matter, producing thought, unthinking; soul
time, 64, 110, 127, 147, 151–6, 202, 230, 289
eventless, 127, 153, 155, 436
tolerance, 461–3
touch, 77, 121f, 124, 135–7
traction (attraction), 60, 66, 123, 125, 130f, 136f; see also cohesion
transmigration of souls, 59, 114, 232f, 239–41, xlv; see also embodiment
transubstantiation, 513–15, lxxiv
truth as correspondence, 397f
moral/metaphysical, 397f

truths, general, 139, 142, 398f
identical, 82, 88, 96f, 101, 345, 361–7, 408f, 414f, 428–30, 450f, xxivf; see also axioms; definition; intuition
of reason/fact, 49–51, 73–81, 86, 88, 173, 238, 301, 361, 367, 374f, 412f, 430, 434, 444, 446f; see also analysis; contingent; demonstrative knowledge; essence/accident; necessity
primary, 73, 75, 170, 361, 367, 408, 411, 491

understanding (Locke, Philalethes), 62, 128, 144, 197, 207, 267, 292, 302, 339
(Theophilus), 173–5, 180, 297, 330, 333; see also innate ideas; reason
'uneasiness', 164, 188
uniformity throughout nature, 71f, 318f, 472, 490, xliv; see also vacuum among forms; for a different sort of uniformity see homogeneity
unity, 51, 129, 132, 231f, 317f, 328, 424, 440; see also aggregates; monad; substance, simple
university, conduct in, 416–22, 519
organization of, 525–7

vacuum, 57, 59, 70, 72, 109f, 126f, 151, 155, 422f, 473f, xliiif, lxxviii; see also time, eventless
among forms, 306f, 321, 323f, 473, *lxxix
fear of, 60, 125, 343
visions, 161, 505f, xxvii, xxx
'volition', 172f, 192
voluntary/involuntary, 172f, 176, 179–82; see also active/passive; freedom of mind; will to believe

warmth, 132f
whole, 151, 157f
and part, 102f, 142, 157, 238, 412f, 486
will, see voluntary
to believe, 182, 359, 456, 516f, 519
to will, 182f, 196f
wisdom, 340, 351, 512
wit, 141

LIST OF EXAMPLES, ILLUSTRATIONS AND ANECDOTES

the time of the earth's rotation, 49f
Hercules in the veins of marble, 52, 80
noise of mill and waterfall, 53f, 116
noise of waves, 54
breaking a rope, 54
tobacco-smoking, 75
moon-worship, 76
a Swedish mathematical simpleton, 78, 353
mortar and hard-core, muscles and tendons, 83f
the infallibility of marble and wood, 87f
Praetor's *album*, 89
cannibalism, bestiality etc., 92
coprophilia, 94
courage under torture, 95
a Vandal king, 101
Hottentot Creed, 104
unconscious plagiarism, 106f
Sleidan's amnesia, 114
trumpet-sound like scarlet, 127
ellipse's resemblance to circle, 131
drawings of medallions, 135
Molyneux's problem, 135–8
a selective madman, 144
the brain like an elastic screen, 144f
chess on horseback, 149
Socrates' itching feet, 165
the *Unruhe* of a clock, 166
wild boar's aggressiveness, 173
a willing prisoner, 176
magic lantern, 177
the drunkard's compulsion, 184
a weak-willed dieter, 187
a slow retreat from alcohol, 187
deception by the Lord of the Mountain, 190f
voting procedures, 193
King Philip's official reminder, 196
throwing peas at pins, 201
how to deter a drunkard, 202
accounting as a model of practical reasoning, 206f
existence of the Antipodes, 209
murdering an old man, 214

map of the land of Tenderness, 215
world, elephant, tortoise, 218
an impudent law-graduate, 219
birds in the sun, 220, 234f
'Is the sun eternal?', 229
hunting for two indistinguishable leaves, 231
repairing Theseus's ship, 231
the Golden Ass of Apuleius, 234f
princess becomes parrot, 235
day-man and night-man, 244
a fictional duplicate world, 245f
nursery lies about childbirth, 253f
Alexander the Great dreams of a plant, 256
trick pictures, 258
what a porter knows about weights, 262
squints, ghosts, and other *idées fixes*, 270f
the false Martin Guerre, 290
the special wickedness of stabbing, 301
the argument of the vanishing heap, 302
a conjecture about pollen, 310, 317
relations with planetary men, 314
the ill-shaped Abbott, 319
the monk named 'Calf', 320
varieties of watch and clock, 326
stripping the clothes off Harlequin, 329
a word with fifty meanings, 331
homicide in English, 346
the definition of 'parabola', 346f
the essence of 'pearls', 348, 408
absurd behaviour by merchants, 349
the 'fanciful shepherd', 350
the two Venuses, 350
painting and music, 350
Ramist logical theory, 356f
testing a chain, 360
training-wheels for stumbling scientists, 371
the Abbé Foucher's misbehaviour in debate, 374
pigeons in a dovecote, 379
an unauthorized reprint, 384f
men are like little gods, 389
if explorers behaved like intellectuals, 390

a heresy to believe in the Antipodes?, 391
invasion by the Australians, 400f
the blur of a spinning cog-wheel, 403
an octogenarian re-founds geometry, 407
a stubborn mathematical sceptic, 408
magic punishment of a child, 412
did Archimedes weigh a wooden para-
    bola?, 416
removing the builders' scaffolding, 417
'What conclusions have they reached?',
    418
unfair weapons in debate, 419
schools turn children into blockheads, 422
travelling blind, 424
two proofs that negroes are men, 427
'Oyster is oyster', 428f
a source of bullets in an emergency, 429
spoiling a neighbour's view, 430
wasting the time of the young, 431
water on the moon, 434
'What can be more sillily arrogant...?',
    435
a prescient dream?, 445
Siamese disbelief in ice, 458, 495
religious discipline of page-boys, 458
the coming revolution in Europe, 462f
an historic question about gambling, 465
how peasants assess land-values, 465
unfounded slander against Grotius, 467
fiction in Cromwell's biography, 467
Sleidan's 'book of lies', 467f
a genealogical question answered, 468
some myths about national origins, 469
a projected history of clothing, 470
differences amongst the planets?, 472
'musical cadences' amongst phenomena,
    473
why we don't encounter animals higher
    than us, 473, 490
'left it to Aristotle to make them rational',
    476

dependence on logical spectacles, 478
amazement over Archimedes' ingenuity,
    489
'How else can we get a conviction?', 491f
debasing the coinage, 492
predicting a volcanic eruption, 493
predicting an eclipse, 493
Why prefer the Bible to the Koran?, 494
'believe it because it is absurd', 495
contradictions admissible in theology?,
    498f
taking the Bible literally, 499f
disputes about Aristotle's salvation, 500f
disputes about the status of Confucianism,
    501f
insanity and religious inspiration, 505
a self-appointed wife of Jesus, 506
the death of a self-proclaimed immortal,
    506f
a dangerous prophet plots against Russia,
    507
'Could the shoemaker make gold?', 507f
the A of theology, the B of mathematics,
    508
Drabicius spreads disaster, 508
Honorius' absurd value-system, 512
'Romanist' becomes 'luthérien', 513n
challenging a learned professor, 514f
Father Fabri on Copernicus and Scrip-
    ture, 515
advantages of committees, 518
absurd effects of sectarian prejudice, 519
rights and duties of teachers, 519f
a dying man keeps the devil at bay, 521
a Moorish woman cures Ximénez's fever,
    523
the biggest book catalogue, 525
ill-treatment of the faculty of Philosophy,
    526f